THEORY AND PROBLEMS OF
SOCIAL PSYCHOLOGY

McGRAW-HILL SERIES IN PSYCHOLOGY

Harry F. Harlow, *Consulting Editor*

John F. Dashiell was Consulting Editor of this series from its inception in 1931 until January 1, 1950. Clifford T. Morgan was Consulting Editor of this series from January 1, 1950 until January 1, 1959.

THEORY and PROBLEMS of SOCIAL PSYCHOLOGY

By DAVID KRECH

University of California

and RICHARD S. CRUTCHFIELD

Associate Professor and Chairman of the Department of Psychology, Swarthmore College

New York   Toronto   London

McGRAW-HILL BOOK COMPANY, INC.

1948

THEORY AND PROBLEMS OF SOCIAL PSYCHOLOGY

XIII

35465

To
EDWARD CHACE TOLMAN

PREFACE

This book is designed for the teacher and the student who are primarily interested in the *science* of psychology as a systematic, interpretive account of human behavior and who are interested in *applying the science* of psychology to current social issues. In attempting to meet these requirements the authors have not found it necessary to keep two sets of readers in mind or to treat the subject matter of this book from two points of view. The basic guiding principle has been that a theoretically sound social psychology is also a practically valid and immediately useful social psychology. Neither the "pure scientist" nor the "man of action" can neglect public opinion survey data or experiments on perceptual organization without running the risk of making his theory truncated and narrow or his program of action superficial and ineffective.

Such a consideration has several implications for maximizing the usefulness of this book to the student and teacher. Basic principles and theory frequently prove bothersome to the teacher whose students are not going to become professional psychologists but who are primarily interested in practical applications. A large section of this book is devoted to such practical applications, but if the student is to "get" that material he must first take the necessary time and spend the necessary mental energy to assimilate and understand the basic principles discussed in the first half of the book. This will not be easy—for either the student or the teacher—but, as experience has demonstrated with a number of undergraduate classes at several colleges and universities, it is not impossible or even unduly difficult. Little is gained by underestimating the capacity or interest of the student in the problems of "theory" or in the basic question of "why?" Conversely, the concern with measurement techniques, public opinion survey methods, sampling problems, and action programs designed to minimize industrial conflict, racial prejudice, and international tensions proves to be of only superficial interest to the teacher whose students are being prepared for fundamental research in psychology, and who wishes to spend his major time with basic principles and with "timeless" questions. A large section of this book is devoted to such basic principles, but if the student is to be in a position to evaluate the *theoretical soundness* of basic principles he must take the time to "spell out" the operation of these basic

vii

processes in the behavior of the leader of a labor union, the politician, the father of a family, and the disciple of a "hate" organization. After all, these basic principles presumably apply to human behavior.

During the past several years a number of major developments have occurred in social psychology that have played an important part in shaping the contents and orientation of this book. In the first place, there has been an increased recognition of the fundamental role that perceptual processes play in man's beliefs, attitudes, thinking, and action. As the reader will note, the theoretical structure of our treatment here leans heavily upon the concepts and experimental findings that have come from the laboratory of the "perception psychologist." In the second place, an entirely new field of research has been opened by the development of *group dynamics*. This exciting and promising approach to the problems of social psychology has been given a prominent place in this book. Third, the activities of psychologists during the war years have resulted in the accumulation and development of new data and new techniques of measurement and investigation in the field. We have tried to exploit these developments here. Finally, the war work of psychologists, psychiatrists, and sociologists has demonstrated the necessity of integrating clinical and sociological data with psychological phenomena. The book reflects this to some extent by the use of concepts developed in the clinic and by the amount of space that it was found necessary to devote to sociological descriptions and data in sketching the backgrounds for our psychological analysis of behavior— especially in the last section.

It is a truism that no book is completely the work of the authors whose names are listed on the title page. Every book is a social product, and the unnamed authors of this book are legion. Among these must be listed Prof. Wolfgang Köhler, whose brilliant experimental and theoretical work has given to psychology a unifying set of basic principles; the late Prof. Kurt Lewin, who saw so clearly and with such great insight the relation between "pure" psychology and "action" and whose research and thinking has made possible the development of "action research" and the whole field of experimental group dynamics; and the authors' teacher, Prof. Edward Chace Tolman, who more than any other psychologist has, in his teaching and his work, helped convince American psychologists of the dynamic, fruitful, and vitalizing effect that theory can have upon experiment and experiment upon theory.

In addition to these great figures in contemporary psychology who must be credited with whatever merit this book may have, the authors' indebtedness to other colleagues in psychology and the social sciences is indeed great. They wish to acknowledge their obligations and thanks to the many research workers whose studies have made possible this book. They have also profited greatly from the interest and criticisms of both the graduate and undergraduate students at Swarthmore College, the University of California, the Washington School of Psychiatry, and the William Alanson White Institute of Psychiatry who have been used as "guinea pigs" in assessing the teachability of the material as organized in this book.

More directly they are indebted to several friends who have read and criticized the first draft of the manuscript incorporated in this book. Among them are Prof. Robert Leeper of the University of Oregon, who has indeed been their best friend and severest critic and whose typically forthright, devastating, but nevertheless helpful criticisms have eliminated many ambiguities and errors; Prof. Robert MacLeod of McGill University, whose scholarship and unwillingness to let the authors dodge too many basic problems have served as their scientific conscience throughout the preparation of this book; Prof. Gardner Murphy of the College of the City of New York, whose persistent concern with contemporary social issues has proved an inspiration for so many social psychologists in America and whose interest in the major objective in writing this book has been a strong rod to lean upon during the tedious and frequently discouraging periods of writing; and to Prof. Karl F. Muenzinger of the University of Colorado, who has always insisted that psychology be taught—whether to the undergraduate or graduate student—as a disciplined science. Prof. Frank C. Pierson of the Economics Department, Swarthmore College, has read and made suggestions relating to the chapter on Industrial Conflict, and Prof. Richard Brandt of the Philosophy Department, Swarthmore College has made a number of helpful contributions in discussions with him concerning the material covered in the first part of the book.

Finally, we wish to express our appreciation to the following journals and publishers who have generously granted permission to reproduce tables, figures, illustrations, and excerpts: *American Journal of Psychology*, American Psychological Association, *American Scientist*, *Annals of the American Academy of Political and Social Science*, Cambridge University Press, Clark University Press, *Common Ground*, Commonwealth Fund, Harper and Brothers, Harvard University Press, Henry Holt, Houghton Mifflin, *Human Relations*, *International Journal of Opinion and Attitude Research*, *Journal of Abnormal and Social Psychology*, *Journal of Comparative Psychology*, *Journal of Experimental Psychology*, *Journal of Personality*, *Journal of Psychology*, *Journal of Social Issues*, *Journal of Social Psychology*, King's Crown Press, Alfred A. Knopf, Macmillan Company, *New York Times*, Princeton University Press, *Psychological Bulletin*, *Psychological Monographs*, *Psychological Review*, *Public Opinion Quarterly*, Reinhold Publishing

Corporation, *Saturday Review of Literature, Science,* Social Science Research Council, *Sociometry, Survey Graphic,* University of Chicago Press, John Wiley, and Yale University Press.

DAVID KRECH
RICHARD S. CRUTCHFIELD

PEACHAM, VT.
August, 1947

CONTENTS

xi

PART TWO. SOCIAL PROCESSES

PART THREE. APPLICATIONS

Supports for distorted beliefs about others. Dominant role of national leaders and special interests. The dependence of international relations on national politics. The lack of certain prerequisites for international unity. Basic ideological conflicts. *A Program for Reducing International Tensions.* Preliminary considerations. Ten steps in a program for peace. A United Nations Institute of the Human Sciences. The leverage of atomic energy for peace. *Summary.*

PART ONE

BASIC PRINCIPLES

CHAPTER I

THE FIELD AND PROBLEMS OF SOCIAL PSYCHOLOGY

Social psychology is no longer an "infant science." As a scientist, the social psychologist feels that he has much to offer to a world beset by ills which are universally ascribed to difficulties of interpersonal relationships. As a responsible citizen of his society, he is eager to apply the science of social psychology to a solution of these problems. But many leaders of society—government administrators, legislators, businessmen, labor leaders, and others—are reluctant to give to social psychology the support it needs for its further development, and they resist the application of a scientific social psychology to vital current world problems. What are the reasons for this?

In the first place many people have the attitude that scientific social psychological research is unnecessary. Almost every politician, business-man, military leader, religious leader, or advertising expert considers him-self a good social psychologist and believes that he already knows the essential facts and principles of human behavior on the basis of his own experience in dealing with people. Unquestionably these individuals, as well as most people who live for any length of time in a complex society, have learned a great deal, in a practical way, about how people behave. And, in a pragmatic sense, what they know about human nature may be adequate to handle many of the problems that they meet in everyday activities. But it is just as obviously true that they do not know enough to deal with some of the most significant social problems of their day. Despite the vast store of good will found among men the world over, they lack the knowledge of how to convert this good will into international understanding and permanent peace. Industrial unrest, racial prejudice, crime, and delinquency continue to be major problems of most of the countries of the western world. But even where "practical knowledge" is adequate to deal with the problems involved, it must be pointed out that there is an important difference between that kind of knowledge and scientific knowledge about human behavior.

The major objective of science is not primarily to control and predict, but to *understand*. Effective control is a reward of understanding, and accuracy in prediction is a check on understanding. The African savage who tips his spear with poison and succeeds in killing his game or human victims thereby has practical knowledge about physiological chemistry, but none of us would think of calling the savage a "physiological chemist." He can control with some efficiency, and he can predict with some degree of accuracy, but he does not understand what he is doing or why his prediction is correct when it happens to be so. This lack of understanding reflects itself in his frequent failure of control and his frequent errors in prediction. On the other hand, the advertising man, the propagandist, or the politician who has a similar (and sometimes just as lethal) effective knowledge about psychology and who, through this practical knowledge, can sometimes control and predict is quick to call himself a "social psychologist," and most laymen are ready to accord him that recognition. Thus, for example, many people unhesitatingly accorded Hitler the distinction of being a "master social psychologist." Yet as far as understanding is concerned, he was no more of a social psychologist than is the savage a physiological chemist.

Of course, the African savage and the common-sense social psychologist will assert that they do understand. But their "understanding" fails to meet any of the requirements of science and must eventually lead to wrong predictions and failure in control. Thus, the savage will aver that the reason his poisoned spear kills is because it was tipped in the food of an evil god—a food that is fatal to the enemies of that particular god. The politician, the propagandist, or the huckster can also ascribe reasons for his frequently successful control and prediction. His "explanatory" generalizations are also taken from the lore and superstitions of his culture. Thus he will quote the following explanatory principles:

Repeat a lie frequently enough and people will believe it.
Clothes make the man.
You can't teach an old dog new tricks.
Out of sight, out of mind.
East is east and west is west and never the twain shall meet.

The dubious value of such "explanatory principles" is immediately seen when we realize that for each one there seems to be an equally accepted and "time-tested" generalization which is directly opposite in meaning. Thus for the above "truths" there are found the following opposites:

The truth will always prevail.
You can't make a silk purse out of a sow's ear.
Never too old to learn.
Absence makes the heart grow fonder.
Brothers under the skin.

These "explanations," if they have any value at all, are merely convenient summary statements to describe what *has* happened in a given case. If the next time the same reaction does not occur, then the alternative and opposite "explanation" is used!

The danger in failing to differentiate between scientific understanding of behavior and practical knowledge about behavior is great. It inhibits the careful study of the facts of social psychology and their systematization into a set of basic principles that can be generally applicable regardless of the specific nature of the concrete social problem. Recent world history has well demonstrated this. When man turns his attention to new and difficult social problems, the complete and tragic inadequacy of his common-sense knowledge, his rule-of-thumb reasoning, and his tradition-based explanation is revealed in all of its disastrous consequences.

While many people in our society nevertheless continue to show an indifference to the scientific study of social psychology because of this dangerous and unfounded belief that it is unnecessary, many others have a resistance to scientific psychology because they feel that *psychology does not know enough*. Unlike physics, psychology deals with problems that are of immediate and important concern to all people. Most people know the significant questions to ask of psychology, but they do not know the significant questions to ask of physics. Thus, for example, how many laymen are aware of the "shocking" fact that physics knows very little about the behavior of aperiodic crystals?[1] Very few people are aware of it, and would not care much if it were called to their attention. But everyone soon discovers, when he seeks the answers, that psychology does not know all that should be known about the causes and cure of schizophrenia, about racial tensions, war and peace, crime, etc. The impatience of many people with psychology derives from a disappointment in what psychology seems to be able to offer in the face of pressing problems. This disappointment is in part due to the fact that psychology, like all sciences, does not now have all the answers—it is still seeking them. Moreover their very impatience with psychology results in their refusal to support its attempts to know more. There is a tendency on the part of the man of affairs to take the attitude, "First show me what you have to contribute to my major problems, and then I'll support you and seek your advice." Here the social psychologist faces a dilemma, for it is in the very nature of the case that even in the initial stages he must do research in laboratories which are the neighborhood, the school, the industrial plant, the city,

[1] For a discussion of the limitations of the physicist's knowledge about periodic and aperiodic crystals and the significance of this problem to biology, disease, and heredity, the student is referred to Schroedinger's (1945) provocative book, *What Is Life?*

and the state, and for this work he must have the acceptance and support of the man of affairs even before he begins to turn out results.[1]

But if many people are impatient with psychology because it does not know enough, perhaps just as many people resist a scientific psychology because of a fear that *psychology knows too much.* In so far as social psychology attempts to gain an understanding of social thinking and behavior, it must perforce delve into the nature of the basic goals of the various individuals of society. In so doing, it is likely to uncover facts that are difficult for some people to take, and it may violate strongly ingrained prejudices, beliefs, and vested interests. Every science has found this type of resistance. Physics challenged some of the accepted doctrines and beliefs of members of certain religious groups, and the study of physics, as well as the lives of individual physicists, was frequently threatened. The same has been true of astronomy and biology. But this is even more true for psychology, since psychology concerns itself with *all* beliefs and goals—not only with religious beliefs or beliefs about the physical world. This difference may help explain the order of development of the different sciences. Society's resistance to a science may reflect the differences in the number and class of people and ideas jeopardized by the body of knowledge built up by the science. Philip Wylie (1947) makes somewhat the same point when he says:

The branches of science have emerged, I submit, in the order in which they have done least damage to man's prestigious illusions concerning himself. Mathematics came first because it hardly hurt human vanity. Physics came next because, although it diminished human illusions of terrestrial grandeur, it left "miraculous man" unimpaired. Biology was put off because it involved an examination of man as an animal—when he insisted on remaining a god. Psychology is being avoided today because, with its acceptance, a thousand prideful institutions will vanish, myriad sacred tenets even of scientists will dissolve.

These are some of the major reasons for the resistance society has shown to the promotion and exploitation of the science of social psychology. However, the fault is not all with the layman's lack of understanding of the nature of science or his impatience or his fears. Often the social psychologist himself has failed by refusing to address himself to the acute problems involved in current social issues. He has sought the refuge of the laboratory and the safety of so-called "pure" research. He has been too unwilling to seek the advice of society as to the special problems on which he should concentrate his attention.

[1] For a fuller discussion of this dilemma in which the social psychologist finds himself vis-à-vis the man of affairs, see Krech (1946).

TWO ASPECTS OF SOCIAL PSYCHOLOGY

Perhaps more important than the reluctance of the social psychologist to tackle problems of social significance has been the relative unavailability of a set of scientific principles that would permit him to understand the specific social problems with which he must concern himself. Such principles would have to be systematically integrated from pure research in social psychology and psychology in general. This lack of theoretical structure has limited the advance of social psychology at two points. (1) It has limited the value of the social psychologist's "practical" research by making possible only a rather narrow understanding (sometimes a wrong understanding) of the implications of his data. (2) This poverty of theory has tended to repel the more theoretical-minded psychologists from concerning themselves with problems of social psychology. Social psychology has lacked status among the more "scientific" psychologists.

Whether we are interested in social psychology as a basic science or in the immediate applications of social psychology, a set of scientific principles is essential. To understand the role of such principles we must next examine these two aspects of social psychology.

Social Psychology as a Basic Science.—Among the sciences of society only social psychology deals primarily with the whole individual. Economics, political science, sociology, and the other social disciplines have as their subject matter the structure and function of social organizations and the kinds of institutional behavior displayed by people within the confines and forms of specific institutions. Social psychology, on the other hand, is concerned with *every aspect of the individual's behavior in society.* Social psychology may therefore be broadly defined as the science of the behavior of the individual in society.

Social psychology and general psychology.—As a basic science, social psychology does not differ in any fundamental way from psychology in general. This identification of social psychology with general psychology follows from three closely interrelated considerations. In the first place, as a basic science, social psychology has as its goal the establishment of universal laws of the social behavior of the individual. If we are to take seriously the problem of understanding this behavior, we must examine such fundamental processes as how the individual achieves his social goals, how he perceives his social environment, how he learns his social behavior. And what we shall discover is that the principles of "social motivation," "social perception," and "social learning" are identical with the principles of motivation, perception, and learning found everywhere in the field of psychology. This identity between social psychological principles and general psychological principles will be expressed in our treatment of motivation, perception, and learning. Examples of the application of the basic propositions with respect to these functions will be drawn with equal freedom from so-called social and nonsocial situations.

In the second place, not only do the same fundamental principles apply to both social and nonsocial behavior, but the general psychologist as well as the social psychologist is literally forced to study the behavior of man as a social being. Whether we are studying the behavior of a man in a laboratory, in the clinic, or in a crowd, whether we are studying his perception of colored papers, his performance on an intelligence test, or his decision about participating in a lynching, we are studying the behavior of a man as influenced by his perception of the social world. There probably exists no such being as an individual in isolation. The effects of a man's group membership, of his experience with other men, of his past and present interpersonal relationships reach into each of his psychological activities no matter how simple or apparently remote. As a consequence every man lives in a social world, and no psychologist, whatever his interests, does or can study the behavior of an asocial man. From this practical point of view, then, two psychologies cannot emerge from the psychologist's laboratory—social and nonsocial—but only one.

In the third place, not only does every psychologist perforce study the behavior of social man, but a more fundamental consideration of what constitutes a "social field" will indicate that there is no theoretical distinction which can be drawn between a "social field" and a "nonsocial field." Although there are, to be sure, special areas within the whole domain of psychology that are commonly (and, for practical purposes, usefully) designated as "social," in terms of theory there is only a continuum from simple (nonsocial) to complex (social) fields. This consideration is of sufficient importance to merit some extended discussion.

The social psychological field.—What, from the point of view of the individual, is a social field? The most obvious answer is that a social field is characterized by the presence of people—in the sense either that they are directly and immediately present or that their presence is represented in the existence of psychological events (percepts, memories, fears, etc.) which are connected with people. That is, social behavior would be said to be that behavior which takes place in direct reference to other people as in any kind of face-to-face situation or that which takes place in the absence of people but is affected by reference to other people. If when Mr. Arbuthnot is physically alone at the moment he is choosing a tie to wear for the day he is influenced in his choice by what he considers the reactions of his wife might be, he is behaving with reference to other people and is therefore in a social field. It should be noted that what is being implied here is *psychological* presence of Mrs. Arbuthnot and not *physical* presence. And conversely, although an external observer may find an individual in the midst of other persons, he cannot legitimately conclude, without other evidence, that these other persons are psychologically "present" for the individual.

Since the commonly accepted formulation asserts that it is the psychological presence of other *persons* which uniquely characterizes a social field, it is necessary to ascertain what especially significant properties these "person objects" have in governing behavior. In what essential respects are these person objects different from other objects in the psychological field? Analysis will reveal that person objects differ from other objects in an individual's field and are especially important in determining behavior because they have, among other characteristics, the properties of *mobility, capriciousness, unpredictability;* because they are the perceived loci of a great deal of *causation;* because they are perceived to have *power* qualities—to provide rewards and threaten punishment; because they are perceived as *sensitive* and *reciprocally reactive.* None of these properties depends upon the fact that the individual apprehends these person objects as being like himself. And the person objects need not, of course, be human. If Mr. Arbuthnot were raised with animals only (as in the case of the mythical "wolf boy" who is discovered living in India every time the Sunday feature writer needs a space filler), he would still exhibit behavior that we should call "social." He would still imitate, be suggestible, cooperate, etc.—though perhaps he would never see the similarities between himself and the animals. This is probably what happens also with animals. They are probably also not aware of the other animals in their fields as being like themselves but simply react to those essential properties of the animals which have been mentioned above—capriciousness, mobility, loci of causation, power qualities, reciprocal reactivity. And, of course, for this reason their behavior in an animal environment differs from that in a nonanimal environment.

In addition to the above defining characteristics of person objects, people may, of course, have other perceived characteristics. Among the most important of these properties is the one of similarity to the perceiver. It is easier, for example, for Mr. Arbuthnot to identify himself with a native American than it is for him to identify himself with a Frenchman, and it is easier for him to identify himself with a Frenchman than with a Chinese. The more similarity there is between the perceiver and the perceived person object the greater the degree of empathy and understanding and identification that is possible. Mr. Arbuthnot, reading in his newspaper about the torture and death of hundreds of African natives, is not nearly so moved as when he reads an account of a gruesome accident in which an American family of five was killed—even though the members of this family were complete strangers to him. The essential factor is that he can think of the American family as being like himself, whereas he would see far fewer similarities between himself and the African natives. However, should Mr. Arbuthnot one day find himself in the presence of these African natives, his behavior would be partly determined by the essential properties of these person objects and he would be in a "social field." Whether these objects were Americans, Frenchmen, Chinese, Africans, animals, or anything else, as long as they had the essential properties of person objects, they would have a unique effect on Arbuthnot's behavior.

Theoretically it is not even necessary that the other objects in the perceiver's environment be animal; they might be plants or even inanimate objects. For example, we know that many natural, nonliving phenomena contain some or all of the essential properties we have been discussing. Clouds and storms and winds are excellent examples of objects in the psychological field that carry the perceived properties of mobility, capriciousness, causation, power of threat and reward. So, too, the sea and the river and the ocean. So, too, the volcano, the glacier, the fire, and the earthquake. Thus a man living in an environment completely without animate objects might still exhibit some types of behavior that we ordinarily think of as social. He might punish a "malicious" stone that trips him, try to appease thunder and lightning, imitate the noises of the waves, etc.[1]

The critical point of all the above observations, then, is that the behavior of the individual in the presence of these and other similar natural phenomena is different from his behavior when not in their presence. Certainly this fact does not justify the need for two separate basic sciences: one a

[1] The fact that all sorts of objects, inanimate as well as animate, have these interesting properties is of singular relevance to the phenomenon of "animism." This widespread phenomenon is often explained as an "illogical" process by which the primitive or the child imputes to inanimate objects the properties he finds in human beings. The adequacy of this explanation is questionable in view of the argument presented above. People—whether "savages" or children—can and do perceive the dynamic properties of mobility, capriciousness, power, etc., as immediately and directly inherent in inanimate and non-human objects as well as in human beings. The perception of capriciousness in a windstorm, for example, does not depend upon reasoning from experience with human beings. It is directly observed. In that respect the capriciousness of a human individual and that of a windstorm are immediately seen as similar. No complicated logical or illogical reasoning process need be involved.

science of the individual in the presence of these objects (social psychology) and the other a science of the individual in the absence of these objects (nonsocial psychology). The real point is that much of what we commonly call "social behavior" gets its special qualities by virtue of the fact that the individual *is* behaving with respect to objects that are mobile, capricious, etc. It is a kind of accidental circumstance, *as far as basic science considerations are concerned*, that people have these perceptual properties to a much greater degree than other kinds of objects. It appears, therefore, that there is *no* real point of transition between the social and nonsocial. That is what was meant by the statement on page 8 that "in terms of theory there is only a continuum from simple (nonsocial) to complex (social) fields." At the most simple level the psychological field includes only rather static, immobile objects; at the complex level it contains mobile, powerful, capricious, causal objects.

Summary.—In the light of the empirically determined observation that the basic processes of motivation, perception, and learning are the same whether we are discussing social behavior or nonsocial behavior, in consideration of the practical impossibility of observing the behavior of an individual in isolation, and because of the theoretical impossibility of finding a real point of transition between a social field and a nonsocial field, it is apparent that as far as basic science is concerned, there are not two psychologies, but only one. For practical considerations, however, we will refer frequently in this book to "social psychological fields" and "social behavior." This is done for purposes of convenience—as a shorthand device for referring to "peopled fields" and to the behavior of the individual as influenced by other people. But the reader must constantly remember that by saying "social" we do not mean to imply that anything different in the essential psychological functioning of the *individual* is involved. This will help to avoid many of the pitfalls into which both the social scientist and the layman fall when they attempt to dichotomize the individual and the social, the social and the biological, etc.

Applications of Social Psychology.—The task of the social psychologist is not only to establish the basic principles of social behavior but to apply these principles in the analysis and understanding of specific behavior in concrete social situations. In order to understand this aspect of social psychology, we must appreciate at the outset just what it is that the social psychologist (on the basis of the best set of psychological principles he can muster) is to attempt in his role as an applied scientist. We must, further, be clear about the difference between the kind of *research* he does as an applied scientist and that which he does when he is functioning as a pure scientist.

The role of the applied social psychologist.—Exactly what is it that social psychology can contribute to man's problems? Why is it socially desirable to overcome the resistances to social psychology that we discussed at some length at the beginning of this chapter? Is it the role of the social psychologist to *solve* social problems, to be the "master fixer"? Definitely not. The solution of complex social problems requires authority, techniques, and resources that fall far outside the province of the psychologist. The proper role of the psychologist in dealing with social problems is that of the analyst, the diagnostician, the strategist, and the advisor with respect to only *one* feature of the whole problem—the behavior of the individual and groups of individuals who are involved And even here, it should be clearly understood, there are other social scientists (those labeled "sociologists," for example) who must share in this task with the social psychologist.

Take the problem of racial prejudice as an instance in point. The task of the social psychologist (whatever his label) from the point of view of social *analysis* is to ascertain why people are prejudiced, how and why this prejudice forms and changes, what effects such prejudice has on the behavior and personality of the individual who holds this prejudice, what effects such prejudice has on the attitudes, personality, and behavior of the victim, etc. It is *not* a primary function of the psychologist to ascertain the incidence of prejudiced beliefs and attitudes among various groups of people or in various sections of the country. That census job—vitally important for planning any action—is the task of the public opinion analyst and the statistician. It is *not* the psychologist's job to examine the political, economic, and general social consequences of any action—these are the proper functions of the sociologist, the economist, the political scientist.

From the point of view of social engineering and the solution of the problem of racial prejudice, the primary function of the psychologist is to ascertain what people's attitudes and discriminatory behavior would be like under different social circumstances and by what changes in the social situation the desired attitudes and behavior could be engendered. But it is not the job of the psychologist to bring about these necessary social circumstances. That is the function of the social planner, the administrator, and the social action groups. Successful change is dependent upon the diverse political, economic, social, and educational activities of large segments of society.

Social psychology is no cure-all. It can provide indispensable understanding, prediction, evaluation, and advice; but even if at some future time the social psychologist could indeed know all that was necessary to know about the psychological bases of racial prejudice, the actual possibility of the solution of the problem would depend entirely upon the wishes and actions of most of the members of society. It is probably not an exaggeration to say that even in the present state of the science of social psychology, enough is known to enable society—if it so desired and if the necessary resources were available—to solve most of the critical aspects of the problem of racial prejudice.

The research of the applied social psychologist.—We have emphasized the important contribution that a basic science of social psychology can make to the efficient applications of social psychology and have stressed the point that any piece of research in psychology must inevitably have implications for social psychology. However, in dealing with such acute problems as international tensions, economic conflicts, and racial discrimination, general principles and sound theory are not enough. The social psychologist, as an applied scientist, must study each specific social problem in its own right, uncovering the relevant factors, determining the relative potency of these various factors and how they interrelate. He must take into account the facts about the *particular* people who are involved in the problem and the *specific* social atmosphere in which the problem occurs. Only with this knowledge about the concrete details of the problem in his possession can he then bring to bear the basic psychological principles in understanding the problem and the behavior it involves. Obtaining these concrete details requires just as painstaking research, just as carefully planned accumulation of data, just as much ingenuity and skill as are required for "pure" research. In addition, it frequently requires the development of new techniques and the adaptation of standard research methods.

The concrete problems to which the applied social psychologist addresses himself are almost always determined for him by the particular interpersonal and intercultural problems that are of special concern to society. These problems change from time to time; and in this sense, the subject matter of applied social psychology is constantly changing.

THREE LEVELS OF SOCIAL ANALYSIS

Before we can proceed to an investigation of basic social psychological principles, we must clarify two fundamental points. One is the level of analysis that we are to use for our subject matter, and the other is the unit of analysis. These questions are intimately related.

Social phenomena may be analyzed at three different levels: (1) the level of the social behavior of the individual, (2) the level of the behavior of social groups, (3) the level of the operation of social organizations or institutions. The first of these, the social behavior of the individual, will be the primary concern of this book, and it therefore becomes necessary to answer the following questions: Can social phenomena be fruitfully investigated on the level of individual behavior? Are there other, equally promising levels of social analysis? What are the appropriate units of analysis at each of these levels? What are the relations among these several levels of analysis?

Individual and Group Levels of Analysis.—The essential method at the level of the social behavior of the individual is to describe *his* social psychological world and to explain his social behavior in relation to the characteristics of that world. What, one may ask, is the purpose of this sort of analysis? Of what value can it be to study any social phenomenon from the point of view of a single individual? How can this be expected to aid in the understanding of social events which, almost without exception, involve the participation of more than one person?

A simple analogy.—The answer to these and similar questions may perhaps be best approached through analogy with another field of science. Suppose it is wished to ascertain how a certain gas will behave under defined circumstances. Ordinarily, the physicist approaches the problem in a statistical fashion, measuring the over-all behavior of the molecules of the gas taken together as an aggregate.

The kinds of description the physicist gives for the behavior of the gas as a whole might be something like the following: If the volume is held constant, the pressure of the gas against the container increases as the temperature increases. This, as one can see, says nothing at all about the individual molecules. The physicist knows, of course, that statements about the gas as a whole do not provide the only possible way of describing what is going on. Such a description is complete *in the units in which it is given*—volume, pressure, temperature of the gas as a whole. As such, this statement is very useful. It can tell us how gases will behave as a whole in various combinations of temperature, pressure, and volume; it can help us predict the conditions under which our automobile tire will annoy us with a blowout; etc.

If, however, the physicist wishes to predict the behavior of a single molecule, or if he wishes to understand more basically why the observed relations among pressure, volume, and temperature exist, then he is required to examine the situation in another way—from the point of view of the behavior of the single molecule.

The behavior of a swarm of ants.—Let us turn our attention from molecules of a gas to a case of greater complexity, the behavior of a swarm of ants. Schneirla (1941, 1946) has made a series of intensive studies of the activities of the Army ant, and his observations and methods of study throw light on the more general problem of methodology in social psychology. We do not mean to imply that the study of the behavior of a swarm of ants has an immediate significance for our understanding of the behavior of groups of people. It is the methodological similarity we wish to examine.

Schneirla has described the behavior of the swarm of ants as a whole— how the swarm moves on a foray, how it circumvents physical obstacles, how it retreats at night, etc. On the basis of such observations it is possible to arrive at a number of fairly concrete statements about the behavior of swarms, as swarms. There are distinctive patterns of movements, and these patterns may be shown to correlate systematically with various conditions of the surrounding physical environment. These can become laws of the behavior of ant swarms; and on the basis of such laws, it becomes possible to make accurate predictions about how swarms will behave in many varied circumstances.

These laws say nothing definite, of course, about the behavior of any *single* ant. For within the general confines of the pattern of movement of the whole swarm there is an almost infinite number of possible variations of individual movements. Correspondingly, the study of the behavior of a single ant, no matter how complete, cannot yield data sufficient to construct laws about the swarm behavior as a whole. If we could assume that all ants are alike in their behavior potentialities and in their reactivity, then we should still have to know the whole story about the precise patterns of stimulation and reaction that exist in any single moment for each and every ant in the swarm before we could make a precise statement about the behavior of the whole swarm. Under most circumstances it is readily seen that even given these essentials, the task of assembling the individual data would be enormously complex—perhaps impossible.

If one simply wants to describe the behavior of the whole swarm, attention to the behavior of the individual ant may be superfluous. But as Schneirla points out, if one wishes to understand more fully why these laws of swarm behavior hold, then he is required to examine the behavior of the ants as individuals. In so doing, Schneirla found it possible to show that the movement of the whole swarm around obstacles, the advance and retreats characteristic of forays, could be made explicable on the basis of specific reactive properties of the individual ants, such as stereotyped following of the colony chemical.

Furthermore, in the case of the ants in a swarm, we encounter a *field dynamic* state of affairs. This means that *changes taking place at one point in the swarm communicate themselves to all other points in the swarm*, and a constant process of disruption and reestablishment of relationships is involved. Each ant is sensitive to stimuli given by the movements of other ants, and each ant reacts to such stimulation in such a fashion as to stimulate other ants in turn. It is important to emphasize at this point that the swarm behavior has lawful character because a large number of ants are in close spatial and temporal proximity and the various individual ants have the dispositions to stimulate and be stimulated by other ants. The synthesis of the behavior of these individual ants is the behavior of the swarm as a whole.

The behavior of human crowds and groups.—Finally, turning our attention to human behavior, we may trace the same methodological aspects of the study of crowd behavior. If we study the behavior of a crowd of people emerging from a theater, we may be able to state some rather general "laws" concerning the density of the crowd at various moments after the end of the show, its changing configurations, its mode of movement around physical obstacles, etc. If all we wish to be able to do is to describe such total behavior accurately and to predict how such behavior may change under changed conditions, we may be satisfied to study these crowds, as crowds, without any specific attention to individuals within the crowd. But just as Schneirla found it necessary to examine the behavior of the individual ants to account for the behavior of the swarm, so would we be required to study the behavior of the individual crowd member in order to get the underlying explanation of the crowd behavior.

This latter requirement is frequently more compelling in the case of human behavior than it is for the other illustrations we have examined. Often we may wish to predict crowd behaviors in types of new situations that we have not been able to observe in the past. In a few instances we may be able to extrapolate what we know about crowd behavior to include the new situations, but frequently we may not be able to do so. This follows from several important differences between, say, the ant swarm or the gas as a whole and a crowd of human beings. It is because of these differences that an understanding of *individual* behavior may frequently permit us to make better predictions about what the crowd will do.

Some significant characteristics of human groups.—One important difference between the theater crowd and the ant swarm is that there is less homogeneity among human beings than among ants. In studying the theater crowd we may find, for example, that there are certain reversed currents in the general movement out of the theater. Detailed analysis might indicate that this is caused by a certain number of women who have forgotten their gloves. The more women in the crowd the greater the extent of the reversed currents. *Perceptual selectivity* will also play an important role. Men will move in special ways in orientation to young women who are perceived as attractive objects. Without knowing how many men and how many attractive women there are in the crowd or whether these women will be perceived as attractive by the men, we might make some very serious errors in predicting the crowd movements. To know this last fact requires that we know something about the perceptions, goals, and past experiences of the individual men comprising the crowd.

Because of the extent of individual differences among people (by individual differences is meant not only differences in native abilities and structure but, more importantly, differences in the needs, perceptions, and cognitions of people) the laws of crowd behavior will be much more complex than the laws of infrahuman swarms or aggregates of physical objects. But there is a much more significant aspect in which human groups differ from infrahuman ones. One of the most important products of culture is the establishment of somewhat stereotyped modes of interpersonal contacts within any one social group. For example, in the family group there are fairly well-recognized and established types of relationships between the parents and the children, between older and younger members, between male and female. The family, functioning as a group, is not made up of a certain number of equivalent people having identical properties (as in the case of the molecules or the ants) but is made up of a number of individuals, each with his own characteristic need pattern, cognitions, intellectual ability, and structure and each occupying a certain fairly well-established *role* vis-à-vis the other members. This makes for heterogeneity compounded. The army is another good example of such a complex human group. Here we do not find a homogeneous aggregation of men behaving as a group simply in terms of the dynamics of interstimulation. Rather, we find a group having substructured groups within it—the officers and men, different ranks among the officers, different established functions among the men. The interpersonal relationships among all these people are fairly well formalized and codified in the articles of war and other documents.[1]

Despite these differences between human groups and other kinds of grouping, the same methodological considerations hold true: To be able to describe and predict the behavior of human groups, it may frequently be sufficient to study the dynamics of group behavior as such; to understand the underlying bases of group dynamics, the study of the characteristics of individual human beings may be helpful and sometimes essential.

---

[1] For an interesting discussion of the operation of social roles, the work of Linton (1936) is of value. Another study of interest is that of Hyman (1942) which clearly brings out the relationships between the individual's perception of the meaning of his own status and the group within which he holds such status.

Summary.—Thus far we have discussed two general approaches to the study of social phenomena—the study of the behavior of the individual in reference to his individual social psychological field, and the study of the behavior of groups of people as a whole. For convenience, in later discussion, the first of these approaches will be referred to as the *psychological* and the second as the *group dynamic*. Enough has been said about the first to require no further amplification at this point. Concerning the second, group dynamics, a little more should be added.

Group Dynamics.—First, let us define more precisely what will be meant by the term *group*. A group does not merely mean individuals characterized by some similar property. Thus, for example, a collection of Republicans or farmers or Negroes or blind men is not a *group*. These collections may be called *classes* of people. The term *group*, on the other hand, refers to two or more people who bear an *explicit psychological relationship to one another*. This means that for each member of the group the other group members must exist in some more or less immediate psychological way so that their behavior and their characteristics influence him. Some illustrations may make this distinction clearer.

A given Republican in California may have no psychological existence for another Republican in New York. Neither of them know of each other or are ever aware of each other. These two Republicans, then, do not form a group. They are, of course, both members of the *class* of Republicans. On the other hand, two people who are friends, members of the same family or of the same face-to-face club, occupants of the same train compartment (especially in the event of a train wreck or other intense experience shared by the occupants) may be considered a group. When the term *class* is used, all members of that class are identical with respect to the property on which they are being classified. When the term *group* is used, the common denominator is that the various individuals exist psychologically for each other in some significant way. These individuals may be very different in their class properties. In fact, theoretically, they could all differ from one another in class and still constitute a group. Arbuthnot, when drafted into the army, might find himself a member of a barracks where every occupant differed from him in age, income, education, religion, marital status, politics, occupation, etc., and yet Arbuthnot might soon find that he was a member of a strongly knit group.

Recognizing a group.—There are two methods by which a group can be recognized. (1) By investigating the perceptions and cognitions of each of the supposed members of a group, it can be discovered which other individuals exist for him in the immediate situation with which we are concerned. When Arbuthnot talks about his barracks. whom does he have in mind? (2) By study of the supposed group itself and by the behavior of each of its members, it may be possible to determine whether or not a given individual is a member in the sense we have defined it. Does Arbuthnot have any feeling of shame when his barracks is singled out for particularly disparaging comments by the inspecting officer? Does Arbuthnot seek to hide an unshined boot of one of his mates just prior to inspection?

Dynamics.—The criterion that can be applied for recognizing a group, simply stated, is whether or not the behavior of other members of the supposed group seems to have any direct influence on the behavior of the given individual and whether or not *his* behavior, in turn, has direct effect on the other members. This statement of interaction suggests the definition of our second term, *dynamics*. Nothing more esoteric is meant by the word dynamics than the connotation of *adjustive changes occurring in the group structure as a whole, as produced by changes in any part of the group.* It is important that this simple definition be clearly understood. The failure to keep it always in mind will prove a handicap in following much of our later discussion. And it will make it difficult to understand the significance of much of the current work on the psychology of group behavior. But the difficulties that might follow as a result of ignorance of the concept of group dynamics may not be so fatal as the dangers that lie in wait for those who misuse the concept of group dynamics when referring to social behavior. This concept, when properly used, can be an extremely helpful one; when improperly used, it can lead one into scientifically unsound and meaningless arguments by analogy. For example, the above definition, in so far as it points out that the changes which occur in the group structure are adjustive changes, immediately suggests that there is, in a social group, something akin to *self-distribution* in a physical field of forces. Thus, in an electrical field any change in electrical potential at one point automatically results in a change in potential at many other points. These induced changes are of such a nature as to *restore a balance of forces* among the various points in the field. That is, the whole field changes until such a new balance of forces is achieved. This is a sound observation of a dynamic principle relating to electrical fields.

There is a real danger, however, in describing a group of *people* as a dynamic whole, as if that group itself were a field. Field phenomena, as found in physics, depend upon the fact that the processes occurring at one point have effects throughout the field because the medium in which events occur is itself affected. Is this true of "psychological fields" and of "social fields"? Our answer must be "yes" for the former and "no" for the latter. To refer to "psychological field dynamics" when we are referring to the psychological field of the individual is to be on fairly safe ground for the following reasons. First, these supposed dynamic effects can be referred to a physical field, *viz.*, the *brain field* of the perceiving individual. This follows because it is a safe assumption that all of man's perceptions and actions are represented by some sort of corresponding brain activity. Furthermore, we have reason to believe that the brain may so operate that events occurring in one area are reflected in effects occurring throughout the brain because the intervening medium itself is affected.[1]

But when we begin to talk about the social field, or the field of the group, as if it were a *dynamic* field, we must be particularly careful not to imply that there are any real effects going on in the medium—in this case the *spaces* between the individuals forming the group. All that can go on in these spaces is the direct and simple transmission of physical energies which provide the visual, auditory, and other stimuli arising from one member and impinging upon another. *All* the psychological effects take place within the individual members and *must be conditioned by the characteristics of these individuals.*

Dangers resulting from misinterpretation of "dynamics" and "field theory."—There are two common errors made by theorists in the social sciences (including social psychology) who use the now fashionable concept of field theory and dynamics. The first error, failing to refer the behavior of the group to the properties of the individuals comprising the group, is exemplified by the "group-mind" concept.

Originally this concept was a major one in the theoretical equipment of the social philosopher, the social psychologist, and the sociologist. Today the term *group-mind* is in disfavor, but the concept still plays an important role in the thinking of the man in the street, the statesman, many social philosophers, and even some social scientists. Despite its burial at the hands of F. H. Allport and others, the group-mind concept still seems to lead a ghostly life in the thinking of many social psychologists for the simple reason that in doing away with the group-mind, the social psychologist seems to have been left with only the individual as his unit of analysis, and no social psychologist can get along without some unit larger than the individual. Thus we find the use of such terms as *group gestalten*, *dynamic social fields*, etc.—all modern terms, but frequently misused.

It is perfectly legitimate and even indispensable, as we have seen, to consider the group as a unit, to study how its behavior changes are de-

---

[1] The pioneer work of Köhler (1940) and of Köhler and Wallach (1944) is especially promising in its suggestions for the study of the dynamics of brain action involved in perception.

pendent upon external conditions, to study the relation of one group to another. The group is a complex situation, and for some purposes it is simpler to make statistical generalizations about group behavior without regard for the behavior of any single individual. But to regard the group as a unit should not imply that its behavior is not dependent upon the goals, emotions, cognitions, and idiosyncratic experiences of its individual members. The conceptions of some political philosophers of a political "state" beyond and above the individuals comprising it and having "needs" different from the needs of all the members taken together are based on the group-mind notion. In its extreme form this view takes on the flavor of Fascism, where the state is all and the individual is nothing.

The second common error that is found in attempts at writing a field theory of social behavior derives from an uncritical analogy between psychological field principles in *the individual* and social field principles for many individuals. We have said before that one can, theoretically, find basic laws of group behavior—statements of necessary relation- ships in which the group as a whole is treated as the unit of analysis. This is, indeed, the goal of the many able social psychologists who work in the field of group dynamics. But we must constantly remember that when we treat the group as our unit of analysis and seek to discover laws of group behavior, we cannot merely substitute the word "group" for the word "individual" in valid psychological laws and assume that we now have equally valid laws of group dynamics.[1] Every time we change our unit of analysis we must beware of ascribing to one unit the properties that are meaningful for the other unit. Thus, to analyze the behavior of the total individual in terms of his goals has proved to be scientifically useful, but to attempt to analyze the physiology of a single muscle group in terms of the "goals" of that muscle has very little scientific value. Similarly, without independent verification, the laws of interpersonal relationships, for the individual as our unit, cannot be taken over and applied to inter- group relationships for the group as our unit. A scientifically mature approach to group dynamics must seek out new concepts, new properties, new variables with which to characterize the group as a whole.

It should be evident that we can (and must) reject the naive concept of the group-mind and all its modern substitutes, but at the same time we can (and must) seek laws of group behavior where the basic unit of analysis is the group and not the individual. Such laws of group behavior must complement the laws of individual behavior.

[1] Thus, it seems to us that J. F. Brown (1936) in his interesting attempt to write a social psychology in terms of field theory has failed, at several points, to examine critically the applicability to the social field of concepts useful in dealing with the psychological field.

The Institutional Approach.—We have so far examined two different approaches to the study of social phenomena: the social psychological and the group dynamic. We must now turn our attention to the third approach—the *institutional*. In this method the emphasis is upon social organizations and institutions—how they arise, how they change, what their properties are, how they relate to one another. On the basis of data collected in seeking the answers to these questions, generalized laws are then formulated concerning the variables that govern the formation, growth, and change of organizations and institutions. In addition to studying the growth and development of organizations and institutions, this approach also concerns itself with specific forms of behavior of people—*institutional behavior*. By this term is meant behavior that is largely regulated by a body of formal rules, laws, and customs and by a whole complex structure of enforcement set up to make these rules and laws operate. When studying this kind of behavior the sociologist must frequently use groups of people as his unit, for, as Haring (1947) points out:

> Many patterns of cultural behavior are not observable completely in the performance of any individual. Only as numerous persons coordinate their activities are these more complex patterns effected. Such patterns of organization of multi-individual responses appear everywhere, from the conduct of a shamanistic ritual to the administration of a railway or an army.

Research methods.—No one of the three approaches we have discussed has a monopoly on any specific research method. All three, for example, can and do use the experimental approach. No one doubts that psychological experiments can be made. Lewin and his students have amply demonstrated that group dynamics, too, can be subject to rigorous experimental treatment by the use of deliberately created group situations under careful experimental control. Experiments in institutional behavior are also possible. One simple example is given in the study of political behavior in which various kinds of campaign techniques were used in comparable sets of election wards and the results of these campaign techniques evaluated by the votes cast in each ward (Hartmann, 1936).

In the very nature of the case, however, it is clear that at the institutional level of analysis other techniques than the experimental are predominant. The most common method is that of correlation of various institutional indices—such as birth rate, income, votes, immigration, criminality, marriage rate, industrial production—in the effort to arrive at valid generalizations about how various factors affect institutions and social organizations. In addition, the systematic observation and recording of behavior patterns for specific segments of society are valuable and commonly used methods. In this method every technique of field observation is used—interviewing, case histories, analysis of historical documents, etc.

The Three Levels Illustrated.—An illustration may help to clarify the differences among the three approaches to the study of social phenomena. Let us consider the problem of the family, as a particularly important social entity within our culture. How would we go about studying the problem (or what would the problems be) from the psychological, the group dynamic, and the institutional approaches?

The psychological approach.—At the psychological level, the typical problems to be investigated would be the individual's behavior as a function of the kind of family environment in which he exists; the individual's aggressive and submissive reactions to different types of family authority; the effects on the individual of introduction of new family members, as in sibling jealousy; the development, in the individual, of beliefs and attitudes as a consequence of familial training and experiences. All these and similar psychological problems would be investigated by studying the individual's psychological field, discovering the nature of his cognitions about the family as a whole and various family members, his need structure as it relates to his family activities, etc.

The group dynamic approach.—At the group dynamic level, the typical problems to be investigated about the family would be the varying structure and behavior of the family group under various conditions, such as external threat to the family's welfare; the shift in authority relationships at the death of a family member or the gain of a family member through marriage; how the family makes group decisions; how it does work that must be carried out cooperatively; how it participates in group play and recreation. All these and similar problems of group dynamics would be investigated by measuring and correlating indices of group rigidity and flexibility, loci of authority, group atmosphere, etc.

The institutional approach.—At the institutional level, the typical problems to be investigated would be the structure of families in various classes of society, such as rural, urban, wealthy, poor; the strength of the family structure and how it relates to juvenile delinquency, divorce, birth rate; changes in the family institution as related to economic depressions, war, changes in social mores. These typical problems would be investigated primarily by studying the correlations among the various indices of family structure and family strength and the various indices of economic status, religious faith, geographical location, criminal rates, marriage rates, birth rates, the nature of other dominant social organizations, etc.

It should be noted that in the first of these approaches we are primarily interested in Mr. Arbuthnot—his perceptions, his emotions, his goals in relation to his family. In the second approach we are interested in the Arbuthnot family and its members—their interrelationships, their mutual adjustments as reflected in changes in the whole family pattern, their "united front" against external threats. In the last approach we are interested in families and their reactions to all sorts of external events.

Complementary Relations of the Three Levels of Analysis.—A comprehensive analysis of social phenomena will necessarily involve study of *all three of these levels*. The three approaches are complementary and, in many instances, so interdependent as to make the interpretation of data collected at one level impossible without data collected at another level. Thus, for example, the beliefs and attitudes of an individual (a psychological problem) may be difficult to understand unless we know something about his group loyalties and group membership (a group dynamic problem) and something about his social class and the institutions within whose confines he is operating (an institutional or sociological problem).

For certain kinds of answers, however, one of these approaches will be preferable to the others. The principal caution to be observed by the social psychologist or sociologist is to avoid mixing up these three levels of analysis in a meaningless way. This danger is especially apparent when we seek explanations. Thus to assert that the reason Arbuthnot goes to church is given in the observed correlation between churchgoing and the socioeconomic level of which Mr. Arbuthnot is a member is an instance of attempting to answer a psychological question by reference to an institutional law. The reasons for Mr. Arbuthnot's churchgoing are to be found in an analysis of Mr. Arbuthnot's goals and cognitions and not in the characteristics of his social class.

Congruity of laws at the three different levels.—Although each of these three levels of social analysis must be kept conceptually and methodologically clean, we must still seek for meaningful relationships between data on one level and data on another level. Thus the laws of group dynamics must ultimately be brought into congruence with the laws of psychology, and the laws of sociology must ultimately be made congruent with the laws of group dynamics and psychology. The word congruent has been carefully chosen for this statement about the systematic relation of these three levels of social analysis. We do not mean to imply that sociological laws must be "reduced" to psychological laws. Nor do we mean that all three sets of laws must eventually become the same set of laws, any more than that the laws of atomic physics must become the same as the Newtonian laws of mechanics. What we mean is that the laws of sociology must not contradict any predictions that can be made reliably by the laws of group dynamics, which, in turn, must not contradict predictions made reliably by psychological laws.

Psychologists and sociologists.—It might be worth while to note, in passing, that the differences characteristic of the three methods of analysis are not always characteristic of the individual practitioners. Many a sociologist has done genuine psychological research, and many a psychologist has concerned himself with the institutional level of analysis. The nature of the problem, rather than the membership in a university department, determines the method of research and analysis. It would be fruitless to attempt to differentiate among social psychologists, group dynamicists, and sociologists on the basis of the specific research they do or the nature of the data and generalizations they use in their thinking. They, together with economists, political scientists, and anthropologists, are all *social scientists*.

THE PLAN OF THE BOOK

The principal way in which the present book differs from many other books on social psychology is in its insistence upon a *systematic* treatment of the field of social psychology. Our intention is (1) to clarify the basic psychological principles of motivation, perception, and learning and to generalize them so that they can be applied to social situations; (2) to establish the principles that govern the formation and operation of beliefs and attitudes; and (3) to see how these generalizations may be applied to concrete social problems of contemporary importance in order to understand these problems and, if possible, to aid in their solution. These three aspects of the plan correspond to Parts I, II, and III, respectively.

Part I: Analysis in Terms of Principles of Motivation, Perception, and Learning.—Social psychology, we have argued, is coextensive with all psychology, and the explanation of social behavior, like all individual behavior, is given in reference to basic principles of motivation, perception, and learning. The analysis of the individual's behavior proceeds by a determination of the properties of the psychological field of the individual—what his existent goals and his persistent tensions are, what he perceives and how he perceives it, how his perceptions are organized together to make up the cognitive structure of his psychological environment, and how the present organizations give way to subsequent organizations. These field properties, to repeat, can be understood in terms of the basic principles of motivation, perception, and learning, the development of which has been the major task of general psychology. For the most part, though not entirely, these principles have been formulated on the basis of experimental data from the laboratory in situations providing the possibility of strict experimental manipulation and control. Relatively little of this work has been done in the context of critical social situations—situations of interest in their own right and of the sort to which we here wish to apply these principles. Nevertheless it is reasonable to assume, as we do in this book, that such principles, no matter where developed, can be applied in connection with "social" situations. Caution is necessary in such application, of course, to make certain that the situation to which the generalizations are extended does not involve critical psychological features not included in the original laboratory situation.

Our task will not be to derive or substantiate these principles, but to list and illustrate them. The illustrations will be drawn from all areas of psychology. Nor will our task simply be to illustrate by reference to anthropological and other social science data that, for example, social mores or culture patterns "influence" perception. Such an exercise does not integrate fundamental principles with social phenomena. Our task, and it is important for the reader to grasp this objective, is to spell out, for systematic theoretical purposes, the operation of the laws of motivation, perception, and learning in social situations.

Part II: Social Processes.—In our analysis of the social behavior of the individual, we shall find that rather than dealing directly with the relationships between the individual's social behavior and his momentary perceptions, cognitions, emotions, and goals, it is possible—and probably essential—for us to study these relationships as mediated by certain types of enduring mental organizations of the individual, such as beliefs and attitudes. This analysis will be used in addition to the analysis in the first part of the book. As integrated complexes of motivational, emotional, and perceptual factors these beliefs and attitudes serve to regulate and direct the significant behavior of the individual. By dealing with these larger psychological units, therefore, it is possible to simplify the social psychological analysis.

In this part, also, two chapters will be devoted to the problem of the methodology of measurement of beliefs and attitudes. Also, in this section, we consider whether or not certain alleged "higher order" social psychological functions, particularly "suggestion" and "propaganda," are useful and meaningful units of analysis. Finally, we give a brief survey of salient facts and principles relating to the other two levels of social analysis—the group dynamic and the institutional.

Part III: Applications to Contemporary Social Problems.—The systematized set of concepts developed in Parts I and II are then applied in Part III to the analysis of a number of selected social problems of high contemporary significance. These problems include racial prejudice, industrial conflict, and international tensions. In treating these problems, both the analysis and suggested "cures" are presented.

In a real sense the usefulness of the analysis made in this part of the book can provide a measuring rod with which to determine the validity of the principles and theoretical structure elaborated in the first two parts. Valid *theoretical* principles must prove valid when applied to *practical* problems. A discrepancy between the two situations can mean either that our theoretical principles are not sound or that we have not applied them in a logical manner to the practical situation. This test is particularly relevant to a theory of social psychology.

SUMMARY

As a scientist, the social psychologist feels that he has much to offer toward the solution of social problems, but many leaders of society are reluctant to give social psychology the support it needs, and they resist the application of the science to current problems. Why?

Three reasons are suggested: (1) Unaware of the difference between scientific understanding and "common-sense" understanding, some people feel that scientific social psychological research is unnecessary; (2) there are those who are impatient with psychology because it does not already know all the answers; (3) there are those who fear that psychology knows too much and that a scientific analysis of society might jeopardize cherished beliefs and vested interests. In addition, the reluctance of the social psychologist to apply himself to important social questions and the lack of a sound theoretical foundation for his science have tended to decrease the applicability of social psychology to current social problems.

Whether we are interested in social psychology as a basic science or in its applications, an integrated set of principles is essential. To understand the role of such principles, these two aspects of social psychology are then examined.

As a basic science, social psychology, defined as the science of the behavior of the individual in society, does not differ in any fundamental way from psychology in general. This follows from three interrelated considerations: (1) The processes of motivation, perception, and learning are the same for the "social" behavior as for the "nonsocial" behavior of the individual; (2) it is impossible, practically, for any psychologist to study the behavior of a nonsocial man; (3) it is impossible, theoretically, to find a sharp point of transition between a social field and a nonsocial field.

As an applied scientist, the social psychologist operates as an analyst with respect to only one feature of any social problem—the behavior of the people who are involved. To do this, he must collect detailed data about each specific problem. Applying the basic principles of his science to these concrete data of the problem, he can help bring about an understanding of the problem and the behavior involved.

In seeking the basic principles, one can approach the data of social phenomena on three different levels: (1) the behavior of the individual, (2) the behavior of social groups (group dynamics), (3) the operation of social organizations. The first of these is the major method and objective of the present book. The advantages, limitations, and dangers inherent in each one of these methods are discussed. A comprehensive analysis of social phenomena will necessarily involve study on all three levels, but it is scientifically necessary to avoid using a law derived from one level of study in answering questions applicable to another level. Ultimately, however, the three different sets of laws must be brought into congruence with one another.

The plan of the present book differs from many other books on social psychology in its insistence upon a systematic treatment of the field of social psychology. It is intended (1) to clarify the principles of motivation, perception, and learning; (2) to establish the principles that govern the formation and operation of beliefs and attitudes and the functioning of higher order processes; (3) to see how these generalizations may be applied to concrete social problems of contemporary importance in order to understand these problems and, if possible, to aid in their solution.

BIBLIOGRAPHY

BROWN, J. F.: 1936. *Psychology and the social order.* New York: McGraw-Hill.

HARING, D. G.: 1947. Science and social phenomena. *Amer. Scientist,* **35,** 351–363.

HARTMANN, G. W.: 1936. A field experiment on the comparative effectiveness of "emotional" and "rational" political leaflets in determining election results. *J. abnorm. soc. Psychol.,* **31,** 99–114.

HYMAN, H. H.: 1942. The psychology of status. *Arch. Psychol.,* No. 269.

KÖHLER, W.: 1940. *Dynamics in psychology.* New York: Liveright.

KÖHLER, W., and WALLACH, H.: 1944. Figural after-effects: an investigation of visual processes. *Proc. Amer. phil. Soc.,* **88,** 269–357.

KRECH, D.: 1946. The challenge and the promise. *J. Soc. Issues,* **2,** No. 4, 2–6.

LINTON, R.: 1936. *The study of man.* New York: Appleton-Century.

SCHNEIRLA, T. C.: 1941. Social organization in insects, as related to individual function. *Psychol. Rev.,* **48,** 465–486.

SCHNEIRLA, T. C.: 1946. Problems in the biopsychology of social organization. *J. abnorm. soc. Psychol.,* **41,** 385–402.

SCHROEDINGER, E.: 1945. *What is life?* New York: Macmillan.

WYLIE, P.: 1947. (Excerpt from a review of *Modern Woman: The Lost Sex* by Ferdinand Lundberg and Marynia F. Farnham) *Sat. Rev. Lit.,* **30,** No. 5, 13–14.

CHAPTER II

THE DYNAMICS OF BEHAVIOR

The question of motivation is the question of "Why." Why does Mr. Arbuthnot go to church? Why does his brother go out on strike and parade in the picket line eight hours a day? Why did his congressman vote for war in 1917 and again in 1941? Why does his maiden aunt rigorously observe all the cultural taboos of her set? Why has his cousin joined the Communist party and his uncle the Republican party? The answers to these questions are usually given in terms of *individual motivation:* because Mr. Arbuthnot seeks social approval, because his brother seeks economic security, because his congressman was incensed by the actions of a foreign state, because his aunt seeks status security, because his cousin seeks to express his rebellion against the Arbuthnot family rules and regulations, while his uncle is afraid of losing the privileged position he now holds.

In any account of the behavior of people we start our description with reference to some kind of active, driving force: the individual seeks, the individual wants, the individual fears. In addition, we specify an object or condition toward which that force is directed: he seeks wealth, he wants peace, he fears illness. The study of the relationships between these two variables, the driving force and the object or condition toward which that driving force is directed, is the study of the dynamics of behavior, or motivation. And we shall find that the basic principles of dynamics accounting for the behavior of joining a church, going to war, choosing a mate, etc., are the same no matter how simple or how complex the activity.

Such principles, if they are to be helpful in making accurate predictions of individual behavior and in increasing our understanding of social phenomena, must answer such questions as the following: What induces these driving forces of wanting, seeking, fearing in the individual? What determines, for different individuals, the specific nature of the objects or conditions toward which these driving forces are directed? How does it happen that in achieving his goal the individual sometimes carries out this integrated series of acts and sometimes that series of acts? What happens when the individual, no matter how strong the driving force, fails to achieve his goal?

Knowing the answers to such questions we could then say something about other important questions: Does everyone have the same wants, needs, and

29

fears? Can an individual's wants, needs, and fears be changed? Can one goal be substituted for another goal to satisfy the same wants? How can conflicting demands be resolved?

The nature of the above questions suggests that their answers will involve basic principles of perception, thinking, and learning as well as of motivation. For when we talk about goals, we are obviously referring to goals as perceived by the individual, and immediately the problem of perception is involved; and when we talk about the individual doing this and that in order to arrive at the goal, we are talking about *adjustive* behavior and thinking, and immediately the problem of learning is involved. Despite the arbitrary demands of textbooks, man's behavior is not segmental—consisting of a chapter on motivation, a chapter on perception, a chapter on learning, etc. His integrated behavior involves all these processes simultaneously.

In the present chapter on motivation, therefore, we will find it necessary to make occasional forward references to the material of the following chapters on perception and learning and to anticipate briefly some of the discussion found there.

Propositions.—Our discussion of the basic principles of motivation, perception, and learning will take the form of a set of propositions, representing generalizations about available facts and theories that are helpful in understanding social behavior. *In no sense are they intended as comprehensive principles sufficient to account for all aspects of the psychology of motivation, perception, and learning; they are meant as convenient ways of organizing our thinking about and discussion of social behavior, and they cover only those aspects of motivation, perception, and learning which seem essential to an understanding of social behavior.*

The propositions concerning motivation that are presented in this chapter treat emotional behavior as inseparable from the dynamics of behavior. Emotions and emotionality are intrinsic aspects of the motivational process. Strong motives *are* emotional, and fears and loves and hates *do* motivate.

PROPOSITION I

The proper unit of motivational analysis is molar behavior, which involves needs and goals

This first proposition has two values: (1) It establishes the unit of analysis that is the most fruitful to use in studying the behavior of men; (2) it emphasizes the indispensability of needs and goals in a meaningful account of the dynamics of behavior.

Unit of Analysis.—Of first importance in our analysis is the decision as to the units of behavior to be employed. Shall we be concerned with more simple, segmental activities such as muscle twitches, movements of the limbs, swallowing, sweating, swearing, and the like, or shall we be concerned with total *behavior acts*, such as getting married, voting for a political candidate, participating in a lynching? The former is a "molecular" unit, and the latter a "molar" unit.[1] It is with the latter that we shall be concerned in this book.

In the absence of molar units, the description of behavior can be little more than an enumeration of unsystematized bits and pieces of momentary, limited, and unrelated responses. Viewed wholly, in the context of needs and goals, on the other hand, the behavior of the individual can be seen as meaningfully organized. The unity implied in the molar description is not something arbitrarily imposed by the psychologist in viewing the individual as he behaves; the individual is a dynamic unity, a whole person, and it is as such that he takes part in social phenomena.

The distinguishing features of molar behavior are (1) that it includes all the behavior of the individual occurring at the same time (his needs, emotions, thoughts, perceptions, actions, etc.) and (2) that it consists of relatively discrete, unified episodes with a beginning and an end. There are, of course, no discontinuities in the individual's stream of activities; one episode merges into the next. What gives unique character to each episode is the *direction* of behavior, *i.e.*, the tendency for each phase of the episode to succeed the preceding phase in a way that is consistent, bringing the end of the episode (the goal) closer and closer and thus reaching a point where the tensions that initiate and sustain the activity are eliminated. The beginning of Mr. Arbuthnot's lunchtime molar behavior is the onset of feelings of hunger; the end of the episode comes with the completion of eating and the feeling of satiety. Every aspect of his behavior during the episode is influenced and governed by the existence of the need and the goal; each successive step tends in the direction of goal achievement and tension reduction.[2]

The Initiating Bases of Molar Behavior.—Another importance of the first proposition lies in its denial of the explanatory value of such concepts as habit, conditioning, imitation, suggestion, and social custom in accounting for the driving power behind the individual's activity. People's be-

---

[1] The critical significance of the distinction in psychology between "molecular" and "molar" units of behavior was first emphasized by Tolman (1932). Lewin (1936), Murray (1938), Muenzinger (1942), and many others have since stressed whole behavior acts as indispensable units of analysis.

[2] For a valuable attempt to write a complete psychology in terms of "start-end" units of behavior, defined by the initiation of behavior by a need and the cessation of behavior by the achievement of a goal, see Muenzinger (1942).

havior is not initiated by habit or imitation or incorporated social norms; it is initiated through needs and guided by goals. Even those social acts which appear to be the most ritualized and autonomized must be viewed properly in the light of their functional utility for the person. This is not to deny the critical significance of imitation and suggestion, of custom and institution, in the determination of social behavior. They are critical, but their role is in shaping and determining needs, goals, perceptions, and meanings, not in operating directly to cause behavior.

Attitudes of people toward Russia, discriminatory practices against Jews, buying highly advertised brands of cigarettes are not be understood as "due to" habit or propaganda, but rather as adaptive acts which reduce tensions and help achieve goals. Thus, instead of saying that Arbuthnot dislikes the communists because of all the propaganda to which he has been exposed, a more fruitful description might be to say that Arbuthnot dislikes the communists because he has a need to be identified with the more solid members of his community, and one way to achieve such identification is to adopt an anticommunist attitude. Arbuthnot, in his beliefs and attitudes, is to be seen not as a passive victim of blaring propaganda, but as an adaptive individual, actively seeking ways and means, within the limits of his social environment, of achieving certain goals to satisfy certain needs.

The regular churchgoing behavior of people who demonstrate no religious needs may seem, on superficial analysis, to be a kind of meaningless, habitual, unmotivated act. Some atheists may admit that this churchgoer's predecessors, in founding the church, were driven by real needs and goals but will argue that the present churchgoer's behavior is in the nature of an unmotivated carry-over—a reaction to vestigial social norms and institutions. A proper molar analysis of the churchgoer's behavior will reveal it to be, on the contrary, a meaningful, motivated action, fulfilling present needs and goals of gregariousness, social approval, wealth display, rest, or something else. The church has acquired quite different meanings for the contemporary individual from those it had for his predecessors, but the very fact that he goes to church or is willing to support it or defend it or keep it tax-exempt is sufficient proof that it has the character of a goal for him.

In terms of our molar unit, then, the behavior of the individual is always concerned with needs and goals. If, in any given instance, this unit does not appear to be the most meaningful or useful, we must first reexamine the validity of our observations rather than the usefulness of this unit. Often a behavior may seem unmotivated because we have failed to identify correctly the need or goal involved, or because we have artificially abstracted a part of the individual's behavior from its integrated context.

Proposition II

The dynamics of molar behavior result from properties of the immediate psychological field

Our chosen unit of analysis at the psychological level is molar behavior—the whole behavior[1] of the individual. In endeavoring to answer the question "Why?" we shall have to study the dynamics of this molar behavior, *i.e.*, the adjustive changes that take place in any aspect of the molar behavior governed by the influences of other parts. (See the discussion of the term *dynamics* on page 19 of Chap. I.) What must be included in order that we may arrive at a full analysis of the dynamics of molar behavior? What various influences must be taken into consideration? Which ones may be excluded for the purposes of a dynamic motivational analysis?

The Immediate Psychological Field.—In answer to these questions, the above proposition asserts that what must be considered as giving rise to the dynamics of molar behavior are the properties of the immediate psychological field. What is the immediate psychological field? It can be thought of as a cross section, at a given moment, of the psychological existence of the individual. It includes only what is present at the moment, not what was present previously or what may be present in the future. In considering the whole developmental history of the individual, of course, what exists in the immediate present is merely an extension of what existed a moment before and is itself the immediate antecedent of what will exist a moment later. But we are not here concerned with the whole causal chain of events which gives rise to the individual's psychological existence at any moment; we are interested in the nature of the situation at that moment and in its dynamics.

The genetic vs. the immediate dynamic approach.—It is essential to make a clear distinction between the *immediate dynamic* problem—how the needs and goals of a given individual at a given time in a given situation determine his behavior—and the *genetic* problem—how these needs and goals and this situation have come into being in the course of the individual's development.

Lewin (1936) has stressed this difference in referring to the "historical" and the "systematic" concepts of causation in scientific explanation. If,

---

[1] In subsequent discussion, *behavior* will be taken to refer to the totality of the motor action and the perceptual and cognitive functioning of the individual. Thus, any changes in the psychological field that are the result of processes such as cognitive reorganization of the paths to a goal, which are other than the overt action of the person, will also be included under the general term behavior. When reference is simply to overt motor movements of the person, the term *action* will be used.

at a given moment, the psychological characteristics of the individual and the nature and content of his psychological environment are definable it, is possible, as Lewin points out, to arrive at a complete and self-contained explanation of the individual's behavior. This would be the systematic approach. It is permissible to lay aside the historical question, *i.e.*, the genetic problem of how it has come to pass that this particular need is operating at this moment, how this goal has emerged, and how this specific psychological environment has developed for the individual.

A comprehensive explanation of the "causation" of the individual's behavior will, of course, require a consideration of both the immediate dynamic and the genetic problems; but for most efficient analysis and to avoid conceptual confusion, the two should be kept separated. If we know that Mr. Arbuthnot has a need for social approval, that he recognizes that membership in the country club is likely to satisfy that need, and that he sees that one way to achieve membership is by associating with certain people and avoiding certain others, then we can, with considerable assurance, predict how he will behave toward the people and we can understand why he will behave in that way.

The clinician, the psychoanalyst, the child psychologist, the cultural anthropologist, the applied social psychologist may wish to study the developmental and socialization process by which this need for social approval has come into being for this man and why the achievement of a particular social role seems to him to be a way of satisfying his need, but such problems must be segregated from the problem of understanding what he does about it *now that these specific needs and goals exist*.

Confusion of the two approaches.—The failure to separate the two problems has often led to tortuous and incongruous motivational explanations of social behavior. Such explanations may frequently deteriorate into an endless search for the "ultimate," or "first," cause. If it be said that Mr. Arbuthnot seeks membership in the country club because he sees it as a goal of social approval, it is then asked why he seeks that goal. If it is answered that this goal has arisen because of a need for personal security, it is then asked why that feeling of insecurity arose. If it is answered that the feeling of personal insecurity has arisen because of a socially embarrassing speech defect that Mr. Arbuthnot has acquired, it is then asked why that speech defect. The answer may be that the speech defect was a defense against a precocious younger brother. Thus, at this stage, we are to understand that Mr. Arbuthnot seeks membership in the country club because his younger brother was precocious! But why stop here? The analysis can go as far as the ingenuity of the theorist will carry him, without ever really reaching the ultimate, or first, cause.

The above causal sequence may be plausible; but by the time it has been carried back several stages, the original problem of understanding and predicting Arbuthnot's present behavior has been lost sight of, and the analysis now lacks any immediate psychological meaningfulness. On the other hand, it is highly useful for diagnostic and predictive purposes simply to know that Arbuthnot's need for social approval and his recognition of membership in the country club as a means of achieving such approval do now exist. As such they can serve adequately in understanding his present behavior. The historical analysis, whether valid or not, is irrelevant for the problem of understanding present behavior.

Frequently it is assumed that motivational analysis in social psychology must follow the pattern of the "historical" or "genetic" approach. This belief that a motivational analysis is synonymous with a genetic analysis may be acribed in part to the influence of the traditional approach of the psychoanalyst, on the one hand, and of the biologically oriented psychologist, on the other.

The psychoanalytic approach.—The emphasis of the Freudian is primarily upon the genetic problem with the implication that behavior cannot adequately be explained in terms of the properties of the immediate psychological situation but must be referred back to the past history of the person.[1] Thus, to understand why a certain individual is ready to lead a revolt against a political authority, an orthodox Freudian might invoke the Oedipus complex in his historical-motivational analysis of this individual's social behavior. He might point out that in the development of the personality, the Oedipus stage is one through which all boys pass on their way to complete heterosexual maturity. Characterizing the Oedipus stage is the need to kill the father and possess the mother. This need is, of course, repressed, but the hostility against the father may manifest itself in the development of a general aggression against all authority figures and, specifically, against the political head of a state.[2]

Whether or not such an analysis of the *genesis* of a present social behavior is correct, it would seem dubious that it could account adequately for the *dynamics* of the present behavior. What is required, for immediate dynamic analysis, is the full definition of the psychological field of the individual at the present moment, not at critical moments in his past. Psychoanalytic

[1] Modern psychotherapy and analysis, it should be noted, have departed somewhat from the classical Freudian approach and are much more concerned with the immediate present than was Freud. See, for example, the writings of Fromm (1941) and Horney (1937, 1939, 1945).

[2] For an illustrative account of this type by an outstanding orthodox Freudian, see Ernest Jones (1941a) on the motivation of revolutionary behavior and (1941b) on the motivation of quisling behavior.

analysis may, it is true, even contribute something to a definition of what is immediately existent. Sometimes it is convenient or even necessary to ascertain the present needs, goals, and other psychological properties of the individual on the basis of a study of his developmental history. But this, it should be understood, is a mere substitute for more direct methods of ascertaining the relevant properties of the immediate situation.

Psychoanalytic methods have, as has been said, a commanding importance in the study of individual development and may, to the extent that developmental "trends" do operate lawfully, be highly significant in predicting the future development of the individual on the basis of his characteristic past history.

The biocentric approach.—In their treatment of the dynamics of the immediate psychological field there is a curious parallel between the psychoanalysts and the biocentric psychologists. For both, the meaning of present motivation is to be found in something other than what is definable strictly as part of the immediate psychological field. Just as the psychoanalyst directs his attention to the psychosexual past of the individual in the search for motivational meaning, so does the biocentric psychologist direct his attention toward the physiological instigators which he regards as the real source of all motivation.

Stomach contractions, dryness of the throat, swelling of the mammaries, hormone concentrations in the blood stream, and a host of other physiological irritations, deficiencies, and imbalances may, according to the biocentric psychologist, result in adjustive activities which persist until the effects of the physiological initiators are somehow removed. This is considered the basic picture of motivation.

Hunger, thirst, sex, activity, rest, elimination, and several others are called the *primary* drives. In response to these drives the individual learns, through experience, complex patterns of action that serve to reduce the drives. As part of this process, other internal and environmental stimuli come to be associated with, to "stand for," the original internal instigators. By this process of conditioning, these new stimuli become capable of eliciting the learned patterns of action. These, then, constitute *secondary*, or *derived*, drives.

In the biocentric view, these secondary, or derived, drives are relegated to a position subsidiary to that of the primary drives. The primary drives tend to be considered more basic, prior in time, more substantial, more dependable, and superior in potency. The secondary drives are often viewed as sorts of surrogates of the original internal instigators; thus, mother love may be reduced to the stimulating effects of ovarian hormone.

The biocentric view is most closely identified with behavioristic and stimulus-response theories of psychology. It is not likely to be found among motivational theorists, even of these schools, in the stark simplicity described above. But without question, the biocentric approach does tend to emphasize the physiological genesis of all motivation, at the expense of its treatment in the immediate dynamic situation.

The motivational analysis of social behavior, however, is not limited to the methods of the Freudian or of the biocentric psychologist. We can treat all motives as contemporaneous, without respect to their biological foundation or their genesis in the past experiences of the individual.

Feasibility of the immediate dynamic approach.—Is the immediate dynamic approach practicable? Can the psychological field, corresponding to a cross-section slice in time of the continuously functioning person, be abstracted for study of its dynamics? Ideally no, for it is never the case that we may freeze a moment in time, like a motion-picture projector stopped for study of a "still." While we study the moment, the moment is already past and a new psychological field exists.

The practical solution to this obvious difficulty is to examine fairly short intervals of time in the stream of behavior of the individual. Changes in the psychological field are not always so rapid as to escape the experimenter. In some cases, and indeed in most cases of importance for the problems under consideration in this book, the dynamics of the psychological field are relatively slow. It is possible to record and measure dynamics by an observation of the properties of the individual's psychological field at several short, successive stages in time. Even with considerable separation in time it is usually possible to study the revealed dynamics.

What is done, then, is to analyze the structure of a given psychological field and at a later point—sometimes immediately, sometimes remotely—to reanalyze the field. In so far as it has been possible to exclude the intruding effects of any "alien" factors (arising out of the physiological, or external, environment of the person) during this time interval, changes in the field may safely be ascribed to dynamic principles, based solely upon the properties of the field itself.

The meaning of the "psychological field."—Basic to an understanding of the present and the succeeding propositions, is the concept of psychological field. By psychological field is meant a state of neuropsychic processes that are reflected in the form of the *experienced* world of the individual and in the form of *patterns of neural processes in the brain* of the individual. The psychological field is not identical with the experiences of the individual, for there are important constituents of the neuropsychic process that are unconscious, *i.e.*, do not result in immediate experiences by the individual.

From the above definition it can be seen that the psychological field is produced through influences arising from three sources: (1) the external physical environment of the person, (2) his internal physiological state, and (3) neural "traces" of past experiences. The psychological field, at any moment, is a dynamic unity of these various effects, for interaction among these effects is the rule. As a dynamic unity resulting from these effects, however, the psychological field is different from any one of these and must not be identified with them. Thus, what goes on in the neuropsychic processes is different from what exists in the external physical environment— the "real" environment. The real environment of a person is that environment which would be described by an objective observer; the psychological environment is that which would be described by the experiencing person himself. For example, suppose we consider the case of a prisoner at the bar. His real environment might be described in terms of the chairs, railings, people, and other objects that are in the room. His psychological environment might be quite differently described—the people might look "forbidding," the whole room "threatening," the railings suggestive of prison bars. How different this same real environment would appear to the policeman, for example. The very same physical environment can result in radically different psychological environments for two different persons.

Similarly, the real internal physiological condition of the individual, as described by a physiologist, will differ from the individual's perception or experience of his own internal state. The common observation that amputees frequently experience the feeling of pain in the toe of a leg which has already been amputated is a striking illustration of this difference. The physiologist talks of referred pain, i.e., pain that the person experiences in one organ but that the physiologist knows derives from the malfunctioning of quite a different organ.

Finally, the real past history of the individual differs from his present memory of that history. The immediate psychological field is significantly affected by the series of physical situations and physiological states through which the individual has previously passed. These past situations are currently represented by the brain traces of the neuropsychic processes to which they gave rise. That is, the past is carried in the present, in the form of such traces. But it is important to note that these traces differ from the real past in two ways: (1) These traces are not of the real physical and physiological conditions to which the individual was exposed—they are records of the past psychological fields through which the person has passed; (2) the present neural trace may differ radically from the trace that was originally laid down when the event was first experienced; i.e., the process of "forgetting," as it were, has changed the individual's past.

In summary, then, what exists in the real physical environment, the physiological conditions of the internal organs, and the brain traces of past events determine in a lawful manner the psychological field of the person, but there is far from a one-to-one correspondence between these real worlds and the psychological field.

Alien factors.—We have said above that changes in the psychological field may be ascribed to dynamic principles based solely upon the properties of the fields themselves, *but only in so far as we can exclude the intruding effects of alien factors.* Alien factors are changes in the external or internal environments of the person that are not brought about by the operation of dynamic principles but are brought about independently. Thus, for example, suppose we were to study the changes brought about in a person's psychological field as a consequence of his assumption of a new leadership position. On the basis of our dynamic principles, we might be able to predict what this new psychological field would be like—what changes would occur in his interpersonal relations, his attitudes toward authority, law and order, etc.— once he becomes a leader. However, suppose that just after he became a leader some unforeseen catastrophic event occurred in his life—he lost his personal fortune on the stock market, and his doctor told him that he had a cancerous growth. These alien factors would undoubtedly influence his psychological field and throw askew all of our predictions based upon our analysis of his previous field and the operation of dynamic principles. In other words, even having valid dynamic principles is not sufficient to make complete predictions about the future behavior of the individual unless the alien factors also can be predicted.

This is the reason that psychologists cannot be expected to provide *concrete* predictions; all that they can do is to provide *conditional* predictions; *i.e.*, if such and such conditions prevail, the person will do so and so. The prediction of whether or not such conditions are likely to prevail is not the task of the psychologist, but of the doctor, the economist, the sociologist, the meteorologist, the biologist, etc.

General Comments.—Proposition II defines the method of approach that is most useful in analyzing all aspects of the behavior of man—his needs, his perceptions, his action. It stresses the desirability and feasibility of looking for the properties of his behavior in the present nature of the psychological field rather than in the history of their past development. If we wish to explain and predict the behavior of a ball set into motion down an incline, it is not relevant to ask how the ball got to the top. Whether it was pushed there or deposited there or manufactured there tells us nothing about its subsequent action. What is relevant are the properties of the immediate situation: the weight of the ball, the steepness of the incline, the frictional constants, etc. No matter how the ball got to the top of the incline, given these properties, its behavior on free descent (without the intervention of alien factors) will be predictably the same.

In the analysis of tensions, needs, and goals (the major purpose of this chapter) in the succeeding propositions, our concerns will be with the nature of the *immediate psychological field* rather than with the past experiences of the subject (an approach characteristic of the Freudian-minded psychoanalyst) or the assumed "original" physiological instigators of needs (an approach characteristic of the biocentric psychologist).

PROPOSITION III

Instabilities in the psychological field produce "tensions" whose effects on perception, cognition, and action are such as to tend to change the field in the direction of a more stable structure

The pattern of the psychological field is not rigid; it is constantly subject to change due to the dynamic interaction of its parts. This pattern is likely at any given moment, therefore, to be in some way *unstable*. By "instability" is meant that the way in which the various parts of the psychological field are organized is likely to involve some degree of disharmony, discrepancy, imbalance, lack of "closure," and the like. These instabilities are stresses in the imperfect pattern, which are called *tensions*.[1] And it is tensions that lie behind restlessness, anxiety, desires, needs, and demands —in a word, behind that aspect of behavior we refer to as "motivation."

The Effects of Tensions.—Tensions, according to Proposition III, derive from the psychological field and, in turn, effect changes in the psychological field. Tensions are not mere passive conditions; they supply the potential for active forces of readjustment in the psychological field. Their effects are widespread. They are frequently accompanied by significant conscious correlates in the psychological field of the individual; they induce goals that demand action on the part of the individual; they influence the perception and thinking of the individual in such a manner as to make certain paths to a goal outstanding; they result in a higher level of reorganization of the entire psychological field. Each one of these effects will be discussed in detail here and under the following propositions. However, common to all of these effects is the fact that *the changes which tensions produce in the psychological field are all tension reductive.* Some of these changes involve action, which brings about the same effect; some, redistribution and overflow of tension, which also eventuate in tension reduction; and some of these changes can restructure the entire personality, which also

---

[1] The significance of the concept of "tension" in the psychology of motivation was first made clear in a systematic manner by Kurt Lewin. See especially his *Dynamic theory of personality* (1935).

can reduce existing tensions. Illustrations of each of these will be given throughout this chapter and the two following chapters.

While tensions persist until they are dissipated by the removal of the imbalance or instability,[1] it is important to recognize, however, that not all states of tension succeed in reordering the field in a way that will reduce the tension. What characterizes all the effects of tension is the common direction they take, *viz.*, toward tension reduction. Where tension is not successfully reduced, we find ourselves dealing with *maladjustment*. Another point must be made clear in connection with the tension-reductive concept prior to our detailed consideration of it. To say that tension has been reduced in a psychological field is not equivalent to saying that a state of "static equilibrium"—a dead level—has been achieved. To anticipate our discussion of Proposition VI (pages 66*ff.*), it must be clear that the history of the psychological field of the individual does not involve a series of excursions away from a stable state and return to the same state. It is, rather, a history of changing equilibriums, in which the psychological field restructures continuously, never returning to a state in which it existed before. Thus, an individual who, by achieving a certain goal, reduces the tensions that initiated his action toward that goal does not thereby become "satisfied." His very achievement of the goal has so restructured his psychological field as to make possible all sorts of new instabilities and tensions, make desirable new kinds of goals, induce new aspirations, etc.

Conscious correlates of tension.—In some aspects tensions have conscious correlates; in others not. To the problem of unconscious motivation we will turn later.

The conscious correlates of tension take various forms: (1) as vague feelings of restlessness, dissatisfaction, discomfort, tenseness, or anxiety, having no specific reference to any explicit features of the field; (2) as feelings of desires, wishes, wants, needs directed toward explicit features of the field, which are apprehended as desired, wished for, wanted, or needed things; (3) as demands perceived as emerging from explicit features of the field, which are apprehended as requiring something of the person.

1. *Vague feelings.* Often an individual feels restless or disturbed or "moody" without being able to characterize his feelings in a meaningful way, without perceiving any particular source of his feelings, and without

---

[1] Ovsiankina (1928) has shown, for example, in an experiment where subjects worked on a series of tasks some of which they were permitted to complete, and some of which were interrupted prior to completion, that the subjects spontaneously tended to resume the incomplete tasks (when the experimenter went out of the room and left the subjects to their own devices). Here the effect of the persisting tension induced by an "incomplete task" was the direct one of reinstituting action toward completion.

knowing what he wants or what he feels like doing. Sometimes, the basis of such vague feelings is the existence of mild tensions, which often are the forerunners of more intense states of growing tension. As the tension increases, in these instances, the vague feelings may give way to more crystallized feelings of specific needs or emotions, which the individual is able to recognize and to adjust to meaningfully. For instance, Arbuthnot rises in the morning experiencing a vague feeling of anxiety but being uncertain as to the exact nature of his mood, its cause, or what he should do about it. Then, as during the morning the tension increases, he suddenly remembers an important conference that he is to have with his boss later in the day. He now feels a clearly recognizable emotion of dread about the conference, and he rushes off to make some last-minute preparations for it.

Sometimes, these uncrystallized feelings, which have no specific reference to particular features of the field, can be quite intense, and the tensions underlying them quite extreme. Clinical practice abounds in cases of people who experience intense and continuous "free-floating anxiety" and "free-floating aggressiveness," which are not recognized by the individual as relating to any particular features of the field and which do not make manifest any particular way in which the tensions are to be resolved. Such free-floating feelings are likely to spread into all aspects of the individual's personality and to influence all of his behavior.

2. *Needs and goals.* Tensions often manifest themselves in the individual's consciousness as feelings of needs and emotions. And in connection with these experiences of needs and emotions, certain features of the field are apprehended as desired, sought after, needed, etc. These things are called *goals.* Mr. Arbuthnot feels hungry and wants food; he feels loneliness and seeks companions; he feels fear and looks for a place of safety. Food, companions, and a place to hide are goals. Properly speaking, the goals are not food and companions and places, as objects, *but actions with respect to these objects,* viz., eating food, being with companions, and hiding in a safe place. But for purposes of convenience, we will, in referring to goals, speak of the object rather than the desired relation or activity with the object.

3. *Demands.* Not only has Mr. Arbuthnot feelings of need which he seeks to satisfy through the attainment of appropriate goals, he also feels "ordered," or "driven about," as it were, by demanding aspects of his psychological field. Demands may be perceived by the person as arising in objects or people who exist as features of the psychological field *outside* himself, or they may be perceived as arising from *within* his own body. As examples of the former, an unpleasant task is perceived as if it itself demands to be finished; a parental command is perceived as demanding obedience;

a moral conscience is perceived as something "out there" that demands the relinquishment of something which is wanted. As examples of the latter, an insistent headache, perceived as being within one's own body, demands remedy; an uncomfortably full bladder demands relief.

Goals once set up in conjunction with needs may, in time, assume something of this demand character; these goals themselves are perceived as *demanding* attainment, *compelling* sustained effort in their direction. But goals are differentiable from other demanding aspects of the field in that they are perceived as ways of satisfying desires, wishes, needs. Goals and needs are resonant, as it were. Demands, on the other hand, require no supplementary or reciprocal need. It would be redundant in the above examples to introduce a "need" to finish the unpleasant task, to obey, to satisfy the moral conscience, to cure the headache, to micturate. In carrying out these demands the individual does not feel that he is satisfying desires; he feels that he is doing what he "has to."

By what means do some features of the psychological field assume demand-character? For one thing, demand-character is partly intrinsic—insistent pain calls for relief, a novel object demands exploration. For another thing, demand-character is partly dependent upon tensions—food looks more demanding to a starving man than to one only slightly hungry. For a third thing, demand-character depends upon past experiences with the object—a hot stove demands avoidance by the burned child.[1]

Unconscious motivation.—The effects of tensions may be perfectly apprehended by the individual, or they may be hidden from him. In the latter case we speak of unconscious motivation.

Under the influence, partly, of the rationalistic tradition it was for a long time the accepted psychological view that *all* motivation is conscious. Man, as an intellectualizing organism, was assumed to be always capable of properly recognizing his needs and consciously directing his activities toward their satisfaction. Where such analysis did not succeed fully in explaining a behavior, the realm of motivation was left and explanations were sought for in other "mechanisms"—in habit, imitation, suggestion, etc.

The greatest contribution of Freud was in his effective challenge of this traditional view. A great proportion of the motivational life of the individual, Freud asserted, is unconscious. He is not aware of the real nature

[1] This should not be interpreted as a view that demand-character develops through "conditioning," *i.e.*, by the mere accident that the stimulus of the hot stove and the response of avoidance were previously found in close temporal contiguity. It is preferable to consider that the hot stove has, through the previous experience, acquired a "meaning" for the individual. His action with respect to the stove and its demand-character in future situations depends upon that meaning in the context of the whole situation, not upon a conditioned response. Tolman's (1932) concept of "sign-gestalt" is applicable here.

of his tensions or the real meaning of the actions in which he engages. Not only to others, but to the individual himself, his behavior may often appear irrational, purposeless, unorganized. Yet if, through deep analytical procedures, the underlying motivation is laid bare, the behavior of the individual is then understood as meaningful, purposive, and organized. Whether or not the person is conscious of his motives, they seem to work in their own dynamic fashion, guiding his behavior as though independent of conscious direction.

Not only did Freud emphasize the role of unconscious motives in accounting for otherwise inexplicable acts, he went much farther in denying the psychological validity of much of the manifest content of conscious motives. Conscious motives, he warned, should not be accepted at face value. Frequently they serve merely as rationalizing "cover" for the functioning of unconscious motives. Though superficially explicable in terms of conscious motives, a man's behavior may actually be understandable only if the unconscious side is revealed. For if the real motives are of such a character as to be repugnant and to conflict with the individual's moral, social, and ego values, they may be repressed (forgotten or made unconscious), and other more acceptable, but spurious, motives consciously reinstated in their place.

For our present purposes the significance of the concept of unconscious motivation is threefold: (1) It warns against accepting much of the conscious motivation of social action at face value; (2) it points to the necessity for use of deep methods of analysis in the search for the underlying unconscious motives which are so frequently involved in social behavior; (3) it points to the fact that motives often become unconscious because of the social situation, which makes for conflict of motives through the existence of social mores, taboos, etc.

One strong note of caution should be sounded. Freudianism has dethroned the conscious and enthroned the unconscious in its place. In so doing there has probably been an overcorrection of the earlier bias. Because some motives are unconscious need not impugn the meaningfulness of all conscious motives.

Nor does the acceptance of unconscious motives demand allegiance to the general Freudian view of motivation, which in rejecting the functional autonomy of present, conscious needs seeks always to trace the motive back to unchanging, unconscious sources which developed in the psychosexual past of the individual. Unconscious motivation is not inconsistent with our second proposition. Whether conscious or unconscious, motives function now and in their own right, determined by their present nature and regardless of how they came into being. And whether conscious or unconscious, they are expressed in behavior that, by the modification of the person and the psychological situation, may prepare the way for the emergence of new motives.

The Variability of Needs and Demands.—Instinct and neo-instinct theories of motivation assume that the number and kind of man's needs and demands are innately and unalterably fixed. These theories differ among themselves in the number of such basic needs and demands that they postulate and in their classification, but they all agree in asserting the permanent unchangeability of the inventory of needs and in denying the possibility of the emergence of new and different needs, uniquely developed in the course of the individual's socialization. These theories agree that though goals related to needs may change and the psychological environment may change, the fundamental needs and demands remain the same.

The implication of Proposition III, however, is that the number and kind of man's needs and demands are not permanently established but are, on the contrary, constantly subject to change. As new tensions arise, new needs and demands may appear, old ones may disappear, and these new needs and demands do not derive their present driving power from prior needs and demands out of which they developed. This view is congruent with the central part of the doctrine of functional autonomy advanced by Allport (1937). But instead of saying that mechanisms can become drives, as Woodworth (1918) originally expressed it, it would be better to say that mechanisms can so function as to bring about the *conditions for the appearance of new needs and demands*. It is not that activity which is long pursued eventually becomes needed or demanded in its own right but that such activity serves to modify the psychological environment in such a way as to create the essential conditions (instabilities) which establish a new need or demand.

An example.—To take a simple example, dear to the heart of the cynic. A man of great wealth finds that his ruthless business practices have made him an object of hatred and scorn in his country. He grows old, gets religion, and begins to worry about his soul. He needs social approval, and he needs it desperately. On the advice of his friends he hires an eminent public-relations expert, who advises our millionaire to become a great philanthropist—to give large sums of money to churches, universities, research foundations, hospitals, libraries, etc. This is done, and gradually the name that was anathema to the public becomes highly respected. But the millionaire continues to give money to the support and expansion of these many institutions. Why?

The answers of those who take the instinctive or the "mechanisms become drives" approach to motivation might be that this behavior is still an attempt to satisfy the "basic" need that was assumed to be initially responsible for his philanthropic gestures or else that through habitual money giving, this behavior has become a "drive." In terms of Proposition III, however, the answer would be that this behavior may be due to *new* needs or demands not necessarily related to the earlier needs or demands. Our millionaire, in giving money to public institutions, has met theologians, scientists, philosophers, writers, doctors—people whom he had not known on intimate terms before. He may have become interested in new concepts; he has been exposed to new ideas, talked with men of strange enthusiasms. All this could very well have altered his cognitive structure, his range of appreciations, and even his personality structure in such ways as to invoke new needs and demands. As was suggested on page 41, new experiences, arising out of an attempt to meet old needs, may bring about new imbalances and instabilities in the psychological field. These, in turn, may give rise to new needs and demands.

The emergence, full blown, of a need to support public activities and do good may be accounted for, in many instances, in a way that is no more mysterious than the emergence, full blown, of a need for calcium in the pregnant woman. A pregnant woman or lactating mother characteristically experiences a new and sudden need relating to calcium, far more intense than she has ever previously experienced. This need is not an inevitable one in the life of this woman; for if she had not become pregnant, she would never have experienced it in this form and intensity. Nor has the need appeared through "learning." What has happened is that a new organization of neural processes, partly affected by the internal deficits of calcium in the pregnant condition, has given rise to tensions that manifest themselves as needs and demands relating to calcium (or rather to the eating of calcium-rich foods and substances).

Unlimited potentialities of needs and demands.—Tensions (reflected in experience as needs and demands) develop out of instabilities in the total momentary configuration of the neuropsychic system. The importance of this for the question of invariance of needs and demands is in the fact that the very nature of the neuropsychic system can be assumed to be such that it has potentialities of entertaining a vast and perhaps unlimited number of different unstable configurations and hence of different needs and demands.

Whether any or all of these potential ones get set up in the course of a given individual's development depends entirely upon the precise conditions of the physiological and physical environments that have existed. Every change in the physiological picture and every change in the social situation has the potentiality of resulting in new needs and demands. The possible number and their nature are indeterminable, although the number appearing in a single individual's life must be quite limited.

There is no set of fixed needs and demands—limited, immutable, inescapable, universal. The illusion of universality is a consequence of biological regularities characterizing the physiological environments of all people living under similar physical conditions and of socially determined uniformities in the psychological environments of the members of a given culture. Thus, for example, the Eskimo has an almost universal need for blubber and fats, and the German people may show an almost universal acquiescence to the demands of authority. Remove the Eskimo child to a more temperate zone and the German child to a more permissive culture, and these needs and demands may be greatly altered.

Can human nature be changed?—Many lay social psychologists—politicians, military leaders, businessmen—demonstrate their faith in a maxim which seemingly contradicts the view that needs and demands are infinitely variable. This maxim is popularly phrased, "You can't change human nature," and it is used to defend a belief that such motives as those involved in authority, in profit, and in war are universal and unchangeable.

Can human nature be changed? The answer depends, of course, upon what is meant by human nature. If we in our particular culture, society, social group define human nature by what we see of ourselves, in terms our needs and demands and *our* ways of expressing and satisfying them, the maxim, as is indicated by everything that follows from Proposition false. In other cultures, societies, and social groups, there are other teristic needs and demands and other characteristic ways of expressing sfying them. This is fully attested to by a mass of anthropological logical observation. Looked at in this way, there is not one ture, but many—as many as there are cultures, societies, and s.

sense (though this is not what is usually implied in the popular ich human nature can be said to be unchangeable. If by e refer to the basic *principles of dynamics* which govern the psychological field, then it is true to say "You can't change ll people in all cultures behave according to the same es of dynamics. Thus, for example, the existence of rsally to behavior that is in the direction of tension n III); interference with tension reduction does ll indicate) result universally in definable types maladaptive sort.

nands.—As has been previously indicated, lyst and by the biocentric psychologist ic question of the origin and develop- t they are not of primary value in obtaining a description and a measurement of the present needs and demands. Methods by which the present needs and demands can be ascertained and measured fall into three types: (1) those which make inferences from present behavior, (2) those which utilize "introspective" descriptions of the immediate psychological field of the individual, and (3) those employing various kinds of "projective" techniques. These three methods are complementary, and all are likely to be used in any investigation of motivation.

Inferences from behavior.—In the first method, characteristics of the actual behavior of the individual in any given situation are made the basis of inferences about the effective needs and demands that are driving him. For instance, the observation that the cessation of a period of activity is marked by eating food may lead to the inference that a hunger need and a demand for food were operative. A consistent behavior of avoidance of a given object may lead to an inference that a feeling of fear or disgust or dislike of the object was operative.

A list of the different behavioral indices by which existing motives ca[n] be ascertained would include the following:[1]

1. A typical behavioral trend, directed toward and terminating in achievement of a given goal

2. A typical mode of behavior

3. The search for, avoidance or selection of, attention and respons[e] specific object or class of objects

4. The exhibition of a characteristic feeling or emotion

5. The manifestation of satisfaction with the achievement of goal or the manifestation of dissatisfaction when there is failure a specific goal.

Obviously, no one of these indices taken by itself can be exp[ected] an infallible indication of the underlying motives, but some taken together will often prove diagnostic. Thus, for exam[ple] to ascertain the momentary needs and demands of a ma[n] servation of his behavior yields the following facts: [he] about the room, never stopping to talk to anyone, nev[er] place, until finally he stops by another guest—a [celebrity] length to him; he follows the celebrity around the versations in which the celebrity is engaged; he conversation or other activity in which the appears pleased and happy when the cel[ebrity] and dissatisfied when the celebrity tu[rns]

[1] This list is substantially a modification of (1938).

might lead one to the inference that the man was motivated, in this situation, by a need for social prestige and that this need was being served through his identification with the celebrity.

That this reliance upon behavioral indices alone might result in erroneous inferences about motives is clear. Often quite different motives may manifest themselves in behaviors that look alike. Thus, the actual fact might be that the man at the party was not at all motivated, in that situation, by a need for social prestige but by a wish to sell the celebrity some insurance; the party provided him with a good opportunity to get on intimate terms with his victim.

In order to avoid such mistaken inferences, a motivational analysis based on behavioral criteria should be supplemented, wherever possible, by the other two methods—introspective and projective.

The introspective method.—A great deal about motives can be revealed by the introspective method, *i.e.*, use of the person's report of his immediate experience. For each of the behavioral criteria listed above there is likely to be an experienced correlate: The individual can report directly on his feelings of needs and demands, on the existence of perceived goal objects, his emotions, on his feelings of success or failure.

It is not to be assumed, however, that these introspective data necessarily tell the truth about his motivation in a direct way. In the case of unconscious motives, direct conscious correlates of states of tensions do not exist. For example, the member of a local watch and ward society who says that he reads pornographic literature through a sense of duty, because he wants to keep such material from corrupting the innocent, may actually be motivated by unconscious sexual tensions. His direct introspective report might tell nothing about that aspect of his motivation. He is not aware of this manifestation of a sex tension.

In the case of such unconscious motivation, however, a proper analysis of the introspective account, with its description of the appearance of various features of the individual's psychological field, may help the analyst serve to reveal the unconscious dynamics.

Projective techniques.—Projective techniques,[1] supplemented by other

<hr>

[1] Frank gives the following definition of projective techniques: "A projective technique for study of personality involves the presentation of a stimulus situation designed or chosen because it will mean to the subject not what the experimenter has arbitrarily decided it should mean . . . but rather whatever it must mean to the personality who gives it, or imposes upon it, his private, idiosyncratic meaning and organization." For further discussion of the way an individual imposes upon a "stimulus situation" his "private idiosyncratic meaning and organization," see Chap. III. For a comprehensive review of projective techniques and their

sorts of tests, are the other main source of data on the individual's existing motives. By analyzing the individual's perception of a set of standardized ink blots or the meanings he ascribes to a set of ambiguous pictures, it has been found possible to learn a great deal about his present, driving motives. And it matters not whether the motives be conscious or unconscious, for the essence of the projective method is that the individual is unaware of what his responses reveal.

All of the above suggests that a proper description of social behavior (which must start with an analysis of the motivations of people) requires the insights, concepts, and techniques of the clinician no less than those of the social psychologist. Taken together, the behavioral approach, as embodied in the work of descriptive studies; the introspective approach, as embodied in the clinical interview; and the approach by projective techniques and other tests constitute the main avenues for the exploration of human motivation.

PROPOSITION IV

The frustration of goal achievement and the failure of tension reduction n lead to a variety of adaptive or maladaptive behaviors

When progress toward a goal is blocked and the underlying tension solved, we speak of *frustration*. Such thwarting of needful, goal-di behavior is a very common occurrence in all man's social activiti consequences are critical and manifold. New ways of satisfyir occur primarily as a consequence of frustration; changes in perce cognition follow frustration; severe emotional states are enge frustration; the structure of the individual's personality may b by frustration and by his mode of adaptation to successive racial prejudice, gang fights and wars, religious behavior, an tant social phenomena can frequently be understood in ter quences of frustration.

Sources of Frustration.—What frustrates man's m situations that bring about frustrations are, of course. all be traced to four main categories of sources: (1) ment, (2) man's biological limitations, (3) the com logical make-up, (4) the nature of man's social e

The physical environment.—The characteri ment provide the most obvious types of obs thirst need of a man lost on the desert physical absence of water and the ph A farmer in the dust bowl for whom faction of a variety of needs is frustrated by droughts and winds. A lonely man in solitary confinement is thwarted by the walls of his cell.

The biological limitations.—Often the thwarting agents lie not in the physical environment but in the biological limitations of the individual himself— in his motor and mental incapacities, in his structural deficiencies. A man may be a cripple and hence unable to achieve the fame he desires as an athlete; he may be ugly and hence unable to win a lover or a mate; he may lack the necessary intelligence to pass through medical school and hence be unable to satisfy his desire to be a doctor.

Doubtless these biological limitations, particularly those which set off the individual as less able than his fellow men, are potent sources of frustration. Adler (1925) has made of such biological deficiencies the basis of an entire theory of maladjustment and adjustment in the development of personality.

Psychological complexity.—Man is not psychologically "unicellular." He is not subject to only one stimulus at a time or required to make only one response at a time. He is remarkably complex, existing at every moment a number of simultaneous, overlapping psychological situations. The wihness of the psychological field makes possible the arousal of many needs or s many demands at the same time. These needs and demands often of oaete and conflict, and the nature of the situation is such that the satisthen n of one need or demand may mean the frustration of others. A man III, isish to be married and, at the same time, desire not to leave his mother. characc have a need for economic security in a prosaic job and a longing for and satid adventure. He may wish to aggress against a hated rival and and sociur the social disapproval of those who abhor aggression. human naïably safe to say that virtually every need or demand that man social grouṗ the cost of a frustration, however temporary or however mild,

There is a concurrent need or demand.

maxim) in whvironment.—The social environment is probably the most human nature wof deep and persistent frustrations and the most significant functioning of the į Such frustrations are also the most resistant to remedy. human nature." A individual with all sorts of mores, regulations, rituals, set of basic principlequently serve to build up more or less impermeable tension does lead univusfaction of his needs and demands. It sets up an reduction (our Propositicthat man satisfy essential needs through money (as the next proposition with of money a difficult and, at times, impossible of changes of an adaptive ana class systems, preventing or hindering free

Ascertaining Needs and De Ler of one caste or class may be thwarted the methods used by the psychoannnother and to acquire the privileges of may be useful in answering the genet ment of specific needs and demands, bu

The role of society and cultural mores in frustration is at times all important, *in that the very needs which a particular culture itself induces are thwarted by the structures and institutions of that society*. For instance, society may, through its educational philosophy, instill in the Negro a desire for a college education and then, through another of its cultural patterns—the institution of racial discrimination—make it impossible for the Negro to satisfy that desire. It may, through its democratic philosophy, instill a need for individual attainment in politics or social status or business and then through discriminations based on family background, wealth, etc., arbitrarily prevent certain individuals from satisfying these needs.[1]

Among society's most pervasive effects on the individual is the development in him of self-regard. Self-regard, essentially, is the social in man. Self-regard is related to one's conception of himself; his proper role in life; his ideals, standards, and values. And in connection with self-regard some of the most potent demands and needs of the individual develop.

It is just such demands and needs that society, through many of its complex cultural patterns, is best prepared to thwart. Ideals of moral goodness and badness, of right and wrong, run counter to other socially approved practices. The man who believes that shrewd practices and taking advantage of his fellow men are wrong finds himself forced to engage in shrewd practices if he is to satisfy other needs. Lying and insincerity are bad, but lying and insincerity are necessary if he is to live in peace with his neighbors and obey the requirements of social ritual. Discrimination against fellow human-beings is wicked, but discrimination is found necessary if he is to fit in and be accepted by his social set. Thus, Murphy, Murphy, and Newcomb (1937) give an interesting list of certain discrepancies between ideals that are taught to the child in our modern middle-class home and other demands the culture makes upon him:

1. Encouragement to make social contacts with everyone during the preschool period when the child is under constant protection of a parent or nurse

2. Warnings not to talk to strange people or people of another race or social class, not to play with the janitor's children or the children across the tracks

3. Contact with the intellectualism of democratic teachers or liberal churches who foster race and class equality in verbal terms

4. Being caught in the tense stratifications of adolescent social structure where "money" counts

5. Getting into the world of achievement in later high school and college

---

[1] One may speculate on the value of taking the extent to which a society frustrates the needs created by it as one objective and quantitative measure of the psychological goodness or badness of the society.

where success on the football team may cut across race and class lines to a degree

6. Finding that any democracy which may have been developed in college sports and intellectual life becomes a hindrance in the race for success in the business world.

Consequences of Frustration.—The sources of frustration are many. What are its consequences for the individual? The following introductory remarks about the consequences of frustration may be helpful:

1. *The potential consequences of frustration are very numerous.* Frustration may lead to many different types of changes in the psychological field. We shall list and discuss the most important of them. Every individual does, in one situation or another, experience every one of these various consequences, but it is likely that in any given instance of frustration only a limited number of these consequences occur.

2. *The consequences of frustration are dynamically interrelated.* The main implication of our treatment of the dynamics of behavior is that things happening in one part of the psychological field have effects pervading the entire field. Any single consequence of frustration, therefore, has effects upon and is, in turn, guided by other simultaneous consequences. The end resultant of the effects on the psychological field, through these various interacting consequences, is the reduction of tension. This means that the consequences of frustration are in some respects equivalent and substitutable. If frustration has an intense consequence of a certain kind, other consequences may be less likely to appear. Thus, for example, the man who "takes out his frustrations" by direct aggressive behavior against the block to his goal is less likely to engage in such frustration reaction as repression, The substitutibility of frustration reactions can sometimes be socially costly, as we shall see when we discuss *autism* (page 59).

3. *The nature of consequences depends partly upon the severity of frustration.* The intensity and duration of frustration depend upon the level of tension and upon the ease with which barriers to the goal may be overcome. Consequences will vary to some extent with the intensity and duration of frustration. The mild thwarting of a minor need will produce negligible consequences in the individual's behavior.[1] Persistent thwarting of an intense need will result in drastic psychological readjustment.

4. *The consequences of frustration are not necessarily bad.* Frustration is a bad word. It has come, for most people, to connote unhappy, tortured experience and neuroticism. This is unfortunate, and it is possible that a more neutral term, such as *blockage*, should be used. Some frustration does,

---

[1] Though we must not underrate the more severe behavioral consequences sometimes produced by a summation of many minor frustrations whose effects are cumulative.

as we shall see, have unhappy or even dangerous consequences for the person. But most of the blockages experienced by the person in his daily life are not deleterious in their effects; the tensions are resolved without disrupting the successful adjustment of the total person. Were this not the case, life would be virtually intolerable.

Most blockages can, as a matter of fact, be regarded as beneficial and adaptive, for they energize the individual's efforts toward achievement of his goals and cause him to reorient, learn, and grow. Let us turn to a consideration of different adaptive consequences of frustration.

Intensification of effort.—Usually when blocked in the achievement of a goal the individual summons up greater efforts to overcome the barriers; the mounting tension makes possible a greater degree of involvement of the whole person in the problem and the added mobilization of his energies often results in achievement of the goal. Related to this is the experimental evidence of Wright (1937), who found that under some conditions the presence of a barrier to a goal enhances the attractiveness or demand-character of the goal and hence (presumably) intensifies the individual's efforts.

Reorganization of perception of the problem.—One of the most critical consequences of frustration is the influence on the way that the problem of achieving the goal or satisfying the need is perceived. Frustration often leads to insight and reorganization of paths to the goal. This aspect of the effect of frustration or blocking is of such great significance for the understanding of social behavior that we shall devote a major part of Chap. IV to it.

Substitution of goals.—Another adaptive consequence of frustration is the discovery and acceptance of alternative goals, which serve as satisfactory substitutes for the original goal. Thus, for example, a woman who is biologically unable to satisfy her maternal need or an unmarried woman who is blocked by social taboos from having children may achieve a substitute goal of working in a nursery or of founding an orphanage.

Henle's (1942) experimental study of substitution revealed that the effectiveness of a substitute goal, in releasing the tensions resulting from blockage of an original goal, depends principally upon the perceived similarity between the original and substitute goals.

Maladaptive consequences.—Sometimes the nature of the psychological situation in frustration does not permit the reduction of tension through the various adaptive means discussed above. The barriers to goal achievement may be impermeable, even in the face of the most intensified efforts of the person to overcome them; the problem of locating a path to the goal may be actually unsolvable; there simply may not exist any possible goal substitutes within the psychological purview of the individual.

In such cases, the frustration persists and intensifies; and eventually, consequences of a less adaptive sort occur. It is to be strongly emphasized that even for these less adaptive behaviors our general proposition holds true that the effects of tension are such as to tend to change the field in the direction of a more stable structure. Whether adaptive or maladaptive behavior is involved, the constant tendency is toward tension reduction.

However, in the less adaptive reactions to frustrations the form of the dynamic restructuring of the psychological field is likely to be such as to impair the healthy functioning of the whole person and to disrupt his successful adjustment to the society in which he lives. *Tension reduction and adaptive behavior are not synonymous.* Mere tension reduction does not suffice to assure a positive, healthy adjustment of the individual. To be able to handle conflicts and frustrations in such a way as not to jeopardize continuous progress toward remote goals requires that the individual's personality be integrated in the proper way. To this question we shall return later.

Among the maladaptive reactions to frustrations that are of greatest importance to an understanding of social behavior are the following: (1) aggression, (2) regression, (3) withdrawal, (4) repression, (5) sublimation, (6) rationalization and projection, (7) autism, (8) identification.

Aggression.—The accumulated tensions arising out of persistent frustration often find expression in aggressive acts which seem to allay, at least temporarily, the frustrated state. Aggressiveness may take the form of feelings and actions of anger and rage, of actual physical violence against objects and people, of verbal attacks and denunciations and slander, of mere fantasies of violence and attack.

The targets of aggression are not necessarily related logically to the frustrating situation; often they are completely unconnected with the thwarting agent. A man frustrated by a domineering boss may spank his child, berate his wife for domestic extravagance, or burst out with a violent denunciation of the government administration. People whose economic ambitions are thwarted may lynch Negroes and persecute other minority groups. The frustration of sex needs may produce sadistic fantasies or harsh treatment of sexually "loose" people. Under some circumstances the aggression may even be turned inward against one's self.[1]

Regression.—Barker, Dembo, and Lewin (1940) have studied the phenomena of regression as a consequence of frustration. They observe that in certain frustrating situations, the behavior of the individual undergoes a kind of primitivation. His actions become less mature, more childish; the

[1] For a more complete account of the frustration-aggression sequence, including a number of experimental illustrations, the student is referred to Dollard *et al.* (1939).

sensitivity of his discriminations and judgments diminishes; his feelings and emotions become more poorly differentiated and controlled, like those of a child. In general, his psychological field tends spontaneously in the direction of a lower level simplification, which is a reversal of the normal trend toward higher level complexity characteristic of the growth and maturation of the individual.

Barker, Dembo, and Lewin observed that the play behavior of children who were deprived of a highly desired object deteriorated from a more advanced level of constructive play, in which blocks were used to build things, to a more immature level of play, in which the blocks were used merely as things to bang about. On a grander scale the same phenomenon may be observed in the field of international relations. A diplomat may be seeking to achieve international agreement on certain complex issues. He behaves on a mature level, searching for some advanced and sophisticated *modus vivendi* by which common understanding can be achieved, being constantly sensitive to the refinements and subtleties of the problem, not permitting his feelings and emotions to discolor his perspective on the whole issue. Then, at some point in the negotiations, he is severely thwarted in his purpose by serious points of controversy, by the apparent irreconcilability of his confreres. He may, as a consequence of this frustration, "regress" to a less mature level of behavior, now falling back on threats and upon inadequate concepts of security, sovereignty, and isolation; now being unable to perceive and understand subtle distinctions; now permitting his previously controlled feelings of suspicion, fear, anger, and discouragement to flood all of his outlook.

Regression does not necessarily mean a falling back upon the specific modes of behavior that the individual had actually used at an earlier stage in his life. This is regression in the sense that Freud has used the term. This return to earlier modes of behavior may sometimes occur in the face of frustration and can be seen as a special case of the more general concept. A scientist frustrated in his search for "logical" meaning in the universe may fall back on the religious beliefs of his youth.

It is not infrequently the case that both such a return to earlier modes of behavior and regression, in the sense of a deterioration from higher level to lower level behavior, may be involved at once, since it is often true that earlier modes of behavior are likely also to be more primitive in structure.

Withdrawal.—Frustration may often be resolved by a psychological withdrawal from the frustrating situation. Sometimes the escape may involve a change in the physical environment itself. The farmer in the dust bowl gives up the struggle against the natural barriers to making a living, packs his goods and family in a car, becomes an "Okie," and leaves for California.

In other situations the individual may be unable to leave the physical scene of his frustration; instead, he erects psychological fences that cut him off from contact with the situation. The "tired liberal," frustrated in his attempts at political reform, loses all interest in politics, refuses to read political news in the paper and to participate in political activities or discussions.

Repression.—Freud has particularly stressed the importance of repression as a consequence of frustration. In repression, unsatisfied needs are apparently subjected to forces that render them inaccessible to consciousness; the individual "forgets" the unsatisfied need. It seems that those needs and demands which conflict with social mores and taboos as reflected in the moral ideology of the person are the most susceptible to repression. A puritanical individual may never be consciously aware of sex desires; a son may never be consciously aware of his feelings of hostility toward his father.

It has been pointed out previously that motives may function unconsciously as well as consciously. That the effects of tensions are repressed, therefore, does not mean that they are made impotent or that the tensions are resolved. The further fate of such repressed effects is to be seen in many ways, among them in sublimation and in rationalization and projection.

Sublimation.—By sublimation is meant the unconscious process in which the tension associated with the repressed needs is deflected to new objects, new goals, new activities of an apparently unconnected sort. Usually, these new objects, goals, and activities are—unlike the repressed needs— socially approved. The puritanical person who has repressed his sex desires becomes an ardent community reformer; the son who has repressed his hostile feelings toward his father becomes a member of the Ku Klux Klan.

Freud makes much of the concept of repression in speaking of the diversion of sex-repressed impulses into nonsexual and socially useful goals. More generally, it can be said that the tension of any repressed need—sexual or nonsexual—may often find expression in what seem to be remote and unrelated activities.[1]

Rationalization and projection.—Since tensions are the product of the structure of the psychological field, including cognitive structure, it is evident that tensions may also be reduced by appropriate cognitive restructuring. It may be assumed that—other things being equal—the existence of frustration will tend spontaneously to lead to cognitive changes which help to reduce tension.

[1] Freud would regard the sublimated activities as forever dependent upon the original, basic sexual sources, whereas the point of view of this book would be that sublimated activities, like other activities, may eventually become functionally autonomous.

Some of such cognitive changes are called rationalizations. The inaccessible goal looks less attractive: the fox and the "sour grapes." An available but less preferred goal begins to look more attractive: the "sweet lemon." Socially unacceptable behavior is redefined and given more acceptable meaning: War is valuable because it builds loyalty, moral stamina and "makes a man out of you."

Rationalizations are rarely conscious deceptions. They are believed in by the individual; he does not apprehend the distortion in his perceptions and thoughts that is caused by the frustration.

Quite commonly, in cases of frustration, there occurs another form of cognitive modification, called *projection*. In projection the individual's perception of the situation is so altered that he assigns blame for his own failures and frustrations to other parts of the field; he "projects" the blame. The tennis player muffs a stroke and looks at his racket for the offending "hole." The incompetent man who fails to get ahead in his job blames those who "are against him." The man who feels moral guilt projects it on others and finds sin in them.

In their study of anti-Semitic college girls, Frenkel-Brunswik and Sanford (1945) found that their subjects (of middle-class American families) had repressed the expression of certain aggressive and sexual impulses, with the result that these needs were projected onto others, especially groups low in social status, such as Jews and Mexicans. When asked to interpret an unlabeled picture of a boy (dressed in a zoot suit) and a girl, these subjects apparently tended to perceive these "inferior" people as aggressive and generally uninhibited. "Uninhibited sex life," write the investigators, "is regarded as a pleasure for a low type of person." Examples of the responses of their subjects are

It is a young girl and her boy friend. They are lower class people, and don't know any better than to do this sort of thing. I have an aversion for the things such people do . . . .

.I think they will marry young but will divorce before long. They allow their emotions to get too much in their way . . . .

This girl and her boy friend are zoot-suiters and I don't approve of them. She goes out to dances, etc. She is finally caught and brought into court . . . .

. . . the girl is the typical type of jitterbug—the kind who hangs around the USO. The couple has a nice time at the dance; that is, in that kind of way.

As Frenkel-Brunswik and Sanford point out,

These sentences express contempt and at the same time envy for the "lower class sexuality." An important tendency of the girls high on anti-Semitism is thus to keep one's basic impulses repressed, to keep oneself pure and reputable. Primitive needs are rendered ego-alien and projected onto an alien group.

Autism.—Closely related to the cognitive changes characteristic of rationalization and projection is another form of reaction to frustration known as *autism*, or *autistic thinking*. This refers to thinking that is almost completely dominated by needs and emotions, wherein no attempt is made to "check" the content of the thinking with reality. In autism, the individual comes to behave on a plane of "irreality" instead of on the reality level. There is, in a sense, a kind of withdrawal or escape from the uncompromising facts of the real world.

The individual who cuts himself off from communications with another person or group and then proceeds to "think" about that person or group without bothering to check his thinking with the facts of the case is engaged in autistic thinking. Recently, Newcomb (1947) has stressed the importance of autism in the development of hostile attitudes. As he puts it,

Hostile impulses commonly arise . . . when status-relationship is so perceived that another is viewed as threat. Such a perception arises through interaction, and it is likely to persist until modified by further interaction. If, as a result of a hostile attitude emerging from the newly perceived status-relationship, communication with the other person is avoided, the conditions necessary for eliminating the hostile attitude are not likely to occur.

Therefore, he concludes,

. . . the likelihood that a persistently hostile attitude will develop varies with the degree to which the perceived interpersonal relationship remains autistic . . . .

Autism, in Newcomb's example, is seen as a consequence of withdrawal from a dangerous or frustrating situation. Other autisms can be seen as operating more directly to reduce tensions. Daydreaming and other fantasies are such autisms. By such means there is imaginary gratification of unfulfilled needs and the overcoming of frustrating barriers to goal achievement. Socially, this kind of behavior may be very "expensive." The individual who has a need for seeing social justice done but gratifies it by fantasy or daydreaming thereby dissipates his energy in socially useless autism, even though he himself may, by this means, get temporary satisfaction of his need.

Identification.—A common and apparently highly effective avenue for the resolution of some types of frustration is through a process of identifying oneself with another person or with a group of persons. The amorous achievements of the screen actress become the conquests of the frustrated suburbanite; the successes of the Nazis became the successes of the frustrated and chronically failing "little people" of Germany.

The process of identification is singularly important in understanding group morale and leadership and will be discussed in detail in Chap. X on Group Dynamics.

Facilitative and Disruptive Effects of High Tension.—High levels of tension and the emotionality with which they are associated often have positive value for adaptive action. The intensely stirred up state of the individual may prepare him for stronger, faster, and more decisive action. In states of anger there can be a reinforcement of attack against the frustrating obstacle; in states of fear there can be a strengthening of necessary defensive action.[1]

But it is also commonly observed that strong states of emotion can bring about disruption and maladaptation in the individual's behavior. The paralysis, or "freezing," in extreme fear and the hysteria of panicky fear may interfere fatally with the individual's prompt adjustment to an emergency. Violent outbursts of anger in fits of "blind rage" may render the person completely helpless to deal properly with the immediate situation.

Adaptive and disruptive states of fear.—An indication of how an emotion of fear may operate either in a "healthy," adaptive way or in an "unhealthy," disruptive way is given in the following statement concerning public fears about the problem of the atomic bomb:[2]

Atomic energy is producing an international fear psychology. But such a fear is not necessarily bad, for human fear releases great psychological energies. When the source of the fear is well understood and a constructive solution is seen, these energies serve as powerful supports of well-directed efforts to overcome the danger. But when the source is not well understood, and no clear solution is seen, these energies lead to a general, vague anxiety accompanied by panicky behavior, helplessness or despair.

Our fear of the atomic bomb does stem from a real and frightful danger. This danger comes from the fact that there is no military defense against the atomic bomb. This fact must always be kept clear and our first objective must be to mobilize a healthy, action-goading fear for effective measures against the real danger—war.

---

[1] The pattern of physiological changes accompanying emotions, such as fear and rage, has been experimentally ascertained to be of such a nature as to mobilize the resources of the organism for quicker, stronger, and more effective physical response. Cannon (1929) has made this fact the basis for an "emergency theory of emotion," which stresses the evolutionary development of emotional behavior in terms of its functional utility.

[2] From "Psychology and atomic energy," a statement by the Committee on International Peace of the Society for the Psychological Study of Social Issues (1946).

The other kind of fear, however—the intangible, unhealthy fear—threatens our achievement of this objective . . . .

In an individual, vague fear soon leads to a sick individual. The fear spreads and influences all his thinking. Then, he either behaves in an immature and helpless manner or he becomes panicky and destructive.

If we as a nation become victims of such a fear we may seek relief in escapist thinking. We will then try to find comfort in the pronouncements of dubious "authorities" that the bomb is not dangerous. We will indulge in wishful-thinking that some defense against the bomb will be developed—*despite what scientists say*. We will hope unrealistically that we can always keep the secret of its manufacture, or we will feel secure in the knowledge that we are accumulating more and more bombs. These immature and escapist reactions can only hinder the constructive solution of this problem at the very time when such solution is most needed and most possible.

Or, what is equally fatal, we may become frantic in our precautions against this unknown danger. We will then accept the suppression of freedom of speech, of research, and of criticism in our own country because we will have become "spy conscious." And like the sick patient ridden by an ill-understood fear, we will see threats to our safety everywhere. We will support a national policy of universal conscription, militarism, and political isolation. This panicky and destructive thinking is just the mental preparation which sets the stage for international conflict and violence.

The above statement indicates how intense fear may result in wishful, escapist, and destructive thinking. Fear and other intense emotions may also produce other deleterious effects on the individual's cognitive organization, especially in the direction of narrowing and rigidifying it.

"Narrowing" and "rigidifying."—What is the implication of the common phrases "blind fear" and "blind rage"? To say that these extreme emotions may "blind" is a way of pointing to the critical fact that in states of strong emotion there is often a "narrowing" of the cognitive organization at the moment; the individual loses broader perspective, he no longer is able to "see" essential aspects of the situation, and his behavior becomes, consequently, less adaptive.

Intimately associated with such effects on cognitive organization is a tendency in states of intense emotion for the flexibility or malleability of cognitive organization to decrease. The cognitive structure becomes rigid, and the adaptability of the person is seriously impaired. The details of this process of rigidification will be discussed in Chap. IV.

Catharsis and tension reduction.—It is commonly observed that the reduction of excessively high tensions through emotional outbursts may be followed by periods of calmness, in which the individual is enabled to regain perspective on the situation and to resume a more normal and reasonable

attitude.   Emotions thus often act as "safety valves" through which the
person can "blow off steam" and restore the kind of equanimity necessary
for solution of his problem.

An interesting example of this cathartic effect of emotionality has been
reported by Allport (1945).   In attempting to teach a course in race relations to a group of public officials in an eastern city, he found that from the
beginning the members of the group indulged in hostile and emotional dis-
course directed at him.   The origin of the anger was in the circumstance
that these officials were being required by orders of their superiors to take
this course and felt that their attitudes and capabilities were being impugned and their dignity impaired.   Their anger came quite naturally to
be directed at the lecturer since he was the outside expert brought in to tell
them how to behave.   By not challenging but rather permitting and even
encouraging this emotional outburst in the beginning sessions and allowing
it gradually to wear itself out, Allport found that the psychological
atmosphere was cleared up, the attitude of the group members became
more friendly, and positive progress in the group discussion was then
facilitated.

PROPOSITION V

*Characteristic modes of goal achievement and tension reduction may be learned
and fixated by the individual*

Just as the types of psychological field situations that may give rise to
tensions (and thence to feelings of need) are extremely varied, so are the
possibilities of different goals in relation to these tension states almost limitless.   It is in the very nature of the complex psychological world in which
the human being lives that there is a multiplicity of functionally equivalent
ways of reducing tensions.   A feeling of sexual desire may find expression
in marital intercourse or prostitution or masturbation or perverted erotic
practices or in manifold other ways, many of them quite indirect.   Feelings
of hostility may be expressed in war, in lynching, in rumor mongering, in
daydreams of hurting others, or in giving a bigger and better dinner party
than that given by your social rival whom you hate.[1]

The fact that this extremely wide range of potential ways of reducing
tensions exists does not imply that all of them exist as psychological realities
for any single individual.   In connection with a certain need in a given
individual, only a limited number of goals may exist that satisfy the need.

---

[1] This last way of expressing hostility has been described by anthropologists as involved
in the "potlach" behavior of the Kwakiutl Indians of Vancouver Island.   Anthropological
literature is exceedingly rich in its accounts of the enormous diversity among cultures in
the characteristic ways that needs are reduced.

And these goals may not all be equal in demand-character or in the degree to which they will satisfy the need. What is characteristic is that the goals relating to a certain need occupy a preference hierarchy, which is unique to the individual. Certain ways of satisfying his needs are preferred to others; certain goals have higher demand-character than others. Given a free choice, he will seek the more preferred goal. Only if the achievement of the more preferred goal is thwarted will he turn to less preferred goals.

Goal preference and intensity of need.—The degree of discrimination among the various goals within the preference hierarchy is influenced in an interesting way by the momentary intensity of the need. When his need is mild, the individual may pay considerable attention to his relative preferences for various goals; when the need is acute, goal preferences become less significant.[1] Strong needs also tend to extend the range of acceptable goals. In starvation, substances previously considered inedible may be eagerly eaten.

Goal preference and "past experience."—The demand-character and preferability of a given goal as a way of satisfying a need depend, among other things, upon the individual's past experiences with it. A goal that has proved satisfactory for need reduction in the past may now tend to be perceived by the person as a good way to satisfy his present need; ways of behaving that proved inadequate as satisfiers of need in the past may now tend to be avoided.

It is to be emphasized that there is nothing mechanical in this process. The effect of past experience on present goals is mediated by cognitive processes. Whether a mode of response that was successfully utilized in the past resolution of a need will function as a preferred way of satisfying that need in the present situation depends upon how the present situation is perceived and the "meaning" of the response as determined by the entire psychological field of the moment.[2]

One of the most important contributions of past experience to the development of new goals lies in the opportunity that such past experience has afforded the individual to become acquainted with the psychological properties of new aspects of his world. By engaging in new activities and having

---

[1] One is reminded of the *New Yorker* cartoon in which a man perishing of thirst on the desert drags himself up to a soft-drink stand in an oasis and remarks in outrage, "What! No strawberry soda?"

[2] In the form of the classic "law of effect," Thorndike (1911) and many others after him have argued that modes of response which were successful in reducing needs in the past experience of the individual will tend, automatically and necessarily, to be called out when the situation again occurs. For a convincing experimental demonstration that, instead, the operation of the law of effect depends upon the meaning of the past response in the context of the present psychological situation, see Wallach and Henle (1941).

commerce with new objects, the individual comes to apprehend previously unsuspected attractions (or repulsions) in them; in this way they gradually acquire demand-character (or the reverse) for him. Mr. Arbuthnot, in allaying his feelings of loneliness, joins a fraternal lodge. Gradually, on the basis of repeated experiences in this lodge, he discovers all sorts of convivial attractions about it and comes to love it. Now it compels his convivial behavior in many significant ways. This particular lodge is no longer equivalent to other social groupings; it has unique demand-character. It calls out strong emotions in Mr. Arbuthnot; it may even become for him an object of *fixation*.

Development of "attitudes."—The high tension of the individual in emotion seems to be an auspicious condition for the genesis and reinforcement of such fixations or dispositions toward objects, people, and events. When objects or people or events have been involved in emotional situations in the individual's past, there are likely to be left permanent "traces" in the form of enduring predispositions for or against the objects, people, or events. A child who has frequently experienced fear, frustration, and anger in the presence of an overbearing father may acquire an enduring *attitude* of hate toward the parent.[1]

Detailed consideration of the critically important topic of attitudes will be taken up in Chap. V. We may anticipate that discussion in one particular to note that a special consequence of the process of development of enduring emotional dispositions, or attitudes, toward objects is that the *words* which one uses in referring to the objects may become capable of arousing emotion and activity in their own right. The significance of this fact in the social psychology of propaganda will be clarified in Chap. IX.

Individual Differences in Goals and in Tension Reduction.—Since the nature of the preferred goals depends partly upon the pattern of past experiences to which the individual has been exposed, it is to be expected that typical goals will differ from individual to individual and from culture to culture. The physical and social environment of the person limits and shapes the goals he may develop. Some cultures simply do not provide the opportunity for the appearance of certain goals, which may be almost "universal" in other cultures; and within a culture, the pattern of social organization may be such as to channel the life and experiences of the individual along relatively rigid, predetermined lines, excluding the possibility of development of goals that are available to other members of the culture who exist in different social stratifications. For an illiterate American, the

---

[1] The prime significance of these emotional dispositions has been greatly emphasized by McDougall (1923) in his doctrine of sentiments.

goal of becoming a teacher or a writer, as a means to satisfy his need for being socially useful, cannot be expected to develop. This dependence of available goals upon the social stratifications of society makes especially important the data that anthropologists and sociologists collect on the details of social structure of a society, such as that of contemporary America.

In connection with Proposition IV, a number of different dynamic processes by which tensions may be reduced were discussed. It is likely that every one of these processes does occur at one time or another for every individual, regardless of his past experiences or his cultural environment. But just as the environment of the individual governs the accessibility of various goals, so may his environment tend to govern the relative importance of these various possible avenues to tension reduction. In a society in which aggression is considered bad and in which acceptable targets for aggression are not supplied, it is probable that the tensions of people will be regularly released through other means than aggressive behavior. A person who lives in a highly protected environment, where his everyday needs are automatically cared for and where he is absolved of and prohibited from assuming important personal responsibilities, may fall easily into the pattern of tension reduction through autistic, withdrawal, and regressive behaviors. A puritanical society may serve to encourage sublimation and repression at the expense of other more direct modes of tension reduction.

Tension reduction and "personality."—It may be a suggestive approach to the analysis of the individual to describe his personality in terms of the pattern of tension-reduction processes that are characteristic of him. This pattern would be the resultant of the individual's growth within the confines of a given culture and environment and of the past history of his experiences of success and failure with these various adaptive processes. Thus, we might come to speak of people whose personalities are predominantly of the "regressive" type or of the "repressed" type or the "aggressive" type, etc. And we might even speak of cultures whose members are likely to be personalities of the "autistic" type, the "sublimated" type, etc.

Such characterizations of the personalities of individuals and of the typical members of a culture are entirely relative. No individual is ever completely and solely regressive or repressed or aggressive. He may be *more* of one of these than the average of people; of all tension-reduction behavior in which he engages, one of these modes of response may be predominant and the others subsidiary. But all individuals are to some extent regressive and repressed and aggressive and so on. It is the *pattern of relative importance* of these various adjustments to tension that characterizes the unique personality of the individual.

PROPOSITION VI

The trend of behavior often involves progressively "higher" levels of stable organization of the psychological field

In order to discuss this proposition we must first examine certain questions concerning the nature of stable organizations, or equilibria, of the psychological field.

Equilibrium.—In Proposition III it was asserted that under the influence of tensions, which are the product of imbalances and instabilities in the structure of the psychological field, the field tends to change in the direction of a more stable structure. In other words, the configuration of all the forces existing in the psychological field tends toward a balance, or *equilibrium*, of forces. One is reminded of certain simple mechanical systems and of certain physiological systems,[1] which tend toward states of equilibrium. But one cannot, by direct analogy, extend what is known about such simpler systems to the complex problem of human motivation without taking great care to avoid certain pitfalls. For one thing, there is the question of whether or not the attainment of equilibrium can be regarded as a real goal of the individual. For another thing, there is the question of whether or not the equilibrium states themselves change.

Equilibrium as a goal.—That there is a constant tendency for the psychological field to change in the direction of reduction of tension *does not imply that the achievement of a state of equilibrium is the goal of the individual's action.* A man may eat because the food looks inviting and without any intent to arrive at a condition of satiety in which the feelings of hunger or the appetizingness of the food will no longer have the power to evoke action in him. The goal in this case is eating food, not escaping hunger or reaching satiation. It may be true that by eating the food the individual will arrive at an equilibrium condition in which he is no longer impelled to eat, but that fact does not necessarily have relevance for his immediate motivation.

A useful analysis of motivation must take account mainly of the psychological properties of the moment, including the experienced needs and demands and goals. The individual's behavior is best understood in reference to these determinants, not in reference to others that lie behind and beyond them in a *logical* but not psychological fashion.[2] As MacLeod (1947) points out,

[1] Cannon's (1932) theory of "homeostasis" argues that the physiological system of the human organism is in very important respects self-regulating and self-balancing. For a penetrating analysis of the "fittingness" of organic change, see Chap. VIII in Köhler's *The Place of Value in a World of Facts* (1938).

[2] Heider (1939) has offered a useful analysis of this distinction between "distal" and "proximal" determinants.

. . . to assert that the goal of an act is to attain a final state of equilibrium or of maximum happiness, or to preserve the species, or even to escape from conflict, is to impute a directedness to behavior which may not be present as such to the individual.

Changes in equilibria.—If an elastic object is stretched out of shape and then released, it springs back to its original shape, *i.e.*, to its initial position of equilibrium. The concentration of CO_2 in the blood of a resting person stands at a given level. If the person begins to exercise the CO_2 concentration rises. This automatically induces faster breathing, which persists until the CO_2 concentration is reduced to its initial level, *i.e.*, to the equilibrium condition.

These simple analogies of systems tending toward equilibrium may be decidedly misleading if applied directly to the dynamics of the psychological field. In these relatively simple systems the final state of equilibrium is the same as the initial state of equilibrium. In the psychological field, on the contrary, the final and the initial equilibrium states are commonly, thought not invariably, different. By a change in the situation that induces tensions and thereby needs and goals, the individual is provoked into action directed at satisfaction of the needs and achievement of the goals. The completion of the action resolves the tension, bringing the individual into a *new* state of equilibrium, different—perhaps markedly—from that which existed before he was provoked into action.

The history of the psychological field of the individual is not one of static equilibria, which involves a series of excursions away from a stable state and return to that same state. It is, rather, a history of changing equilibria, in which the psychological field restructures continuously, never returning to a state in which it existed before. These changes in equilibria are often observed to be progressive, *i.e.*, involving progressively "higher" levels of stable organization of the psychological field.

"Higher" Levels of Stable Organization.—The growth of the human individual—physically, mentally, and psychologically—can be regarded as a process of simultaneous differentiation and integration. In other words, the individual is constantly growing more complex, and at the same time the complexities are becoming better synthesized. (Growth is, in this sense, the exact opposite of regression as discussed on page 55.) What is the significance of this increased complexity in our understanding of motivation?

The complexity of the psychological field.—The individual is not a single-tracked, single-minded animal. He functions not in only one situation at a time but in several overlapping situations, which differ in their relative "potency" for him, *i.e.*, some have more effect on him than others—he pays more attention to them and is more deeply involved in them. And in each of the different situations there is a high degree of complexity due to the very richness and detail of the kinds of physical and social worlds in which we live.

There is, moreover, the fact of what has been called "time perspective," *viz.*, that the individual's immediate psychological field includes not only the present situation but also representations of past and future situations.

The complexity of each single situation, the overlapping of situations, and the intrusion of past and future situations, all contribute to the extreme complexity of the whole psychological field. Such complexity, in the absence of a high order of integration of the field, must eventuate in chaotic behavior. The welter of concomitant demands, needs, and goals arising out of all these overlapping situations will, without such integration, be unmanageable. What is the nature of the necessary integration?

Organization of needs, demands, goals.—In view of the heterogeneity and frequent incompatibility of needs, goals, and demands, any adaptive functioning of the individual must involve an organization of the needs, demands, and goals in such a fashion as to set up *priorities and hierarchies of importance* among them. For the integrated personality, many potential conflicts are resolved by the fact that one need or goal or demand takes automatic precedence over others. Thus, for example, a man may always direct his behavior first toward the economic welfare of his family and only secondarily toward his own needs for a happy type of job.

Integration of the personality also involves the dominance of remote over immediate goals. It is a characteristic of the mature individual that he is better able to postpone immediate gratifications for more important ultimate ones. Thus, for example, a young man puts off marriage so that he can get a college education and a good job and then have a happier marriage.

Ideals, ideology, values.—Such integration of needs, demands, and goals is accomplished through the development of a system of ideals, ideology, and values within the individual. This system of ideals, ideology, and values (however developed) serves as a governing framework for the various needs, demands, and goals. It controls the behavior in such a way as to ensure the highest amount of need satisfaction and goal achievement consistent with the total functioning of the person. An integrated personality is one in which the needs, demands, and goals—instead of functioning as separate, segmented parts of the behavior—work together optimally in a way that is self-consistent, mutually reinforcing, and nonconflicting. And this integration is mainly possible through the individual's system of values, ideals, and ideology.

Values, ideals, and ideology are the criteria in terms of which the individual judges himself. Thus, his feelings of self-esteem, self-regard, self-respect, and the like, depend upon these standards and upon how he perceives himself in relation to them. And such feelings give rise, of course, to actions directed at achieving a desired position for the self. This is well illustrated in connection with the "level of aspiration."

Level of aspiration.—It is characteristic of the growing, advancing individual that he continuously sets for himself new levels of accomplishment (his levels of aspiration) that are above those of his present achievements.[1] Viewed segmentally, this phenomenon seems to contradict a simple theory that behavior tends toward equilibrium; here it seems that an equilibrium is voluntarily abandoned and a tension deliberately set up. The person seems to be pulling himself up by his own bootstraps.

Actually, when viewed in the perspective of the whole person, the level of aspiration phenomena provides a striking illustration of our proposition that there is often a trend in behavior toward higher levels of stable organizations. There is nothing mysterious in the phenomenon. When the individual achieves a desired level of performance, his *standards are thereby changed*, and this immediately calls out new action toward higher levels. Aspiration endlessly leads achievement in much the way that the carrot, dangling from a pole tied to the head, leads the donkey.

Defense of the self.—Some of the most potent of all needs and the most effective of all goals have to do with the defense of the self, *i.e.*, with the adjustment of the field in such a way as to enhance feelings of self-esteem, self-regard, etc., or to remove threats to self-esteem and self-regard. The numerous means by which tensions may be reduced, discussed under Proposition IV, can be viewed as operating in such a way as to be maximally defensive of the self. This is particularly obvious in connection with such processes as projection, in which blame is transferred from the self to others; rationalization, in which repugnant or immoral or unacceptable actions of the self can be—by cognitive changes—"explained" away; withdrawal, in which the self is protected by being removed from the scene of the threat or problem or conflict; autism, in which self-gratification is imagined.

Involvements of the self.—The self is the most important structure in the psychological field, and it is likely, under normal conditions, to be one of the strongest structures. It has, therefore, a role of unparalleled significance in the determination of the organization of the field. The nature of the relationships of the self to other parts of the field—to other objects, to people, to groups, to social organizations—is of critical importance in understanding the individual's perception of a connection between various objects, individuals, and groups and himself. He is proud of his garden and becomes

[1] The first laboratory experiments on level of aspiration were those of Hoppe (1930). A review of much subsequent work can be found in Gould (1939).

angry when the neighbor's chickens invade it; he loves his son and strives to provide him with a college education; he feels loyalty to his country and goes to war to defend it against external threats. Without such feeling of *self-involvement* in the garden, the son, and the country, his tensions and needs would be markedly different.

The normal process of growth and socialization of the individual is one of development and multiplication of various self-involvements with objects, people, groups, and social organizations in the world about him.[1] The involvements of the self in these more and more complex social relationships give birth to new needs, new demands, and new goals as the horizons, interests, and concerns of the individual continuously expand.

SUMMARY

The question of motivation is the question of "Why." In order to answer this question we must study the basic principles of the dynamics of behavior, including perception and cognition as well as motivation.

The discussion of motivation is centered around a set of propositions, which represent generalizations about the available facts and theories essential for our understanding of social behavior.

Proposition I: The proper unit of motivational analysis is molar behavior, which involves needs and goals. Behavior in molar units includes all of the behavior of the individual occurring at one time, and it consists of relatively discrete, unified episodes with a beginning and an end. Each episode has a consistent direction, defined by the existent need and goal. Molar units are used in studying man's behavior because they yield the most fruitful analysis of it.

This proposition denies the explanatory value of such concepts as habit, custom, conditioning, imitation, etc., in accounting for the driving power behind the individual's activity.

Proposition II: The dynamics of molar behavior result from properties of the immediate psychological field. It is first essential to distinguish clearly between the *immediate dynamic* problem—how the needs and goals of a given individual at a given time in a given situation determine his behavior—and the *genetic* problem—how these needs and goals and this situation have come into being in the course of the individual's development. Both of these

---

[1] Sherif and Cantril's *Psychology of Ego-Involvements* (1947) presents a good account of experimental and concrete social illustrations of the genetic formation of the self, the reformation of the self in adolescence, self-involvements and identifications in group situations, and breakdowns of the self under conditions of stress.

problems are significant, but they must be kept separated. Failure to do so may result in futile attempts to find the explanation of immediate behavior in the past history of the individual instead of in the properties of the immediate dynamic situation. Motivational analysis need not follow the method of the psychoanalyst—in which the historical emphasis is uppermost—or the method of the biocentric psychologist—in which the emphasis is primarily upon internal physiological instigators. *All motives can be treated as contemporaneous.*

The psychological field is a state of neuropsychic processes which are reflected in the form of the *experienced world* of the individual and in the form of *patterns of neural processes* in the brain. It is a dynamic unity of influences arising out of (1) the external physical environment, (2) the internal physiological environment, and (3) the neural traces of past experiences. However, this dependence is not simple. There is far from a one-to-one correspondence between the psychological field and these "real" worlds (external, internal, and past).

The dynamics of the psychological field can be lawfully analyzed only if the effects of alien factors are excluded. Alien factors are changes in the internal or external environments of the person that are not brought about by the operation of the dynamic principles of the field itself but are brought about independently. The psychologist can make only predictions that are conditional, *i.e.*, those which do not take account of the possible intrusion of alien factors.

Proposition III: Instabilities in the psychological field produce "tensions" whose effects on perception, cognition, and action are such as to tend to change the field in the direction of a more stable structure. The organization of the psychological field at any given moment is likely to involve imbalances, instabilities, and other imperfections of patterns, which give rise to *tensions.* Tensions persist until resolved, and their influences are widespread in causing behavior that serves to reduce the tensions. Such behavior may be action toward a goal, cognitive reorganization, or more general restructuring of the field.

The *conscious* correlates of tension are (1) vague feelings of restlessness, dissatisfaction, "moodiness," etc., having no specific reference to any explicit feature of the field; (2) feelings of needs, directed toward explicit features of the field, which are apprehended as desired, sought after, or needed things (*i.e.*, "goals"); (3) demands perceived as emerging from explicit features of the field, which are apprehended as requiring something of the person.

The effects of tension may be *unconscious;* *i.e.*, their existence and their effects on the person's behavior may not be recognized by him.   Unconscious motives operate, like conscious ones, to reduce tensions.

Needs and demands, therefore, are not rigidly and innately fixed but are as variable as the tensions of the psychological field.   Activities caused by original needs and demands change the psychological field and may thus create new needs and demands independent of the old.   The illusion of universality of needs and demands is a consequence of biological regularities characterizing the physiological environments of people living under similar physical conditions and of socially determined uniformities in the psychological environments of the members of a given culture.   There is not one human nature but many.   Human nature (in the sense of the needs, goals, and demands of people and their ways of expressing and satisfying them) is as variable as the cultures, societies, and social groups in which people live.   But regardless of this variability, the dynamic principles that govern the functioning of the psychological field are absolute and universal.   The specific nature of the needs and demands operating in a present situation may be ascertained by (1) inferences from overt behavior, (2) "introspective" descriptions of immediate experience, and (3) "projective" techniques. All three approaches are complementary in the investigation of motivation.

Proposition IV: The frustration of goal achievement and the failure of tension reduction may lead to a variety of adaptive or maladaptive behaviors.   Frustration of motives may be traced to four sources: (1) man's physical environment, (2) man's biological limitations, (3) the complexity of man's psychological make-up, (4) the nature of man's social environment.   The consequences of frustration are very numerous; they are dynamically interrelated; their nature depends partly upon the severity of frustration; they are not necessarily bad.

Adaptive adjustments to frustration (or "blockage") are found in intensification of effort toward the goal, reorganization of the perception of the problem of how to reach the goal, substitution of an accessible goal for an inaccessible one.   *Maladaptive* consequences of frustration (*i.e.*, those which may occur at the cost of the total healthy functioning of the individual) are found in the form of aggression, regression, withdrawal, repression, sublimation, rationalization and projection, autism, and identification.

High tension in states of emotion and strong motivation may be facilitative in mobilizing the person for stronger, more effective action.   It may also, however, be disruptive in leading to a "narrowing" and "rigidifying" of the cognitive structure, which interferes with the individual's adequate adjustment to his problem.   The overflow of tension involved in emotional outbursts may have a positive cathartic effect in enabling the person to regain perspective on the situation.

Proposition V: Characteristic modes of goal achievement and tension reduction may be learned and fixated by the individual. There are many different goals that can satisfy a person's needs, and they vary in their relative preference. Preferences among goals become less important in states of intense needs. Goal preferences are altered by the individual's experiences with the goals.

States of high tension are auspicious occasions for the development of *attitudes* toward objects, people, and events.

Characteristic modes of tension reduction are learned by the individual as a function of his past experiences of success or failure with them and of the opportunity for employment of them within the confines of his particular culture. *Personality* may be described as the *pattern of relative importance* of these various modes of adjustment to tension which uniquely characterizes the individual.

Proposition VI: The trend of behavior often involves progressively "higher" levels of stable organization of the psychological field. The view that tensions arise out of instabilities of the psychological field and that the trend of behavior is toward reestablishing a stable field must not be identified with theories of equilibriums in simple mechanical and physiological systems. For one thing, the individual may not perceive a state of equilibrium as a goal for his action. For another thing, the successive states of equilibrium in the psychological field are not static but constantly changing, often toward progressively higher levels.

The psychological field of the person is highly complex, due to the very intricacy of a given situation and to the overlapping of several simultaneous situations, including those involving the past and the future. Such complexity would result in chaotic behavior, save for the organization of the person's needs, demands, and goals in such a way that there are *priorities and hierarchies of importance* among them. The integration of needs, demands, and goals is accomplished through the development of a system of ideals, values, and ideology within the individual, which guides and organizes the competing motives.

The individual's feelings of self-regard, etc., arise out of his perception of himself in relation to his ideals, values, and ideology. His wish for self-esteem is seen, for example, in the setting of progressively higher levels of aspiration for himself.

Defense and enhancement of feelings of self-regard, etc., are potent sources of motivation. The various means of tension reduction discussed under Proposition IV may be viewed as operating in such a way as to be maximally protective of the self.

The normal process of growth and socialization of the individual is one of development and multiplication of various self-involvements with objects, people, groups, and social organizations in the world about him.   These self-involvements give birth to important new needs, demands, and goals.

BIBLIOGRAPHY

ADLER, A.: 1925.   *The practice and theory of individual psychology.*   New York: Harcourt Brace.

ALLPORT, G. W.: 1937.   *Personality: A psychological interpretation.*   New York: Holt.

ALLPORT, G. W.: 1945.   Catharsis and the reduction of prejudice.   *J. Soc. Issues,* **1,** No. 3, 3–10.

BARKER, R., DEMBO, T., and LEWIN, K.: 1940.   Frustration and regression: an experiment with young children.   *Univ. Ia. Stud. Child Wel.,* **18,** No. 1.

CANNON, W. B.: 1929.   *Bodily changes in pain, hunger, fear and rage.*   New York: Appleton.

CANNON, W. B.: 1932.   *The wisdom of the body.*   Rev. ed.   New York: Norton.

DOLLARD, J., DOOB, L., et al. 1939.   *Frustration and aggression.*   New Haven: Yale Univ. Press.

FRANK, L. K.: 1939.   Projective methods for the study of personality.   *J. Psychol.,* **8,** 389–413.

FRENKEL-BRUNSWIK, E., and SANFORD, R. N.: 1945.   Some personality factors in anti-Semitism.   *J. Psychol.,* **20,** 271–291.

FROMM, E.: 1941.   *Escape from freedom.*   New York: Rinehart & Co., Inc.

GOULD, R.: 1939.   An experimental analysis of "level of aspiration."   *Genet. Psychol. Monogr.,* **21,** No. 1.

HEIDER, F.: 1939.   Environmental determinants in psychological theories.   *Psychol. Rev.,* **46,** 383–410.

HENLE, M.: 1942.   An experimental investigation of dynamic and structural determinants of substitution.   *Contr. psychol. Theor.,* **2,** No. 3.

HOPPE, F.: 1930.   *Erfolg und Misserfolg.*   *Psychol. Forsch.,* **40,** 1–62.

HORNEY, K.: 1937.   *The neurotic personality of our time.*   New York: Norton.

HORNEY, K.: 1939.   *New ways in psychoanalysis.*   New York: Norton.

HORNEY, K.: 1945.   *Our inner conflicts.*   New York: Norton.

JONES, E.: 1941a.   Evolution and revolution.   *Int. J. Psycho-Anal.,* **22,** 193–208.

JONES, E.: 1941b.   The psychology of quislingism.   *Int. J. Psycho-Anal.,* **22,** 1–6.

KÖHLER, W.: 1938.   *The place of value in a world of facts.*   New York: Liveright.

LEWIN, K.: 1935.   *A dynamic theory of personality.*   New York: McGraw-Hill.

LEWIN, K.: 1936.   *Principles of topological psychology.*   New York: McGraw-Hill.

McDOUGALL, W.: 1923.   *Outline of psychology.*   New York: Scribner.

MacLEOD, R. B.: 1947.   The phenomenological approach to social psychology.   *Psychol. Rev.,* **54,** 193–210.

MUENZINGER, K.: 1942.   *Psychology: The science of behavior.*   New York: Harper.

MURPHY, G., MURPHY, L. B., and NEWCOMB, T. M.: 1937.   *Experimental social psychology.*   New York: Harper.

MURRAY, H. A.: 1938.   *Explorations in personality.*   New York: Oxford.

NEWCOMB, T. M.: 1947.   Autistic hostility and social reality.   *Hum. Relat.,* **1,** 69–86.

OVSIANKINA, M.: 1928.   Die Wiederaufnahme unterbrochener Handlungen.   *Psychol. Forsch.,* **11,** 302–379.

SARGENT, H.: 1945. Projective methods: their origins, theory, and application in personality research. *Psychol. Bull.*, **42**, 257–293.

SHERIF, M., and CANTRIL, H.: 1947. *The psychology of ego-involvements.* New York: Wiley.

Society for the Psychological Study of Social Issues: 1946. Psychology and atomic energy. *Amer. Psychol.*, **1**, 358–359.

THORNDIKE, E. L.: 1911. *Animal intelligence.* New York: Macmillan.

TOLMAN, E. C.: 1932. *Purposive behavior in animals and men.* New York: Century.

WALLACH, H., and HENLE, M.: 1941. An experimental analysis of the law of effect. *J. exp. Psychol.*, **28**, 340–349.

WOODWORTH, R. S.: 1918. *Dynamic psychology.* New York: Columbia Univ. Press.

WRIGHT, H. F.: 1937. The influence of barriers upon strength of motivation. *Contr. psychol. Theor.*, **1**, No. 3.

CHAPTER III

PERCEIVING THE WORLD

Men eat their meals, walk out on strike, play bridge with people they do not like, and sign mimeographed petitions to Congress because by so doing they seek to satisfy various needs and achieve sundry goals. The underlying reason, the *initiating* cause, for behavior is to be found, we have seen, in an analysis of needs, goals, and tensions. But, as we have also seen, a description of the motivated act involves a description of the individual's perceptions. Action is not a formless, disembodied, and meaningless explosion of energy released by accumulated tension. It has direction and content, and the direction and content of action are shaped by the individual's conceptions about his world.

It may be true to say that Mr. Arbuthnot goes to church because he wants to identify himself with the solid citizens of the community. But such a motivational analysis provides only a partial description with which to begin an account of his behavior. Why does Mr. Arbuthnot think that churchgoing will help him achieve his goal? Why that particular church? How does he recognize who the solid citizens are? Only when we know the answers to these questions and many other similar questions can we give a useful analysis of Arbuthnot's churchgoing behavior.

It may appear obvious that the content and direction of action is shaped by knowledge and experience, but this statement is pregnant with problems for the psychologist—problems whose solution is necessary before we can write a scientific social psychology. A few illustrations will make clear the importance and nature of these problems.

BASIC PROBLEMS IN PERCEPTION AND COGNITION FOR THE SOCIAL PSYCHOLOGIST

Let us start with the simple case of the dependence of action on perception. You meet an acquaintance on the street and stop to talk with him. A complete scientific analysis of this bit of social intercourse must begin with your "seeing" him. Had you not perceived your acquaintance at all, there would be no social intercourse to explain. But why have you seen him? This is not a simple question. The answer is not "Because he was there to be seen." Occasionally you walk right by acquaintances without noticing them, without being aware of their presence. You are lost in thought and fail to see what is "there to be seen," or you fail to recognize the package-burdened individual hurrying through a crowd of shoppers as the dignified man of your acquaintance—the president of the university. *What will an individual perceive? What are the laws of such simple perception?*

Another example: Even if we should know under what conditions you will perceive a certain object among all those physically present, we still need to know the properties of that perception. What will the object "look like" to you? A labor leader and the president of an industrial concern with whom he is negotiating the end of a strike pass the picket line around the plant. Do both men perceive the pickets in an identical way? The labor leader may see a group of friendly, earnest men who stand ready to back up his reasonable demands; the industrial leader may see a mob of unshaven, foreign-looking, disreputable men who "look" incapable of thinking for themselves. *What are the contents and properties of an individual's perception? What determines these properties?*

But even with a complete statement of the properties of the immediate experience (or perceptions) of the individual, we should still not have enough for a description of his psychological world. While what we perceive, our "perceptual world," is dependent in a complicated but orderly way on the nature of the physical objects which surround us, it is also dependent upon objects and events not immediately present. How we perceive the world is a product of memory, imagination, hearsay, and fantasy as well as what we are actually "perceiving" through our senses. If we are to understand social behavior, we must know how all perceptions, memories, fantasies are combined or integrated or organized into present *cognitive structures*. Very few percepts exist alone—almost every percept becomes organized together with other percepts. In the perception and thinking of the individual Ku Klux Klan member concerning people who inhabit his cognitive world—no matter how they got there, whether through direct sensory perception or through hearsay and fantasy—how are these people grouped? We may find that he divides his people into four groups— "White, English-speaking, Protestant members of the Democratic party"; "White, damyankee northern Republicans"; "Papists, Jews and foreigners"; "Niggers." On the other hand we may find that the sociologist divides his world into many more and many different groups and subgroups and subgroups within subgroups. To know how individuals will perceive single people we must know how they will group them—we must, as it were, have a "map" of their cognitive world. *What are the structures and substructures of an individual's cognitive world and their interrelations? What are the laws of organization of such structures?*

As indicated by the above questions, there are really two major problems for social psychology in connection with cognitive organization. (1) There is the specific descriptive problem: What are the relevant cognitive structures and their properties in the individual whose social behavior the psychologist is attempting to analyze or to understand or to predict or to change? (2) There is the problem of isolating the general principles or laws that determine the nature of the individual's cognitive world.

The Problem of Description.—In a sense, the first problem is a problem of "applied" psychology. The psychologist who is interested in describing the political attitudes of, say, the small businessman must determine for the members of that class the cognitive contents of their "political world." Without that he cannot make much useful sense out of their expressions of opinions which he may have laboriously recorded during his polls and surveys. As we shall see in Chap. VII and VIII, it is the failure of most public opinion studies to fulfill this requirement that makes their data extremely difficult to interpret.

To get a good description of a man's cognitive world is extremely difficult. Nevertheless, this task is an essential objective for the social psychologist. As was illustrated by the examples we have used and by the analysis of the dynamics of behavior in Chap. II, a psychologically useful description of the behavior of people must start with a description from the perspective of "the other one"—and therein lies the difficulty. We must know what Arbuthnot perceives and what is the nature of Arbuthnot's cognitive world. It will not do to know what the social psychologist perceives or thinks or what the social psychologist, on the basis of his knowledge and theories, thinks Arbuthnot *should* perceive.

Description of direct experience.—In more technical terms, what we need is a good "phenomenological" description of Arbuthnot's cognitive world. The *phenomenological method* (as the term is used by experimenters in perception psychology) can be briefly described as the systematic attempt to observe and describe the world as it appears to the experiencing individual. As MacLeod (1947) describes this method, "It involves the adoption of what might be called an attitude of disciplined naivete. It requires the deliberate suspension of all implicit and explicit assumptions, *e.g.*, as to eliciting stimulus or underlying mechanism, which might bias our observation." In addition to all the other techniques of investigation that the social psychologist must use, the development of a technique by which he can obtain a good description of the individual's direct experience would prove extremely helpful.

There are several major difficulties by which the student of social behavior is persistently plagued when he attempts to infer the relevant cognitive structures of his subjects.[1] The first of these major difficulties derives from a tendency to apply terms taken from one level of analysis to a description of phenomena treated on another level.[2] The history of the psychology of perception is replete with such confusion. For example, because lemonade, as a physical object, could be physically analyzed into substances having the chemical qualities that could separately lead to sensations of sweetness, sourness, and coldness, some early perception psychologists tended to assume that the subject who tasted lemonade should experience the separate sensations of sweetness, sourness, etc. If a subject reported that he did not experience these separate elements but rather that he experienced something describable only as a whole— with a different set of attributes—then the experimenter wrote off that subject as an untrained, naive subject who was worthless for the scientific investigation of "experience." Since laws of experience are no better than the descriptive data upon which they are based, the resulting laws of sensation and perception proved of doubtful value.

In the field of social psychology much the same sort of error can be made. For example, the church or political party that may influence our subject's action is frequently described, not as it is apprehended by the individual whose behavior we are trying to understand but as apprehended by a trained sociologist. The dimensions used by the good sociologist may be completely valid as a *sociological* description (just as the dimensions used by the early psychologist in describing lemonade were valid as a stimulus description), but to describe a single church member's behavior in terms of the sociologist's perception of the church or to describe a specific diplomat's maneuverings in terms of the historian's perception of political events is to confuse the two levels of description and to substitute the observer's cognitive world for the subject's cognitive world.

The second type of error might be called the "logical error." This error involves reading one's logical deductions into the psychological world of the subject. For example, it might be demonstrated that anti-Negro action on the part of Southerners increases with a decrease in the price of cotton. To argue from this alone that the Southerner, when the price of cotton falls, apprehends the Negro as an economic competitor who must be kept "under control" is to commit the "logical error." No doubt, if the above correlation held, we could argue that the economic situation is

[1] A more complete discussion of the pitfalls in the way of a good description of the individual's social world is found in MacLeod's (1947) paper from which the present analysis was adopted in part.

[2] The dangers resulting from such confusion, it will be remembered, were stressed in Chap. I, p. 21.

an important condition for the increase of anti-Negro feelings; but no matter how logical the reasoning might seem to us, we could not argue that the Southerner necessarily sees the Negro as an economic competitor.

We have spent this time on the problem of describing the specific cognitive content of people's psychological worlds, (1) because of its general importance for understanding social behavior and (2) because of its practical importance for public opinion studies. Little has been done by psychologists and other social scientists in this field. Almost the entire task of obtaining a good description of the perceived social worlds of different people remains yet to be done. For the student interested in obtaining insight into the social behavior of people, this whole area offers an exciting and rewarding field of research.

The Problem of Laws.—The second problem facing the social psychologist in the field of perception and cognition is that of discovering general principles and laws. It was pointed out above that "laws of experience are no better than the descriptive data upon which they are based." From this it might appear that since social psychology does not have many sound descriptions of the perceived social world of individuals to draw upon, valid principles of cognitive organization cannot be formulated. This conclusion does not, however, follow. Psychology does have a host of well-verified experimental facts and descriptions obtained from so-called "nonsocial" material—the perception of simple visual forms, auditory stimulus patterns, etc. It is true that if we are interested in the actual cognitive content of any individual's social world, there can be no substitute for descriptive data collected about it specifically. But it is also true that if we are interested in the general operation of the cognitive processes of one's social world, then data collected with almost any cognitive material will do. This is merely repeating what was pointed out at length in Chap. I that there are no processes of "social perception" different from those of any other kinds of perception.

Extending the application of the principles of organization.—Extending the perceptual laws discovered in the laboratory to cover social phenomena involves more than the extrapolation of principles to "new" material. These "principles of organization" must be generalized to cover the phenomena both of sensory perception and of cognition. This extension is based on the theory (and observation) that the mental organization of the individual follows similar laws whether the "data" for such organizations are given perceptually (as technically defined, *i.e.*, through mediation of the senses) or in some other way. In the technical sense we do not "perceive" the shape of an individual's nose from hearing a description of it in the same way that we perceive it when we look at it. Nor do we perceive the action of another country (through our newspaper accounts) in the same way that we perceive a series of dots on a blackboard. But no matter how the data making up our cognitive world "got there" in the first place, the resulting cognitive organizations follow the fundamental organizing principles that hold for sensory perception. It is because of this generality of the organizing principles that we can apply a law which was derived in the first instance from a study of our perceptual organization of sights, sounds, and tactual impressions to our cognitive organization of "ideas."

Although the above may be true, it is necessary, nevertheless, to regard all such laws with some caution. These laws are the best ones which can be formulated at this stage in the development of psychology; and as we shall see in Parts II and III of this book, they are useful in helping us to understand social behavior. With further research it may be discovered that these laws will have to be modified when applied specifically to certain kinds of social material. Here, too, the student of social psychology has a challenging field of research open to him. Each one of these principles of organization should be tested experimentally with social material in significant social situations. Recent work in this direction has already demonstrated experimentally (as we shall see later on in this chapter) that there is some justification for such extrapolation, but much further verification remains to be done.

TWO MAJOR DETERMINANTS OF PERCEPTION

The principles of organization are frequently grouped into two major categories: the principles relating to the *structural* factors of perception and those relating to the *functional* factors involved in perception. Experimental and theoretical literature in perception psychology is replete with discussions as to the relative importance of these two sets of factors.

Structural Factors.—By *structural* factors are meant those factors deriving solely from the nature of the physical stimuli and the neural effects they evoke in the nervous system of the individual.[1] Thus, for the Gestalt psychologist, perceptual organizations are determined primarily by the physiological events occuring in the nervous system of the individual in direct reaction to the stimulation by the physical objects. Though not denying the influence, under certain conditions, of motivation and mental set, they emphasize that the sensory factors are primary in accounting for the "look of things."

To use a very simple and common example, the Gestalt psychologist

[1] The term *autochthonous* is frequently used by the Gestalt psychologist when referring to these factors.

would point out that our perception of the dots in Fig. 1*a* is perforce a perception of two horizontal groupings and not, say, an ungrouped collection of dots or of five vertical groupings, etc. Furthermore, they would insist that the factors which force this organization derive from the spatial relationships among the physical dots themselves as faithfully projected in the sensory region of the brain and are relatively independent of our reasoning, needs, moods, past learning, etc. To repeat: Those sensory factors which are independent of the perceiving individual's needs and personality and which force certain organizations in his cognitive field are referred to as "structural factors of perception." The isolation of

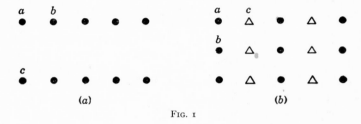

(a)   (b)

Fig. 1

these factors, their careful description, and the laws of their operation have led to the formulation of the "laws of organization."

Functional Factors.—The *functional* factors of perceptual organization, on the other hand, are those which derive primarily from the needs, moods, past experience, and memory of the individual.[1] Thus, for example, in an experiment performed by Bruner and Goodman (1947), two groups of children (one a poor group from a settlement house in one of Boston's slum areas and the other a rich group from a "progressive school in the the Boston area, catering to the sons and daughters of prosperous business and professional people") were asked to judge the size of various coins. The differences in the perceptions of the two groups of children were striking, with the poor group overestimating the size of the coins considerably more than did the rich group. The experimenters suggest that these results indicate the effect of need upon perception, and they formulate the following two hypotheses as possible general laws:

1. *The greater the social value of an object, the more will it be susceptible to organization by behavioral determinants.*

[1] The term *functional* as applied to these factors was first suggested by Muenzinger (1942). In their treatment of these same factors, Bruner and Goodman (1947) suggest the term "behavioral determinants" which they define as ". . . those active, adaptive functions of the organism which lead to the governance and control of all higher-level functions, including perception. . . ."

2. *The greater the individual need for a socially valued object, the more marked will be the operation of behavioral determinants.*

Another illustration of the operation of functional factors is found in an experiment by Levine, Chein, and Murphy (1942). In that experiment, ambiguous drawings, when presented behind a ground-glass screen to hungry college students, were more frequently perceived as food objects (ham sandwiches, salads, etc.) than when presented to college students who had just finished eating. The different perceptions of the hungry and not-hungry students could not be due to "structural" factors, since the same pictures were presented to both groups but could be due only to the differences in need or motivation of the members of the two groups.

While quantitative laws of how these "functional" factors actually operate in perception are lacking, a great deal of experimental work is available that demonstrates their pervasive influence in perception.

Interrelationship between Structural and Functional Factors.— The interaction that is true for most psychological processes is also characteristic of the operation of structural and functional factors in perception. Neither set operates alone; every perception involves both kinds of factors. Although we can experiment with structural factors alone in perception or with functional factors alone, we must realize that this is done only for experimental convenience, that whatever perception is being observed is a function of both sets of factors.[1]

It is important to recognize the interrelationships between these two sets of factors because it is at this point that a necessary rapprochement can be made between the experimental psychologist who tends to analyze man into his component functions and the social psychologist who seeks to treat man as an indivisible entity. The traditional experimentalist has tended to study "cold" perceptions, cognitions, learning, and thinking. He has put aside, when he entered his laboratory, what he knew about the "interference" with these processes by such "nonintellectual" and bothersome processes as emotion, attitudes, needs. On the other hand, the experimentalist in the field of motivation has tended to neglect man's cognitive life. This piecemeal approach may frequently be necessary in the laboratory in order to make manageable the experimental investigation of the particular process that interests the researcher. But when we deal with man in society, when our behavior is of such molar proportions, we cannot deal with disembodied perceptions and noncognitive motives. We

[1] For an experimental demonstration that the structural factors of organization, in the perceptions of animals, seem to be influenced by functional factors, see the experiment by Krechevsky (1938) in which the functioning of the "law of proximity" was studied under various problem conditions, each with its own "demands."

must seek to deal with all these functions as they are found in man in the business world, the family, the political campaign, etc.

In studying the following principles of cognitive organizations, therefore, the student should always bear in mind that each principle refers to the operation of both factors as found in "living" perceptions. No attempt will be made to "tease out" the structural factors from the functional factors or the "learned" organizations from the "unlearned" organizations. In listing, describing, and illustrating the major propositions concerning perception and cognition, no attempt will be made here to justify them or to demonstrate their validity by appeal to experimental evidence. There are available several good summaries of the experimental foundations for the organizational principles used, and the student is referred to them.[1]

PROPOSITION I
The perceptual and cognitive field in its natural state is organized and meaningful

This first proposition affirms that the cognitive field, except perhaps in rare pathological conditions, is never a "blooming, buzzing, confusion" of discrete impressions, unrelated experiences and unitary sensations. Whether we are discussing the initial sensory stimulations of the infant or the experiences of the adult when confronted by new and even bizarre objects and events, the individual's cognitive fields are organized and meaningful. A few examples may clarify the meaning of this proposition.[2]

"Simple" Perception.—A baby is presented, for the first time in his life, with a red balloon on a white table. Considered purely physically, the "balloon" and the "table" can be described only as a visual field consisting of discrete pin points of stimuli consisting of light of varying wave lengths. What is the infant's resulting experience from this conglomeration of physical stimuli? Is it a mosaic of indifferently related kaleidoscopic sensations of reds and whites merging into one another, without form and without clearly defined boundaries, or is the child's experience better described as a perception of a red object having form and solidity against a background of a white object with its own form and solidity? Proposition I would require that the latter situation hold. The infant's per-

[1] Koffka (1935) and Kohler (1947) present the best systematic account of these principles. Ellis's source book (1938) makes available in English many of the experimental papers originally written in German.

[2] For a discussion of the distinction between organized perceptions "without meaning" and organized perceptions "with meaning," see Tolman's (1933) paper. He characterizes the first concept as that held by the "pure Gestaltist," the second as that held by the "sign-Gestaltist."

ceptual field would consist of at least two discriminable, meaningful structures. The meanings might be extremely simple and might even be wrong—but there would be meaning. Thus, the red object might have the meaning that "this object if inserted in the mouth can be chewed and swallowed," and the white object may mean "this object, if pushed, will jiggle." The important thing is that the baby's experiences will be organized and meaningful.

Proposition I does not assert how much of this cognitive structure is due to the previous experiences of the baby or if the meanings are conditioned by hunger and activity needs. All we are concerned with is the nature of his cognitive field when he is stimulated by the balloon and the table.

The Strange and Bizarre.—Or take another example. A savage who has never seen a white man or any of the paraphernalia of the white man's civilization sees an Army airplane descend from the skies and make a three-point landing and sees Second Lieutenant Arbuthnot come out of the plane. Obviously our savage will see the airplane and Arbuthnot as organized objects, but will they, because he has never seen their likes before, be completely meaningless to him? Again, the meaning he experiences may be wrong, but there will be meaning. He may experience the meaning of a "bird" as part of his purely visual percept of the airplane; he may ascribe the meaning of "God" or its equivalent to Arbuthnot, 2nd Lt. AUS. He will not have to wait until he is given instructions or until he has had further and extended experiences with these strange objects before his cognitive field is organized into a meaningful one.[1]

Forming an Impression of a Personality.—A final example: In an experiment reported by Asch (1946) an attempt was made to determine how people form impressions of personality through hearing simple descriptions of the personality.[2] The experimenter read to his subjects (college students) a number of discrete characteristics which were said to belong to an unknown person. He then instructed his subjects to write a brief description of the impression the subject had gained of this unknown person. One such list, for example, was: "energetic, assured,

---

[1] The American school child who listened to his teacher sing various Christmas carols in foreign tongues and when asked to join with her sang "Atomic Bomb, Atomic Bomb" to the tune of "O Tannenbaum, O Tannenbaum" is an amusing and at the same time a somewhat horrifying illustration of the tendency to perceive strange sounds meaningfully. Akin to this is the youngster's remark who, after hearing the hymn that starts "Gladly the Cross I'd bear," asked "Why was the bear cross-eyed?"

[2] This experiment of Asch's is an interesting and valuable illustration of an experimental attempt to apply principles of "pure" perception to social material. See the discussion on p. 80 of this chapter.

talkative, cold, ironical, inquisitive, persuasive." The list was read with an interval of approximately five seconds between the terms. Then the reading was repeated. Below are reproduced two of the typical sketches obtained from the subjects:

He is the type of person you meet all too often: sure of himself, talks too much, always trying to bring you around to his way of thinking, and with not much feeling for the other fellow.
He impresses people as being more capable than he really is. He is popular and never ill at ease. Easily becomes the center of attraction at any gathering. He is likely to be a jack-of-all-trades. Although his interests are varied, he is not necessarily well versed in any of them. He possesses a sense of humor. His presence stimulates enthusiasm and very often he does arrive at a position of importance.

Note how the discrete terms of the list have been organized into a living, meaningful, and even colorful personality. Not only have the individual terms *energetic, assured, talkative*, etc., been perceived in an organized way with an organized meaning, but the resulting organization of the terms has permitted the subject to "perceive" characteristics that were not even mentioned ("He possesses a sense of humor"). Asch summarizes the results of his experiments as follows:

When a task of this kind is given, a normal adult is capable of responding to the instruction by forming a unified impression. Though he hears a sequence of discrete terms, his resulting impression is not discrete. All subjects . . . of whom there were over 1,000 fulfilled the task in the manner described . . . . Starting from the bare terms, the final account is completed and rounded.

General Comments.—What is true about our experiences with objects and people is also true about our experiences with events and ideas. Strange and new social mores, taboos, and relationships are not seen by us as meaningless but are immediately perceived with meaning. We cannot help doing this. Man is an organizing animal. This accounts, in many instances, for our misinterpretation or misunderstanding of the customs, habits, values, and institutions of foreigners and strangers. We cannot say to ourselves, "Hold off any interpretation until you collect all the facts." As soon as we experience *any* facts, they will be perceived as organized into some sort of meaningful whole. This is a universal characteristic of the cognitive process and not a weakness of the impatient or prejudiced individual. In the experiment of Asch's referred to above, an experimental demonstration of the immediacy of this process is provided.

In one of his experimental setups Asch read two different lists of traits to two different groups of subjects and again asked for personality descriptions. The two lists were identical with regard to the traits used but differed in the order of succession. For example, one group heard the following list: "intelligent, industrious, impulsive, critical, stubborn, envious." The other group heard the same words, but in reversed order: "envious, stubborn, critical, impulsive, industrious, intelligent." The descriptions obtained from the two groups of subjects differed markedly, leading Asch to conclude that "When the subject hears the first term, a broad, uncrystallized but directed impression is born. The next characteristic comes not as a separate item, but is related to the established direction."

Our perception of the dots in Fig. 1*a* (page 82) as two sets of horizontal lines and the over-all impression we form of a man's personality from knowing only one or two facts about him are both instances of the same fundamental process of cognitive organization. This principle also helps us to understand the tenacity with which people hold on to "disproved" scientific theories or economic and political dogmas. No matter how much evidence one can bring to bear that a scientific theory does not fit the known facts, scientists are reluctant to give it up until one can give them another integration to take the place of the old. Merely attacking a well-integrated theory cannot be very effective. The old theory does integrate facts for people, does organize discrete experiences. In the absence of some other way of organizing facts, people will frequently hold on to the old, for no other reason than that.

PROPOSITION II

Perception is functionally selective

No one perceives everything that there is "out there" to be perceived. Our mental apparatus is not an indifferent organizing machine ready to accord equal importance to all stimuli that impinge upon our sense organs. The factors that determine the specific organization of our cognitive field and select out only certain stimuli to integrate into that field are frequently at work even before we are exposed to the physical stimuli. Typically, only certain physical stimuli are "used" in making up the organized perception, while other stimuli are either not used at all or are given a very minor role. This is what is meant by saying that perception is "selective."

Proposition II, however, also indicates that this selectivity is functional. The objects that play the major role in the organized perception, the objects that are *accentuated*, *are usually those objects which serve some immediate purpose of the perceiving individual.*[1] As our first motivational proposition has indicated, our basic, most useful unit in understanding the social behavior of the individual is the molar unit—a unit in terms of needs, tensions, and goals. To ask the question, then, "Why are certain objects selected to play a major role in most cognitive organizations?" is to ask the question, "What function does any cognitive organization serve?" The answer to this question not only will tell us what objects will be selected for perceptual organization but will also indicate the meaning with which those objects will be perceived.

Functional Selectivity of Perception and Dynamics of Behavior.— Illustrations of the effects of needs, mental sets, moods, etc., in selecting out certain objects for a major role in perception are commonplace. So, too, are illustrations of the effect of these dynamic processes on the meanings given to the resulting perceptions.

Needs.—Let us take the simple example of two men seated at a lunch-room counter surveying the posted menu on the wall. One is very hungry; the other, only thirsty. Both are exposed to the same physical objects, yet the first will notice the hamburger and tomato-and-lettuce sandwiches, while the "tea, coffee, beer, pepsi-cola" items will be neglected or relatively so. The second man will react in the opposite manner. Ask both men to tell you what they "saw" on the menu, and the first will respond with a list of food items "and other stuff"; the second will enumerate the drink items "and other things." In one case the food items have been clearly and specifically perceived and organized against a background of non-differentiated "other stuff"; in the second case the figure-ground relationships have been reversed.

That needs, rewards, and punishments can even determine in simple visual perception which aspect of a visual field will be selected out as the figure and which as the ground has been demonstrated by an experiment of Schafer and Murphy (1943). In that experiment two somewhat ambiguous figures were presented momentarily to the subjects. Each figure was so designed that part of the picture could be seen as an outline of a human face. Every time one of these faces was presented and seen as a face, the subject was rewarded (with money); every time the other figure was presented and seen as a face, the subject was punished (some of his

---

[1] It should be clear that this does not necessarily mean that *only* those stimuli which serve some function or other will be noticed or seen by the subject. This statement affirms that the functionally significant stimuli will be given the major role to play, although other stimuli may be noticed peripherally, as it were. Bruner and Goodman (1947) make the further interesting suggestion that with habitual selection, the stimuli which are thus selected for major attention tend to become progressively more vivid and achieve greater clarity.

money being taken away). The technique, in other words, was to build up a strong association between certain visual patterns and rewards and between other visual patterns and punishments. After this was done, the "rewarded" pattern and the "punished" pattern were combined into one picture in such a manner as to make it possible to perceive either face as the figure or as the ground. A significantly higher number of the faces that had previously been rewarded, when perceived alone, were now perceived as the *figure* in this combined picture than were faces that had been punished. (Fifty-four out of sixty-seven perceptions were perceptions of the rewarded faces as figures.)

That the meaning of what is selected for major attention in perception is influenced by needs is also apparent. We have already seen both in Levine, Chein, and Murphy's experiment and in Bruner and Goodman's experiment (pages 82*f*.) that the immediate perception of ambiguous objects is shaped by the hunger needs of the subjects and that the perceived size of a coin is determined by the differential goal character of the coins for the poor and rich children. On a more complicated level, Sanford (1936, 1937) has shown that the need for food, in children and in adults of college age, has a significant effect upon word association, interpretation of "neutral" pictures (*i.e.*, pictures having nothing to do, directly, with eating or with food), chain associations, completion of drawings, and completion of words where only the first two letters of a word were given. For example, a picture of a baby, a finger of whose hand was extended, was interpreted to mean "He's sticking his finger in the pie" by some of the hungry subjects, while some of the nonhungry subjects interpreted it as "He's pointing to a toy."

The successful diagnosis of individual need structures by the "projective technique" mentioned in Chap. II (page 49) provides dramatic illustrations of the principles we have been discussing here. For the very use of this technique depends upon the fact that the specific perceptual and cognitive organizations with which the individual responds to pictures and words reflect his basic needs.

Mental Set.—Here, too, illustrations abound in everyday experiences. We see hundreds of men, every day, wearing different suits of clothing— suits that differ in cut, material, color, styling, number of buttons, etc. But usually all we perceive is that they are wearing clothes, and our resulting perceptual organization is not a very clear cut and differentiated one. What is the mental picture you have, for example, of the suit you saw your friend wear yesterday? But if we are on the way to a store to buy a suit, our perceptions of the clothes worn by friends and even strangers change rather remarkably. We notice the colors of the suits; we see shapes of pockets, cuts of lapels, presence or absence of pocket flaps which we never perceived before. With our changed mental set different objects are selected out for perception, and our resulting cognitive structures become much more differentiated and detailed.

A simple experiment by Murray (1933) has indicated how the mental set of the individual influences the meaning of what he perceives. Using girls as his subjects, Murray asked them to describe the picture of a man under two conditions—before these subjects had played a game of "murder" and after. In the latter instance the subjects tended to see much more maliciousness in the man's features than they did in the former instance.

The policeman, the social worker, the ward politician, and the foreign visitor walking through the same slum district not only interpret what they see differently but actually perceive different objects. The mental set of the perceiver can sometimes be of absolute importance in determining selective perception.

Mood.—An ingenious experiment of Leuba and Lucas (1945) provides some striking illustrations of how the mood or temperament of an individual operates to select out different stimuli for perceptual organization and tends to determine the meaning of the stimuli so selected.

The experiment involved the description of six pictures by three subjects when in each of three different moods: happy, critical, and anxious. Each of the three subjects was first hypnotized; the first mood was then induced by the appropriate hypnotic suggestions; and then the pictures were shown. After the subject had observed each picture, he was asked to describe what he had seen. When the six descriptions had been obtained, the subject was allowed to rest for a while, the first mood was removed by suggestion, he was brought back to his "normal" hypnotic state and told that he would forget having seen the pictures and what he had said about them. Then the next mood was induced, and the procedure repeated.

The final hypnotic suggestions for the different moods were as follows:

HAPPY MOOD: "Now you are feeling very happy and you are in a cheerful and joyous mood. You feel as if everything is rosy and you are very optimistic. You have a comfortable feeling of well-being; nothing is worrying you. You feel perfectly at peace with everything and everyone. You are in a very happy, cheerful, and optimistic mood."

CRITICAL MOOD: "Now you are very critical; you are quick to find fault and to condemn unfavorably. Your judgment of others is very harsh and severe. You see failings and faults very clearly. You are very critical and fault finding."

ANXIOUS MOOD: "Now you are quite anxious. You are disturbed over some possible misfortunes. You are disquieted and concerned as to something in the future. You are a little fearful and mildly alarmed. You have a feeling as if you were expecting something disagreeable to happen, yet were not sure that it would. You are quite anxious."

Following are three descriptions that one of the subjects gave for a picture showing "four college men on a sunny lawn, typing, listening to radio." In the happy mood his description read:

"Complete relaxation. Not much to do—just sit, listen and relax. Not much at all to think about."

When this subject was in a critical mood he observed or paid attention to or perceived, different things. Now his description ran:

"Someone ruining a good pair of pressed pants by lying down like that. They're unsuccessfully trying to study."

When in an anxious mood, still other items were perceived:

"They're listening to a football game or world series. Probably a tight game. One guy looks as if his side wasn't winning."

Notice how in the happy mood there seems to be little attention to details. The perceptual structure seems to be fairly simple and undifferentiated. In the critical mood a specific detail—the crease in one man's trousers—seems to occupy a central role in the perceptual field, an item which had not been reported at all in the first description. In the final mood, anxious, the details of the facial expression of one of the men are closely observed and interpreted, and now the cognitive field includes something that is not even physically present—a football or baseball game.

The different moods of the subjects had a directive effect not only on *what* was observed but, even more strongly, on the meaning of what was perceived. Thus, in analyzing some of the descriptions obtained from the subjects, the experimenters write:

The meanings and feelings attached to the activities shown in the pictures and the probable causes and results of those activities are usually different from mood to mood. In a happy frame of mind the Ss see the soldier in picture III (wounded man being carried on a litter by soldiers to aeroplane) as being "well taken care of" and as being taken "back to safety" or "a transport plane." When in an anxious mood these same Ss say the soldier "is in bad shape," "may not live," "an emergency case," "it frightens me."

Things are very rarely what they seem. The emotions, moods, personalities, and temperaments of people color and determine what they see "out there." The entire cognitive world of the individual who has an overriding need for security will be organized on quite a different basis from the individual who does not seek constant reassurances. "Wishful thinking" and "wishful perception" have similar sources. The man who fears a war and seeks peace will perceive political events, people, speeches, diplomatic forays, and production figures quite differently from the man who welcomes a war. The selectivity of perception is in large measure determined by the dynamics of behavior.

Functional Selectivity of Perception and Culture.—What we perceive, as well as how we interpret what we perceive, is not only a function of those processes which can be specifically defined as motivational ones. Our immediate perceptions are also a function of the "higher order" cognitive organizations—of beliefs, of social ideals, of morals, of cultural frames of reference. The effect of these higher order cognitive organizations will be examined in more detail when discussing Proposition III, but for purposes of completeness a simple illustration at this point might be helpful.

Take, for example, the perceptions of an American tourist and a native Mexican at a Mexican bull fight. The American is likely to perceive and stress the pain to the animal, the messiness of the scene, and the flies. The Mexican fan, on the other hand, might perceive and stress the skill of the performer, his daring or fearlessness, the fine technical points involved, and even the fine spirit of the bull in putting up such a good fight.

What is selected out for perception not only is a function of our perceiving apparatus as physiologically defined but is partly a function of our perceiving apparatus as colored and shaped by our culture.

Functional Selectivity of Perception and Structural Factors.—We must always remember, however, that in addition to the various factors discussed above, the physical distribution and qualities of the stimuli also help determine which stimuli, of the welter of stimuli impinging on our sense organs, will be selected out for perception. The familiar figure-on-background or "isolation" experiment of the perception laboratory illustrates this factor in operation. A single red dot, among many black dots, will "stand out" in perception. A single Negro in a crowd of white people is much more likely to be noticed by a neutral perceiver than if that individual were seen among many other Negroes. The slogan most frequently repeated (and most loudly) is also more likely to come to the attention of the individual than the infrequently mentioned one.

The "structural" factors involved in the creation and presentation of propaganda and educational material are sometimes quite important in determining what perceptions the "victims" or "students" will experience, as we shall see when we discuss those subjects. We must be constantly on guard against neglecting these structural factors in our attempt to pay proper attention to the functional factors. The physiological functioning of the nervous system in response to the nature of the distribution of the physical stimuli in space and time also operates so as to make perception selective.

General Comments.—The failure to understand the implications of Proposition II, that perception is functionally selective, has led to much misguided effort and heartbreaking disappointment on the part of teachers, parents, religious missionaries, and leaders of "causes." Take a child on a slumming trip to teach him the facts of social life, and show him how haggard, lean, scrawny, and undernourished the children are, and what does he "see"? He may perceive only the interesting alleys and inviting fire escapes that these children have to play with as compared with the clean, sterile, and uninteresting playrooms he has at his disposal. Show a documentary film of life in Russia to an insecure and hostile American, presenting pictures of Russian factory workers doing the same sort of things that Detroit factory workers do, Russian farm hands going through actions similar to those of Iowa farm hands, Russian traffic policemen gesticulating very much the way New York City "cops" do. Will he perceive all these similarities? Probably not. He will have noticed the large tractor factories which could so easily become converted to tank factories, he will have been impressed with the "militaristic" bearing of the policemen and with the "ruthless scowl" on the face of the Russian general who appeared for a few feet in the film.

On the occasion of the 1946 reprinting of Upton Sinclair's *The Jungle*, R. L. Duffus, reviewing the book in *The New York Times* of Oct. 13, 1946, gives an interesting illustration of how functional selectivity of perception can subvert the best intentions of the social reformer. Duffus writes:

After this book appeared, four decades ago, quite a number of Americans temporarily stopped eating meat . . . . They just didn't care for meat after they had read young Mr. Sinclair's fictionalized account of how meat was handled in the Chicago stockyards. This was not Mr. Sinclair's intention. He was a socialist and an ardent friend of the underpaid and overworked. He did not foresee that the American people, after reading of the misfortunes of his Lithuanian hero, would clamor, not for a cooperative commonwealth, but for a pure food law . . . . Young Mr. Sinclair admired the strong peasant stock that was pouring into this country so hopefully at the turn of the century. He hated to see it abused, as it was. He hated the cruelty which ground the lives out of men. He hated child labor. He hated the growling tyranny that fired and blacklisted when men formed unions to better their lot. He hated the cheating and the foul corruption that battened on the innocent. So he spent some seven weeks observing how people lived "back of the yards" and then wrote this book . . . . He . . . threw into it his burning indignation, lighted it with his ingenuous hopes of a world redeemed by socialism, and got it into print . . . it became a best seller, it has been translated into twenty-seven languages, it led to reforms in the handling of meat.

Upton Sinclair was a socialist, and the facts he perceived demonstrated, to him, the need for socialism. So he saw them, and so he wrote them down. The vast majority of his readers, however, were not socialists, but they were meat eaters, and they perceived his facts in their own way and read therefrom their own lesson. They selected out for major attention, not the stories about the little Stanislovs who were forced to work in the packing houses or the men like Jurgis who averaged a weekly salary of $6.65, but the other stories—about the workmen and stockyard rats who had fallen into lard vats and had gone out to the world as "pure leaf lard." Accordingly, his readers did not conclude from Sinclair's facts that the world must be redeemed by socialism but merely that a new pure food act was required.

There are no impartial "facts." Data do not have a logic of their own that results in the same perceptions and cognitions for all people. Data are perceived and interpreted in terms of the individual perceiver's own needs, own emotions, own personality, own previously formed cognitive patterns.

PROPOSITION III

The perceptual and cognitive properties of a substructure are determined in large measure by the properties of the structure of which it is a part

To know that experience in its natural state is organized and meaningful (Proposition I) and that the nature of the organization is determined functionally (Proposition II) is not enough. Our mental world is a structured or organized one, and it can also be seen as broken down into hierarchies of structures. Our cognitive field does not consist of completely independent organized structures; each of our perceptions is not an experience that "lives a life of its own," as it were. Every perception is embedded in an organization of other percepts—the whole going to make up a specific "cognitive structure." Each of these cognitive structures, in turn, can be broken down into several related substructures. Thus, when we perceive a politician, our perception of that particular politician is influenced by all our other percepts involving politicians. But the major structure, politicians, may have substructures: Democratic politicians, Republican politicians, honest politicians, etc. What we need for an adequate understanding of any one perception is knowledge about the interrelationships among the structures and substructures of our cognitive fields. Proposition III is designed to answer the questions raised by this point and states that the perception of a single object or group of objects is determined by the nature of the cognitive whole in which the percepts of these objects will be embedded.

Illustrations from Simple Visual Perception.—Figure 2 is usually perceived as a simple figure of three lines meeting at a center point *O*. Each angle made by any two adjacent lines, say angle *AOC*, can be described as a substructure of the figure. That is, the perception of that angle is of an organized figure "in its own right," but it is also perceived as a part of a larger figure—the whole of Fig. 2. Each of these angles is usually perceived as an obtuse angle, *i.e.*, larger than a right angle. What would happen to our perception of angle *AOC* if we added a few lines so as to induce a change in our perception of the *whole* structure without,

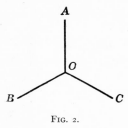

FIG. 2.

in any way changing the lines that make up angle *AOC*? The answer is immediately given if we look at Fig. 3. Now we perceive the substructure, angle *AOC*, as a right angle! Although we have not done anything physically to angle *AOC*, it "looks" different. It looks different because the *whole* figure, of which angle *AOC* is a part, looks different.

The same dependence of the perceptual properties of a part on the whole is seen in the *contrast* and *assimilation* experiments in visual perception. The results of these experiments can be summarized by the following statements: (1) Substructures of a major structure will tend to look either as much alike as possible (assimilation) or as much unlike as possible (contrast). (2) Assimilation appears when the differences between the substructures and the major structures are small; contrast appears when the differences are large. Thus, a series of black dots, in a single row, will all appear equally black despite the existence of minor differences in shade among them. Each dot, as a substructure of the row of dots, is assimilated, and the minor differences in blackness are not usually perceived. Conversely, if one dot were much brighter than the others, then that dot would be perceived as a light gray by virtue of being a member of a black contrasting series.

Now suppose that all you could see were angle *AOC* of Fig. 2 or only the single dot in our last illustration and you were told that a given person insisted that he perceived angle *AOC* as a right angle or that another individual perceived the dot as light gray. Would it not appear to you either that these people had defective vision or that they were inaccurate in their descriptions of their own perceptions? This would be a logical deduction if you could not see the whole of Fig. 2 of which angle *AOC* was a part or if you could not see the entire set of dots. What is true for simple visual perception is also true for other instances of perceptual organization. We cannot understand an individual's perception, or interpretation of an event that is part of a larger organization for *him*, unless

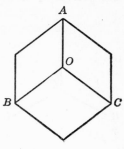

FIG. 3.

we also know what that larger organization is. This frequently accounts for the apparently incomprehensible perceptions and judgments of people and our failure to "understand" such people.

Perceiving Traits of Individuals and of Groups.—A reformulation of this whole-part principle, in more specific social terms, might be helpful at this point. Such a reformulation is given in the following statement: *When an individual is apprehended as a member of a group, each of those characteristics of the individual which correspond to the characteristics of the group is affected by his group membership, the effect being in the direction of either assimilation or contrast.* Among other uses, this formulation can be helpful in aiding us to understand why, in our perception of people, we frequently are "biased" or "unjust."

Assimilation and contrast.—Suppose you were told that Arbuthnot is a member of the Communist party. Now suppose, also, that your cognitive field corresponding to "Communists" consists of the following characteristics: Communists speak with foreign accents, are always ready to incite to riot, and are unkempt in their appearance and dress. Let us now assume that Arbuthnot is, actually, somewhat poorly dressed. How will you perceive his dress? Most probably (if you do have that simple and stereotyped picture of Communists) you will perceive his clothing as "unkempt"; whereas if you had apprehended Arbuthnot as a member, say, of the "genteel poor," you might have perceived his dress as being "worn, but neatly and cleanly patched." What you would have done in the first instance is to have perceived Arbuthnot's dress in terms of the corresponding characteristics of the larger group of which he is a part (Communist), and, by assimilation, you would have ascribed the qualities of the group to the individual. In the second instance, your perceptual processes would have been of the same order, only this time your perception of Arbuthnot's dress would have been assimilated to a group having different characteristics.

Suppose, on the other hand, that Arbuthnot were dressed in the neat and intact dress of most of your acquaintances. Now, how would you perceive Arbuthnot? Most probably as being a "very well-dressed Communist." You would not have thought to use the phrase "very well-dressed" if you had apprehended Arbuthnot as a member of the Republican National Committee. In that case you would merely have perceived that he was "properly dressed." But since you know that Arbuthnot is a Communist, you have perceived his dress in terms of the corresponding characteristics of the group of which he is a part; and this time by contrast, he would seem "very well-dressed."

In the same way do we judge the personality traits and motivations of individual Jews, Republicans, Negroes, Catholics, Russians, etc. Because so many Americans ascribe characteristic personality traits to these groups, as groups, their perceptions of the individual members of these groups usually show typical biases. Thus, many Americans, through the operation of the assimilation phenomenon, tend to overestimate the shrewdness of a particular Jew, or the inscrutability of a somewhat reticent Russian— because they believe Jews to be shrewd and Russians to be inscrutable. Because of contrast, they tend to overestimate the intelligence of a Negro who is normally intelligent and to underestimate the religious conservatism of a Catholic who is liberal in some of his religious views. Again, the reason appears to be due to the stereotyped notion that Negroes are stupid and that Catholics are extremely conservative believers. The common observation, during the war, of the tendency of the American soldier to regard any normally decent German as a "very good guy" is an instance of the contrast phenomenon, since many of our soldiers had been indoctrinated concerning the extreme ruthlessness and inhumanity of the Nazi and had generalized it to Germans.

The critical point to remember is that this way of perceiving people is not a fault found among the prejudiced few. It is to be found universally and is due to the very nature of our perceptual and cognitive processes. As long as we continue to organize people into groups on the basis of certain supposed "personality traits," our perceptions of specific individuals will tend to be "distorted" and influenced by the nature of such major cognitive structures. Although we may never be able to avoid organizing people into groups in our cognitive field (Proposition I), there is no reason why such organizations must be based on skin color, religion, or nationality. And certainly there is no reason demanding that only certain defined personality traits should be perceived as "belonging" to any specific grouping based on such differentia.

Our perceptions of angle AOC as a right angle, our judgment of Arbuthnot's grooming, our estimate of a particular Russian's integrity, and our appraisal of a businessman's motivations are but special instances of the general principle that the properties of a substructure are determined in large measure by the properties of the whole structure of which it is a part.

Constancy of the cognitive field.—This general whole-part principle has so many ramifications in our cognitive and social life that it might be useful to reformulate it in still another way. Frequently we are forced to pay attention to new facts, facts that seem not to fit in with our existing structures or that even contradict them. At times, this results in a fairly radical reorganization of the existing major structures of our cognitive field, but frequently such a reorganization does not take place despite our perception of contradictory facts. For example, if we have a very strongly structured field in which the Jew is always penurious, we will not easily see any single Jew as a philanthropist, no matter how philanthropic his activities may be. In some way or other this disturbing Jew is "assimilated" into our rigidly structured organization. However, close analysis will reveal that such facts as these are encompassed by our original generalization. To comprehend what frequently happens when "contradictory" perceptions occur, it is useful to reformulate Proposition III in the following way: *Other things being equal, a change introduced into the psychological field will be absorbed in such a way as to produce the smallest effect on a strong structure.*

The formulation of the whole-part principle in terms of *constancy* is a helpful way of describing what we universally experience in simple visual perception. It is this very tendency of strongly structured fields to assimilate "new" facts and make them fit into the existing structure which makes it possible for us to identify objects at all. People, automobiles, trees, dogs, books, etc., are seen in different illuminations, from different distances, at different angles almost every time we look at them. If there were no "object constancy" in our perceptual life, all objects of our world would look radically different every time we saw them and we would be unable to recognize them as the "same" objects.

We can use some data collected by Asch in the experiment already described (see page 85) to illustrate how this principle operates in the perception of the traits of people. In one of his experiments, two lists of personality traits were read to two different groups of subjects. The first three terms of the lists were opposites; the final two terms, identical. Thus, the subjects of Group A heard the following list: List A: Kind, wise, honest, *calm, strong*. The subjects of Group B, on the other hand, heard the following: List B: Cruel, shrewd, unscrupulous, *calm, strong*.

It will be noticed that the italicized words were common for both lists. The instructions given to the subjects of both Groups A and B were the same. After hearing their list, the subjects were told, "Suppose you had to describe this person in the same manner, but without using the terms you heard, what other terms would you use?" In other words, the subjects were required to give synonyms for the terms they had just heard.

The differences between the synonyms given by Group A and Group B were striking. Thus, for example, the word "calm" was given as equivalent to "cold, frigid, calculating" twenty times by the subjects of Group B (those who had heard the list "cruel, shrewd, unscrupulous, calm, strong"), whereas these synonyms *never* appeared in the responses of Group A. On the other hand, the subjects of Group A (those who had heard the list "kind, wise, honest, calm, strong") gave the following synonyms for the word "calm": "soothing, peaceful, gentle, tolerant, mild-mannered." Similar results were obtained for the key word "strong." Where Group A listed such synonyms as "fearless, helpful, just, forceful," Group B gave "ruthless, overbearing, hard, inflexible, dominant."

The description of what happened to the perceptions of the subjects in Groups A and B is easily made in terms of our last reformulation of Proposition III. When the subject heard the first two or three terms read, he immediately organized them into an integrated "personality" (Proposition I. See especially the discussion on page 87). When the words "calm" and "strong" were introduced, they were perceived according to the already existing perception of the individual. If they "fitted in," they were perceived with their usual meaning; if they did not fit in, they were perceived in such a manner as to produce the smallest effect on the already existing structure; *i.e.*, they were "reinterpreted." Thus, the first term of list B, "cruel," set up an initial organization that predetermined the way the succeeding words would be perceived; and in so doing, the perception of the word "calm" did not result in a radical reorganization of the original structure.

Many similar illustrations can be drawn from our everyday social experiences. Suppose your perception of Russia's foreign policy is one of imperialism and aggression. And suppose you read that her foreign minister has appealed for international good will and peace. Will you change your conception of Russia's foreign policy, or will your perceptions of what you have read be of such a nature as to leave intact your original organization? Probably the latter. You will "interpret" the foreign minister's statement as a "lie" or as "diplomatic double talk." Or suppose that a Frenchman who firmly believes that all Germans are cruel and untrustworthy meets a German who acts kindly and honestly. Will that change the Frenchman's concepts of Germans in general? Again, probably not. He may ascribe some "ulterior" motive to this German who will then be perceived as a "make-believe 'honest' German." This will result in no change in his major structure about the nature of Germans.

The lack of change in organization of the major structures in the above cases can be ascribed to their strength, or "rigidity." As we have seen in Chap. II (page 61), a strong need or emotion can lead to a rigid cognitive structure. And, it will be recalled, the "constancy" reformulation of Proposition III refers to "strong" structures.

Frequently the major structure retains its constancy through the creation of new substructures. Thus, for example, in the above illustration of the Frenchman who meets a kind and honest German, the Frenchman may perceive this German as an "exception." In such an event we can see that some restructuring has occurred in that a new substructure has been differentiated (exceptional cases), but his major structure, "Germans in general," remains intact.

Just as it is fortunate that object constancy is the rule in visual perception, so is it fortunate that our more complex cognitive field also tends to maintain its *major* organizations despite apparently contradictory facts and experiences. If this were not true, there could be little stability in our cognitive life with respect to our most central beliefs and attitudes. Stability, of course, can become rigidity; and when that happens, as we have seen in the discussion of the dynamics of behavior and the influence of emotion on adjustment, we frequently get into trouble with the world of reality—our perceptions, as it were, fail completely to pass the reality test.[1]

---

[1] A more extended discussion of rigidity in cognitive organization as related to problem-solving behavior is given in the following chapter.

Frames of Reference.—The whole-part principle can be summarized in still another way: Any stimulus is perceived in relation to other stimuli with which it is organized. This formulation, as Sherif and Cantril (1947) point out, is the basic definition of the term *frame of reference*, a term that they define as follows: "The term 'frame of reference' is simply used to denote the functionally related factors (present and past) which operate at the moment to determine the particular properties of a psychological phenomenon (such as perception, judgment, affectivity)."

Sherif (1935, 1936) has made this formulation of our Proposition III his major concept in social psychology and has generalized it to account for many varied processes. As Sherif and Cantril point out, in the volume cited above,

The scale of magnitudes against which subsequent stimuli of a similar kind are judged, the organized perceptual whole which determines the particular relative properties of its parts, the established social status in relation to which responses to other individuals and groups are shaped are all specific cases of frames of reference.

Illustrations of the frame-of-reference phenomenon abound in psychophysical experiments. Thus, for example, Wever and Zener (1928) have shown that when subjects are required to judge the weight of a series of objects as "light," "heavy," etc., the judgment of each weight is a function of the total series, since if the series itself is changed from a light series to a heavy one, the same object that was formerly judged heavy will now be judged as light.

Similar results are obtained when the judgments to be made are of a much more complicated sort and are directly related to social material. As an instance of such experiments the work of McGarvey (1943) can be cited. McGarvey had her subjects rate the "social prestige" of various occupations and found that the judged desirability of any given occupation was determined by the entire series of occupations to be judged.

Helson (1947) has attempted to treat this phenomenon of relativity of perception and judgment in terms of his theory of adaptation and has suggested a carefully worked-out mathematical formulation to help understand and predict the "universality of shifts in scale-value with change in comparison-stimulus." Because his theory goes beyond the mere observation that the perception of any single stimulus is changed as the related stimuli are changed, and because his theory is designed to predict some specific properties of the perception of certain stimuli, it is of some importance to see the implications of his formulation for social psychology. Briefly, his theory can be stated in the following way:

The effects of stimulation result in an organized perception (our Proposition I). For every such organized perception there is assumed a stimulus that represents the pooled effect of all the stimuli that gave rise to the organized perception. The individual may be said to be "attuned or adapted" to this central stimulus. That is, stimuli that are near this value (in intensity or affective value, etc.) will be perceived as "indifferent, neutral, doubtful, equal, or the like, depending upon the context . . ." of the judgment involved. Stimuli that are perceived in that way or judged in that way are said to be at "adaptation level." Stimuli that are above the adaptation level "are assumed to establish positive gradients" with respect to the adaptation-level stimulus and will be perceived as "good," "loud," or "strong." Similarly, stimuli that are below the adaptation level "establish negative gradients" with resulting perceptions of the opposite kind. If, now, new stimuli are introduced, which are above the adaptation-level stimulus, a new adaptation-level stimulus will gradually be established and all subsequent stimuli will then be perceived in terms of this new level.

The value of the above formulation to social psychology can be indicated by applying the adaptation-level theory to an analysis of certain propaganda techniques designed to change judgments of people. What would be the effect of publicizing *extreme* statements concerning any social issue? Let us choose racial prejudice, and let us assume that the stated opinions and beliefs available to an individual (opinions and beliefs that are publicly held by other people) range from an extremely prejudiced set to a rather mildly tolerant one. His adaptation level will then be such as to lead him to perceive a rather weak prodemocratic statement as "adequate, acceptable, or reasonable." Now, if the range is altered by adding extreme prodemocratic statements, it is highly likely that the individual will acquire a new adaptation level and he will judge as "acceptable and reasonable" a more strongly stated prodemocratic proposition than he formerly had. In other words, the sheer reiteration and publicity of strong, prodemocratic expressions can result in a shift in scale, or "framework," that can change a person's judgment in the direction of democracy.

PROPOSITION IV

Objects or events that are close to each other in space or time or resemble each other tend to be apprehended as parts of a common structure

If we are to know just why certain perceptions are organized together with other perceptions to make one cognitive structure, we must have some general understanding of what determines why an individual will organize the perceptions of object A with that of object B into one common structure rather than the perception of object A with that of object C. Why, for example, do some people have a cognitive structure in which socialism and Christianity are organized together, while other people have a cognitive structure in which socialism and atheism are found together? Proposition IV attempts to indicate the major factors that determine the contents of a single structure.

Proximity and Similarity.—In visual perception, experimental literature is replete with demonstrations that proximity and similarity are important organizing factors. Fig. 1a, which was used to illustrate the structural factors in perception, can serve to illustrate that in simple perception those objects which are close to each other in space (proximity) tend to be organized together in perception. Dot A is perceived as belonging to dot B rather than to dot C simply because A is closer to B than it is to C. A simple measurement of the physical distances among the different dots, everything else being equal, would permit us to predict, with a high degree of accuracy, which dots would be organized with which other dots. Similarly, Fig. 1b can be used to illustrate the principle of similarity. Here, dot A will be organized with dot B rather than with dot C because A is more similar (in shape) to B than it is to C.

This does not mean that Proposition IV is a purely "structural" proposition, that we can predict which organization will eventuate in the cognitive field of the individual merely by a description of the physical stimulus or the physical relationships existing among the stimuli. The terms *proximate* and *similar* must always be understood, of course, in a psychological sense, *i.e.*, as perceived by the individual. Two novel objects that are perceived as similar by one individual will not necessarily be perceived as similar by another individual and will therefore not give rise to the same cognitive structure. All the factors that we have discussed in the previous propositions will affect the perception of any object and therefore the nature of the resulting structure. The needs of the perceiver, his moods, his past training, etc., often play a determining role in defining what is proximate and what is similar. Thus, for example, a zoologist, because of his mental set and his previous cognitive organizations, might select out for perception, when viewing a new species of animal, the presence or absence of mammaries. All animals having this anatomical feature would be perceived as "similar," and so, in the cognitive field of the zoologist, horses, human beings, and whales might be organized together. Other people might see no similarity among these instances of land animals, human beings with souls, and fish. Or take another illustration: The child who has just received a spanking at the hands of his father may organize "fathers, bullies, and castor oil" into one structure of "evil" because these three objects have been perceived with a common characteristic. Yet if his father had never spanked him, such an organization might never take place. The individual who has read about the Nazis' racial theories and who has experienced racial prejudice at the hands of an American court might also perceive the Nazi and the American policeman as similar.

Culture and similarity cues.—The specific cues that are selected by us for major attention and will therefore determine our cognitive structures are, in turn, a function of our culture. Thus, if our culture and training emphasize signs of wealth as important cues to perceive at all times, we will perceive those cues most readily and will group people according to similarity of "wealth signs"—the kind of houses they live in, the automobiles they ride in (*e.g.,* "the station-wagon set"), the schools they send their children to, etc. If our culture or educational influences emphasize pigment of skin, we will group people into Negroes and whites; if the Maori culture emphasizes the importance of tattoo marks, people who have similar tattoo marks will be seen as similar and will be organized together in the perceiver's cognitive field.

The similarities, obviously, need not rest on visual signs alone. If similar *labels*, or descriptive words, are applied to different people, there will be a tendency to organize those people together in perception. If different people or objects play the same frustrating role in our experience, we may tend to perceive them together.

Proximity.—Proximity in time and space also works in very much the same way. The birth of twin cows occurring at the same time as a calamitous flood can be organized together as indications of the work of the devil. An increase in the divorce rate of a country, occurring about the same time as the outbreak of war, can be organized into one picture of Divine retribution.

Perceiving Cause and Effect.—Perhaps one of the most important kinds of cognitive structures is that involved in "causal organization," *i.e.,* our perception of one object or event as a "cause" of another object or event. Some people perceive the Jews as the "cause" of depressions; others perceive the munitions manufacturer as the "cause" of war; still others perceive the current political administration as the "cause" of every national difficulty and calamity. What determines which cause will be organized together with which effect in our cognitive field? This is an extremely important question because so much of our social action is shaped by the way we perceive cause and effect.

Proximity and perception of cause and effect.—Duncker (1945), in his analysis of the thinking process, gives some compelling illustrations of how proximity may determine our perception of causations:

Someone comes home of an evening. A gust of wind slams the door shut behind him. At the same moment at the other end of the corridor, the light goes on in a room whose door is ajar. Although one knew ever so well that no causal connection exists between the door's blowing shut, and the light's going on, that rather someone in that room has turned on the light, by chance at exactly the same moment—still he would be unable to escape the compelling impression of causal relations . . . *the time and place of cause coincide phenomenally with the time and place of the effect.*

The point is not that all of our final or sophisticated statements of cause and effect are unequivocally determined by the temporal coincidence of two events but that in a new situation or in an ambiguous one, our immediate perception of cause and effect is largely determined by this factor. Knowing this, we can predict fairly accurately the causal relations that will be perceived by the child and the unsophisticated—whether we are concerned with the individual's perception of the cause of a "licking," the cause of war, or the cause of economic depressions.

Similarity and the perception of cause and effect.—For an illustration of the factor of similarity in the perception of causality, we can again quote from Duncker:

At least as important for man's dealing with causation as those spatial and temporal correspondences of *position* are certain correspondences of *form* between cause and effect . . . . An example of temporal correspondence of form: the rhythm of the sounds of knocking corresponds to the rhythm of the motions of knocking . . . heavy things make "heavy" noises, dainty things move daintily.

On a more complicated level, as in the perception of "human causation," Fritz Heider (1944) in his very helpful analysis of the perception of causality points out that the perception of responsibility (*i.e.*, the attribution of a crime to a person) can be due to several types of similarity:

A crime can be blamed on a person because of a physical similarity "he looks as if he could have committed this crime." Or he can be held responsible for it because of "spiritual" similarity, that is, a similarity between a crime as a moral event and the natural disposition of the "responsible". . . .

In his discussion, Heider refers to the well-known experiment by Zillig (1928) to illustrate this point. In that experiment two groups of children performed calisthenic exercises before an audience of their classmates. One of the performing groups was composed of children who were almost uniformally disliked by their classmates, and the other group, of children who were liked. The experimenter had trained the liked group to make mistakes deliberately and the disliked group to perform the calisthenics letter perfect. At the end of the two performances the experimenter discovered that the audience had "seen" the disliked group as having made the mistakes. A mistake, it appears, is much more likely to be organized together with disliked people than with liked people. As Heider says, "A bad act is easily connected with a bad person." The perception of cause and effect, in other words, is very definitely determined by our value judgments, our needs, our emotional reactions.

General Comments.—The politician and the propagandist seem frequently to illustrate in their actions their awareness of our Proposition IV. In a critical political or economic situation, the politician may seek to avoid taking power and refuse a seat in the government. Why? Because he knows that if his administration coincides with a disastrous national occurrence, both of these events (his being in power and the national calamity) will tend to be perceived by many people as causally related— no matter how conclusively he can demonstrate that he was not at fault. He will be perceived as having been responsible for the military defeat or the economic depression just as certainly as Duncker's man perceived the door's being shut as the cause of the light's going on. The Jew or the Republican or the Catholic, if he is regarded as a "bad" person, will be perceived as the cause of a "bad" event.

This tendency to organize objects or events together on the basis of proximity or similarity is a universal one. It is not something that only the poor logicians do. This does not mean that we can never change our perceptions of causality and integrate objects and events originally perceived as unlike into a common structure, but it does mean that initially and prior to any corrections, our cognitive structures will be organized in terms of objects or events which are perceived as similar or in proximity.

SUMMARY

The fundamental importance of perception for social psychology is clearly indicated when we realize that all of man's molar action is shaped by his "private" conceptions of the world. This sets two major problems for the social psychologist: (1) the description of the social world as perceived by the specific individual (or individuals) whose social behavior we are interested in understanding and (2) the discovery of general principles of perception and cognition.

Without the description indicated in (1) above, the psychologist cannot interpret correctly the formalized expressions of beliefs and attitudes (whether verbally obtained or through observation of action) of the people whom he is studying. It is at this point that many current "attitude" and "opinion" studies are limited in their usefulness.

The second problem is of primary importance to the scientist who wishes to have a fundamental understanding of the processes underlying the beliefs of people. To obtain such principles, recourse can be had to the laws that have been formulated on the basis of the experimental study of "simple" perception. The primary purpose of the present chapter is to generalize these laws of organization for social as well as nonsocial material and for both perceptual and cognitive processes.

In doing so, no attempt is made to prove each proposition. The student is referred to numerous experimental demonstrations of their validity in simple perception. However, illustrations, experiments, and analyses drawn from social material are provided that indicate the applicability of these propositions to such material. Furthermore, no attempt is made to distinguish between structural and functional factors as determinants of the perceptual and cognitive processes. The first of these refers to factors deriving solely from the nature of the physical stimuli and the neural reactions they evoke in the nervous system of the individual (the "autochthonous" factors of the Gestalt psychologist); the second refers to those factors which derive from the needs and past experiences of the individual. The position is adopted that these two sets of factors are intimately related and that every perception is a function of both. When we deal with man in society, we cannot deal with structural principles of perception where *functional* principles are held constant or with functional principles of perception where *structural* principles are held constant. The propositions stated in this chapter are designed to encompass both sets of factors in unifying statements.

Proposition I: The perceptual and cognitive field in its natural state is organized and meaningful. This first proposition, which is basic to an understanding of perception, is illustrated by the nature of man's perceptions of the novel and the bizarre; the manner in which an individual forms an integrated impression of another's personality from only a few facts about the other person; the tendency of people to jump to conclusions; and the reluctance of many to discard a disproved theory in science, religion, economics or politics in the absence of an alternative integrating theory.

Proposition II: Perception is functionally selective. The second proposition points out that no one perceives everything that is "out there" to be perceived but that only certain objects play a major role in one's perceptual organization. The objects thus accentuated in perceptual organizations are usually those which are functionally significant to the perceiving individual. Illustrations are given of the influence of needs, mental sets, and moods in selecting objects for perceptual organization. The effects of the individual's culture on his cognitive organization, and of the physical distribution of the objects are also discussed. The significance of this proposition for propaganda and education is briefly indicated, and the general observation is suggested that data do not have a logic of their own which results in the same perceptions and cognitions for all people.

Proposition III: The perceptual and cognitive properties of a substructure are determined in large measure by the properties of the structure of which it is a part. Each of our perceptions does not lead "a life of its own" but is embedded in an organization of other perceptions—the whole making up a specific cognitive structure. Proposition III indicates the nature of the relationship between any given perception and its cognitive structure. In generalizing this basic perceptual proposition, two reformulations in more specific social terms are given:

1. *When an individual is apprehended as a member of a group, each of those characteristics of the individual which correspond to the characteristics of the group is affected by his group membership, the effect being in the direction either of assimilation or of contrast.* This reformulation is illustrated by an analysis of how our tendency to group people into religious or ethnic or racial groups influences our perceptions of specific individuals.

2. *Other things being equal, a change introduced into the psychological field will be absorbed in such a way as to produce the smallest effect on a strong structure.* This second reformulation takes cognizance of the stability of man's strongest beliefs despite the prevalence of facts contradicting such beliefs and despite personal experiences with such facts and is illustrated by analysis of the reason why contradictory facts are not always effective in changing our appraisals of the motives and actions of people.

Finally, the concept of "frame of reference" as used in social psychology is discussed in terms of Proposition III. The value of the adaptation-level theory as applied to the phenomena subsumed under the frame-of-reference concept is illustrated in the field of propaganda. On the basis of this theory the suggestion is made that an individual's judgment of what is fair and reasonable can be shifted by the sheer reiteration and publicity of extreme positions.

Proposition IV: Objects or events that are close to each other in space or time or resemble each other tend to be apprehended as parts of a common structure. The final proposition indicates why certain perceptions are organized together with other perceptions to make up a single cognitive structure. In isolating similarity and proximity as two of the major determining factors, it must be understood that these are to be defined as perceived by the individual. The role of culture and training in the determination of what is to be perceived as "similar" (and therefore what will be organized with what in perception) is discussed. Then an analysis of the perception of causality is given in terms of this principle. Its implications for our understanding and prediction of how people will perceive the causes of social events and whom they will tend to hold responsible for such events are indicated.

BIBLIOGRAPHY

ASCH, S. E.: 1946. Forming impressions of personality. *J. abnorm. soc. Psychol.*, 41 258–290.

BRUNER, J. S., and GOODMAN, C. C.: 1947. Value and need as organizing factors in perception. *J. abnorm. soc. Psychol.*, 42, 33–44.

DUNCKER, K.: 1945. On problem-solving. *Psychol. Monogr.*, 58, No. 5.

ELLIS, W. D.: 1938. *A source book of Gestalt psychology.* New York: Harcourt Brace.

HEIDER, F.: 1944. Social perception and phenomenal causality. *Psychol. Rev.*, 51, 358–374.

HELSON, H.: 1947. Adaptation-level as a frame of reference for prediction of psychophysical data. *Amer. J. Psychol.*, 60, 1–29.

KOFFKA, K.: 1935. *Principles of gestalt psychology.* New York: Harcourt Brace.

KÖHLER, W.: 1947. *Gestalt psychology.* New York: Liveright.

KRECHEVSKY, I.: 1938. An experimental investigation of the principle of proximity in the visual perception of the rat. *J. exp. Psychol.*, 22, 497–523.

LEUBA, C., and LUCAS, C.: 1945. The effects of attitudes on descriptions of pictures. *J. exp. Psychol.*, 35, 517–524.

LEVINE, R., CHEIN, I., and MURPHY, G.: 1942. The relation of intensity of a need to the amount of perceptual distortion. *J. Psychol.*, 13, 283–293.

MACLEOD, R. B.: 1947. The phenomenological approach to social psychology. *Psychol. Rev.*, 54, 193–210.

MCGARVEY, H. R.: 1943. Anchoring effects in the absolute judgments of verbal materials. *Arch. Psychol.*, No. 281.

MUENZINGER, K.: 1942. *Psychology: The science of behavior.* New York: Harper.

MURRAY, H. A.: 1933. The effect of fear upon estimates of the maliciousness of other personalities. *J. soc. Psychol.*, 4, 310–329.

SANFORD, R. N.: 1936. The effects of abstinence from food upon imaginal processes. *J. Psychol.*, 2, 129–136.

SANFORD, R. N.: 1937. The effects of abstinence from food upon imaginal processes: a further experiment. *J. Psychol.*, 3, 145–159.

SCHAFER, R., and MURPHY, G.: 1943. The role of autism in a visual figure-ground relationship. *J. exp. Psychol.*, 32, 335–343.

SHERIF, M.: 1935. A study of some social factors in perceptions. *Arch. Psychol.*, No. 187.

SHERIF, M.: 1936. *The psychology of social norms.* New York: Harper.

SHERIF, M., and CANTRIL, H.: 1947. *The psychology of ego-involvements.* New York: Wiley.

TOLMAN, E. C.: 1933. Gestalt and sign-Gestalt. *Psychol. Rev.*, 40, 391–411.

WEVER, E. G., and ZENER, K. E.: 1928. The method of absolute judgment in psychophysics. *Psychol. Rev.*, 35, 466–493.

ZILLIG, M.: 1928. Einstellung und Aussage. *Z. Psychol.*, 106, 58–106.

CHAPTER IV

REORGANIZING OUR PERCEPTIONS

The fundamental processes of motivation and emotion, which were discussed in Chap. II, and those of perception and cognition, which were discussed in Chap. III, are the same for all people and for all social orders. Yet the one most general characteristic of people—and this is an observation which is obvious and compelling—is that people differ widely among themselves in their needs, in their goals, in their perceptions, in their cognitions, and in their actions.

There is, of course, no contradiction between the universality and constancy of the fundamental laws of motivation and perception on the one hand and the heterogeneity and changing nature of the motives and cognitions actually found among people on the other hand. The solution of the apparent contradiction lies in the fact that the same process, operating with different material or in different media, will give us different end results. We look for the explanation of differences in behavior among men in the different environments of men, and not in different innate, fundamental characteristics. We assume that people differ in their goals and beliefs because of differences in the kind of physical world in which they have lived, in the kinds of problems they have had to solve, in the various educations to which they have been subjected. In other words, the differences in behavior among men—white, black, or yellow; Russian, American, or Swiss; Catholic, Jewish, or Moslem—are due to the differences in the personal histories of these men.

What is true of differences among men is also true for the single individual. The perceived world of every individual is a structured one, but it is also an ever-changing one. The perception of a triangle for the beginning student of geometry is quite different from his perception of the same triangle after a semester's study. The perceptual properties of a voter's "political field" can change radically if the voter were to take an active part in civic affairs, join a political party, run for office, and lose the election as a result of questionable vote-tallying procedures. The little boy may perceive his social world as structured into "little boys," "little girls," and "grownups." Later, this world may become structured into "tough boys," "sissies," "girls," "baseball players," and "all others." Still later his perceived social world may become extremely complicated and differentiated. He may add racial, religious, political, economic, national, and cultural dimensions as the basis on which to group people. The conventional answer to the question, "Why does this happen—why does an individual's cognitive structure change in its properties and in its complexity?" is that the individual "learns" or because he is "taught"—appeal is made to the history of the individual's experiences.

Our interest in social behavior, however, is not confined to tabulating differences in behavior and correlating them with differences in the histories of the individuals. Both as pure scientists and as applied scientists we want to know the fundamental processes that lie behind the correlations. The applied social psychologist may want to know how to change cognitive structures in certain predetermined directions. He may want to know, for example, how to change the cognitive structure "good Americans *vs.* bad foreigners" into "one world." To be able to do so efficiently, the social psychologist must understand the basic principles of behavior change.

CHANGE IN BEHAVIOR AND COGNITIVE REORGANIZATION

The term *behavior change* is not synonymous with the term *learning* or *education* or *training*. As we have seen in Chap. II, pages 45 *ff.*, an individual's goals and needs may change without learning or training. Thus, the need of the millionaire to support research, in that illustration, can be understood as a consequence of his changed personality, due to the various experiences he had been subjected to, but it cannot be understood as a consequence of specific habit formation. The new need for calcium, on the part of the pregnant woman, can be understood in the light of the woman's changed physiological condition, but certainly this need was not learned. The need developed as her physiological condition changed.

The term *behavior change*, then, covers more than the term *learning*. The behavior of the individual can change when (1) the individual is placed in a problem situation, (2) when significant changes occur in his physiological state, and (3) through the operation of the dynamic factors involved in retention. The differences between the first two types of change have already been indicated. The third type can be illustrated by the discrepancy that is frequently found between what we testify to having seen several years ago and what we actually perceived at the time the event occurred. This type of behavior change, as we shall later see in this chapter, is particularly important in understanding the phenomenon of rumor.

Principles of Cognitive Reorganization.—There is something that is common, however, for the three different change-inducing conditions listed above. In each one of them, *cognitive reorganization* occurs. The processes of thinking, problem solving, learning,[1] forgetting, and the "sudden" appearance of new goals and insights, all become special cases of the process of cognitive reorganization.

When the problem of behavior change is seen in this light, the possibility of integrating the large number of fields of learning becomes apparent. The experimental psychologist has chopped up the study of behavior change into a large number of different parts. Some experimentalists distinguish between *acquisition* and *fixation;* others between *memorizing* and *reasoning;* still others between *habit formation* and *thinking.* All such distinctions serve useful purposes in the laboratory, and each one of the above processes can be defined relatively independently and investigated separately. However, as already indicated, all of the above processes involve cognitive reorganization and can therefore be treated from a common point of view.

The propositions that will be discussed in this chapter are not to be understood as learning propositions only but as generalized statements of cognitive reorganization. Phrasing the problem of change in behavior in terms of cognitive *reorganization* immediately suggests that many of the propositions to be examined will be similar to the propositions of cognitive *organization* discussed in the last chapter. To a very considerable extent this is true, for in many respects a law of cognitive change is essentially a law of cognitive organization *as it operates through a series of situations.* It involves adding the dimension of time to the laws of cognitive organization. This point will become clearer as we examine each of the following propositions. One more point should be clarified before turning our attention to the propositions themselves. We will not be concerned, in this chapter, with a discussion of the problem of motor learning or the acquisition of motor skills. The psychological problems involved there are of only peripheral interest to the social psychologist.

PROPOSITION I

As long as there is blockage to the attainment of a goal, cognitive reorganization tends to take place: the nature of the reorganization is such as to reduce the tension induced by the frustrating situation

This first proposition serves two major ends: (1) It defines one of the most characteristic situations in which cognitive reorganization occurs; (2) it stresses the dependence of much of cognitive reorganization on the needs, goals, and tensions of the individual. In a sense, of course, this proposition is a restatement of the material discussed under the fourth proposition in

---

[1] For a detailed discussion of learning as a reorganization of the cognitive field, the student is referred to D. K. Adams' valuable paper "A restatement of the problem of learning" (1931).

Chap. II,[1] but the relationship among goals, obstructions, and change in behavior is so intimate and important that it is essential to begin any systematic formulation of the cognitive reorganization process with a clear statement of this relationship.

The Nature of the Reorganization.—The block to the goal may be of many different kinds. It may be a physical barrier, it may be a long waiting period, it may be an unsatisfactory personal relationship which blocks the achievement of various goals. As Adams (1931) writes, "The obstruction may be anything from a barbed wire fence when the need is to pick up a shot grouse on the other side, to the weight of tradition when the need is to reformulate a scientific problem." Similarly, the nature of the cognitive reorganization that will enable the individual to remove the block and achieve his goal may also vary from the very simple to the very complex. Thus, Adams' hunter, who perceives the barbed-wire fence as a block to his goal, will not solve his problem until his perception of the spatial relations is reorganized so that a very circuitous route of several hundred feet around the barbed-wire fence is perceived as a direct path to the grouse (this is the kind of cognitive reorganization involved in the typical *Umweg* learning experiments of the laboratory). And Adams' scientist may be required so to reorganize the whole conceptual structure of his science as to perceive a formerly respected scientific theory as, for example, mere "naive pre-Einsteinian thinking."

Frequently the nature of the reorganization may involve the *differentiation* of a major structure into component parts. Apprehending all members of the Democratic party, for example, as constituting one major undifferentiated structure may be adequate for a person who wishes to elect his party to power. However, for the attainment of certain goals, such as the election of Congressmen friendly to labor, such a cognitive organization may be inadequate, and the reorganization that is required may involve breaking up the structure Democratic party into the substructures New Deal Democrats, Southern Democrats, etc.

Needs, blocks, and distorted cognitive organizations.—While the existence of a goal and a block to that goal typically initiate cognitive reorganization, it must not be assumed that the resulting cognitive reorganization will be adaptive in every case. Frequently the effect of the tension upon the cognitive reorganization can be distorting, in the sense that the resulting cognitive organization diverges radically from reality. Thus, as we have seen in Chap. II, the frustration of needs can lead to fantasies and bizarre thinking which do not aid the individual in adjusting to the situation. But

---

[1] See Proposition IV, p. 50: "The frustration of goal achievement and the failure of tension reduction may lead to a variety of adaptive or maladaptive behaviors."

no matter how bizarre and how "irreal" the cognitive reorganization may be, it can always be understood, from the point of view of the subject himself, as being in the direction of reduction of need tension.

(Whether a blocked goal will lead to a distorted cognitive organization or to an adequate and useful one seems to depend upon a number of factors, among which are the strength of the need tension, the individual's characteristic manner of responding to frustration, and the perception of the block to the goal.)

Strength of the need.—Two experiments, one with the problem-solving behavior of the chimpanzee and the other with human subjects, give some illuminating illustrations of the relationship between the strength of needs and the adequacy of the cognitive reorganization that takes place in response to those needs.

Birch (1945) studied the effects of different degrees of food deprivation on the problem-solving ability of six young chimpanzees. The problems given to the animals were the familiar string-pattern and stick problems used in experimental work with those animals. In these problems, the solution requires the perception of the relationships between crossed strings and food objects attached to some of the strings; it requires the ability to perceive roundabout paths (*Umweg*), the use of sticks far removed from the goal objects as tools to rake in the food, etc. The need conditions of the animals were varied by depriving them of food for 2, 6, 12, 24, 36, and 48 hours.

(The results of this experiment clearly indicated that with excessive tension (induced by too long a period of food deprivation) the perceptual processes of the animals were so interfered with as to reduce considerably their problem-solving efficiency.) Thus, as Birch summarizes his results,

When motivation is very low, the animals are easily diverted from the problem by extraneous factors . . . . Under conditions of very intense motivation, the animals concentrated upon the goal to the relative exclusion of other features of the situation which were essential to the solution of the problem. Also, the frequent occurrence of frustration responses, such as tantrums and screaming . . . hindered the animals in their problem-solving efforts. Those animals . . . under the intermediate conditions of motivational intensity behaved in a manner which indicated that, although the food acted as a central factor in determining the direction in which they organized new patterns of response, they were not so dominated by . . . the food that they were incapable of responding to other relevant features of the problem situation.

In the now classic experiment of Dembo (1931), human subjects were given the task of reaching for a flower, which was four feet away from a marked square on the floor in which the subject stood and from which he was not allowed to move. Although there were only two possible ways of reaching the flower, the subjects were told that there were three ways. After having used the two available methods, the subjects found themselves in a frustrating situation. Because of the insistence of the experimenter, the tensions induced in the subjects became very intense. The anger that followed from this, for many of the subjects, resulted in striking cognitive distortions. As time went on, all sorts of bizarre perceptions were reported by the subjects. One subject, for example, "saw" the room as filled with water and the flower floating to her. Some rings, which had been placed near the square, were picked up again and again, and attempted use was made of them, although they were obviously of little value in solving the problem. Because of the nature of the experimental situation, no cognitive reorganization could help achieve the goal, yet there was no dearth of reorganizations.

In terms of the propositions already examined in this book, the results of the above two experiments can be summarized as follows: (1) Cognitive reorganization will take place when a blocked goal exists in the individual's field; (2) at any given moment, the objects in the problem situation that will be perceived and hence available for the cognitive reorganization will be selected in terms of the need (Proposition II, page 87); (3) under conditions of intense need, the resulting cognitive reorganizations may prove to be inadequate or bizarre; (4) but whatever the nature of the cognitive reorganization, it can be seen as directed toward tension reduction.

Characteristic individual manners of responding to frustration.—The nature of the cognitive reorganization that takes place under the influence of a blocked goal is also due to the pattern of tension-reductive processes that is characteristic of an individual. Chapter II, it will be remembered, suggested that as a resultant of the individual's growth within the confines of a given culture and environment and the past history of successes and failures with various adaptive means of reducing tensions, he may come to react to frustrations in an "aggressive" manner, an "autistic" manner, a "regressive" manner, a "sublimated" manner, etc. Each one of these ways of reacting will help determine the functional selectivity of his perceptions in any problem situation and, therefore, the nature of his cognitive reorganization. Thus, for example, the individual who has adopted an aggressive manner of reacting in frustration situations will perceive the block to his goal as "a thing to be attacked," and his cognitive reorganization will differ widely from the individual who typically adopts a sublimated approach. In some problem situations one of these manners may lead to useful and adaptive cognitive reorganizations, whereas in other problem situations it may lead to non-adaptive reorganizations.

An individual who sees a certain economic practice as standing in the way of his achieving economic security may perceive this economic practice as a thing to be attacked and will look for (and find) specific individuals and groups against whom he might aggress. His cognitive reorganization is typical of the direct actionist. Another person, in the same situation, may react in a sublimated manner and seek roundabout ways of achieving the same goal. His cognitive reorganizations may be typical of the evolutionary rather than the revolutionary. Sometimes one of these cognitive reorganizations is the more adequate, sometimes the other. The significant point to be made here is that the adequacy of a cognitive reorganization is a function not only of the existence of a blocked goal and the intensity of the need but also of the characteristic tension-reductive process of the individual.

Perceiving the block.—Finally, of very great importance to determining the nature of the cognitive reorganization that will occur when a goal is blocked is the individual's perception of the block. It will be seen that Proposition I lists a blocked goal as one of the conditions for cognitive reorganization. While by very definition the *goal* is always perceived by the individual, the perception of the block frequently offers difficulties. Sometimes the individual *does not perceive the block at all*—he does not know, for example, why he cannot apply himself to his work. More frequently, however, the *wrong* object is perceived as the block. Thus, "grasping tendencies" of the labor unions may be seen by some businessmen as the block to national prosperity. In either case, the adequacy of the cognitive reorganizations that will eventuate—all in the direction of achieving the blocked goal object—will reflect the accuracy with which the correct block is perceived. The more wrong the perception of the block the more inadequate will be the cognitive reorganization. The significance of this relationship will be demonstrated in greater detail in the discussion of the other propositions that we shall examine in this chapter.

General Comments.—The significance for social behavior of the relationships among needs, tensions, blocks, and cognitive reorganizations cannot be overemphasized. In our attempt to understand the learning of people and their thinking, we must constantly remember that *learning or thinking is not a cold affair but is intimately related to the dynamics of behavior.* Needs and emotions not only initiate learning and thinking, but their effects are present in determining the resultants of learning and thinking.

It is difficult to teach an individual to adopt a new attitude concerning national sovereignty, for example, unless we can first produce a situation where his concept of national sovereignty is no longer adequate for the achievement of his own goals. It is doubtful whether any amount of education will be effective unless that is done first. The education will not "take"—his cognitive structures will tend to resist reorganization unless some tension is involved. On the other hand, if people are too highly motivated, it is dangerous to assume that they will achieve an adequate reorganization of their social concepts. The angry man is not the best social planner. New and workable patterns of economic activities cannot be expected of people on a starvation diet. The brave new world cannot be built by highly frustrated people of the old world. Such people can become violent, like Birch's 48-hour starved chimpanzee; they can engage in fantasy and achieve distorted cognitive reorganizations, like Dembo's students; but they will probably not achieve a workable and efficient solution of their major problems.

Most learning and thinking that takes place in man in society—whether it is his adoption of a new attitude toward religion or his failure to see the new dangers of warfare for his very survival, whether it is the incorporation into his "self" of a new set of values or his failure to reorganize his world of "many sovereignties" into a structure of "one world"—each major reorganization or lack of it can best be understood if we remember that needs, tensions, blocks, and the process of cognitive reorganization are intimately related.

PROPOSITION II

The cognitive reorganization process typically consists of a hierarchically related series of organizations

This proposition extends to the *reorganization* process Propositions I and III of perceptual organization.[1] In so doing, it points to two very significant and frequently neglected aspects of learning, thinking, and other cognitive reorganizations. In the first place, by describing the entire cognitive reorganization process in terms of a *series* of *organizations*, it asserts that each successive step in the learning, or thinking, process is meaningfully organized. In the second place, it states the nature of the relationships that exist among these successive steps. And the knowledge of this relationship can aid us, as we shall see, in predicting the nature of the *final* cognitive reorganization by knowing something about the nature of the *initial* cognitive organization.

Process and Continuity in Cognitive Reorganization.—Throughout our discussion we have referred to the process of cognitive reorganization. Implied in the phrase *cognitive reorganization process* or the *learning process* is the notion of a continuous event extending over a period of time. Thus,

---

[1]These propositions, it will be remembered, are (I) "The perceptual and cognitive field in its natural state is organized and meaningful" (p. 84) and (III) "The perceptual and cognitive properties of a substructure are determined in large measure by the properties of the structure of which it is a part" (p. 94).

for example, when we speak of a child "learning" the multiplication table or the rituals of prayer or how to get along with people or the importance of paying attention to the various "status roles" that different individuals may have in his society, we assume that his *final* cognitive organization reflects the contributions of almost every single experience he may have had with those objects. His learning process begins with his first lesson and ends with his last lesson.

The "three-stage" view of continuity.—But there are two different ways of viewing the continuity of the cognitive reorganization process. One point of view seems to be that with each lesson, trial, or experience, the individual adds a little bit more to his developing cognitive structure until finally it is completed and meaningfully organized. According to this concept, the reorganization process is described as if the individual, in the process of changing his beliefs or concepts, passes through three different stages: (1) a stage where his cognitive structure is an organized and meaningful one (the original structure) through (2) a period of change that consists of unorganized, meaningless, unrelated perceptions and associations, which gradually, through repeated experiences, again reach (3) the stage of organized, meaningful structures (the new idea, concept, or belief). To use an analogy, the cognitive reorganization process is seen very much like the process in tearing down a brick building and using the bricks to construct another, quite different building. As each brick is transferred, the new building begins to take shape, but only when almost all of the bricks are in place does the new edifice begin to take on shape and form and become a completed structure.

The series view of continuity.—The second way of viewing the continuity of the cognitive reorganization process is to conceive of it as consisting of a series of meaningful organizations, wherein certain specific events which influenced any one of these organizations may have had relatively little to do with the final, resulting structure. To illustrate with another analogy, the cognitive process is here seen very much like the process a girl goes through in trying to decide on the ensemble she will wear for an important social engagement. She may first consider a simple black dress with a few "touches of white"—but then gives that up because she feels that such a costume would be too severe for the occasion. Then she may try another combination and give that up because she suddenly remembers that her hostess does not approve of low-cut dresses. She may then try some other combination and another until she finally hits upon "just the thing"—if her wardrobe is extensive enough. Her final solution was preceded, in other words, by a number of different but *complete* ensembles—it was not built up piecemeal, in the way we erect a brick building.

This view was first summarized by Koffka (1925) as follows:

To cut a long story short, we find at the beginning, in our most elementary reactions . . . in training and in intelligent performances, unitary, articulate, meaningful wholes . . . . Development starts with structures. Development proceeds by transformation of such structures. Gradually, by a number of leaps and bounds we achieve different orders, different articulations, different meanings.

Nevertheless, even from this point of view, the different cognitive organizations that occur, one after the other, before the final cognitive organization is arrived at can be said to belong to one process because they all reflect the activities of the same individual, who is attempting to solve the same problem, created by the desire to achieve a single goal.

There are now available a number of experimental verifications of this description of the learning process in both animal and human behavior.[1] The history of the cognitive reorganization process is not a sequence from order through chaos to order, but from one order to another. The distinction between these two descriptions of the reorganization process is an important one, because of the different implications that follow from each— several of which we can now consider.

The laws of frequency and effect.—The description of the cognitive reorganization process as consisting of a series of unitary organizations denies the validity of the assumption that specific cognitive organizations are built up by the simple succession of event plus consequence and that only after several such repeated successions does the cognitive organization begin to take shape and acquire goal-directed meaning. This is another way of saying that our present Proposition II denies the validity of the law of frequency and the law of effect as those laws are usually stated.[2] Since the final organization is only one organization, in a series of organizations, the perceived cause-and-effect events that shape it may be relatively independent of the events that shaped the preceding structures. Repeated experience provides the opportunity for repeated cognitive reorganizations, but it does not, through a cumulative process, gradually build up the final structure. Each successive structure is a function of what the individual

---

[1] For discrimination learning in rats, there are the experiments of Krechevsky (1932a, 1932b); for learning in chimpanzees, Spence (1934); for conditioned responses in dogs, Girden (1938); for concept formation in human beings, Heidbreder (1924) and Hanfmann and Kasanin (1937).

[2] For a discussion of the experimental evidence and the theoretical considerations that indicate the untenability of these laws, see Tolman (1932). For an attempt to revise these laws so as to make them applicable in certain limited learning situation, see Spence (1937, 1945).

perceives at that time and is organized in those perceived terms. A child who is punished every time he wets the bed does not necessarily learn that it is bad to wet the bed. He may learn, instead, that his mother is an everpunishing and disagreeable person. This may follow if he has not yet reached the stage where a wet bed is a significant percept in his world. The *frequent* succession of "wet bed" followed by "punishment" may be perceived by him at one stage in his social learning as "mother-in-room" followed by "punishment." Only when he begins to perceive the wet bed will the sequence "wet bed" followed by "punishment" begin to be effective.

Learning from experience.—The generalization that it is not the frequency of occurrence of an event or the objective sequence of cause and effect which determines the nature of the resulting cognitive organization but that only those things which are perceived and attended to will play a role in the new cognitive organizations[1] can help us to understand the apparent failure of people to learn from experience. Let us assume that certain monopolistic practices of business are responsible for economic depressions. No matter how many times an individual may live through the sequence monopolistic practices—depression, there is nothing in the situation to guarantee that he will finally arrive at the cognitive reorganization "Monopolies lead to depressions." If the depression is deep enough and his goals are being blocked thereby, his cognitive structures may reorganize again and again but may never arrive at the correct organization. The first time it happens, he may "learn" that depressions are caused by the Republican party; the second time, that they are caused by the Democratic party; the third time, by the Jews, etc. In each case his cognitive field has undergone a reorganization—he has "learned" and has "profited from experience," but in each case he has arrived at the wrong solution, *because his cognitive structure was reorganized in terms of the particular events that were dominant in his perceptual field at that moment.* Not until he experiences monopoly practices as an important percept will he be able to learn from experience. If that does not happen, then no matter how frequently he lives through the same sequence, he will not achieve the adequate cognitive organization. (In this connection, see the discussion of the role of perceiving the block, in learning and thinking, page 116, and the perception of causality, page 104.)

The failure to understand this has led to much unwarranted criticism and cynicism about the social behavior of people and their learning capacities. "Can't they learn from experience!" is the oft-repeated cry of the exasperated

---

[1] At this point the question of incidental learning may be raised, *i.e.*, learning where no attention has been paid to that which is eventually learned. Postman and Senders (1946) show that a close analysis of such unattended learning indicates that the lack of attention is more apparent than real.

social changer. "Repeat a lie frequently enough and people will believe it!" is the maxim of many a propagandist. Neither is correct. People do learn from experience, but not from the sequence of events as experienced by the political scientist, by the economist, or by the social changer. (People learn from the sequence of events that they themselves perceive—and their perceptions may not include monopolies or imperialism or graft.) People do *not* believe a lie simply because it is repeated frequently enough and loudly enough. If they come to believe a lie, it is because the lie seems to meet a need, because the insistent repetition of the lie brings it to their attention, and because an alternative set of meanings is not made available to them.

Whether we are discussing the discrimination learning of an animal, the inculcation of toilet habits in children, the solution of political problems by the citizens of a country, the adoption of a new way of viewing international relations, or any other cognitive reorganization process, we must remember that the entire process, at each stage, will consist of organized structures, and the particular organization that will occur will be a function of what the individual perceives at that time.)

The function of education and guidance.—It is at this point that deliberately directed educational efforts assume their vital significance in learning and reeducation. We have seen that major cognitive structures of people will not necessarily change through the presentation of new facts. But that does not mean that the propagandist or the educator has an insignificant role to play in determining behavior change. If the conditions are present that will encourage the initiation of the cognitive reorganization process (*e.g.*, a blocked goal, a significant change in the physiological state of the individual, etc.), then the presentation of new concepts, the directing of the attention of people to new relationships, can become of absolute importance. Guidance, instruction, information, and education, by making the individual conscious, or aware, of new relationships, can determine the nature of his cognitive reorganization. A complete understanding of the cognitive reorganization process gives a major role to the public educator and to the propagandist.

Relationship among Cognitive Organizations in the Reorganization Process.—Up to this point we have discussed only one implication of Proposition II—that the cognitive reorganization process consists of a series of organized, adaptively designed structures. But these various structures are not entirely independent. For one thing, as we have seen, they are all parts of a single process. (But, more specifically, each structure is frequently found related, in a fairly definite and systematic manner, to the other structures in the series.) Proposition II defines this relationship and describes the sequence of the cognitive reorganizations as leading from the more general to the more specific. This sequence is especially characteristic in problem situations.

An animal experiment.—In analyzing Krechevsky's data on the discrimination learning of the rat, Tolman and Krechevsky (1933) suggested the following description of what takes place when a rat finally learns that a lighted doorway means food: (1) When first introduced into the discrimination box, the animal adopts a *general hypothesis* with which he attempts to solve his problem. This general hypothesis usually is one involving exploration; *i.e.*, the animal explores the box rather than, say, sleeping in the box or squealing in the box, etc. (2) The next step in the cognitive reorganization process of the animal involves a *specific hypothesis* within this general hypothesis. This specific hypothesis may involve the exploration of the alleys only rather than of the restraining walls of the box or the floor of the box. But this cognitive reorganization, that "the alleys alone contain food and should be explored," reflects the nature of the first general hypothesis. If the first general hypothesis had been of an entirely different nature, then the next hypothesis would not have involved exploration of the alleys. This process of the occurrence of new cognitive reorganizations, *each one conditioned by the previous hypothesis and each one "narrowing" down the field of attention of the previous hypothesis, continues until the "correct" hypothesis is achieved or until a new general hypothesis is adopted, which in turn is followed by its succession of specific hypotheses.*[1]

An experiment in human thinking.—According to Duncker's analysis of problem solving in people (1945) the first cognitive organization that occurs can be described as a general "range" *within which* the solution is then sought. This range involves the perception of either some general property of the sought-after solution or some general method by which to arrive at the solution. Within such a range various functional solutions are arrived at which Duncker described as specifying the demands that the solution would eventually have to fulfill. The final cognitive reorganization is called a "specific solution" by Duncker and comes as an application of the functional solution to the available data of the situation, supplemented by one's store of particular experiences.

The above general description of Duncker's data and analysis can be clarified by an illustration from the protocol of one of his subjects.[2] In his

[1] For the experimental and theoretical justification for the use of such words as "hypotheses" when referring to the behavior of the rat, see Krechevsky's (1932a) original paper.

[2] The description is based on the presentation made by Duncker and Krechevsky (1939) in their joint paper where they indicated the similarity between the problem-solving behavior of the rat and the "creative thinking" of the human being.

experiment he presented the following problem to his subjects (students at the University of Berlin): *"The problem:* To cure a man of a tumor in the stomach by applying certain rays which if sufficiently strong can destroy organic tissues. The problem then is to destroy the tumor without at the same time destroying the healthy tissue surrounding the tumor." The following is a description of the cognitive reorganization processes for one of his subjects: (1) *General range,* inquire into the nature of the conflict here presented, *i.e.,* that rays can both harm and heal. (2) *Functional solutions,* transmit the rays through the "good" tissues so that the rays would do no harm to them. (3) *Final solutions,* send several bundles of weak rays from points outside the body, all these weak rays converging at the point of the tumor.

Maier's (1931) concept of "direction" in thinking, it should be pointed out, is very similar to Duncker's concept of "functional solution." Actually, Maier's analysis of "reasoning" is congruent with the analysis presented here of the cognitive reorganization process.

Illustrations from thinking about social problems.—That part of Proposition II which generalizes the interrelationships among the successive structures in the cognitive reorganization process can be seen as extending to the process of reorganization, our Proposition III of perception. The latter proposition stated that the properties of a substructure are determined in large measure by the properties of the structure of which it is a part. Each successive cognitive reorganization can be seen as a substructure of a major organization. Thus, just as our perception of an individual's personality traits is determined by our cognitive structure of the group of which he is a member, so our various cognitive reorganizations (hypothesis, functional and specific solutions, etc.) are influenced by the more general cognitive structures that preceded them.

This proposition aids considerably in our understanding of the kind of thinking frequently found in attempts to solve social problems. Let us assume that we are interested in understanding and predicting the thinking of a political leader who is wrestling with his country's economic difficulties. If we know that this political leader believes all evil to be due to the willful activities of "bad" people (the "devil theory of history"), then we can make some fairly reliable predictions as to the sequence of his cognitive reorganizations. As a consequence of this most general cognitive organization, he will, as he seeks to find the solution to his country's problems, reorganize his field so as to blame, say, the "Communists." If this does not work, then he will achieve the reorganization, "The Jews are at fault"; then, perhaps, "the English"; etc. It is unlikely that he will proceed from his initial cognitive organization to one in which the fault is ascribed to the basic economic relationships that exist in his country or to the pattern of world trade. The apparent randomness of his successive hypotheses can now be seen as systematically determined.

Frequently, this major structure, which conditions the successive reorganizations, may be so basic and firmly established as to escape notice. The individual, in critically examining his own thinking, may never go so far as to question his basic assumptions—and yet these basic assumptions may be influencing his thinking without his recognizing it. For example, diplomats of various countries meet around the peace table after a catastrophic world war. They all seek the solution to the problem of war. They may all be intelligent men and genuinely seek peace. The cognitive reorganizations, as the diplomats wrestle with this problem, are many and varied. "War can be prevented if my country has so large an army and navy that no other country, or combination of countries will dare attack it." When that solution does not seem possible, then, "We will ally ourselves with the two or three biggest countries, so that we will be an unbeatable combination." If that, too, does not seem feasible, then "We will withdraw from international affairs and avoid contact with other countries." When that is demonstrated to be an irreal solution, then, "We will fight a preventive war now in order to avoid a bigger war later," etc. All of these cognitive organizations are organized, attempted solutions, and some of them may seem quite practical. What is at fault? We shall understand little if we write off these diplomats as being either stupid or men of ill will. They may be neither. They are merely illustrating again that specific hypotheses can be determined and limited by the major cognitive structure. Once having started with an unexamined general cognitive structure—that there exist ambitious, sovereign, and completely independent states, each jealously guarding its sovereignty, relentlessly motivated in its desire to increase its sphere of influence—their succeeding cognitive reorganizations reflect this at every point. Had they reexamined this basic cognitive organization or had they started their solution attempts with the general cognitive organization that people exist who happen to live in different geographical areas, who happen to speak different languages, but who have many common goals, needs, and beliefs that have nothing to do with sovereignty and spheres of influence, they might have come upon other suggestions and other solutions.

On the positive side, Proposition II indicates that if we wish to control or influence the thinking process of people, we must "start where they are" and attempt to direct their thinking from that point. This may involve changing some of their fundamental beliefs before we can change specific beliefs, or it may involve phrasing the belief we wish them to adopt in terms of their fundamental beliefs. But if we have no information on what their major, general cognitive organizations are, we cannot understand or predict or control their subsequent thinking. The thinking process, despite the fact that it consists of a series of complete cognitive organizations, is a unified, interdependent one.

PROPOSITION III

Cognitive structures, over time, undergo progressive changes in accordance with the principles of organization

Proposition I was primarily concerned with cognitive reorganization that occurs in reaction to a blocked goal. However, as was pointed out in the introduction to this chapter, not all changes are due to tension-reductive activities consequent upon the blocking of a goal. Some very important cognitive reorganizations occur when a period of time intervenes between the moment a cognitive organization is formed and the moment it again functions in the behavior of the individual. An understanding of the cognitive reorganizations that occur in this manner will permit us to understand the psychology of rumors, testimony, and "forgetting." And it is this kind of cognitive reorganization with which the present proposition is concerned. Although the proposition is phrased in terms of time, it must be clear that time, per se, cannot have any effect. Time merely provides an opportunity for other events to affect and change the original cognitive organization.

Retention, Forgetting, and Cognitive Reorganization.—To phrase the problem in terms of time suggests that we are here primarily concerned with the retention or forgetting processes. In a sense, of course, this is correct, but the concept of "forgetting," as it is sometimes described, carries along with it certain misleading implications. One common notion of the nature of the forgetting process can be phrased in the following way: Retention is a function of the physiological processes occurring in the nervous system of the individual with the passage of time. Once a cognitive organization is achieved, it tends to persist for some time. However, due to various events and influences, this pattern slowly disintegrates and parts of the pattern are gradually lost. Thus, this description would imply that the changes which occur would all be in the same direction; *i.e.*, the cognitive structure would be gradually lost, or parts of it would drop out. This view of the forgetting process has been characterized as the "decay" concept. We would know less about a perceived event after a long interval of time than after the immediate experience of the event.

The facts that can be mustered to support the above description are frequently valid. Thus, for example, the forgetting of a piece of poetry or a list of names that has been memorized seems to indicate that after a time all we can do is to recall only one or two lines or one or two names—the other lines and names having disappeared from memory. However, such changes are not the only ones that occur. In attempting to recall a piece of poetry memorized during our school years, we may frequently include in our recitation verses from two different poems, or we may remember our list of names incorrectly. The effects of forgetting, in other words, are displayed not only in errors of omission but frequently in errors of commission as well.

The formulation of the forgetting process in terms of Proposition III is more useful than the one given above, because, as we shall soon see, it is a more generalized statement of what happens to cognitive organizations with the passage of time. In terms of this statement, the facts that can be subsumed under the common formulation of the forgetting process are seen as a special case of cognitive reorganization over time. According to Proposition III, several kinds of change in a cognitive structure are allowed for. It does not specify that the original structure must gradually disappear. Thus, since Proposition III states that the nature of the change is determined by the principles of organization, we can predict (on the basis of such principles and the specific nature of the original cognitive structure) that in certain cases the original cognitive structure may become more stable and more resistant to forgetting as time goes on. In other cases we can predict that the original cognitive organization will change to a radically different one—involving properties that were not at all present in the original structure. And under some circumstances we can predict that the original organization may disappear completely. The specific conditions that will permit us to make one or the other prediction will be discussed in some detail later in this section. But we first want to examine some of the experimental evidence for the suggested formulation of the nature of changes that occur over time and, second, to point to some of the implications of this formulation for an understanding of the systematic and predictable changes that rumors undergo as they are passed from individual to individual.

Retention of visual forms.—Our first illustrative experiment is taken from Friedrich Wulf's (1922) pioneer study of the "memorial" fate of simple visual perceptions. In this experiment Wulf used as material 26 figures drawn upon pieces of white cardboard. The subjects were instructed to look at the drawings (each drawing being presented separately for an exposure period of 5 seconds) with the intention of reproducing it some time later. The first reproduction test was given 30 seconds after the card had been removed. The subject was then requested not to think of the figures after he left the laboratory. After 24 hours, the subject was called back for another recall test. A third test was given after one week; and for some subjects, a fourth recall test was given after two months. The subject's task was to draw the entire figure as he remembered it.[1] In analyzing the reproductions obtained from his subjects it appeared that in all but eight of the reproductions the reproduced drawings showed a systematic and progressive change from the original irregularly formed figures toward figures that were "sharper" or "smoother" (see Fig. 4). In other words, a simple figural perception, over time, changes in the direction of simpler or more sharply defined forms. The change, then, is not haphazard, nor is it partial in the sense that some elements of the original structure are retained and some forgotten—with the result that the remembered figure is an incomplete one. The entire perception has changed from one organization to another. And, it must be emphasized, this change cannot be ascribed to the operation of needs or the existence of blocked goals. We have here an instance of organizational factors (for the most part structural factors) operating over time so as to produce the same effects that those factors induce in immediate perception.

This experiment of Wulf's has been repeated several times, with variations. Thus, Gibson (1929) and Carmichael, Hogan, and Walter (1932) have investigated the effect of word labeling on the change in the memory of a perceived figure. In these experiments it was demonstrated that the word which is attached to a perceived figure operates so as successively to change the memory of that figure to one that is more congruent with the word. Here we have instances of organizational factors (for the most part functional factors, since the meaning of words is dependent upon the individual's training and experience) operating over time so as to produce the same effect that those factors induce in immediate perception (see Fig. 5).

Retention of verbal material.—Bartlett, in his book on memory (1932), was the first to generalize these observations and extend the principle to the remembering of more complicated material. Bartlett's book is replete with experimental demonstrations of this effect. In one of his recall experiments he used a story, approximately 300 words in length, with his Cambridge University students as subjects. The story, "The war of the ghosts" was drawn from the folklore of a culture that was foreign to his subjects and dealt with seal hunting, war parties, canoes, ghosts, etc. Each of Bartlett's subjects was allowed to read the story through twice, and then, after varying

[1] This experiment has been justly criticized on the grounds that by asking each subject for repeated reproductions—after varying intervals of time—Wulf was not studying "pure" memory but memory as influenced by practice. However, this practice was not of a corrective nature, since the subject never knew how well he had done on any one test. What we have here is something quite similar to what happens in "real life," *i.e.*, an occasional recall (without checking on the accuracy of the recall) of an event that has occurred in the past.

intervals, the subjects were asked to reproduce the story in writing as accurately as possible.

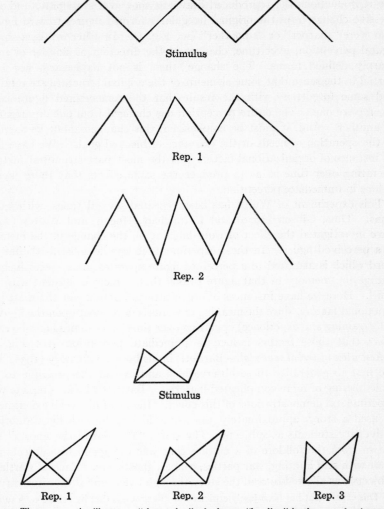

FIG. 4.—The upper series illustrates "sharpening"; the lower, "leveling" in the reproductions over time. (*After Wulf.*)

Bartlett found that with the passage of time, the reproductions all showed systematic and orderly changes that could be accounted for by the sharpening and leveling tendencies, by the cultural frame of reference of the subjects, by the speech patterns of the Cambridge students, etc. As instances of the latter effects, the more familiar word "boat" replaced the original "canoe"; "hunting seals" became "fishing." Such modern, journalistic phrases as "refused on the ground of family ties" replaced the original phrase, "I will not go along. I might be killed. My relatives do not know where I have gone." It should be pointed out that these were real errors due to the forgetting process, since Bartlett's subjects were trying to reproduce the story literally.

As an instance of the leveling or sharpening effect—the tendency of the recalled reproductions to become simpler and better organized—the pro-

| Stimulus | Eyeglasses | Dumbbell |

FIG. 5.—Stimulus figure and reproductions by two different subjects. The first subject, when presented with the stimulus, was told that it looked something like "eyeglasses"; the second subject, was told that it looked like a "dumbbell." (*After Carmichael, Hogan, and Walter.*)

gressive changes that occurred in the subjects' reproductions frequently reached a point where merely the form of the material remained and nothing else. Thus, as Bartlett himself summarizes this effect,

In fact, response to a general scheme, form, order, and arrangement of material seems to be dominant . . . no sooner was a story presented than it was labelled, said to be of this or that type . . . . The other details were omitted, rearranged, or transformed . . . . The form, plan, type, or scheme of the story seems, in fact, for the ordinary, educated adult, to be the most dominant and persistent factor in this kind of material.

The form of the original cognitive structure that remains—long after the details have been leveled out and much of the content has disappeared—nevertheless frequently bears some relation to the original structure. As William James (1890) has pointed out in his lively description of our experience when we try to recall a forgotten name,

The state of our consciousness is peculiar. There is a gap therein; but no mere gap. It is a gap that is intensely active. A sort of wraith of the name is in it, beckoning us in a given direction, making us at moments tingle with a sense of our closeness. If wrong names are proposed to us, this singularly definite gap acts immediately so as to negate them. They do not fit into its mould. And the gap of one word does not feel like the gap of another . . . the rhythm of a lost word may be there without a sound to clothe it; or the evanescent of something which is the initial vowel or consonant may mock us fitfully, without growing more distinct.

Illustration from an analysis of a rumor.—Allport and Postman (1947), in their analysis of the basic patterns of distortion that occur in the transmission of rumors, show how the various structural and functional organizing factors of perception can so operate through time as to convert the perception of a simple and innocent event into an exciting story.

We choose a trifling rumor incident and select it almost at random from the wartime crop of stories current in a rural Maine community in the summer of 1945, shortly before Japan's surrender.

A Chinese teacher on a solitary vacation drove his car into the community and asked his way to a hilltop from which he could obtain the pleasant view pictured in a tourist guide . . . . Someone showed him the way, but within an hour the community was buzzing with the story that *a Japanese spy had ascended the hill to take pictures of the region.*

In comparing the objective event with the resulting rumor, they suggest that the following factors were at work:

1. *Leveling.* Omitted from the rumor are many details . . . the courteous and timid, but withal honest, approach of the visitor . . . the fact that the visitor's precise nationality was unknown although he was certainly Oriental . . . the fact that the visitor had allowed himself to be readily identified by people along the way; and . . . that no one had seen a camera in his possession.

2. *Sharpening.* The rumor agents accentuated certain features while minimizing others . . . . What in the original situation was Oriental became specified as Japanese; what was merely a "man" became . . . a "spy" . . . . The truth that the visitor had a picture in his hand (the tourist guide) became sharpened into the act of "taking pictures."

3. *Assimilation.* In the Maine countryside resident natives have had little contact with Orientals . . . . They had only one available rubric for Orientals, firmly implanted in their minds by wartime news and stories: the "Japanese spy". . . . The novel situation was perforce assimilated in terms of the most available frames of reference.[1]

In summarizing their analysis, Allport and Postman point out that there were obvious dynamic, or motivational, factors present which also shaped the forgetting and distortion process. The war was important to these residents of the Maine community, hatred for the Japanese was intense, and a desire to protect America, coupled with a suspicion of foreigners in general, all tended to make the residents alert for possible danger. Guided by such motivational factors and in response to the various perceptual processes we have discussed in the previous chapter and the present chapter, the original incident became a war rumor.

[1] In this connection see our discussion, p. 94 of Chap. III, of the whole-part principle in perception.

Just as immediate perception is not a true reflection of what is "out there" to be seen, so is the remembered event not simply a "pale" reflection of the original structure. The original structure is ever-changing, acquiring new meanings, shaping and fitting itself in response to structural and functional organizing factors.

There are several subpropositions that follow from our major Proposition III. These subpropositions can help us to specify the exact nature of the change that will occur, in memory, in the original cognitive structure.

Relation between the Original Structure and the Process of Reorganization.—The first subproposition concerns itself with the relationship that exists between the properties of the original cognitive structure and the changes that take place, over time, in this structure. In its most general form, this subproposition can be stated as follows: *The specific changes that a cognitive organization undergoes in retention are a function of the structural and functional properties of the original cognitive organization.*

This subproposition can be illustrated by several examples. One of the structural organizing principles states that an object will be perceived in terms of the most stable organization possible (leveling and sharpening). If, now, the original perception is simple and well organized, there can be no marked changes in the direction of sharpening and leveling. Thus, if Wulf's subjects had been presented with simple figures instead of the irregularly formed figures, their memory of the original forms would have been much more accurate, after even a long interval of time, than it was under the conditions of his experiment. On the other hand, if the original perception is of a figure that lacks form and organization, then, during the retention process, such sharpening and leveling will tend to take place. Similarly, if you recount a very detailed and complicated story of a riot or accident or any other incident, your hearer will "trim down" the story to a simple, well-organized, and meaningful whole. If you wish your story to be repeated essentially as you told it, you must make it coherent, simple, with only the essentials included. It is not a question of how much can be remembered but what will be remembered. Thus, as Allport and Postman summarize their experiments on the recall and transmission of reports of pictures observed by their subjects,

It is often assumed that rumors become embroidered in the telling, or that they become enlarged like a rolling snowball. This is a misconception. Though we certainly find many insertions of reasons and circumstantial detail, they seem to occur only in the interest of sharpening. Elaboration which serves neither the purpose of coherency nor emphasis on the main point of the story seldom occurs—never in our experimental situations.

What is true of *structural* factors is also true of *functional* factors. We have seen, in Chap. III, that we tend to perceive objects and events in terms of our needs, moods, cultural frames of reference, etc. If the original cognitive structure is such as to fit in with these factors, then the reorganizations that will take place over time will be minimal; but if it does not fit in, then there will be relatively extensive reorganization. In other words, it appears that what our needs and moods cannot accomplish during the original perception of the event, they will accomplish during the retention period. This process can result in the invention of facts and in the exaggeration of details during retention. Thus, for example, if you see an altercation between a group of pickets and police, and if you believe, to begin with, that the police are always the first to initiate violence, you might "remember," in your later retelling of the scene, that the police struck first—even though your original perception of the event may have been a relatively confused one. Such an invention is an honest error due to "forgetting." Your cognitive structure has undergone a change to conform with the functional determinants that were present to begin with and persist in your mental make-up. Exaggeration is also frequently a consequence of the same process. If you hate the policeman whom you have seen handle the picket somewhat less than gently, you will "remember" him as having been particularly brutal.

Dynamics of Behavior and Selective Memory.—The effect of needs on memory shows itself in still another way—in selective memory or selective forgetting. Just as in perception we have seen that the needs of the individual help determine which objects will be *selected out for perception,* so do needs continue this selective process and help determine which of all the objects originally perceived will be *selected out for retention.* One of the first experiments in this area is that of Zeigarnik (1927). Her experiments were conducted with 164 subjects (students, teachers, children). The instructions were "I shall give you a series of tasks which you are to complete as rapidly and correctly as possible." They were then given from 18 to 22 tasks—one at a time—which consisted of manual work (constructing a box of cardboard, making clay figures, etc.). Half of these tasks, in random order, were interrupted before the subjects could complete the tasks. Following the entire series of tasks (interrupted and completed) the experimenter asked, "Please tell me what the tasks were upon which you worked during the experiment." In addition, introspective reports were requested from the subjects, and such questions were asked as which tasks were the most interesting, least interesting, most pleasant, etc.

Zeigarnik's results indicated that the unfinished tasks were remembered approximately twice as well as the completed ones. On the basis of further control experiments and the reports of the subjects, Zeigarnik concluded that the recall value of the unfinished task was higher because at the time of testing for recall there still existed an unreleased tension with respect to the unfinished tasks. It is not that the tasks were unfinished which was crucial, but that the subject was not content with his performance on those tasks and therefore had built up a persistent tension with respect to them. Thus, in a more recent experiment by Alper (1946) it is demonstrated that items learned under conditions of "ego involvement" (*i.e.*, where the completion of the task satisfies self-regard needs) are much better remembered than when the same tasks are learned under conditions of "task involvement" (*i.e.*, where the completion of the task is regarded impersonally and is done only to satisfy the experimenter).

This selectivity of memory becomes particularly important in helping us to understand the cognitive world of many people and the nature of the data they use to support many of their beliefs and attitudes. As we have pointed out in the introduction to Chap. III (page 77), the cognitive field of the individual is made up not only of what he perceives here and now but also of what he remembers and of what he imagines. But it now appears that he will not remember *everything* he has ever perceived *or even a representative and random sample of the events* that he has experienced. He will remember only a *selected sample*. He will retain events in which he was frustrated or insulted or "cheated" by foreigners, for example, but he will forget events where foreigners did not play such disagreeable roles; he will retain events in which he was deeply involved, and he will forget others. This "sampling error" of experiences can thereby result in a distorted cognitive field.

Intervening Events and Cognitive Reorganization.—Thus far we have described forgetting as an orderly, continuous, and even creative process of change that occurs in response to the various organizing factors as they operate on the original cognitive structure. But this process is very rarely allowed to continue without the intervention of new perceptions. That is, we now know that an original perception, *without any further new experiences occurring in the life of the individual*, will undergo systematic changes. But the time interval that transpires between the original perception and the recall is not an empty time interval. While the cognitive reorganizations are going on under their own steam, as it were, the individual is perceiving new objects and events, is acquiring new needs and goals, is experiencing new emotions and feelings. These new experiences will, in many cases, influence the orderly changes thus far described. This follows from our basic perceptual concept that no perception (old or new) lives a life of its own but that it interacts with almost every other similar perception. To take specific cognizance of this process, Proposition III can be formulated in the following subproposition: *The specific changes that a cognitive organization undergoes in retention are a function of the relation between the properties of the original structure and the intervening perceptions.* This formulation, it can be readily seen, encompasses such facts as are usually investigated in the laboratory under the technical term of *retroactive inhibition.*

The typical laboratory experiment used to demonstrate this effect is to have two groups of subjects memorize, say, a list of nonsense syllables (list A). Then the experimental group is given a second list to memorize (list B), while the control group is permitted to rest during this interval. At some later time both groups are tested for their retention of list A. Any difference in the recall scores that may be found between the performance of the experimental group and that of the control group is then assumed to be due to the influence of the mental processes involved in learning list B on the retention of A.

Frequently, the result of the influence of an intervening perception upon an old perception is such as to create an entirely new cognitive organization. Two similar perceptions do not merely become attached to each other but interact with each other. That is why one can sometimes refer to "creative forgetting." This frequently happens in our social memories. Thus, suppose that Arbuthnot's wallet is stolen by a pickpocket in city *A*. He discovers it a few minutes later and is quite distressed. Shortly thereafter, let us assume, Arbuthnot finds occasion to spend some time in the Italian quarter of that city. For some reason or other, entirely unrelated to his loss of the wallet, Arbuthnot has a very unpleasant experience with the Italians in that community. A year or so later Arbuthnot may "remember" that his pocket was picked in the Italian community of city *A*. In other words, the *unpleasant* experience in one part of city *A* can become organized with a subsequent *unpleasant* experience in another part of the city, with the result that the interaction of these two experiences (similar in their "unpleasantness") has created a new cognitive structure. This would be more likely to happen, of course, if Arbuthnot, to begin with, had an anti-Italian prejudice, but it is in this way that many "honestly" recalled events reinforce original prejudices.

The intervening event need not be a perception, in the narrow sense. The memorial fate of a cognitive structure can be redirected by the coming into being of new goals, new tensions, new needs. In other words, the original perception or cognitive structure will change not only in terms of the originally existing needs but also in terms of later developing needs. Thus we can remember the same event in one way at one time and in quite an opposite way at another time.

Proposition IV

The ease and rapidity of the cognitive reorganization process is a function of the differentiation, isolation, and rigidity of the original cognitive structure

The three preceding propositions have concerned themselves with some of the conditions that initiate cognitive reorganization (Proposition I), with the interrelationships among the various successive structures (Proposition II), and with the nature and direction of change as a function of intervening events and the operation of the organizational factors over time (Proposition III). There remain, however, several additional important characteristics of the reorganization process which are not adequately dealt with in those propositions. For one thing we know that the rate of the cognitive reorganization process differs not only from person to person but also from problem to problem for the same individual. We have all heard the common expression, "He's very quick about catching on to a lot of things but is awfully slow about changing his mind where the Democratic party is concerned." It is also a commonplace observation to find situations where a blocked goal exists but where no cognitive reorganization apparently takes place. In other words, in addition to all the other characteristics of the cognitive reorganization process, we must know something about the property of ease or rate of change.

Frequently the concept of individual differences in native intelligence is used to explain differences in rate of cognitive reorganization among people, and the concept of specific native abilities is used to explain differences in rate of cognitive reorganization in the same individual. Differences in the tempo of cognitive reorganization are thus viewed as reflections of some biologically determined (and frequently innate) capacities that are inherent in the physiological organism rather than in the psychological field in which the organism is operating. Thus, when one citizen arrives at a new insight into the nature of political activity more quickly than another citizen, some of us are likely to explain the difference by saying that the first citizen is more intelligent than the second. If the first citizen, on the other hand, seems to be slow about solving certain mechanical problems which the second man can do quickly, one can then say that the first man does not have much mechanical aptitude whereas the second does.

Undoubtedly, in many instances, the biologically determined capacities of the individual are important in understanding differential rates of cognitive reorganization, but that is far from the whole story. In many instances this explanation is erroneous. Proposition IV suggests that a better understanding of the problem of ease and rate can be gained from an analysis of the properties of the cognitive structures involved than from the supposed biological nature of the individual who harbors these structures.[1]

Differentiation and Isolation of the Cognitive Field.—We have seen, in our introduction to the concept of cognitive structures, that cognitive fields can differ with respect to the property of *complexity*. Some individuals for example, may have a simple, undifferentiated cognitive structure relating to religious objects and events. All religions are seen as alike; all religious people are grouped together without any differentiation. Some people, on the other hand, may have highly differentiated and complex cognitive structures relating to religion. Thus, they may differentiate between "good" and "bad" religions, between Catholics, Protestants, Jews, Moslems, etc. They may differentiate the organized church from the spiritual creed of any religion; the rank-and-file members from the official clergy. In addition to this property of complexity or differentiation, there is the property of *isolation* which characterizes cognitive structures. This property refers to the interrelationships and interdependencies that exist among various structures in the cognitive field. The term *intercommunication* has been suggested as a descriptive phrase for this property. Thus, although it is true that no structure exists in complete isolation from all the other structures in the cognitive field, nevertheless the degree of interrelationship, or intercommunication, among the structures does vary. For example, for one individual the structure relating to religious phenomena may be relatively isolated from his structure relating to economic matters. The changes that may take place in his economic thinking may have very little influence on his religious thinking. Another individual, on the other hand, may have a high degree of communication between his religious and his economic structures, and a reorganization of one is immediately reflected in a reorganization of the other.

It is obvious, from the illustrations given above, that these properties of cognitive structures will influence the rate of cognitive reorganization, creative thinking, and ingenuity in problem solving. This relationship, however, is not a simple one.

Let us return to our example of the two individuals with differing religious cognitive structures. Suppose that each one of them were presented with an apparently significant new argument relating to religion. Since every cognitive organization is determined by the relations existing among all the individual parts, a single new perception would have a relatively decisive effect on a major structure that was simple, undifferentiated, and isolated

---

[1] For an interesting analysis of the effects of frustration upon cognitive ability which leads the author to conclude that "intellectual ability varies with the psychological situation of the individual." see Barker (1938).

from other structures, but it would have a relatively minor effect on a complexly differentiated structure that was in communication with other structures. Thus, a man who believes that "religion is good" and does not differentiate further and does not "see" the connections between religious events and political or economic events might be persuaded that all religion is "bad" by a single decisive argument or by a strongly unpleasant experience with a church official, a religious person, or the manifestation of a religious practice. On the other hand, a man who had a highly differentiated religious cognitive structure, which was in communication with his economic and political structures, could easily assimilate a strong argument or an unpleasant experience without involving a change in his major religious structure. It might, for example, affect one of his religious substructures ("church officials" or "religious ceremonies") but permit his major structure to remain relatively intact. Second, since his religious structure is not isolated from other structures, it is determined not only by religious percepts but also by political and economic percepts. Therefore this new, single argument or experience could have little relative effect on the religious organization; it would, as it were, "be lost in the shuffle." Our first man, then, under the conditions described here would show more rapid cognitive reorganization than our second man.

Creative thinking and ingenuity.—On the other hand, just the reverse effects would be expected if we examined the rate of cognitive reorganization consequent upon the presentation of a nonreligious argument or experience. The reason is obvious and follows from the analysis made above. An economic or political perception, for the person with the isolated religious structure, cannot result in reorganizing his religious structure simply because there is no communication between the two sets of perceptions. For our second man, however, the possibility of such reorganization exists. For him, as it were, there are more avenues of approach to his religious structure. A block to a political goal or an economic goal may thus result in the reorganization of his religious beliefs. This may frequently result in strange reorganizations, but it will also result in many more ingenious (and sometimes more adequate) reorganizations in a problem situation than would be true for the first man.

Perhaps another way of phrasing the difference between an isolated structure and a nonisolated one would be to say that in the former, the *focus of attention* is narrower than in the latter. Fewer different items are involved, and those items are more definitely segregated from the rest of the field. Thus, in a typical problem-solving experiment with chimpanzees, the food may be outside the cage, just out of reach of the animal, and can be obtained only by the use of a stick that is hanging from the ceiling at the back of the cage.   If the animal restricts his attention to the food and the bars that intervene, we may say that he has a narrow focus of attention.   His cognitive structure of the problem situation is simple and clear-cut: There is the food out there, there are the bars in front of him, and that is all that is relevant to the situation.   On the other hand, if the animal's attention includes more items in addition to the above two—the experimenter at some distance away, the light bulb on the ceiling near the window, the stick hanging in the rear of his cage—he has a less simple structure and his focus of attention is wider.   The ingenuity of the solutions that the chimpanzee with the simple structures can achieve will be considerably poorer and less adaptive than in the case of the chimpanzee with the wider field of attention.   In the first case he may reach for the food between the bars—and fail.   He will try that again and again.   His goal is blocked, but the nature of his original cognitive organization is such that it cannot readily undergo reorganization.   It is as if there were no other "materials" with which to develop a new organization.   On the other hand, for the chimpanzee who has a wider, less isolated structure of the problem situation, the initial hypothesis, that food can be obtained by reaching through the bars, can be more readily reorganized.   If unsuccessful in his first approach, he may next attempt "begging" the experimenter to get it for him; if that fails, he may try using the stick that is hanging from his ceiling as a tool to rake in the food, etc.

Whether we consider the problem-solving behavior of the chimpanzee or that of man when up against various social problems, it is generally true that the more simple, undifferentiated and isolated any cognitive structure is the less available it is for reorganization and the less creative and ingenious will the solution attempts be.

Factors That Determine Differentiation and Isolation.—Whether an individual's cognitive structures are simple or differentiated, isolated from other structures or integrated with them is extremely important.   What factors determine these properties of the cognitive structure?   There are, of course, a number of specific factors that can be responsible, but the most significant ones seem to derive from four major sources: (1) the biologically determined capacities of the individuals, (2) the operation of the principles of organization, (3) the manner and frequency with which the original structure is experienced, and (4) the motivational and emotional factors of behavior.

Biologically determined capacities.—There can be little doubt that individuals differ in the capacity to organize and maintain structures of varying complexity.   A rat cannot organize into one structure as many different perceptions as can a man. The same is true among different individuals of the same species. Some people can organize more items together, into more complicated and interrelated structures, than can others. And these differences are frequently due to hereditarily determined differences in the structure or functioning of the nervous systems. Not all men are created equal. The existence of a blocked goal will not lead all people to an equally efficient or equally rapid reorganization of their cognitive structures.

There will always be people who will be ahead of others in their thinking. No amount of training and wise application of psychological principles can eliminate the differences in the complexity and interrelatedness of cognitive structures due to biological differences. However, as was indicated before, not all differences in these properties of cognitive structures are due to biological factors, and perhaps most of the difficulties society experiences as a consequence of retarded cognitive reorganization can be ascribed to other factors.

Operation of the principles of organization.—The very operation of the principles of organization that make cognitive reorganization an orderly process can be such as to promote simplicity in structure and isolation of one structure from another. It is because of this that we frequently find, even among the most intelligent of people, a resistance to cognitive reorganization. Repetitive errors are not only characteristic of the stupid— they are universal.

The net result of the operation of organizational factors is to create a structured, differentiated, meaningful cognitive field. The operation of the similarity and proximity principles create different structures and substructures and tend to isolate one from another. Organization, in other words, is a two-edged sword. Without such organization, our mental world would indeed be a blooming, buzzing confusion; with organization, our mental world tends to lose its fluidity. Some of the retarding effects of the factors of organization, however, can be vitiated if we take advantage of what we know about the relationship between the speed of cognitive reorganization and the conditions under which the original organization was acquired. We now turn to a discussion of this significant relationship.

Conditions determining formation of original structure.—Two conditions are important here: (1) the manner of presentation of the stimulus situation that leads to the original cognitive organization and (2) the frequency with which that stimulus situation is presented.

The student who is taught economics in isolation from everything else that he learns, to whom the laws of economics are presented in a simplified, clear, well-structured manner, but without reference to all of his other concerns and knowledge, is thereby encouraged to build up a relatively isolated cognitive structure. It may not be simple and undifferentiated, but it may be in little communication with his other cognitive structures. The presentation of pro and con arguments concerning a proposed tax program solely in terms of the demands of a balanced budget may result in an isolated cognitive structure which will make it difficult to see the solution of other social problems through manipulation of the taxing scheme of a country.

The second factor, frequency, is perhaps not more important than the first, but its effects are usually more dramatic. In general it appears that the more frequently a given organization is experienced the stronger is the tendency of that organization to become simplified and isolated from other structures in the cognitive field. Thus Luchins (1942) in his study of the effect of drill upon mechanization found that as a consequence of excessive drill with a specific method of solving problems, the pupil's perception of a problem became the perception of a much narrower and isolated phenomenon, *i.e.*, "This is another instance of the old method."

From this point of view, the oft-quoted maxim "Repeat a lie frequently enough and people will believe it" acquires an additional interpretation to the one we have already suggested (see page 121). Not every lie will be accepted and incorporated by people into their thinking because of frequent repetition; but once a lie is accepted (for reasons discussed on page 121), then repetition of the lie becomes effective. Thus suppose that the propagandist in a foreign country were to spread, via newspapers, radio, motion picture, rumors, the statement that the United States was deliberately creating an economic blockade against his country. If the economic conditions of the country were bad enough, if no other explanation for those conditions were made available, then some people of that country might accept the lie. However, if at that time, the United States could initiate counterpropaganda, point out the falsity of the reasoning that ascribed the difficult economic conditions to a "nonexistent" blockade and indicate other reasons for the difficulties, then some of the people might drop their belief in the lie. But if such counterpropaganda were prohibited and the original lie were repeated and repeated, eventually, as a *consequence of frequency*, the original belief in the lie would become a simplified, isolated cognitive structure in the mental life of the individual. It would be relatively immune to attack by "reason"; it would resist all reorganization that might be initiated through the individual's perceiving the apparent inconsistencies between the lie and other facts. It would begin to lead, relatively, "a life of its own." At that point, only insistent attacks on the "lie" itself could hope to have any effect. Cognitive structures are not immune to reasoned attack until they have become simplified and isolated, and frequency of repetition is one way of doing just that.

Needs, emotions, and rigidity of cognitive structure.—We have already seen, in discussing our first proposition of cognitive reorganization, that the strength of a need may influence the character of the cognitive organization. One such effect can be to make the organization simplified and isolated. In Birch's experiment, (page 114), it will be recalled, the very hungry chimpanzee could not leave the field of vision in which the food was located, with the result that it became almost impossible for him to organize the stick, which was behind him, together with the food, which was in front of him. Under the stress of great need, the cognitive organization involving the goal object and the most obvious and immediately perceived possible route to the goal object becomes simplified and isolated from all other objects and events in the individual's field of experience. The immediately perceived barrier to the goal becomes a more and more dominant object, attention tends to become centered on this one object, and the result is a very narrow, isolated, rigid organization. The stronger the tension, the stronger the emotional "tone" of the situation, the less likely that cognitive reorganization will occur. A man desperately in need of food will persist in maintaining his original notion of how to get the food— he will not be able to "think through" new solutions, discover new roundabout routes. The maxim "Necessity is the mother of invention" is true only if the necessity is not too great.

General Comments.—A consideration of the implications of Proposition IV will make it clear why we should expect to find in many situations that people repeat their errors and "butt their heads against the wall." As long as a need exists, people will strive to satisfy it. They will act. But we know that their actions will be determined by their cognitive structures. If their cognitive structures are isolated and rigid and thus do not change, their actions cannot change—their strivings to achieve their goals will be characterized by stereotypy. One man may continue to seek justice and security within the confines of a political and economic system that consistently frustrates his attempts, because he is not intelligent; another, because his thinking about each aspect of that system is isolated from the others and he cannot see the interrelationships and the necessary over-all changes that must be made; and a third, because of the rigidity of his concepts induced by his emotional thinking about the "system." In most cases, a situational analysis will tell us whether a man will or will not display cognitive reorganization, and it can tell us what must be done if we wish to encourage cognitive reorganization.

SUMMARY

We know that differences in social behavior among men reflect differences in their cognitive structures.   And we know that differences in cognitive structures are, in turn, due to the differences in the kind of physical worlds in which people live, in the kinds of problems they meet, and in the various trainings to which they are subjected.   What is true of the differences among men is also true for the individual.   Cognitive structures are not static.   They are constantly changing—in response to the individual's changing situations (learning), his changing physiological state, and through the effects of the dynamic factors involved in retention (forgetting).   Phrasing the problem of behavior change in terms of cognitive reorganization stresses the similarity between the propositions discussed in this chapter and those discussed in the chapter on cognitive organization.   In many respects a law of cognitive reorganization is a law of cognitive organization as it operates through a series of events.   The four propositions discussed in this chapter concern themselves, then, with all kinds of cognitive reorganization—those which are involved in learning, thinking, problem solving, as well as those which occur in response to changes in the physiological condition of the organism and through forgetting.   However, the problem of the acquisition of motor skills is not discussed.   The psychological problems involved there are of only peripheral interest to the social psychologist.

Proposition I: As long as there is a blockage to the attainment of a goal, cognitive reorganization tends to take place; the nature of the reorganization is such as to reduce the tension induced by the frustrating situation.   This proposition serves to define one of the most characteristic situations in which cognitive reorganization occurs, and it stresses the intimate relationship that exists between the cognitive reorganization process and the dynamics of behavior as defined in Chap. II.   A number of factors are discussed that help determine the adaptive value of the resulting cognitive organizations.   Among these are the strength of the need, the individual's characteristic manner of responding to frustration, and the perception of the block to the goal.   It is concluded that intense needs, by distorting and narrowing the field of perception, can lead to bizarre, irreal, and unadaptive reorganizations; the adaptive value of a characteristic manner of responding to frustration varies with the nature of the problem.   The failure to perceive the block at all or to perceive the wrong block can also lead to nonadjustive cognitive restructuring.

Proposition II: The cognitive reorganization process typically consists of a hierarchically related series of organizations.   This proposition, by describing the entire cognitive reorganization process in terms of a series of organizations, asserts that each successive step of the learning process is meaningfully organized. The implications of this for the laws of frequency and effect, learning from experience, and the role of education and guidance are discussed. It is pointed out (1) that repeated situations provide the opportunity for continued cognitive reorganization but do not, through mere cumulative effects, gradually build up the final structure—as the traditional laws of frequency and of effect would have it; (2) that only that which is perceived and attended to will play an important role in determining the nature of the resulting reorganizations—people do learn from experience, but only from their own perceived experiences; (3) that consciously directed education, therefore, assumes vital significance in shaping the cognitive reorganization of people.

Proposition II further states that although the reorganization process consists of a series of separately organized structures, nevertheless these structures are frequently related to each other in a uniform manner, wherein the sequence can be described as leading from the more general to the more specific. Some illustrations of this relationship are taken from animal experiments and studies of creative thinking among human adults. This principle is then further illustrated by a discussion of the problem-solving process as it frequently occurs in critical social situations. Throughout, the point is stressed that the thinking process, despite the fact that it consists of a series of cognitive structures, is a unified and interdependent one.

Proposition III: Cognitive structures, over time, undergo progressive changes in accordance with the principles of organization. Not all cognitive reorganization is due to tension-reductive behavior consequent upon the blocking of the goal. Some very important changes occur during the interval of time between the moment a cognitive structure is formed and the moment it functions again in the behavior of the individual, without respect to needs. Proposition III is concerned with these changes. This proposition, as phrased, treats the forgetting process as a cognitive reorganization process in which the changes can be of various kinds and in various directions. It does not require that all forgetting must result in the dropping out of items or the decay of the original structure. Experimental evidence from the retention of simple visual forms, verbal material, and rumor analysis, which is given to support this formulation of the forgetting process, suggests that organizational processes, operating over time, tend to produce the same effects that those factors induce in immediate perception.

In discussing the conditions that determine the specific pattern of reorganization which a cognitive structure will undergo in retention, the relations (1) between the original structure and the process of reorganization and (2) between the intervening events and the process of reorganization are examined. The first relationship is formulated as follows: The specific changes that a cognitive organization undergoes in retention are a function of the structural and functional properties of the original cognitive organization. Examples are given of the operation of this principle from the analysis of rumors and the role of elaboration, invention, and exaggeration in rumor development, as well as from experiments dealing with selective memory. The effect of the sampling error of retained experiences upon the structure of our cognitive world is also discussed.

The second relationship is formulated in the following terms: The specific changes that a cognitive organization undergoes in retention are a function of the relation between the properties of the original structure and the intervening perceptions. Examples are given from the traditional retroactive inhibition experiments of the learning laboratory and from the "creative forgetting" which frequently serves to reinforce and give support to social prejudices.

Proposition IV: The ease and rapidity of the cognitive reorganization process is a function of the differentiation, isolation, and rigidity of the original cognitive structure. This proposition deals with the problem of the rate of cognitive reorganization. The general point is made that a better understanding of the problem of speed of reorganization and that of individual differences in the ease and rapidity of the process can be gained from an analysis of the properties of the cognitive structures involved than from the biological nature of the individual who harbors these structures. The properties of differentiation and isolation of the cognitive field are defined and discussed, and the relationship between these properties and ease of cognitive reorganization is formulated. The conclusion is made that simple and isolated structures are more amenable to reorganization by direct attack whereas differentiated and interdependent structures are more amenable to restructuring by indirect attack. In addition, it is pointed out that in the latter case, the cognitive structure is more available for new, creative recombinations.

The factors that determine differentiation and isolation of cognitive structures are then discussed, and the following ones are examined: (1) the biologically determined capacities of the individual, (2) the operation of the factors of organization, (3) the conditions that determine the formation of the original structure, and (4) needs and emotion. In connection with the third factor, the two most important conditions are described as (a) the manner of presentation of the stimulus-situation which leads to the original cognitive organization and (b) the frequency with which the stimulus situation is presented. This last condition is discussed with reference to certain important implications for the propaganda process.

Finally, a brief discussion is appended on the effects of needs and emotions on the rigidity of cognitive structures. References are made to the material discussed under the first proposition, and the point is stressed that the stronger the tension and emotion of the individual when attempting to solve a problem the more rigid, narrow, and isolated will be the cognitive structure.

In considering the implications of Proposition IV it is pointed out that we can expect to find people in many situations repeating their errors and "butting their heads against the wall" in their attempts to solve the problems that confront them. This is not to be explained away as a characteristic of the stupid but is explicable from an analysis of the nature of cognitive structures formed under various conditions.

BIBLIOGRAPHY

ADAMS, D. K.: 1931. A restatement of the problem of learning. *Brit. J. Psychol.*, **22**, 150–178.

ALLPORT, G. W., and POSTMAN, L.: 1947. *The psychology of rumor.* New York: Holt.

ALPER, T. G.: 1946. Task-orientation vs. ego-orientation in learning and retention. *Amer. J. Psychol.*, **59**, 236–248.

BARKER, R. G.: 1938. The effects of frustration upon cognitive ability. *Character & Pers.*, **7**, 145–150.

BARTLETT, F. C.: 1932. *Remembering.* London: Cambridge.

BIRCH, H. G.: 1945. The role of motivational factors in insightful problem-solving. *J. comp. Psychol.*, **38**, 295–317.

CARMICHAEL, L., HOGAN, H. P., and WALTER, A. A.: 1932. An experimental study of the effect of language on the reproduction of visually perceived form. *J. exp. Psychol.*, **15**, 73–86.

DEMBO, T.: 1931. Anger as a dynamic problem. *Psychol. Forsch.*, **15**, 1–144.

DUNCKER, K.: 1945. On problem-solving. *Psychol. Monogr.*, **58**, No. 5.

DUNCKER, K., and KRECHEVSKY, I.: 1939. On solution-achievement. *Psychol. Rev.*, **46**, 176–185.

GIBSON, J. J.: 1929. Reproduction of visually perceived forms. *J. exp. Psychol.*, **12**, 1–39.

GIRDEN, E.: 1938. Conditioning and problem-solving behavior in dogs. *Amer. J. Psychol.*, **51**, 677–686.

HANFMANN, E., and KASANIN, J.: 1937. A method for the study of concept formation. *J. Psychol.*, **3**, 521–540.

HEIDBREDER, E.: 1924. An experimental study of thinking. *Arch. Psychol.*, **11**, No. 73.

JAMES, W.: 1890. *Principles of psychology.* I. New York: Holt.

KOFFKA, K.: 1925. Mental development. In Murchison, K. (ed.), *Psychologies of 1925.* Worcestor: Clark Univ. Press.

KRECHEVSKY, J.: 1932a. Hypotheses in rats. *Psychol. Rev.*, **6**, 516–532.

KRECHEVSKY, I.: 1932*b*   "Hypotheses" vs. "chance" in the pre-solution period in sensory discrimination learning.   *Univ. Calif. Publ. Psychol.*, **6**, 27–44.

LUCHINS, A. S.: 1942. Mechanization in problem solving.   *Psychol. Monogr.*, **54**, No. 6.

MAIER, N. R. F.: 1931.   Reasoning and learning. *Psychol. Rev.*, **38**, 332–346.

POSTMAN L., and SENDERS, V. L.: 1946.   Incidental learning and generality of set.   *J. exp. Psychol.*, **36**, 153–165.

SPENCE, K. W.: 1934.   Systematic versus random responses in the solution of multiple choice problems by the chimpanzee.   *Psychol. Bull.*, **31**, 688–689.

SPENCE, K. W.: 1937.   Discrimination habits in chimpanzee.   *J. comp. Psychol.*, **23**, 77–100.

SPENCE, K. W.: 1945.   An experimental test of the continuity and non-continuity theories of discrimination learning.   *J. exp. Psychol.*, **35**, 253–266.

TOLMAN, E. C.: 1932.   *Purposive behavior in animals and men.*   New York: Century.

TOLMAN, E. C., and KRECHEVSKY, I.: 1933.   Means-end-readiness and "hypotheses." *Psychol. Rev.*, **40**, 60–70.

WULF, F.: 1922.   Über die Veranderung von Vorstellungen.   *Psychol. Forsch.*, **1**, 333–373

ZEIGARNIK, B.: 1927.   Über das Behalten von erledigten und unerledigten Hendlungen. *Psychol. Forsch.*, **9**, 1–85.

PART TWO

SOCIAL PROCESSES

CHAPTER V

BELIEFS AND ATTITUDES OF MEN

Both the Jews and the Catholics have beliefs about the proper head-dress when praying to God. Because of these beliefs, the orthodox Jew keeps his hat or skullcap securely in place when he enters his synagogue whereas the Catholic uncovers his head when he enters his church. Both the Russian and the American political leaders assert their belief in polit-ical democracy. To the Russian this belief involves, among other things, the right of an individual to vote for or against a candidate for public office, but only one name and one party (claiming to represent the interests of all the people) must appear on the ballot; to the American, a belief in democracy means, among other things, a belief in the right to vote for one of a number of candidates, each from a different party, and each claiming to represent all the people.

There are some Frenchmen who have violent attitudes with respect to Germans—they hate them, they believe them to be uncivilized and dishonest, and, in certain circumstances, they may take action against them. There are some Americans who have strong attitudes with respect to their coun-try—they love their country, they believe it to be beautiful and just in its dealings with other countries, and, in certain circumstances, they may even be willing to take extreme action in protecting it against danger.

People, in other words, direct their actions—whether the actions involve religious ceremonies, ways of earning a living, political activity, or violence—in terms of their beliefs and attitudes. The very fact that beliefs and atti-tudes play such a prominent and seemingly significant role for the individual argues strongly for the indispensability of beliefs and attitudes in the analysis of social behavior.

BELIEFS AND ATTITUDES DEFINED

The argument behind the four chapters of Part I was that the social behavior of the individual is explicable in terms of motivational, emotional, perceptual, and learning processes. However, it is neither convenient nor perhaps possible to describe, analyze, and predict the individual's social behavior by reference to those fundamental processes considered singly. Behavior, we have pointed out several times, is a dynamic resultant of all those processes operating simultaneously. Moreover, behavior is a function not only of the immediately present stimuli and their momentary perceptions, but of more enduring dispositions. It is therefore more profitable and more realistic to work with a higher order of psychological unit than needs or perceptions. These higher orders are the enduring organizations of perceptual, motivational, and emotional factors known as *beliefs* and *attitudes*. A complete picture of a man's beliefs about and attitudes toward various aspects of his social world will yield highly reliable predictions about his behavior in various social situations.

Beliefs and attitudes do not, of course, function in a psychological vacuum. In order to predict behavior in a given situation it is not enough to know the relevant beliefs and attitudes pertaining to that situation. We must also take into account the specific needs and perceptions existing at the moment. But here again it is proper to stress the dynamic character of the psychological field. The needs and perceptions that operate at the moment are not indifferently connected with the beliefs and attitudes of the individual. How an immediate situation is perceived is determined, as we have seen in Chap. III, partly by the preexisting beliefs of the individual, and the needs operating in the immediate situation are partly affected by the individual's preexisting attitudes. It is because of this that we found it convenient, in all the preceding chapters, to make constant reference to beliefs and attitudes, and it is also because of this that we shall find much of our discussion of the nature of beliefs and attitudes to be dependent upon the propositions covered in those chapters.

Beliefs and attitudes, though similar in that they are both the end results of motivational, perceptual, and learning processes, are significantly different one from the other. They have different attributes and different implications for action, and it is therefore important that we distinguish clearly between them if we are to make sound scientific use of these two concepts. In our illustrations given in the opening of this chapter, some of the differences have already been indicated. Attitudes, since they involve motivational or emotional factors (*e.g.*, the Frenchman *hates*, the American *loves*), can frequently be seen at the bottom of violent or intense action.

Beliefs.—Because beliefs constitute such an intrinsic and inseparable part of our psychological fields, it is somewhat difficult to find a logical starting place for a discussion of them. We can begin by a definition, the full significance of which will have to be evaluated by the specific characteristics of beliefs to be discussed in this and the following chapter. *A belief is an enduring organization of perceptions and cognitions about some aspect of the individual's world.* A belief is a pattern of meanings of a thing;

it is the *totality* of the individual's cognition about the thing. In so far as a perception or a cognition is in itself an organization, a belief is, as it were, *an organization of organizations*. As such, it is structured and complete. It is a product of original perceptions, of the reorganization those perceptions have undergone, of the cognitions created by such reorganizations, etc. For example, a man believes that the earth is spherical. This is equivalent to saying that his belief involves several different kinds of related cognitions. He conceives of the earth as having certain properties of shape; and although he has never seen the earth as a sphere, he "knows," or believes, that if he were to be placed far enough out in space away from the earth, he would see it to be spherical in shape, like a ball or an orange or the moon. He knows, or believes, that to travel in a straight line in any direction on the earth's surface would eventually return him to his starting place—and he may even have done this. If he is a mathematician, he may also include in his belief the cognition that if he were to perform certain mathematical computations involving the distribution of the mass of the earth, these computations would be satisfied only by assumptions of the mass as being spherically distributed.

Or, to take another example, a child may believe that there is a Santa Claus. This is again equivalent to saying that the child's belief involves several different kinds of related cognitions: The child conceives that there is a being who "looks" in a certain way, white beard, ruddy face, tasseled hat; that this being acts in a certain way and is given to specific kinds of judgments; *e.g.*, if the child behaves, Santa Claus will reward him on Christmas; if the child misbehaves, Santa Claus will stay away from his home on Christmas.

Belief as a Generic Term.—The term *belief* will be used in a generic sense to include *knowledge, opinions,* and *faith*. There are observable differences among what we call knowledge, opinion, and faith, but there is a common set of factors governing them, and a common set of characteristics in terms of which they can be described. This general use of the term belief corresponds closely to the way the word is used in everyday speech. We commonly say "We believe . . . " when we mean more explicitly that we have *knowledge* or that we are of the *opinion* or that we have *faith*. For example, we "believe" that the earth is spherical, that the atomic bomb would be safer under international control, that God is guiding our actions.

Attitudes.—As we have already indicated, attitudes lie behind many of the significant and dramatic instances of man's social behavior. It is for this reason that many psychologists regard the study of attitudes as the central problem of social psychology. In common with beliefs, attitudes can be conceived of as integrations mediating between the fundamental psychological processes and action.   More specifically, an attitude can be defined as *an enduring organization of motivational, emotional, perceptual, and cognitive processes with respect to some aspect of the individual's world.* The similarities and differences between this definition and the definition given for beliefs are clear.   Beliefs can be seen as the *cognitive* embodiment of attitudes.   All attitudes incorporate relevant beliefs about the object of the attitude, but we cannot say, conversely, that all beliefs are part of attitude structures.   Beliefs, as such, are motivationally and emotionally neutral, though, of course, motivational forces may have played a role in the process of the formation of the beliefs.   But when beliefs are embedded in attitudes, they are thereby subject to special dynamic pressures.

The object of an attitude, under certain conditions, is frequently perceived as having a goal character, as demanding action.   The Frenchman with an anti-German attitude perceives the German as "bad"—the very sight of the German may impel the Frenchman to do something about him.   The object is far from neutral.   The objects of attitudes, in other words, have many of the same characteristics as emotional objects.   It is this which helps give attitudes their insistent, dynamic, stirred-up, driving character.

But we know that an emotional object cannot be defined in terms of itself, but only in terms of the entire psychological field.   Thus, for example, a tiger may evoke fear in a person if the tiger should be met in the jungle.   The same tiger, safely behind the bars of the cage, does not arouse the same degree of tension in the observer, is not perceived with the same emotional attributes.   The tiger "looks" different.   The tiger is to be feared or is to be run away from only under certain conditions.   The very same considerations hold for the objects of attitudes.   Only under certain conditions will the object of the enduring organization we call an attitude have goal character or demand action or evoke a feeling of emotion.   Thus, a Southerner who has a strong anti-Negro attitude may, under certain conditions, experience the emotion of hate or fear when he perceives a Negro.   However, when this same Southerner is seated in the barber chair and a Negro is shining his shoes, he need not experience either of the above emotions.   To characterize an attitude as a driving force does not mean that an individual who has an intense attitude will always find himself in a state of tension when in the presence of the object of his attitude. Whether he does or not depends very much on the context in which he perceives the object.

The "sign" of attitudes.—However, the fact that in certain situations an attitude does involve tension and that the object of an attitude is frequently perceived as demanding action on the part of the individual differentiates attitudes in a very important way from beliefs. It is for this reason that attitudes can be designated as either "pro" or "anti" while beliefs are conceived of as "neutral." We speak of a pro-British attitude or an anti-Russian attitude, but we do not speak of pro or con when we are describing a man's belief about the spherical nature of the earth.

THE FUNCTIONAL SIGNIFICANCE OF BELIEFS AND ATTITUDES

A human psychological existence without beliefs is virtually inconceivable, for it would be an existence without continuity. One of the major roles that beliefs play in the individual's personality is in providing structure and continuity for his psychological world. Beliefs can be seen as the building blocks of his world; and for all practical purposes, the pattern of his beliefs and attitudes may be taken as equivalent to the pattern of his psychological world. The continuity from one psychological situation to the next is given primarily by the enduring pattern of his beliefs and attitudes (among which are the very important beliefs and attitudes that he holds about himself). In the absence of such enduring structures, the individual would be a "new" individual in each situation; his behavior would tend to be organized only in terms of the immediate pattern of concomitant stimuli and his momentary needs.

In addition to this general organizing role which beliefs and attitudes play, they are also related in an intimate functional way to man's general and specific needs.

Beliefs and Attitudes and the Search for Meaning.—The fundamental processes of cognitive organization and reorganization operate so as to make the development of beliefs inevitable. They do not wait upon the explicit intention of the individual to construct a meaningful world for himself. If man is an organizing animal as far as his perceptions are concerned, as it was pointed out in Chap. III, then it is also true that man is a believing animal. The same forces that result in organized perceptions result in organizations *of* perceptions. Frequently, and almost necessarily as we shall see, these beliefs and attitudes fail to check with objective facts, but nevertheless the process of organization and reorganization goes on—to establish beliefs and to change them.

Although beliefs inevitably develop, the intention of the individual can and does facilitate this process. Many psychologists have pointed to the insistent nature of man's strivings after meaning. Thus, Bartlett (1932) points out, "It is fitting to speak of every human cognitive reaction—perceiving, imagining, thinking, and reasoning—as an effort after meaning." The tensions driving the individual toward better understanding can be conscious as well as unconscious. Thus, a man may actively search for meaning, for the further development of beliefs in areas of his psychological world that are only vaguely structured. He may also strive deliberately to change his beliefs in some particular area. But this active, conscious search for beliefs is a mark of sophistication found only among some individuals and under certain fairly well-defined circumstances. Ideally, the educational process is one in which the individual is actively motivated and set in pursuit of new and more adequate meanings and understandings. And there are particular phases in the educational process where such conscious strivings after beliefs are most likely to occur. In response to exposure to new ideas, new facts, new relationships, the college student often comes for the first time in his life to question many of his beliefs and to realize the emptiness of large areas of his psychological world. A man searching for an ideology or a life philosophy is also driven by an explicit need for understanding.

The need for meaning and personal crises.—In our society, at least, such cases of conscious search for understanding are relatively exceptional. More commonly, beliefs grow and change only to the minimal extent that is called for by the exigencies of the individual's immediate situation in life and through the operation of the "automatic" factors of organization and reorganization. All that is required is that his daily perceptions and daily actions have meaning and integration. However, when his usual stock of beliefs no longer can encompass his recurrent experiences, when his perceptions will not fit into "neat, meaningful, useful categories"—as Allport and Postman (1947) describe beliefs—then he will seek new beliefs. A man may be thrown out of a job and for the first time may feel the need to understand the workings of the economic system. Such crises may never occur for some individuals, and for them the story of the growth of beliefs is a relatively undramatic one in which most of their beliefs develop according to a fairly regular pattern set by the uniformities of their culture, without the spur of conscious search.[1]

Beliefs and Attitudes in the Service of Other Needs.—The individual's beliefs and attitudes may help him to achieve various goals. He develops these beliefs and attitudes in response to problem situations; and in so far as they are enduring cognitive organizations, they may remain with him and be useful in the solution of a number of different problems. Thus, for example, in acquiring beliefs and attitudes about scientific theories,

---

[1] For a further discussion and illustration of the relation of crises to the growth of beliefs and their function in the need for meaning, see Cantril's (1941) discussion of the "critical situation" which he defines as arising when "an individual is confronted by a chaotic external environment which he cannot interpret and which he wants to interpret."

the CIO, the Catholic Church, or the Negro, the adult can use these beliefs and attitudes in meeting his needs for group acceptance, in solving practical problems, or in achieving economic security. Several studies are now available that indicate this type of functional relationship among beliefs, attitudes, and needs.[1]

Illustrations from a study of beliefs and attitudes of internationalism. Queener's study (1947) of the development of beliefs and attitudes of internationalism is replete with case histories of individuals who demonstrate the functional value of their beliefs and attitudes concerning peace and internationalism. Queener collected his data through extended interviews with some fifty adult men. In his interviewing he attempted to get some psychological insight into the general life histories of his subjects, in addition to the specific histories of their beliefs and attitudes about internationalism. His results indicate the following generalizations:

1. *Beliefs about internationalism can be seen as cognitive reorganizations which develop in response to the need for group acceptance.* Queener presents the case history of one of his respondents, a fifty-four year old business executive, who seems to have been dominated throughout his career by a strong need for group acceptance. In summarizing the history of this man's beliefs and attitudes about internationalism, Queener points out,

If it is correct that a dominant value in interviewee 35's history is adaptation to the dominant group, and he himself is conscious of this as a skill ("I'm very adaptable"), a number of fluctuations would be expected as he moves from one group to another. This is actually the case, shifting from the isolationism of his home community to the internationalism of his college days back to the semi-isolationism among the Mormons, and now to the internationalism of "liberal, educated" men.

It is important to understand that these fluctuations do not necessarily signify pretended changes of opinions or beliefs or attitudes, but may be genuine cognitive reorganizations in attempting to satisfy a basic need.

2. *Beliefs about internationalism may be supported through all sorts of extrinsic rewards.* One of Queener's respondents, a strong believer in internationalism, is described as follows:

. . . after suffering an impressive list of professional frustrations [he] at last finds his dramatic skills and economic independence of use to an international peace organization, and has since been fully employed by it. In this work he meets many "interesting people," finds his antagonists mainly in lawyers "interested only in their professional (corrected to "political") careers, . . . and gets a "thrill" from leaving an organization where there previously was none.

[1] For a suggested formulation, in terms of theory and experimental implications, of the problem of attitudes as a problem of the psychology of learning, see Krech (1946).

3. *Beliefs and attitudes about internationalism may be rewarded by permitting the individual to exercise certain "personality motifs."* This type of functional value of a belief or attitude is of particular importance, since it indicates that the reduction of certain unconscious tensions can also be served by beliefs and attitudes. Thus, an "almost-pacifist" holds beliefs and attitudes that Queener describes as follows:

> The content of this attitude might be characterized . . . by its projection of aggressive motives into other persons (no confidence in peace-by-law), next a projection of the subject's own means of aggression control into them ("fear" utility), and finally an interpretation of the world scene in terms of one's own adjustment.

This same point is emphasized by Sanford (1946) in his psycho-analytic study of an "American quisling" when he points out, "In this one case, then, an important and not uncommon pattern of social attitudes is seen to rest upon the deepest factors of personality."

General Comments.—Beliefs and attitudes serve several important functions in the individual. They give continuity to his personality, they give meaning to his daily perceptions and activities, they serve in his attempted achievement of various goals. Any single belief or attitude may serve various goals, and different needs can give rise to the same enduring organizations. This consideration, together with the considerations discussed in Chap. II—in particular, that many of man's tensions do not have conscious correlates, that man frequently responds simultaneously to a host of conflicting needs and demands, and that behavior indices of motives are often misleading—indicate that the task of determining the functions of beliefs and attitudes is far from a simple one. The superficial connections that seem to exist between the person's needs and his beliefs and attitudes are frequently not the real functional ones. For the critically important job of determining the functional nature of beliefs and attitudes (since if we are to change these beliefs and attitudes, we must understand their functions) the study of beliefs and attitudes must therefore involve the integrated efforts of many psychologists with different approaches. The insights and techniques of the clinical psychologist, as well as those of the "learning" psychologist and social psychologist, are essential. Attitude tests and opinion polls by themselves fall far short of giving understanding of the beliefs and attitudes of men that lie behind their social behavior. However, the same note of caution must be sounded here that was emphasized in our discussion of motivation in Chap. II. In analyzing the functional nature of beliefs and attitudes we must not make the historical, or genetic, error. We must avoid ascribing a past function to a current belief or attitude.

JUDGMENTS

Before proceeding with a more detailed discussion of the characteristics of beliefs and attitudes, their relation to objective facts, their resistance to change, etc., it is essential to consider an important aspect of behavior which is closely related to beliefs and attitudes, *viz.*, judgment.

Beliefs and attitudes, we have seen, are enduring organizations. As such they enter into every momentary psychological event and provide a fixed basis for the structurization of the perceptions and cognitions immediately present. The particular way the immediate perceptions and cognitions are organized at any given moment often becomes revealed in judgments. A judgment can best be defined as a process of characterizing objects in terms of certain categories. Thus, a person judges that this line is short or that this man is sincere or that this governmental policy is a good one.

Judgments, Beliefs, and Attitudes.—As we have seen in Chap. III, our perceptions and therefore judgments are usually determined by more than the immediate stimuli being judged. The whole range of stimuli that affect us—the "frame of reference"—determines any given judgment. We have also pointed out in that connection (see pages 101*ff.*) that frames of reference can be equated to cognitive structures. Therefore, judgments are intimately related to beliefs and attitudes in the sense that these latter often play a major role in governing an individual's judgments. What an individual believes about a thing or his attitude with respect to a thing must inevitably influence the judgments he makes about it under various circumstances. If an individual believes that businessmen are reactionaries, he will be more likely to judge any given act of a businessman as reactionary.

There is one important research consideration that follows from the intimate relationship between judgments and beliefs and attitudes. We can frequently gain much insight into an individual's beliefs and attitudes by placing him in various situations requiring momentary judgments. Since these situations are easily contrived, they serve as short cuts to the study of the person's beliefs and attitudes. As we shall see when we concern ourselves with the problem of measuring beliefs and attitudes, most of the experimental work uses this method of observing the person's beliefs and attitudes.

The terms judgment and opinion are often used almost interchangeably. But such use is inconsistent with our definitions and with the characteristics of the two behaviors referred to by those terms. Judgment, as we have indicated, refers to the momentary product of perceptions, beliefs, and attitudes.   Opinions, as special kinds of beliefs, refer to such products as they may persist in a stable way for the individual over a period of time. A man's opinions will exhibit themselves in his momentary judgments; a series of judgments may eventually be consolidated into fixed opinion.

CHARACTERISTICS OF BELIEFS AND ATTITUDES

In order to make analytic use of beliefs and attitudes in the study of man's social behavior, we must know not only their functional values for the individual and the way they display themselves in the momentary behaviors we call judgments but also know many of their other characteristics.   Since beliefs and attitudes are enduring organizations in the psychological field, it is to be expected that the characteristics of beliefs and attitudes will be similar to those of perceptual organizations which have already been discussed in Chap. III.   However, there is some advantage in rephrasing those characteristics so as to make them directly applicable to these higher order structures.   In addition, we shall find that certain characteristics apply only to these higher order organizations.

The characteristics of beliefs and attitudes can be grouped into four categories: (1) referring to the nature of the objects involved, (2) referring to the nature of the cognitive structure involved, (3) referring to the strength and importance of the belief or attitude, and (4) referring to the characteristic of verifiability.

The Objects of Beliefs and Attitudes.—In this section we shall concern ourselves not only with the various objects that are involved in different beliefs but also with respect to the contents of different beliefs.   The object of a belief determines its *kind;* the contents of beliefs refer to the various cognitions that are organized together around a specific kind of object.

Beliefs and attitudes differ in kind.—The beliefs and attitudes of man are as varied in kind as the objects of his psychological world.   Thus, he has a vast range of beliefs relating to the physical world that surrounds him— beliefs about the nature of substances, the spatial and temporal relations among objects, the laws of the behavior of physical objects.   Under certain circumstances (as in the case of a scientist whose theories are under attack), he may even acquire attitudes about these objects and relations.   Man has perhaps even a more imposing array of beliefs and attitudes about the *social* world in which he lives.   He has beliefs and attitudes about the nature of other people and groups of people, about social organizations, and about political and economic events.   He has a variety of beliefs about art, philosophy, God, and the Hereafter.   And he has many beliefs and attitudes about himself as an object in the psychological field.

No one has ever undertaken the ambitious (and probably thankless) task of cataloging all of a single individual's beliefs. Merely to contemplate the extent of the prodigious task is sufficient to convince one of the impressive range in the variety of a man's beliefs and attitudes. But the number of any individual's beliefs and attitudes is finite. He can have beliefs and attitudes *only with respect to those objects which exist in his psychological world*. In so far as his psychological world is limited, the kinds of beliefs he has will be limited. Not every American, for example, has beliefs about atomic fission; not every American has attitudes about trade barriers or the gold standard. Yet this simple fact is frequently forgotten (as we shall see in the following chapter on the measurement of beliefs and attitudes) by many attitude testers or public opinion pollers. We cannot assume that simply because we have a reliable attitude- or belief-measuring device, we can therefore measure the beliefs and attitudes of all men with respect to any belief or attitude. The failure to recognize this fact has led to frequent misinterpretations of the results of these tests. People can respond, in some way, to any test, but that does not mean that they therefore have the belief or attitude in which the investigator is interested.

Beliefs and attitudes differ in content.—It is almost too obvious to merit mention that beliefs and attitudes differ in their *content*. The perceptions and cognitions involved in the layman's beliefs about water may differ from those involved in his beliefs about steel; his perceptions involved in his attitudes toward Russia may differ from those involved in his attitudes toward the British.

The generalization that different beliefs and attitudes have different contents is equally valid for the contents of the beliefs and attitudes of *many* people about the same object. Thus, for example, the religious Jew and the religious Catholic may both believe in God, but the nature of the Jew's cognitions about God—the characteristics he ascribes to God, the role he thinks God plays in man's world, the attributes of God, etc.—may be quite different in several respects from the nature of the Catholic's cognitions about God. The specific contents of these two sets of beliefs differ. What is true of the difference between the Jew and the Catholic may also be true, though not to the same degree, of the difference between one religious Catholic and another or one religious Jew and another. This suggests that when we attempt to measure the "same" belief or attitude of different people, we are, strictly speaking, analyzing different beliefs and attitudes. However we can, with some justification, treat these different beliefs as if they were the same. For in one very important respect they are the same. Although the specific contents of the beliefs about God, for example, may differ from person to person, we would find, in the instances given above, that the more general aspect of the beliefs would be identical. Thus all religious Jews and all religious Catholics would include in their beliefs the cognition of a supernatural deity who has supernatural power and influence over their lives. It is this general content which usually identifies the belief. Nevertheless, when we want a detailed analysis of the beliefs about God among a group of people, it is important to take into account the individual differences in specific contents. The implications of this for the analysis of the beliefs and attitudes of groups of people will be made clearer in later chapters when we deal with such matters as economic, racial, and political beliefs in the United States and their relationships to the actions of large masses of people.

The Structure of Beliefs and Attitudes.—In common with all cognitive structures, beliefs may differ in *precision* and in *specificity*. The first of these refers to two slightly different attributes of beliefs: (1) the clarity of the individual perceptions and cognitions involved in any one belief and, (2) the degree of differentation in the structure of the belief (see the discussion of structural differentiation, pages 136*ff.*). The second characteristic, specificity, refers to the intercommunications between one belief or attitude and other beliefs and attitudes (see the discussion of isolation of structures, pages 136*ff.*).

Beliefs and attitudes differ in precision.—Some of man's beliefs, like some of his perceptions, are clear, explicit, highly differentiated; others are vague and poorly structured. And the same is true for his attitudes. He may, for instance, have clear and precise notions about the way the stock market operates or what makes his automobile go or the role of religion in modern life; on the other hand, his notions about nuclear fission, democracy, economics, and women's coiffures may be vague, fuzzy, and confused. Every belief can be placed at some continuum of clarity between the one extreme point of utmost clarity, as exemplified by the belief that two plus two equals four, and the other extreme of utmost vagueness, as exemplified in a scarcely verbalized "feeling" that the theory of evolution has "something or other to do with monkeys or something like that."

Similarly, a man may have highly differentiated beliefs about science and poorly differentiated beliefs about God. Thus, he may distinguish between science and scientists, between laws of science and data of science, between the role of science in one sphere of man's life and the role of science in another sphere. On the other hand, his beliefs about God may be undifferentiated—he may not differentiate between the Church as an organized institution and religion as a "way of life," between the forms of worship and the spirit of worship, between one religion and another. Every belief, in other words, can be placed not only on a continuum of clarity but also on a continuum of degree of structurization. As we shall see in the next chapter, some studies are now available that have examined both these aspects of beliefs (see especially the study by French (1947) on page 185).

The precision of beliefs and attitudes is a particularly significant characteristic to know when predicting the effects of education and propaganda. A large number of experiments is now available that trace the relationship between the clarity of a perception and belief and its resistance to "suggestion." However, the precision or ambiguity of a belief or attitude should not be confused with its strength or importance for the individual. The two are related; but as we shall see, they refer to different characteristics of the structures.

Beliefs and attitudes differ in specificity.—Not only may beliefs and attitudes vary in their clarity and degree of detail and differentiation within the single belief structure, but they may differ in their specificity, *i.e.*, in the sense of being isolated, nongeneralized, or not connected with other beliefs and attitudes.

A man may have a strong conviction that depressions always follow wars, but this belief may not be connected in any close fashion with other economic beliefs that the man has. It stands virtually alone, as something perhaps clear and strong, but yet cut off cognitively from other beliefs—a sharply defined element floating around in a foggy area of the man's psychological world. In contrast, another of the same individual's beliefs may be highly generalized, fitted in a tight structure with a whole body of related beliefs and attitudes, and its influence reaching out in many directions in the psychological structure of his world. Thus he may believe that the Catholic Church is the only true church of God, and this belief may be buttressed by a large number of related beliefs and attitudes—about political systems, science, poetry, art, family relationships, etc. These areas of his psychological world will be organized and structured in a way thoroughly congruous with his belief about the Catholic Church. We have already discussed at some length the significance of this characteristic of specificity for creative thinking and problem solving (see pages 135 to 141), but we wish now to discuss its implication for the pattern of beliefs, for the integrated nature of man's personality.

Few beliefs and attitudes can be thought of as existing in a state of isolation from other beliefs. Most of them are parts of constellations, and these constellations may in turn be synthesized with other constellations. A man's attitude toward the Turks is likely to be intimately bound up with his beliefs about other nationalities, about foreigners in general, about immigration policies, about harems, about Mohammedanism and a welter of other things.

The degree to which the beliefs and attitudes of a person are embedded in an orderly pattern may be taken as the degree of unity of the individual's personality. A unified totality of beliefs and attitudes is an *ideology*, or *life philosophy*. Only rarely will an individual exhibit such a high degree of unity of beliefs and attitudes that we are justified in saying that he has a single ideology. More commonly, an individual's political, religious, artistic, and scientific ideologies are somewhat separable. But even this statement needs qualification. To assume that for every area of human thought which we can label with a distinct name there exists a corresponding pattern of beliefs is to commit the "stimulus error," *i.e.*, confusing the objective stimulus with the perception evoked by that stimulus (see the discussion on page 79, Chap. III). It is more likely that for a given person some of his religious and some political and some scientific beliefs, for example, will form one unified cluster. Thus, as Stagner (1936) has indicated, the ideology of the fascist is not solely a "political" ideology but involves an integration of beliefs and attitudes about nationalism, militarism, racial antagonism, and "middle-class consciousness."

With a great many people, perhaps the majority, the organization of beliefs is at a still lower level of synthesis, where it would be scarcely proper to speak of ideologies at all. The reasons for this lack of integration are many. It is true that almost all organizing processes work toward unification of various structures into consistent, simple systems. But the very complexity of the physical and social worlds in which we live makes this task of unification an almost impossible one. That an individual's beliefs and attitudes are confused, inconsistent, and unsynthesized is largely because the demands upon him are too great. He usually has neither the intelligence nor the information to make complete sense out of the welter of experienced data with which he is bombarded. When unity of high degree is achieved, it can usually be explained either by the fact that the person is of extraordinarily high ability and motivation in his search for meaning or by the fact that the world in which he lives is a relatively simple one. This latter circumstance can come about in two ways— either the person lives in a narrow, withdrawn, encapsulated existence and hence avoids the complexities of the world, or he lives in a society that is highly organized and stable and that by its "official ideology" makes relatively easy a synthesis of the beliefs of its individuals. The first of these possibilities is exemplified by the integrated beliefs of the ignorant (whose world of percepts is extremely limited) or by the blind fanatic (who perceives only a strictly selected sample of events). The second is exemplified by the individual who has lived his whole life in a rigidly controlled, integrated state where music, politics, history, economics, and science are all interpreted for him in terms of the official ideology.

Strength and Importance of Beliefs and Attitudes.—Although all beliefs and attitudes have functional utility for the individual, they do not have equal significance, nor are they all equally responsive to the changing needs and demands of the person. A discussion of the factors that make for difference in strength and importance will be reserved for a section of the next chapter. We wish here to specify only what is meant by these dimensions.

Strength of beliefs and attitudes.—One belief may be observed to endure unchanged for a long period of time and throughout a great variety of experiences by the individual and to be resistant to change in the face of other, contradictory beliefs or under the pressure of motivational forces. Another belief held by the same person may be observed to exist only relatively temporarily, to change readily in the face of contradictory evidence, to yield easily to motivational pressures. The former we call a *strong* belief, and the latter a *weak* belief. We have already seen in Chap. IV that the rigidity of a cognitive organization is related to the degree of emotional tension associated with it. This would immediately suggest that the rigidities or strengths of *attitudes* differ in a general way from the strengths of beliefs. Although it is true that attitudes may be relatively strong or relatively weak, nevertheless many attitudes will be stronger than many beliefs. This follows from the very definition of the differences between attitudes and beliefs—attitudes involving, *within their very structures*, needs, demands, tensions.

Importance of beliefs and attitudes.—Not all of man's beliefs, no matter how strong or weak, are of equal importance for his daily behavior. A man's belief that two plus two equals four may be precise and may be strong, yet it may be of little importance in accounting for most of his behavior in the world. On the other hand, a man's belief about democracy may not be very precise, but it may be of tremendous importance in accounting for much of his social and political behavior. Frequently, as we shall see in the chapter on measurement of beliefs, the saliency of beliefs is taken as an indication of the importance of beliefs. Although this is sometimes a valid measure, it is not always so. Saliency refers to the fact that not all of a man's beliefs stand out with equal prominence in his cognitive field. He may be more acutely aware of certain of his beliefs than others, they may enter his thoughts more readily, they may be more frequently verbalized—they are, in a word, salient. However, many of the most important and most functional of man's beliefs may be of low saliency. They may have receded from his immediate attention through a process of habituation, of being taken for granted, of existing unchallenged. They are so deeply rooted and have endured so long that they are in the nature of fundamental "givens" about his world. They are not things he normally speaks of, because there is no reason for him to speak of them. Nevertheless they may play a decisive role in almost all of his thinking and actions.

Attitudes, too, differ in importance and in saliency, and here again the correlation between the two is not perfect. Perhaps one way of regarding the saliency of attitudes is to think of different attitudes having different "thresholds." Since the objects of attitudes have demand-character about them only under certain conditions (see page 152), a highly salient attitude can be thought of as one where these conditions are relatively easily satisfied; an attitude with low saliency, where these conditions are relatively infrequently satisfied. Both attitudes may be strong and important for the individual. Thus, for example, a man may have a religious attitude of low saliency and a political attitude of high saliency. His religious attitude may express itself in his behavior only when some particularly effective event occurs—when the picture of hell or paradise is dramatically and effectively portrayed or when his church is maliciously and foully desecrated. Under these circumstances, if his religious attitude is an important one, he may take action that will be of key importance for the rest of his life. On the other hand, his political attitude, equally important, may be, as it were, "on the top of his mind" and may display itself in every possible political situation—being highly salient.

In general, beliefs and attitudes are likely to be more important when they are functionally related to the more central characteristics of the individual's personality structure, when they are well organized and generalized, and when they are based upon needs for identification with other people and groups. They are likely to be more salient when they are newly formed or when they are in process of change or when they are being subjected to challenge by other people or by apparent logical inconsistency with other newly developing beliefs and attitudes.

Verifiability of Beliefs and Attitudes.—All beliefs, whether they be in the nature of knowledge, opinion, or faith, may be described in terms of the foregoing dimensions of kind, content, precision, specificity, strength, and importance. The fact that knowledges, opinions, and faiths vary along the same dimensions is part justification for the use of the term *belief* in the generic sense with which we have defined the word. However, there is another important attribute of beliefs—verifiability—which must now be considered. The verifiability of beliefs (and of the belief aspect of attitudes) is an important characteristic to examine because (1) it helps define the problem of the relation between beliefs and objective facts and (2) it points to some significant differences among knowledges, opinions, and faiths. The first problem will be discussed in the next section of this chapter. The second problem, the differences among the various types of beliefs, is of direct concern here because it is this dimension of beliefs which, more than any other dimension, justifies our making any discrimination at all among the terms *knowledge, faith,* and *opinion.*

Belief, knowledge and verifiability.—The term *verifiability* refers to the individual's conception of his object of belief as being relatively accessible or inaccessible to proof and to its having been subjected to proof. Thus, beliefs about life after death concern matters that most people conceive of as being nonverifiable—it is not accessible to proof and therefore, obviously, has never been proved. Beliefs about the properties of water, on the other hand, concern matters that are verifiable—water is accessible to proof, and many proofs have been made about the properties of water. Those beliefs which the individual conceives of as being verifiable and verified he refers to as *knowledge.* He believes (*i.e.,* has knowledge) that an unsupported body will fall, because he has observed this phenomenon repeatedly in his own experience. Similarly, he knows there is a country called Canada because he may have read and been told a consistent body of details about it, because he may communicate with someone who lives there, because he may have seen pictures of it, and, most of all, because he may actually have traveled there. In the same sense, he may "know" that the British Labor government is communistic, because he has been told a number of supporting details by a lecturer who has spent one week-end in England, he has read certain newspaper accounts of its "communistic" practices, he has been shown printed documents "proving" it. In all these and other cases of belief as knowledge, the distinguishing feature is that the belief has been subjected to proof.

We must not, of course, confuse this kind of proof with scientific, objective proof. We are here discussing proof as it is acceptable to the *individual whose beliefs we are examining.* For him, what he knows is what he has proved to his own satisfaction. This he may have done through some sort of observations, through reasoning, through intuition, or through the acceptance of "expert" pronouncements. There is no necessary relation between such perceived "facts" and the true objective facts to which the beliefs pertain. Actually, as we shall see in the next section, there are many compelling factors that make for significant discrepancies between perceived and objective facts. The significant thing to remember, however, is that *beliefs, as "knowledge," are restricted to such matters as can be regarded by the individual as verifiable and verified.*

Belief, faith, and verifiability.—Those beliefs of the individual which he himself recognizes as intrinsically unverifiable are referred to as matters of *faith.* He believes (*i.e.*, has faith) that an omnipresent, all-knowing God exists, although he himself may never, in the very nature of his conceptions about God, "prove" the validity of his belief to his own satisfaction. In the same sense, he may believe that an ideal socialist society (a society that because of "practical" considerations he believes will never come into being) would make for universal happiness. But since he recognizes that this belief is not susceptible to real test, his belief is a faith. Of course, both of these beliefs, held by another man, might be matters of "knowledge." That is, in both cases the individual might feel that he has proved to his own satisfaction the validity of his concepts about God and the ideal socialist society.

Belief, as faith, also has the characteristic of being unequivocally accepted by the individual. The fact that he knows he cannot prove his belief does not make it any less strong; but as a matter of fact, its very unverifiability makes it unchallengeable and removes the possibility of proving him wrong.

Belief, opinion, and verifiability.—Somewhere intermediate on the scale of verifiability are those beliefs we call *opinions.* Opinions have neither the proved property of knowledge nor the intrinsically unverifiable property of faiths. From the point of view of the individual, calling his belief an opinion is a recognition on his part that the belief is still to be verified. It is also a recognition that other people may entertain other opinions about the same object and that the relative validity of the various beliefs (or opinions) is not yet fully determined. When, for the individual, the opinion is verified, then it becomes a matter of knowledge; when it is accepted completely without verification and he no longer recognizes that opposite opinions may be just as valid, then his former opinion becomes a matter of faith.

Frequently opinions exist in this unverified way because they refer to data that are difficult of accessibility. For one thing, beliefs about future events may be of the nature of opinions because the individual feels that it is impossible to know what will happen. For example, people may have different opinions about whether or not it will be possible to develop a defense against the atomic bomb or who the next President will be. For another thing, opinions exist in connection with controversial issues that usually involve the selection of one of a number of different alternatives, the rightness or wrongness of which must await future test or which may never, in the very nature of the problem, come to a test. Thus a man may entertain an opinion that the Republicans would have been more successful in handling the last depression than the Democrats or that the Democrats would be more successful in handling national problems than would the Republicans—in the next Administration. These opinions may be strong and persistent, but the very fact that the man himself refers to them as "opinions" indicates that they are not of the same essence as knowledge or faith. The central difference among these lies in the comparative amount of verifiability.

General comments.—Although all three of these are beliefs and as such will play a determining role in man's social behavior, nevertheless it is important to know whether any specific belief is a matter of knowledge, faith, or opinion. They will affect man's behavior differentially, and the proper methods of changing them will vary according to which type of belief is involved.

Beliefs, Attitudes, and "Facts."—In our discussion of the characteristics of beliefs and attitudes, thus far, we have concentrated entirely upon beliefs and attitudes as they exist *psychologically for the person holding them.* But for purposes of social analysis we must know more than this psychological side. We must also know how the beliefs of the individual relate to the "real" world in which he lives.

Correlation between beliefs and objective facts.—Everything we have discussed about perception in Chap. III has pointed to the fact that there is no one-to-one correspondence between the stimulus object and the perception evoked by that stimulus object. In consideration of this, the easiest and most valid generalization that can be made is that *there is not a one-to-one correlation between beliefs and objective facts.* At one period in history most people held a clear, strong belief that the world is flat. It was for them a "fact"—a matter of direct observation and knowledge. Today in America many people take it as a clear, unquestioned "fact" that Negroes are inferior to whites in innate intellectual capacity. We need hardly point out the discrepancy in these examples between what people "know" and the real facts of the matter.

It is of special significance that beliefs which show a discrepancy with the objective facts can nevertheless be just as strong and be associated with just as high a degree of certainty as those which more accurately correspond with the realities of the situation. A man who believes the Negroes are inferior in native intelligence may be as certain of this "fact" as he is certain that the sun will rise tomorrow. A man may believe that the number 13 is unlucky just as surely as he believes that number 13 falls between 12 and 14. Thus, for example, Carlson (1931) found a correlation of only .20 between the objective facts that 357 college students knew about presidential candidates (in the 1928 election) and their certainty of opinions concerning these facts. Actually, he found that those students who were best informed were below the average in certainty. Further analysis revealed that students who were one-party persons in their political behavior—never split a ticket—were much more certain of their beliefs than other students, although they were not superior in their knowledge of objective facts. We may express this second generalization by saying that *strength of belief does not necessarily depend upon the degree of correspondence with objective facts.*

Rationality of man's beliefs.—What do the above generalizations imply about the "rationality" of man's beliefs? Many of the popular notions about man as an "irrational" animal are based upon just such observations that there is an obvious and marked discrepancy between many beliefs and the objective facts to which the beliefs refer. But characterizing a belief as irrational is applying a *sociological* criterion to a *psychological* phenomenon, and this confusion of levels of analysis can lead to confusion in understanding. Often what appear to be irrational beliefs when viewed by the outside observer—the physicist, the economist, the political scientist, the sociologist—are seen to be quite rational from the point of view of the experiencing person himself.

From the psychological point of view, man is not quite the irrational being he is often made out to be by the cynic and the propagandist. That he is not is supported by the great extent to which man's beliefs resist change, by the extent to which his beliefs change meaningfully, and by the deep-rooted need for clarification which makes an active search for facts one of the outstanding features of man's mental life. In other words, this rationality of man's cognitive processes is seen in his distortion and selection of facts to make them appear reasonable (see discussion, Chaps. III, IV) just as well as in his more adjustive and objectively successful thinking. To illustrate this we might examine the significance of "logic-tight" compartments characteristic of some mental processes, rationalization, superstitions, delusions, prejudices, and stereotypes.

Logic-tight compartments.—The tendency toward making beliefs and attitudes logically coherent within themselves by the distortion or exclusion of contradictory elements points to a rationality that demands internal consistency. The mind of man is often stigmatized as consisting of logic-tight compartments. There is merit in this description, for unquestionably man is able to entertain many actually contradictory beliefs. As Murphy, Murphy, and Newcomb (1937) point out in summarizing the investigations of interrelationships among beliefs,

Evidence abounds . . . to suggest that the most freakish assortments of opinions and beliefs are commonly held by single individuals. The prevalence of irrational beliefs, even among those at college levels, has more than once been amply demonstrated. Belief in various tokens and omens, particularly those portending "bad luck," is admitted even by those who make high scores in tests of information in various fields of science. "Rational" and "irrational" ideas may evidently be the best of bedfellows.

But it should be noted that *within* each of these apparently inconsistent and "freakish assortment" of logic-tight compartment (*i.e.*, within each belief system) man demonstrates a need for consistency. That beliefs containing contradictory elements can exist side by side can be ascribed to the fact that for the individual, these various belief systems are not in communication, they are not organized together as subparts of a more comprehensive belief system which would tend to force the removal or alteration of the contradictory elements. When such integration, however, is achieved, a fundamental change in beliefs frequently occurs.

"Rationalization" as "Rationality".—The meaning of the phenomenon of "rationalization" has been much misunderstood. It has commonly been regarded as evidence for man's irrationality, whereas in truth it should rather be taken as evidence of just the opposite. If man showed no such strong tendencies toward rationalization—justification in terms of "reasons"—then we might be justified in calling him irrational. The existence of rationalization is one of the clearest demonstrations of the need for and striving after the only kind of logic that is available to the individual—the logic of his own psychological world. The real significance of the phenomenon of rationalization is in what it indicates concerning the dynamic character of the basic cognitive and perceptual processes— the mutually adaptive and integrative adjustment of the various mental organizations to one another, beliefs, attitudes, needs, emotions, and perceptions.

Superstitions, delusions, prejudices, and stereotypes.—The confusion that must follow from describing psychological processes (beliefs) in terms of objective analyses (facts) has resulted in the misunderstanding of the significance of many different so-called "types" of beliefs—superstitions, delusions, prejudices, and stereotypes. As we shall see, in some cases these terms are given objective definitions; in some cases, psychological; and in some cases a combination of the two. If the above terms are to have any scientific usefulness at all, we must be clear about their use.

1. *Superstitions.*—What we call "superstitious beliefs" are those which (*a*) have been demonstrated to be at variance with the objective facts, (*b*) are likely to be shared among many members of a society, and (*c*) frequently involve a disposition to ascribe phenomena that admit of a

natural explanation to such occult or supernatural causes as "fate," "luck," and the "devil." It should be noted that, as stated, the concept is essentially an objective and statistical one, stressing as it does the fact of incidence in a society of a set of erroneous beliefs and measuring them by such cultural phenomena as the commercialization of "charms," hotels with missing thirteenth floors, dream books for lottery games, etc.[1]

From a purely psychological point of view, such beliefs are not unique. Superstitious beliefs admit of the same description and the same explanation as all other types of beliefs—knowledge, faith, opinion. *That they are set off by a special name is largely the result of the viewing of them by an external observer.* As such, they may be useful for certain *sociological* analyses, but not for psychological analyses. A so-called primitive who treasures his own toenail clippings for fear they will fall into the possession of other people who will then be able to harm him may not regard this belief as of a different order from his belief (knowledge or faith or opinion, as the case may be) that if he eats of a certain poisonous fruit, he will die. And a farmer who plants his potato crop in the moonlight considers this precaution no more peculiar than rotation of crops. He may "know" both to be valid—he may have observed the poorness of his neighbor's crop and remembers that his neighbor planted it in the daytime.

2. *Delusions.*—Delusions are deeply rooted, often morbid beliefs and attitudes which depart widely from the objective facts. But here again, as with superstitions, these delusions are explicable in the same psychological terms as other forms of beliefs and attitudes. To the external observer it may sometimes seem incredible that a person can entertain a strong belief or attitude that serves to govern a great part of his behavior, a belief that he is a subject of a plot, that people are out to get him, that he is being constantly followed, that he is a victim of planned persecution, when as far as the external observer can judge, this belief is entirely unfounded on fact. Yet from the perspective of the deluded person himself, such a deep-seated belief is confirmed by his perceptions. He loses his job; his friends fail to invite him to a party; there are always people behind him when he walks along the street, but when he looks closely at them, they pretend to pay no attention to him; and when he sits in a restaurant, he observes people whispering about him. And sometimes these people are all "Communists" or "Jews" or "Catholics" conspiring together. All these perceptions are "facts" and obviously go to support his firm conviction that he is indeed the victim of a plot.

Such delusions are typically systems or patterns of beliefs, internally

[1] For a study of the prevalence of superstitions among students, see Lundeen and Caldwell (1930).

consistent and based upon a whole host of confirmatory "facts." To call these beliefs irrational is, from the point of view of the individual, contradictory, inasmuch as he is actively searching for evidence that will prove the validity of his beliefs and is seeking to make each fact congruent with every other fact he uncovers. The logical character of these beliefs is vividly demonstrated by the impossibility of the psychiatrist to out-argue the deluded individual—the patient can bring a new fact to support his belief as fast as an old one is demolished.

3. *Prejudices.*—Strictly speaking, prejudice means prejudgment; a man who has prejudices has beliefs that are established prior to the revelation of the pertinent objective facts and that by their strength tend to pre-determine the way in which new perceptions will emerge. But in the very nature of the case, *all* beliefs partake to some degree of prejudice. It could not be otherwise. As we have pointed out in Chap. III (page 86), "Man is an organizing animal. . . . We cannot say to ourselves: 'Hold off any interpretation until you collect all the facts.' As soon as we experience *any* facts, they will be perceived as organized into some sort of meaningful whole. This is a universal characteristic of the cognitive process." And once such an organization is made, each new perception will be predetermined in its characteristics.

But commonly in social psychology, the term *prejudice* is used more specifically to refer to attitudes and beliefs that serve to place the objects of the attitudes and beliefs at an advantage or disadvantage. In our discussion of racial prejudice in Chaps. XII and XIII, for example, the notion of prejudiced beliefs and attitudes stresses the consistent direction of the discrepancy between objective and perceived facts. When people are "prejudiced" against the Catholic or the Russian, it means only that the perceptions they have about the Catholic or the Russian will tend to deviate in an unfavorable direction from the objective facts. In any event, their prejudices, psychologically considered, must be understood like all beliefs to be matters of knowledge, faith, or opinion—and not something psychologically unique.

4. *Stereotypes.*—The concept of stereotype, which has been influential in the thinking of many social scientists, refers to two different things. (1) It may refer to a tendency for a given belief to be widespread in a society. This is a sociological and statistical concept and can be illustrated by the studies that count the number of people who believe, for example, that blondes are less intellectual than brunettes or that workers are more honest than capitalists. (2) The concept may refer to a tendency for a belief to be oversimplified in content and unresponsive to the objective facts. This is a psychological concept. But as we have seen, all organi-

zations show the leveling and sharpening effects (see page 127), and therefore all beliefs are to some extent stereotypes.

These two uses of the word "stereotype" are not wholly unrelated. The more simplified a belief tends to be, the more likely it is to find wide acceptance among members of a society without substantial variation in its content. (See the discussion of the factors making for change in rumors as they are passed down from individual to individual, page 130.) Nevertheless, for analytical purposes, the two uses must be carefully distinguished; otherwise we may unduly obscure the true psychological processes through which the stereotyped belief (so-called) is generated within each individual and how it operates for him. For example, the statistical fact may correctly be stated that the majority of the people in America believe the Jew to be "shrewd," but that fact alone tells us nothing about the *immediate functional significance* of this belief for any given individual who may hold it. And if we are interested in changing this individual's belief, the mere knowledge that many other Americans hold it does not tell us why he holds it or how he can be induced to let go of it.

Restatement of the problem.—It appears then that superstitions, delusions, prejudices, and stereotypes are stable, enduring cognitive organizations, internally consistent and logical in the sense that they are constructed of a set of perceived "facts." From the point of view of the psychologists they are matters of knowledge, faith, or opinion and must be understood and analyzed as such. But such explaining away of the differences between a knowledge and a delusion, on the basis of their essential psychological similarity, does not absolve the psychologist from further special concern with superstitions, delusions, prejudices, and stereotypes. *These beliefs present specially important social problems because they do differ so widely from the realities of the situation and thus may eventuate in behavior inimical to the rest of society.* The psychologist must and can say more than that they are merely "interesting variations" of beliefs and that, in essence, man is "rational." He can rephrase the problem of man's rationality as follows: *Why is it that in any given case the beliefs and the objective facts do not agree?* Formulating the problem in this way directs his attention to specific cases where the discrepancy is great between objective facts and beliefs but does not require him to treat these beliefs as "sociological" phenomena (he still remains within the concepts of his own science). Nor does it require him to assume that these beliefs are psychologically unique and therefore require a whole new set of psychological principles.

The answer to the question when formulated this way requires a knowledge about the development of beliefs and attitudes and the factors involved in the reorganization (or resistances to reorganization) of beliefs and attitudes. To this major problem we shall address ourselves in the next chapter.

SUMMARY

It is pointed out that it is neither convenient, nor possible, to analyze the individual's social behavior by reference only to the momentary effects of the motivational, emotional, preceptual, and learning processes discussed in Part I. Instead, it is suggested that it is more profitable to work with more enduring and complexly integrated psychological units—*beliefs* and *attitudes*. People direct their actions—praying, working, politics, love, or violence—in terms of their own beliefs and attitudes.

Beliefs and attitudes, though similar in that they are both enduring products of motivation, perceptual, and learning processes, have different implications for action, and it is therefore necessary to distinguish between them if we are to make sound scientific use of these concepts.

A belief is defined as *an enduring organization of perceptions and cognitions about some aspect of the individual's world.* It is the totality of the person's cognitions about an object. It is, as it were, an enduring organization of organizations. The term *belief* is to be used in the generic sense to include all varieties of enduring organizations as above defined, *i.e.*, knowledge, opinions, faith.

An attitude is defined as *an enduring organization of motivational, emotional, perceptual, and cognitive processes with respect to some aspect of the individual's world.* This definition is then clarified by comparing and contrasting attitudes with beliefs. All attitudes incorporate beliefs, but all beliefs are not part of attitudes; beliefs are motivationally relatively neutral but, when embedded in attitudes, are subject to special dynamic pressures. The object of an attitude, under specified conditions, is perceived with the attribute of a goal. All these characteristics of attitudes help give them their insistent, dynamic, stirred-up property.

The functional significance of beliefs and attitudes is then discussed, and it is pointed out that they give continuity to the individual's personality, meaning to his daily perceptions and activities and serve in his attempted solution of various goals. In the light of this, it is suggested that the proper study of beliefs and attitudes requires the insights and techniques of the clinical psychologist, as well as those of the learning and social psychologist.

Closely related to beliefs and attitudes are judgments—the process of assigning objects to categories. Judgments are seen to reflect the directive influence of beliefs and attitudes, and thus the study of an individual's momentary judgments provides a feasible technique for the study of beliefs and attitudes.

Finally, the common characteristics of beliefs and attitudes are examined in some detail, and the following are isolated, illustrated, and discussed: kind, content, precision, specificity, strength, importance, and verifiability. In terms of this last characteristic, the differences among knowledge, faith, and opinion are discussed. This discussion leads to an examination of the relationship among beliefs, attitudes, and objective facts. Two generalizations, deriving from the propositions listed in Part I, are drawn: (1) There is no one-to-one correlation between beliefs and objective facts, and (2) the strength of beliefs does not necessarily depend upon the degree of correspondence with objective facts. In considering the bases and implications of these generalizations it is suggested that man is not quite the irrational being he is often made out to be if we measure rationality in terms of the relationship between man's beliefs and his perceived facts. Superstitions, delusions, prejudices, and stereotypes are then examined from this point of view, and it is concluded that, psychologically, these can be seen as knowledges, faiths, or opinions and not as unique psychological processes requiring a special set of laws and principles. However, such beliefs present important social problems because they differ so widely from the realities of the situation and thus eventuate in behavior inimical to the rest of society. To understand and "cure" people of these beliefs and attitudes, we must seek to determine why there is such a discrepancy between the objective facts and certain beliefs. This requires a knowledge of the processes of belief development and change. These processes will be examined in the next chapter.

BIBLIOGRAPHY

ALLPORT, G. W., and POSTMAN, L.: 1947. *The psychology of rumor.* New York: Holt.
BARTLETT, F. C.: 1932. *Remembering.* London: Cambridge.
CANTRIL, H.: 1941. *Psychology of social movements.* New York: Wiley.
CARLSON, H. S.: 1931. Information and certainty in political opinions. *Univ. Ia. Stud. Charact.*, 4, No. 1.
KRECH, D.: 1946. Attitudes and learning: a methodological note. *Psychol. Rev.*, 53, 290–293.
LUNDEEN, G. E., and CALDWELL, O. W.: 1930. A study of unfounded belief among high-school seniors. *J. educ. Res.*, 22, 257–273.
MURPHY, G., MURPHY, L. B., and NEWCOMB, T. M.: 1937. *Experimental social psychology.* New York: Harper.
QUEENER, E. L.: 1947. The development of internationalist attitudes directed toward peace. Graduate School, Yale Univ. Ph. D. Dissertation.
SANFORD, R. N.: 1946. Identification with the enemy: a case study of an American quisling. *J. Person.*, 15, 53–58.
STAGNER, R.: 1936. Fascist attitudes: an exploratory study. *J. soc. Psychol.*, 7, 309–319.

CHAPTER VI

DEVELOPMENT AND CHANGE OF BELIEFS AND ATTITUDES

To know the characteristics of beliefs and attitudes and the role they play in personality is to know a great deal. It enables us to understand the actions of man in society. But that is not enough. If we are to *predict* behavior of people over extended periods of time, or if we are to *control* the actions of people, we must also know something about the development of beliefs and attitudes and the processes involved in changing beliefs and attitudes once they are developed. This is, of course, one of the major concerns of the applied social psychologist and the social action groups. Educators, leaders of causes, reformers, politicians, minority-group leaders, and businessmen are interested in more than knowing the general nature of attitudes or even what specific beliefs and attitudes people already hold. They are also very much interested in knowing how to develop beliefs and attitudes that people do not now have and how to change the beliefs and attitudes that they do hold. The National Association of Manufacturers wants to strengthen the traditional beliefs and attitudes against government control of industry; The Friends of the Soviet Union wants the Americans to adopt beliefs and attitudes that are favorable to Russia; The American Jewish Congress wants to change anti-Semitic beliefs and attitudes to tolerant beliefs and attitudes; educators want to abolish superstitions and replace them with more rational beliefs.

Here, as almost everywhere in psychology, the prediction and control of behavior is a concern of the social psychologist both as a "pure" scientist and as an "applied" scientist. For it is obvious that any program of action designed to change attitudes must be based upon an understanding of the fundamental processes involved in the change, and it is at this point that the pure scientist enters the problem.

In this chapter we shall examine the various forces that determine the development of beliefs and attitudes and control their change. Among such determinants we shall examine the cultural factors, the functional factors and their interrelationship to the cultural factors, the role of facts in determining the growth of beliefs, and the specific characteristics of beliefs and attitudes that tend to make them self-preservative and resistant to change. On the basis of this analysis we shall then outline some basic programmatic steps which can be used as guides for those who are interested in controlling and changing beliefs and attitudes.

CULTURAL DETERMINANTS

We have already seen that the formation of beliefs and attitudes is an inevitable consequence of the operation of all the factors making for perceptual and cognitive organization. These fundamental psychological processes, however, do not operate in a vacuum. The nature of the psychological field, as was pointed out in Chap. II, is dependent upon the nature of man's "real" environment—internal and external—in a systematic, even if not simple, manner. Sociologists, educators, and many others have laid a great deal of emphasis upon one aspect of this real environment in attempting to account for the development of specific beliefs and attitudes in the individual, *viz.*, the cultural influences. Thus, for example, correlational studies have been made (both by psychologists and by sociologists) of the correspondence between the presence of certain beliefs and attitudes and the schooling of the individual, the religion of the individual, his socioeconomic status, and the beliefs and attitudes of his parents, siblings, friends, teachers, etc.

As illustrative of such studies, the following might be cited. Carlson (1934) found that the religious background of the university students was an important determinant of the students' beliefs about a number of social questions. His results indicate that Jewish undergraduates held the most liberal beliefs about God, war, and birth control; Protestants were intermediate; and Catholics, the most conservative. Similarly, Harris, Remmers, and Ellison (1932) found a statistically reliable difference in the conservatism of students who reported no religious affiliation as compared with those who indicated some church preference—those with religious affiliation being more conservative. In Stagner's study (1936) of the difference in Fascist attitudes of students attending expensive colleges vs. those attending middle-class colleges, he found that the students from wealthier backgrounds tended to be more pro-fascist than did students from lower socioeconomic classes. Defining cultural influences in terms of interpersonal relationships, Newcomb and Svehla (1938) report positive correlations between children and parents in their beliefs about internationalism. Morgan and Remmers (1935), working with the same attitudes and beliefs, have shown a correlation between students and teachers; Winslow (1937), between friend and friend. The number of correlational studies of this kind is almost limitless, practically every cultural influence having been subjected to study.[1] Actually, almost every good survey of public opinions and attitudes

---

[1] For a good summary of many of these studies, see Murphy, Murphy, and Newcomb (1937).

includes such correlational analyses. Thus in a study conducted under the auspices of the Social Science Research Council (1947) on public reactions to the atomic bomb and world affairs, the following relationships between cultural determinants and opinions about armed imperialism were found.

TABLE I.—RELATIONSHIPS BETWEEN VARIOUS CULTURAL DETERMINANTS AND ATTITUDES TOWARD ARMED IMPERIALISM*

Answers to the following question: "Some people say we should use our Army and Navy to make other countries do what we think they should. How do you feel about that?"

	General approval, per cent	General disapproval, per cent	No response, per cent	Number of cases
Subjects with				
Grade-school education......	19	57	24	500
High-school education.......	13	77	10	455
College education..........	8	83	9	213
Subjects earning annually				
Under $2,000..............	19	58	23	440
$2,000 to 3,999.............	16	73	11	478
$4,000 and more...........	8	86	6	216
Religion:				
Protestant................	14	70	16	855
Catholic..................	18	68	14	245

* Adapted from SSRC, 1947, Table 1-35.

There can be little question that cultural determinants of belief are effective, but correlational studies, such as those reviewed above, are difficult to interpret for purposes of shedding any light on the basic processes involved in belief and attitude formation. Frequently these studies are misinterpreted. To evaluate the significance of these studies and to understand the role and limitations of cultural determinants require a closer analysis of the fundamental psychological processes involved.

Cultural and Psychological Factors.—That the particular culture in which a man finds himself will help shape the specific beliefs and attitudes he develops not only is supported by the above empirical studies but also follows from basic theoretical considerations. The specific tensions, needs, demands, emotional experiences, and perceptions of man are definitely conditioned, as we have pointed out, by the nature of his real world, by the stimulus patterns to which he is subjected. But no man's real world is such that he is immersed in a random sample of stimulus patterns. Man typically, and perhaps always, lives in a "contrived" world—a world of stimulus patterns which are designed so as to encourage the emergence of only certain kinds of needs, certain kinds of emotions, certain kinds of goals, and certain kinds of perceptions. (See, in this connection, the discussion of individual differences in goals and tension-reduction, page 64, Chap. II.) Most "real" worlds in which the individual finds himself and in response to which he must develop beliefs and attitudes are characteristic of a particular cultural pattern, are filled with people, objects, and events of a particular kind. It is to be expected, therefore, that cultural differences among societies will be reflected in differences in beliefs and attitudes among the individuals in those societies.

But exposure to a characteristic and defined range of stimulation does not, in itself, result in the growth of a uniform set of beliefs. (1) Because the very process of perception is selective (Proposition II, page 87), (2) because cognitive organizations develop primarily in terms of the individual's perceptions (Proposition II, page 117), and (3) because the development of any specific cognitive organization is intimately related to the needs of the individual (Proposition I, page 112), beliefs cannot be expected to reflect faithfully the nature of the stimulus pattern or the cultural pattern. Beliefs and attitudes, in other words, develop selectively. Only within those areas of greatest importance for the person's own needs are beliefs and attitudes of any form developed and extended. And the specific form taken by those beliefs and attitudes is also governed to a marked degree by the purposes such beliefs and attitudes will serve.

This selective nature of the formation of beliefs and attitudes acts as a limiting factor on the effectiveness of the cultural pattern. It limits the number, kind, and content of the beliefs and attitudes. At the same time, of course, the "contrived" or specified range of the pattern of stimulation to which man is characteristically exposed also acts as a limiting factor. It is because of these limitations that the effect of cultural influences upon the formation of beliefs and attitudes is not a simple and direct one; it is because of them that we cannot expect to find very high correlations between cultural influences and beliefs and attitudes of individuals; and it is, finally, because of them that the study of such correlations, taken by themselves, can give us but little scientific understanding of the development of beliefs and attitudes in people. The fundamental fact that in the last analysis, the cultural influences are effective only in so far as they are perceived by the individual, interpreted by him, and "used" by him makes inevitable that we can never hope to predict, with any great degree of accuracy, the formation of beliefs and attitudes as a function of such influences.

However, quite aside from all this, the very heterogeneous nature of culture and society itself is such as to make for wide individual differences in the formation of beliefs and attitudes. That is, even if the beliefs and attitudes of man automatically mirrored his objective stimulation, we would still find it difficult to predict his beliefs and attitudes in terms of his culture. We would still find tremendous individual differences within the same culture. The reasons for this lie in the heterogeneous nature of the pattern we call culture.

That individual differences in beliefs, attitudes, and action are found even among the relatively homogeneous cultures of the so-called "primitive" societies is indicated by the study of Hallowell (1937) who writes

Individuals are not completely moulded to a common pattern despite the forces at work which tend to produce this result . . . . Gross similarities must not be allowed to obscure the minutiae of genuine differences in thought and conduct . . . . Indeed, the very nature of culture allows for such variations. It is not a die which stamps out succeeding generations of individuals indistinguishable in all their habits and beliefs.

The heterogeneity of cultural influences.—Too frequently it is assumed that culture or cultural pattern is a unitary variable that can be correlated with other unitary variables. But the cultural influences to which people are subjected are heterogeneous and frequently contradictory. This is true whether we consider *one* individual or a group of individuals living in the same society. Take the case of the single individual. What do we mean when we refer to Arbuthnot's "educational influences"? Obviously we cannot mean by that phrase only the formal schools to which Arbuthnot has been sent. In our society and every society, there are a vast number of formal and informal educational agencies. These educational agencies include Arbuthnot's parents, his friends, his neighborhood gang, the books he reads, the movies he sees, the radio programs he listens to, the church he attends, and many other people, groupings of people, and products of people. It includes every functioning, stimulating person and object within Arbuthnot's ken. It would be extremely unlikely, even for the most sheltered of Arbuthnots, that every one of these educational agencies would evoke the same or even noncontradictory needs, emotions, percepts, and therefore beliefs and attitudes in Arbuthnot.

This heterogeneity of cultural influences is even more marked when we examine a group of people within the same society. What, for example, are the American cultural influences as they operate among individual Americans? What are the common influences that operate on the "poor white" of the South, the resident of Park Avenue in New York, the automobile worker in Detroit, the farmer in Kansas, the itinerant worker in Colorado? How do their schools, their companions, their reading matter, their entertainment, their churches differ? Obviously, while we can tease out a number of common educational influences—and very important ones, as we shall later see—there are tremendous differences.

An illustrative analysis—beliefs, attitudes, and the family.—Perhaps among the most significant of the cultural influences in our society is the family. As Murphy, Murphy, and Newcomb (1937) point out,

... attitudes of individual parents are part of, and shaped by, larger streams of cultural influences. While parents are the immediate sources of attitudes and patterns of social behavior, they are also mediators of values and emphasis in the culture as a whole, and much of their function as mediators may be quite unconscious .... Parents are thus the immediate educational device of society, although society through the school, the church, the playmates and other specific relationships maintains supervision of the parents' activity, both to prevent the parent from presenting an unorthodox code and to prevent the child from readily accepting heterodoxy should a parent propose it.

Murphy, Murphy, and Newcomb cite the study of Horowitz (1936) as illustrative of the process of parental mediation of attitudes. Horowitz investigated the formation of race attitudes among rural Tennessee children. Among the questions that Horowitz asked the children were "Who tells you what you should do?", "What kind of children does she (the mother) like you to play with?", "What kind of children does she tell you not to play with?". Following are some of the typical responses collected:

First-grade girl: Mamma tells me not to play with black children, keep away from them. Mamma tells me, she told me not to play with them . . .

Second-grade girl: Colored children. Mother dosen't want me to play with colored children. . . . I play with colored children sometimes and Mamma whips me.

Second-grade boy: Colored children, mother and daddy tell me. They tell me not to play with colored people or colored persons' things.

Third-grade girl: Mother told me not to play with them because sometimes they have diseases and germs and you get it from them.

In addition to this kind of individual analysis, there is a number of correlational studies which also indicate the operation of parental mediation of beliefs and attitudes. Thus Queener (1947) in summarizing the studies that examined the correlations among family members as far as beliefs and attitudes about internationalism and peace are concerned, writes,

Taken together, and allowing for a great variety of methods and an occasional contradiction, the studies indicate that a subject is more likely to be internationalist (including anti-warist) if his parents are internationalist . . . if one parent is foreign-born, if both parents are foreign-born . . . if the brothers and sisters are internationalist . . . if the older brothers and sisters have college education.[1]

There can be little doubt, then, that most social scientists look to the family as one of the most important of cultural influences. Yet a more detailed examination of the data reveals some serious limitations of this outstanding cultural influence upon the formation of beliefs and attitudes.

Limitations upon family effectiveness.—One of the limiting factors we have pointed to is the individual's selective responses to the various influences of his culture. A study by Hirschberg and Gilliland (1942) on parent-child relationships in beliefs and attitudes provides some illustrative data on this limiting factor. These investigators administered three "attitude scales"[2] to 200 Northwestern University students, and copies of these scales were sent to their parents. They found the following parent-child correlations: Attitude (or belief—no clear differentiation being made between beliefs and attitudes) toward God, +.29; toward the New Deal, +.59; about the depression, +.42. It will be noted that although all the correlations are positive and thus indicate some relationship between the beliefs of the parents and the beliefs of their children, none of these correlations is very high and, what is particularly significant for the present discussion, *the degree of correspondence varies widely* (from +.29 to +.59) *from one kind of belief to another.* As the investigators point out,

A relationship between the attitudes of parents and those of children does exist, but the degree of relationship depends upon (1) the home situation, (2) the subjects tested and (3) the attitude studied. The home is a source for the development of attitudes but in some cases the influence is stronger than in others. The child's attitude may or may not be largely influenced by the home depending upon the attitude and the home . . . . The high correlation on the New Deal scale may be explained by the fact that institutional influences affect the family as a whole and thus influence the attitude of each member.

In other words, to say that the family is important in shaping attitudes or beliefs is not equivalent to saying that the child will take over attitudes and beliefs ready-made from the parents. The influence is possible, but whether the child will develop or not develop the same belief as his parents hold depends upon the importance and meaning of that belief for the child himself.

The other limiting factor derives from the heterogeneity and multiple nature of the cultural influences to which the child is subjected. Here the study of Newcomb and Svehla (1938), to which we have referred several

[1] Sample studies that Queener gives for the above conclusions are Newcomb and Svehla (1938), Droba (1933), Kulp and Davidson (1933), and Eckert and Mills (1936).

[2] These were Thurstone's *Attitude toward God* scale; Stagner's *Opinions about Depression* scale; and Lomas's *Attitude toward the New Deal* scale.

times, merits more detailed consideration. In their investigation of intra-familial correlations with respect to beliefs and attitudes, they observed that the correlations for certain beliefs and attitudes were higher for those groups in which the parent-child correlation on beliefs and attitudes toward the church were high. In other words, the family is effective in shaping the beliefs and attitudes of the children *in proportion to the degree to which other cultural influences operate in the same direction.*

General Comments.—Cultural influences, because of the relationship between the real and psychological worlds and as is shown by empirical evidence, do have an effect on the individual's beliefs and attitudes. But these cultural agents do not operate by "giving" beliefs and attitudes to individuals. The influence of the family, the school, the neighborhood companions, or the church is more indirect and complex. Each agency does not operate in a piecemeal fashion, but in terms of the pattern of influences. These cultural influences create and limit the situations for the individual out of which arise his needs, emotions, and perceptions which are organized into beliefs and attitudes. The relationship between the influence of cultural agencies and the resulting beliefs and attitudes is so complex that in some instances the effect of the parent's influence can be seen to account for the rise of a belief or attitude that is in opposition to the parent's belief. Thus, the behavior of the parent may induce a need for revolt against parental authority. This need, in turn, may express itself through the adoption of a belief about God or militarism or alcohol that is directly (and even perhaps deliberately) opposed to that espoused by the parent. Once adopted for that reason, that belief or attitude may remain as a strong belief of the person in the service of other needs. In such cases, of course, the correlation between parents' beliefs and children's beliefs will be negative; in other cases, positive. Therefore the existence of a low correlation or even no correlation at all tells us very little about the influence of parents' beliefs on children.

Nevertheless, although the effect of cultural influences on the formation of beliefs and attitudes is indirect, complex, and limited by the needs and demands of the individual, the patterns of culture do influence such beliefs and attitudes, and a proper recognition of this influence is essential if we are to understand the conditions that must be fulfilled before we can change an individual's beliefs and attitudes. The significance of this will be shown later in this chapter, in the section devoted to the problem of change.

FUNCTIONAL DETERMINANTS

We have seen in the preceding chapter that beliefs and attitudes are characterized by their functional value for the individual. But the immediately preceding discussion has indicated the difficulty and theoretical impossibility of making any sharp division between *cultural* determinants and *functional* determinants. By functional determinants is meant such factors as the needs, demands, emotions of the individual. But these needs, demands, and emotions derive from the situation conditioned by cultural agencies. This is merely a restatement of Proposition III in the chapter on motivation (page 40) to the effect that needs and demands arise out of instabilities in the psychological field of the individual and that these instabilities, in turn, can arise out of changes in the external and internal real worlds of the person.

Beliefs, Attitudes, and Specific Personality Traits.—In addition to the various daily needs that an individual attempts to satisfy and in the course of which he may develop certain kinds of beliefs and attitudes (see, for example, the illustration taken from Queener's study cited on page 155), some attention has been paid by psychologists to the effects of such specific personality traits as introversion-extraversion and ascendancy submissiveness on the development of beliefs and attitudes. As illustrative of a large number of studies in this field, we can refer to those of Dexter (1939) and Vetter (1930).

Dexter, in examining the introversion-extraversion characteristics of a group of "radical" students (women), found them to be more introverted than the total group of students, more self-sufficient, and more dominant and to show more feelings of inferiority. She suggests that because of these personality traits, these women can more readily adopt beliefs and attitudes that depart from the accepted group norms and therefore tend to develop radical beliefs and attitudes.

On the other hand, Vetter found that his radical students were more submissive (using the Allport ascendancy-submission test) than all the other students he examined and at the same time more introverted than the reactionary students. In keeping with Dexter's later findings, Vetter also found his women radicals more ascendant.

The significance of such studies has frequently been misinterpreted (and sometimes maliciously so). Even if we do accept the possibility that such traits as ascendancy, introversion, etc., are valid ways of characterizing a person, the data do not mean that an introverted individual will necessarily end up with radical political beliefs and attitudes or that the extroverted individual will end up as a reactionary. Just as we saw that cultural agencies do not "give" specific beliefs and attitudes to people, so personality traits do not determine the specific nature of their beliefs and attitudes. Here again, the relationship is indirect and complex. It is nonsense, in theory and in fact, to attempt to label all political radicals as neurotic introverts or all political reactionaries as neurotic extraverts.

However, just as we have seen that the parent's beliefs may result in the adoption of the same or opposite belief in the child and just as we have pointed out that in either case to understand the development of the belief we must take into account the parent's belief, so must we take into account the possibility of such personality traits in accounting for the development of beliefs and attitudes. One individual, in response to the effects of the trait of introversion, may develop radical beliefs and attitudes; another individual, in response to the same trait but under different cultural influences, may develop reactionary beliefs and attitudes. Actually, Vetter found, in the study cited above, that when he combined radicals and reactionaries, the combined group of subjects was more submissive and more introverted than the middle-of-the-road subjects. Here again, simple correlational studies cannot tell us much. What we need are careful clinical case studies of the development of beliefs and attitudes in relation to these personality traits.

Such studies, fortunately, are now being made in connection with the over-all personality structure of the individual. We have already referred to two such studies—that of Queener (see page 155) and that of Sanford (page 156). We wish now to turn our attention to other such intensive studies.

Beliefs, Attitudes, and General Personality Pattern.—Perhaps the pioneering study of the clinical approach to the development of beliefs and attitudes is that of Murray and Morgan (1945) in which the personality structures of 11 college men were studied intensively in an attempt to tease out the relationships among personality structure, cultural influences, and sentiments[1] about God, war, the family, and sex.

In line with the attempt to examine specific beliefs and attitudes as related to general personality are the studies of Rabin (1945) who examined a number of extreme pacificists (conscientious objectors during the war) by means of the Rorschach test and that of French (1947) who studied religious sentiments. Although such studies as these (especially that of Murray and Morgan and that of French) spell out the significance of general personality structures for the development of beliefs and attitudes and contribute greatly to our understanding of the intimate dynamic relationships between general personality structures and beliefs and attitudes, it must be emphasized again that to seek for invariant and simple correlations between even the most general personality structures and specific beliefs and attitudes is to pursue a will-o'-the-wisp. In so far as these studies take more factors into account than studies that concern themselves with a specific personality trait, there is greater probability of obtaining useful correlations. But it would be

---

[1] Murray and Morgan use McDougall's term *sentiments* to refer to much the same concept that we have defined as *attitude*.

unjustified "name calling" to attempt to label all anti-Semitic or anti-Negro people, as some clinicians are wont to do, as being this or that kind of personality.

French's study, referred to above, is a very nice illustration of just this point. In addition to a careful attempt to characterize the differentiation, clarity, intensity, and integration of the religious beliefs and attitudes held by her subjects, French also attempted an exhaustive analysis of her subjects' general personality structures by the use of over twenty tests and devices, among them being the Thematic Apperception Test, Study of Values scale, intensive interviews, written autobiographies, and other clinical procedures, as well as the Scholastic Aptitude Test and various "intelligence" measurements. She found that the most meaningful analysis of her data could be made in terms of the general organization of the religious beliefs rather than in pro or con terms. The personality structures of her subjects who had highly organized[1] religious beliefs were noticeably different from the subjects who had less highly organized beliefs, *whether they were religious, agnostics, or atheists.* That is, the atheist and the very religious individual might have the very same personality structure. Thus, she summarizes her data as follows:

. . . the "highs" may be described as persons of firm ego structures, persons who consciously recognize and accept both strengths and weaknesses as parts of their selves. The "less highs," on the other hand, are characterized by weak ego structures and strong superego structures; they are persons who accept only what is "good" as part of their selves and who suppress or repress what is "bad."

French's study illustrates yet another point made in the present discussion. We have stressed the dynamic relationships that must exist among needs and beliefs. Each influences each other. In recognition of this relationship, French undertakes to examine the influence of the degree of organization of religious beliefs upon personality:

Less highly organized philosophico-religious sentiments function as a part of the strong superego-structures of the subjects who possess them, governing basic needs. The cleavage between the "good" and the "bad," between what is consciously acceptable and what must be kept out of consciousness, in these sentiments sets the pattern for other sentiments, for example, the sentiments for the parents . . . . Highly organized philosophico-religious sentiments, on the other hand, are an integral part of the ego-structures of the subjects who possess them. The conscious ambivalence and ambitendency which character-

[1] A "highly organized" sentiment was one that had greater differentiation, greater integration among the substructures of the belief, less unconscious components, less intensity, etc., than did the "less highly organized" sentiments. Compare these criteria with those listed in the previous chapter.

ize them characterize other sentiments as well . . . . Thus, highly organized philosophico-religious sentiments are ego-standards, orienting the individuals who possess them in a positive way, whereas less highly organized philosophico-religious sentiments have a defensive function, serving as ego-shields.

"FACTS" AND THE DEVELOPMENT OF BELIEFS AND ATTITUDES

The cultural factors can be seen as providing the "facts" that are involved in the development of beliefs and attitudes, and the functional factors can be seen as partly responsible for the manner in which those facts will be used. And as we have already seen, the relation between facts and beliefs is not a simple one. It is therefore important to examine in some detail the discrepancies between facts and the beliefs and attitudes of the individual. This problem has an additional importance. As was pointed out at the end of the previous chapter, certain beliefs and attitudes develop among men (such as superstitions, delusions, prejudices, and stereotypes) which are characterized by their *wide* divergence from the real facts. Because these beliefs frequently result in troublesome social action, an analysis of the reasons for the discrepancy between real facts and beliefs assumes a high priority.

Sources of Facts in the Development of Beliefs and Attitudes.— Where does the individual get his facts for incorporation into the structures we have called beliefs and attitudes, and how adequate are these sources? A brief examination of this question will immediately show why we can expect a certain amount of discrepancy between the real facts and the beliefs and attitudes upon which they are presumably founded.

The relative lack of available objective facts.—The first factor responsible for discrepancies between the objective facts and a belief is the almost inevitable lack of objective facts that are available to any individual about the given aspect of his world. A great many of the beliefs held by people are in error simply because the people are not sufficiently well informed. The facts that they do possess are sadly inadequate to represent the totality of the facts of the case. Even if the few facts that a person does possess are substantially correct, a lack of knowledge of related facts can distort the significance of the correct facts. Beliefs are compounded of many facts; and as we have so frequently pointed out, the meaning of a single fact is never independent of the other facts with which it is associated. As long, then, as the repertory of facts possessed by the ignorant or ill-informed person fails to include certain of the essential facts about the situation, his correct facts will be distorted and the corresponding belief will be wrong. In this sense it might be paraphrased that "a few facts are a dangerous thing." Thus, for example, to know that a certain study has indicated that

Southern Negroes score lower on intelligence tests than do whites is to know a correct objective fact. If, however, one did not know at the same time some of the other essential facts about the study—that the Negro subjects had had very little schooling whereas the white subjects had had measurably more schooling or that the Negro subjects were not motivated to do well on the test whereas the white subjects were well-motivated—this could (and very frequently does) lead to a completely erroneous interpretation of the one correct fact available to the person, and on the basis of this fact he may eventually construct a wrong belief. He may become prejudiced.

Authorities as a source of facts.—It is inevitable that in the complex world in which we live no single individual can hope to ascertain, at first hand, all the objective facts pertaining to any given object. He must necessarily depend, in considerable degree, upon what the "experts" tell him. For the child, the experts are mainly his parents; for the student, they are his teachers and his books; for the very religious person, they are his priests, ministers, or rabbis; for the scientist, they are other specialists in the field. For all individuals, then, facts are frequently mediated by other people as authorities, and the amount of discrepancy between the real facts and the individual's perception of those facts will be dependent upon the validity of the authority's assertions. The authority may be honestly mistaken about his facts; or as a propagandist, he may deliberately falsify the facts for his own ends.

All this does not imply, however, that facts offered by the authority will be taken over by the individual wholly, blindly, and undigested. Not only will the individual's needs be of greatest importance in governing his manner of acceptance and incorporation of the facts offered by the authority (as we have already seen in various discussions), but other factors will also play a determining role. Among these are the factors that determine who will and who will not be accepted as an authority or reliable source of information by the individual. The prime significance of this factor will be manifest in the analysis of suggestion and propaganda in Chap. IX, but we might illustrate the general point under discussion here by some data from the *Atomic Bomb and World Affairs* study (SSRC, 1947) referred to previously. In this study an attempt was made to discover something about people's sources of information about the atomic bomb. Among the findings were the following: (1) "The number of sources of information a person has is closely related to his education and income"; (2) "people with better than average education and income tend to consider magazines their most trustworthy source"; (3) "the poorly informed tend to trust the radio more than the newspapers; the well-informed trust them equally"; and (4) "radio is trusted because it gets the news quickly, magazines because of their detail."

Although the above generalizations are essentially sociological statements and tell us more about the cultural determinants of authority selection than about the psychological determinants, nevertheless they indicate the complexity of the factors that are responsible for such selection.

The critical point to remember is that we do live in a complex world, that we must depend upon authorities for many of our facts, and therefore it is highly probable that discrepancies between the facts and our beliefs will frequently occur.

The creation or invention of facts.—The lack of relevant facts and the frequent conflicting facts provided for us by different authorities frequently operate so as to force the creation or invention of facts that may bear no real relation to the external situation. Those pressures which work toward the formation of beliefs work in the absence of adequate data and may force the emergence of facts that support and are congruent with the beliefs.

But even in the absence of such pressures, we have already seen that all cognitive organizations undergo change over time (Proposition III, page 125) and so do beliefs. And as they change, facts are created through the process of creative forgetting. It is to be regretted that virtually no research which might be comparable to Bartlett's research on the modification of memory traces over time has been done in connection with such changes in beliefs. We know very little about the precise changes in content that occur in specific beliefs under various conditions. All that can be asserted with reasonable confidence is that such changes do take place. Knowledge of the general motivational and perceptual principles discussed in Chap. IV can make it possible to give rough predictions of the nature and direction of the changes that will occur in the facts involved in various beliefs.

Appearance and Reality.—Our great dependence upon the evidence of the senses is obvious. It is a truism that people are most likely to believe the things they can see and hear and touch. In most instances this dependency upon the senses is fully justified. Those Scholastics whose zoological beliefs were rooted in Aristotelian tradition might readily have arrived at beliefs in better accordance with the objective facts had they simply gone out and looked at animals. The physical nature of the object *is* related to our perception of it despite the influence of beliefs on the perception of objects. The prime method of experimental science *is* observation via our senses. Some of us who have wrong beliefs about the Chinese, the Negroes, the Jews, the British can change our beliefs (if they are not too firmly grounded and rigid) merely by going out and observing these people. The significance of this will become apparent when we examine the role of "contact" in belief and attitude change.

Although all the above is true, nevertheless appearances *are* often illusory. People frequently accept the direct perception of things as indicative of the real nature of things. We are not referring here to the distorting influence of need factors on perception but merely to the frequent lack of correspond-tnce between the looks of things and the nature of things. Thus, for example, most people would perceive a piece of steel as "solid." Yet, the more sophisticated scientist knows that he cannot trust his senses in this case—that actually the steel is not a solid piece of matter but is made up of many atoms widely separated in space. If he were to build his theory on the basis of his simple, unaided perceptions, he would end up with wrong beliefs about matter. Köhler (1937) stresses this naive realism of many primitive peoples, in basing their beliefs upon the appearance of things, as explanatory of the beliefs that some anthropologists (see, for example, Levy-Bruhl, 1923) often regard as characteristic of the "prelogical mentality" of the savage mind. Thus, the savage who dreamed that he had committed a murder was certain that he did, in fact, commit the murder.

To the extent, therefore, that the substance and the superficial appearance of things do differ, the facts about the object and the corresponding beliefs will be discrepant—unless, of course, the person takes into account the possible deceptiveness of appearances. The man who appears to be kind and considerate may be cruel; the politician who is seen and heard behaving nobly may be behaving meanly. That is why the scientist tends to be cautious about mere appearances. He tries to dig deeper than the surface, he uses all sorts of independent checks upon his senses, and wherever possible he uses instruments that go beyond his senses in that they give him perceptions which his unaided eye or ear or taste buds cannot give him. It is of interest to point out, however, that this tendency of the scientist or of the "sophisticated" to avoid dependence upon mere appearances may tend to produce a kind of exaggerated skepticism about facts of all kinds. There were many people during the war, for example, who dismissed as "propaganda" the photographs of atrocities in concentration camps. Having been fooled too many times by mere appearances and having learned the value and necessity of being skeptical about appearances, people may refuse to accept even those facts which are truly represented by appearance.

General Comments.—The discrepancy between facts and beliefs, then, is due to a number of factors, both functional and cultural. The individual who has strong needs that must be satisfied by the development of appropriate beliefs and attitudes, will get his facts where he can. Living in a complex world, he is at the mercy, for much of the raw material of his beliefs, of various authorities. These authorities are frequently unreliable, through ignorance or through maliciousness. In addition, the individual himself is frequently unschooled in discerning substance from appearance; and where he does pick up his facts by himself, he again runs the risk of being fooled. Finally, where he can find no facts (either in authorities or first hand), he must, as long as there is any functional necessity for the development of a belief, invent facts himself. All of this suggests that the incidence of superstitions, delusions, stereotypes, and prejudice will be related to the reliability of the authorities we must depend upon (teachers, newspapers, books, broadcasts), the training in scientific method we have had, the range of experiences to which we have been subjected, and the degree to which our major needs and demands can be adequately satisfied.

SELF-PRESERVATION OF BELIEFS AND ATTITUDES

We know that beliefs and attitudes show constant change in many of their characteristics. Yet we also know that once beliefs and attitudes are developed in response to the many cultural and functional factors we have already considered and on the basis of the facts as available to the individual, these beliefs and attitudes frequently show *resistance* to change. This is especially true for the "sign" of an attitude or the direction of a prejudiced belief.

In our examination of the nature of cognitive reorganization we have discussed the basic processes that lie behind such resistances, but the self-preservation tendencies of beliefs and attitudes are so important that it is of some value to rephrase the operation of these forces as they apply specifically to beliefs and attitudes.

We can group some of the more common factors responsible for this tendency of beliefs and attitudes into four categories: (1) the selective nature of perception, (2) the operation of the "constancy principle," (3) the withdrawal behavior frequently induced by certain beliefs and attitudes, and (4) the social support which many beliefs and attitudes receive.

Tenacity of Beliefs and Attitudes and Selectivity in Perception and Memory.—Because perception is functionally selective, and because beliefs and attitudes play a role in determining the nature of this selectivity, new data physically available to an individual but contradictory to his beliefs and attitudes *may not even be perceived*. Since cognitive reorganization is frequently dependent upon the perception of new data, any process that results in dropping an "iron curtain" on new data will inhibit reorganization. In this sense we can say that attitudes and beliefs contain within themselves a mechanism that operates toward self-preservation.

But frequently people are forced to perceive data that are contradictory to their beliefs and attitudes.   Children are forced to hear tolerance lectures or see "educational" movies, and some facts may be too obvious to escape at least momentary notice even by the most prejudiced.   The iron curtain, as it were, is lifted through cultural influences.   But if the belief or attitude involved is a strong one, the effect of such perceptions may be fleeting, for we know that not only is perception self-selective but forgetting, too, is selective.   Very soon after exposure, people may have "forgotten" the contradictory facts.   A number of experiments can be cited which indicate that people remember better those items which are in accordance with their beliefs and attitudes, than those items which contradict them.   An instance of such experiments is the one performed by Levine and Murphy (1943) in which students who had both favorable and unfavorable beliefs and attitudes about communism were presented with passages of reading matter some of which were favorable and some of which were unfavorable to the Soviet Union.   The students were later tested for retention of the content of these passages.   The experimenters found that those students who were favorable to communism remembered the pro-Soviet Union material much better than those who held beliefs and attitudes unfavorable to communism, and vice versa.   In memory, as in initial perception, then, beliefs and attitudes have self-protective devices.

Tenacity of Beliefs and Attitudes and Cognitive Constancy.—It will be remembered that in discussing Proposition III of perception, it was found helpful to reformulate the proposition in the following terms: "Other things being equal, a change introduced into the psychological field will be absorbed in such a way as to produce the smallest effect on a strong structure." In the discussion there, examples of how this tends to make beliefs and attitudes self-preservative were given (page 100).

Beliefs are enduring cognitive structures, and attitudes, including as they do motivational and emotional factors, involve perhaps the strongest of our cognitive organizations.   It is to be expected, therefore, that beliefs and attitudes not only will *select* our perceptions but will also tend to determine the meanings with which we will experience the perceptions.   The new items, in one way or another, will be assimilated, and the basic beliefs and attitudes will not have changed.

Tenacity of Beliefs and Attitudes and Withdrawal.—Attitudes and beliefs operate in still another way to protect themselves against change. They help create an idiosyncratic world for the individual where contradictory items are not even physically present.   This is done through the behavior pattern of *withdrawal*.   The individual with a given belief or attitude frequently withdraws himself, sometimes physically, from exposure to contradictory data.   If he is successful in so doing, he cannot, of course, perceive the contradictory data, and his beliefs and attitudes remain safe and inviolate. (For the basic considerations involved here, see Chap. II, pages 56, 59.)

For example, the individual who is anti-Catholic will not attend Catholic gatherings or read pro-Catholic literature. The anti-New Dealer will not tune in his radio to a pro-New Deal broadcast. Beliefs and attitudes, in other words, in influencing the actions of people can result in limiting their experiences and thereby decrease the probability of new experiences resulting in changes in beliefs and attitudes.

Tenacity of Beliefs and Attitudes and Social Support.—We have seen in a previous section in this chapter that the developments of beliefs and attitudes reflect the cultural pattern in which the individual has been immersed. By and large, the members of any one cultural class or subclass will have beliefs and attitudes that are similar in kind and content. We should expect, for example, that the attitudes of the Russian people with respect to Germans would be relatively homogeneous and would differ in some generally consistent way from, say, the attitudes of the Argentinians with respect to Germans. Likewise, the attitudes of the Park Avenue residents with respect to labor unions would differ, on the whole, from the corresponding attitudes of the residents of a mining town.

The correlation between the patterns of culture and patterns of beliefs and attitudes operates so as to give social support to any one individual's beliefs and attitudes. His attitudes frequently operate to meet his needs of social acceptance and approval (see the case study taken from Queener's study, page 155). This situation operates in such a way as to inhibit any tendency toward change in belief or attitude. Thus the suburbanite finds that his anti-New Deal attitudes help establish him as a member of the bridge club on the commuter's train. The same is true of the anti-Trotsky attitude of the Communist party member. To change a socially approved attitude in the face of a need for group acceptance is extremely difficult and can be done, in some instances, only by changing the goal of the need itself, *i.e.*, the particular group with which the individual will seek to identify.

General Comments.—A study that illustrates several of the above self-preservative forces inherent in beliefs and attitudes is that of Cooper and Jahoda (1947). The study, based on several experiments and investigations performed by the Department of Scientific Research of the American Jewish Committee and by the Bureau of Applied Social Research of Columbia University, undertakes to answer the question of what happens to a prejudiced person when, in an experimental situation, he is involuntarily confronted with antiprejudice propaganda.

Several "Mr. Biggott" experiments were performed. In these studies, the person who has prejudiced beliefs and attitudes is presented with a series of cartoons lampooning a character named "Mr. Biggott" who holds the same beliefs and attitudes that the subject has. The subject is then interviewed, and his reactions to the cartoons are examined. The writers point out,

What the producers of the cartoon intended was roughly this: The prejudiced reader would perceive that Mr. Biggott's ideas . . . were similar to his own; that Mr. Biggott was an absurd character . . . . He would then, as the final stage in this process, presumably reject his own prejudice, in order to avoid identification with Mr. Biggott.

The study showed a very different result. Prejudiced respondents . . . went to such lengths to extricate themselves from identification with Mr. Biggott[1] that in the end they *misunderstood the point of the cartoon.*

Cooper and Jahoda then give several illustrations of this process of "derailment of understanding." In one series of experiments a cartoon was shown to the subjects in which Mr. Biggott is shown lying in a hospital bed and saying to a doctor that he wants only "sixth-generation American blood" for his blood transfusion. The follow-up interviews demonstrated how selective attention and reinterpretation of data can operate so as to preserve major attitudes. Some subjects selected for their attention Mr. Biggott's social inferiority, proclaiming that one who was *only a sixth-generation American* was a *parvenu* and had no right to pretensions! This led to a loss of focus on the real problems of the cartoon, and the attention of the subject became deflected from the problem of racial prejudice and turned to the problem of snobbishness. Other subjects perceived Mr. Biggott as a foreigner or as a Jew and thus avoided identification.

In another cartoon, a congressman is seen interviewing an applicant for a job. The applicant has brought a letter of recommendation saying that he has been in jail, has started race riots, has smashed windows. The congressman seems pleased and says, "Of course I can use you in my new party." The respondents showed various and ingenious reinterpretations of the cartoon so that in the end their own beliefs and attitudes remained unaffected. Following are some of the responses of the subjects to this and similar cartoons:

It might be anything crooked . . . might be a new labor party. That shady character makes me think so.

It's about a strike . . . about trouble like strikes . . . . He is starting a Communist party.

It's a Jewish party that would help Jews get more power.

[1] See the discussion in Chap. II, p. 69, on defense of the "self."

As the authors sum up this series of experiments:

The only cue these respondents took from the cartoon was the fact that it tried to show up a bad politician. The rest they supplied themselves by identifying the Congressman with whatever appeared to them to be "bad politics." Thus they imposed their own ideology on the cartoon and arrived at an interpretation satisfactory to them.

Self-preservation and self-reinforcement.—Not only do the various processes we have discussed and illustrated tend to make beliefs and attitudes self-preservative, but they make beliefs and attitudes self-reinforcing. Attitudes and beliefs create, as it were, the fuel upon which they grow. A pro-British attitude, by determining that the individual will perceive only the strengths and virtues of the British people, provides ever-fresh data that all Englishmen are models of the good and virtuous. An anti-Russian attitude that results in the withdrawal of the individual from all contact with things Russian can lead to distorted and irreal thinking about the Russians. As this autistic thinking goes on, unchecked by reality, the Russians become worse and worse and the anti-Russian attitude becomes more and more intense. Vicious circles are created. Beliefs and attitudes not only twist and warp data and thus maintain themselves but create new data for self-incorporation and thus grow in intensity.

HOW TO CHANGE BELIEFS AND ATTITUDES

Despite the significant influences of cultural factors on the development of beliefs and attitudes, despite the deep-rooted functional nature of many beliefs and attitudes, and despite the inherent tendency of beliefs and attitudes to preserve themselves, beliefs and attitudes *can* be changed. The experimental literature in social psychology presents a number of successful instances of such change. In the area of race relations alone, Rose (1947), in a review of the studies in reduction of prejudice, lists 26 different investigations that sought to determine the effectiveness of school courses, specific propaganda, and personal contact in changing attitudes toward minority groups. A number of these indicated some degree of success. Among the more successful ones he cites the study by Mapheus Smith (1939), Remmers (1936, 1938), and F. Tredwell Smith (1943).

Mapheus Smith tested the effect of the course Immigration and Race Problems, given at the University of Kansas, on attitudes toward the Negro. The experimental group was tested with the Bogardus and Hinckley scales before and after the course and showed a significant increase in favorableness toward the Negro. The control group, which took a general introductory sociology course with less than 6 per cent of the time spent on race problems, showed no change after the course.

Remmers and his associates at Purdue University studied the effectiveness of specific reading matter[1] on attitudes toward Negroes and Jews. His subjects were pupils from four Indiana high schools. In all schools there were large and significant changes immediately after the reading of the selections. Follow-up studies indicated that after two months and, in another case, after six months most of the attitude change remained.

In an excellent study by F. Tredwell Smith, the effect of personal contact on attitudes toward the Negro was investigated. The experimental subjects were 46 graduate students at Teachers College, Columbia University, who volunteered to spend two week-ends on a conducted tour of Harlem. The control subjects were matched with the experimental subjects in attitude scores (toward the Negro), age, sex, and geographical origin. The tour through Harlem included participating in several teas and dinners with Negro hosts. After the tour a number of attitude tests were given to both control and experimental subjects. The first retest (immediately after the tour) showed a large increase in favorableness toward the Negro among the members of the experimental group; none, among the control. Eleven months after the conclusion of the experiment, 40 members of the original experimental group were again retested. Of these, 25 had kept all their gains and only a few had shown any significant drop.

Turning to other kinds of beliefs and attitudes, Sims (1938) has shown that written propaganda was effective in changing the attitudes of students either for or against the TVA (depending upon the nature of the propaganda used). Three months after exposing the students to the propaganda, its effects were still measurable.

Rosenthal (1934) has reported a change in the beliefs and attitudes of students toward socioeconomic issues consequent upon their viewing a propagandistic motion picture that favored the USSR as compared with life in a "capitalistic" country. He found that only those beliefs and attitudes which were specifically dealt with in the motion picture showed such an effect.

Although all of the above studies are limited by various considerations (such as the relative unimportance for the individual of the beliefs and attitudes which were changed, etc.), nevertheless they suggest that the efforts of those whose major objective is the control of beliefs and attitudes need not always go unrewarded. The effectiveness of any procedure adopted,

[1] These were (1) excerpts from W. E. B. DuBois's *Dark Water*, (2) a short biography of G. W. Carver, and (3) "So Lucille went to college," a short story by Charles Carson.

however, will be proportional to the theoretical soundness of the measures taken and not to the energy expended. The objective of this section is to outline the major considerations that must be kept in mind when planning such belief- or attitude-change programs. In a later chapter (Chap. XIII) these principals will be applied concretely to one specific kind of belief and attitude—racial prejudice in the United States.

Objectives in the Control of Beliefs and Attitudes.—Usually the efforts of those who are interested in controlling or changing beliefs and attitudes are directed at one of the following objectives: (1) to remove certain beliefs and attitudes altogether, *e.g.*, change an anti-Negro attitude so that the individual is "objective" about Negroes, having neither pro nor anti beliefs and attitudes about them; (2) to change the sign of an attitude, *e.g.*, change an antidemocratic attitude to a prodemocratic attitude; (3) to prevent the development of certain beliefs and attitudes, *e.g.*, so bring up a child as to prevent his adoption of an antidemocratic attitude in the first place; (4) to encourage the development of a belief or attitude, *e.g.*, so bring up a child as to assure his eventual adoption of a prodemocratic attitude; and (5) to change the content and specificity of a belief or attitude, *e.g.*, change an anti-Franco attitude to a more generalized anti-fascist attitude.

Each one of the above objectives may present different problems and may demand different control programs. In any attempt to control beliefs and attitudes it is first essential that we analyze clearly just what our objective is. Once the objective is determined, it then becomes essential to diagnose the nature of the belief or attitude that is to be changed, developed, or prevented from developing.

The Problem of Diagnosis.—In diagnosis, there are several questions that must be answered: (1) What needs do these beliefs and attitudes meet for the individuals who hold them, or what needs can such beliefs and attitudes serve for the people who are to be induced to hold them? (2) What emotional processes are involved or can become involved? (3) What is the nature of the content and interrelationships of these attitudes and beliefs? (4) What is the nature of the social support for these attitudes and beliefs?   *are the supports coming from the social environment*

The relevancy of these questions for a proper diagnosis of beliefs and attitudes should be obvious from our entire discussion in this and the preceding chapter. However, it might be of some value to emphasize here several common errors made by action groups, propagandists, and educators in their attempts to diagnose beliefs and attitudes.

Errors in diagnosing needs and emotions.—The first error is failing to realize the important functional value of beliefs and attitudes. Too frequently educational agencies assume that undesirable beliefs or attitudes reflect the inherent "cussedness" of human nature, or else they assume that these beliefs and attitudes reflect only the effects of conditioning or bad training. The service performed by these beliefs and attitudes *for* the individual is neglected.

Another error derives from the attempt to discover one universal need or emotion that holds for all people harboring any given kind of belief or attitude. The history of attempts to control beliefs and attitudes is replete with instances of this error. To some Marxists, for example, all people harboring an anti-Negro attitude are reacting to the need for economic security; to some psychiatrists, all such people are suffering from repressed sex needs. Correspondingly, the control measures that have been suggested by such analysts have been simple and unitary in character. Do away with economic insecurity, and racial prejudice will disappear; or teach people to live a healthy sex life, and all aggressive attitudes will disappear. Such analyses and cures do hold for some people but are certainly not valid in all cases.

Finally, another common error in this connection is the historical error in which the needs and emotions that are ascribed to beliefs and attitudes are seen from the historical perspective rather than from that of the immediate psychological field. Thus it is suggested that the person who has a strong antireligious attitude has this attitude now because as a child he was forced to attend church service at the expense of playing with other children.

Errors in diagnosing contents of beliefs and attitudes.—Similar errors are frequently made in the diagnosis of the contents of attitudes and beliefs. We cannot assume, for example, that everyone who has an anti-Russian attitude includes in his attitude a common set of percepts. For some, the important aspects of the content of an anti-Russian attitude may involve political percepts; for others, religious; for still others, racial; etc. Nor can we assume that the contents of an antimilitaristic belief or attitude remain constant from time to time within the same individual.

Errors in diagnosing the nature of social support.—As was pointed out, the cultural pattern is not a homogeneous one. To know that an individual is an American or a Frenchman or a German is not enough to enable us to say which of his beliefs and attitudes will be supported by his society and which will be frowned upon. We must know what kind of an American, Frenchman, or German he is and what his socioeconomic grouping is—that of a worker, a manager, a professional, etc. And much more important, we must know who his immediate associates are, what sort of school he goes to, and who are his "prestige figures." What do his teachers believe, and what are their attitudes, and what do his parents believe and his coworkers?

Research in diagnosis.—As will be indicated in Chap. XIII, there is no royal road to diagnosis, nor are general principles enough. Proper diagnosis necessitates intensive diagnostic research with the particular individuals involved and with the particular beliefs and attitudes. The specific tools and techniques available for such research will be discussed in the next two chapters.

Problems in Programs of Action.—Once we have an adequate analysis of the beliefs and attitudes we wish to eliminate or change or encourage, then we can plan our control measures. The most important initial generalization that can be made about the problem of control is that our program must recognize the complexity and diversity of the contents and functions of beliefs and attitudes and of the diversity of their bases of social support. We must, in other words, avoid seeking for a simple panacea in the treatment of any troublesome beliefs and attitudes. We must be catholic in our approach. If beliefs and attitudes are to be controlled, all the characteristics of beliefs and attitudes must be operated upon. A successful program will attempt to control the perceptions involved in beliefs and attitudes no less than the needs and emotions.

Changing the perceptions involved.—A major part of any program of control is that of controlling the percepts involved in beliefs and attitudes. To achieve this objective we must know how to translate the general principles of perceptual and cognitive organization into specific and effective control measures. If we know why one Mexican appears similar to another Mexican in the perceptions of the prejudiced person, then we know the target for the application of our general perceptual principles; we know, for example, which characteristics of similarity and proximity to seek to modify. This does not necessarily mean (as is so often assumed) that we can work only on the perceiving individual, on the prejudiced person's perceptions. As has been pointed out in Chap. III, *both* structural and functional factors are involved in every perception. It is quite possible to change the prejudiced person's perceptions by removing or changing certain environmental supports. The full significance of this point, that perceptions can be controlled through control programs aimed either at the perceiver *directly* or at the *object* of his perception, will be made clear in our discussion of how to control racial prejudice (Chap. XIII). It is necessary only to emphasize here that such control is essential if we are to change beliefs and attitudes.

One more point must be made. Frequently, as we have seen, individuals with strong attitudes withdraw themselves from exposure to the objects of their attitude, and thus it becomes difficult to change their percepts by manipulating the objects. The solution to this problem, though difficult to achieve in practice, is straightforward. Ways and means must be found for destroying such barriers to fresh stimulation. Just as any step that will change the environmental supports for perceived similarities may change the content of beliefs and attitudes, so any step that will minimize autistic thinking may help change the contents of beliefs and attitudes. The significance of this point lies in its suggestion that sometimes even *enforced contact among antagonistic people can induce changes in their beliefs and attitudes vis-à-vis each other*. As we shall later see, there is both experimental and observational evidence for this in the area of racial beliefs and attitudes.

Controlling the emotional and motivational factors.—However, even if we do make some significant changes in the environmental supports that lie behind certain undesired perceptions, we will not, thereby, do away with the undesirable belief or attitude. Facts can be *created* by the individual, as we have seen, to support a strong belief or attitude. The above procedures can accomplish some change, but other steps must be taken. They are those which are necessary for controlling the emotional and motivational factors involved in beliefs and attitudes. These steps can be grouped into two general categories: (1) measures designed to inhibit the initial appearance of certain needs, demands, and emotions or measures designed to encourage the appearance of certain of these processes; (2) measures designed to remove or lessen the intensity of certain needs and demands already present and to remove the lasting after-effects of past emotional experiences in the present psychological field of the person.

It is true that no one need or demand is always found to be at the base of any given belief or attitude, but it is also true that in a statistical sense, such correlations do exist. For example, although the need for wealth or the emotion of envy may sometimes lie behind "desired" beliefs, most frequently they are found associated with undesirable beliefs and attitudes. Similarly, although the need for love and the emotion of joy may sometimes be served by socially undesirable beliefs and attitudes, they most frequently are found to be functionally related to desirable beliefs, attitudes, and action. From the point of view of changing beliefs and attitudes of many people, therefore, it would be desirable because of this to encourage certain needs and discourage others.

That such a program is theoretically possible follows directly from the considerations we have examined in the chapter on motivation. We have seen there that needs, demands, and emotions arise out of the properties of the psychological field of the individual. It should be possible, by manipulating his environment, therefore, to determine his specific needs and emotions. The task of effectively manipulating the environment is not a simple one. Such "manipulation" frequently involves changing the practices in the nursery, the home, the school, the church, the place of work, etc.

The critical point, however, is that many of the needs and emotions which lie at the root of the beliefs and attitudes we wish to control are not inevitable. To those who are interested in controlling beliefs and attitudes this is a very heartening fact. Beliefs and attitudes do not reflect the eternal "cussedness" of human nature.

Two Major Programmatic Guides.—All the measures suggested in the preceding pages depend, in final analysis, upon our effective manipulation of the individual's environment. The problem of changing beliefs and attitudes has been aptly summarized by Lewin and Grabbe (1945) in their statement that *"the re-educative process has to fulfill a task which is essentially equivalent to a change in culture."* It cannot be emphasized too strongly that the task of changing beliefs and attitudes involves working through most, if not all, of our formative agencies—whether formal institutions, individual people, or even objects. This consideration directs our attention to several important general guides which must be observed if we are to carry out our educational process successfully.

The necessity for integration.—Any attempt to change only one set of the factors involved in beliefs and attitudes can have but limited effect. Lewin and Grabbe, in the paper referred to above, after surveying many attempts of well-meaning attitude changers, have this to say:

Methods and procedures which seek to change convictions item by item are of little avail in bringing about the desired change of heart. This is found to be one of the most important experiences for those engaged in the field of re-education. Arguments proceeding logically from one point to another may drive the individual into a corner. But as a rule he will find someway—if necessary a very illogical way—to retain his beliefs.

This does not mean that the educational process cannot be analyzed into different problems, each with its own objective. Actually, we have done just that in the preceding analysis. Nor does it mean that changing the environmental supports behind perceptions alone has no value at all. What it does mean is that the program should be a multidimensional one. There should be a constant recognition that a change in the environmental supports lying behind percepts can be influenced by a coordinated change in the environmental supports lying behind needs and emotions and both of these can be influenced by a change in the nature of the social support that beliefs and attitudes receive.

Necessity for group identification.—Most beliefs and attitudes receive social support. This not only tends to make beliefs and attitudes resistant to change, as we have already seen, but can also help induce change. Effective measures designed to control beliefs and attitudes must seek, wherever possible, to create new group identifications for the people it would change to the end that social support for the new beliefs and attitudes will be forth-coming.[1] Social support for beliefs and attitudes is effective only in so far as the individual is or wants to be a member of the group that has those beliefs and attitudes.

However, the same considerations that indicate the usefulness of group identification also point to some very important limitations. Where no proper group exists for such identification, it becomes difficult, if not impossible, to establish certain beliefs and attitudes. The range of available cultural patterns within any society tends to limit the range of possible beliefs and attitudes that individuals in that society can hold. If the German culture, for example, were homogeneously militaristic, if there were no significant groups of Germans who had antimilitaristic beliefs and attitudes, if there were nothing in the German cultural history that could serve as a prop to support an antimilitaristic attitude, if most Germans were kept from contact with antimilitaristic cultures elsewhere, then it would be a long and difficult task to educate the German so that he would achieve or hold an antimilitaristic attitude.

Fortunately, however, very few cultures are that homogeneous. What the above does mean, practically, is that in attempting to change the beliefs and attitudes of the individual, we should seek the social approach. We must attempt to educate the individual as a part of a group, and we can do that by taking advantage of the diversification within our cultural pattern.

SUMMARY

To know the characteristics and functions of beliefs and attitudes is not enough to enable us to control the actions of people. We must also know something about the processes behind the growth and change of beliefs and attitudes. In discussing the determining influences of the growth of beliefs and attitudes, both the cultural environment and the functional factors (those unique to the person) are examined.

It is pointed out that there are both theoretical reasons and empirical data to indicate the formative influence of the cultural environment. Man's psychological field, it is recalled, is a function of his real world. But this real world is a contrived one in the sense that the available stimulus patterns are limited within a specifically defined range; *i.e.*, man's real world is characteristic of a particular cultural pattern. It is to be expected, therefore, that differences in cultural environments (an aspect of the real world)

[1] For a discussion of methods of inducing group identification and the influence of such identifications on beliefs and attitudes, see Chap. XI.

LUNCHEON TECHNIQUE

will be reflected in differences in beliefs and attitudes (an aspect of the psychological field). Several correlational studies are then cited to indicate some of the relationships that have been found between cultural determinants and specific beliefs and attitudes.

However, it is then pointed out, exposure to a characteristic and defined range of stimulation does not result in the growth of a uniform set of beliefs. Because of the functional factors, beliefs and attitudes develop selectively within the possible range. The growth of beliefs and attitudes is thus a complex function of both cultural and functional factors. This accounts, in part, for the individual differences in beliefs and attitudes to be expected of people even within the same culture. These differences are also due to the heterogeneous and frequently contradictory elements within the cultural patterns themselves.

In the light of all of the above, the value of correlational studies between specific cultural indices and beliefs or attitudes is questioned. This last point is illustrated by an analysis of the data concerning family influences on various beliefs and attitudes of children.

In discussing the functional determinants, investigations that seek to correlate specific personality traits and general personality structures with specific beliefs and attitudes are reviewed. It is concluded that although such studies contribute greatly to our understanding of the intimate dynamic relationships between personality factors and beliefs and attitudes, nevertheless to expect invariant and simple correlations between them is not theoretically justified nor are such expectations supported by the data. The functional determinants play an important role in the growth of beliefs and attitudes but do so within the limitations of the cultural environment. Certain kinds of people do not always hold certain kinds of beliefs and attitudes.

Since the cultural environment provides most of the facts for beliefs and attitudes and the functional factors are primarily responsible for the manner in which these facts are incorporated, the relation between facts and the growth of beliefs and attitudes is then examined. In this discussion it is pointed out why we can expect discrepancies between the facts of the case and the corresponding beliefs and attitudes. Four responsible causes are isolated: (1) the relative lack of available facts, (2) the necessary dependence upon authorities for facts, (3) the tendency of the organizing process to create facts where the environment does not provide adequate facts or where the individual's needs are frustrated, (4) the individual's unschooled and thus indiscriminate dependence upon the appearance of things.

In terms of the various influences that determine the kind and content of beliefs and attitudes, the following factors are discussed as operating in the direction of the self-preservation of the developing beliefs and attitudes:

the selective nature of perception, the operation of the constancy effect, the withdrawal behavior frequently induced by beliefs and attitudes, and the social support that many beliefs and attitudes receive. Some of these factors are then illustrated by studies designed to investigate what happens to a prejudiced person when he is involuntarily confronted with antiprejudice propaganda.

Despite the self-preservative forces inherent in beliefs and attitudes, however, the efforts of those who would change beliefs and attitudes need not always go unrewarded. A number of studies that indicate this are then reviewed. The major considerations to be kept in mind in planning effective belief- and attitude-control programs are outlined. The following topics are discussed: (1) the differing objectives possible in the control of beliefs and attitudes and the necessity of specifying these objectives; (2) the problem of diagnosis and the common errors that are made in diagnosing the needs, emotions, contents, and the social support involved in beliefs and attitudes; (3) the problems in programs of action. In connection with this last topic, two major programmatic guides are suggested. The first stresses the necessity for an integrated approach. It is emphasized that changing only one of the factors involved in beliefs and attitudes can have but limited effect. There must be a constant recognition that a change in the environmental supports lying behind percepts can be influenced by a correlated change in the environmental supports behind needs and emotions, and both of these can be influenced by a change in the nature of the social support that beliefs and attitudes receive. The second guide calls attention to the necessity for group identification. The point is made that in attempting to change beliefs and attitudes of the individual, we should employ the *social* approach. We must create new group identifications for the people whose attitudes we would change to the end that social support for the new beliefs and attitudes would be forthcoming. To educate the individual as part of a group we must take advantage of the diversification within our cultural pattern.

BIBLIOGRAPHY

CARLSON, H. B.: 1934. Attitudes of undergraduate students. *J. soc. Psychol.*, **5**, 202–212.

COOPER, E., and JAHODA, M.: 1947. The evasion of propaganda: how prejudiced people respond to anti-prejudice propaganda. *J. Psychol.*, **23**, 15–25.

DEXTER, E. S.: 1939. Personality traits related to conservatism and radicalism. *Character & Pers.*, **7**, 230–237.

DROBA, D. D.: 1939. Why war? *World Unity*, **11**, 270.

ECKERT, R. E., and MILLS, H. C.: 1936. International attitudes and related academic and social factors. *J. educ. Sociol.*, **9**, 142–153.

FRENCH, V. V.: 1947. The structure of sentiments. *J. Person*, **15**, 247–282; **16**, 78–108.

HALLOWELL, A. I.: 1937. *Handbook of psychological leads for ethnological field workers.* Division of Anthropology and Psychology, National Research Council, Washington, D. C.

HARRIS, A. J., REMMERS, H. H., and ELLISON, C. E.: 1932. The relation between liberal and conservative attitudes in college students, and other factors. *J. soc. Psychol.*, 3, 320–335.

HIRSCHBERG, G., and GILLILAND, A. R.: 1942. Parent-child relationships in attitudes. *J. abnorm. soc. Psychol.*, 37, 125–130.

HOROWITZ, E. L.: 1936. The development of attitudes toward the Negro. *Arch. Psychol.* 28, No. 194.

KÖHLER, W.: 1937. Psychological remarks on some questions of anthropology. *Amer. J. Psychol.*, 50, 271–288.

KULP, II, D. H., and DAVIDSON, H. H.: 1933. Sibling resemblance in social attitudes. *J. educ. Sociol.*, 7, 133–140.

LEVINE, J. M., and MURPHY, G.: 1943. The learning and forgetting of controversial material. *J. abnorm. soc. Psychol.*, 38, 507–517.

LEVY-BRUHL, L.: 1923. *Primitive mentality.* New York: Macmillan.

LEWIN, K., and GRABBE, P.: 1945. Conduct, knowledge and acceptance of new values. *J. soc. Issues*, 1, No. 3, 53–64.

MORGAN, C. L., and REMMERS, H. H.: 1935. Liberalism and conservatism of college students as affected by the depression. *Sch. & Soc.*, 41, 780–784.

MURPHY, G., MURPHY, L. B., and NEWCOMB, T. M.: 1937. *Experimental social psychology.* New York: Harper.

MURRAY, H. A., and MORGAN, C. D.: 1945. A clinical study of sentiment. *Genet. Psychol. Monogr.*, 32, 3–149, 153–311.

NEWCOMB, T. M., and SVEHLA, G.: 1938. Intra-family relationships in attitudes. *Sociometry*, 1, 180–205.

QUEENER, E. L.: 1947. *The development of internationalist attitudes directed toward peace.* Graduate School, Yale Univ. Ph.D. dissertation.

RABIN, A. L.: 1945. Rorschach test findings in a group of conscientious objectors. *Amer. J. Orthopsychiat.*, 15, 514–519.

REMMERS, H. H.: 1936. Further studies in attitude, Series II. *Stud. in Higher Educ.*, 31, *Purdue Univ. Bull.*

REMMERS, H. H.: 1938. Further studies in attitude, Series III. *Stud. in Higher Educ.*, 34, *Purdue Univ. Bull.*

ROSE, A. M.: 1947. *Studies in reduction of prejudice.* Chicago: American Council on Race Relations.

ROSENTHAL, S. P.: 1934. Change of socio-economic attitudes under radical motion picture propaganda. *Arch. Psychol.*, No. 166.

SIMS, V. M.: 1938. Factors influencing attitude toward the T. V. A. *J. abnorm. soc. Psychol.*, 33, 34–56.

SMITH, F. T.: 1943. *An experiment in modifying attitudes toward the Negro.* New York: Teachers College, Columbia Univ.

SMITH, M.: 1939. A study of change of attitude toward the Negro. *J. Negro Educ.*, 8, 64–70.

Social Science Research Council: 1947. *Public reaction to the atomic bomb and world affairs.* Ithaca: Cornell Univ.

STAGNER, R.: 1936. Fascist attitudes: an exploratory study. *J. soc. Psychol.*, 7, 309–319.

VETTER, G. B.: 1930. The measurement of social and political attitudes and the related personality factors. *J. abnorm. soc. Psychol.*, 25, 149–189.

WINSLOW, C. N.: 1937. A study of the extent of agreement between friends' opinions and their ability to estimate the opinions of each other. *J. soc. Psychol.*, 8, 433–442.

CHAPTER VII

THE MEASUREMENT OF BELIEFS AND ATTITUDES

The measurement of beliefs and attitudes has become a major American industry. Every American, no matter what his financial means, can now buy information on "attitudes." For the price of a daily newspaper he can avail himself of the results of public opinion studies carried on regularly by various local and national polling agencies. If he can afford a larger expenditure to buy "slick-paper" magazines and journals, he can get more specialized attitude studies. And if he wishes to spend a great deal of money, he can buy the services of commercial agencies which will make a custom-built attitude survey for him to meet his own business or political needs.

The basis of this demand for information about people's beliefs and attitudes is not hard to find. By knowing the beliefs and attitudes of people it is possible, as we have seen in the two previous chapters, to do something toward the prediction and control of their behavior. And for many groups in our society, such prediction and control of the behavior of other people are important desiderata.

If a political party knows the attitudes and opinions of the American people toward its party platform, it is better able to predict the behavior of people at the polls and to devise a platform that meets with greatest general favor. If the State Department knows the beliefs and attitudes of people in the area of foreign affairs, it can predict the support or resistances that will appear among the citizens of the country toward proposed foreign policies. If the members of a minority group know the attitudes of the rest of the community toward the minority group, they are better able to foresee and thereby perhaps to forestall aggressive acts against the minority group. If public health officials know the details of people's beliefs, and particularly their erroneous beliefs, about venereal diseases, they can institute an intelligent educational campaign about VD. If the manufacturer of a beauty cream wants to increase his sales, it is useful for him to arrange price, packaging, and promotion in terms of what he can find out about people's opinions toward his product.

The above "applied science" uses of attitude and opinion information as well as the needs of the social psychologist as a "pure" scientist require the measurement and quantification of various aspects of beliefs and attitudes, so that the necessary experimental and statistical manipulation of variables is possible.

Basic social science and its applications are likely to differ in the kind of measurement of beliefs and attitudes they demand. For the former, it is often possible to work with small, selected samples of people in laboratory or classroom or clinical situations and to measure their beliefs and attitudes by the use of specially designed instruments. For the various social applications, on the other hand, it is usually necessary to work with larger samples of the entire population or defined segments of it in the field (*i.e.*, in their homes, in their places of work, on the street, etc.). And the measuring instruments designed for the laboratory, the classroom, or the clinic may be entirely inappropriate for use here. Completely different technical problems of measurement of beliefs and attitudes may arise, and different instruments are required.

This chapter and the following will reflect, to a certain extent, the above difference in emphasis and technique in measuring beliefs and attitudes. The present chapter will be concerned with a discussion of general issues involved in all measurement of beliefs and attitudes and with types of scales and rating methods that are particularly—though not exclusively— applicable to the measurement of selected samples under controlled conditions.

The chapter that follows, on public opinion research, will be concerned mainly with technical problems involved in the measurement of beliefs and attitudes on large-scale samples and in the field.[1]

THEORY OF BELIEF AND ATTITUDE MEASUREMENT

Before proceeding to a discussion of the details of measurement of beliefs and attitudes, we must first clarify a number of theoretical points involved in such measurement, we must note what various attributes of beliefs and attributes are to be quantified, and we must outline the various types of measuring instruments.

General Considerations.—The measurement of beliefs and attitudes, like the measurement of all psychological variables, presents unique and frequently very difficult problems. The following general considerations will be helpful guides to an understanding of some of these technical problems:

1. *The measurement of beliefs and attitudes is necessarily indirect.* Beliefs and attitudes are enduring organizations of perceptual, motivational, and

[1] For an important critical review of opinion-attitude methodology, see McNemar (1946).

emotional processes (see Chaps. V and VI), which are influential in the direction and guidance of behavior. They cannot be observed or measured directly; they can be measured only indirectly on the basis of inferences drawn from the individual's behavior and immediate experience. A negative attitude toward labor unions may be revealed by crossing a picket line or by a feeling of anger when seeing John L. Lewis in a newsreel. A belief in the contagious nature of infantile paralysis may be revealed by a behavior of keeping children out of public places during an epidemic or by what people say about infantile paralysis.

Since beliefs and attitudes must necessarily be measured indirectly, it is obvious that there are many different ways to make these measurements. At the proper point in this chapter we will discuss each of these main techniques in detail; at this point we wish merely to indicate the variety of means that have been used. Not all possible approaches to attitude and belief measurement have been utilized thus far in social psychology, and it is entirely possible that new and much superior techniques will be developed.

Attitudes and beliefs may be reflected either in the behavior of the individual or in his immediate experience. Hence, both behavioral analysis and introspective analysis can be utilized for measurement. In connection with the former, measurements can be made by quantifying relevant aspects of the individual's behavior toward the object itself. Thus, for example, a man's attitude toward the Mexican may be measured in terms of his actions of approach or withdrawal, his practice of discrimination, etc. Or the behavior may be merely verbal, as in the responses to items on a questionnaire that refer to the Mexican. Or the behavior may not be directed at the object itself, but at some other object related to it. For example, a man may behave in a certain way toward a Mexican's dog (*e.g.*, kicking it) and thus reveal his attitude toward the Mexican. Or he may respond in a certain fashion to items on a test that make no direct references to the Mexican, but that are, nonetheless, diagnostic of his attitudes toward the Mexican. These latter may be referred to as "projective" behaviors.

On the introspective level, the individual himself may, in terms of his immediate experiences, be able to provide data for the measurement of his beliefs and attitudes. His perceptions, feelings, and emotions relating to Communism may be highly diagnostic of his beliefs and attitudes about Communism. Also, his perceptions, feelings, and emotions about other objects that are in some way connected with Communism may, "projectively," reveal his beliefs and attitudes toward Communism. There has been, on the whole, a traditional tendency to discount the "introspective" data as a basis for attitude and belief measurement, but there is not, as this book repeatedly emphasizes, any theoretical reason why techniques utilizing the data of immediate experience cannot be as reliable and as informative as other more objective techniques of measurement. Allport (1942) has put it in the following way:

> If we want to know how people feel: what they experience and what they remember, what their emotions and motives are like, and the reasons for acting as they do—why not ask them? This is the simple logic of the introspectionist's position that commends itself to many in spite of the scorching displeasure of behaviorists and objectivists.

2. *The manner in which beliefs and attitudes reflect themselves in behavior and experience is governed in part by the nature of the momentary situation.* The individual's reaction to a given object is a dual function of (a) his enduring attitudes and beliefs about the object and (b) the nature of the immediate situation. As the situation varies, his reaction toward the object will also show variation, even though his belief or attitude toward the object may be thought of as invariant. The significance of this fact for the theory of measurement of beliefs and attitudes is very great, for it implies that the psychological situations under which the belief or attitude is measured must be carefully controlled and standardized if the measurement on one occasion is to be comparable to the measurement on another occasion. It is a corollary of this that the statistics of measurement of an attitude or belief are difficult to interpret unless accompanied by a statement of the precise conditions under which the measurement was taken.

3. *The required precision of measurement of beliefs and attitudes may vary.* "Measurement" does not necessarily imply a highly refined degree of quantification; in some cases the crudest possible degree of differentiation is sufficient, as seen, for example, in a mere dichotomy of prolabor or antilabor or of more intense or less intense. The essential requirement is that the particular dimension involved shall be susceptible to a high enough degree of differentiation and with a sufficiently high level of reliability that the necessary experimental and statistical treatment is made possible. The usefulness of measurement of beliefs and attitudes seems sometimes to be impugned on the basis of an alleged lack of precision. The truth is, however, that although the highest degree of precision may be an ideal toward which to work, crude measurement of beliefs and attitudes is often adequate for fruitful use of these psychological variables. When the effects in which one is interested are small, more precise measurement is required; when the effects are large, lower precision may suffice.

4. *Belief and attitude measurement, like all measurement, demands reliability.* The usefulness of measures of beliefs and attitudes is strictly limited by the level of reliability of such measures, *i.e.,* the extent to which a meas-

urement repeated under the same conditions will yield the same values.) If repeated measurements of something that is presumed to be the same give inconsistent results, the measurements can have no systematic value for analysis. A fallible measuring instrument for beliefs and attitudes is as worthless as a capriciously elastic ruler. Any measurement of beliefs or attitudes must be construed in terms of the reliability of the measuring instrument.

5. *The validity of measurement of beliefs and attitudes can be determined only indirectly, in terms of predictions of behavior based on such measurements.* The validity of a measuring instrument is the extent to which it measures what it purports to measure. Attitude and belief measurement, as we have said, is necessarily indirect. There is, therefore, no direct mode of validation of measurements. The best that can be done is to make use of the measurements in predicting how the individual will behave in various circumstances and then to see how well these predictions are borne out in fact. To the extent that the predictions are verified, the measurements of the relevant beliefs and attitudes may be considered valid.)

There are, as we shall see later in discussing the problem of validity, several other less rigorous approaches to a determination of validity.

The Measurement of Individual Beliefs and Attitudes.—It seems to be accepted that only common beliefs and attitudes, *i.e.*, those held in common by numbers of people, are susceptible to measurement whereas individual beliefs and attitudes, *i.e.*, those held only by single individuals, are not.) As Allport (1935) has stated it, with the concurrence of Murphy, Murphy, and Newcomb (1937): ". . . Measurement requires a scale and there is no scale which does not depend upon the central tendencies and dispersions of opinions expressed by *many* people."

This point of view seems to us to be highly debatable. Many important aspects of an attitude or belief, such as direction, intensity, and importance, seem capable of being characterized in an absolute manner for an individual and not dependent upon their relation to norms established by the attitudes and beliefs of other people. The essence of an attitude's sign, for instance, is in psychological approach to or withdrawal from the object of the attitude, and in no conceivable sense can the determination of whether or not there is such approach or withdrawal be said to depend upon norms of other people's attitudes toward the object. Unless this were the case, it would be impossible for all people to have a negative attitude toward an object (since negativity and positivity would have to be relatively determined), and this is manifestly absurd. Intensity of our own attitudes, as manifested, for example, in the degree of emotionality with which an object is charged for us, obviously need not be measured by comparison with other people's feelings.

We know that we are angry and whether it is mild or intense anger by intro-spective observation alone, without any comparison with norms of anger set up for people in general. And our judgment of other people's emotions (and hence the intensity of their attitudes) tends likewise to be absolute rather than relative. We shall see later on that strength of an attitude or opinion might be measured by the amount of change produced in it by forces of persuasion, information, etc., brought to bear against it. If the strength of the forces applied could be measured objectively, there would be no need to invoke group norms in stating the strength of the attitude.

Measurable Attributes of Beliefs and Attitudes.—In Chap. V (page 158), a number of characteristics of beliefs and attitudes were examined, among them being "sign," content, clarity, specificity, strength, importance, and verifiability. Each of these attributes or dimensions of beliefs and attitudes is psychologically significant, and no adequate investigation of beliefs and attitudes may neglect any of them. The accuracy of predictions of behavior based upon a study of people's beliefs and attitudes depends heavily upon the care in taking account of each of these dimensions. It is essential, therefore, that methods for the quantification of each of these dimensions be available.

Types of Measurement of Beliefs and Attitudes.—As indicated previously, the inherent indirection involved in belief and attitude measure-ment means that there is a wide variety of ways in which beliefs and atti-tudes can be measured. One principal classification of measuring instru-ments is the attitude or opinion *scale*. Different types of scales are those developed by Thurstone, Likert, Guttman, Bogardus, and several others.

Another principal classification of measuring instruments is the *rating* of opinions and attitudes. The sources of data for rating and the types of ratings vary widely.

MEASUREMENT BY SCALES ·

Of all methods of measurement of beliefs and attitudes, by far the most prominent, the most widely used, and the most carefully designed and tested is the attitude or opinion scale. In essence, the method of scaling requires that the individual react verbally with expressions of approval or disap-proval, agreement or disagreement to a set of carefully standardized items or propositions. The pattern and summation of reactions to the set of items provide a way of inferring the individual's opinion or attitude concerning the object to which the items refer and permit the individual to be assigned a position along a quantitative scale of pro-ness or con-ness.

Scales differ markedly in type and in method of construction, but in every case their objective is identical—to assign an individual a numerical position along a scale that extends from one extreme of approval or acceptance to the other extreme of disapproval or rejection.) The relative scale positions occupied by various individuals may be taken, therefore, as indicative of the relative favorableness or unfavorableness of their opinions and attitudes.

The method of scale measurement does not measure opinions and attitudes directly. What it requires of the individual is a set of judgments of the acceptibility or unacceptibility of a series of verbal propositions.) As we have seen in Chap. V, page 157, judgments are immediate cognitive processes that are partially governed by those existing predispositions of the person which we call beliefs and attitudes. (The pattern and summation of a set of judgments, then, can be expected to throw light on the nature of the underlying predispositions.)

In the construction of the typical scale the objective is to select a set of items or propositions in such a fashion that the acceptance or rejection of each one will imply a different degree of favorable or unfavorable attitude.) Thus, for example, three of the 22 items from one form of the Thurstone-Droba scale for measurement of attitudes toward war (Droba, 1930) are as follows: "The benefits of war outweigh its attendant evils." "Compulsory military training in all countries should be reduced but not eliminated." "It is difficult to imagine any situation in which we should be justified in sanctioning or participating in another war."

It is obvious that a person who agrees with the first item is in the prowar direction, one who agrees with the second item is in the intermediate position, and one who agrees with the third item is in the antiwar direction.

(The separate items in such scales are not customarily of interest in themselves. That is to say, we are not interested in the reaction to a specific, single item, but only in how the reaction to this item can be summed with those to many other equivalently weighted items to derive a final scale position.) There is, of course, nothing to prohibit the analysis of reactions to a single item, but the usefulness of a scale does not stand or fall on the basis of the validity of any single item. Any set of items will do as well as any other set, merely providing that they render the same final total score on the particular dimension in question.

Criteria for the Selection of Scale Items.—In determining which items shall be included in a scale, which ones shall be excluded, and how many items are required, the following criteria are relevant:

(*Diagnostic function.*—The item must bear some diagnostic relationship to the attitude or opinion for which measurement is being sought. That is, the item must serve some discriminative function, so that people of different belief and attitude complexion will respond to the item in systematically different ways.)

Sometimes the diagnostic relationship of the item to the belief or attitude in question can be clearly assured by making the manifest content of the item bear directly on the object of belief or attitude. For example, to ascertain opinions about Russia's good faith in international affairs an item might be chosen as follows: "Russia is sincerely trying to make the United Nations work." If it can be assumed that an individual gives an honest answer of assent or dissent to that proposition, it is very likely that his answer will reveal something about his opinion of Russia's good faith. In many attitude scales, particularly in the Thurstone type, the items are chosen to have such manifest reference to the object in question. This may be important in helping to ensure that all people being measured are reacting to the same object; otherwise comparative scale scores for different individuals would be psychologically meaningless if the objects toward which the beliefs or attitudes refer were not the same for the different individuals. Also, the very mechanics of scale construction may require that the manifest content of the item refer rather directly to the object in question. This, it will later be seen, pertains especially to the Thurstone scale.

Sometimes, however, the content of an item may not bear such manifest relationship to the object in question. By the very nature of the complex dynamic functioning of the individual and the integration of his perceptual, cognitive, and motivational processes, it is to be expected that his underlying beliefs and attitudes will reach out to influence a great many of his judgments, some of which refer to things only indirectly related to the objects of belief or attitude. Thus, for example, an item in a scale for measurement of attitude toward Communism might take the following form: "Religious values are of the highest importance in a person's life." Assent or dissent to this proposition might be discovered to be markedly related to one's attitudes about Communism, and hence the item could be used as one diagnostic item of the scale, even though its manifest reference was to religion rather than to Communism. Many items in attitude and opinion scales, especially in the Likert type, are chosen solely on the basis of discriminative value. They may often have hidden meanings, which make responses to the item lead to correct inferences about the thing being measured, even though in surface meaning they seem indifferently related to the belief or attitude in question.

Sharpness of discrimination.—Not only must an item call out responses that are psychologically related to the beliefs or attitudes in question, it must also differentiate sharply among people who fall at different points along the dimension being measured. Ideally, the response to an item should be perfectly correlated with the underlying belief or attitude. All those assenting to the proposition should be found to be more extreme along the scale than those dissenting. (There should be no overlap.) This meaning of sharpness of discrimination becomes clear in another context. During the recent war in the Pacific, American soldiers imposed a modern "shibboleth" test on Japanese who were, under the cover of darkness, attempting to infiltrate American lines. By using "lallapalooza" as a password, they were able to discriminate the friend from the foe, whose response was likely to be "rarraparooza."

This test undoubtedly provided a fairly sharp discrimination, though not perfect. Some Japanese "passed" the test, and some unfortunate Americans probably "failed" it. In the same way, no item on an attitude or opinion scale will be found to be a perfect discriminator. (There will always in practice be cases of overlap, in which people who assent to a given proposition are actually lower on the scale than some who dissent.)

(In selecting items for a scale, those which show the smallest overlap and are, therefore, the sharpest discriminators are chosen.) There are several alternative ways in which the sharpness of discrimination of an item can be ascertained, and we shall presently review them.

Discrimination along the entire scale.—(Items must be meaningfully related to the attitude or opinion being measured, they must discriminate sharply among people, and they must be chosen so as to discriminate at every point along the dimension.) Not only is it necessary to be able to separate the sheep from the goats, the friends from the foes, the pros from the antis, it is also usually desired to be able to make much finer differentiations. (Ideally, all shades of opinion and attitude from one extreme to the other should be discriminable.)

(What this requires is that items be chosen so as to serve discriminatively at various points on the scale, so that, for instance, extreme anticommunists can be separated from those a trifle less extreme, etc.) The number of items that are to be utilized in the final scale will depend, for one thing, upon the desired degree of refinement of differentiation. Assuming perfect items, the number of attitude or belief categories in which people can be separated is equal to the number of items. If a simple dichotomy is sufficient, one perfect item will do the job. If highly refined dimensions are desired, many items will have to be included.

The degree of differentiation may vary at different places in the scale. Thus, shades of difference among people who fall toward the middle of the scale may be measurable, while similar differences among people falling near the extremes may be obscured. (Frequently, scales suffer a "truncation" at the extremes; beyond a certain degree of attitude for or against the given object, there is no distinction made among people.) The *rabid* reactionary is not differentiated in a measurable way from the *strong* reactionary. The social implication of this shortcoming of attitude and opinion scales may, in some applications, be serious. It is often the most extreme, rabid bitter-enders who play the critical role in social phenomena, and it is these people whom scales need also to measure adequately. That scales are often inadequate in this aspect is probably accounted for by the technical difficulties involved in finding items which will truly discriminate at the very extremes of a scale.

Minimal number of items for reliability.—It was pointed out above that with perfect items, the minimal number to be included in a scale is determined by the desired level of refinement of measurement. Items are, however, never perfect. There are always special factors entering which reduce the discriminability of any item—unique meanings ascribed to it by different people, accidental misunderstandings, etc. There are, as well, other sources of random or accidental variation in the responses people make to an attitude or opinion test. All these influences will tend to reduce the reliability of the scale, *i.e.*, the consistency with which it differentiates people along the dimension.

The remedy for the imperfections of items and the random and accidental variations in the way people respond to the items is to increase the number of items. The greater the number of items the higher the reliability, because the irrelevant "errors of measurement" tend to be canceled out. Though the individual ascribes unique meaning to one item in a way that distorts the measurement of his attitude, it is less likely that he will do so in the same way to a considerable number of items. However, considerations of efficiency and practicability in testing sharply limit the total number of items that can be comfortably accommodated in an attitude or opinion scale.

Summary.—The criteria for selection of scale items are that the items must be psychologically related to the belief or attitude being measured, that they must discriminate sharply among people, that they must discriminate in all parts of the dimension, and that they must be sufficiently numerous that random and accidental imperfections in the items and in the testing are canceled out. These criteria should be kept in mind as the various types of scales are now discussed.

The Thurstone Method of Scale Construction.—Thurstone and his coworkers (Thurstone, 1929 and 1931; Thurstone and Chave, 1929) have developed certain widely used methods of attitude scale construction. They have published a number of specific scales for the measurement of attitudes and opinions toward war, the church, capital punishment, evolution, the Negro, birth control, censorship, the Chinese, and many other social objects. Other investigators have utilized the Thurstone method in producing scales concerned with a very wide range of objects. Theoretically, such scales could be developed to measure attitudes toward any social object or issue, and this seems to have provided social psychologists with an almost inexhaustible field of applied research.

Steps in construction of the scale.—The essential steps involved in the Thurstone technique are (1) the amassing of a very large number of simple statements or propositions about the object or issue in question; (2) the judging of each of these items by a sizable group of experts as to its proper diagnostic position on an attitude continuum between one extreme and the other and the rejection of those items for which there is insufficient agreement among the judges as to proper scale position; (3) the assignment of a scale score to each remaining item, computed as the median scale position for that item given by the group of judges; (4) a final selection among the remaining items so that they will spread more or less evenly along the scale from one extreme to the other.

The original set of statements or propositions is collected from various sources. The principal criteria in choosing them are that they should be phrased in simple, unambiguous terms and that they should refer rather directly to the object or issue in question. Involved wordings cause disagreements among the judges' placements of the items, and it is also obvious that the more directly the item refers to the object or issue in question the higher the agreement among judges is likely to be. Probably all judges would rate the item, "Use of alcoholic beverages in any amount is likely to be injurious to the health" as toward the proprohibition extreme, but they would probably disagree on the exact diagnostic significance for attitude toward the Negro of an item, "All men are created equal."

The group of judges must be large—usually in excess of one hundred—but its make-up does not have to depend upon the personal attitudes or opinions of the judges themselves. The task for the judge is to place each item in one of 11 piles which appear to be equally spaced from one extreme of the scale to the other. That is, the judge must decide whether assent to the given item would indicate an extreme favorable attitude, a neutral attitude, an extreme unfavorable attitude, or some intermediate position among these.

Out of the original large set of items, only those are selected about which there is high agreement among the judges as to scale position. An item that is assigned with almost equal frequency to all 11 piles obviously fails to command a communality of meaning for the judging group and can be expected to lead to similar ambiguity in its discrimination of people's attitude. On the other hand, an item that falls in almost all cases in piles 8, 9, or 10 might be expected to carry a fairly uniform significance for people responding to it. There is never perfect agreement among the judges as to the placement of an item; the items showing highest amount of agreement are selected for further consideration.

The *median* position assigned an item by the various judges is taken as the scale value of that item.   In other words, assent to an item would mean that the individual's attitude could be considered as falling at that scale position along the continuum.

Finally, the scale is made up of a limited number of items (approximately twenty in the typical Thurstone scale) so chosen as to have scale values that spread along all parts of the continuum.   It would be undesirable to have a heavy preponderance of items with scale values falling in one limited region of the dimension and none or very few in other regions.

Illustrative items selected in the above fashion are reproduced below. They are 7 items chosen from among the 22 that constitute one form of Droba's (1930) scale for measuring attitude toward war.   Listed with each item is the *scale value*.

Scale Value	Item
1.3	1. A country cannot amount to much without a national honor, and war is the only means of preserving it
2.5	2. When war is declared, we must enlist
5.2	3. Wars are justifiable only when waged in defense of weaker nations
5.4	4. Peace and war are both essential to progress
5.6	5. The most that we can hope to accomplish is the partial elimination of war
8.4	6. The disrespect for human life and rights involved in war is a cause of crime waves
10.6	7. All nations should disarm immediately

Scoring of the scale.—In taking the test, the individual is instructed to check each of the items (randomly presented) with which he agrees.   His attitude score is then computed as the median of the scale values of the items he checks.

Complete internal consistency of the set of items would require that an individual should check only items immediately contiguous in scale value, *e.g.*, items 3, 4, and 5 in the above illustration.   In practice, however, it is usually found that although the checks do cluster around a given point in the scale, there are some scattered ones at other points in the scale, often quite remote.   Thus, in the above illustration for example, a person might check items 3, 4, and 5 and also item 7, without checking other items having scale values intermediate between item 5 and item 7.   That this happens is a reflection of the unreliability of the items, resulting from the not surprising fact that it is difficult—if not impossible—to construct a set of items with identical scale values for each person measured.   As we have already said, the difficulty is largely avoided by using a fairly large number of items, thus tending to balance out individual inconsistencies.

Generalized Thurstone-type scales.—In order to escape the laborious task of constructing separate scales for measuring attitudes and beliefs about whatever object that might be of interest, Remmers and Silance (1934) proposed to develop "master" scales. The Thurstone scaling technique was followed; but instead of making the various propositions refer only to a single object in each scale, the statements were generalized, so that they could be applied with equal meaning to a wide variety of objects.

The advantage of such master scales is obvious. They permit the measurement of attitudes and opinions toward virtually any object, without the time-consuming and expensive process of constructing and standardizing a scale adapted solely to that object. There is, also, a tendency in the development of generalized statements to make them fairly simple. This may help to make the scales more easily understood by the less well educated.

Remmers and his coworkers have made extensive use of such master scales in measuring attitudes toward a very wide variety of social institutions, policies, racial and national groups, occupations, etc. In many instances the reliabilities of such measurements have been approximately as high as those made on the basis of scales designed directly for a single object. In some cases, however, the reliabilities have been below minimal acceptable levels. One reason for this may lie in the difficulty of making any set of generalized statements apply with equal meaning to a wide variety of objects. A more serious cause may be in the rather indiscriminate application of such master scales to the measurement of all sorts of possible objects and issues. Certain attitudes and beliefs may simply not exist for most people (see our discussion on page 159 of Chap. V) despite the ardent wish of the experimenter to measure them. Measurement of such non-existent beliefs and attitudes will not, of course, yield high reliabilities. The implication of this latter point is clear, and it is important for an understanding of attitude measurement. The actual attempt to quantify an attitudinal dimension should follow rather than precede the ascertaining of whether or not the dimension does meaningfully exist. And this ascertaining will usually necessitate an investigation of the cognitive structure of the individual pertaining to the object in question, by the analysis of reports of his immediate experience, by indirect indications in his behavior, or by whatever else. This is, of course, as true of the use of individual scales as it is of master scales.

Murphy, Murphy, and Newcomb (1937) point out that the tendency toward simplification in the wording of generalized statements for the master scales if carried to its logical extreme might lead to such items as, "I think . . . is lovely," "I think . . . is terrible." We see how in fact the master scale tends to converge on the method of self-rating (see below) in which the individual reports directly on the status of his belief or attitude.

That the master scale when applied to a given object does not necessarily measure the same thing as a scale specially designed to measure that object is seen in the study of Dunlap and Kroll (1939). They found that a generalized Remmers scale applied to measurement of attitude toward war correlated only .28 with scores on the Droba scale.

The Likert Method of Scale Construction.—A somewhat different approach to the scaling of attitudes has been made by Likert (1932) in his study of attitudes toward imperialism, toward internationalism, and toward the Negro. His procedure, which differs from the Thurstone technique in several important ways, involves the following steps: (1) the collection of a large number of statements or propositions either referring directly to or considered by the experimenter as likely to relate to the object in question; (2) the applying of these statements to a group of subjects who indicate for each statement their reaction of *strongly approve, approve, undecided, disapprove,* or *strongly disapprove;* (3) the summation for each individual of responses to all the items, by scoring the above five categories 5, 4, 3, 2, and 1, respectively; (4) the examination of the amount of correlation between each item and the total score; (5) the elimination of items that fail to correlate to a substantial degree with the total score, *i.e.,* that do not hang together with or measure the same thing as the other items in the test.

It has been observed above that the necessity for agreement among the experts as to the proper scale placement of the item requires that the manifest content of an item refer rather directly to the object of measurement. In the Likert method, on the other hand, this necessity is not so great. Even if the manifest content of an item does not refer directly to the object in question, it can—by its correlation with the total score of the other items—be proved diagnostic and included in the scale.

The Likert approach is somewhat more pragmatic than the Thurstone. The latter technique seeks to develop a rational scale, whereas the former selects items in terms of how well they work. The difference can be seen, in one way, in Likert's study on attitudes about foreign affairs. He started with many propositions referring to foreign affairs, and on the basis of the intercorrelation of items with other items he discovered that the entire set of items could be separated into two constellations, one referring to attitudes about imperialism and the other referring to attitudes about internationalism. The correlation between these two clusters was .63.

Comparative value of the Thurstone and Likert methods.—The relative merits of the Thurstone and Likert methods of scale construction can be examined in several aspects: ease of construction and use, amount of information, reliability and validity, meaningfulness of scores.

As to ease of construction and use, it is doubtful that either one has an appreciable advantage over the other. One requires an original group of judges; the other requires a preliminary group of subjects on whom the items are to be statistically intercorrelated. The scoring of neither method is particularly laborious.

As to amount of information, the advantage seems to lie with the Likert approach, which gets a five-point judgment on each item rather than the mere acceptance or rejection of the Thurstone item. This may permit a certain amount of use of the individual items for specific analysis of their content. The items in a Likert scale, that is, can be made to serve a dual function—to provide data on the individual's opinions and attitudes about the specific issue covered by the single item as well as a total score on the attitude or opinion dimension being studied. The Thurstone items cannot readily serve this double function.

As to reliability, there is no sharp difference in the methods, with the Likert method perhaps holding a slight edge. Concerning the more important question of relative validity, there is little definitive evidence. Both methods have been widely used in experimental investigations of all sorts, and both methods have demonstrated their usefulness.[1]

As to meaningfulness of scores, there would appear to be a real difference. The scores yielded by the Likert method have little absolute significance. Scale scores can be interpreted only in terms of where the individual falls in relation to the total distribution of such scores. Extent of pro-ness or con-ness is purely relative to the population of people that has been measured. Thurstone-scale scores, on the contrary, may be regarded as somewhat more absolute and more rational, having meaning independent of the scores of other people in the population.

This point requires some elaboration. That the Thurstone-scale scores can be regarded as having something of this absolute and rational significance depends upon the objectivity of the original judges in their placement of the items. Is the scale value, in other words, a function of the absolute meaning of that item as viewed by the judge in relation to the entire dimension of the attitude lying between one extreme and the other? That is, of course, the intended task of the judge. But we must ask the additional and significant question, can the judge actually make such absolute judgments, *regardless of his own attitude on the question?* To put it more directly: A scale may be asserted to have a higher degree of absoluteness to the extent that there is agreement among the judges *regardless of their own attitudinal bias* as to the place on the scale that each item belongs. Whether or not judgments of scale position are actually independent of the judge's attitude is obviously a matter for experimental investigation.

[1] One of the most comprehensive uses of the Likert-type scale was in the research of Rundquist and Sletto (1936) in measuring attitudes of morale during the depression.

There have been a number of investigations of this question, and the results of these studies are consistent. Studies by Hinckley (1932), Ferguson (1935), and Pintner and Forlano (1937) are representative. In the Hinckley investigation a group of Southern white students who were prejudiced against the Negro and a group of Northern white students who were favorable toward the Negro each sorted 114 statements about the Negro into 11 piles, supposed to be indicative of various degrees of favorableness and unfavorableness. The correlation between scale positions of the items assigned by the two antagonistic groups was .98. Unquestionably the attitude of the individual judge had nothing to do with his judgment as to the proper placement of an item on the attitude continuum.

(This demonstrated independence of scale position of items and attitude of the judge lends considerable weight to the view that the Thurstone items and the Thurstone-scale scores have some degree of absolute significance for the attitude continuum, without reference to the scores of the population as a whole) But in a larger sense they are still *relative* to the general cultural frame of reference. What is "extreme" in one culture may not be so in another.

This finding, also, bears in an interesting way on the question of the feasibility of measurement of individual attitudes (see the discussion on page 209). (For an individual to be able to rate his own individual attitude in a useful way as far as measurement is concerned means that he should be able to do it in reference to some absolute standards, independent of his own attitude. The above evidence seems to argue that individuals do, indeed, have such absolute standards.)

The Guttman Method of Scale Construction.—Recently, in connection with War Department research on the morale of American soldiers, Guttman has developed a new technique for the scaling of attitudes.[1] (The prime objective of this scaling technique is to determine first whether or not the attitude in question is "scalable," *i.e.*, if a sufficiently large proportion of the population being measured responds to the scale items in a consistent way. *The criterion of consistency is that endorsement of a given item is accompanied by endorsement of all other items that are less extreme and rejection of all items that are more extreme.* The Guttman method includes a "scalogram" device for ascertaining the degree of consistency that is present)

(When sufficient consistency of this sort is demonstrated by the set of items the scale is obviously undimensional and can be expected to yield reliable measures. If a set of items is found to lead to inconsistent responses, on the other hand, the inference is that there is more than one dimension underlying the scale.) In this case, the method provides a means whereby

---

[1] Detailed description of the method can be found in Guttman (1941, 1944). The best critical appraisal of the method is by Festinger (1947).

the offending items can be eliminated and the scale purified until it meets the criterion of consistency. Often in practice this means that the final set of items may be in the nature of very slight variations on the same theme. As Festinger (1947) remarks, this may limit its practical usefulness:

Limited experience with its use in public opinion research with civilian populations has tended to show that it becomes an unwieldy instrument. In interviewing people, maintaining good rapport and the interest of the interviewee are important considerations. The process of asking as many as ten questions, all of which are, to a large extent, rephrasings of the same thing, is a considerable strain on relations between interviewer and interviewee. Most of those engaged in this type of research will probably find the inclusion of a series of questions which could be subjected to scale analysis not feasible from practical considerations. In connection with standard paper and pencil attitude tests, however, scale analysis offers the promise of considerable improvement in our measuring instruments.

It should be noted that the above criticism pertains with equal force to other scale methods, such as those of Thurstone and Likert, inasmuch as they, too, depend upon the asking of a considerable number of closely related questions about the same thing. How this difficulty is avoided in large-scale public opinion measurement will be seen in the following chapter.

The Bogardus Social Distance Scale.—Early in the work on attitudinal measurement Bogardus (1925) designed a now classic technique for the specific purpose of measuring attitudes toward nationalities and especially to compare attitudes toward different nationalities. His so-called social distance scale was made up of a number of statements selected, on an a priori basis, to elicit responses indicative of the threshold of acceptance of any nationality group.

The instructions for the scale read as follows: "According to my first feeling reactions, I would willingly admit members of each race (as a class, and not the best I have known, nor the worst members) to one or more of the classifications under which I have placed a cross." For each nationality to be measured, seven classifications are offered, *viz.*,

1. To close kinship by marriage
2. To my club as personal chums
3. To my street as neighbors
4. To employment in my occupation
5. To citizenship in my country
6. As visitors only in my country
7. Would exclude from my country

The classifications progress in an orderly way from that implying a willingness to accept a fairly close degree of relationship with the nationality to that implying a willingness to accept only an extremely remote relationship or none at all. (The individual's attitude toward the nationality is then measured by the closeness of tolerated relationship. In practice, in applying the scale, it has been found that there are relatively few reversals, *i.e.*, cases in which a nationality is accepted by an individual for a closer relationship and rejected by him for a more remote relationship (*e.g.*, accepting Turks to close kinship by marriage but rejecting them as neighbors on his street).

It is possible with the social distance scale to compare different people's attitude toward the same nationality or to compare a single individual's attitudes toward various nationalities. It has been widely and successfully used for these purposes in social psychological research, and without drastic modification.[1]

Evaluation of the Bogardus scale.—How, theoretically, does the social distance scale differ from the Thurstone-type or Likert-type scales? Does it measure the same things but simply in another manner, or does it measure something entirely different? Is there an advantage in this technique over the others or not? Can this technique be used where the others do not apply? Let us evaluate the social distance scale in light of such questions.

First, let us observe that the Bogardus scale does not involve judgments of the general negativity or positivity of an object (*i.e.*, the nationality group) by the individual. All it does on the manifest level is to elicit expressions of the degree of feeling of social distance from the object. Now, of course, to the extent that there is a correlation between social distance and general attitude toward the object, the Bogardus scale will yield attitudinal measures as well. And to this extent the relative placement of a nationality group on a social distance continuum should correspond to the placement of the nationality on a continuum of the Thurstone or the Likert type.

Without question such a correlation is positive, but far from perfect. Social distance from an object may in some cases be markedly independent of the general affectivity of the object. In most applications of the Bogardus scale, the English are found to be less distant than the French, yet it is quite apparent that at times, at least, the degree of negative feeling toward the English is much more intense than toward the French. Social distance is a complex quality, related in the most intimate way to the ego standards of the individual, his conceptions of prestige in the eyes of the group, etc. Even though a man may hate the English and place them in an extreme negative position on an attitude scale of the Thurstone or Likert type, he might not reject them as residents in his own street. On the other hand, he might feel an indifferent affectivity toward "Brombinians" (a non-existent group which might be asked about by the experimenter) but would

---

[1] Bogardus (1933) has presented certain revisions in the scale.

place them far down on the social distance scale, being unwilling to see them on his own street or perhaps even in his country because he considered them "foreign." ⟨ *The one would involve no feeling of lowered social prestige, whereas the other would.*⟩ One of the important technical features of the scale is that it requires the person to make judgments in terms of life situations that involve a relation to himself.

With appropriate modifications, this type of scale might be developed for use with practically any kind of object. One adaptation of the Bogardus technique has been made by Crespi (1944) in the form of a "Social Rejection Thermometer" for measurement of attitudes toward conscientious objectors. The scale statements were as follows:

1. I would treat a conscientious objector no differently than I would any other person, even so far as having him become a close relative by marriage.
2. I would accept conscientious objectors only so far as having them for friends.
3. I would accept conscientious objectors only so far as having them for speaking acquaintances.
4. I don't want anything to do with conscientious objectors.
5. I feel that conscientious objectors should be imprisoned.
6. I feel that conscientious objectors should be shot as traitors.

It is notable that in building this scale Crespi found it necessary to include steps 5 and 6, which go beyond a mere statement of psychological "distance" from the object. This confirms our general point that the social distance scale is really not a pure attitudinal measure. The most extreme negative *attitude* requires something more than mere remoteness of the object; it also involves (as is implied in items 5 and 6 above) a desire for punishment or hurt or destruction of the object.

Another variant of the social distance scale is that of Dodd (1935) who constructed the following five-step scale to measure attitudes toward 15 national, 11 religious, 5 economic, and 3 educational groupings in the Near East:

1. If I wanted to marry, I would marry one of them.
2. I would be willing to have one as a guest for a meal.
3. I prefer to have one merely as an acquaintance to whom one talks on meeting in the street.
4. I do not enjoy the companionship of these people.
5. I wish someone would kill all these individuals.

The social distance scale as it now stands seems to include two different types of reactions of the individual: (1) his relative willingness or unwillingness to be exposed to the object, (2) his relative willingness or unwillingness to be identified with the object.) If Iranians are rejected from the person's club, it may be that he does not want to be forced into contact with them or that he does not want people to identify him with them or both. The latter aspect seems to show the greatest promise for further methodological exploitation. A generalized scale for measurement of the threshold of tolerated closeness of identification with a wide variety of objects might be developed.

What such a technique could provide would be measures that reflect genuine attitudinal dispositions beyond mere opinions. Opinions (as was pointed out in Chap. V) may be quite free of self-involvement and emotionality; objects or issues with which the person rejects or welcomes personal identification are probably those involving emotion and hence are in the nature of attitudes.

The Rank-order Scale.—In making comparisons of the relative negativity or positivity of attitude or opinion toward a set of similar objects, such as nationalities, political ideologies, politicians, occupations, etc., it is possible to employ a method of *ranking*, in which the individual ranks the objects from most favored or approved or accepted to least favored or approved or accepted. This method is particularly useful when it is desired to obtain relative attitudes or opinions among a whole set of objects, and it may sometimes be useful in a special way if it is desired to elicit opinions toward a single object without revealing to the individual the especial interest in that object. For example, a workman might be asked to rank all his working associates in order of efficiency, with the real object of determining only his opinion toward his foreman's efficiency.

The rank-order method is limited to cases that permit such a meaningful ranking of a number of comparable objects, as, for example, in preferential voting for a set of political candidates.

The Method of Paired Comparisons.—Related to the method of ranking is another technique in which the individual makes a series of judgments as to the relative favor, approval, or agreement of a number of objects taken a pair at a time.[1] To start with the simplest case of only two objects, such as two nationalities, the technique would require a judgment of which of the two is held in higher favor. This then would provide for an ordering of these two objects. With more objects than two, each object is compared separately with each other object, and a final scaling of the objects is possible on the basis of how each object stands in relation to all the rest.

With a sizable number of objects, the method becomes unduly laborious. Thus, for example, in Guilford's (1931) study in which 15 nationality groups

---

[1] The method of paired comparisons in attitude measurement was first developed and applied by Thurstone (1927, 1928).

were rated, a total of 105 separate comparisons had to be made by each person.

The method of paired comparisons can yield for the whole group of subjects not only the ranking of the various objects but something in addition about the distance between any two objects on the scale. This is done by taking the percentage of overlap in paired comparisons of the two objects as a measure of distance on the scale. Thus, if the percentage of people judging Turks to be less preferred than Armenians is the same as the percentage judging the French to be less preferred than the Irish, it might be said that the scale distance between Armenians and Turks is equal to that between Irish and French. In order to be clear about what is implied by "equality" of scale units we shall have to turn our attention to this and certain other problems in the interpretation and use of scales.

Problems in the Interpretation and Use of Scales.—We have seen that there are certain differences and certain similarities in the Thurstone, the Likert, the Guttman, the social distance, the rank-order, and the paired comparisons scales. In interpreting and using all these varieties of scales it is necessary to consider several problems: the equality of units on the scales, the zero point of the scales, the unidimensionality of the scales.

Equality of units on the scales.—Equality of units along an attitude scale is, for obvious reasons, an important desideratum. Thurstone attempted to achieve equality of units by requiring his judges to place the items in 11 piles at "equally appearing" intervals along a continuum. By this procedure it was hoped to make the final scale values of the items reflect this homogeneously spaced scale. It is probably safe to say that the Thurstone technique does help to make for greater equality as conceived by judges. Whether or not this "judged" equality of units of an attitude dimension carries other implications of equality is a moot question.

"Equality" might be defined in quite different ways. For example, it might be defined in terms of the degree of change along the attitude continuum under the influence of some standard force. That is, if it were established that under the influence of a uniformly applied piece of suggestion or propaganda or educational material people shifted from point A on an attitude scale to point B as readily as other people shifted from point C to point D, it might then be asserted that the scale distance between A and B is equal to that between C and D. This definition of equality would clearly not be comparable to the judged equality of the Thurstone scale. The superiority of one definition over the other would depend upon the particular use and interpretation one wished to make of the scale scores.

There is no attempt to ensure equality of units in the Likert scale or in the Bogardus social distance scale. In the latter, for instance, there is no reason to suppose that the difference between accepting a nationality to one's street as neighbors and accepting them to employment in one's occupation is equal to the difference between accepting them to employment in one's occupation and accepting them to citizenship in the country.

There seems, in general, to be no good evidence to argue that we are dealing with truly equal units in the attitude scales now in use. A unit difference at one place on the scale is not necessarily equal to a unit difference at another place. That this is true makes difficult the quantitative manipulation of scale scores; we are not entitled, for instance, to average the the scale scores for a given individual from several different scales; nor are we permitted to compare positions on one scale with positions on another, except in a rather crude fashion.

What, then, it may be asked, does such scaling accomplish? What is the use of such scales if we cannot compare scores on two different scales, if we cannot average scores from several scales, if we cannot say that difference of a given amount in one region of a scale is the same as that scale difference in another region?

The answer is that these scales do provide, at the very least, a reliable way of differentiating people in rank order along an attitude or opinion continuum. Thus, if a scale is reliable, it is possible to say with assurance that individual A is more extreme than individual B, who is, in turn, more extreme than individual C, and so on. There is some justification, moreover, for the averaging of the scale scores of groups of people, so that one group can be compared with another group. Such averaging should usually be done by computation of the median, which is the scale score that exactly divides the group into halves.

It is possible, therefore, to compare the attitude or opinion score of individuals and of groups of individuals. Also, it is possible to evaluate changes in the scores of individuals or groups, as a result of experimentally induced effects or of other influences tending to modify opinions and attitudes.

But in making such comparisons it is important to remember the inherent limitations of scales without equal units. An individual with an attitude score of 8 cannot necessarily be assumed to fall exactly halfway between two other individuals having scores of 6 and 10. Nor can he be assumed to have twice as strong an attitude as an individual with a score of 4. Suppose, for another example, that we wish to compare the average attitude scores of two groups before and after the application of opposite types of propaganda. To begin with, the two groups are equal in average scale score. Following the propaganda, one group is observed to have moved three points in one direction, and the other group three points in the opposite direction. We are not entitled to conclude that the opposing types of propaganda have been equally effective in changing attitudes, since we do not know for certain that a shift of three scale points in the minus direction is equal to a shift of three points in the plus direction. All that we can safely infer is that the effect was opposite in direction. On the other hand, suppose that the two effects are in the same direction, one being three units and the other five units. In this case, we can safely conclude that the one effect was greater than the other (subject, of course, to the usual statistical tests of significance of the difference) because a shift of plus five involves the same plus three units of the one group in addition to two more units of shift.

The zero point of scales.—It has been pointed out in Chap. V (see page 152) that one attribute of an attitude is its sign. (A person's attitude may always be characterized as pro or anti, for or against the object. Opinions, similarly, are usually separable into two classes, in favor of or opposed to, accepting or rejecting, the object of belief.)

The very existence of sign in attitudes and opinions implies that there must be a point on each scale where the sign changes. This point is the zero point, or neutral position, of the scale. To one side of the zero point attitudes grow more positive; to the other side they grow more negative. Right at the zero point, attitudes can be characterized as neither positive nor negative. *In fact, having no sign they cannot be called attitudes.* Attitudes are always positive or negative in some degree.)

(The precise determination of zero points of scales is of considerable importance in the measurement of attitudes and opinions. Whether a person's attitude or opinion falls slightly to the positive or slightly to the negative side of the zero point may make for critical differences in his behavior.) Just as an iota of added weight on one side of an object in balance may bring the object tumbling down in that direction, so may a slight increment in the negative attitudinal direction result in a negative vote against a political candidate. (The zero point has something of the character of a point of unstable equilibrium.) It may often be decisive for further attitude and opinion development just where in reference to the zero point, whether slightly to the left or slightly to the right, the person's opinion falls. And this may be particularly true under the sudden influence of a new situation in which a crystallization or polarization of attitudes and opinions is called for. (A person standing slightly to the left may tend in a crisis situation, other things being equal, to swing more strongly to the left than to the right, and vice versa.)

(Not many people will be expected to fall precisely *at* the zero point in a scale; that is why it can be called a point of unstable equilibrium.)(There seems to be something in the nature of a natural process of crystallization or polarization in attitude and opinion formation that works against the maintenance for long of an entirely neutral opinion or of an attitude that is only very slightly positive or negative.[1]

The types of scales we have reviewed, *e.g.*, the Thurstone and Likert types, do not satisfactorily meet this requirement of determination of a zero point. The Thurstone scale does, to be sure, make an attempt in this direction. It will be recalled that in ascertaining the scale values of items, the original judges assigned the items to 11 piles, including a middle, or neutral, pile. It can be argued, therefore, that middle scores in the Thurstone-type scale are an approximation of zero points. But how psychologically meaningful are such middle scores? Will middle scores on a Thurstone scale correspond to a point of psychological neutrality as perceived by the individual himself? To these questions Riker (1944, 1945) addressed a study that compared the scores of college students on six Thurstone scales (attitudes toward the Negro, the Germans, the treatment of criminals, capital punishment, evolution, and Communism) with their scores on an 11-point self-rating scale. The scores from the two types of scales showed sufficiently large differences to imply that the neutral, or zero, point in the two might not be identical. That is, a group with an average scale position defined as neutral on the Thurstone scale might not rate themselves as neutral in the attitude. It should be granted, nevertheless, that the presumptive evidence favoring the assumption of the middle score as a true zero point is, as McNemar (1946) has said, "far greater for the Thurstone type of scale than for the less rational scales for which the neutral points are arbitrarily designated as the mid-point of the possible scoring range."

In the Likert and other "less rational" scales, the interpretation of a zero point becomes highly ambiguous. The middle point of the possible scoring range is arbitrarily determined as a function of the assignment of scores of 5, 4, 3, 2, and 1 to the five categories of response to each item and as a function of the weighting of the various items. And the score of a given individual, who falls at the middle point of the scoring range, can be achieved in two quite different ways: (1) by taking a neutral position on most or all of the items; (2) by taking a strongly favorable position on some items and a strongly unfavorable position on other items.

This leads us to a consideration of how a zero score is to be psychologically interpreted once it is established on any of our scales. For attitudes, a

---

[1] An investigation by Thouless (1935) throws light on this process of "polarization." He has found that in the case of beliefs about religion people tend to fall into a bimodal distribution, either clearly accepting or rejecting religion. Few people in his study tend to assume a neutral, or zero point on the scale.

zero score simply means there is no attitude. For opinions, it would seem that zero score might mean any one of the following: (1) that the person is truly "neutral"; he is neither pro nor con, he is undecided; (2) that the person is strongly in favor of some aspects of the issue and strongly opposed to others, thus his position balances;[1] (3) that the person has no opinion whatsoever, *i.e.*, the object of the belief does not even exist for him.

It is the first of these meanings of "neutral" which is most appropriate for psychological analysis. The second introduces another problem—the unidimensionality of the scale. A neutral score which is obtained by a nice balancing of pro and con judgments may represent an artifact as far as the particular scale is concerned. It may mean that the total score is a combination of two scores, relating to two different opinions. Thus, the scale is not unidimensional.

The third of the above interpretations of neutral, or zero, point raises the most serious problems. It is obviously meaningless to measure something that does not exist, yet that frequently happens in opinion and attitude measurement as a result of the indiscriminate application of all sorts of scales to all sorts of people without an adequate preliminary analysis of their beliefs and attitudes. People will cooperate (in the classroom, laboratory, and clinic they are frequently coerced to do so) in filling out questionnaires, making marks on paper, etc., even concerning things about which they know nothing or feel nothing.

The upshot of our foregoing discussion is that the neutral, or zero, points of attitude and opinion continua cannot be ascertained in a direct way from the scales themselves. For crude purposes, of course, it may be sufficient to know that individuals falling somewhere approximately in the middle of a scale are probably fairly close to the region of the zero point. But for refined determination this will not suffice. To arrive at a more precise and more logical determination of the zero point, it is necessary to consider certain other related attributes of attitudes and opinions.

It is a matter of both empirical observation and logical analysis that there is a lawful relationship between the scale position that a person holds between the two attitudinal extremes and the intensity of his attitude. A person holding an extreme attitudinal position is likely to feel more intense, more emotional about it, than someone who holds a less extreme position. And similarly, a person holding a more extreme opinion is likely to feel more "certain" about it than one who holds a less extreme opinion. This relationship would be expected to be symmetrical in the positive and the

[1] This alternative is reminiscent of the definition of a "liberal" as one who is reactionary with respect to some issues and radical with respect to others—his final total position being "in the middle."

negative directions. If we were to plot the scale scores on the horizontal axis and the corresponding intensity or certainty values on the vertical axis, a U curve would result, intensities being lowest in the middle and highest at the extremes.

Guttman and Suchman (1947) make this relationship between scale position and intensity the basis for a refined way to establish the zero point of the scale. Their method involves the scaling of items by a new technique (see the discussion of the Guttman scale, page 220) and the ascertaining of the average intensity or certainty with which each item is approved or rejected by the sample of people being measured. The average intensity or certainty is plotted against the scale position of the item. As noted above, a U curve results. The zero point of the scale is then taken by Guttman and Suchman as the point where the lowest part of the U curve occurs. This approach to the establishment of a zero point of a scale is by far the most convincing that has yet been proposed. Its introduction of the intensity dimension in this connection makes particularly good psychological sense.

Unidimensionality of the scale.—The purpose of scaling and other methods of measuring attitudes and opinions is to arrange individuals in progressive order along some single continuum. People who obtain the same score on the scale are meant to be equal in the particular attitude or opinion that is being considered. If the items of the scale reflect other attitudes, in which the individuals differ, then the measurement of the desired attitude is likely to be imperfect. No single item, of course, could possibly be expected to reflect only one single attitude or opinion. The judgment of approval or disapproval of the item, "The government should provide free medical services for all people," for example, might be determined simultaneously by attitudes about socialism, bureaucracy, and humanitarianism, as well as beliefs about economic practicability, the state of public health, and the quality of the medical profession. This item might find a legitimate place in a scale devoted to the measurement of any one of these attitudes and opinions.

But if a scale is to measure attitude toward socialism, say, and this item is included, care must be taken not to include many other items that also might reflect some of these additional beliefs and attitudes covered by this item. Without this precaution, the final scale might turn out to measure attitude toward bureaucracy, for example, as well as attitude toward socialism. In such a case, it would be unclear whether two individuals with the same score on the scale were actually equal in attitude toward socialism or their apparent equality was a mere artifact of the one's stronger attitude toward bureaucracy balancing his weaker attitude toward socialism. Even if it is true that attitudes toward socialism and toward bureaucracy are positively correlated to a considerable extent, a measure based partly on one and partly on the other is not likely to be really satisfactory as a measure of either.

The greater the incidence of cases of checking noncontiguous items on a Thurstone scale the more it may be suspected that the scale departs from unidimensionality. That is, if the items are being reacted to on the basis of more than one attitude or opinion, it is not to be expected that the order of items measuring one attitude or opinion will be exactly the same as the order in measuring the other attitudes or opinions. This would produce the apparent inconsistencies in the checking of noncontiguous items. Dudycha's (1943) study of a Thurstone-type scale on attitudes toward war revealed that there were numerous instances in which items at disparate parts of the scale were endorsed by the same individual. That the Thurstone-type scale may sometimes suffer a lack of unidimensionality was also demonstrated in another way by Ferguson (1938) who by factor analysis found that more than one factor was necessary to account for the variability in individual scores on the above war scale.

The kind of item analysis involved in the Likert-type scale may be expected to aid in achieving unidimensionality. By intercorrelation, only those items which have something in common are retained for final inclusion in the scale. Sometimes, even the elementary precaution of this statistical approach to the purification of scales is neglected. It is not uncommon to find attitude "tests" or "scales" that are mere conglomerations of items chosen on an a priori basis as presumably referring to the attitude in question. Constructed in this hit-or-miss fashion, they are not likely to be reliable or valid, nor can they be expected to exhibit unitary character, measuring a single dimension of belief or attitude.

It should be understood, however, that there is nothing intrinsically improper in having an attitude test cover several different aspects of the attitude or belief, *providing these aspects are part of a constellation making up the belief or attitude*. In measuring a man's belief about democracy, for instance, we may necessarily include aspects relating to economic opportunity, political equality, and the rights and dignities of the human being, because all these go to make up his belief about democracy. They are not all the same thing, but they all combine to form the over-all belief. The scale is unidimensional in so far as it measures beliefs about economic opportunity, political equality, etc.

To put it another way, no one would object to a measurement of physical height of people that depended upon the number of inches from head to toe. Yet this total height is made up of heterogeneous parts: the lengths of the leg, the torso, the neck, etc. And these lengths are to a certain extent independent of one another. This scale is unidimensional when used to measure height of the whole person; it is multidimensional if used to infer the lengths of various parts of the body.

(What is to be avoided in a scale (and this is the reason for insistence upon unidimensionality) is the inclusion of irrelevant and confusing sources of variability.) We should not want our scale for the measurement of the man's belief about democracy to reflect in a systematic way his beliefs about religion, about foreigners, about education, or about anything else that was not for him an intrinsic and inseparable part of his belief about democracy. If it did so, it would be like a measuring instrument for height that yielded measures partly dependent upon the width of the object.

The Refinement of Scales.—(What is required in order to construct a simplified and purified scale is a careful preliminary analysis of the psychological object as it exists for the people to be measured. The aim of such analysis is to determine the relevant properties of the object, the different aspects in which it is viewed, and the interrelations of these aspects. This can best be accomplished through a study of the immediate experience of people in regard to the object, *i.e.*, through "introspective" reports elicited by questioning. (On the basis of such preliminary analysis of a sample of people, scales can be drawn up that are designed to measure attitudes and opinions concerning the object in such a way as to conform most closely to the relevant aspects of the object as it exists psychologically for people) Consistent with the continuous stress in this book on the perceptual and cognitive side of social analysis is the very great emphasis we place in attitude measurement upon the psychological description of the object. Little careful work has been done in this direction, and it constitutes one of the most promising and urgent fields for future research.

What such preliminary exploration of any object is likely to reveal is, as we have seen in Chap. V, that people differ among themselves in the aspects of the object which are psychologically present for them, in the relative importance of these aspects and in their interrelatedness. Take attitudes toward Soviet Russia, for example. A great many American people will be found to score strongly anti-Russian on an attitude scale. But the object of attitude may vary widely among these people. For some, Russia is the seat of communism and social chaos; for others, an imperialist threat to the rest of the world. For some, Russia is the organized menace to religion and godliness; to others, a ruthless dictatorship denying human individuality and freedom. People may, from these divergent points of view, agree in the intensity of their anti-Russian attitudes. But to lump them all together, without consideration of the aspect of the object that is uppermost for them and largely determining their attitudinal reaction, is meaningless and often positively misleading. For people are able to see most objects from several points of view; and as their frame of reference shifts, so may their attitudinal reactions. (In the prediction and understanding of the social behavior of an individual it is absolutely essential to consider which particular aspect is functional at the moment and what attitudinal dispositions are related to that aspect.)

One practical implication of the above arguments for refinement of scales is that the number of scales required for the measurement of a single object will require substantial increase if we are to be able to measure large and heterogeneous populations of people and to measure the various possible aspects in a pure and simple fashion. In practice, the task of such complete measurement may indeed become prohibitive. The solution may lie in reserving the use of pure attitude and opinion scales for the refined measurement of just those few aspects which, on the basis of cruder and less costly methods of preliminary exploration, have been isolated as the variables requiring very precise measurement. It will be pointed out in the next chapter that the method of intensive interviewing in public opinion research is especially helpful in ascertaining the general dimensions of attitudes and opinions as they exist in the population at large and thus setting the stage for the application of more precise measuring instruments at the critical points.

Is "reliability" a measure of "purity" of scales?—It seems often to be supposed that the purity of a scale may be ascertained by its statistical reliability, *i.e.*, by the consistency with which individuals score on different forms of the scale or on repeated applications of the same form. (It should be pointed out, however, that the mere fact that a scale has high reliability cannot argue anything about its purity, *i.e.*, whether or not it is measuring the same thing for all the people being tested.) A scale may be impure—measuring different things for different people—yet it may maintain these differences in a consistent way if repeated or if tested in comparable forms. Statistical statements of reliability are not adequate substitutes for psychological analysis of the object to which the scale is meant to pertain.

The naming of scales.—If the aim in purifying the scales is to make the object of measurement as homogeneous as possible for all the people being tested, should not the person be told what it is that the scale is supposed to measure? Would not this tend to ensure greater uniformity? These questions raise several points.

For one thing, it would indeed seem likely that the clear specification to the individual as to what is to be measured should in many cases ensure a selectivity among the beliefs or attitudes that determine the judgment of each item of the scale. That is to say, if the individual is informed what is the objective of the measurement, he will be better "set" in such a way as to bring only the relevant belief or attitude into play in making judgments of the items rather than permitting other, irrelevant ones to operate.

There is another important consideration, however. If the belief or attitude being measured is one involving repression by the individual or a desire to conceal his true feelings or a wish to conform to socially accepted stereotypes concerning the object, it may be poor procedure to name the scale. In connection with attitudes and opinions about sexual practices, religious matters, patriotism, etc., the individual might be expected to give more honest and more diagnostic responses to the scale items if he were unaware of the intention of the test. Thus, Stagner (1936a, 1936b) and Raskin and Cook (1938) have shown that some individuals who express a negative attitude toward Fascism itself will endorse items denoting a "fascist" attitude when the items are placed in a scale named "Opinions about the Depression."

A final point: It is sometimes argued, on the basis of such evidence as Stagner's above, that attitude scales should never be labeled. Such labeling, the argument goes, merely calls out stereotyped reactions to the word rather than revealing "real" attitudes. This argument is faulty in that it fails to recognize the importance, and often the critical importance in social behavior, of attitudes and opinions toward these "word" objects. The measurement of people's attitudes and opinions about fascism (and it is not to an empty word they are reacting, but to a whole pattern of real meanings to which this word is for them attached) may be of singular value in helping to understand and predict their social behavior. Whether the meanings they attach to fascism are the same or different from those ascribed to the term by political scientists, say, is a quite different problem. People may regard fascism as a bad thing and may have—if measured on a fascism attitude scale—a strong anti-fascist attitude; yet at the same time they may also accept and support specific things that someone else may characterize as fascist. Depending upon his objectives, therefore, an experimenter may wish to use a scale unlabeled, labeled, or both.

MEASUREMENT BY RATINGS

The essence of the scale method of measurement of attitudes and opinions is the objective scoring and summarization of the individual's responses to a considerable number of carefully standardized items. Another quite different approach to the measurement of attitudes and opinions is the method of rating, in which the quantification of the individual's belief or attitude is based upon the judgment of an expert, *e.g.*, a clinician, an interviewer, or a coder. Such measurement may be based on ratings by a single judge or on the average ratings of a group of judges.

The analogue of the scale method of measurement is the true-false examination, the scoring of which is an entirely objective and mechanical process. The analogue of the rating method is the essay examination, in which the scoring of the individual is done subjectively by the judging of the essay material by the person reading the examination.

Sources of Data for Ratings.—Ratings of opinions and attitudes may be made on the basis of data drawn from widely varied sources: (1) nonverbal behavior toward the object, (2) verbal statements relating to the object, (3) secondary expressive cues, (4) responses in clinical-type interviews, (5) personal documents, (6) responses on "projective" tests, (7) immediate experience.

Nonverbal behavior.—In certain obvious respects, ratings of attitudes and opinions based upon the overt, nonverbal behavior of the individual toward the object would seem to be the most attractive. What the person feels and thinks may be expected to be revealed in a simple and significant way in his direct behavior.

There are, unfortunately, rather serious limitations upon the applicability of this method of rating. The chief drawback is the virtual impossibility of relying upon the casual everyday behavior of the individual to provide significant instances of reaction toward the object in question. It may be nothing more than coincidental that the person is led in his daily activities to behave in a way revealing of the particular attitudes or opinions we wish to measure. A man's normal behavior might be observed faithfully over a long period without its providing concrete manifestations of his attitudes or beliefs toward Communism, the Good Neighbor Policy, or the theory of evolution.

There are, of course, exceptions to this. Some attitudes and opinions of social interest are concerned with objects likely to be involved in people's regular activities. There is ample opportunity in the usual behavior of many people to express attitudes and opinions by displaying positive or negative reactions toward such common social objects as policemen, foreigners, Jim Crow customs, picket lines, etc. Even in these special cases, however, there are additional difficulties. For one thing, although a great many people will normally be found in contact with the object of desired measurement, not all people in the sample may be. What is more serious, the specific nature of the psychological situation in which the object is encountered will differ from person to person. We know that behavior depends upon much more than attitudes and opinions, and hence we cannot rely upon behavior as a direct indicator of attitudes and opinions without a careful consideration of other aspects of the psychological situation. One man may be observed to talk good-naturedly to a colored bootblack, and another to refuse to ride in an elevator with a Negro. The former could not safely be rated as more favorable toward Negroes than the latter. The situations in which they were observed were incomparable.

We need then, ideally, the existence of overt behavior toward the given object by all people in the sample and under psychologically standardized conditions. An added practical requirement is that the actual observation of the behavior be feasible.

There are relatively few instances in which these three requirements are satisfactorily approximated, but in exceptional cases the very nature of social organization does make this kind of approach to measurement of attitudes possible. Voting behavior is a good example. Attitudes and opinions about political parties, candidates, and issues are expressed in the overt behavior in a polling booth on election day. And this is done by large proportions of the population and in a fairly standardized situation.

The attitudes and opinions of people toward various social rules, customs, and institutions may also be inferred on the basis of the conformity behavior with respect to them. F. H. Allport (1934) has been particularly interested in the measurement of such conformity behavior. Under his influence studies have been made of such behaviors as stopping an automobile at a red light, arriving at a place of work on time, and performing appropriate ritualistic acts on entering a church. There are difficulties in inferring attitudes directly from the observed strength or weakness of such conformity behaviors. Sometimes conformity to a social institution may signify a positive attitude, but sometimes not. Under repressive social forces an individual may conform unwillingly, being intensely negative in attitude. And nonconformance, though often indicative of a negative attitude, may sometimes really reflect a negative attitude toward the authorities who attempt to enforce conformity, rather than toward the institution itself.

How else may overt behavior be used as a basis for ratings of opinions and attitudes? One possibility is the observation of the person under contrived and standardized conditions of a quasi-laboratory or quasi-clinic nature. Considerable research has been done on the rating of the child's personality characteristics by observing his behavior in play situations and other "natural" situations involving other children, adults, and various other types of objects.[1] These techniques could doubtless be adapted to

---

[1] One of the earliest of such behavioral investigations was that of Hartshorne and May (1928), who observed children in standardized real-life situations designed to reveal traits of honesty and deceitfulness.

the rating of the child's attitudes toward given social objects (*e.g.*, Negroes) which are introduced into the situation.)

Wartime programs of assessment of the personality of men (OSS Assessment Staff, 1948) included the observation of behavior under standardized conditions, which approximated the psychological character of real-life situations. With appropriate modifications, as MacKinnon (1946) points out, such techniques could also be of value in revealing attitudes and opinions by inducing overt behavior toward given social objects under standardized and natural conditions.

Verbal statements.—(Many social objects toward which overt behavior is infrequent or impossible are of such a nature as to command verbal statements pertaining to them by the individual.) A man may rarely be in a position where he can, in overt, nonverbal terms, express his attitudes toward John L. Lewis, and he may never, because of its very abstractness, express his opinion about the Holy Ghost in terms of direct, overt action. But he can talk about these things, and what he says may be expected to provide a basis for rating his attitudes and opinions toward them.

Some of the same limitations that apply to the use of nonverbal behavior as a basis of ratings pertain also to the use of verbal material. It may not be possible to under ordinary everyday conditions enough instances where the individual expresses himself verbally about the object in question. The situations in which he does express himself, moreover, are not likely to be standard from person to person, and this makes difficult the direct inference of attitude from verbal statement. For these reasons, as well as the imposing technical difficulties in observing people's verbal behavior in everyday life, the practicability of this approach—like that of the use of overt behavior—is severely limited.

Just as in the case of overt behavior, the verbal statements can be elicited in a standardized way, *e.g.*, as in a questionnaire or interview. We will discuss this approach to ratings in a separate section.

Secondary expressive cues.—(Facial expressions, gestures, tone of voice, subtle nuances of phrasing, etc., constitute important sources of material for rating attitudes and opinions. It is commonplace that *what* a man says may be less revealing than *how* he says it.) These secondary cues are utilized in making ratings only in conjunction with the other sorts of data, such as overt verbal and nonverbal behavior toward the object or the answers in clinical and public opinion interviews or the responses to "projective" tests. It is frequently the case that the clinician or the interviewer places greater reliance on these secondary cues than he does upon the manifest content of what the individual says. As we shall presently see, it is one critical advantage of ratings made by public opinion interviewers over those made by coders on the basis of the interview reports that the interviewer is able to observe these secondary cues.

There seems to be little or no promise of objectifying the scoring of such cues in the measurement of attitudes and opinions in the way that there are hopes of objectifying the scoring of answers to questions, responses to projective tests, etc.   The meaning of secondary cues is intrinsically dependent upon the entire psychological context, and the proper meaning is likely to be best judged by an expert observer on the scene who can get the feel of the situation as it exists for the person.

Clinical-type interviews.—One of the most promising methods available for the rating of attitudes and opinions is the free, intensive, clinical-type interview.   In this method, the individual is guided by skillful nondirective techniques to discuss the objects in question and thus to reveal—often indirectly and unconsciously—his dispositions of attitudes and beliefs.

For the determination of all sorts of *personal* attitudes and sentiments, such as attitudes toward one's parents, toward oneself, etc., this method is widely used by clinical psychologists and psychiatrists.   It has been less widely used for the rating of *social* attitudes and opinions of a relatively impersonal sort.   A highly significant adaptation of the clinical-type interview to the measurement of attitudes and opinions of cross-section samples of the general public is found in the use of the "open-end" interview in public opinion research (see page 277).

Personal documents.—Allport (1942) has discussed the considerable potentialities inherent in personal documents of the individual as a basis for evaluation of numerous features of his personality.   As he considers it, the term *personal document* embraces among other things autobiographies, letters, diaries, and artistic and literary works.   As such, they comprise only one class of case study materials, *viz.*, documents in the "first person."   Allport writes:

As a self-revealing record of experience and conduct the personal document is usually, though not always, produced spontaneously, recorded by the subject himself, and intended only for confidential use.   Its themes naturally revolve around the life of the writer, its manner of approach is naturally subjective (phenomenological).   Such documents vary greatly in candor, scope, authenticity, and psychological value.   Sometimes they are deceptive and trivial; but sometimes they represent distillations of the most profound and significant experiences of human life. . . .   Personal documents are for the most part introspective protocols, adapted especially to the study of complexities of phenomenal consciousness.   Their use seems natural enough to psychologists who happen to be interested in complex phenomenal states.

Generally speaking, personal documents have been employed by psychologists in the diagnosis of personality problems.) Relatively little use has been made of them for the rating of the individual's attitudes and opinions toward social objects and issues.   There seems, however, to be no inherent prohibition upon this possible use, though the practical difficulties may be paramount.   Allport lists some of the major shortcomings in the use of personal documents, which would apply with equal force to the use of such personal records as the basis for ratings of opinions and attitudes: unrepresentativeness of the sample, nonobjectivity of the data, difficulty of ascertaining validity, intentional and unintentional deception by the person, unreliability due to momentary circumstances in which the person writes, relative scarcity of records, and expense of the method.

This last objection is particularly imposing if one is interested in large-scale attitude and opinion measurement, but it may not be irremediable if we are interested in a smaller scale study of a selected group of subjects for whom records are available.   This might be particularly true in an investigation of attitudes among a limited and known group of people as an attempt in "pure" social psychology to gain light on some basic principles concerning attitudes.

That not all of the other above difficulties are impossible to overcome for the use of personal documents in the evaluation of attitudes may be illustrated in two studies.   The first was by Stouffer (1930), who collected topical autobiographies from 238 subjects.   These 238 autobiographies were rated by four judges on a "graphic rating scale" (see page 245) in respect to the autobiographer's attitude toward prohibition.   An average intercorrelation of .96 was found among the judges' ratings.   The composite rating for the four judges was correlated with the scores on an objective attitude scale which measured attitude toward prohibition, and the "validity" coefficient was found to be .81.   The implication of the study is that independent judges can agree remarkably well on their ratings of an attitude based on personal document material and that their ratings coincide fairly well with another type of measurement of the same attitude.

The second illustrative study was concerned with the analysis of captured German civilian mail to ascertain various attitudes of people being subjected to strategic bombing.[1]   A random sample of mail originating in selected German cities was coded and rated for attitudes toward the Allies and toward the Nazi leadership and for opinions about the course of the war, the probable outcome of the war, etc.   The typical attitudes and opinions for a given community were then correlated with the objective facts about the extent and kind of bombing to which that community had been subjected

[1] This study by the Morale Division of the United States Strategic Bombing Survey in February, 1945, was under the direction of Dr. Herbert H. Hyman.

by the Allies. By this analysis a number of important relationships between bombing and attitudes were tentatively established. After cessation of hostilities the findings were verified on the basis of direct and more intensive interviewing of a cross section of the German civilian population.

It would seem that in special, and probably exceptional, circumstances personal documents may provide a basis for the rating of attitudes and opinions.

Projective methods.—Much attitude measurement and rating, especially that based on simple scales and on direct questioning, has been criticized as superficial, as dealing only with manifest verbal content, and as failing to reach into the deep, often unconscious dynamics of attitudes. This criticism is especially justified in connection with the measurement of those attitudes which are (1) asocial and hence not willingly revealed in public by the individual or (2) which have components that are repressed, being unacceptable to the individual's values and standards and hence not readily accessible to consciousness.

This same methodological problem arises in the study of motivation and personality in general. A partial solution there has been the development of *projective techniques.*[1]

It has been suggested that projective techniques might also be profitably used in the measurement of social attitudes, particularly those which prove inaccessible to other means of measurement. Very little work has, as yet, been done along this provocative line. The following studies constitute the principal research applications that have been made.

Proshansky (1943) adapted the Thematic Apperception Test[2] as a projective technique for the measurement of attitudes toward labor. He selected from magazines and newspapers a number of pictures that depicted various social conflict situations involving labor and that were ambiguous as to outcome as far as labor was concerned, *i.e.*, indicating neither victory nor defeat for the labor cause. Subjects (college students) were shown the pictures briefly one at a time and after each exposure were instructed to give a detailed account of what the picture represented and to make up a story about it. As Proshansky remarks,

This method clearly permitted autistic distortion at the time of the original perception, or retrospective falsification as attitude got in its work upon memory, or sheer elaboration of the meaning of the picture, consciously going beyond anything that the picture actually offered.

[1] See Chap. II, p. 49, for a discussion of projective methods in the study of motivation.
[2] Description of the Thematic Apperception Test and its use may be found in Murray (1938).

Two examples of responses to the same picture reported by Proshansky demonstrate the effectiveness of the technique in eliciting diagnostic remarks:

Home of a man on relief—shabby—dresses poorly. Scene is probably of a shack down South. Also might be the home of some unemployed laborer. Horrible housing conditions. Why don't the government provide for these people. The ordinary worker is always forgotten and allowed to rot.

Picture of one room, very messy, stove in center, woman on the left, man standing next to stove, couple of children near them. This is a room of what we call "poor people." They seem to be messy, sloppy people, who seem to enjoy dwelling in their own trash.

The responses to the pictures were rated by three expert judges as to the degree of antilabor or prolabor attitude revealed. These ratings for each subject were then correlated with his score on an attitude scale devised by Newcomb (1939) to investigate attitudes toward organized labor. The correlations between the projective test ratings and the Newcomb scale scores were .87 for one group of subjects and .67 for another group. It may be concluded, then, that such a projective technique involving perception and interpretation of pictures does serve to a substantial degree to differentiate people in the dimension of attitude toward labor also exemplified by the Newcomb scale.

Fromme (1941) has also tried out a set of pictures in the conventional Thematic Apperception Test technique of presentation and has found favorable comparisons with scores on a standardized attitude scale—the Survey of Opinion on Methods of Preventing War. The regular set of Thematic Apperception Test pictures has been profitably used by Frenkel-Brunswik and Sanford (1945) in their study of personality factors in anti-Semitism. They also experimented with four additional pictures designed to elicit direct reactions to racial problems. One of them represents Jewish-looking people in a poor district; another, an older Negro woman with a young Negro boy; the third, a young couple in zoot suits; and the fourth, a lower class man, apparently in great fear, confronted by a policeman holding a billy club.[1]

In a rather different approach to the use of projective techniques, Dubin (1940) found that it was possible to make fairly good predictions of scores on attitude scales toward labor, toward government, and toward war on the

---

[1] An earlier use of reaction to pictures was made by Horowitz (1936) who measured children's anti-Negro prejudice by their expressed readiness to participate in various kinds of depicted activities in which Negroes were present. Murphy and Likert (1938) presented photographs and motion pictures, the reactions to which were used for the measurement of attitudes. Both of these specific approaches were limited in that the visual material was well structured and allowed too little opportunity for the kind of free restructuring essential to the projective method.

basis of the individual's play construction with a set of toys, when instructed to represent "the world as you see it" and "the world as you would like to see it."

The most comprehensive use of various types of projective tests in the study of attitudes has been that involved in the program of personality exploration by Murray and his coworkers (1938). As part of this program, some attention was paid to the measurement of sentiments concerning such social matters as war and religion. Murray and Morgan (1945) describe the use of a variety of projective techniques in this measurement, including the standard Thematic Apperception Test pictures. In the study of religious sentiments by French (1947), already discussed (page 185), the Thematic Apperception Test pictures were used.

A more ambitious and more refined application of the interpretation of pictures as a projective technique in the measurement of attitudes is planned by Loeblowitz-Lennard and Riessman (1946). Their objective is the standardization of a set of ambiguous pictures dealing with all phases of social interaction. They would hope to be able to develop perfectly objective categories for the scoring and evaluation of responses to the pictures.

The studies reviewed above suggest rather clearly that projective techniques can serve to differentiate people with respect to their social attitudes. On a priori grounds, at least, it is to be expected that through such projective tests unconscious components of attitudes or secretly held attitudes can be measured more validly than by the conventional attitude questionnaire. To be useful as a mass testing instrument for attitude research, however, the projective technique must be developed and refined in two ways: (1) It must be simplified and standardized so that it can be applied economically and easily to people representative of all parts of the general population and in everyday, nonlaboratory situations; (2) its scoring must be objectified so that the attitudes of large numbers of people can be readily determined without the need of expert ratings of the projective responses by highly trained judges. Even if these two refinements prove impossible, however, and projective techniques prove impractical for large-scale use, such as in public opinion research, they will still, of course, be of critical value in the small-scale clinical and laboratory measurement of attitudes.

Immediate experience.—The immediate experience of the individual himself—his feelings, emotions, thoughts, perceptions—provides a unique and especially important source of data for the ratings of attitudes and opinions. These data are, of course, directly accessible only to the experiencing individual himself, and ratings based upon them must be *self-ratings*.

Self-ratings of Beliefs and Attitudes.—Among the various ways of measuring attitudes and opinions by ratings, *self-rating* occupies a place by itself. In self-rating, the individual himself is the judge, or "expert"; his task is to place himself at what he considers to be the proper point on the dimension of the belief or attitude being measured.)

The advantages of self-rating may also be its disadvantages. (Because of the very nature of the case, the individual is in the most strategic position to observe how he feels, thinks, and acts in relation to a given object, but for the very same reason he is also more susceptible than anyone else to being deceived by his own needs and his own point of view in trying to appraise his attitudes and opinions in an objective way.) For the rating of many of his attitudes and opinions, the judgment of the individual may be far superior to that of any other judge. In rating certain others, the individual's capacity for self-deception and distortion may be boundless.

(Self-rating is likely to break down when the rating is strongly governed by immediate needs of the individual. If an attitude is repressed, for instance, self-rating is obviously useless.) If the individual is unwilling to reveal his true attitude because he would regard its publication as prejudicial to his welfare, self-rating is, again, meaningless. (Thus, antisocial attitudes are poor material for self-rating, and one would not expect a personnel psychologist to ask prospective employees to rate themselves on undesirable attitudes toward the job, the employer, etc.) And if it fits the immediate needs of the person to believe that he is of one attitudinal persuasion rather than another and this causes "rationalization," "projection," and other "autistic" processes to occur, the self-rating will be distorted.

Another source of difficulty in self-ratings is that the individual, even if he is able to rate himself objectively, may not use a scale or standard that is comparable to that of other people who rate themselves. (His self-rating may be too high or too low as determined by the frame of reference of his judgment (see page 101, Chap. III, on the influence of frame of reference or adaptation level on judgments). A man may rate himself as "radical" in his political views, because his frame of reference is determined by the narrow range of political opinions in his restricted social environment, let us say that of his Republican business associates. Whereas, in terms of the norms of the population as a whole, the man might be rated by external observers as nothing more radical than "slightly left of center."

(Self-ratings that are made in terms relative to the attitudes and opinions of others may, as in the above example, be faulty because the person has a restricted sample of people around him who determine his norm.) They may also be faulty simply because the person is not able to make accurate judgments of other people's attitudes and opinions. In a Bennington College study, Newcomb (1943) found that students' judgments of the political attitudes and opinions of their classmates were often at wide variance with the facts.

Despite these various difficulties and limitations, self-ratings have been used widely and successfully in getting measures of the direction of attitudes and opinions, the intensity and certainty with which attitudes and opinions are held, the importance of the object or issue to the person, etc. For the measurement of some of these attributes of opinions and attitudes, the method of self-rating has proved to be the only satisfactory approach yet developed.

Types of Rating Scales.—Rating scales may be either *relative* or *absolute*. As examples of the former there are (1) the rank-order scale, and (2) the percentage of population scale; examples of the latter are (3) the graphic rating scale and (4) the specific category scale.

The rank-order scale.—In this type the judge is simply required to place the people being rated in a rank order from high to low on the attitude or opinion in question. A given individual's scale position is, therefore, relative to other people in the sample. The units of this scale are, of course, unequal; *i.e.*, the difference between third place and fourth place is not necessarily equal to the difference between fourth place and fifth place.

The principal usefulness of this type of rating is in studying the causes and correlates of gross differences of rank of people along such a dimension. It may be adequate, for example, in a study of the correlates of anti-Semitism to be able to class people of a given group as either more anti-Semitic or less anti-Semitic. These two differentiated classes may then be compared on a variety of relevant dimensions of other sorts and correlations determined. If the range of anti-Semitism within the whole group is slight, such relative differentiation by ranking may be too insensitive to reveal correlations that actually exist.

The percentage of population scale.—If we wish to rank only one person (as in self-rating) or each of a few people, ranking can be done by ordering the person to his proper percentage position in the whole population of such people. This is technically equivalent to assigning him a percentile score, which states what proportion of the entire population of such people the individual exceeds in that given dimension. Just as we characterize an individual as falling at the 90th percentile in scholastic aptitude, so may we judge him as falling at the 73d percentile in his anti-Semitism (*i.e.*, he is more anti-Semitic than 73 per cent of the people in the given population).

The main difficulty of this type of rating is that it requires the judge to have a fairly clear conception about the range and distribution of this attitude or opinion in the population as a whole.

The graphic rating scale.—If the rating is to be made in absolute terms, *i.e.*, without reference to group norms, one device is to require the judge to place a check mark at the appropriate position along a line that runs from one extreme of the attitude or opinion to the other. The simplest graphic scale provides labels for the end points and perhaps the neutral point. Others may have a number of distinguishing labels at regular intervals along the scale. The check mark can be placed at any point on the line.

The specific category scale.—Unlike the graphic scale, this type of scale requires that the rating be made in terms of a limited number of defined categories. The number of categories may vary, but usually scales of this kind consist of three, five, or seven categories, an equal number falling on either side of the neutral category.

Sometimes the description of the categories is no more than a verbal statement of different degrees of pro-ness or con-ness. For example:

1. Very much in favor of disarmament
2. Moderately in favor of disarmament
3. Uncertain about disarmament
4. Moderately opposed to disarmament
5. Very much opposed to disarmament

In other cases, the categories may be described in a way that includes more specific reference to the content of the attitude or opinion. For example:

1. Feels that disarmament should be carried out at once, that it is the only way to ensure peace; sees no good whatsoever in being armed
2. Feels that disarmament is probably a good idea, is for it on the whole but sees some dangers in it too
3. Feels that there is something to be said for disarmament, but just as much against it, undecided
4. Feels that on the whole disarmament is a dangerous thing to do, though recognizes that there are some good things to be said for it
5. Feels that disarmament would be entirely wrong, that it would endanger the country, that safety lies only in being armed

Although it is often difficult to phrase such verbal statements in a way that will make them easily applicable to all people who are to be rated, they usually prove of considerable help to the judge in his ratings and also help to make the standards for his ratings comparable to those of other judges.

"INDIRECT" METHODS OF MEASURING BELIEFS AND ATTITUDES

It was pointed out in the introductory discussion of this chapter (page 206) that "the measurement of beliefs and attitudes is necessarily indirect." This is true, but there are also *degrees* of indirection. Some methods of measurement involve an explicit, frontal approach to the attitude, such as in the scaling techniques, where the individual is required to respond to verbal items that refer directly to the object of the attitude or opinion, or such as in those rating techniques in which the individual reacts overtly to the object or makes direct verbal statements about it or rates himself.

Other methods of measurement may be relatively more "indirect," involving a concealed, flanking approach to the attitude or opinion. Instead of observing the manifestations of the attitude or opinion in governing action and judgments directly relating to the object, these indirect methods study the manifestations of the attitude as it affects action and perception and judgment of other objects which are somehow functionally connected with the object in question.

Indirect means of measuring attitudes are particularly crucial in the experimental investigation of the change of attitudes (see Chap. VI). The prototype of a study on attitude change has the following elements: (1) a measurement of the given attitude in the experimental group, (2) application of experimental conditions calculated to modify the attitude, (3) remeasurement of the attitude to establish the amount of change. The technical difficulty here is obvious. If the subject is aware that his attitude is being measured, it is unlikely that there can be a fair test of the experimental effect. What is needed is an "indirect" measurement.

A study by Asch, Block, and Hertzman (1938) gives an excellent illustration of an indirect measurement of change of opinions. The objective was to measure the change in people's opinions of the intelligence of an occupational group (*viz.*, politicians) under various conditions of suggestion. The technical problem was how to do this without revealing the intent of the experiment to the subject. The solution was made possible by the fact that opinion about intelligence of the occupational groups was found to be substantially correlated with opinion about the idealism, social usefulness, conscientiousness, and stability of character of these groups. These latter opinions could then be taken as indirect indicators of opinion about intelligence, and the results of experimentally induced changes in opinions about intelligence could be observed indirectly in changes in opinions about these correlated traits.

One of the principal advantages of such measurement by indirection is that it enables the experimenter to measure without tending to produce an effect on the attitude itself; direct measurements may be thought in some instances to produce changes of the thing being measured (a not uncommon problem in the general science of measurement). A second principal advantage lies in the possibility of concealing from the individual the intent of the measurement; this again may make for better determination. In all kinds of scientific measurement such an indirect approach is found useful.

What are its specific possibilities in the measurement of beliefs and attitudes?

We have already discussed one of the most important of the indirect methods, *viz.*, projective tests (page 240). Here the attitude or belief is measured in terms of the spontaneous organizing effects that it has on the perception of indifferently organized material. And it may be assumed that this projective process has no particular effect on the attitude itself and that it is relatively unconscious. Closely related to such projective measures are others that have to do with the effects of attitudes and beliefs in distorting logical material. A number of experimental studies have demonstrated that even such highly structured material as syllogisms may be markedly affected. That the course of syllogistic reasoning may be diverted by the attitudes and opinions of the individual has been used by Morgan and Morton (1943, 1944) and Morgan (1945) as an actual measurement device.

But such techniques as these do not in their present stage of development provide good means of quantifying beliefs and attitudes. They may serve to indicate the presence or absence or the sign of beliefs and attitudes, but they are too crude to provide quantitative measures of intensity and strength of the attitudes, etc.

There have been singularly few attempts to use these and other methods of measurement by indirection in the study of beliefs and attitudes. It would seem that this is an extremely fruitful area for future methodological research.

THE MEASUREMENT OF VARIOUS CHARACTERISTICS OF BELIEFS AND ATTITUDES

We have seen that the quantitative placement of a belief or an attitude along a dimension between the two extremes may be accomplished by scaling, by rating, and by indirect methods. Various other characteristics of beliefs and attitudes were discussed in Chap. V: kind, content, clarity, specificity, strength, importance, and verifiability. Each of these characteristics must be evaluated if the knowledge about an individual's beliefs and attitudes is to lead to the understanding and prediction of his behavior. The measurement of these various characteristics raises a number of technical problems which we shall now consider.

The Measurement of Kind, Content, Clarity, and Specificity.—The method *par excellence* for the determination of these aspects of beliefs and attitudes is that of questioning the individual and analyzing his introspective reports of his immediate experience (the "phenomenological" approach). What is required is to arrive at a full picture of the specific cognitive structure as it relates to the object of the belief or attitude and of the broader cognitive structure as it relates to the interconnections of this belief or attitude with other beliefs and attitudes.   No other technique seems even remotely to be able to meet the demands of this sort of comprehensive description of the cognitive structure.   To arrive at anything approaching a complete account of what the "Negro" or "Communism" or "free enterprise" means to the individual by simply observing his behavior or by asking him to respond to 20 scale items would be manifestly impossible.   What is needed is the most intensive, searching, and prolonged investigation of cognitive contents, and there is no short cut to this goal.   The contents of an individual's beliefs and attitudes about a single object, Adolf Hitler, for example, might be so detailed and complex as to require many hours to describe.   And not only is it necessary to ascertain the contents and the clarity of the contents, it is also important to ascertain the structure of relationships of this belief and attitude toward Hitler with the other beliefs and attitudes that the individual holds, *i.e.*, to determine how specific or how generalized, how isolated or how interconnected this belief or attitude is.   The psychoanalyst spends hundreds of hours eliciting material that serves to describe the individual's emotional complexes.   It does not seem extravagant to suppose that several dozen hours might be profitably devoted to the building up of a full account of the individual's beliefs and attitudes about some important social object.

There has not, to our knowledge, been any study of beliefs and attitudes that approached this intensive degree of investigation of the nature, clarity, and specificity of cognitive contents.   The reason is not hard to find.   The technical problems involved are most formidable.   For one thing, the expenditure of time and energy on this kind of investigation of the beliefs and attitudes of a very small number of people about a very limited range of objects would be considerable.   For another thing, methods for the analysis and synthesis of such large quantities of specific information about beliefs and attitudes have not been developed.   And for a third thing, it would seem unlikely that the beliefs and attitudes of all kinds of people in the population could be investigated to this degree of comprehensiveness, simply because there would be no easy basis for obtaining the cooperation of people in general.

As a compromise between this ideal of very full investigation of cognitive structure of beliefs and attitudes and no such investigation at all, there has been developed in public opinion research the technique of the open-end, intensive interview (see page 277).   And for the investigation of certain questions of a "pure" scientific nature about the psychology of beliefs and attitudes, these above limitations are not so critical.   It is perfectly feasible that a small number of persons might be intensively studied over a long period of time in the laboratory or clinic, in an attempt to answer theoretical questions about how beliefs and attitudes develop, how they change, how they interrelate with other beliefs and attitudes, how they affect behavior, etc. It seems possible that the next major advance in the field of belief and attitude research will come along these lines.

An interesting step in this direction is a proposed study by Smith, Bruner, and White (1947) on the dynamics and measurement of opinion about Russia. The objective of this group research project is to arrive at a deeper understanding of the dynamics of opinion, its dimensions, its organization, and its function in personality and to develop methods suitable for studying these dynamics in opinion polling situations. The procedure of the study involves the intensive study of 10 adult subjects concerning their opinions about Russia and related topics. These subjects are each given about thirty hours of testing and interviewing, a considerable part of which is designed to throw light on the broader aspects of the individual's personality. Opinions about Russia are studied by a variety of techniques, including a lengthy open-end interview; an information test on Russia; a typical life history written by the person; an opinion-poll questionnaire; projective tests, including political cartoons about Russia; a stress interview in which the person's opinions are attacked; experimental social situations in which the person can be observed as he expresses his opinions normally. The data are appraised by a group of social psychologists, clinicians, and anthropologists. The importance of the study is summed up by Smith, Bruner, and White as follows:

If the present research program has distinctive merit, it lies in the wedding of the clinical and survey approaches. The intensive study of ten cases alone could establish few general conclusions about the dynamics of opinion. Yet from such a study which is truly exploratory, may emerge insights which can broaden the scope and usefulness of briefer opinion survey procedures. Understanding the nature and roles of opinion in a few well-studied individuals should raise the pertinent research questions to be attacked in the study of the wider group, as well as suggesting appropriate techniques for answering them.

An additional word might be said about the measurement of specificity of beliefs and attitudes. To study specificity is to study systems of beliefs and attitudes. One approach to this is the direct one of having the individual describe the relationships he perceives among his beliefs and attitudes, how he apprehends them as forming meaningful clusters and constellations. Another quite different approach is the *statistical* one, in which the various beliefs and attitudes of people are intercorrelated and their patterns thereby revealed. This method has the advantage that it can get at patterns about which the individual is unaware. But it has the disadvantage that patterns which are unique to the individual cannot be discovered. Both the introspective and the statistical approach to the measurement of specificity would seem essential.

The Measurement of Strength.—Beliefs and attitudes vary in strength, *i.e.*, in tendency to resist change. For all of the practical and theoretical problems concerned with change of beliefs and attitudes, it is obvious, therefore, that the measurement of this attribute of strength is exceedingly important. Strength is clearly not entirely independent of all other attributes of beliefs and attitudes, and to a certain extent the degree of strength may be inferred from these other measures. (For example, strength is probably positively correlated with extremeness of opinion or attitude; *i.e.*, attitudes and opinions falling toward the extremes of the scale are more resistant to change than those falling in the middle of the scale.) But there is no experimental evidence to support a view that strength and extremeness are perfectly correlated.[1]

(Strength of attitudes may also be assumed to correlate positively with intensity or importance; the more central the attitude to the individual the more deeply connected with his needs, and the greater the degree of emotionality associated with it the more the attitude is likely to resist change.) Similarly, the strength of a belief may be expected to correlate positively with the degree of certainty with which it is held. But there are other determinants of strength of attitudes and beliefs in addition to these, and hence an independent measurement of strength is required.

This poses something of a methodological dilemma. Since indirect indicators of strength—extremeness, intensity, certainty, etc.—are apparently not entirely adequate, there seems to be but one logical alternative —*to measure strength by subjecting the attitude or belief to stresses designed to change it.* To our knowledge there has been as yet no significant methodological contribution in this direction. One reason is probably the technical difficulty involved in setting up some kind of standard "strength test" that could be practically applied to the measurement of strength of many different beliefs and attitudes among many different people. How would one, for instance, equate the standard "force" that is to be brought against the belief or attitude from person to person? Another reason is that this procedure would violate the requirement that the measurement be done in such a way not to affect the thing being measured. In the engineering laboratory the

---

[1] If an alternative method of measuring scale units previously mentioned (see p. 225) were followed, in which equality of units along the scale was measured by ease of change, the dimensions of strength and of extremeness would not, of course, be independent; they would, in fact, be identical.

strength of materials may be tested by subjecting them to increasing stress until they break. But with beliefs and attitudes we wish to retain the original condition unaffected by the measurement.

It occurs to us that one approach which might avoid some of the latter difficulty would be to test strength of an attitude or belief in terms of its effectiveness *in producing modifications in something else.* Strength is, after all, a relative matter—a relation of internal forces to external forces. Rather than the application of a standard force to attempt to bring about a change in the attitude, we might reverse the procedure by measuring the amount of effect the attitude would have in changing standard material. Amount of perceptual or cognitive distortion caused by an attitude or belief under standard conditions might, thus, provide a measure of the strength of the attitude or belief. This is the essence of many projective techniques.

In order to develop a strength test in this direction, it would be necessary to work up a standardized set of materials which vary stepwise in their degree of internal strength of structure.

The Measurement of Importance.—In our discussion of the nature of attitudes (Chap. V), we have emphasized the critical significance of the motivational component. Attitudes differ in importance to the individual in proportion to the importance to him of the needs and emotions with which they are connected. Of the whole inventory of attitudes that he has, some are of the greatest possible importance to him, influencing almost all of his activities; others are somewhat less important to him, influencing some of his activities and not others; and still other of his attitudes are of relatively little functional significance to him, coming into play only on rare occasions and in restricted contexts.

The degree to which an attitude is important or central to the individual is one of the most critical attributes requiring measurement. In understanding and predicting the individual's behavior it is at least equally necessary to know how important or central the attitude is to him, as it is to know its "sign," how extreme it is, etc. The measurement of importance or centrality of attitudes has been relatively neglected in conventional attitude measurement. We can touch only in a tentative way upon some preliminary developments of technique and to certain possibilities of future exploration along these lines.

Importance or centrality of attitudes may be revealed in several different ways. For one thing, the intensity with which the person feels about the object or issue is highly related to its importance to the person. For another thing, the saliency of the object or issue to the person, *i.e.*, the extent to which it occupies his attention, is likely to be related to its importance to him. And for another thing, the individual's feeling of self-involvement in the object or issue is probably related to its importance to him. All three of these probable relationships may be made the basis of measurement of importance or centrality of the attitude.

Intensity.—The most common devices for the determination of the intensity of an attitude or opinion are (1) self-rating by the individual on how strongly he feels about the question and (2) rating by the interviewer on how strongly the person feels about the question as judged from what the person says, various secondary expressive cues, etc.

These and certain other devices for the measurement of intensity have been studied by Katz (1944). His conclusion was that intensity is a reliably measurable dimension and that different devices designed to gauge intensity all seem to tap the same essential dimension. He was also able to demonstrate the usefulness of the intensity measure in predicting people's opinion about other related questions. That is, people who held a given position on the question, but with varying degrees of intensity, gave predictably different answers on certain other questions. Knowledge of intensity, in other words, is helpful in understanding and predicting attitudes and opinions.

An investigation by Cantril (1946) throws additional light upon the measurement of the intensity function. He asked the following question of a national sample of adults: "Which one of the following statements best expresses what you think should be the relationship between business and government when the war is over?" A card was handed to respondents with the following printed alternatives:

1. There should be as little government regulation of business as possible.
2. Some government regulation of business is necessary but there should be less regulation than we had under the New Deal before the war.
3. The government should continue to regulate business about the way it did before we got into the war.
4. There should be more regulation of business than there was before the war.
5. The government should own and control all big industries, banks, and natural resources.

This question was then followed by the further question: "How strongly do you hold this opinion—very strongly, fairly strongly, or don't you care much one way or the other?"

The scale value for each of the five alternatives had previously been determined by the Thurstone procedure of asking 80 judges to place each item along the scale. The percentage of people who answered "very strongly" to the intensity question was plotted against the scale position for that alternative. This relationship between extremeness of opinion and intensity with which it is held is shown in Fig. 6.   As Cantril concludes, on the basis of this relationship: ("The more extreme an attitude is in its direction, the more intensely it is likely to be held."[1])   Such a generalization seems reasonable in light of the fact that extreme positions on issues and extreme attitudes are much more likely to appear in cases in which the individual is deeply involved.   The phenomenon of "polarization," previously mentioned (page 228), would probably be speeded up in connection with objects and issues important to the person.   It is more difficult to maintain a somewhat detached point of view, to delay committing oneself definitely to one side or the other, when the issue is one of intense importance to the person.

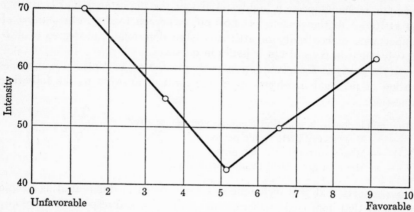

Fig. 6.—Intensity and extremeness of opinion about government control of business. (*Taken from Cantril*, 1946.)

As a rather different approach to the measurement of intensity of attitude, an adaptation might be made of Thorndike's (1940) technique for determining the amount of money that the individual says he would have to be paid to do various unpleasant things.   Money values were placed by people upon doing such undesirable acts as "Have to live all the rest of your life in Japan," "Eat a quarter of a pound of human flesh," "Spit on a crucifix." The amount of money demanded by the individual to behave in contradiction to an attitude might be taken as a measure of the intensity with which the attitude is held and hence as a measure of the importance or centrality of the attitude to the individual.   Thus, if a man asserts that he would have to be paid ten thousand dollars to entertain a Negro in his home and another man asks only one thousand dollars, it might be assumed that the first man had a more intense attitude about the Negro than the second man.

[1] See also our previous discussion of Guttman's work on the relation between intensity and extremeness (p. 230).

The necessary assumption in this form of the technique is, of course, that the need or desire for money is relatively equal for all people measured. This presents one technical shortcoming. Another is that this method would be easily applicable for measuring intensity of only negative attitudes, though for some purposes it might be turned about by asking how much the individual would pay to see certain positive things accomplished.

Self-involvement.—Sherif and Cantril (1947) have placed great emphasis upon the "ego-involvement" aspect of attitudes. Their stress is entirely consistent with our own theoretical treatment which points to needs and emotions as primary components of attitudes. The degree of ego-involvement is without question highly related to the importance and centrality of attitudes to the person. Hence, one approach to the measurement of importance or centrality of attitudes is to determine the degree of self-involvement in the objects or issues in question.

In the study of Katz (1944) previously mentioned, use was made of a self-rating of personal involvement, in the form of answers to the following question:

How much does this question mean to you personally?
———Means very little to me personally.
———Means something to me personally.
———Means a great deal to me personally.

Katz reports that this technique did not succeed in differentiating people in a way that improved predictions of how they would respond to other key questions related to the issue. Despite this one negative indication of the usefulness of this technique, it seems worthy of further exploration. Possibly the difficulty in the form of self-rating used here was a failure to make clear to the individual what was intended to be meant by "meaning" something to him.

Saliency.—Some attitudes and opinions are more salient than others for the individual, in the sense that they are more easily elicited, more readily verbalized, more prominent in the cognitive field. Under many circumstances it is probable that the more important the beliefs and attitudes the more salient they are. In these circumstances, therefore, saliency can be taken as a measure of importance.

In the intensive, open-end type of interviewing (see page 277), which permits free, conversational responses to rather general questions, it is possible to go about measuring saliency of given attitudes or opinions in terms of the readiness with which they appear "spontaneously" in the answers of the individual. The interviewer keeps the person talking within the general area of the problem, but without mentioning the specific attitude or opinion in which he is interested. *This mention must first and naturally come from the respondent, in his own words and in his own frame of refererence. Those attitudes and opinions which appear readily and frequently are considered salient; those which appear only after a considerable time or after direct probing by the interviewer are considered less salient.*

We shall give three examples of the actual research use of this technique of measuring saliency. The first is from a study of the reasons for buying war bonds, made during the war by the Program Surveys Division of the U. S. Department of Agriculture. It was desired to determine what were the opinions of people in general about the need for buying bonds—what, in other words, were their beliefs about the function of bond buying? The method of questioning was to start off with questions about different areas, such as inflation, the progress of the war, etc., and then gradually to bring the discussion around to the buying of bonds. A supplementary method was to start off with general questions about reasons for bond buying, then to observe what different reasons were mentioned. No reasons were suggested to the individual; they were to emerge spontaneously. If at the conclusion of the general questioning certain reasons had not been mentioned, these were specifically asked about.

The results of this study were such as clearly to indicate that reasons for bond buying differed markedly in their saliency for the same individual and that a given reason differed in saliency among different people. This was shown, moreover, not to be due to the complete *nonexistence* of the belief for the individual. Many beliefs about bond buying that could be shown on direct probing to be psychologically existent for the person failed to emerge at all under prolonged nondirective questioning. For example, some people who failed spontaneously to mention the prevention of inflation as a reason for buying war bonds did, under direct questioning, demonstrate that they believed this to be a reason. It is probably not unreasonable to assume that those reasons which appeared most saliently were more important and central to the individual than those which were less salient.

The second example of research use of saliency is taken from the study of German civilian morale under Allied bombing, made by the United States Strategic Bombing Survey (1946). It was desired to obtain some quantitative measure of the saliency of bombing for different groups of people—such as the heavily bombed, the unbombed, the Nazis, the non-Nazis, etc.—in their retrospective accounts of their experiences, opinions, and attitudes during the war.

People were questioned at length (by open-end questions) about their attitudes toward the progress of the war, their leadership, the Allies, unconditional surrender, etc., *without any mention by the interviewer of bombing.*

There were in all some 35 questions asked (requiring over an hour on the average) before the interviewer himself introduced the question of bombing. A measure of saliency was then possible on the basis of how early in the interview the respondent himself spontaneously mentioned bombing and how frequently spontaneous references to bombing occurred. This was then essentially a method for measurement of the threshold of mention of bombing under the assumption that the more salient the attitudes and opinions concerning bombing the more readily they would appear in the interview. It was possible by this approach, moreover, to study the relative saliency of bombing in different contexts, *e.g.*, thoughts of surrender, pessimism about outcome of the war, distrust of leadership, hatred of the Allies, etc. Complete methodological analysis of these data has not yet been made, but enough has been done to indicate the presumptive value of this technique for the measurement of saliency of bombing, *i.e.*, in differentiating people for whom bombing was more important and more central in affecting their morale and behavior under varying conditions of bombing attack from those for whom it was less important and less central.

Our third example is drawn from a recent study under the auspices of the Society for the Psychological Study of Social Issues (1947) of the attitudes of the American people toward Soviet Russia. It was desired to measure the importance of attitudes and opinions toward Russia as related to the basic needs, hopes, and fears of the individual. How salient, in other words, are the attitudes and opinions toward Russia in the everyday personal life and outlook of the individual? How central are such attitudes and opinions in the need-emotion structure of the individual's personality?

The technique employed in this study was rather similar to that of the German bombing morale study described above. In a lengthy interview schedule (of the open-end type) consisting of approximately thirty questions, no mention is made of Russia until question 23. In the previous questions the individual is asked about his personal plans, hopes, needs, and fears concerning himself, his country, and the world as a whole. These questions provide ample opportunity for mention of Russia to emerge spontaneously in one or more of these contexts. Here again, the quantitative measure of saliency (and hence of importance of the attitude to the individual) is given simply by the readiness and frequency of spontaneous reference to Russia.

We have pointed out several times in the foregoing examples that the saliency of an attitude or opinion in one context may differ markedly from that in another. The general theory of attitudes and beliefs we have advanced in Chap. V would lead us to expect such variations in saliency depending upon context. The arousal of different needs in different situations produces a differential significance of attitudes and beliefs. The implication is that measurements of saliency to be meaningful must be related to the particular psychological context.

Under some circumstances saliency is probably not a good measure of importance or centrality of attitudes and beliefs. This is especially true when the attitudes or opinions are of a nature as to be subject to repressive pressures or pressures for concealment. Though such attitudes may be exceedingly important to the individual, they may not appear readily in his consciousness or may not be easily revealed in his spontaneous discussion. Some important beliefs may also be so thoroughly built into the structure of the individual's world, so much taken for granted, that they will not tend to appear readily in his thoughts.

If the individual is well aware of his important attitudes and they are then salient in his consciousness, they may—even if antisocial—be brought into the open by a skillful interviewer under good conditions of rapport, the assurance of anonymity, etc. But if the individual is unaware of some of the components of these important attitudes, saliency may not be valid indication of importance, and recourse must be taken to the clinical methods of projective techniques and the like, which enable us to uncover the repressed material.

The Measurement of Verifiability of Beliefs.—It was pointed out in Chap. V that beliefs differ critically in respect to the attribute of *verifiability*, *i.e.*, the degree to which the individual regards the particular belief as accessible of "proof." Whether a particular belief held by a man is considered by him as something he "knows" or as something about which he has an "opinion" or as something about which he has "faith" makes for great difference in how this belief will affect his behavior and how this belief may be subject to change. What is needed are techniques for ascertaining objectively the degree to which a given belief constitutes a matter of knowledge, opinion, or faith for the individual. No explicit methodological work has been done along this line. One suggestive approach would be through the intensive questioning of the person about his belief—why he held the belief, the evidence he had for it, whether he felt it necessary or desirable to search for further evidence, etc.

Certainty of belief.—Intimately related to the question of the verifiability of a belief is the question of how *certain* the person feels about it. To know something or to have faith implies, of course, that there is complete certainty, and in such a case there is no need to measure certainty. But in matters of opinion, on the contrary, certainty may vary all the way from zero to complete certainty. Here it is necessary to measure degree of certainty by whatever means may be available.   One obvious approach, which has been used in opinion research, is simply to ask the individual to rate the degree of certainty of his belief.

THE RELIABILITY AND VALIDITY OF MEASUREMENT OF BELIEFS AND ATTITUDES

The ultimate consideration concerning any measurement technique is its validity, *i.e.*, the extent to which it measures what it purports to measure. Invalid measures of beliefs and attitudes are, of course, worthless for the understanding and prediction of behavior.   The validity of a technique is dependent in an intimate way upon its *reliability*, *i.e.*, the extent to which it yields *consistent* measures.   Obviously, a measurement technique cannot be more valid than it is reliable (though the opposite does not hold).   Before we can turn to the critical question of validity, therefore, we must first consider the reliability of measurements of beliefs and attitudes.

Reliability.—Repeated measurements of an individual's belief or attitude may give different results.   Such variation may be indicative of internal unreliability of the testing instrument itself, or it may arise from two other sources of variation: (1) *apparent* variation in the attitude or belief, which is caused by changes in the psychological condition under which the measurements are made; (2) *true* variation in the attitude or belief over time.   It might be found that an individual's scores on an anti-Semitism scale would differ when he was tested publicly and when tested anonymously.   And it might be found that his scores on this scale would be different before and after some personal experience with Jews.   Neither of these findings would necessarily impugn the reliability of the scale itself.   In order to evaluate the reliability of the measuring instrument itself, these two other types of variation must be segregated.

Ways of measuring reliability.—Internal unreliability of a measuring instrument may be ascertained in three different ways: (1) the test-retest method, in which the measurement with the given test is repeated, immediately or after a lapse of time, and the two measurements compared; (2) the equivalent forms method, in which measurements on two comparable forms of the same test are compared; (3) the split-half method, in which the score on one half the test is compared with that on the other half.   The degree of reliability is customarily expressed as the coefficient of correlation between the two sets of measurements.   Reliabilities determined in these three different ways will not necessarily be equal, and the decision as to the most appropriate way to determine the reliability of a given test must depend mainly upon the specific nature of the test and the manner in which it is to be used.

There are certain systematic tendencies in the coefficient of reliability yielded by the three methods. In the test-retest method the coefficient may be spuriously high due to memory factors if the time interval between test and retest is short. On the other hand, if the time interval is quite long, genuine changes in the attitude may have occurred, and hence the coefficient would be spuriously low. In the split-half method, it is argued that the coefficient is likely to be spuriously high, since one measures consistency under artificially perfect conditions of identical motivation, instructions, test situations, etc., for the two halves. Such perfect conditions are not likely to prevail in any actual application of the test for comparative purposes. In general, the coefficient of reliability yielded by the equivalent forms method can be expected to be slightly lower than those by the other methods. For this reason it is often preferred, as erring, if at all, on the side of an overconservative estimate.

Sources of unreliability.—The sources of unreliability are manifold. Practically anything that goes wrong in the content of the test, in the way it is administered, or the way it is taken may be expected to reduce reliability. Among the principal sources of unreliability, which we shall simply list without further discussion, are the following: complex and ambiguous items in the attitude scale which cause misunderstandings; items having special meanings not common to all the people; items that are inconsistent with one another, *i.e.*, not lying along a single dimension; mechanical errors in reading, marking, and scoring the items; inadequate and nonuniform instructions in administering the test; variable and disruptive factors in the measurement situation, such as distractions or poor rapport.

The above sources of unreliability pertain particularly to attitude and opinion scales. In connection with ratings, unreliability may arise out of some of the above factors as well as the following: deficiencies in the structure of the rating scale; complexity of the variable to be rated; noncomparability of rating criteria among judges; "halo" tendency in ratings, wherein judgments of one variable affect judgments of other variables; insufficiency of data upon which rating is based, including lack of direct contact with the individual. Self-ratings are prone to unreliability in a unique way because of the pervasive and variable influences of such subjective factors as needs, emotions, self-biases, moods.

The reliability of a scale may change over a period of time, as a function of altered meaning of some of the items. As events transpire, the diagnostic significance of a single item may change, sometimes radically. Farnsworth (1943) has found significant changes in the scale values of items on Thurstone-type opinion scales between 1930 and 1940.

How to increase reliability.—The most obvious and direct approach to improvement of the reliability of techniques of attitude measurement is the correction of the various types of deficiencies listed above. Scales can be markedly improved by elimination of complex and ambiguous items, by intercorrelation analysis of the items leading to removal of those which are internally inconsistent, by clarifying the instructions, by standardizing the conditions under which the scale is applied, etc. The reliability of ratings can be enhanced by improving the structure of the rating scales, by simplifying the definition of the variable to be rated, by establishing common criteria among the judges, etc.

Aside from these technical improvements, the most effective way to increase reliability of a scale is to increase the number of items. As was pointed out previously (page 214), the effects of random and accidental variations in responses to the items will be better canceled out as the number of items increases. In so far as constant errors are not involved, reliability goes up as a direct (though not linear) function of number of items. Assuming only that enough such similar items are available, there is no theoretical limit to the level of reliability that may be achieved. There is, however, an extremely important practical limitation. If a scale is too long, it may be uneconomical and, what is worse, it may require more time and more cooperation than the subject is willing to give to it. A typical Thurstone scale includes approximately twenty items. With forty such items the reliability would be appreciably increased, but it would be practically unwieldy. The proper approach to construction of a reliable attitude scale is first the improvement of the items and elimination of deadwood rather than the indiscriminate accumulation of a large number of items, each of dubious diagnostic value.

The reliability of ratings is also definitely dependent upon the amount of material upon which the ratings are based. Longer and closer observation, more intensive interviews, a larger supply of personal documents and projective results will all serve to make for higher reliability of rating. The multiplication of judges who make the ratings will also raise reliability. But this expedient is often not practically feasible; and in the case of self-ratings, it is, of course, impossible.

Minimal adequate levels of reliability.—It is a fairly common rule of thumb that the minimal adequate level of reliability is in the neighborhood of .90 or .95 for *individual* measurement and .50 for *group* measurement. This distinction between individual and group measurement is an important one. The former refers to the situation in which we wish to make predictions about the individual and to study changes in his score. For example, we might wish to use a given individual's attitude score to predict how he would behave in a certain situation. Or we might wish to determine if and how much his attitude changed as a function of a certain influence. Unless the reliability of our measuring instrument is .90 or .95 or better, there would be such a large degree of accidental variation in the individual's score that we could not make predictions or evaluate changes with confidence. We would never be sure whether the observed variation was due to a real change in the individual's attitude or due simply to unreliability of the scale.

In group measurement, on the other hand, we are not interested in single individuals, but in the average attitude score of a group of individuals. For example, we might wish to predict the average behavior of a group on the basis of the average attitude score of the group. Or we might wish to determine the average amount of change in the group attitude under the influence of some given experimental conditions. It is understandable that under these circumstances a somewhat lower level of reliability may be tolerated, since the random variability in the individual scores will tend to cancel out in the group average. Even with an attitude scale having a reliability as low as .50, therefore, it may be possible to arrive at useful conclusions about predictions and changes of the group average. But we could not use such a scale for the study of single individuals.

It need scarcely be emphasized that we are talking about minimal acceptable levels of reliability. There is nothing magical about .50 or .95. The aim should always be to work toward the highest reliability possible within practical limitations.

It is fortunate that most of the research requiring measurement of attitudes and beliefs is concerned with groups rather than individuals. Both in pure and applied social psychology this is true. As pure science, the concern is with the establishment of basic principles about attitudes and beliefs—the laws of their development and changes. The required method is largely that of the comparison of control and experimental groups under controlled conditions. As applied science, the main concern is with the attitudes and opinions of various defined groups of people, how they change under given circumstances, etc. The public opinion analyst deals with the average attitudes and opinions of Republicans, college graduates, skilled workers, and the like. The expert on race relations deals with the attitudes of certain groups within the community toward other groups. The propagandist deals with the opinions of large segments of the population, caring nothing about the opinions of individuals taken singly.

Illustrative reliabilities of various techniques.—In light of the above comments on reliability it may be helpful to list here a few representative figures on reliability of some techniques of attitude measurement that have been used. This is nothing more than an arbitrary sampling, and the interested student is advised to go to the original publications on the various techniques to study the details of their reliabilities.

Likert, Roslow, and Murphy (1934) computed the median of the reliabilities of 10 Thurstone-type scales to be .76 by the equivalent forms method. The median of reliabilities of a set of Likert-type scales was found to be .85. Some reliabilities are much higher. Likert (1932) reports a coefficient of .92 for one of his scales, and precisely the same coefficient is reported by Thurstone and Chave (1929) for their attitude toward the church scale and by Nystrom (1933) for a scale measuring attitudes of Filipinos toward America. The generalized or "master" scales of Remmers seem to yield a median reliability of about .70.

When the Bogardus Social Distance scale was used on 21 nationalities to arrive at a score for general attitude toward out-groups, the split-half reliability was found to be .95. Guilford's (1931) use of the paired comparisons technique for determination of racial preferences yielded remarkably high reliabilities varying from .967 to .995. A scale on attitudes toward fascism made up of 35 items which were not combed out for internal inconsistency had a split-half reliability of .77 (Stagner, 1936). This is not high for a scale of this length and indicates the indispensability of careful construction of a scale.

In Stouffer's (1930) study of attitudes toward prohibition, the average intercorrelation of six judges' ratings of case histories was .87. As to self-rating, Ewing (1942) reports rate-rerate reliabilities (one-week intervals) of about .80, and Riker (1944) reports the reliabilities of self-ratings of 13 issues to range between .50 and .86 and for self-ratings of *intensity* between .66 and .99.

Proshansky (1943) does not report reliabilities of his projective technique utilizing the Thematic Apperception Test (see page 240), but the correlations of scores on this test with those on an attitude scale of the objective type were found on two groups to be .67 and .87, indicating a fairly respectable reliability of this projective method.

Validity.—Once the reliability of an attitude-measurement technique has been established as satisfactory, the remaining problem is to ascertain the validity of the technique. As we have previously mentioned (page 209), the determination of validity is necessarily indirect. There are several such indirect approaches: (1) the measurement of "known" groups, or of types of people who on a priori grounds should differ in an expected way in their opinions and attitudes; (2) comparison with other measurements of the opinions and attitudes; (3) study of the accuracy of predictions of behavior based upon the measurement of the attitudes and opinions.

Measurement of "known" groups.—There are often a priori grounds for assuming that if a scale or other measure of attitudes and opinions is valid, it should differentiate certain defined types of people in an expected direction. We should probably have little confidence in a method of measuring attitude toward war if typical members of peace organizations did not score toward the extreme antiwar position or in scales of attitude toward the Negro if members of the Ku Klux Klan did not fall toward the anti-Negro pole or in scales of attitudes toward Russia if members of the Friends of Soviet Russia did not score more in the pro-Russian direction than members of the Committee on un-American Activities. Membership in various types of organizations whose objectives are ideologically clear may obviously be taken as one convincing way of validating opinion and attitude tests. This is true, of course, only on a group or average basis. Not every single member of an organization will be in complete ideological sympathy with its objectives; there are other possible reasons for joining. But on the whole, we should expect groups of such people to score differently on the relevant attitude scale from nonmembers or members of opposing organizations.

There are several shortcomings in this validation method, which limit its usefulness. One is that people who join organizations are likely to be different in many psychological respects from people who are not "joiners." Therefore, the scale may be valid in differentiating organization members but not other people who have attitudes just as extreme. Another difficulty is that even though a scale may validly differentiate people of *extreme* attitudes, such as organization members, it may not be equally valid in distinguishing among people who are of more moderate opinion. It is not likely that one can find organizations that ideologically represent *all* scale positions on an attitude continuum, since organizations are almost always centered around fairly extreme positions. A third practical difficulty is that for some attitudes and opinions for which scales are to be built, there are not likely to be easily found any organizations that ideologically represent the various extremes.

Though it is perhaps more striking to validate against *formal* groups of people, for whom an overt behavior of joining was required in support of their attitude, it is also often convenient to validate against *types* of people, distinguished in terms of sociological classification rather than in terms of organizational membership. Thus, Sims and Patrick (1936) applied a Thurstone-type scale for measuring attitude toward the Negro to different groups of college students, with the following results (high score indicating positive attitude):

	Average Score
Northern students	6.7
Northern students living in the South	5.9
Southern students	5.0

Several illustrative studies validating against "known" groups or against sociological types are as follows. Pace (1939) constructed a scale, using verbally stated situations calling for a hypothetical behavior response, to measure "social-political-economic" liberalism. The validity of the scale was attested to by the fact that it differentiated perfectly between 25 known radicals and 25 known conservatives (*i.e.*, none of the conservatives scored more toward the liberal end of the scale than any of the radicals). Raskin and Cook (1938) developed a scale for measurement of attitude toward fascism, which yielded the following average scores for members of several political groups (minus end of scale being the anti-fascist pole):

Republicans	1.5
Democrats	− 3.7
Farmer-Laborites	−16.5
Socialists	−21.3
Communists	−30.0

A scale for measuring attitude toward the TVA (Sims, 1938) was validated by applying it to various groups of people who might be expected to show differential approval of a government utility program of this sort. The groups scoring most extremely (a high score indicating disapproval) were as follows:

N. Y. Edison Co. employees	75
Stockholders in private power companies	68
Merchants in the TVA region	34
Government employees in Washington, D. C.	23

Comparison with other measurements.—Another general approach to validation is through comparison of individuals' scores on the given scale or test with their scores derived from other quite different techniques designed to measure the same attitude or opinion. For example, in the study of Stouffer (1930), previously mentioned (page 239), it was found that the correlation between a Thurstone-type test of attitude toward prohibition and ratings based on case histories was .81 (.86 corrected for unreliability of the two measures). This provides some presumptive evidence of the validity of both these measures. And similarly, in the study by Proshansky (1943) projective tests of attitudes toward labor correlated highly with scores derived from an attitude scale. Here again it would seem to be indicated that the two methods had validity.

It can be argued with considerable justification, however, that this general approach is not really a validation procedure at all but is merely another way of determining reliability. That two techniques agree may demonstrate their consistency but not necessarily their accuracy in measuring what they are purported to measure. It is, nevertheless, a source of considerable confidence about the applicability of an attitude or opinion test that its scores agree with those determined by other, quite different methods, such as case history analysis, interviewer's ratings, or projective tests.

Accuracy of prediction of behavior.—The ultimate practical test of the validity of opinion and attitude measurement lies in the usefulness of these measurements for the understanding and prediction of the individual's behavior. If his opinions and attitudes have been correctly assayed, it should be possible to make accurate predictions about how he will behave toward the object of the attitude or opinion in various situations, both verbally and overtly, both directly and indirectly.

There are, on the whole, very few good examples of this sort of validation. As one example, Telford (1934) examined the average scores on a scale measuring attitude toward the Church made by people who reported different frequencies of church attendance and discovered the following clear-cut relationship:

Frequency of Church Attendance	Average Score
Regularly	1.91
Frequently	2.48
Occasionally	3.50
Seldom	4.95
Never	6.75

This would seem to constitute a reasonably sure validation of the attitude scale, but it should be observed that the behavior was not ascertained independently, but through the individual's own report.

Another important example of validation through prediction of behavior is given in the election forecasts of the various public opinion polling agencies, such as Gallup, Fortune, etc. On the whole, such forecasts, made on the basis of the expressed opinions of a sample of the voting populace, have proved highly successful. Apparently there is a fairly simple relationship between verbal expression of preference for a candidate and actually voting for him. Political opinions ascertained by such methods do seem, therefore, to be valid. Even here, however, it should be noted that we do not have a straightforward case of validation of an individual's opinion through his behavior. All that is done is a kind of statistical validation, predictions being made in terms of the percentages of people who will vote a certain way, and not in terms of how a single individual will vote.

It is unfortunate that there has not been more work in the direction of validation of attitude measures in terms of predictions of behavior. There are, of course, critical difficulties in this sort of experimental work. For one thing, it is often impossible to make the necessary behavioral observations. For another thing, it may not be clear *what* behavior one should predict from the existence of an attitude or opinion, even if it is perfectly validly measured. The failure of accurate prediction in any given instance may not necessarily be a sign of invalid measurement of the attitude concerned but may merely reflect our ignorance about how that attitude will govern behavior in the given situation. We must not naively assume that an attitude which is genuinely experienced by the individual will be translated *directly* into overt action in a fashion that looks appropriate to the external observer. Corey (1937) found, for example, that scores on a scale designed to measure attitude toward cheating correlated virtually zero with actual cheating behavior. This does not necessarily argue that the scale was invalid. Perhaps it did accurately reflect the individual's attitudes about cheating, but the behavioral situation was not from his point of view one in which his beliefs about cheating had any relevance. The "Negro" on an attitude scale may be quite a different psychological object for the person than a Negro acquaintance met in a face-to-face situation. Only to the extent that there is psychological identity of the objects in the two cases must we expect that there will be congruence of the attitude and the behavior. And this relationship may be, let us again emphasize, a very complex one.

Concerning overt behavior as a validation of attitude measurement, Murphy, Murphy, and Newcomb (1937) make the following observation:

Actions are no more inherently "valid," in the first place, than words. The following remarks seem to us patently true: "Actions are frequently designed to distort or conceal 'true' attitude quite as fully as verbal behavior . . . . *All* behavior is subject to modification in the process of execution from considerations of courtesy, expediency, or other social pressures." And it is furthermore apparent that when verbal behavior is used to distort or conceal the "true" attitudes, the distortion commonly conforms to everyday behavior. The reasons for concealing "true" attitudes are the same for both verbal and "overt" behavior. If conditions of secrecy, and preferably of anonymity, are observed, there is more reason to expect free and complete expression of attitudes through words, thus freed from social pressures, than from behaviors which are open to all beholders. There are other methods, both psychological and sociological, for measuring what people *do;* here we are discussing attitudes, and observable behavior presents a weaker case for validity than "merely verbal" behavior, under proper safeguards. And, finally, it may be observed that a man's categorical agreement or disagreement with a strongly stated opinion about the Chinese, or Jews, or Rotarians, or Communists, is in everyday life regarded (if the man is sincere) as a *significant* part of his behavior. There seems to be no reason why this behavior should suddenly become *non-significant* when it is made the subject of careful inquiry, particularly if motives for insincerity are reduced to a minimum.

SUMMARY

The measurement of beliefs and attitudes is essential both in various applications and in the pure science of social psychology. Such measurement, being necessarily indirect, can be accomplished by a variety of means which utilize the behavior and immediate experience of the individual as diagnostic data. In measuring beliefs and attitudes, account must be taken of the fact that the manner in which they are reflected in behavior and experience is governed in part by the nature of the momentary situation. The required precision of measurements may vary, but the techniques must be both reliable and valid. The determination of the validity of measurements can be done only indirectly. "Individual" beliefs and attitudes are also measurable, since there is a considerable degree of absoluteness possible in the quantification of various attributes, and hence the meaning of such measurements does not have to depend solely upon relative norms of the group.

One of the most widely used and best tested methods of measurement is the attitude, or opinion, scale. The scaling method requires that the individual react with verbal expressions of endorsement or rejection of a set of carefully standardized items or propositions. The summary pattern of his judgments of the items reveals the properties of his underlying beliefs and attitudes. The separate items of a scale are not usually analyzed individually.

There are several criteria in selecting items for a scale. The items must (1) be psychologically related to the attitude or opinion being measured, (2) discriminate sharply among people, (3) discriminate in all parts of the dimension, (4) be sufficiently numerous so that random and accidental imperfections are canceled out.

The main types of scales are as follows: the *Thurstone* scale, in which the scale values of the items are determined by taking the median of the judgments of a large number of judges; the *Likert* scale, in which the items are chosen so as to have the best intercorrelations with the total score and are judged by the subject in five categories of approval or disapproval; the *Guttman* scale, in which the items are chosen so that they represent a unidimensional scale, *i.e.*, endorsement of a given item must be accompanied by endorsement of all other items that are less extreme and rejection of all that are more extreme; the *social distance* scale, in which the subject indicates the degree of feeling of psychological distance from a nationality (or other) group; the *rank-order* scale, in which a set of objects are ranked from most approved to least approved; and the *paired comparisons* scale, in which the relative scale position of each of a number of objects is determined by its successive comparison with each of the other objects.

The Thurstone scale attempts to ensure equality of units on the scale by having the original judges make their judgments in terms of equal appearing intervals. But no scales can be assumed to have real equality of units, so that care must be taken in the manipulation and interpretation of scale scores. The zero point of a scale is the place where no attitude exists or where the opinion is either entirely neutral or is nonexistent. The zero point cannot be determined unambiguously from the scale itself. One independent method of establishing the zero point is to locate it at the point on the scale where the intensity of feeling or the certainty of opinion is at a minimum. To be most useful, scales should be *unidimensional; i.e.,* they should measure only one attitude or opinion at a time. Many attitude scales fail to be unidimensional and include within them irrelevant and confusing sources of variation. Scales should be simplified and purified until they are unidimensional and measure only the psychological object to which they are supposed to pertain.

The refinement and purification of scales require a careful preliminary analysis of the nature of the psychological object as it exists for people. Adequate reliability of a scale is not alone sufficient to guarantee unidimensionality. Scales may measure different things depending upon how the scale is named.

Another quite different approach to the measurement of beliefs and attitudes is the method of rating, in which the quantification of the belief or attitude is based upon the judgment of an expert or an interviewer. The sources of data for ratings are various: (1) nonverbal behavior toward the object, (2) verbal statements relating to the object, (3) secondary expressive cues, (4) responses in clinical-type interviews, (5) personal documents, (6) responses on "projective" tests, (7) immediate experience. *Self-ratings* are uniquely important, but they may be especially susceptible to biasing effects due to needs, subjective frame of reference, etc. Rating scales may be *relative,* as in (1) the rank-order scale or (2) the percentage of population scale, or *absolute,* as in (3) the graphic rating scale or (4) the specific category scale.

Indirect methods of measurement are important when it is desired to conceal the intent of the measurement from the person or to study attitude and opinion change in which the measurement process cannot be permitted to affect the attitude or opinion. Several examples of such indirect methods are given.

All the various attributes of beliefs and attitudes must be measured if there is to be a full understanding and prediction of the individual's behavior. The measurement of *kind, content, clarity, and specificity* of attitudes and beliefs is accomplished mainly through intensive questioning of the individual and analysis of his introspective reports. Belief and attitude systems may also be studied through statistical intercorrelation.

One possible approach to the measurement of *strength* of a belief or attitude is by determining the amount of effect it will have in modifying something else. *Importance* of beliefs and attitudes may be revealed in various ways including (1) the intensity with which the person feels about the object, (2) the saliency of the object to the person, (3) the degree of feeling of self-involvement in the object. Experimental examples are given of each of these approaches.

Verifiability of beliefs must be ascertained in order to be able to distinguish among matters of knowledge, faith, and opinion. This can best be done by intensive questioning of the person. Degree of certainty of an opinion may be measured through self-rating.

In order to be valid, measurements of beliefs and attitudes must be reliable, *i.e.*, consistent. *Reliability* can be measured by comparing scores in three ways: (1) test-retest, (2) equivalent forms, (3) split-half. The sources of unreliability are such things as complex and ambiguous items, inconsistent items, mechanical errors in taking and scoring the test, inadequate and nonuniform instructions, variable and disruptive factors in the test situation. Ratings may also be unreliable because of complexity of the variable, noncomparable standards of judging, "halo," etc. Reliability may be increased by correcting the above deficiencies and by increasing the number of items in the scale or the amount of material upon which ratings are based. Minimal levels of reliability for individual and group measurement are indicated, and some illustrative reliabilities of various techniques are presented.

Validity, i.e., the extent to which the instrument measures what it purports to measure, can be ascertained in three ways: (1) the measurement of "known" groups, who on an a priori basis should differ in expected ways in their opinions and attitudes; (2) comparison with other measurements of the opinions or attitudes; (3) study of the accuracy of predictions of behavior based upon the measurement of the attitudes and opinions. Experimental illustrations of the three methods of validation are given, and difficulties in the use of behavior as a validation of measurement are indicated.

BIBLIOGRAPHY

ALLPORT, F. H.: 1934.   The J-curve hypothesis of conforming behavior.   *J. soc. Psychol.*, **5,** 141–183.

ALLPORT, G. W.: 1935.   Attitudes.   *In* Murchison, C. (ed.), *A handbook of social psychology*, Worcester: Clark Univ. Press.

ALLPORT, G. W.: 1942.   *The use of personal documents in psychological science.*   New York: Social Science Research Council, No. 49.

ASCH, S. E., BLOCK, H., and HERTZMAN, M.: 1938.   Studies in the principles of judgments and attitudes: I. Two basic principles of judgment.   *J. Psychol.*, **5,** 219–251.

BOGARDUS, E. S.: 1925.   Measuring social distance.   *J. appl. Sociol.*, **9,** 299–308.

BOGARDUS, E. S.: 1933.   A social distance scale.   *Sociol. & soc. Res.*, **17,** 265–271.

CANTRIL, H.: 1946.   The intensity of an attitude.   *J. abnorm. soc. Psychol.*, **41,** 129–136.

COREY, S. M.: 1937.   Professed attitudes and actual behavior.   *J. educ. Psychol.*, **28,** 271–280.

CRESPI, L. P.: 1944.   Attitudes toward conscientious objectors and some of their psychological correlates.   *J. Psychol.*, **18,** 81–117.

DODD, S. C.: 1935.   A social distance test in the Near East.   *Amer. J. Sociol.*, **41,** 194–204.

DROBA, D. D.: 1930.   *A scale for measuring attitude toward war.*   Chicago: Univ. Chicago Press.

DUBIN, S. S.: 1940.   Verbal attitude scores predicted from responses in a projective technique.   *Sociometry*, **3,** 24–48.

DUDYCHA, G. J.: 1943.   A critical examination of the measurement of attitude toward war.   *J. soc. Psychol.*, **18,** 383–392.

DUNLAP, J. W., and KROLL, A.: 1939.   Observations on the methodology of attitude scales.   *J. soc. Psychol.*, **10,** 475–487.

EWING, T. N.: 1942.   A study of certain factors involved in changes of opinion.   *J. soc. Psychol.*, **16,** 63–88.

FARNSWORTH, P. R.: 1943.   Shifts in the values of opinion items.   *J. Psychol.*, **16,** 125–128.

FERGUSON, L. W.: 1935.   The influence of individual attitudes on construction of an attitude scale.   *J. soc. Psychol.*, **6,** 115–117.

FERGUSON, L. W.: 1938.   An item analysis of Peterson's "war" scale.   *Psychol. Bull.*, **35,** 521.

FESTINGER, L.: 1947.   The treatment of qualitative items by "scale analysis".   *Psychol. Bull.*, **44,** 149–161.

FRENCH, V. V.: 1947.   The structure of sentiments.   *J. Person.*, **15,** 247–282; **16,** 78–108.

FRENKEL-BRUNSWIK, E., and SANFORD, R. N.: 1945.   Some personality factors in anti-Semitism.   *J. Psychol.*, **20,** 271–291.

FROMME, A.: 1941.   On the use of certain qualitative methods of attitude research: a study of opinions on the methods of preventing war.   *J. soc. Psychol.*, **13,** 429–459.

GUILFORD, J. P.: 1931.   Racial preferences of a thousand American university students.   *J. soc. Psychol.*, **2,** 179–204.

GUTTMAN, L.: 1941.   The quantification of a class of attributes: a theory and a method of scale construction.   *In* Horst, P., *et al.*, *The prediction of personal adjustment.*   New York: Social Science Research Council, No. 48.

GUTTMAN, L.: 1944.   A basis for scaling qualitative data.   *Amer. sociol. Rev.*, **9,** 139–150.

GUTTMAN, L. and SUCHMAN, E. A.: 1947.   Intensity and a zero-point for attitude analysis.   *Amer. sociol. Rev.*, **12,** 57–67.

HARTSHORNE, H., and MAY, M. A.: 1928.   *Studies in deceit.*   New York: Macmillan.

HINKLEY, E. D.: 1932. The influence of individual opinion on construction of an attitude scale. *J. soc. Psychol.*, **3**, 283–296.

HOROWITZ, E. L.: 1936. The development of attitude toward the Negro. *Arch. Psychol.*, **28**, No. 194.

KATZ, D.: 1944. The measurement of intensity. *In* Cantril, H., *Gauging public opinion.* Princeton: Princeton Univ. Press.

LIKERT, R.: 1932. A technique for the measurement of attitudes. *Arch. Psychol.*, No. 140.

LIKERT, R., ROSLOW, S., and MURPHY, G.: 1934. A simple and reliable method of scoring the Thurstone attitude scales. *J. soc. Psychol.*, **5**, 228–238.

LOEBLOWITZ-LENNARD, H., and RIESSMAN, F.: 1946. A proposed projective attitude test. *Psychiatry*, **9**, 67–68.

MACKINNON, D. W.: 1946. The use of clinical methods in social psychology. *J. soc. Issues*, **2**, No. 4, 47–54.

McNEMAR, Q.: 1946. Opinion-attitude methodology. *Psychol. Bull.*, **43**, 289–374.

MORGAN, J. J. B.: 1945. Attitudes of students toward the Japanese. *J. soc. Psychol.*, **21**, 219–227.

MORGAN, J. J. B., and MORTON, J. T.: 1943. Distorted reasoning as an index of public opinion. *Sch. & Soc.*, **57**, 333–335.

MORGAN, J. J. B., and MORTON, J. T.: 1944. The distortion of syllogistic reasoning produced by personal convictions. *J. soc. Psychol.*, **20**, 39–59.

MURPHY, G., and LIKERT, R.: 1938. *Public opinion and the individual.* New York: Harper.

MURPHY, G., MURPHY, L. B., and NEWCOMB, T. M.: 1937. *Experimental social psychology.* New York: Harper.

MURRAY, H. A.: 1938. *Explorations in personality.* New York: Oxford Univ. Press.

MURRAY, H. A., and MORGAN, C. D.: 1945. A clinical study of sentiments. *Genet. Psychol. Monogr.*, **32**, 3–149, 153–311.

NEWCOMB, T. M.: 1939. Labor unions as seen by their members: an attempt to measure attitudes. *In* Hartmann, G. W., and Newcomb, T. M. (ed.), *Industrial conflict.* New York: Cordon.

NEWCOMB, T. M.: 1943. *Personality and social change.* New York: Dryden.

NYSTROM, G. H.: 1933. The measurement of Filipino attitudes toward America by the use of the Thurstone technique. *J. soc. Psychol.*, **4**, 249–252.

OSS ASSESSMENT STAFF: 1948. *Assessment of men.* New York: Rinehart.

PACE, C. R.: 1939. A situations test to measure social-political-economic attitudes. *J. soc. Psychol.*, **10**, 331–344.

PINTNER, R., and FORLANO, G.: 1937. The influence of attitude upon scaling of attitude items. *J. soc. Psychol.*, **8**, 39–45.

PROSHANSKY, H. M.: 1943. A projective method for the study of attitudes. *J. abnorm. soc. Psychol.*, **38**, 393–395.

RASKIN, E., and COOK, S. W.: 1938. A further investigation of the measurement of attitude toward Fascism. *J. soc. Psychol.*, **9**, 201–206.

REMMERS, H. H., and SILANCE, E. B.: 1934. Generalized attitude scales. *J. soc. Psychol.*, **5**, 298–312.

RIKER, B. L.: 1944. A comparison of methods used in attitude research. *J. abnorm. soc. Psychol.*, **39**, 24–42.

RIKER, B. L.: 1945. Comparison of attitude scales—a correction. *J. abnorm. soc. Psychol.*, **40**, 102–103.

RUNDQUIST, E. A., and SLETTO, R. F.: 1936. *Personality in the depression; a study in the measurement of attitudes.* Minneapolis: Univ. Minnesota Press.

SHERIF, M., and CANTRIL, H.: 1947. *The psychology of ego-involvements.* New York: Wiley.

SIMS, V. M.: 1938. Factors influencing attitude toward the T. V. A. *J. abnorm. soc. Psychol.*, **33**, 34–56.

SIMS, V. M., and PATRICK, J. R.: 1936. Attitudes toward the Negro of northern and southern college students. *J. soc. Psychol.*, **7**, 192–204.

SMITH, M. B., BRUNER, J. S., and WHITE, R. W.: 1947. A group research project on dynamics and measurement of opinion. *Int. J. Opin. & Att. Res.*, **1**, 78–82.

Society for the Psychological Study of Social Issues: 1947. Unpublished survey on attitudes toward the Soviet Union.

STAGNER, R.: 1936a. Fascist attitudes: an exploratory study. *J. soc. Psychol.*, **7**, 309–319.

STAGNER, R.: 1936b. Fascist attitudes: their determining conditions. *J. soc. Psychol.*, **7**, 438–454.

STOUFFER, S. A.: 1930. An experimental comparison of statistical and case history methods of attitude research. Ph.D. Thesis. Univ. Chicago.

TELFORD, C. W.: 1934. An experimental study of some factors influencing the social attitudes of college students. *J. soc. Psychol.*, **5**, 421–428.

THORNDIKE, E. L.: 1940. *Human nature and the social order.* New York: Macmillan.

THOULESS, R. H.: 1935. The tendency to certainty in religious belief. *Brit. J. Psychol.*, **26**, 16–31.

THURSTONE, L. L.: 1927. The method of paired comparisons for social values. *J. abnorm. soc. Psychol.*, **21**, 384–400.

THURSTONE, L. L.: 1928. An experimental study of nationality preferences. *J. gen. Psychol.*, **1**, 405–425.

THURSTONE, L. L.: 1929. Theory of attitude measurement. *Psychol. Bull.*, **36**, 222–241.

THURSTONE, L. L.: 1931. The measurement of social attitudes. *J. abnorm. soc. Psychol.*, **26**, 249–269.

THURSTONE, L. L., and CHAVE, E. J.: 1929. *The measurement of attitudes.* Chicago: Univ. Chicago Press.

United States Strategic Bombing Survey: 1946. *The effects of bombing on German morale.* Washington: Government Printing Office.

CHAPTER VIII

PUBLIC OPINION RESEARCH

The use of such attitude- and opinion-measuring devices as scales, case studies, projective tests, clinical interviews, and the like, is—for rather obvious reasons—restricted to situations where the individuals being measured are readily available and able to cooperate. The common criticism that the major part of attitudinal theory has been based on data provided by the college sophomore is a product of this practical limitation. Special types of persons, such as college students, the institutionalized abnormal, soldiers, and others readily accessible for controlled measurement, have been given disproportionate emphasis in the development and use of attitude- and opinion-measurement techniques. The average, normal member of society has, in consequence, suffered neglect. Relatively few attitude studies have been based on truly random samples of the whole population of a given society or social group, and this fact has two consequences: (1) Estimates of the incidence of various attitudes and opinions in specific populations are largely inadequate; (2) general theoretical principles of attitude formation and change may not be validly extensible to the entire population but may merely reflect special factors to be found in the restricted samples upon which the research has been conducted.

There has been traditionally something of a neglect of techniques of measurement adapted to the study of samples of the public at large in nonlaboratory and nonclinic situations. With this there has gone a tendency to avoid certain types of problems, whose solution depends upon the study and measurement of all kinds of people under all kinds of conditions.

DEVELOPMENT OF LARGE-SCALE METHODS OF MEASUREMENT

The answer to these traditional shortcomings has been the development of methods of large-scale public opinion measurement. As we have pointed out at the beginning of the previous chapter, such public opinion research has by now become a major mass industry in America. Business, industry, labor, and government have shared in this development. Among the national public opinion research organizations, some well-known ones are:

The National Opinion Research Center—NORC

The American Institute of Public Opinion—the Gallup poll

The Fortune poll (Elmo Roper)

During the war a number of governmental and military research organizations conducted large-scale attitude and opinion studies. Among these the most prominent were:

The Program Surveys Division, U.S. Department of Agriculture

The Surveys Division, Office of War Information

Research Branch, Morale Services Division, War Department

Office of Civilian Requirements, War Production Board

Morale Division, United States Strategic Bombing Survey (Germany and Japan)

There is in operation an increasingly large array of private and commercial opinion research organizations, having more limited objectives in connection with the activities of marketing, labor, industry. There are regional and local polls sponsored by newspapers. There are numerous research centers attached to universities, including the following:

Survey Research Center, University of Michigan

Bureau of Applied Social Research, Columbia University

Office of Public Opinion Research, Princeton University

On the international scene there are growing activities, with nation-wide polls in France, Mexico,[1] Sweden, Australia, Canada, and England, which also has its well-known Mass Observation.[2]

The objectives of the work of these different agencies are diverse. Quite apart from the mere measurement of attitudes and opinions per se, they are often concerned with the evaluation of the effectiveness of programs; the study of specific political, economic, and social problems; the analysis of morale; the search for theoretical principles governing attitudes and opinions; the census of facts and figures. An imposing body of methodology is growing in connection with this research.

Especially relevant to the present discussion are those methodological issues concerned with type of question, interviewing, sampling, analysis of data, and study design. We shall consider each of these problems in turn. Before doing so, we must say something about the general nature of the tools of measurement in public opinion research.

Reliance on Single Questions.—McNemar (1946) has characterized the

---

[1] An *International Journal of Opinion and Attitude Research* has recently been established, edited by L. Radvanyi, University of Mexico.

[2] See Ferraby (1945) for an account of the Mass Observation technique, which includes covert observation by trained investigators, of the everyday behavior and conversations of people.

research of public opinion agencies as depending mainly upon single questions rather than upon the multiple items of the sorts of scales described in the previous chapter. On the whole this distinction is a valid one. Obvious practical considerations make it difficult or impossible to apply tedious tests and scales to the average respondent sampled in a large-scale survey. His cooperation is essential, and his interest must be maintained at a high level. He is not likely to appreciate the methodologist's wish to obtain high reliability of measurement by asking a whole battery of questions that are overlapping and repetitious. Nor is he likely to assent to the request of a strange interviewer at the door that he sit down and mark the numerous items of an attitude scale of the typical variety. The average respondent may be willing to talk informally to the door-to-door interviewer, but he is likely to regard a printed questionnaire or scale or test that he must read and mark as something more formidable, more "official," and more suspicious. He is likely to be "too busy," "not interested," "just going out," or has "misplaced my glasses." Sometimes, even, the last is a delicate euphemism for the fact that he cannot read, and it should be remembered that the illiterate in America constitute a not inconsiderable segment of the population.

Moreover, practical limitations of time in an interview militate against a large battery of questions all directed at the measurement of a single attitude or opinion variable. In any study of the effectiveness of a program or the complexities of a political or economic or social issue, it is necessary to measure each individual on more than one dimension of attitude and opinion. One cannot afford the luxury of obtaining high reliability of a single measure at the cost of not obtaining other essential data from the individual. Without such varied data from each respondent, correlational analysis is impossible and the meaningfulness of the single measure becomes dubious.

Because of both the need for rapport with the respondent and the need for measurement of a number of variables, then, precise scaling methods must be abandoned in public opinion research in favor of single questions designed to provide the basis for measurement.

The integration of single questions.—What has just been said should not be taken as a justification for the inclusion in an interview schedule of a heterogeneous mass of single questions each directed at a different and unrelated objective. This dubious practice has been common in a great deal of public opinion research. The respondent may be asked, in the course of a 15-minute interview, his opinions about a wide range of issues, from relations with Russia to municipal corruption, from tax reduction to compulsory military training. Better practice demands that the interview schedule as a whole center about one problem, that it consist of a series of integrated questions directed at various related aspects of the problem.   This permits the measurement (even if not with the utmost precision) of a number of essential variables required in a complete analysis of the problem.   It serves to minimize the danger that the respondent will answer superficially, that he will fail to understand the interviewer or that the interviewer will fail to understand him.   Katz (1946) has expressed several of the above points clearly:

No single survey finding has much meaning in and of itself.   It can be properly interpreted only within a well-defined framework, either one that has been established by the experimental design of the study or one which the respondent has been allowed to establish for himself.   Practically, this means that an adequate study must explore a problem thoroughly; it must not ask a single question but a whole series of questions.   It must approach the problem from many angles, ask the dependent questions, explore the reasons why, seek the relevant objective background material and personal data.   In many cases it must be repeated in time to give trends.

The greatest weakness in opinion research has been the failure to set up thorough studies of the problems under consideration.   Poll operators often attempt to cover between 6 and 10 major problems in one questionnaire.   A number of issues of high "attention value" will be summarily treated with a single question.   Any one of these issues can be appropriately studied only through an integrated survey with many interlocking questions with full exploration of the significant dimensions of the problem.   Without a well-constructed framework of hypotheses, survey findings can be interpreted to mean anything and everything.

Too often public opinion polls assume that the complexities of a problem can be met by finding some neutral and unambiguous wording of a single question.   Somehow such wording is expected to achieve both adequacy and objectivity of interpretation.   Although question wording is important, the assumption that there is some magic by which a single question can be so well phrased with so little suggestive bias that it will furnish adequate and valid answers to a complex question is naive.   The emphasis upon the neutral wording of the single question should be shifted to the adequate experimental design of a well-integrated study.

TYPES OF QUESTIONS

We have not thus far mentioned the *nature* of such single questions.   This is one of the most significant of all methodological issues in public opinion research, and it has been the focus of vigorous controversy.   Although the separation between them is by no means complete, the two principal types of questions that are used are the *poll* question and the *open-end* question.   We shall examine each of these and compare them.

The Poll Question.—The poll question is so designed as to elicit a choice by the respondent of one of a set of presented alternative answers. (For this reason the poll question is sometimes referred to as the "fixed-alternative" or "fixed-response" question.) For example, the poll question may ask, "Which party do you think would do a better job of running the government during the next few years—the Republicans or the Democrats?" The respondent's opinion is simply recorded as favoring the Republicans or as favoring the Democrats or as undecided.

Other examples are "Would you like to see more control over labor unions, less control, or about as much as there is now?" "Do you think the United States should join an international organization for the maintenance of peace, or should it not join?" In all such questions the sole requirement for the respondent is to choose among the stated alternatives. There is no provision for any other answer.

The poll question developed naturally out of the methodology of psychophysics in the experimental laboratory and out of psychological testing, in both of which the subject was called upon to respond in terms of fixed categories—"lighter" or "heavier" in weight comparisons, "yes" or "no" on test items. The very name "poll" question points to another root in the development of this type of question, *viz.*, voting behavior. The Gallup poll originated as a straw-vote device for predicting elections, and indeed its greatest successes have been in this connection. It was an easy step from "voting" for candidates to "voting" on various types of public issues.

The Open-end Question.—In sharp distinction to the poll question, the open-end question is so designed as to elicit a free response not restricted to predetermined categories. For example, open-end questions may be phrased as follows: "What do you think about the Republican party?" "How do you feel about control over labor unions?" "What do you think the United States should do to try to maintain world peace?"

The unique feature of the open-end question is that the respondent is given no predetermined structure for his reply and hence is permitted to answer naturally and spontaneously in whatever terms and whatever frame of reference he chooses. The interviewer, in so far as possible, makes a verbatim record of the respondent's replies.

The poll question came out of the experimental and testing laboratory; the open-end question may be said to have developed from the psychological clinic. The clinical interview demands a free, informal questioning atmosphere, in which the patient is encouraged to talk in his own terms and thus reveal most easily the underlying dynamics of his attitudes and needs and emotions. The role of the clinician is not that of an inquisitor or cross examiner but that of a friendly and interested listener, who only by subtle and unobtrusive means guides the interview along the desired channels. Much of the tremendous value of the nondirective clinical interview approach has been retained in the adaptation of this type of intensive questioning to the needs of public opinion interviewing.[1]

But the clinician is usually not interested in *quantifying* his interview data or in adding up the results of given questions in one clinical interview with results of those same questions in other interviews. He may, therefore, ask questions of each individual with complete freedom, unhindered by the necessity for getting from each patient precisely comparable material that can be tabulated commonly for all patients. In public opinion research, on the other hand, it is essential to quantify and tabulate and hence to follow what is virtually a fixed schedule of questions. The demand for a fixed schedule is met very easily, of course, in the polling technique. How it can be met in the use of open-end questions is at first sight not so obvious.

As adapted for public opinion research the open-end question technique has endeavored to combine the advantages of a fixed schedule of questions to be asked of all respondents, with the advantage of the free, unstructured reply. This has been accomplished (though not yet perfectly) by a great deal of attention to the construction of the open-end interview schedule. In order that the answers from all respondents in the sample be susceptible to classification and summary in a set of common dimensions, it is necessary to construct clusters of questions that follow smoothly and naturally from one to another and can unobtrusively guide the respondent to talk in the specific areas and in the specific contexts desired by the interviewer. The same open-end questions are asked (in the same order) of each respondent. The task of the interviewer is to get full answers by nondirective means, *i.e.*, by encouraging the person to talk without asking additional questions not in the fixed schedule. The interviewer may, of course, employ as he wishes such nondirective probes as "Why?", "Will you tell me more about that?" etc. But this nondirective interviewing must be done in such a manner as not to prejudice the respondent's answers in any way, such as by suggesting possible replies to him or by asking new questions not in the schedule which may steer the respondent in a direction not common to the other respondents.

[1] The work of Carl Rogers (1942) has been particularly influential in the extension of clinical interviewing techniques to nonclinical samples. More than any other, the name of Rensis Likert has been associated with the application of intensive interviewing and the open-end question to public opinion research, first in the work of the Program Surveys Division of the U.S. Department of Agriculture and currently in the work of the Survey Research Center at the University of Michigan.

"Funnel" structure in open-end questions.—In order to guide the respondent's discussion along the desired channels without the use of direct questions, the clusters of open-end questions are frequently constructed in a funnel structure, proceeding by degrees from more general questions to narrower questions. Thus, the first question in a cluster may indicate the general area in which the respondent is urged to express himself, the second question indicates a narrower area within the total area, the third a still narrower area included within the second, etc., until the respondent is finally brought to the point where he addresses his discussion most directly at the objective of the cluster of questions. No matter how wide or how narrow the scope of the open-end question, it is still open-end; it still avoids indicating answers to the respondent. Thus, open-end questions may vary in scope all the way from, "How are things going with you these days?" to "What do you think about the proposal to eliminate billboards from highways?"

An example of a cluster of questions that exhibits the funnel shape is as follows:[1]

1. How do you feel about the general idea of having an organization like the United Nations?

2. How satisfied are you with the way the United Nations has worked out so far?

3. Do you think the United States has given in too much or has had its own way too much in the United Nations?

This "funnel" approach is especially valuable in measuring the *saliency* of a belief or attitude (see page 254), inasmuch as a more salient belief or attitude may be expected, other things being equal, to manifest itself earlier in the stepwise progression from general to specific questions. In the above cluster, for instance, a person who feels very strongly that the United States is being taken advantage of in the United Nations would be more likely to reveal that feeling in the first two questions, even before that particular aspect was referred to by question 3.

Coding of open-end questions.—The use of the open-end question necessitates a process of *coding* not required by poll questions. In the poll question the responses are precoded; *i.e.,* the interviewer has simply to check the appropriate category for each question in accordance with the respondent's choice. Responses from all interviews are tabulated, and the percentages of answers in each category computed. In the use of open-end questions on the other hand, each interview consists of a detailed verbatim record of the respondent's discussion of each question. Before tabulation and analysis can proceed, it is necessary to code each interview

[1] Taken from the SSRC (1947) study on the atomic bomb.

on each question, *i.e.*, to assign each one to its proper place in a scheme of classification.   This requires the services of an expert staff of coders, who perform a function analogous to that of the clinician when he makes judgments about various aspects of the individual's personality on the basis of the content of the clinical interview.   The process of coding introduces a number of methodological problems which we shall presently discuss.

Comparison of the Poll and the Open-end Question.—On the surface, at least, the poll question has certain obvious advantages over the open-end question.   It is relatively simple to use in the interview situation, even by minimally trained interviewers.   It ensures comparability among various respondents in the question asked.   Its coding is objective.   It lends itself to succinct reporting of results, as in the newspaper or on the radio.   It is, unquestionably, cheaper in time and money than the open-end question.   Were these considerations the only or the principal ones, there would be little argument in favor of the more expensive, more elaborate, more highly technical methods involved in the use of open-end questions.

The fact is, however, that the above considerations, though important, are secondary to the matters of *validity*, *depth*, and *comprehensiveness*. The poll question, as it must be used practically, seems inherently limited in these critical aspects.   The rigid structure that it imposes upon the respondent's answer almost invariably tends to produce a distortion in the answer.   This is particularly true because the same question with its same arbitrary structure must be applied to all people in the sample being interviewed.   This is the common justification for the poll question— that it requires each person to respond to the *same* question in terms of the *same* list of prescribed alternative answers.   But this may achieve superficial similarity at the sacrifice of psychological similarity.   How the question is perceived and what it means to the person will inevitably be governed by motivational and cognitive factors which may differ markedly from person to person.   Thus, not only may people differ (because of their varying beliefs and attitudes) in their answers to a question that is psychologically equivalent to them, they may also differ in their interpretations of the question, even when it is stated in precisely identical words.   The difference in answer, therefore, may reflect a difference in interpretation rather than a difference in belief or attitude.   Without a knowledge of the respondent's own interpretation of the question, the poll answer he gives is meaningless to the analyst.

An experiment on interpretations of questions.—The critical importance of the respondent's interpretation in determining the significance of his reply has been demonstrated in a study by Crutchfield and Gordon (1947).

These investigators found that (1) there may be marked heterogeneity in the interpretations that a sample of respondents puts upon a poll question, (2) different types of people may tend to give certain interpretations rather than others, and (3) apparent differences in the expressed opinions of different types of people to the same poll question may not reflect real differences in their opinions (about a psychologically equivalent question) but may reflect differences in their interpretations of the poll question.

The procedure of the study was first to ask the respondent a poll question in the standard polling manner and then to encourage him to enlarge and explain his answer by free discussion of the nondirective type. The question (repeated from a Gallup survey) was "After the war, would you like to see many changes or reforms in the United States, or would you rather have the country remain pretty much the way it was before the war?" It was found that only 60 per cent of the respondents interpreted the question as apparently intended by Gallup (*viz.*, in terms of domestic changes or reforms). The remaining 40 per cent of interpretations referred to technological improvements, changes in basic political-economic structure, foreign affairs, immediate war conditions, and personalized conditions, all of which were irrelevant to the question as intended. Men were found to differ from women in their original answers to the poll question, but it was shown that this apparent difference in opinion was a mere artifact caused by the difference between men and women in their interpretations of the question. When only those men and women who interpreted the question as intended (*i.e.*, in terms of domestic changes or reforms) were compared, it was found that the apparent difference in their poll answers disappeared completely.

Superiority of the open-end question in ascertaining interpretations.—The implication of the above findings is that without a knowledge of the respondents' interpretations of the question it is illegitimate to sum up the polled answers and to draw conclusions about these totals. But it is just at this point that the poll question is at its weakest; it is practically impossible by the poll technique alone to ascertain the exact frame of reference in which a question is being answered. At best, one can hope to minimize the heterogeneity in interpretations by exhaustive pretesting of the poll question and by placing it within a framework of preliminary questions in the interview schedule in such a way as to make the intended context of the question clear to the respondent. Regardless of the care with which these two safeguards are applied, they can never suffice to give an adequate solution to the problem of question interpretation.

The open-end question, on the other hand, is just so designed to make greatest allowance for individual differences in interpretations, by permitting the respondent to answer the question in his own terms and by encouraging him to answer fully in a way that facilitates a judgment of the meaning of his answer. Throughout this book we have stressed the need for an approach to social psychology that makes use of the individual's own perceptions and cognitions of his psychological world. As applied to public opinion research, this approach is embodied in the use of the open-end question, providing, as it does, the utmost opportunity for the individual to express his opinions in his own terms and from his own point of view.

Not only, of course, does the open-end question elicit answers that make the respondent's interpretation clear and hence enable the analyst to place the answer in a meaningful context, but it also helps to tell the interviewer when the question is being misunderstood and allows him to correct the respondent on the spot by bringing the discussion around to the intended interpretation. This is not possible in the poll-type interview.

Biasing factors in the poll question.—The mechanical rigidity of the poll question renders it particularly susceptible to a wide variety of biasing influences. Slight differences in wording often produce marked variation in the answers. McNemar (1946) summarizes this issue cogently:

Even if a simple yes-no question is clear, calls for the same frame of reference, and has a cognitive level low enough for all respondents, it entails other difficulties which can be subsumed under the *mechanics of questioning*. Some of the factors which may affect the answers are: positive versus negative statements of the question; loading by introducing emotionally charged words or phrases; the presence of contingent or conditional ideas; the influence of juxtaposed questions; suggestive elements; alternate wording; prestige elements; personalization of the question; stereotypes; technical words; biased wording; etc. Research directed at these factors indicates definitely that the percentages of yes (or no) responses can be varied. For example, Cantril shows that "interventionist sentiment" between May and September, 1941, showed an apparent variation from 78 per cent down to 8 per cent mainly as a function of the question asked.[1] Which is the correct percentage? No one knows.

The commonly attempted remedy for these problems of question wording is intensive pretesting of alternate wordings until an "unbiased" form of the question is found. But as McNemar properly remarks, there is really no objective basis for the determination of what the unbiased form is. Another expedient is the "split-ballot," in which different forms of the

[1] The reference is to Cantril (1944). The two questions giving the extreme percentages were (1) So far as you, personally, are concerned, do you think the United States has gone too far in helping Britain, or not far enough?   (2) Should the United States go into the war now and send an army to Europe?

question are asked of subsamples of the whole sample and the over-all percentage for the question computed by averaging the percentages obtained from these different forms. This is advantageous in that not "all the eggs are put in one basket," so that in the long run the average of a number of split ballots is likely to be less biased than the separate forms. But it is disadvantageous in that it reduces the sample when making cross tabulations of answers to the question against other variables.

Relative vs. absolute significance of poll answers.—Perhaps the safest solution to the problem of biased wordings of questions is to accord relative rather than absolute significance to the percentages of answers based on these questions. In other words, if a given poll question about the manufacture of atomic bombs splits 60 per cent in favor of continuing manufacture and 40 per cent opposing, it should not be assumed that these two figures necessarily represent the correct distribution of sentiment on the issue. Rather, it should simply be assumed that those people (the 60 per cent) who assented are as a whole more strongly in the direction of believing that manufacture should continue than are those people (the 40 per cent) who dissented. If another poll question with slightly altered wording were asked, the two percentages might now become 80 and 20. Obviously both this set of figures and the previous set cannot be right in an *absolute* sense, but they both can be meaningful in separating people *relatively.*

To refer back to our discussion of scale items (see page 211) in the previous chapter, it will be recalled that each item served to discriminate between more extreme and less extreme opinion or attitude and each item made this discrimination at a different place along the continuum. No one item could do more than separate the group into a dichotomy, and the point of separation had nothing more than relative significance. A poll question is really quite similar to a single item on an attitude scale. And so it also separates people into a dichotomy (or into several more classifications if the poll question provides more than two alternative answers) and can do so at quite different points along the continuum. One important difference is that in constructing the poll question there is usually an endeavor to arrive at a formulation which seems most likely to differentiate at or near the zero point, or neutral point, of the scale. As we have said, the neutral point is the most significant single point on a scale, separating these negatively inclined from those positively inclined. An unbiased wording is assumed by most people to be a wording that makes the question come closest to discriminating at the neutral point. The task of ascertaining just what specific wording will accomplish this is a most difficult one.

In this connection the technique for determination of the zero point proposed by Guttman (see page 230) becomes particularly relevant. By use of correlated intensity measures Guttman establishes a zero point in an objective way. This point he takes to be the true point of division of sentiment in the issue. And in order to measure change in sentiment over time, he simply measures the zero point anew to ascertain if and how much it has shifted. Now it will be recalled that the Guttman technique necessitates the use of a number of questions, not one, in order to establish a scale. For purposes of public opinion questioning he has tried to reduce the required number to four or five. But, as he would emphasize, the number cannot be reduced further if the zero point is still to be determinable. The clear implication of Guttman's argument is that the use of a single poll question is almost certain to be unsatisfactory if one wishes to arrive at an absolute interpretation of the poll answers.

What use can be made of poll questions on a relative basis? In the first place, a single poll question can be of use in trend studies. By repeating the same question (whether biased or unbiased) over a period of time, it may be possible to measure changes in level of opinion. This method has been widely used in trend studies of public opinion on a variety of issues, especially by Cantril (1944) and Bruner (1944). In the second place, single poll questions may be of use in comparing different groups or kinds of people. That is, if the same poll question is asked of different groups they may be compared on a relative basis. But it should be noted that for both of these uses—in trend studies and in comparisons of groups— the assumption has to be made that the biasing factors, whatever their nature, remain constant in their effects from time to time and from group to group. And whether or not this assumption is fulfilled cannot, of course, be ascertained from a study of the single question itself.

The search for reasons.—Another important aspect in which poll and open-end questions differ is in depth. The poll question tends to remain on a superficial level of "voting" for an alternative as stated. Reasons for the opinion, which are largely instrumental in making sense and predictive value out of the ascertained opinions, are not readily uncovered by the poll technique. Nothing is easier, on the other hand, than to obtain reasons by the open-end question technique. The nondirective interviewer assumes that a follow-up question "Why?" is implicitly attached to every open-end question. It is the cardinal sin for the nondirective interviewer to ascertain a bare statement of opinion without encouraging the respondent to reveal the bases of the expressed opinion, either directly or indirectly.

The poll technique has developed an expedient that helps to overcome the nakedness of the poll answers. Often a follow-up question is asked of the form, "Which of the following is the reason for your answer?" A list of reasons is presented (usually on a printed card) from which the respondent selects the most appropriate. To construct such a predetermined list of reasons it is necessary to conduct a thorough pretest, employing intensive, full-answer questions of the open-end variety. If assembled on a purely a priori basis, the list probably will not suitably fit the reasons that various members of the sample wish to express. There are several drawbacks to this expedient. For one thing, it is difficult, if not impossible, to be sure that the list of possible reasons is sufficiently exhaustive. A pretest made upon a nonrepresentative sample may not yield the full range of possible reasons. And sometimes it is just the most unexpected reasons that become the most interesting for analysis. An added expedient here is to add a cateogry "Other reasons" to the list, which the individual may specify as he wishes.

For another thing, and this is to be stressed, a fixed list of reasons, no matter how representative, can be expected to bias the respondent's choice. Such a list suggests reasons to him of which he would not have spontaneously thought. Although no definite research is available on this point it is probable that for many questions the tabulation of reasons obtained by the polling method, in which the person merely checks reasons on a predetermined list, would differ markedly from the tabulation obtained by the open-end method, in which the individual himself is required to express the reason.

It is perhaps significant that there is a growing practice among those who employ the poll-type question to include open-end questions to elicit reasons. This is undoubtedly advantageous in obtaining more data on reasons, but it cannot be expected to yield the same type of material as that obtained in a regular open-end question schedule. The poll schedule sets the individual to respond in a yes-no fashion, which is not conducive to the eliciting of full, explanatory discussion on an occasional open-end question inserted among the poll questions.

Crystallization of the issue.—Katz (1946) makes the important observation that the relative usefulness of poll and open-end questions should partly be judged in terms of the degree of *crystallization* of the issue toward which opinion is being measured. In the case of a controversial issue upon which people have arrived at opinions with a high degree of certainty and strength, it may well turn out that the results obtained by the poll method do not differ significantly from those obtained by intensive, open-end questioning. People's opinions are stabilized, the reasons for their opinions are more explicit and simplified, the context in which they consider the issue is more rigid, the biasing effects of wordings of questions are reduced.

Subtle, nondirective methods are not required because the cognitive structure is relatively clear and strong.

But in the case of issues that have not been fully considered and about which people have vague, relatively unformed opinions, the poll question, by providing the respondent with a predetermined set of alternatives and a list of reasons, may seriously prejudice his answer. For the uncrystallized opinions, the method of open-end questions seems indispensable.

Katz suggests that a combination of the two types of questions be employed—poll questions in connection with highly structured opinions or matters of fact and open-end questions for less well structured opinions. It has, in truth, become increasingly common in public opinion research for both types of questions to be employed. The better poll-type schedules usually include some open-end questions, and virtually all intensive, open-end interviews contain some direct, fixed-alternative questions.

The value of direct questions.—Nondirective interviewing by open-end questions is critically important in that it permits the individual to express himself in the way he chooses. This questioning method does not, however, serve all purposes. Although it is true that the skillful interviewer can, by nondirective means, guide the respondent to discuss various desired aspects of a problem, it is not always possible to force the respondent to come to grips with the issue in the intended way. He may talk all around the point, without committing himself, or he may refuse to budge from a particular frame of reference in which he talks about the problem. The interviewer may still, somewhat indirectly, help to force the issue by summarizing what the person has said and asking him if that is what he means. If this device fails, the interviewer may have finally to fall back on direct questions.

Such direct questions should probably be asked only after nondirective open-end questions have been exhausted. By this means the context for the answer to a direct question is established beforehand and the meaningfulness of the answer is likely to be enhanced. There is, in this connection, an interesting methodological point, about which there seems to be no available research evidence. The question is how the answers to direct questions when asked alone would compare with answers to these questions when they have been preceded by open-end questions.

Not only may direct questions be a final expedient when open-end questioning fails to pin the respondent down sufficiently, direct questions may also have positive value in their own right. The clinician sometimes finds it useful to abandon the nondirective atmosphere and to force the patient to answer specific questions, to challenge his answers, to subject him to "stress." Similarly, in the public opinion interview, direct questions may sometimes serve an important function in arousing, challenging, and forcing the respondent.

Complementary use of poll and open-end techniques.—An interesting proposal for the complementary use of the poll and intensive interview methods has been offered by Lazarsfeld (1944), who argues for three stages in a public opinion study: (1) a pilot study of a small subsample using intensive, open-end questions to uncover the essential dimensions of the problem and to aid in the construction of critical poll questions; (2) interviewing of the entire sample with the poll questions; (3) further intensive interviewing of a small subsample using open-end questions to study more deeply those few areas of the problem which have been, on the basis of analysis of the poll results, revealed as highly significant in the problem.

There have been no published accounts of studies conducted according to this plan, so that its merits have not been established. A recent study on attitudes toward the problem of atomic energy (SSRC, 1947) did employ both the poll and the intensive interview approach, national-sample studies being conducted by both methods. But the two studies were not coordinated in the systematic manner proposed by Lazarsfeld.

Productivity of the two techniques in analysis.—The data of poll and open-end questions are equally applicable to correlational analysis; *i.e.*, the answers to one question may be cross tabulated by the answers to other questions or may be broken down against factual data relating to the individual, etc. And both types of questions lead to data that can be utilized in pattern analysis, in which the answers to a set or cluster of questions can be combined into a scale or index. Thus, for example, an index of dissatisfaction with the operation of the rationing program during the war could be constructed on the basis of the answers to 10 poll questions or on the basis of the coded answers to 10 open-end questions.

But the open-end question is clearly superior in analysis in that it may also provide data which are the basis for ratings (by the coder or by the interviewer) on various attributes of opinions and attitudes. We have seen in the previous chapter (page 238) that the full verbatim transcripts of intensive interviews do serve in this way as a basis for ratings. Ratings can be made on a single open-end question or (more usually) on a cluster of open-end questions or on the entire interview. The important point is that the same set of questions may provide the data for making different ratings, including some that may not even have been anticipated in the original design of the study.

Summary comparison of poll and open-end questions.—The open-end question is potentially capable of providing validity, depth, meaning, and comprehensiveness in attitude and opinion measurement in a degree that the poll question cannot hope to equal. The open-end question is superior in ascertaining the respondent's interpretations, in being less dependent upon specific biasing wordings, in determining the reasons for opinions, and in providing fuller data for analysis. In the study of issues upon which opinions are highly crystallized or in determining matters of fact, the poll question—because of its greater simplicity and economy—may be preferred. The two methods may be profitably used together, the open-end question to explore the dimensions of the problem and to establish the context and reasons, the poll question to measure certain specific dimension.

PROBLEMS OF INTERVIEWING

No matter what type of question is asked in a public opinion survey, it must be asked by an interviewer, and we must consider some of the more important problems relating to the interviewer and the interviewing process. Among these are the problems of the functions and training of the interviewer and the reliability of interviewing.

Functions of the Interviewer.—The first job of the interviewer is to choose a respondent, *i.e.*, to sample. As we shall see in discussing details of the sampling process, the amount of latitude allowed the interviewer in selecting whom he will interview varies according to sampling technique, but in any case he does have a critical responsibility. The second job is to get the cooperation of the respondent and to establish rapport. The third job is to ask the questions and record the answers. The final job is to make the required judgments or ratings of factual characteristics of the respondent, such as age, economic status, and education, and psychological characteristics, relating to intelligence, personality, beliefs and attitudes, etc.

The open-end interviewing method involves a somewhat different problem of establishing cooperation and rapport than does the poll technique. In the former the interviews are necessarily long, often lasting more than an hour, and the respondent must be prepared to sit down and talk freely and at length. He cannot be caught "on the run" or interviewed satisfactorily on the doorstep. This is an added hurdle for the intensive interviewer, but in some ways it serves as an advantage. The respondent is approached in a more serious way, and he is more easily convinced of the importance of the interview. His answers are, on the whole, likely to be less superficial. That the approach necessary for intensive interviewing technique is a successful one can be seen by the very low level of refusals to be interviewed that are encountered. Over a period of time and for various studies, the level of refusals in the interviewing of one organization[1] using the intensive approach was about 1 or 2 per cent. In one polling study (Cantril, 1944)

[1] Program Surveys Division, U. S. Department of Agriculture.

the level of refusals was 14 per cent. The difference is probably partly a function of the difference in the atmosphere of a request to sit down and talk things over from that of a census-type interview and partly a function of the higher level of training and skill required of the interviewers who are doing intensive interviews.

In the poll technique the actual interviewing process is not overly complicated. But in asking open-end questions, the interviewer's role is a difficult one requiring a high level of skill. It is his job to keep the person talking, to guide the discussion along the desired channels, to prevent the discussion from wandering off the track, to move smoothly from topic to topic; he must make judgments as to the proper place to terminate the respondent's discussion of a given question, when to repeat a question, when to probe, when to restate and summarize. Difficult as this task would be under any circumstances, it is made especially hard in that he must operate continuously under two prohibitions: (1) that he shall not deviate in any appreciable way from the fixed interview schedule, not rewording questions as he sees fit, not inventing new questions on the spur of the moment, but keeping the discussion going only by nondirective techniques; (2) that he himself shall not enter into the discussion in an active role, not expressing his own opinion, indicating neither agreement nor disagreement with what the respondent says. And during the entire interview he is also kept busy making a verbatim record!

Training of the Interviewer.—As it may be guessed from what has been said above concerning the different functions of the interviewer, the requisite skill and training of the interviewer depends somewhat upon the type of interviewing technique employed. In general it may be stated that the level of experience and the quality of performance demanded of the intensive interviewer are much greater than that required of the poller. In the work of the Program Surveys Division, for instance, the interviewing staff was made up of full-time highly paid expert interviewers, who benefited from numerous training sessions, close field supervision, etc.

Poll agencies, on the whole, depend upon part-time field personnel with some, though not intensive, training and supervision. One of the important sources of difference in expense between the open-end and poll method lies in the difference in quality of interviewing personnel. Although it may be perfectly true that the average poller is sufficiently well trained to ask the fairly mechanical poll questions, it would be dangerous to assume that interviewers with no more training and skill than this could gradually undertake intensive interviewing. There is, unfortunately, a paucity of experimental evidence on the effect of training on interviewer reliability.

Reliability of Interviewing.—Under this heading we can include discussion of all those factors connected with the interview situation and with the interviewer and his conduct of the interview which make for bias and inconsistency in the responses of the individual. We can also include interviewer unreliability in the recording or rating of the individual's beliefs and attitudes.

The biasing effect of the interviewer's opinions.—It has been indicated in several methodological investigations that the opinions held by the interviewer may bias the results of his interviews, especially on certain types of issues.[1]   Cantril (1944), for instance, found that there were, in a poll study made in October, 1940, appreciable differences in the percentages of "yes" and "no" answers obtained from the respondents of interviewers who took opposite sides on the question: "Which of these things do you think is more important for the United States to try to do—to keep out of war ourselves or to help England win, even at the risk of getting into the war?" Interventionist interviewers tended to get a predominance of "help England" answers, whereas isolationist interviewers tended to get the reverse. One suggested remedy for this kind of interviewer bias has been to make the interviewing staff as closely representative as possible of the whole population, thus tending to cancel the effects of the bias. A better solution would seem to lie in greater attention being paid to the quality, training, and supervision of the field staff.

The biasing effect of the interviewer's appearance.—The appearance of the interviewer, in terms of race, socioeconomic status, etc., has also been shown to bias respondents' answers. Robinson and Rohde (1946) studied this effect in a poll study in New York City by having two poll questions relating to anti-Semitic opinions asked of comparable samples by four groups of interviewers: (1) Jewish-looking, (2) non-Jewish-looking, (3) Jewish-looking who introduced themselves with Jewish names, (4) non-Jewish-looking who introduced themselves with non-Jewish names. The two questions were:

1. Do you think there are too many Jews holding government offices and jobs?

2. Do you think that the Jews have too much power in the United States?

The percentages of "yes" answers to these two questions obtained by the four different groups of interviewers are shown in Table 2. It is clearly evident that the interviewers who looked Jewish and identified themselves as Jewish elicited markedly lower anti-Semitic responses.

A National Opinion Research Center poll during 1942 demonstrated the difference of expressed opinion among Negroes in a southern city when interviewed by Negroes and by whites. To the question, "Do you think

[1] See Blankenship (1940), Katz (1942), and Udow (1942) for studies along these lines.

it is more important to concentrate on beating the Axis or to make democracy work better here at home?" the Negro interviewers elicited 39 per cent "beat Axis" answers whereas the white interviewers elicited 62 per cent. Apparently the white interviewers were unable to establish the same degree of rapport and to obtain as sincere replies as were the Negro interviewers.

As to socioeconomic differentials, Cantril (1944) reports that a discrepancy between interviewer and respondent on the grounds of class seems to hamper rapport and make for distortion of poll answers. Working-class interviewers reported more radical views on labor questions than did white-collar interviewers.

TABLE 2

Group interviewed by	Percentage of "yes," question 1	Percentage of "yes," question 2
Jewish-looking..........................	15.4	15.6
Non-Jewish-looking......................	21.2	24.3
Jewish-looking with Jewish names..........	11.7	5.8
Non-Jewish-looking with Non-Jewish names..	19.5	21.4

The effect of secrecy and anonymity.—That the answers given openly to the interviewer may deviate from those given secretly has been shown in several studies. Cantril (1944) compared the answers to 12 poll questions when asked under two conditions: (1) by regular interview, (2) by having the respondent mark a ballot privately and drop it into a padlocked box carried by the interviewer. Significant differences in answers were found for a number of the questions, especially those which involved matters of social prestige or social approval. Another indication that on questions involving social prestige or approval the public answer of the respondent may be distorted is in Hyman's (1944) finding that in wartime 17 per cent of 243 people known to have cashed in war bonds answered that they had not cashed in any and that the correlation between absenteeism records and workers' admissions of absenteeism to interviewers was only .60.

The influence of secrecy and anonymity cannot, of course, be separated from that of rapport. It seems logical that the better the rapport that can be established the more willingly will the respondent reveal his sincere opinions and attitudes. McNemar (1946) points out that it was the experience in the Research Branch of the Morale Services Division of the War Department that face-to-face interviewing was able to ascertain data with the same degree of reliability as by anonymous written questionnaires. And it is certainly the consensus of experienced interviewers who have used the intensive open-end methods that skillful interviewing can establish the degree of rapport and confidence in the respondent necessary to elicit sincere answers.

The reliability of interviewers' ratings.—One of the important functions of the interviewer is to rate the respondent on factual characteristics and on certain psychological characteristics. There are, for obvious reasons, extreme technical difficulties in determining the reliabilities of such ratings, and few good studies are available especially in connection with the rating of the psychological variables, which are the more important and unquestionably the more difficult. On the rating of income, Cantril (1944) reports that different poll interviewers rating the same respondents agreed to the extent of a correlation of .63. Peak (1945) reports that interviewers' ratings on identification of German civilians with Nazism correlated .65 with similar ratings made by highly trained professional coders of the interview data. When the middle category was omitted (neither acceptance nor rejection of Nazism), the agreement was found to be remarkably high, with only 10 per cent disagreement in ratings.

International Applicability of the Interviewing Method.—The above findings about matters of rapport, secrecy, anonymity, etc., raise interesting questions about the general applicability of the methods of polling and intensive interviewing to people in other countries. It has sometimes been argued that these methods are especially adapted to the American scene and cannot be successfully applied elsewhere. The answer to this seems to be given in the general success of polling operations in various countries of the world over a period of years and in the successful wartime experiences of the Morale Division of the United States Strategic Bombing Survey (1946). Methods of intensive interviewing with open-end questions developed in America were applied with great success and without substantial modification to the intensive interviewing of more than seven thousand civilians in Germany, Austria, and Japan, representing a cross section of the population.

One validity check on the honesty of answers in these intensive interviews is presented by Peak (1945). She reports that estimates of total Nazi party membership based upon the admissions of party membership by respondents in the intensive interviews tallied extremely closely with best available independent estimates.[1]

It should be pointed out, of course, that methods of public opinion research are applicable only to the extent that the general political atmosphere is permissive. If people live under dictatorial or authoritarian regimes and

---

[1] The exact figures reported by Peak are 5,646,000 estimated from the intensive interviews as compared with 6,000,000 from independent records and estimates.

are afraid to express their opinions and attitudes, no method of public opinion research is likely to succeed. Nor is it likely that public opinion research of an objective sort would be tolerated by the authorities.

SAMPLING

Every study of opinions and attitudes involves *sampling, i.e.,* the selection from the whole population of a smaller group to be investigated. The measurements of characteristics of the smaller group—the sample—are the basis for inferences about these characteristics in the population. The precision with which these inferences can be made depends upon the *size* of the sample; the accuracy (lack of bias) in the inferences depends upon the *representativeness* of the sample. In this section we must consider some of the technical problems that arise in connection with sampling.

The Necessity for Sampling.—To measure an entire population—such as all adult Americans or all employed women or all homeowners in Chicago —is an enormous undertaking. For technical reasons it may be virtually impossible to do; and even if practicable, its cost may be prohibitive.[1] Only extremely rarely is the complete precision of a total census required in social measurement, and it is never required in the measurement of attitudes and opinions (except in the case of voting in elections).

The alternative to a complete count of the population is sampling. Instead of asking all eligible voters in the country for whom they expect to cast their ballots, the pollsters query a carefully chosen sample of the eligible voters. In order to determine the opinion of labor union members about a proposed labor law, a selected sample of union members is interviewed. Sampling methods are applied in virtually every field of measurement. As Stock notes, "Engineers work out the strength of certain materials by testing samples of them in the laboratory; the quality of the contents of a grain elevator is determined by a small sample; . . . a doctor determines the blood count of a single patient from a small blood sample."

Definition of the Population.—The first step in the sampling process is the definition of the population. What group, in other words, is presumably being studied? When it is reported that 65 per cent of the people favor a given issue, does this refer to 65 per cent of the entire American population —men, women, and children—to adults only, to eligible voters only, or to whom? When it is stated that a certain per cent of American workers holds a given attitude, does this refer to every American who works or only to skilled workers or only to union members or to the officers of unions or to

[1] Stock (1944) points out, for instance, that the 1940 census cost about $50,000,000 and that the unemployment census of 1937 cost $1,986,595.46. The reader will find the article by Stock a particularly valuable discussion of the sampling problem.

whom? And if a research article reports that the correlation between attitude toward Russia and attitude toward England is .40 for a group of 75 college sophomores, to what population is this supposed to be generalizable —to all college sophomores, to all college students, to all Americans, or to whom?

The necessity for precise definition of the population to be sampled is perfectly obvious, but it is neglected with surprising frequency in all sorts of social research. It is not uncommon for the attempt to define a meaningful population to follow rather than precede the selection of a sample. It need scarcely be added that such a procedure is rarely of much significance. In public opinion research, fortunately, the need for precise definition of the population has been fairly consistently appreciated.

Representativeness of the Sample.—Once the population is defined, the next step is to decide on an appropriate sample. What is of utmost importance is that the sample shall be unbiased, or representative of the population. Such representativeness can be assured by the application of a logical method for choosing the people who are to be included in the sample. The basic scheme for selection is *random sampling*, in which every person in the population shall have an equal chance of being included in the sample. How to achieve this ideal is the big technical problem of sampling.

Stratified sampling.—A sample may be drawn randomly from the entire population; this is called an *unstratified* random sample. Or the population may be divided up into subpopulations or strata, and a sample drawn randomly from within each of these strata; this is known as a *stratified* random sample. The two may be illustrated in a situation in which it is desired to sample the employees in a factory half of which are men and half women. An unstratified sample would be obtained by giving each employee (regardless of sex) an equal chance of inclusion. Thus, the total sample of 100 might come out with 46 men and 54 women. In a sample stratified by sex, however, 50 men and 50 women would be randomly chosen. (If the population distribution of men and women was not equal, of course, the numbers of men and women in the sample would not be equal but would be proportional to the respective numbers in the population.) The advantage of stratification is that the sample is less likely to deviate widely from the population distribution in the stratified respects (and in other characteristics which are correlated with the modes of stratification). For example, if men and women employees have different opinions and if by chance a random sample includes more than its proper proportion of men, the opinions of the sample as a whole will be loaded toward the male view.

There can be multiple modes of stratification. To arrive at a sample of the adult American population, for example, the sample might be stratified by state, by rural and urban areas, by sex, by age, by socioeconomic level, etc. In order to do this requires that the proper proportions of all these classifications in the whole American population be known beforehand.

Pitfalls in sampling.—It is commonly assumed that if a sample is large enough, it is likely to be free of bias. Thus, the congressman reads his avalanche of mail and computes percentages pro and con. Or a national magazine sends out ballots to its thousands of subscribers and determines what people think. In neither case is there any assurance that a truly random sample of the American people has been obtained; in fact, these are almost certain not to be representative samples since people who write to congressmen and subscribe to magazines are unique in many characteristics. Mere size of sample is not an indication of representativeness.

Even a deliberate attempt to go out to find all sorts of people from all walks of life is not necessarily successful. Poll interviewers left to their own devices are likely to accost respondents in railroad stations, to visit homes that are conspicuous, etc. Yet large segments of the population do not travel, and they live in unlikely places in inaccessible neighborhoods. Some kinds of people are simply hard to find. Hilgard and Payne (1944) have demonstrated that people who are found at home only after several callbacks may differ systematically from those found on the first call.

Statistics computed on the basis of mail questionnaires are subject to bias, due to the fact that it may be difficult to mail to a representative sample and that those who reply to mail questionnaires are by no means typical.[1]

Methods of Sampling.—Keeping the above pitfalls in mind, we turn now to a review of the principal ways that representative sampling can be done.

Sampling from files.—When a complete file of the names of the population is available, the most direct method of sampling is to select every nth name. Examples of such files are lists of employees, city directories, property lists, subscription lists, public-utility records, etc. Studies of employee morale have utilized samples drawn from pay-roll lists. Studies of reasons for bond redemptions have been made from Treasury lists. In the United States Strategic Bombing Survey study of civilian morale of Germans under bombing, the sample was drawn from up-to-date ration lists in each community.

[1] The most comprehensive consideration of mail questionnaires as a research problem will be found in Franzen and Lazarsfeld (1945). Other relevant references are Cahalan and Meier (1939), Stanton (1939), Suchman and McCandless (1940), Shuttleworth (1941), and Reuss (1943).

It is exceedingly important to determine if such lists are inclusive of the whole population being studied. The *Literary Digest* presidential poll fiasco in 1936 was caused by a dependence upon lists of telephone subscribers as representative of the voting population. Property lists, public-utility files, etc., are often likely to overrepresent the higher socioeconomic strata.

Area and block sampling.—When complete lists are not available, randomness can be achieved by a geographical method. In essence, this involves the predetermination of the home or farm to which the interviewer is to go to get his interview, on the basis of a randomly placed point on a rural map or a randomly chosen house in a randomly chosen block from a city map. The details of this process are too technical for discussion here,[1] but several implications of this method should be noted. By largely restricting the freedom of the interviewer in selecting his respondents, it goes far toward the avoidance of bias in the sample. It has been shown to yield samples that check well against census figures for sex, age, rural-urban residence, race, and socioeconomic level. But it is an expensive method, requiring more travel, callbacks, etc.

Quota control sampling.—The method of sampling most widely used by polling agencies is a combination of methods of stratification and of selection of respondents by the interviewer. The central office determines what proportion of the total sample should fall into certain strata—age, sex, socioeconomic level, geographic region, etc. The interviewer is then instructed to fill his quota in each of these set categories by getting people at random. That is, he may be required in a given study with a quota of 20 interviews to find 10 men and 10 women, 12 people below forty and 8 over forty, 18 whites and 2 Negroes, etc. He will, of course, be instructed to find his respondents in a given community or in one part of a community.

We have mentioned above that one of the pitfalls in sampling is the biased choice by the interviewer of his respondents. Though the quotas imposed upon him do serve to restrict the amount of such bias, he is still permitted fairly wide latitude in the persons he will pick to fill a given cell. That such bias does tend to occur in the quota sampling is seen in the repeated findings that when such methods are used in national polls, there is a consistent upward bias in education and socioeconomic level. This is also found in Gallup's election polls, reflected there as an overrepresentation of Republican sentiment.[2]

The method of quota control sampling has been universally used by public opinion polling agencies because it is cheap, fairly simple, and has not in the

---

[1] The interested reader may refer to Hansen and Hauser (1945) for details.

[2] See Katz (1941, 1944) for cogent analyses of some of the sampling shortcomings of the public opinion polls in the presidential elections of 1940 and 1944.

past been subject to gross bias. That it is not so accurate a method as is desirable, however, has become increasingly apparent, and the polling agencies have begun to tighten up their procedures, to reduce the amount of freedom in interviewers' choice of respondents, etc. But the quota control method still falls considerably short of the accuracy of the more costly area or block sampling.

Choice of sample points.—For nation-wide studies both block and quota control sampling are carried out in a limited number of sample points, *i.e.*, in certain communities and certain counties. The interviews obviously cannot be spread out randomly over the whole country, nor is this statistically necessary. What is done is to use techniques for the random selection of a limited number of communities and counties in which all individual sampling is carried out. Choice of sample points is usually done by stratification; *i.e.*, all communities and counties in the country are classified into various categories—size, industrialization, region, etc.—and then the sample points are selected randomly and in the proper proportion from these cells.

Checking the sample.—The representativeness of a sample, however chosen, can be checked in one way by comparing the percentages of certain characteristics in the sample against the known percentages of these characteristics in the population. The correct population figures may be ascertained through the census and other independent sources. The fact that a sample checks in certain characteristics does not, of course, ensure that it is unbiased in other aspects.

The use of panels.—For certain research purposes, such as studying changes in opinions and attitudes, a panel technique may be valuable. By reinterviewing the same panel of respondents, sometimes repeatedly, it may be possible to reduce some of the random sampling errors and hence to increase the sensitiveness of the measurement of change.[1]

Size of Sample.—Even assuming that a sample is chosen in an entirely random fashion, *i.e.*, so that every person in the population has an equal chance of being included, it cannot be expected that the sample value will coincide precisely with the population value. Purely by chance some people will be included and others not, and so the sample value may fall below or above the population value. The fewer the number of cases in the sample the more probable is it that a wide deviation from the population value can occur. For example, if we were to choose 10 people perfectly randomly from the whole population of a city, it would sometimes happen that the proportion of men would be more or less than the proportion of women.

[1] A critique of the panel method can be found in Lazarsfeld and Fiske (1938) and Lazarsfeld (1940), and example of its application in Lazarsfeld, Berelson, and Gaudet (1944), *The People's Choice.*

Sometimes the proportion might be as high as 8 men to 2 women. But if we were to take a random sample of 100 cases in the city, the likelihood of getting 80 men and 20 women would be much less, though it would—on very rare occasions—happen.

Assuming an unbiased sample, therefore, the larger the sample the more likely is it that the sample value will approximate the population value. As size of samples goes up, precision increases very rapidly at first, then more slowly. In general it may be stated that the precision of a sample increases in proportion to the square root of the number of cases. A hypothetical case may clarify the point. Assume that in a random sample of 100 cases we obtain 40 per cent "yes" answers. It can be shown that with a confidence of 99 out of 100 we can state that the limits within which the population percentage of "yes" might fall are from 28 to 52.5 per cent. If the sample were 200 cases, the confidence limits would be 32 to 49 per cent. Table 3 shows the rapidly narrowing range of limits within which the population value might fall as the size of sample increases.[1]

TABLE 3

Sample Size	Confidence Limits, Per Cent
100	28.0 to 52.5
200	32.0 to 49.0
500	34.5 to 45.5
1,000	36.0 to 44.0
3,000	37.5 to 42.5
10,000	38.5 to 41.5

It will be noted that with a sample of 500 the range of possible error is only slightly more than 5 per cent in either direction. And it is also to be emphasized that this is true regardless of how large the population may be. Sometimes it is erroneously believed that if the population is large, the sample must be proportionately large. But, in fact, assuming randomness of sampling, a sample of 500 will give just about as precise results for a study of the whole of the United States as it will for a survey of a single large city.

The determination of the exact size of sample to be used in any public opinion study rests mainly upon two considerations: (1) the desired precision of the results and (2) the kind of analysis to be made of the results. In regard to the first point, the size of sample will be adjusted so that the percentage figures can be considered correct within 1 or 2 or 5 per cent or whatever else is desired. To obtain a crude picture of how sentiment on an issue lies, it may not be important whether the population figure is 70 or 65 or 80 per cent. Hence, the sample need not be large. In an election poll, on the other hand, it may be decisive whether sentiment for one party

[1] Figures taken from chart presented by Wilks (1940).

is 49 or 51 per cent, and in this case the size of sample must be appropriately larger.

In regard to the second point, it is usually the case that the survey data are to be broken down into various subclassifications in order to ascertain the opinions of different categories of people. Also, it is customary that the answers to one question are cross tabulated against the answers to other questions. To the extent that such breakdowns are envisaged, the size of sample must be made large enough so that the precision of measurement within any single subgroup will reach the required levels. If figures are to be reported for the nation as a whole, a smaller sample will suffice than if they are to be reported region by region or state by state or occupation by occupation.

Precision of a sample increases as the square root of the number of cases, whereas cost of increased samples goes up almost in direct proportion. This means that there is pressure to keep samples as small as possible, consistent with required precision. The samples used in most public opinion polls are quite small. This is sometimes the basis of unjustified criticism of the accuracy of polls. But quite at variance with popular belief, it is a statis‐tical fact that the relatively small samples yield remarkably high precision.

PROBLEMS OF ANALYSIS

Before analysis proper can begin, it is necessary to categorize and tabulate the data from all the interviews. We have already seen that for poll questions the coding process is automatic, since the respondent himself indicates the specific category into which he is to be placed. For the full, narrative answers to open-end questions, however, the coding process is an important step, the details of which we must now consider.

Coding and Tabulating.—The aim of coding is simply to assign each interview to its proper category in each of a large number of dimensions. The types of dimensions are numerous, including, among others, the follow-ing: (1) *sociological* variables, such as sex, age, rural-urban residence, geo-graphical location, race, occupation, education, and income; (2) other *factual* characteristics, such as type of house, membership in a given organ-ization, possession of a car or radio; (3) *psychological* variables, such as level of information (general or specific), group identifications, economic dissatis-factions, personality traits, political preferences; (4) *opinion and attitude* variables, such as approval or disapproval of a given object, belief or disbe-lief of a specific sort, "yes-no" answers to specific questions, intensity and other attributes of opinions and attitudes; (5) *reasons* for opinions and attitudes, either those expressed by the respondent or those judged by the coder.

The particular scheme of classification for each of these variables will, of course, be determined by such things as the number of occupational categories to be used, the number of levels of information desired, the number of degrees of approval or disapproval in the attitude rating, and the variety of reasons that may be offered.

Code construction.—The skeleton for the codes of a study should ideally be fixed in advance; *i.e.*, the variables to be coded should have been decided upon, as well as the main categories of these variables. This makes possible a great deal of "precoding" by the interviewer himself with respect to factual and sociological variables and even ratings of psychological characteristics. When a sample of interviews is returned to the central office, the coding staff can try out the skeleton codes in a preliminary way, decide where they need revision, put "flesh on their bones" in the form of specific categories of reasons, etc. Once a workable **code** has been established, the actual final coding process can begin.

Problems in coding.—The coding of intensive interview data requires the services of a well-trained coding staff. Many of the judgments required in coding psychological variables are subtle and difficult ones requiring a high order of psychological insight. The coder must be sensitive to the meaning and the context of the words as well as their obvious content. The data in intensive interviews are often insufficient to make for clear-cut judgments. Sometimes the interview seems not to be classifiable with respect to the rigid code, and often a particular code category seems inapplicable because of the coexistence of other aspects in the reply which alter its significance.

Reliability of coding.—All of the foregoing problems work, of course, to reduce the reliability of the coding process. Reliability of coding is always ascertained, as the coding progresses, by "check coding," in which a selected sample of all interviews is independently recoded by another coder or sometimes by the coding supervisor. Such checking serves two functions: (1) to reveal sources of discrepancy in the way various coders are making their judgments, thus enabling them to arrive at better common standards and definitions, (2) to inform the analyst of the approximate reliability of the over-all figures tabulated from a given code, so that he may interpret and manipulate the data with the proper degree of caution.

As might be expected, reliability over many intensive surveys has been found to be highest with the more factual variables and lowest with the more subtle psychological variables. Reliability may be increased in a number of ways. First, it is increased by the attainment of common standards and definitions among coders. This is sometimes accomplished by an intensive preliminary "round robin" in which a small sample of interviews is coded and compared and discussed by all the coders. Second, coding

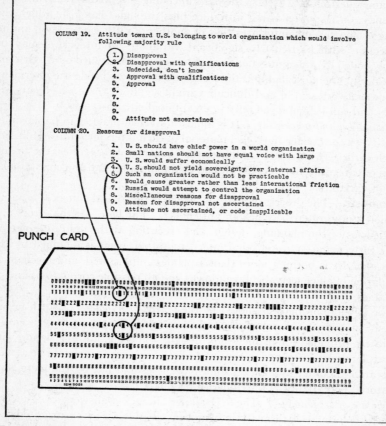

QUESTION

Q. 8: How would you feel about this country belonging to a world organization where we would have to follow the decisions of the majority of the nations?

ANSWER

"No, American people don't want laws from someone else. We want to make our own and live by them. We do pretty well by ourselves. It's fine to have an organization to settle fighting and war -- but leave America out of everything else. We've got it pretty good here, and we don't want to change. You said the majority of the nations. What if they gang up on us? Then we're liable to have to do pretty near anything. Look at how Europe followed Hitler -- he'd have had lots of votes. We don't want any messing with our government. Anyway, that kind of organization wouldn't work. You couldn't get the nations to follow what was decided. They'd walk out on what they didn't like, just the way Russia's been doing."

COLUMN 19. Attitude toward U.S. belonging to world organization which would involve following majority rule

    1. Disapproval
    2. Disapproval with qualifications
    3. Undecided, don't know
    4. Approval with qualifications
    5. Approval
    6.
    7.
    8.
    9.
    0. Attitude not ascertained

COLUMN 20. Reasons for disapproval

    1. U. S. should have chief power in a world organization
    2. Small nations should not have equal voice with large
    3. U. S. would suffer economically
    4. U. S. should not yield sovereignty over internal affairs
    5. Such an organization would not be practicable
    6. Would cause greater rather than less international friction
    7. Russia would attempt to control the organization
    8. Miscellaneous reasons for disapproval
    9. Reason for disapproval not ascertained
    0. Attitude not ascertained, or code inapplicable

PUNCH CARD

Fig 7.—An illustration of the coding of open-end questions, showing a typical open-end question, a verbatim answer, the codes relating to the question, and the manner in which the appropriate columns in the punch cards are punched to indicate how the answer is coded. Column 20 is double-punched (4 and 5) because both these reasons are found in the answer.

301

reliability will reflect the care with which the original questionnaire was constructed. For a variable to be codable, it is essential that there be foresight in providing the proper questions to elicit the diagnostic material. Third, the adequacy of the performance of the interviewer is reflected in coder reliability. Often the interviewer fails to "follow through" on a question, fails to elicit the context and the underlying reasons. He simply does not give the coder sufficient information. Fourth, coding reliability may often be enhanced by extending the scope of material on which the given variable is rated. Thus, the coder may make his judgment on the basis of a cluster of questions or of the whole interview instead of a single question. But if the same questions are used as the basis of coding several different variables, this may, on the other hand, introduce bias through "halo," in which the rating of one variable influences that of another. Fifth, on occasion and in connection with particularly significant variables, all interviews may be doubly coded by different coders and the discrepancies ironed out. Or even more rarely, the most highly trained expert analysts will code the interviews on one or two essential and difficult variables. Both these expedients are costly and can be employed only in exceptional circumstances.[1]

Tabulation and machining.—It is almost universal practice in public opinion surveys to transfer the coded material of each interview onto a Hollerith punch card. This greatly facilitates the counting of categories, the breakdown of categories by different factual characteristics, and the cross tabulation of variables.

Analysis.—The process of analysis, which is the logical climax of a public opinion study, often becomes an anticlimax. For here, all the errors and deficiencies of the planning, design, and execution of the study become all too clearly manifest. And here, much too often, what is dignified by the term *analysis* is nothing more than a planless, uninspired, and mechanical tabulation of all conceivable breakdowns and all possible correlations among variables.

The keynote of analysis should be the *testing of hypotheses*, which means the study of certain breakdowns and cross tabulations that have been deliberately provided for in the study design. There is nothing wrong with the exploration of new and unexpected relationships, but it should be a planful search, dictated by hunches and hypotheses and not by the mere combinatorial potentialities of a Hollerith machine.

The use of breakdowns.—The over-all percentages of answers for the whole population provide little analytic significance. What is necessary is to break down the data into subclassifications, so that they can be compared and

---

[1] Such expert coding was used for the determination of attitude of German civilians toward Nazism in the study described by Peak (1945).

correlated. In this way the psychological and sociological "determinants" of opinions and attitudes may be revealed.

The principal types of breakdowns are as follows:[1]

1. Breakdown of opinions and attitudes by age, sex, geographical region, education, income, and other sociological and factual characteristics

2. Breakdown of opinions and attitudes by level of information, political preference, personality traits, economic dissatisfactions, and other psychological characteristics

3. Breakdown of opinions and attitudes by other opinions and attitudes

4. Higher order breakdowns, which break by three or more variables at once

5. Pattern breakdowns in which answers to many questions are used simultaneously to develop a scale or index

Which of these types will be used in any given study depends upon the particular hypotheses to be tested and the particular kinds of information that are to be reported. Several generalizations about the relative usefulness of these types of breakdowns can, nevertheless, be made. First, breakdowns by sociological variables are not likely to be so discriminating and so meaningful as other types of analyses. The differentiation of opinions and attitudes is not likely to take place primarily along lines of age, sex, place of residence, occupation, etc., except in special circumstances. That these breakdowns do often yield differences is usually an artifact, based on the circumstance that the sociological variables are, for other reasons, partially correlated with the basic determining variables. And even if correlations with sociological data can be found, they may not merit reporting. What, for instance, is the value of reporting that people over forty are more in favor of a reduction on tax than people under forty? Sometimes, of course, the sociological break may be of primary interest in a study. Thus, in order to design and direct propaganda most effectively, it may be useful to know which occupational groups, which racial groups, which geographical groups, which income groups hold certain opinions and attitudes.

Second, breakdowns by psychological variables are likely to be especially productive. Opinions and attitudes are psychological entities, and as such their basic determinants and governing conditions are to be sought in other psychological factors. The psychological group identifications of an individual are more important than his formal occupational or class membership. His feelings of economic insecurity and dissatisfaction are more important than the objective facts about his income. One study, for example,

---

[1] See Chap. 13 in Cantril (1944) for a more detailed discussion and illustration of such breakdowns. Also, see McNemar (1946) for a critical analysis of some problems in the "quest for correlates."

showed that anti-Semitic attitudes were more highly correlated with the discrepancy between an individual's income and the income he desired than with the absolute level of his income.[1]   Many studies have shown that information is a more significant correlate of opinions and attitudes than is formal education.

Third, higher order breakdowns are likely to be more informative for analysis than simple ones.   Complex interaction is the rule in psychological processes, and the relationship between any two variables may only be understandable if other variables are also taken into account.

Pitfalls in interpretation.—The final stage in a study is the interpretation of the relationships that have been discovered in the process of analysis. In many respects it is this stage which is the most susceptible to error. Techniques of question formulation, interviewing, sampling, coding, and analysis are constantly undergoing refinement, and the reliability of these successive steps is being improved.   But at the point of interpretation, the public opinion researcher must become more than a technician; he must become a social scientist.   Many public opinion "experts" have gained reputations through technical competence, but this does not qualify them to make pronouncements upon social, political, psychological, and economic problems.

Some of the pitfalls in interpretation relate to quite specific matters.   For one thing, relationships that are found in analysis may be presented without an adequate test of their statistical significance.   For another thing, relationships that are found to be statistically significant may be presented as having *social* or *psychological* significance, whereas in fact they may be too small to be important.

Other errors are made in inferring causation from correlation.   That one variable is found to be related to another is sometimes taken to mean one causes the other.   Such observed relationships are often, in fact almost always, spurious; *i.e.*, the true psychological causation is to be found only in other more basic factors or in complex combinations of factors.

We have already mentioned (page 283) the dangers inherent in imputing absolute significance to simple percentages of answers to questions.   Somewhat related to this error is that noted by Katz (1946) in which problems of fact are confused with problems of opinions about fact.   Thus, he gives the example of a public opinion poll release during the war which carried the implication that there was in fact a great deal of unwarranted absenteeism on the basis of people's answers to the loaded question, "What do you think should be done with workers in war factories who are regularly absent from work without a good excuse?"

[1] Campbell (1947).

Another common error in interpretation consists in failing to take account of the differences in social influence of people expressing opinions. The usual polling practice is to weight all people's opinions equally. Yet this is clearly contradictory to the fact that for many expressions of opinions and attitudes, some people are more important than others. Some individuals and some groups may play an especially decisive role in certain social actions; some people are community or group leaders, and their opinions affect those of many other people; some people are experts on the issues and their opinions may carry extra weight. Proper analysis and interpretation of results must take account of these facts, and the design of a study and the definition of the population should consider them.[1]

Trend analysis.—A good deal of public opinion research is concerned with changes in opinions and attitudes over time. Changes in the answers to a question asked repeatedly may be taken to demonstrate basic psychological shifts, and these shifts are then "explained" on the basis of important social happenings during the period. Errors in interpretation are particularly common here because of a failure to establish real psychological connection of the events and the attitude changes, because of failure to take account of changes in the meaning of the question over time, because of slight (but decisive) changes in the wordings of the questions, etc.

THE STEPS IN A PUBLIC OPINION SURVEY

It may be worth while at this point to summarize the eight steps involved in a public opinion survey and to indicate some of the details of these steps not yet discussed.[2]

1. *Statement of problem, hypotheses, and objectives.*—The first and most essential step is to understand the particular problem as it exists in a practical form for the government administrator, the labor relations expert, the propagandist, or the economist. Then the problem must be analyzed and broken down into relevant subproblems. For each of these problems, hypotheses must be formulated; *i.e.*, it is conjectured that this variable is related to that, that a change in one factor will cause a change in another, etc. It is decided just what measurements will be needed in order to test the various hypotheses. And finally, in this first stage of the study, the population to be studied is defined.

2. *Design of study and sample.*—With these required measurements in mind the next step is to decide on the strategy of the study. How can

[1] One approach to this general problem is the study of samples of leaders, and another is the poll of experts. See in this connection the work of Kornhauser (1947).

[2] The reader may refer to Maccoby and Holt (1946) for a more detailed description of how surveys are made.

the measurements best be made?   Will a comparative analysis of two groups or two communities or two industrial plants be the most effective?   Or will it be necessary to measure a single group periodically?   Can the problem be studied experimentally; *i.e.*, may not a group be subjected to experimental effects and then compared with a control group?   Will poll questions or open-end questions or both be required?   At what date will the interviewing be done?   What kind of a sample will be drawn and where?

3. *Construction of interview schedule.*—Questions are then built to elicit the data needed for the various measurements.   Care must be taken in the wording of the questions, in their ordering in the schedule; "icebreakers" must be provided at the beginning; etc.   A number of alternative questions designed to measure the same variables may be developed.

4. *Pretest and pilot study.*—The interview schedule is next tried out on a small sample of respondents, poor questions are changed, new ones added, until the schedule works smoothly as an interviewing instrument.   An important feature of the pretest is the coding of interviews on the spot, to see if the questions do yield the data required to make the necessary measurements.

A further step at this point, which is all too rarely used in public opinion research, is a pilot study.   The pretest is elaborated to the point that a sufficient number of interviews on the final form of the schedule are collected. These interviews are coded, and an abbreviated analysis of the data is made. In this way it is possible to discover which areas of the problem have not been adequately analyzed, where more attention should be placed, which variables require more refined measurement, which ones can be dropped, etc.   It is probable that the expense of such a pilot study is repaid manifold in the increased efficiency and productiveness of the final large-scale study.

5. *Field work.*—The next step is the training and assignment of interviewers and their interviewing of the sample of respondents.   The interviews are collected in the central office where the final steps (6) *coding and machining*, (7) *analysis*, and (8) *preparation of report* are carried out.

SOCIAL SIGNIFICANCE OF PUBLIC OPINION RESEARCH

The significance of public opinion research to pure social psychology in its search for understanding of principles of opinions and attitudes and to applications of social psychology in obtaining insights and facts necessary to the solution of practical problems requires no elucidation.   But it may be worth while to review some of the broader social implications of public opinion research.

Public Information.—The greatest significance of public opinion research probably lies in its potentialities for apprising the individual citizen of the opinions and attitudes of other citizens. One important source of social tensions of all kinds is the relative ignorance of the average person about what other people think. He carries about a burden of misconceptions and stereotypes; he leads a kind of "autistic" life (see page 59) in which he is insulated from the reality of other people's existences. The usual media of mass communication—newspapers, magazines, radios, motion pictures— are inadequate to pierce this fog of ignorance and misconception. In many ways, in fact, they function so as to worsen it. They do not provide un- biased pictures of what other people think, and they talk only about certain kinds of people; *i.e.*, their sampling is biased.

Wide dissemination of the results of public opinion studies can play a positive role in helping to correct this situation. By proper techniques of sampling, the opinions and attitudes of all segments of the population can be publicized. And by proper techniques of interviewing, analysis, and reporting, these opinions and attitudes can be made understandable in terms of the context, the underlying reasons, and the point of view of the people holding them.

International understanding.—What is true of one country is true of the world as a whole. Public opinion research on the opinions and attitudes of people in one country can be of inestimable value in increasing understand- ing of them by people of other countries. One source of international ten- sion is the misunderstanding of other peoples, and what is urgently required is the widespread dissemination of more facts. There have been some de- velopments on the international scene in this direction. Public opinion polls are being instituted in numerous countries, and there are proposals for international public opinion research agencies.[1]

The obstacles to this development on the international scene are obvious. Some authoritarian governments are unwilling to permit the people of their countries to know what other segments of their civilian population are thinking. And many countries may be afraid to allow the world as a whole to be well informed on the opinions and attitudes of their people and even more afraid to allow their people to be apprised of what people in other countries really think.

Democratic Leadership.—Another social significance of public opinion research lies in its capabilities of keeping the leaders of a country (or of any social organization) in close touch with the people (or the rank-and-file members). Leadership cannot be democratic unless means are available by which the leader can be constantly and closely informed concerning the opinions and attitudes of the people. Lobbyists, official spokesmen, news- papers, letters to congressmen, etc., cannot be depended upon to be unbiased

[1] For one such proposal, see Dodd (1946).

or comprehensive in their reporting of public opinion.   Properly conducted, public opinion research can supply a great need here.

Nielsen (1946) makes the interesting observation that this function of public opinion research is not to be found in countries where democratic leadership is absent.   In Germany and Japan, public opinion research was never developed as a tool for keeping the leadership in close contact with the "will of the people."   In these countries any study of opinion had the function of determining only whether or not the people were obeying the policies that their leaders had laid down.   Nielsen writes:

> The evidence which is available suggests that for very basic reasons totalitarian governments cannot use attitude research for "good" purposes, *i.e.*, adjusting policy to the nation's desires.   Moreover, they have the greatest difficulty in using the technique even for purely expedient purposes, *i.e.*, achieving some objective appraisal of the effectiveness and adequacy of their own programs.   It appears that the useful application of attitude research by government requires considerable tolerance for criticism within the bureaucratic structure, and mutual confidence between governors of the state and the people.   These premises did not obtain in Germany and Japan, and opinion research took the degenerate form of police spying.

Government Administration.—Before and especially during the war methods of public opinion research, particularly of the intensive survey variety, established their value as an aid in government administration. Campbell (1946)[1] lists some of the types of questions that surveys have been intended to answer in connection with the appraisal of Federal programs and the development of new programs: (1) How well is the public informed on the subject matter of informational campaigns, and how much does it know about the details of specific programs?   (2) How does the public feel about actions the government has taken?   (3) How will the public feel about new government action that is being planned?   (4) What is the public doing in connection with specific programs?   (5) What is the public planning to do in the future?   (6) Are there public needs on which the government should take action?

These questions are complicated ones and require highly developed research techniques.   As Campbell remarks: "It must be apparent that a survey designed to examine a complicated program of this kind bears little resemblance to the polls of public opinion to which newspaper readers are accustomed.   Most government agencies are concerned with problem

---

[1] See also Truman (1945) for a statement of the range of administrative problems that might be subject to attitude research and Woodward (1944) for an account of some of the difficulties encountered in making such attitude research bear on actual administrative operation.

analysis rather than polling and require much more highly developed procedures than are used in most polls."

A good example of survey research designed to help solve problems of government administration is a series of studies undertaken during the war for the Treasury Department. In the four years following Pearl Harbor this Federal agency was required to borrow through the sale of government bonds a net total of more than two hundred billion dollars and to raise this huge sum in a way that would minimize the danger of wartime inflation. To do so, billions of dollars of war bonds had to be sold to the rank and file of the population; the spending habits of the nation had to be greatly changed almost overnight.

Treasury officials called upon the Division of Program Surveys to conduct periodic surveys to assist in designing and evaluating the program of education and selling set up to sell war bonds. In these surveys all the types of questions mentioned by Campbell were investigated. After each drive, for example, survey results revealed how well informed the public was about its activities, popular reactions of approval or disapproval of selling techniques were determined, attitudes toward proposed quotas were discovered, the number of people who bought extra bonds during the drive was ascertained, people's plans for the use of money invested in bonds were found out, and the public's needs for improved facilities for buying and redeeming bonds were uncovered.

Through a thorough analysis of the successes and failures of past programs and of the reasons for each, new programs were constantly being designed with increasing efficiency. As a result of the use of this research the sale of war bonds was greatly increased and the cost of the program to the taxpayer significantly reduced.[1]

Dangers in Public Opinion Research.—The social significance of public opinion research is very great, but like any highly productive scientific technique it has potentialities for evil as well as for good.

Misleading the public.—As public confidence in and reliance upon public opinion research grows, there is an increased responsibility on those conducting and reporting the research for careful, honest, and impartial work. The printed reports of national public opinion agencies have often seemed to go beyond and to misinterpret the actual poll data. There has often appeared to be bias in the issues chosen for study, and in the way the questions on these issues are formulated. The reporting of technical procedures employed has been grossly inadequate. And there has been no assurance that the published results represent more than a fraction of the data that have

[1] A comprehensive account of public opinion research in the wartime activities of the Treasury Department is given in a forthcoming book by Cartwright.

been accumulated. To the extent to which these criticisms hold, the public is misled, perhaps unintentionally, but misled nonetheless.

In its very nature public opinion research is potentially corruptible, and in the hands of special-interest groups and propagandists it might become the tool of misinformation rather than information. The insurance against such misuse lies for one thing in the improvement of technical aspects of the research, the tightening up of the procedures, and the growth of a sizable body of social scientists who feel professional responsibility for this research. There are many heartening advances along these lines. Problems of the impartial publication of such research are of a different order. Objective standards are needed, and it has even been proposed that, borrowing a leaf from the Federal control of foods and drugs, there should be a "pure polls" act which would establish proper safeguards in the publication of public opinion research data.

Emasculating leadership.—Although democratic leadership may benefit from the use of public opinion research, this does not mean that good leadership consists in simply *following* every twist and turn of public opinion. Cartwright (1946) states the problem clearly:

What do we want of our leaders in a democracy? What should they do for us? Certainly they should represent the will of the majority; we all agree to that. But they should do more. We want men who will lead as well as follow the public will; we want experts who know more about the subject than anyone else; we want men of vision who can invent new solutions to our problems. No doubt a poll of the American people would reveal support of each of these propositions. If the public really accepts these functions of the leader, however, it then follows that leaders should by no means always abide by the results of the polls. There are certain circumstances under which they are obliged to disregard them.

Among the circumstances mentioned by Cartwright are (1) that people may be polled on technical issues about which they are little informed and on which their answers may be meaningless, (2) that people may be asked to suggest new solutions to problems or new policies and the lack of suggestions may be taken as a mandate to the leader to do nothing, and (3) that though people may select poll alternatives presented to them, they may feel little conviction about the issue and the sharpness of the separation of answers may fail to reflect the essential confusion of thought which exists.

The danger that democratic leadership may, by its reliance on public opinion research, come to follow rather than to lead is not merely a hypothetical one, as is demonstrated by the increasing use of poll data in political campaigning. Some political candidates seem to have come to rely in disconcerting degree upon the results of public opinion studies for the stand they take upon issues, for the platform they uphold, and even for the details of the wording of the political speeches they make.[1]

Public opinion research used in this fashion can weaken leadership; used properly, it can sustain, strengthen, and make truly significant the term *democratic leadership*.

SUMMARY

It is pointed out that the applicability of the measuring devices discussed in Chap. VII is restricted to special groups of people and that the disproportionate emphasis in the use of these techniques has therefore resulted in the neglect of the average member of society and of the investigation of some socially important problems. In answer to this situation methods of large-scale public opinion measurement have been developed, and a number of national and international organizations are briefly described whose major function is the conduct of such measurements. However, this type of measurement raises many methodological problems, and the objective of this chapter is stated as the examination of these problems.

First some general comments are made on the tendency of public opinion polls to include single questions relating to varied issues within one interviewing schedule and their dependency on the single question to provide the basis for measurement. The practical considerations that encourage this procedure and the dangers inherent in this practice are discussed, and it is concluded that better practice demands that the interview schedule show more careful experimental design, center about one problem, and consist of a series of integrated questions directed at various related aspects of the problem.

The *type of question* to be used in public opinion surveys is then taken up for discussion. Two different kinds of questions are described, discussed, and compared. These are the *poll* question and the *open-end* question. The first is characterized as being designed to elicit a choice by the respondent of one of a set of presented alternatives; the second, to elicit a free response

---

[1] It is also significant, in this connection, that editorial policy may ultimately come to depend upon public opinion polls for a guide as to what line should be taken. This abdication of editorial leadership is implied in the recent statement by a professor of journalism who argues for the use of public opinion polls as tools to prevent "errors of editorial judgment." In his words: "A publisher is smart to take a poll before he gets his neck out too far. Polls provide a better idea of acceptance of newspaper policies."

This proposed expedient of saying only what the public wants to hear is not unrelated to the current trend in radio programming which, by its slavish dependence upon market research in public opinion, sacrifices the possibility of progressive leadership to the goal of discovering the least common denominator of public approval.

not restricted to predetermined categories. It is concluded that the open-end question is potentially capable of providing validity, depth, meaning, and comprehensiveness in attitude and opinion measurement in a higher degree than the poll question. The open-end question is superior in ascertaining the respondent's interpretations, in being less dependent upon specific biasing wordings, in determining the reasons for opinions, and in providing fuller data for analysis. In the study of issues upon which opinions are highly crystallized or in determining matters of fact, the poll question—because of its greater simplicity and economy—may be preferred. The two methods may be profitably used together, the open-end question to explore the dimensions of the problem and to establish the context and reasons, the poll question to measure certain specific dimensions.

The second methodological problem discussed is that centering around *interviewing*. Here an examination is made of the *functions* of the interviewer, the *training* of the interviewer, the *reliability* of the interviewer, and the *international applicability* of the interviewing method as these problems appear in connection with both the polling surveys and the open-end, non-directive interviews. In discussing these problems the experimental data relating to each are examined, and some specific cautions and guides for reducing bias and unreliability due to interview sources are suggested.

In discussing the problems related to *sampling*, the necessity for using sampling procedures in public opinion studies is first pointed out, and the importance of defining precisely the population to be sampled is emphasized. After that the various common sampling techniques are discussed, and the difficulties with each are pointed to. Among the sampling techniques used by public opinion studies, the following major two are examined: (1) stratified sampling, (2) unstratified sampling. Either method, however, involves the problem of getting a representative sample. To achieve this representativeness, the following technical procedures are described: (1) sampling from files, (2) area and block sampling, (3) quota control sampling. Then some discussion is given over to the choice of sample points, checking the sample, and the use of panels. In discussing the size of the sample, the various considerations that determine the optimal size are considered, and it is emphasized that relatively small samples can yield high precision.

The process of *analysis*, which is the logical climax of a public opinion study, is then discussed. The problems and pitfalls in analysis that are characteristic of both the polling procedure and the open-end interviewing method are examined with respect to coding and tabulating, the use of breakdowns, and interpretations. With respect to the first of these, it is pointed out that the open-end method requires more care and is subject to more errors than is the polling method. However, with respect to the last two of these, the superiority of the open-end method is demonstrated by the fact that breakdowns in terms of psychological determinants rather than sociological determinants are more readily available and a more insightful interpretation of cause-and-effect relationships is possible. Several common errors in interpretaion of public opinion studies are isolated for special examination.

The steps involved in a public opinion survey are then summarized. These are (1) clearly stating the problem, hypotheses, and objectives; (2) designing the study and sample; (3) constructing the interview schedule; (4) pretesting and conducting pilot studies; (5) doing the field work; (6) coding and tabulating the data; (7) making the analysis; and (8) preparing the report.

The last section of this chapter concerns itself with the social significance of public opinion research. It is pointed out that its values lie in its potentialities for apprising the citizen of the opinions and attitudes of his fellow citizens, in increasing international understandings among people of various countries, in its capabilities of keeping the leaders of a country (or of any social organization) in close touch with the people (or the rank-and-file membership), and in aiding government administration. However, it is also pointed out that public opinion research has potentialities for evil as for good. Public opinion research is potentially corruptible, and in the hands of special-interest groups and propagandists it might become the tool of misinformation rather than information; and second, it is pointed out that the grave danger exists that democratic leadership, in its reliance on public opinion research, may come to follow rather than to lead the people. Public opinion research used in this fashion can weaken leadership; used properly, it can sustain, strengthen, and make truly significant the term *democratic* leadership.

BIBLIOGRAPHY

BLANKENSHIP, A. B.: 1940. The effect of the interviewer upon the response in a public opinion poll. *J. consult. Psychol.*, 4, 134–136.

BRUNER, J. S.: 1944. *Mandate from the people.* New York: Duell, Sloan & Pearce.

CAHALAN, D., and MEIER, N. C.: 1939. The validity of mail ballot polls. *Psychol. Rec.*, 3, 2–11.

CAMPBELL, A.: 1946. The uses of interview surveys in federal administration. *J. soc Issues*, 2, 14–22.

CAMPBELL, A. A.: 1947. Factors associated with attitudes toward Jews. *In* Newcomb, T. M., Hartley, E. L., *et al.* (ed.), *Readings in social psychology.* New York: Holt.

CANTRIL, H.: 1944. *Gauging public opinion.* Princeton: Princeton Univ. Press.

CARTWRIGHT, D.: 1946. Public opinion polls and democratic leadership. *J. soc. Issues*, 2, 23–32.

CRUTCHFIELD, R. S., and GORDON, D. A.: 1947.   Variations in respondents' interpretations of an opinion-poll question.   *Int. J. Opin. & Att. Res.*, **1**, No. 3, 1–12.

DODD, S. C.: 1946.   Toward world surveying.   *Publ. Opin. Quart.*, **10**, 470–483.

FERRABY, J. G.: 1945.   Planning a mass-observation investigation.   *Amer. J. Sociol.*, **51**, 1–6.

FRANZEN, R., and LAZARSFELD, P. F.: 1945.   Mail questionnaires as a research problem. *J. Psychol.*, **20**, 239–320.

HANSEN, M. H., and HAUSER, P. M.: 1945.   Area sampling—some principles of sample design.   *Publ. Opin. Quart.*, **9**, 183–193.

HILGARD, E. R., and PAYNE, S. L.: 1944.   Those not at home: riddle for pollsters.   *Publ. Opin. Quart.*, **8**, 254–261.

HYMAN, H.: 1944.   Do they tell the truth?   *Publ. Opin. Quart.*, **8**, 557–559.

KATZ, D.: 1941.   The public opinion polls and the 1940 election.   *Publ. Opin. Quart.*, **5**, 52–78.

KATZ, D.: 1942.   Do interviewers bias poll results?   *Publ. Opin. Quart.*, **6**, 248–268.

KATZ, D.: 1944.   The polls and the 1944 election.   *Publ. Opin. Quart.*, **8**, 468–482.

KATZ, D.: 1946.   The interpretation of survey findings.   *J. soc. Issues*, **2**, 33–44.

KORNHAUSER, A. W.: 1947.   Problems and possibilities in polling experts on social issues. *Amer. Psychol.*, **2**, 329.

LAZARSFELD, P. F.: 1940.   Panel studies.   *Publ. Opin. Quart.*, **4**, 122–128.

LAZARSFELD, P. F.: 1944.   The controversy over detailed interviews—an offer for negotiation.   *Publ. Opin. Quart.*, **8**, 38–60.

LAZARSFELD, P. F., BERELSON, B., and GAUDET, H.: 1944.   *The people's choice*.   New York: Duell, Sloan & Pearce.

LAZARSFELD, P., and FISKE, M.: 1938.   The "panel" as a new tool for measuring opinion. *Publ. Opin. Quart.*, **2**, 596–612.

MACCOBY, E. E., and HOLT, R. R.: 1946.   How surveys are made.   *J. soc. Issues*, **2**, 45–58.

McNEMAR, Q.: 1946.   Opinion-attitude methodology.   *Psychol. Bull.*, **43**, 289–374.

NIELSEN, W. A.: 1946.   Attitude research and government.   *J. soc. Issues*, **2**, 2–13.

PEAK, H.: 1945.   Observations on the characteristics and distribution of German Nazis. *Psychol. Monogr.*, **59**, No. 6.

REUSS, C. F.: 1943.   Differences between persons responding and not responding to a mailed questionnaire.   *Amer. sociol. Rev.*, **8**, 433–438.

ROBINSON, D., and ROHDE, S.: 1946.   Two experiments with an anti-Semitism poll.   *J. abnorm. soc. Psychol.*, **41**, 136–144.

ROGERS, C. R.: 1942.   *Counseling and psychotherapy*.   Boston: Houghton.

SHUTTLEWORTH, F. K.: 1941.   Sampling errors involved in incomplete returns to mail questionnaires.   *J. appl. Psychol.*, **25**, 588–591.

Social Science Research Council: 1947.   *Public reaction to the atomic bomb and world affairs*.   Ithaca: Cornell Univ.

STANTON, F.: 1939.   Notes on the validity of mail questionnaire returns.   *J. appl. Psychol.*, **23**, 95–104.

STOCK, J. S.: 1944.   Some general principles of sampling.   *In* Cantril, H., *Gauging public opinion*.   Princeton: Princeton Univ. Press.

SUCHMAN, E. A., and McCANDLESS, B.: 1940.   Who answers questionnaires?   *J. appl. Psychol.*, **24**, 758–769.

TRUMAN, D. B.: 1945.   Public opinion research as a tool of public administration.   *Publ. Admin. Rev.*, **5**, 62–72.

UDOW, A. B.: 1942. The "interview effect" in public opinion and market research surveys. *Arch. Psychol.*, No. 277.

United States Strategic Bombing Survey: 1946. *The effects of bombing on German morale.* Washington: Government Printing Office.

WILKS, S. S.: 1940. Confidence limits and critical differences between percentages. *Publ. Opin. Quart.*, 4, 332–338.

WOODWARD, J. L.: 1944. Making government opinion research bear upon operation. *Amer. sociol. Rev.*, 9, 670–677.

CHAPTER IX

PERSUASION THROUGH PROPAGANDA

Man's greatest achievement, his crowning glory, and the sign that first and foremost distinguishes him from the great ape is language. Philosophers, psychologists, anthropologists, philologists, and educators have regarded language as that which makes possible the formation of societies among men, the creation and transmission of cultures, and the sharing of experiences. Man's appreciation of his own capacity for speech has been equaled only by his awe at the power of language to mislead him. Propaganda (vocal and written) has attained high eminence among the "forces" that control man. It has been seen as a weapon of warfare more deadly than the atom bomb and as an instrument of peace more effective than the United Nations. Among the virtues of propaganda, as a control technique, have been listed its relative cheapness, its subtlety, and its almost unlimited potentialities. Thus one psychologist (Biddle, 1931) has pointed out,

Many forms of coercion create emotional disturbances in the coerced, resentments, over-compensations or desire for revolt. Propaganda is different in that it controls without occasioning antagonistic emotions. Each individual behaves as though his responses were his own decision. Many individuals may be coerced to behave alike, each apparently guided by his own judgment.

And Lasswell, in the *Encyclopedia of the Social Sciences* (1935), characterizes propaganda as follows:

Propaganda in the broadest sense is the technique of influencing human actions by the manipulation of representations . . . . As proposals for action along new lines arise to compete for moral and physical support of the masses, propaganda attains eminence as the one means of mass mobilization which is cheaper than violence, bribery or other possible control techniques.

What is implied by many who use the concept of "propaganda" is that here man has a unique "force," that somehow through the use of language he can tap powers of control different from ordinary psychological processes, that the changing of beliefs and attitudes through propaganda and suggestion merits special consideration and treatment. It is the purpose of this chapter to examine, in some detail, the processes of changing beliefs and attitudes through propaganda and to determine whether propaganda is indeed a special kind of psychological phenomenon or instead, propaganda effects are completely describable in terms of the basic propositions of *cognitive reorganization*. Propaganda, however it may operate, is important in social life, and it is therefore essential to have a sound understanding of the basic processes involved.

LANGUAGE—THE MAJOR TOOL OF PROPAGANDA

Language, whether written or vocal, is the chief medium through which propaganda operates. To many people, indeed, "controlling beliefs and attitudes through language" is equated with "propaganda." However true it may be that language operates as a social factor in individual thinking,[1] it is in social control, in persuasion, that language plays its greatest role and has its greatest interest for the social psychologist. To understand the processes involved in propaganda, therefore, we must first examine some of the characteristics of language.

PATTERNS OF SPEECH

The efficiency of speech in persuasion is frequently influenced by matters that are somewhat peripheral to the meanings of the words, phrases, and sentences used by the speaker. The use of language, because it so frequently involves direct social intercourse, occurs in a dynamic situation where empathies, likes, and dislikes that arise between speaker and listener play an important role in determining how effectively speech can operate.[2] Some of these peripheral influences are completely independent of speech behavior—as when we form a dislike of a speaker before he even begins to speak, because of the clothes he wears or because of the way he approaches the platform or because of the kind of car in which we saw him drive up when we entered the hall or, perhaps, because of who we know him to be, *e.g.*, his religious, political, or social affiliations. But many of the peripheral influences are intrinsically related to the speech behavior itself—as when we form a like or dislike of the speaker because of his pleasing or harsh voice, his use of "ain't" or his use of such words as "phenomenological." All these factors determine the individual's speech pattern. Speech is a highly standardized form of action, and its specific patterns differ from person to person, from subculture to subculture, from society to society.

[1] "Language," writes Krout (1942), "is the primordial stuff of mental behavior. Man can no more get away from language, once trained in its use, than he can dismiss his memories." For an interesting analysis in the way speech, through the "form of talking to one's self," can influence thought, see Tolman (1932), especially p. 239*ff.*

[2] For a valuable treatment of language from the psychological point of view, see Kantor's (1936) *An Objective Psychology of Grammar*.

Since all language must be acquired by the individual from his culture, the specific pattern of speech any one person may display will reflect both his own *individual characteristics* and the *characteristics of the society* in which he acquired his language. The listener will usually be influenced by both these sets of characteristics. Thus, Arbuthnot, in listening to a radio forum, may judge a speaker to be a "stable" or an "emotionally unreliable" man, an honest son of toil, or a spoiled child of the rich—depending on whether the speaker spoke slowly or rapidly (individual characteristic) and whether he pronounced "neither" as "neether" or "nyther" (cultural characteristic).

Individual Language Patterns.—Individual speech patterning is determined by both biological and personality factors that are peculiar to the person. Thus, certain anatomical factors may be primarily responsible for the "sound" aspects of speech—squeaky voices, resonant voices, etc.,— while the general personality structure of the person may influence such voice and speech traits as vigor, intensity, and the tendency to use extravagant phrases. Some experimental evidence is available showing that speech and voice traits are significantly correlated with personality traits as they manifest themselves in various expressive movements of the individual,[1] but what is most significant for our present concern is that *listeners tend to judge a speaker's personality (whether correctly or wrongly) by his individual speech pattern.* These judgments of the listener cannot fail to influence the persuasive capacity of the speaker. This has become particularly important in recent times, when so many of the socially important speech events— campaign addresses by presidential candidates, for example—are broadcast over the radio where the listener cannot see the speaker, does not know the speaker, but can only hear his voice. As Allport and Cantril (1934) have pointed out,

Each member of an ordinary congregate audience receives a clear impression of the personality of the speaker. Complex visual perceptions of his physical build, posture, clothes and movements, in addition to auditory perceptions derived from his speech and voice, make this impression seem more accurate and complete. Over the radio, the rich and informative visual pattern is absent; only the voice and speech remain . . . . In spite of such hazards, however, probably most people who listen to radio speeches feel assured that some of their judgments are dependable. Often the impression is nothing more than a feeling of favor or aversion, but sometimes it represents a surprisingly definite judgment concerning the speaker's physical, intellectual and moral qualities.

Voice patterns and personality judgments.—Among the many experiments that have put this question to test, *i.e.*, if listeners judge a speaker's personality by his individual speech pattern and how adequately they make such

[1] See, for example, the study by Allport and Vernon (1933).

judgments, is that of Allport and Cantril (1934).[1] These experimenters restricted their investigation to individual patterns by having their speakers use uniform material read from typewritten texts whereby differences in vocabulary, fluency of speech, and grammatical accuracy were eliminated. Eighteen male speakers and over six hundred judges took part in the experiment. The subjects who served as judges did not know or see the speakers but merely listened to their voices as they were broadcast and were then asked to match certain personality data about the speakers (which were provided them) with the voices of the speakers. Thus, for example, the subjects would be given a list of several vocations, political preferences, ascendance-submission scores, photographs, extroversion-intraversion scores, etc., belonging to the various speakers and were required to assign the personality score or vocation or photograph to the correct voice. In one experiment the single personality features were combined into a brief thumbnail sketch of each speaker, and the judges attempted to match the proper thumbnail sketch with the proper voice. On the basis of the matchings obtained from the subjects, the investigators drew the following conclusions:

1. *Voice alone conveys some correct information concerning the outer characteristic (e.g.,* age, complexion, appearance in photograph) *and inner characteristic (e.g.,* ascendance-submission score) *of personality.* The majority of the judges' matchings were better than chance, and 47 per cent of them were better by large margins.

2. *Judgments of personality based on voice alone, even when the judgments are erroneous, do not represent mere guesses.* A voice seems to arouse a more or less uniform impression among the different members of a group of listeners even when the impression is incorrect. For the various features of personality, some preconceptions of the type of voice to which these features correspond are associated in the minds of the judges.

3. *The more significant personality traits are judged more consistently and more correctly than the specific "outer" characteristics.* Thus, for example, the ascendance-submission scores tended to be judged more correctly than the individual's appearance in photographs. In addition, the matchings between voice heard and the complex pattern of personality as described in the thumbnail sketches were better than the matchings with single personality features.

4. *If a voice of a speaker arouses a "stereotype" in the perception of the*

[1] Other similar experiments are those reported by Pear (1931) who worked with radio audiences in England, Wolff (1943) who relates his results to various forms of personality expression, Taylor (1934) who was primarily interested in the degree of social agreement of such judgments, and McGehee (1944). For a valuable and comprehensive discussion of these and related experiments, together with an analysis of the theoretical implications of the data, see Zucker's (1946) paper "Psychological aspects of speech melody."

listener, it is likely that several features of personality will be subsumed under that stereotype. This "totalizing" effect again illustrates the operation of the organizing factor in perception that we discussed on page 94; *i.e.*, the perceptual properties of a substructure are determined in large measure by the properties of the structure of which it is a part.

General comments.—Although a number of experiments, then, in addition to the one just described, have indicated that listeners do judge personality traits of speakers on the basis of individual speech patterns and that such judgments are more consistent and correct than chance alone would allow, we must be careful not to give undue weight to this factor in evaluating the efficacy of speech in persuasion. Too frequently the efficiency of a speaker or a "propagandist," a lecturer or a leader has been ascribed to the voice and sound characteristics of his speech. We cannot characterize the leader or the influential teacher in terms of his "resonant voice." As we shall see in the chapter on Group Morale and Leadership, the status of the influential person in a group is determined by much more than these matters. And even where we confine ourselves to *speech* effectiveness, we shall soon see that the individual speech pattern fades into relative unimportance when compared with the roles played by the other, more basic factors. However, for a complete analysis of the role of speech in the control of beliefs and attitudes, we must give some weight to the individual speech pattern of the speaker. In some instances, the individual pattern plays a major role. Thus, one broadcasting official characterized the late President Roosevelt's voice as follows:[1] "It expresses the character of the man. President Roosevelt's voice reveals sincerity, good-will, and kindliness, determination, conviction, strength, courage and abounding happiness." It does not matter whether this is a valid character analysis of President Roosevelt or not, but it does indicate the importance that a man whose business is "voice" can ascribe to the personality-revealing characteristics of an individual speech pattern.

Cultural Speech Patterns.—The distinction between individual speech patterns and cultural speech patterns cannot be a sharp and simple one. Here, as elsewhere, all factors interact in determining the behavior of the person. In general, however, the individual patterns can be seen as those primarily responsible for the *differences* and the cultural patterns as those responsible for *similarities* among the people of the same culture.

The cultural pattern of the individual's speech is characterized by a number of attributes. Among the more important ones can be listed vocabulary, word construction, dialect, word taboos, and ratio of gestures

[1] Quoted by Allport and Cantril in the study described above and taken from *The New York Times Magazine*, June 18, 1933.

to vocalizations. Thus the Chinese and the Turk will use different words to express the very same thought, and so, in many cases, will the resident of New York's East Side as compared with the denizen of Park Avenue. The American in his word usage will follow the process of the *isolating technique* of word construction and will say, "widow of the director of the brewery company," where the German will frequently employ the *intensive synthetic technique* and say, "Aktienbrauereidirektorswitwe"—all in one word. The Italian and the Jew will accompany their speech with a generous dose of gestures, shoulder shrugs, and hand movements, where the Englishman will be relatively immobile.

Social origin of gestures.—That expressive gestures which accompany speech have a cultural etiology and do not reflect the basic "emotionality" of the person is demonstrated in a study by Boas, Efron, and Foley (1936). These investigators studied the gestural behavior patterns of three groups: "(1) traditional Italians living in 'Little Italy,' New York City; (2) traditional Jews living in the East Side Ghetto, New York City; and (3) assimilated Italians and Jews, both living in similar 'Americanized' environments." Two of their conclusions are of significance for our discussion. In the first place they discovered that the "traditional" Italian and Jewish groups had fairly *uniform* and *distinctive* gesture patterns. There was, in other words, a typical Italian gesture pattern and a typical Jewish pattern. Second, they found, however, that in the assimilated group these uniform and characteristic gesture patterns were missing for *both* the Italians and the Jews. In other words, "cultural stimulation rather than 'racial' descent is operative."

Cultural patterns in speech events.—Although the pattern is culturally determined, it is *perceived* by the listener as inherent in the individual speaker. When a speaker shrugs his shoulders at every other sentence or flings out his hands, the listener reacts to it as part of the speaker's speech and not as a cultural stereotype which has nothing to do with the speaker's personality. Each one of these culturally determined speech traits— whether it be gesture or the use of a forbidden word or a "southern" pronunciation—is usually ascribed some significance by the listener. It means something to him and will influence the speech event. Thus we tend to characterize a Chinese as being "impassive" whereas an Italian is labeled as "emotional" because of the relative differences in these culturally determined modes of expression. And some people, for example, find the pronunciation of the American Southerner as being "very funny"—it is therefore difficult for them to take seriously a serious speech delivered by a Southerner.

General comments.—The one generalization that can be made concerning the relationship between speech patterns and the persuasiveness of the speech event would seem to be this: The efficiency of speech in influencing beliefs and attitudes is to a measurable degree dependent upon the comparability of the pattern of speech employed by the speaker and that usually accepted by the listener. It should be clear that the speech pattern of the effective speaker need not be the same as that used by the listener but rather one that is accepted by the listener. Frequently the listener will be much more impressed and susceptible to the arguments of a speaker who uses a speech pattern that is "superior" to that used by the listener himself. Speech patterns have different prestige values as well as different personality implications. In a psychological analysis of speech and language all these factors must be given adequate weight, for we must view the use of language as a social act involving adjustive, interpersonal behavior.

SPEECH, WORDS, AND MEANING

The above "peripheral" aspects of a speech event are important factors to take into consideration when analyzing the influence of speech in persuasion, but the meaning of the words used in speech plays an even more significant role. These meanings, obviously, depend upon the mental processes of the listener when he is stimulated by a written or spoken word. The same word, as an objective stimulus, has different meanings for different people and even for the same person in different situations. As we have seen in Chap. III, the perception evoked by a stimulus is a function of both *structural* and *functional* factors—of factors that derive from the objective nature of the stimulus pattern and of factors that are dependent upon the perceiver's needs, past experience, etc. (see page 81). To understand the meanings with which people perceive words, therefore, we must examine words in terms of their structural as well as their functional characteristics.

Invariant Meanings of Words.—While for perhaps 99 per cent of the meanings we get out of words we must appeal to such functional factors as the needs and knowledges of the hearer, the very physical characteristics of words as stimuli seem to "force" certain perceptions and meanings in the same way that the arrangements of the dots in Fig. 1 (page 82) force certain visual perceptions. Such words will have relatively *invariant* meanings in the sense that people of widely differing needs and cultural backgrounds will perceive these words in much the same way. In addition, some words are relatively invariant because their meanings are dependent upon experiences that are universal to people of a given society. These words have, as it were, "acquired" structural characteristics that "force" certain perceptions.

Sound and sense.—According to some students of language, there are some words that determine the perceived meaning because of their very sounds.[1] These are the familiar onomatopoetic, or "echoic," words which seem to imitate the sound of the objects to which they refer—such as the word "quack" when used to refer to the call of the duck. Whether or not such onomatopoetic words do force invariant meanings upon people completely unfamiliar with them is debatable, but in certain situations their sound qualities may be of great aid in establishing their meanings. As Thorndike (1946) points out,

... how many of these ten words would Arabs, Finns, or Chinese define correctly from merely hearing them—*blob, chatter, chuckle, flick, giggle, ping, slap, swish, thump, yap?* Per contra, a slight, even imagined similarity of a word's sound to its meaning may make the meaning easier to get and remember. If it seems as fit and proper that maladroit persons should bungle and ebullient persons blurt, as that dogs should bow-wow and cannon boom, then mere sounds of bungle and blurt may help to carry their meanings as much as do the mere sounds of bow-wow and boom.

Aside from the sounds of *words*, there seems to be some evidence that the sounds of specific letters, when incorporated into words, force a common meaning. Thus there is Orr's (1944) hypothesis that the front vowels (*e.g.*, the short *i* as in "little") contrasted with the back vowels (*e.g.*, the broad *a* as in "large") carry a meaning of "minuteness, slenderness, and other kindred notions." In support of Orr's hypothesis, Thorndike (1946) refers to the following observation:

I have verified Orr's hypothesis as regards modern English words by a comparison of monosyllabic words having *I* (as in bit) or *i* (as in machine) as their vowel sound with monosyllabic words identical with them save in vowel sound. I have made less extensive comparisons using Greek, Hungarian, and Finnish words. All agree in showing *I* and *i* to occur in a disproportionately large number of words meaning small things or sounds of high pitch and small volume, though the differences are much less than in modern English.

As Orr (1945) himself suggests in a second paper, if a businessman "were naming two products, similar in character but dissimilar in volume or power,

[1] Orr (1944) points to the following verses from Pope's *Essay on Criticism* as illustrative of the poet's recognition of the importance of the structural factors involved in word meaning:

" 'Tis not enough no harshness gives offense,
The sound must seem an echo to the sense.
Soft is the strain when Zephyr gently blows,
And the smooth stream in smoother numbers flows;
But when loud surges lash the sounding shore,
The hoarse rough verse should like the torrent roar"

he would be well-advised to give the name 'Thugon' to the stronger or more massive of the two and 'Thigeen' to its weaker brother." As further illustrations of his hypothesis Orr points to the compelling differences in meanings that front vowels carry with them: "silly giggle" as opposed to "hearty laugh," "mincing titter" vs. "loud guffaw," or the well-known Scottish phrase which contains words many of us may find difficult to define yet which all of us find easy to understand: "Mony a mickle makes a muckle."

Culturally determined invariance.—At the other extreme from the above illustrations, but still within the category of "relatively invariant" words, are those words which tend to evoke the same meanings for a people of a *given culture*. Strictly speaking, of course, these words owe their meaning to people's experience with them rather than to any structural factors inherent in the words. But they are invariant in the sense that the experience upon which they are dependent is so common to all the people of the culture that the words no longer depend upon specific contexts. Each culture has "bad" or "good" words, "happy" or "sorrowful" words. The invariance of these words is of much more interest for the understanding of persuasion than are the types of words and sounds discussed above. This is clearly indicated in Sargent's study (1939) of the use of words by *The Chicago Tribune*.

Sargent chose *The Chicago Tribune* for analysis because, in his opinion, that newspaper, more than almost any other large American newspaper, violates the policy of keeping editorial comment out of its news reporting. As he points out, even in its presumably objective news accounts, "It labels its *betes noires* with adroit adjectives that arouse negative emotional reactions in readers. Similarly it attaches flattering phrases to favored policies or persons." His data substantiate this charge.

Sargent selected 40 terms from the news columns of *The Chicago Tribune*, 20 of which had been commonly used by that newspaper when referring to policies that it did not support and 20 when referring to policies it approved. Thus the words "Czarism, dictatorship, regimentation, agitator, brain trust" were found among news stories referring to activities of the Democratic Administration or to labor union events, while the phrases "freedom, right to work, taxpayer, cooperation, and recovery" were used by the newspaper when it had occasion to report on the activities of the Republican party or the National Association of Manufacturers.

To the 40 terms thus chosen, Sargent added 10 neutral terms, and all 50 words were arranged in a mixed order. The reactions of six groups of subjects, totaling 231 people, were studied: (1) a large PTA meeting, (2) a high-school alumni fraternity, (3) beginning college students, (4) advanced college students, (5) a workers' forum, and (6) a "middle-class" community forum. Each subject was first given a sheet on which the 50 words were mimeographed and was told that the purpose of the experiment was to get his immediate emotional reactions to various sounds and phrases. As the experimenter read the terms, one at a time, the subject checked on his sheet whether he "liked," "disliked," or "had no feeling" about the word. The subjects did not know the source of the words.

Sargent's results indicate clearly that many terms arouse standardized feeling tones. Using a system of scoring that permitted him to assign a feeling-tone value ranging from plus 100 ("liked") to minus 100 ("disliked") for any word, he found, for example, the following values:

Czarism	−84	Cooperation	+95
Dictatorship	−84	Freedom	+92
Domination	−79	Reemployment	+88

In comparing the various subjects' responses, Sargent found that "marked similarities of reactions exist among the different groups. Rank order correlations ran from .81 to .96 between all groups except the workers' forum. The correlation between its responses and the others, about .40."

In the next part of his study Sargent took 12 terms having possible emotional values from *The Chicago Tribune's* news columns and 12 parallel terms used by *The New York Times* in reporting the *very same events* and then obtained the feeling tone values for these 24 terms as indicated above. Table 4 presents some of the results:

TABLE 4.—COMPARISONS OF FEELING-TONE VALUES BETWEEN TERMS TAKEN FROM *Chicago Tribune* AND *New York Times.**

Source of term	Term	Feeling-tone value
Chicago Tribune	Radical	−53
New York Times	Progressive	+92
Chicago Tribune	Regimentation	−53
New York Times	Regulation	+32
Chicago Tribune	Government witch hunting	−38
New York Times	Senate investigation	+57
Chicago Tribune	The dole	−35
New York Times	Home relief	+27
Chicago Tribune	Alien	−35
New York Times	Foreign	0

*Based on data in Sargent (1939).

There can be no doubt that *The Chicago Tribune* was selecting words with invariant emotional feeling tones in its attempt to influence the beliefs and attitudes of its readers, but it should be pointed out that *The New York Times* did not find it possible to avoid such "emotionally loaded" words either. Words carry with them emotion-evoking characteristics, and it would indeed be difficult to obtain a sufficient number of neutral words to carry on any extended speech event.

General comments.—Although the overwhelming majority of the words and sounds we use in speech events (as is true for all objects in our real world) derive their meanings and evocative powers from their total context and the psychological state of the listener, some words and sounds, as a consequence either of their intrinsic nature or of constant patterning, are perceived with relatively invariant meanings for most people. Usually such invariant meanings carry with them emotional and feeling-tone connotations. A thorough analysis of the process of persuasion through language must take such sounds, words, and phrases into account. Words are not always neutral and do not mean simply whatever they are "paid to mean" as Humpty Dumpty in *Through the Looking Glass* would have it.

Variable Meanings of Words.—Language is effective in controlling beliefs and attitudes because words evoke meanings beyond the feeling tones discussed above. And the meanings with which most words will be perceived are determined in large part by the hearer's knowledge about those words. But to say that the past experiences and training of the hearer (the sources of his knowledge about words) help to determine the meaning of speech can be and frequently has been misinterpreted. As has already been pointed out, the same word can have different meanings for the same individual in different situations. The study of the dictionary meaning of words, except for certain genetic problems, is relatively useless to the psychologist. It is therefore essential that we examine the significance of the statement, "The past experiences and training of the hearer help to determine the meaning of speech."

Learning and meanings of words.—The critical contribution made by experience and learning to the meaning of words can best be understood by the "thing character" of words. Our knowledge about a thing, *e.g.*, a "real" chair, is dependent in large measure upon our experiences with real chairs. What we know about chairs and the meaning with which we perceive chairs reflect our *use* of chairs in the past. We may have used chairs as things to sit upon, as stepladders, as weapons, as fuel, as temporary tables, etc. Each one of these uses has added to our meanings and beliefs (*i.e.*, "knowledge") about the chair. In a sense, therefore, our perception of a chair is dependent upon our past adjustive reactions to various problem situations in which the chair played a role.

All this is also true about our perception of words. Our knowledge about words is dependent upon the adjustive speech events in which those words have been involved. Our perceptions of a word vary tremendously; many of them are unique to us and reflect our own past needs, emotions, problem situations. The word "chair" may be perceived as a stepladder, a weapon, a desired academic position, or an office in a political organization. Our beliefs, or knowledge, about words are *varied* and *flexible* and are *resultants of past experiences and learning*, but they are not "conditioned responses" unequivocally evoked by a "conditioned stimulus."

Context and meanings of words.—But, as we know, perceptions are determined by much more than the "traces" of past experience. Present needs and present contexts interact with past traces to determine the nature of the present perception. This is also true of our perception of words. People therefore can and do perceive words in entirely novel ways, depending upon the present psychological field of the individual. To understand the meanings of words, then, we must know the individual's present psychological field, which, through traces, includes his past training concerning a given word. Also, just as no one physical object is perceived in isolation, so will no one word be thus perceived. That is why we can frequently understand a completely new word when it is embedded in a sentence that is meaningful or spoken by a person whose actions are meaningful. Our understanding may turn out to be wrong, but we shall have perceived the word in terms relevant to the major structure of which it is a part.

Words as Objects in the Real World.—Words are perceived as existing in their own right, and the laws of perception and organization applying to other objects apply to words. One of the reasons for the frequent misinterpretation of the function of words in our behavior is the tendency to think of words only as "symbols" and to assume that all language behavior is somehow "substitute" or "vicarious" behavior. But all that we know about our perception of words indicates that words are perceived in the same immediately meaningful way in which we perceive other objects. When we perceive a chair, to return to our previous example, we react directly to the chair. We experience certain perceptions, and we do certain things to the chair or with it. We do not behave as if the chair were a symbol for something else—for something "real" which is not actually present. When we hear a sudden loud noise, we react immediately to that noise—we are startled or frightened by the noise itself. The noise is perceived meaningfully—we do not perceive it as a "symbol" for something else. In much the same way do we adjust to words. When we hear a word or a sentence or see a word or a sentence in a newspaper, we frequently perceive meanings directly and immediately, and we react to these words, phrases, or sentences as we would to any other object in our real world.[1] The function of a word in an individual's behavior is similar to the functions of other equally real objects in his real world. As a listener it is an object to which he adjusts as a pedestrian must adjust to a speeding automobile in his environment, and as a speaker it is an object that he uses as a rider uses the automobile to get about in his environment.

An environment of words.—These considerations mean that man lives in a world of word objects as truly as he does in a world of any other kinds of objects. *An individual listening to a speaker or reading a pamphlet is immersed in the special real world created by the words and sentences as truly as he is living in a real world created by chairs, tables, and sidewalks.* Man can frequently alter another's world by introducing *words* in the other's environment, just as he can by introducing cows, automobiles, and buildings. Whether or not changes in this real world (no matter how accomplished) will affect the individual's psychological world is, of course, dependent on many other factors, but the possibility remains that through changing an individual's environment via words, we can theoretically accomplish the same kinds of changes in an individual's beliefs and attitudes as through changing an individual's environment through manipulation of other objects. It is because of this that language can be effective in changing beliefs and attitudes and in evoking needs and emotions.

Differences between words and other objects.—While we have emphasized the functional similarity between words and other objects, there are some important differences—differences that are of particular significance in understanding the unique value of words as persuasive tools. In the first place, words are not limited by the same temporal and spatial factors that limit other objects. The speaker can, through words, immerse the hearer in one environment and a moment later change that environment completely. The speaker can create an excessively sparse environment— simple and devoid of many objects—or a completely "full" environment. Second, perceptions evoked by words can be greater in number and more varied in kind than those evoked by other objects. This is partly due to our greater experience with words (once we have acquired language) than with other objects and partly because it is physically easier for us to manipulate words. Consequently almost any word can be experienced in juxtaposition with any other word, and thus novel and bizarre perceptions can

---

[1] A compelling illustration of the "thing character" of words is found in the so-called "magic" words or "holy" words. What, for example, can one say the word "abracadabra" symbolizes to the believer in its efficacy?   Abracadabra itself is perceived as having magical effects.

be more easily evoked. It is these qualities which give to speech events their unique power. But other than that, speech is effective or ineffective in controlling beliefs and attitudes in the very same way that other environmental changes result in changes in beliefs and attitudes.

General Comments.—The significance of the analysis made in this chapter of language, of the role of past experience and present context in determining the meanings of words and of the similarities and differences between words and other objects in man's real world, suggests a different perspective from which to view the power of language in controlling beliefs and attitudes from that frequently taken. It suggests that we should expect to find that the same principles which apply to cognitive reorganization in general apply to the perception of words. This means, in turn, that to discover how and why speech is effective in persuasion we must seek for the answer in the cognitive, motivational, and emotional processes of the listener as well as in an analysis of the word objects used in persuasion. A fruitful propaganda analysis would be only partially concerned with the analysis of the words used, the clever phrases, the repetition of slogans, etc. It is actually more concerned with the current beliefs, needs, percepts, attitudes of the listener. Thus, in a sense, we can anticipate the answer to the question that we posed at the beginning of this chapter: Changing beliefs and attitudes of people through speech or propaganda involves no special principles or unique processes. The principles outlined in Chaps. IV and VI will be adequate for "propaganda" analysis. However, to determine if the empirical studies check with such an analysis, we shall now turn to an examination of data dealing specifically with propaganda.

PROPAGANDA—SOME GENERAL CONSIDERATIONS

Almost every student of propaganda has offered his own definition of the term. Although the definitions may differ in several particulars, there seems to be agreement as to the objectives of the propagandist and the kind of response evoked by propaganda. It is commonly assumed that the propagandist seeks to influence people's beliefs and attitudes and, thereby, their actions. It is also generally assumed that the specific beliefs and attitudes which the propagandist seeks to induce are not valuable or socially desirable in their own right but that they are sought by the propagandist because of some ulterior or antisocial purpose that he has in mind. Finally, it is also frequently assumed that the successfully propagandized person's response is an *uncritical* or *unreasoned* one.

Propaganda and Education.—The above characteristics of propaganda are occasionally set against the characteristics of education. Thus, it is assumed that education seeks to add to an individual's knowledge, and it is assumed that the specific knowledge which education seeks to make available to people is valuable and desirable in its own rights and will lead to socially desirable action—the educator having no ulterior motives. Finally, it is assumed that the successfully educated individual's response is a *critical* or *reasoned* one.

Some writers have indicated that it is not easy, in every case, to distinguish between propaganda and education primarily because some educators may be guilty of "unconscious" propaganda. Considerable discussion has taken place as to whether propaganda can be unconscious or whether we must restrict the term only to "conscious" propaganda. Such discussion emphasizes that in the minds of many, one of the distinguishing characteristics between the propagandist and the educator lies in the *purposes* and *consciously employed techniques* of the two practitioners rather than in the fundamental psychological processes involved. From this point of view, "propaganda" is not considered to involve any psychological processes differing from, say, those involved in learning arithmetic, how to play the piano, or the solution of the problem box in the laboratory. As has already been anticipated, this characterization of propaganda is similar to the one that will be employed in this chapter. The term *propaganda* does not refer to a process genuinely different from other processes of cognitive reorganization but is an *epithet* applied by some people to certain persuasive techniques.

Conscious and Unconscious Propaganda.—There can be little doubt that people differ in the degree to which they are aware of the effects of their activities upon others, but this is hardly justification for the assumption that therefore the activities themselves are different. Thus, for example, a certain experiment may be described by a psychology lecturer with a conscious intent to induce a favorable attitude in the students toward cooperation as a mode of life. The very same experiment, on the other hand, may be described by a lecturer with the conscious intent of only teaching certain experimental techniques. Both speakers may use identical material and even the very same words, and the responses of the students may be identical—an increased favorable attitude toward cooperation. *The difference in intent of the two speakers may make very little difference in a psychological analysis of the cognitive reorganization that has taken place among the hearers.* Differences in intent become important only if our problem is an analysis of the psychology of the speaker or propagandist, but not if our problem is an analysis of the process of persuasion.[1]

---

[1] Perhaps the only instance where "intent" may become significant is if the *listener* perceives the speaker's intent or suspects the speaker of having a hidden motive in his speech. The mental set with which a listener approaches a speaker or writer, as we have seen, may be a very important variable to consider in assessing the speech event.

An illustrative case.—The above conclusion is strikingly illustrated by a comparison of an analysis of Thorndike's *Arithmetic*, Book II, and an experiment in propaganda performed by Meyers (1921). In analyzing Thorndike's arithmetic textbook (which was written by Thorndike without any conscious intent to influence economic or political beliefs and attitudes), Freeman points out that in some two-hundred pages Thorndike presents 643 arithmetic problems that accept and stress familiar capitalistic notions. Each of these arithmetic problems involves buying and selling at a profit, employing others for wages and profiting thereby, loaning out money at profitable interest rates, etc. This, Freeman suggests, tends to strengthen the beliefs and attitudes of the children about certain economic practices. To emphasize his conclusions, Freeman asks what would happen if the arithmetic textbooks we used in our grade schools contained problems such as the following: Suppose that among the workers in a Southern cotton mill, one out of every hundred has pellagra because of inadequate wages paid. How many new cases would appear if the mill added one thousand workers at the same wages? If a family, to maintain an adequate nourishment level, needs $20 a week for food, what is the degree of undernourishment in such a family when its relief funds are but $5 a week? Freeman answers his own question as follows: "Books containing such problems, although they taught the abstract relationship of numbers as well as any others, would be dismissed as propagandistic and unworthy of the dignity of pure arithmetic."

Compare Freeman's analysis of Thorndike's *Arithmetic* with the following experiment conducted by Meyers, which Meyers appropriately titled "Control of conduct by suggestion: An experiment in Americanization." In this experiment Meyers attempted to teach English letter writing to foreign-born soldiers in the American Army. His teaching was done through the medium of "model letters." But not only were these model letters designed to teach the soldiers how to write letters—form of salutation, etc.—but, quite consciously, specific opinions and facts were inserted in the model letters which Meyers thought should become part of the soldiers' beliefs and attitudes. This was *concealed* but *conscious* propaganda. After the letter-writing course, Meyers found that his model letters not only improved the writing ability of his students, but they had also succeeded in influencing their beliefs and attitudes.

What is the essential psychological difference between Thorndike's *Arithmetic* and Meyers' model letters? The former has been labeled by Freeman as "unconscious propaganda"; the latter would be labeled by many people as "conscious propaganda." But these distinctions distinguish only between the purposes of Thorndike and Meyers, not between the effects of the arithmetic book or the English composition models and not between the nature of the cognitive reorganization processes that occurred among the students.

The term *propaganda* as it has been defined above can be applied by different people, with equal legitimacy, to arithmetic textbooks, comic strips, sermons, spelling books, paintings, political pamphlets, and history books. Whether material or events are propagandistic in nature, it must be emphasized, does not inhere in the conscious intent of the creator or initiator of the materials or events but in whether the person who applies the term approves or disapproves of the possible effects of the material. From a strictly scientific analysis, there is no way to distinguish between the fundamental processes involved in propaganda and nonpropaganda. However, as we shall later see, there are certain specific techniques that admitted propagandists usually employ, whereas alleged nonpropagandists avoid such techniques. It may be of some practical value to examine such special techniques; but again, the different techniques employed do not necessitate different explanatory principles to account for their effects.

Propaganda and Suggestion.—The belief that the understanding of the effects of propaganda does involve the invoking of special explanatory basic processes is a reflection of the thinking about the concept of "suggestion"— since propaganda is but a special case of suggestion. In turn, the belief that suggestion refers to a unique type of psychological process has its source in the work and theorizing of the early hypnotists and that of Mesmer and the investigators in the field of abnormal psychology. The concepts about hypnotism and suggestion developed by those early workers were taken over by the sociologists (notably Tarde and LeBon) who saw in the "force" of suggestion something that could explain most, if not all, of social behavior. From these early sociologists the concept was borrowed by later sociologists and psychologists until at one time it could be truthfully said that for most sociologists the concept of suggestion and its twin, imitation, were the basic explanatory concepts for all of social behavior.[1] Today, however, social scientists are revising their views of suggestion and imitation, and current research tends to destroy the belief that suggestion and imitation exist as distinct psychological forces.

Suggestion as a unique force.—Many of the early concepts about suggestion involved two assumptions: (1) that a type of response to stimulation exists that is different in nature from other kinds of responses, these special events being called "suggestion"; (2) that individuals vary in the tendency or capacity to make this special type of response and that these individual

[1] For an interesting historical survey of the concept of suggestion as it was used in social psychology—both theoretical and experimental—see Coffin (1941), p. 1–22.

variations reflect differences in a fundamental personality trait which can be called "suggestibility." Frequently these two assumptions were involved in circular reasoning to support each other. Thus, the type of response called suggestion was generally defined as the acceptance of a proposition in the absence of logically adequate grounds. The reason why an individual accepted such a proposition was ascribed to the individual's suggestibility. In other words, the first assumption was supported by assuming the second, and the second was supported by appropriately defining the first. Much the same analysis was made for "imitation." Imitation also involved a special type of response, and the reason people imitated was to be found in the propensity of the individual to imitate.

Influenced by these concepts, propaganda was given a similar treatment. Thus, propaganda was conceived as a special form of stimulation which, when effective, resulted in the process of suggestion. The individual's susceptibility to propaganda was explained by the special nature of the stimulation (the kind of words used, the repetition, etc.), and by the individual's "suggestibility." This theoretical analysis determined the nature of research in propaganda until very recent times. Institutes were organized to analyze the words and special tricks of the trade used by propagandists. Second, tests were devised to measure an individual's suggestibility or gullibility. The differences in suggestibility among various types of people were measured: between men and women, between college students and noncollege students, between people of different ages, and between people suffering from different mental disturbances. Some of these investigations will be examined later in this chapter.

All the above research has helped accumulate a great deal of useful descriptive data which are relevant to the problem of propaganda analysis; but despite the massiveness of the data, the validity of the theoretical assumptions behind the investigations has not been established. If anything, this research, as so frequently happens in the history of science, has indicated a need for a sharp reorientation of the basic principles that initiated the research in the first place.

An alternative view of suggestion.—As alternatives to the older assumptions about suggestion are the following: (1) The behavior usually termed *suggestion* follows the same laws of cognitive reorganization as do other tension-reduction processes; there is no special kind of response to stimulation that can be called suggestion. (2) The suggestibility of the individual is a function of the person's immediate psychological field; there is no basic personality trait, constitutionally determined, that can be called suggestibility.

These two alternative assumptions do not deny the facts that have been subsumed under the older assumptions but indicate a different explanation of those facts. Thus, it is obvious that some speakers or writers make suggestions. It is also obvious that some listeners accept these suggestions and some do not. It is, finally, equally true that some people tend to accept suggestions more easily than do others. But the description and analysis of these observations, in terms of the two alternative assumptions listed above, would go something like this: Propaganda (whether involving speech events or other events, conscious or unconscious) is one of many ways of changing the environment of the person. When this environmental change is of such a nature as to be capable of resulting in a new belief or attitude, this environmental event can be called a "suggestion." If the structural and functional factors determining the individual's mental processes are such as to lead to a change in belief congruent with the suggestion, he can be said to be "suggestible"; if the dynamic factors of the psychological field do not permit such reorganization, he can be said to be "nonsuggestible."

This indicates an entirely different research approach to the problem of propaganda. Instead of analyzing the tricks of the trade, the emphasis is placed upon the needs, emotions, and beliefs of the person to be propagandized. Instead of looking for different degrees of suggestibility among different kinds of people, we must look for differences in the immediate psychological fields of all people.

How do the actual data correspond to these two alternative theories about suggestibility?

PROPAGANDA—SOME EXPERIMENTAL INVESTIGATIONS

The experimental study of propaganda involves, necessarily, the investigation of specific methods of inducing or changing beliefs and attitudes of people. Sometimes the beliefs and techniques of persuasion are extremely simple—as, for example, the experiments that seek to induce a belief in the person that one line is shorter than another, through appropriate hints given by the experimenter. Sometimes these beliefs and attitudes are more socially significant—as, for example, the studies that seek to change an individual's beliefs about the Negroes or prohibition or Communism. For the most part, the techniques of studying the effect of propaganda in persuasion involve the study of changes in *momentary judgments of people* rather than in any more direct measurement of beliefs and attitudes. The justification for this technique, as has been indicated in Chap. V (page 157), lies in the fact that since momentary judgments reflect the beliefs and attitudes of the individual, the study of judgments can give us data on the person's beliefs and attitudes. As further justification there is the practical consideration that the propagandist is often interested only in momentary judgments—as in the case of voting or in crowd action.

The Trait of Suggestibility.—The data usually cited in support of the proposition that suggestibility is a trait of the personality are of two kinds. (1) There are the experiments that seek to determine if certain types of people are more prone to accept a suggestion than other types. Much of this work has been done with patients in mental hospitals, perhaps because it is believed that different mental diseases reflect basically different personalities. The second kind of experiment seeks to determine if an individual's readiness to accept a suggestion in one situation is correlated with his readiness to accept a suggestion in another situation, since, if suggestibility is a personality trait, we should expect to find a high consistency in the behavior of individuals in different situations.

Suggestibility and personality types.—Typical of the first type of experimental data are such researches that seem to indicate that catatonic dementia praecox patients are negatively suggestible, that schizophrenics are nonsuggestible, that "pyknics" among all the body types are the least suggestible, that Negroes are more suggestible than whites, that delinquent girls are more suggestible than girls who have not come to the attention of the court, etc. Thus, for example, in an experiment conducted with patients in a mental hospital in Sweden, Lindberg (1940) concludes that his data show that:

Suggestibility is associated with bodily types in such a manner that the pyknics . . . have the lowest percentage of suggestibles . . . . The connection between bodily types and suggestibility also indicates that suggestibility (or resistance to suggestibility) is, partly, at least, constitutionally determined.

Usually these experiments are based on group differences in some simple suggestibility test of the type best illustrated by the careful study of Reymert and Kohn (1940) in their investigation of suggestibility in children. In that experiment a pseudo-thermal apparatus was devised which contained no heat, but the nature of its appearance and the type of instructions given by the experimenters were such as to lead the subjects to assume that heat would be generated by the apparatus. For example, when certain lights on the apparatus were turned on, steam was seen to be escaping from the apparatus and the subject was told to report when he could "feel" the increase in heat. When the subject reported that he did feel the heat, he was judged as having accepted the suggestion.

The difficulty with all the data summarized above as supporting evidence for the assumption that suggestibility reflects a basic personality trait is that the correlations between suggestibility and types are only alleged. For almost every positive correlation that has been reported between personality type, body build, or racial type and suggestibility, some other researcher has reported a negative correlation or a zero correlation, Thus. where Cushing and Ruch (1927) report that delinquent girls are more than normally suggestible, Hull (1933) reports them as being much less than normally suggestible. Where Hull finds that schizophrenics are nonsuggestible, Travis (1922) had reported schizophrenics negatively suggestible.[1] The same contradictory results seem to exist with respect to other types of correlations, *e.g.*, suggestibility against sex, intelligence, or age. Thus, although in general the experimental data seem to indicate that suggestibility decreases with age among children, other factors than age seem to be the significant variables. In the Reymert and Kohn experiment cited above, for example, the personality of the experimenter was an important factor which changed the correlations with age—one experimenter getting different results from another. The data on intelligence and sex are also inconsistent. Thus, although most studies [but not all, *e.g.*, the investigation of Otis (1924)] seem to indicate that girls are more suggestible than boys, the differences are relatively small and the individual differences within either sex group are more significant than the differences among the groups.

Generality of suggestibility.—The second type of experiment (determining correlations among various suggestibility tests) has also led to consistently inconsistent results. Some experimenters have reported positive correlations, some zero correlations, and some negative correlations. Thus Estabrooks (1929), who tested elementary-school boys on a number of different suggestibility tests, reported correlations ranging from +.23 to −.08. Here, too, as many writers have emphasized, the specific test situation is much more important than any hypothesized personality trait. It should be pointed out, moreover, that even if we were to find consistently high correlations among various tests, that in itself would not be sufficient proof of a suggestibility trait. It is quite possible for a person to accept (or refuse) suggestions consistently, but the reason for this consistency may be due to the operation of a number of different factors in the person's psychological field. Thus he may have learned to adopt a submissive set to certain individuals or kinds of individuals (*e.g.*, to professors, scientists, political leaders, priests); and wherever such a person is the source of the suggestion, he may consistently accept the suggestion. Or in situation after situation he may perceive that the easiest means to the achievement of

[1] For a good summary of the data in this area, see the paper by Coffin (1941) previously referred to.

a desired goal object is the acceptance of expert or authoritative suggestions—and again he will consistently (in those situations) accept suggestions. At best, then, consistently high correlations among various tests and situations can be considered as a necessary but not sufficient requirement for demonstrating suggestibility as a basic personality trait. But even this requirement is not met by the available data.

General comments.—Extensive experimental work has failed to supply unambiguous data to support the assumption that suggestibility is a personality trait and that individuals can be differentiated with respect to that trait independently of the situation in which it is presumed to appear. Almost all the data available can be much more readily interpreted to mean that whether or not an individual accepts a suggestion is a function of the total psychological situation. We might thus speak of suggestibility as a "trait" *of the situation* rather than of the person. This conclusion, by removing suggestibility as an acceptable explanation of suggestion and pointing to the conditions of the psychological field of the person as the locus for explanatory principles, leads us next to an examination of these specific conditions.

Prestige Suggestion.—"Prestige suggestion" has occupied the major attention of propaganda analysts, has accounted for many of the experiments in the field of propaganda, has been frequently cited as a prime example wherein an individual will change his beliefs about an object without "adequate grounds" or without "reasoning," and, in controlling the beliefs of people, has been the advertiser's favorite technique.

One of the first experiments in this field was that of Bridges (1914), in which he found that when a subject was asked to judge the comparative aesthetic qualities of picture cards and was told which cards the majority of people usually chose as "best" or "worst," the subject's judgments tended to agree with the majority choices more frequently than when he was not given such suggestions. This effect was labeled the "majority prestige" effect. Since that early experiment a large number of prestige experiments have been performed—the effect of majority and expert prestige has been studied on the judgments of political slogans, paintings, facial expression of emotion, literary merit of passages of literature, the judgment of lengths of lines, tastes of food, etc. And, as has been indicated, the usual interpretation was that the subject, under the influence of prestige, submitted to the suggestion from the prestige source and changed his judgment to conform with the suggestion.

An alternative interpretation.—Perhaps the first experimenter to challenge the usual interpretation and to suggest that many instances of prestige suggestion could be understood in terms of perceptual principles was Duncker

(1938) who, on the basis of his work on the modification of children's food preferences through suggestion, pointed out that

> If an object is found to undergo a change of valuation on being presented as the work or favorite of some admired personality, this "suggestion by prestige" is often treated as though on an otherwise unchanged object there has been "grafted" another value. On closer inspection, however, one may find that the object had by no means remained unchanged. To anyone but an ignorant "snob" a "big name" may give a new meaning or inner profile—the more readily the more ambiguous the object was in the first place.

In other words Duncker suggests that under conditions of prestige suggestion we do not change our beliefs about the same object as originally perceived but rather that the prestige suggestion adds to our knowledge about the object, the object is therefore perceived differently, and consequent upon a change in the perception there must be a change in valuation or judgment. This reinterpretation is significant because (1) it places changes in judgment following prestige suggestion in the same category as judgments based upon reasonable grounds and thus (2) it again points to the applicability of the basic principles of perception, learning, and thinking to the phenomena of prestige suggestion.

It will be remembered that in the chapter on the growth of beliefs it was pointed out that in the development of almost all of our beliefs, we are necessarily dependent upon authorities for our facts (page 187). As we obtain new facts from the people we accept as authorities, these facts are incorporated into our beliefs, and the belief system must necessarily show a change. To call one such sequence of events "prestige suggestion" and another a "reasoned change" seems unwarranted. Duncker then goes on to outline several ways in which prestige suggestion may bring about a change in the perception of the object being judged. In the first place, he points out, the perception of the object may be modified by presenting a new context, or frame of reference, for the object. This, as we have already seen, can result in a changed perception. In the second place, the effect of a prestige suggestion may be such as to accentuate certain aspects of the object or point out certain favorable elements in the object that had formerly escaped the perceiver's attention, and by these means the perception of the object may be changed.

An experimental illustration.—The first experiment we shall discuss is that of Asch, Block, and Hertzman (1940). In this experiment four different groups of college students were asked to rank 10 professions[1] for the following characteristics: intelligence required, social usefulness, conscientiousness,

[1] These professions were accountancy, business, dentistry, engineering, journalism, law, medicine, music, politics, and teaching.

stability of character, and idealism. Group I did its ranking without being subjected to any suggestions; Group II operated under majority prestige and was told that five hundred college students had previously ranked the profession of politics as top with respect to the five characteristics. Group III was told that the five hundred college students had ranked politics *lowest* for the five characteristics, and Group IV was told that the students had ranked politics highest in social usefulness, lowest in intelligence, etc.

The resulting rankings of politics as a profession with respect to intelligence and social usefulness is presented in Table 5.

TABLE 5.—EFFECTS OF MAJORITY PRESTIGE SUGGESTION ON RANKINGS
OF THE PROFESSION OF POLITICS.*

Group	Average rankings for intelligence	Average rankings for social usefulness
I	8.1	8.2
II	4.1	4.1
III	9.1	8.5
IV	8.9	4.9

* Adapted from Asch, Block, and Hertzman (1940).

It will be noticed that Asch and his coworkers found a striking prestige suggestion effect. The control group (I) ranked politics very low in both intelligence and social usefulness. All the other groups showed ranking consistent with the majority prestige suggestion: Group II raised the politicians from eighth place to fourth place for both characteristics, Group III lowered the politicians to ninth place for intelligence and to a position midway between eighth and ninth place for social usefulness, and Group IV raised politicians for social usefulness and lowered them for intelligence. Thus far the above data confirm the usual results obtained in such experiments. But the experimenters did not stop there. They next asked the subjects, "What particular group or groups of politicians did you have in mind when making the judgments?" The typical replies given clearly indicate that the term *politics* carried *distinctly different meanings* for the subjects of the different groups and that the four groups did not differ in the way they judged the same objects but differed in the objects they chose to judge. Thus, for example, the subjects of Group II gave the following responses: "National politics—Roosevelt, Hull, Stimson"; "More statesmanship than politics"; "Politics as a career—Lehman, LaGuardia, etc." The subjects of Group III, however, answered "Politicians," "Tammany Hall underlings," "Usual neighborhood politicians."

As further support for the above analysis, the experimenters point out that when later the subjects were further questioned most of them denied that they had been influenced by majority prestige suggestion, despite the obvious fact that they had. As the investigators suggest, however, this did not mean that the subjects were lying but rather that "the subjects were not aware of a change in their response because such changes did not occur. What they do fail to recognize—and this has important consequences—is that the standard has to a large degree determined for them the object of judgment."

Differential value of prestige sources.—Closely related to the proposition that prestige suggestion operates by changing the nature of the object judged are the experiments indicating that different sources of suggestion have different prestige value. As was pointed out on page 187 (Chap. VI), beliefs and attitudes change in accordance with the facts as provided by authorities, *but not all "authorities" are given equal acceptance by people.* Thus, for example, we should expect to find that an economist's suggestion about economic matters would be more effective in changing the perception of an economic event (and therefore will show more prestige suggestion effect) than would an economic suggestion of a poet. But this would hold only where the person clearly recognized economics and poetry as two different areas and where his knowledge about each included differentiation among authorities. Where the belief systems are but vaguely organized, we should not expect to find such a marked degree of differential prestige value according to source. Thus, where the child "knows" that the parent is an expert on all matters, most of the parent's suggestions may be readily accepted—no matter what the object—but where the adult "knows" that Mr. Tycoon is an expert only on mass production, his perceptions will be influenced by Mr. Tycoon's suggestions only in the realm of mass production and not, say, in the realm of race relations.

In summarizing the experiments that compare the relative effectiveness of majority vs. expert prestige suggestion, Coffin (1941) points out

The effectiveness of group opinion as compared with expert opinion appears also to depend on the issue being judged. The more closely the issue relates to "social norms," the more influential the group opinion, while problems relating to "personal norms" are less influenced by group judgments. Expert opinion may operate more strongly in certain "technical" matters. However, the prestige value of various "expert" sources depends again upon the problem at issue.

Again we find, then, that prestige suggestion is responsive to the very same conditions which are influential in the normal process of belief and attitude change.

Prestige suggestion and needs.—Although prestige suggestion frequently operates through first changing the nature of the perceived object, not all prestige effects can be so described. Some instances of prestige suggestion operate in a different sequence. A prestige suggestion may be accepted because of the *need of the individual to agree with the person making the suggestion.* In such cases the individual first accepts the suggestion, and then the perceptual qualities of the object are changed. This will typically occur where there is close identification between the suggestor and "suggestee." A thorough analysis of the way prestige suggestion operates must allow for these cases.

A striking instance of the neglect of this possibility is found in Lewis' analysis (1941) of some of her experimental results. In that experiment groups of college students were asked to rank 10 political slogans of contemporary interest (the experiment being done in 1938 to 1939) for five characteristics: compellingness to action, social significance, personal inspiration, author's intelligence, and approval. In addition, each subject was asked to state, anonymously if he preferred, his political party affiliation. The control group did its rankings without any prestige suggestions; the experimental group was told how various political leaders (Roosevelt, Hoover, Browder, etc.) had previously rated these slogans at a "press conference."

In analyzing one of her experimental groups, the members of which had said that they were Communists, she found that Browder's alleged rankings had influenced their judgments. In keeping with the analysis we have just discussed, Lewis concluded that in these cases "The subjects did not simply 'change their minds'. . . . Rather, the slogan they were judging appeared in ᴧ new light, acquired a new meaning, and thus demanded a new judgment." Despite the soundness of such an analysis for most cases of prestige suggestion, one of the specific examples given by Lewis does not seem to be amenable to such an interpretation. Thus, "For example, . . . *Balance the Budget* had meant, on the first test (for the control group), 'Abolish relief' and was ranked low. Now (for the experimental group which had been told that Browder had rated that slogan high) it meant: Lower war appropriations, (higher) undistributed surplus taxes, more relief money—in short, balance the human budget." (!)

Such a strained interpretation seems to neglect completely the interpersonal relationships that sometimes hold in prestige suggestion. A more believable interpretation of Lewis' results might be something like this: The authoritative suggestion made it necessary for the subject to change his judgment consciously because of his need to agree with Browder. This necessity, in turn, created a situation where the subject was forced to seek for new meanings and rationalize his behavior. In other words, there are two sequences characteristic of prestige suggestion: (1) Prestige suggestion leads to changes in judgments which lead, in turn, to changes in perception. (2) Prestige suggestion leads to changes in perception which lead to changes in judgment.

These two sequences have been observed in various experiments. Thus Luchins (1945), in an experiment on the effects of suggestion in the perception of drawings (which we shall discuss in greater detail later), concludes on the basis of his data that

> Both external conditions (the nature of the drawing) and internal conditions (attitudes of the subjects) were relevant in bringing about the results . . . . The comments revealed the operation of subjective factors such as *a desire to see what other individual said he saw*, a belief that one *had to see* what the other said in order to be "correct," an acceptance of the other's description as a kind of challenge—"If she can see it, so can I."[1]

What is true for all belief and attitude change is equally true for change consequent upon prestige suggestion. The functional value of beliefs and attitudes plays an important role in determining their development and change. And this may become especially important in person-to-person suggestion situations. It will be remembered that we pointed to the importance of such factors as speech patterns and other "peripheral" matters when discussing the effectiveness of speech events in persuasion. The mental set toward the person making the suggestions may be of crucial significance and can evoke a need to agree *even before the suggestion is made* by the speaker. Such needs as "the need for submission" and the need "to be in harmony with others" do exist, can be very strong needs, and will, therefore, influence behavior. When they operate in so-called propaganda or suggestion situations, they are no different from when they operate in other situations.

Summary and general comments for prestige suggestion.—Prestige suggestion, by changing the individual's environment through manipulation of either word objects or other objects, can result in a change in the nature of the perceived object. As a consequence of this change, the beliefs and the judgment of the object may be changed. The occurrence of these processes is in part determined by the acceptability, to the person, of the authority making the suggestion. Thus, a change in the belief about an object consequent upon prestige suggestion follows the same principles that hold for all changes in beliefs and attitudes.

Prestige suggestion, however, can operate still another way. The "prestige suggester" may stand in such an interpersonal relationship to the recipient of the suggestion as to evoke a need for agreement on the part of

[1] Italics our own.

the recipient. Where the suggestion is counter to the belief already held by the recipient, the recipient will first change his judgment and then seek to rationalize the object perceived so that it is congruent with his new judgment. Here again the net result is a change in the perceptual qualities of the original object, since rationalization frequently involves genuine cognitive reorganization. This sequence of events is seen, then, as a special case of the influence of needs upon belief formation.

Lundholm (1938), in contrasting the effectiveness of propaganda that involves an appeal to submission needs as compared with propaganda based on other appeals, makes this judgment:

> Submission to authority itself is unlikely to induce enduring belief . . . . Whenever you wish to swing the opinion of an individual or group, appeal to submission is far less effective than appeal to other impulses or appeal to rational considerations . . . by dignity and domination one might temporarily impress one's opinion upon an audience, but if this impression is to be of enduring effect, its content itself must be endowed with emotional or rational appeal that is independent of the psychological presence of the propagandist.[1]

Other Instances of Suggestion.—Not all persuasion or propaganda involves prestige suggestion. Thus, for example, the suggestion that is alleged to take place in a crowd situation or even under the influence of inanimate objects plays an important part in changing beliefs and attitudes although the prestige element is not involved. We shall next examine some experimental data involving more general suggestion situations to determine if the same basic analysis made for prestige suggestion also holds here.

The effects of "social suggestion" on visual perception.—The experiment of Luchins, already referred to, examines the effect of a suggestion made by one individual in a social situation upon the simple visual perceptions of another individual. This experiment is of interest for several reasons. In the first place, because it deals with the visual perception of a specified object, it enables us to follow the processes we have outlined in the preceding discussion in a relatively simple situation and therefore may help to clarify the nature of these processes. In the second place, it emphasizes the importance of an additional factor that must be taken into consideration when analyzing the potential effectiveness of suggestions or propaganda— the *ambiguity* of the object concerned.

Luchins presented his subjects with a series of drawings that began with a

---

[1] Lundholm, in the same paper, presents an interesting analysis of the two famous speeches from Shakespeare's *Julius Caesar*—that of Brutus and of Antony—concluding that Antony's success was probably due to his careful avoidance of appeal to submission whereas Brutus' failure was probably due to his strong emphasis of such an appeal.

very ambiguous design and in which, with each successive card shown to the subjects, the contours of a bottle gradually evolved until on the last card there was a complete and clear sketch of a bottle.[1]   The drawings preceding this last card had various added lines and curlicues which might be perceived as outlining the profile of a face or feature of a face.   The members of his control group (school children ranging in age from eleven to thirteen years) were asked with each card, ". . . tell me everything you see in it," and then, "Are you sure that this is all you see?"   The test was administered individually to each control subject.   For his experimental group (made up of children of the same age range and I.Q. as the control group) the same test was administered to two children at a time.   One of these two children was the experimenter's confederate who had been instructed to say that she saw a "face" *in every card*—and nothing more.   The confederate's answer always preceded that of the subject (the second child of each pair) and was overheard by the subject.   For other experimental groups, the confederate said that she saw a "bottle"; for others, a "battleship"; for still others, "an automobile"; etc.   Luchins sums up the results obtained as follows:

. . . some subjects were influenced in their perception of a drawing by another's reaction.   With the exception of a few subjects, the influence was not in the nature of a blind reiteration of what the confederate had reported.   The subjects examined the drawings.   They looked in them for the object reported by the confederate.   When a characteristic of the design compatible with the confederate's statement was found, it became for some subjects the only aspect of the design to which they paid attention.   The remainder of the drawing was ignored.   In other cases, the discovered feature became the focal point around which the entire drawing was reorganized . . . in a drawing which contained a *clearly structured object, subjects tended to describe this object regardless of what the confederate said* . . . .   When a drawing did not lend itself easily to organizations . . . compatible with the confederate's reaction (*e. g.*, when the confederate said "Battleship") the children usually reacted to some characteristic of the design itself.

Note how closely Luchins' results follow the analysis Duncker had previously proposed for prestige suggestion (see page 338).   Suggestion changes the perceptual nature of the drawing through accentuation, through discovery of new features previously unattended to, etc.   However, it should also be noted that there are limits to this effect.   If the drawing is ambiguous and not well structured, then this process seems to proceed readily enough; but if the drawing is clear, or if there is no element in the objective drawing that can serve as a focal point for reorganization, then social suggestion seems to be ineffective.

[1] See Fig. 8.

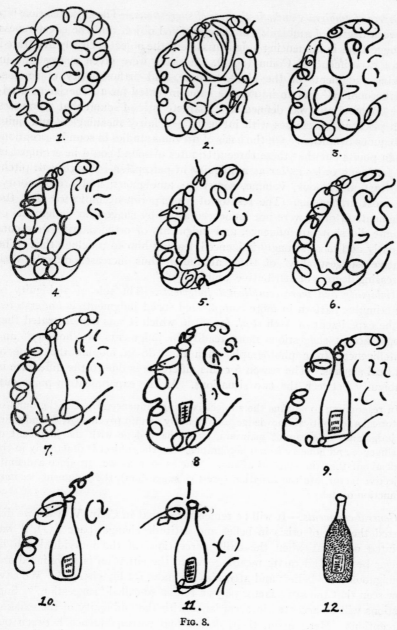

Fig. 8.

Degree of ambiguity and effectiveness of suggestions.—The close relationship between degree of ambiguity of the perceived object and the effectiveness of suggestions in influencing judgments about the object is clearly illustrated in an experiment of Coffin (1941). Subjects were given suggestions in making judgments of the pitch, volume, and orthosonority of sounds. "Orthosonority" was an impressive name invented for a nonexistent attribute of sound and was defined as a characteristic of sound that "increases with pitch and decreases with intensity"—a fairly meaningless and quite ambiguous definition. On the basis of previous studies in sound perception, Coffin points out that these three attributes of sound could be arranged in the following order as far as ambiguity in perception is concerned: pitch, the least ambiguous; volume, somewhat ambiguous; and orthosonority, the most ambiguous. The results of his experiment indicated that the judgments of pitch were not influenced at all by suggestion, judgments of volume did show an influence, and judgments of orthosonority were consistently and most strongly influenced, leading him to conclude that "The relative 'suggestibility' of these attributes thus increases directly with increasing degrees of attributive 'ambiguity.' "

Ambiguity and more complicated judgments.—The role of ambiguity of the stimulus pattern in more complicated social judgments is underscored in the experiment of Asch *et al.* (1938) in which it was demonstrated that people accept suggestions more readily in judgments of "honesty" and "intelligence" from photographs than they do in judging the value of political slogans. The reason for this difference is due to the difference in ambiguity between the two situations. As the experimenters point out,

In responding to slogans the subject is being influenced by a background of historical and political knowledge, as well as by certain psychological tendencies of judgment. We cannot maintain, as we have done with the judgment of intelligence and honesty from photographs, that the subject is practically in the dark about the true state of affairs. Now as soon as we introduce a definite objective factor into the situation (prestige suggestion), the judgment becomes a function of it.

General comments.—It will be remembered that in Chap. V, when we discussed the role of crisis in belief and attitude change (page 154), it was pointed out that when the daily perceptions of the individual can no longer be given adequate meaning—when the situation is a confused and ambiguous one—beliefs and attitudes are more readily changed. We have now seen that the same factor plays a role in so-called "suggestion." Suggestions will be accepted in accordance with the ambiguity of the existing perceptions. Here again, then, do we find correspondence between our general principles and the data from suggestion and propaganda experiments.

The fact that the more general types of suggestion follow the same process which prestige suggestion follows, *i.e.*, changing the perception of the object and then the judgment, has some interesting implications in the understanding of the use of irony in propaganda and persuasion. The words of an ironical statement are deliberately at variance to the meaning intended; yet when skillfully employed, irony can be a powerful persuasive technique. From our analysis one of the reasons for this seems to be that the ironical statement may cause the listener to perceive a new aspect of the situation. As a consequence of this new perception, the listener himself draws the conclusion that was intended by the speaker, without the speaker's ever having explicitly "suggested" it. He has merely altered the listener's environment, and the rest occurs naturally. Another illustration of this can be found in the so-called "concealed" propaganda. A political party may distribute leaflets ostensibly prepared by the Communist party urging all citizens to vote for a given candidate. The hope of the propagandist is that the citizen, in reading the leaflet, will see that candidate in a new light and will then vote against him. This is not a hypothetical example but has occurred a number of times in our political history. It may be profitable to reread the quotation from Biddle, given on page 316 of this chapter, in which he points out that one of the values of propaganda, as opposed to other forms of social control, is that each individual so controlled is left with the impression that his responses follow his own decision. This is not only an "impression" but a true statement of the event.

Suggestion and the context of needs and belief systems.—Many incidental observations and analyses of somewhat relevant data point to the validity of the proposition that specific suggestions are more readily accepted or that propaganda is more effective when the specific needs of the individual are thereby met. This indicates that the efficacy of propaganda is determined by the same tension factors as are involved in any process of belief or attitude change. But unfortunately, there have been no well-planned experiments that have specifically investigated the dynamic relationships between needs and propaganda effectiveness. Among the experiments that have at all concerned themselves with this relationship are such studies as that of Hartmann (1936a) and the investigations seeking to demonstrate that suggestions which are accepted as a consequence of propaganda tend to be in harmony with some larger system of beliefs or some already existing predisposition and therefore, presumably, with the major needs and interests of the subjects (Knower, 1936; Coffin, 1941).

Hartmann conducted his experiment during the election campaign of 1935 in the city of Allentown, Pa. For experimental purposes the city was divided into three types of wards: "1, an 'emotional' area in which all resident adults received leaflets written in a vigorous advertising style urging support of the Socialist ticket; 2, a 'rational' region, in which a more academic type of persuasion was used; and 3, a control district where nothing was distributed." After the votes for the Socialist ticket had been counted, personal post-election interviews were conducted with 45 house-holders chosen at random from districts 1 and 2. Although this study was admittedly preliminary and Hartmann's summary seems based on impressions rather than adequate data, he feels that the data justify the following conclusion: "Those ideas will be most readily assimilated by the voter which fit in with his present, 'apperceptive mass,' which are joined with some prepotent wants, which meet him on his own level and lead him on from where he is."

Knower, in his investigation of the effect of a printed argument in changing beliefs and attitudes about Prohibition, first determined the already existing beliefs of some four-hundred summer school university students and then subjected various groups of these students to printed propaganda for and against Prohibition. His conclusions indicate that "When subjects read two arguments, one which defends their previous attitude and one which opposes it, more subjects changed in the direction of an intensification of their previous attitude . . . than changed in the opposite direction."

The purpose of Coffin's study was ". . . to investigate . . . the influence of motivational or attitudinal factors in suggestions, with explicit reference to the relationship between pre-existing attitudes and the content of accepted suggestions." The experiment, conducted in the winter of 1939 to 1940, took advantage of the war in Europe as it was reflected in the diversified opinions on the issues of the war among college students.

Coffin selected 25 propaganda items from current newspapers and magazines, items which those sources had labeled as rumors or propaganda. His subjects were asked to indicate whether they thought each ietm to be "true, false, probable, improbable." On the basis of their responses, the subjects were assigned scores ranging from 25 (complete acceptance of pro-Allied propaganda) to 0 (complete rejection of pro-Allied propaganda).

The subjects were then given an "attitude test" designed to measure their attitudes toward the European belligerents and permitting Coffin to assign to each subject an "attitude score" ranging from $+16$ (strongly pro-German) to -16 (strongly pro-Allies). The results indicated a close relationship between "attitude" and readiness to accept pro-Allied propaganda, the correlation being $+.79$. Coffin concludes,

. . . the acceptance of propaganda is closely related to attitude. Among individuals of widely varying attitude toward a social situation, their acceptance of propaganda concerning the situation varied with their attitudes. Individuals expressing similar attitudes may be grouped together and the groups may be characterized as being "suggestible" to specific propagandas and "unsuggestible" or negatively suggestible to other specific propagandas.

So important is this relationship between attitudes and suggestibility that it may operate even where a suggestion or a propagandistic statement is specifically labeled "rumor." Thus, for example, in an experiment performed by Smith (1947) students were given 13 pro-Russian and 13 anti-Russian items and were asked to indicate their belief as to the truth of each statement. Some of the statements were labeled "actual facts," and some, "unverified rumors." The students were then given a Russian attitude scale, and the correlations compared. One of the findings is summarized by Smith as follows:

Under all labels, scores on the belief scale were correlated positively with scores on the attitude scale: *i.e.*, the pro-Soviet people showed the highest degree of belief on the pro-Soviet items and the anti-Soviet people the lowest, etc.

The above studies are valuable, but what is needed in addition are some clinically oriented researches into important need structures of people and their readiness to accept various suggestions, researches such as we have quoted in the chapter on belief development (see especially page 184). However, the data that are available and the host of general observations that have been made support the conclusion that the same relationships that hold for needs and belief development also hold for needs and propaganda effects. No special psychological principles seem to be indicated.

Propaganda and Its Special Techniques.—Up to this point we have concerned ourselves with the basic psychological processes involved in persuasion through propaganda. For a complete analysis we must also discuss the contributions made to the effectiveness of propaganda by the special techniques commonly used by the propagandist. As we have indicated in the introduction to the discussion of propaganda, it is these techniques, more than anything else, which set propaganda apart from other persuasive devices.

A fairly large number of studies are available that have investigated the relative effectiveness of the media used in propaganda (newspapers, magazines, movies), of the different techniques for using a given medium (nature of appeals used, physical make-up of the propaganda, etc.), of emotional vs. rational types of propaganda, etc. Although these studies have some practical value, it must again be emphasized, before turning to a consideration of some of the results, that the reasons for the effectiveness or ineffectiveness of the various techniques studied lie in the basic processes we have already examined.

Some empirical studies.—Annis (1939) studied the relative effectiveness of militaristic and pacifistic cartoons and editorials in changing the beliefs and attitudes of college and high-school students. He reports that college students were more easily persuaded by editorials and high-school students by cartoons. Another of these studies is that performed by Asher and Sargent (1941) who studied the effectiveness of an argument accompanied by a "complimentary" or "uncomplimentary" cartoon. The arguments concerned themselves with various socially significant matters—politicians, socialism, etc. They found that of the three methods used—(1) presenting words on blank cards, (2) speaking the words aloud, and (3) presenting the same words as labels of complimentary or uncomplimentary cartoons—the third was the most effective in bringing about a shift in judgments among college students.

Cantril and Allport's (1935) book presents the results of a study designed to compare the relative effectiveness of listening to the radio, listening to a speaker, and reading. They conclude, among other things, that (1) the more difficult the material the less effective is auditory presentation and (2) radio-listening can more easily evoke responses congruent with the suggestions being made whereas the reading of the material may evoke critical responses. In line with these results is the conclusion of Knower (1935) that individual, face-to-face presentation of propaganda is more effective than if the same arguments are presented to the subject when he is merely one member of a large audience listening to a speaker.

Cantril and Allport also report that short sentences are more effective (in broadcasting) when the material is factual and uninteresting but lose their superiority as the material becomes more interesting, that the optimal speed of broadcasting is between 115 and 160 words per minute, and that repetition is desirable.

Many analysts have shown the importance of using words with invariant meaning or feeling tones (see page 324) in making propaganda effective. Thus Hartmann (1936b) has shown in an interview study that many people favor public ownership of natural resources and increased social security insurance. But these same respondents rejected these proposals when they were tagged as being "socialist."

Slogans.—Slogans, as "capsules" of propaganda, offer a convenient object for examination of many of the special techniques usually labeled "propagandistic." A slogan, as a tool of propaganda, should be distinguished from a commercial catch phrase, and Bellak (1942) suggests the following useful definition of a slogan: "Directive phrases as having the characteristics of brevity and timeliness, use the imperative, are identified with a certain group, and can be considered essentially as battle- or rallying-cries."

This definition emphasizes both the external structure of the slogan and the meaningfulness of the slogan in terms of the current social situation. The external structure of a successful slogan is so designed as to maximize its attention-getting value, *i.e.*, make it stand out as a noteworthy object in the environment, and to maximize its memory value so that it can be remembered easily and be repeated frequently. The first of these objectives (making it stand out as a figure against a background) is frequently achieved by a number of devices. Thus, alliteration of sounds is sometimes used, *e.g.*, "Keep cool with Coolidge," or a ringing repetition of sounds is employed, "America for Americans," or puns are resorted to, "Don't be a N.A.M. fool!" To increase the memory value of a slogan, simplicity, brevity, and rhyming schemes seem to be the favorite techniques: "Had enough? Vote Republican!"; "Sound Money"; "Tippecanoe and Tyler Too!"

Words with invariant meanings or feeling tones are frequently used to guarantee that the hearer will perceive the slogan with a favorable mental set: "Liberty, Fraternity, Equality" or "The right to work." However, a slogan, no matter how cleverly designed in terms of structure, will not "catch on" if it does not appeal to a particular need or demand of the hearer. This does not mean, of course, that effective slogans necessarily formulate the true and correct solution to these needs and demands, but they must appear to do so and must "stand out as short-cut characterizations of the direction and temper of the time and situation" (Sherif, 1937).

General comments.—All of the above data and "rules of the game" can be helpful in making persuasion through propaganda effective. The method of presentation of the suggestion is important. The personality of the individual making the suggestion, his clothes, his appearance, and his speech patterns are all contributory factors to the efficacy of propaganda. But these are also important in determining the efficacy of any other form of persuasion—"reasoned persuasion," education, etc. The good educator knows this and deliberately attempts to exploit these techniques. He dramatizes his material, he chooses his words carefully, he attempts to establish a proper interpersonal relationship between himself and his student, and he pays attention to the emotional and motivational processes involved in learning. He does not regard the educational process as a "cold" intellectual process.

But in the final analysis, all of the above matters are somewhat secondary. Propaganda will be effective or ineffective only in so far as it is congruent with the principles that determine all belief and attitude change.

PROPAGANDA PROPHYLAXIS

The analysis made in this chapter of the processes involved in persuasion through propaganda become particularly significant when dealing with the very practical social problem of how to "protect people against the power of propaganda." This problem is of great concern to educators and propagandists alike. Much of the activity of people concerned with this problem seems, however, to emphasize the nature of propaganda *material* and *techniques* rather than the nature of the intended victim, in their efforts to protect the victim. As we have pointed out earlier, more attention has been paid to an analysis of the words and tricks used by the propagandist than to the needs and belief systems of the man at the receiving end. Thus, for example, the Institute for Propaganda Analysis made the assumption that if the public could be taught how to recognize propaganda, the public would become immune to its effects and would react more rationally. The acceptance of this assumption is illustrated by the following quotation from Sargent (1942):

Thousands of subscribers to *Consumers' Research* and *Consumers' Union* have become aware of the tricks of advertisers and have learned to depend upon scientific analysis in selecting and buying their products. The Institute for Propaganda Analysis . . . announced in its final issue (discontinued because of the war) of its bulletin that its monthly circulation has been 10,000 and that, in addition, 18,000 copies of annual volumes have been sold. Since a large proportion of subscribers were libraries, schools, colleges, editors, clergymen, lecturers, and the like, the influence of the Institute upon American thought has been considerable. The most concrete illustration is the widespread use of the Institute's "Seven Devices" in analyzing potential propaganda.

The analysis of propaganda and suggestion made in this chapter would seriously question the enthusiastic claims made above. Undoubtedly the work of *Consumers' Research*, *Consumers' Union*, and the Institute for Propaganda Analysis has affected the thinking of many people, has changed some of the buying habits of some consumers, and has enabled the detection of specific propagandists. And undoubtedly there are "rules of evidence" that, if applied by people, can help them to distinguish between sound and unsound argument. But this is far from saying that the thousands of subscribers to these services have become immune to propaganda. The above techniques are of limited value. As we have seen, there is no fundamental distinction between propaganda and nonpropaganda. We might pick out one specific piece of material, label it propaganda, and then describe it in great detail. But that will by no means protect us against a piece of propaganda that might appear in the form of an arithmetic book, a lecture by a famous scientist, or a newspaper dispatch. As long as certain needs exist unsatisfied among people and certain belief systems are held and certain authorities remain the source for our facts, propaganda can be effective.

Thus, while sound propaganda prophylaxis would include exposing current propaganda and the most popular tricks of the propagandist and would include education in rules of evidence and scientific method, the most effective part of such a program would consist of (1) *providing aggressive counterpropaganda* by attempting to induce the beliefs and attitudes we want rather than permitting the other propagandist to induce the beliefs and attitudes he wants and, above all, of (2) *doing something about the needs, demands, and larger belief systems that are responsible for making the "wrong propaganda" so readily acceptable.*

Experimental Data.—Although the above generalizations follow from our analysis of propaganda, again unfortunately, there are not now available clear-cut experimental data to support this theoretical deduction. The two best experiments in this field (Biddle, 1932; Collier, 1944) yield somewhat ambiguous results.

The study by Biddle was designed "to teach resistance to organized autistic thinking." His procedure consisted of presenting nine lessons to high-school pupils which encouraged them to take a more critical and "reasoned" approach toward social problems. The pupils were then "propagandized" by editorials and speakers. When tested for susceptibility to this propaganda, they seemed to show increased resistance. These results suggest the value of attempting to train people to be "propaganda wise" and indicate the usefulness of including such training in any program of propaganda prophylaxis. However, Collier criticizes Biddle's conclusion on the grounds that the propaganda material used may not have been very "effective" propaganda and that the subjects of Biddle's experiment were exposed to this inadequate propaganda only once, whereas in real life people are exposed to the same propaganda repeated over a long period. In addition, Collier might have pointed out that Biddle's study dealt with issues that were probably not central to the personality structures of the high-school students.

When the above factors are varied, however, Collier's study seems to show that propaganda training has very little value in immunizing the individual against the propaganda effect. The practical significance of this conclusion is so important that the study demands detailed analysis.

The specific purpose of Collier's experiment was to determine whether or not the beliefs and attitudes of individuals would be affected by propaganda material *even if the individuals were clearly aware of the purpose behind the propaganda* and even if they were consciously examining the content of the material *critically*. Approximately three-hundred university students served as subjects, although the major analysis was based on an experimental group of 34 and a control group of 75. Both these groups were given an opinion test prior to the start of the experiment. The items for this test were based directly on propaganda literature published by the German Library of Information—a registered propaganda agency of the Nazi government operating in the United States in the years immediately preceding the war. (The experiment was conducted during the early stages of the war and before the United States had become a belligerent.) The students were asked to rate the items on the test from a plus five, indicating "firm and resolved agreement," through zero, indicating "doubt, indifference, or neutral attitude," to a minus five, indicating "firm and resolved disagreement." Such items as the following were used:

The German people are generally happier under the Nazi regime than before 1932. Foreign workers in Germany enjoy the same protection and the same privileges as the German workers.

The Nazi leaders seem sincerely interested in a more equitable distribution of wealth for all European countries.

A high positive score on this test was taken to indicate a pro-Nazi belief or attitude; a high negative score, an anti-Nazi belief or attitude. Both control and experimental groups were given the test at the same time, and nothing further was done with the control group until they were retested after an interval of four weeks. The experimental group, however, was exposed to certain propaganda material between their first and second testing.

The experimental group (students of Collier's course in Applied Psychology at the University of Vermont) took the first test one week before the problem of propaganda was discussed in the class as part of its regular work. Propaganda was dealt with in Collier's lectures in the following way: First he lectured on the definition and nature of propaganda. He then discussed the various devices used by many propagandists and the characteristics by which some propaganda could be detected. To illustrate this discussion he examined, for the class, several specific pieces of German propaganda literature and indicated just how each piece of literature had used certain propaganda devices. The material he used for these illustrations was that issued by the German Library of Information and consisted of several issues of *Freude und Arbeit*, a beautifully produced picture magazine which consistently attempted to suggest (although indirectly) that (1) Nazi leaders were friendly, benevolent, and frequently expressed common human sympathies (*e.g.*, pictures were shown of Nazi leaders kissing babies and growing flowers in their gardens at home); (2) Nazi leaders were strong and wise; and (3) the Nazis had a more workable and humanitarian plan for Europe than had hitherto been proposed. In addition he used *Facts in Review* (a more sober German journal ostensibly presenting "news analysis"), the document titled *Polish acts of atrocity against the German minority in Poland*, and, finally, the *German White Paper*.

After the completion of his series of lectures, Collier announced to his class that they would be responsible for a paper (in three weeks) on an analysis of German propaganda. To help them obtain material for this paper, he told them that the samples of German propaganda he had used in his lectures would be available, in a reference room, for their study. Thus the students, in this way were to be exposed to German propaganda for a period of approximately three weeks. But, it must be emphasized, they approached this propaganda after a series of lectures on the nature of the propaganda, after the propaganda itself was "debunked," and they were to read the propaganda critically, with a view to writing an analytic paper on the material.

After four weeks from the beginning of the experiment, these students were given the opinion test again. The comparison of the first and second test results for the control and experimental group would indicate, Collier hoped, what effect, if any, the exposure to the propaganda material had on the beliefs and attitudes of the members of the experimental group.

The comparisons between the two groups revealed that the changes in opinions or beliefs which took place were in *opposite* directions. The experimental group started with an average score of −1.29 and ended with a score of −0.91. It will be remembered that the higher the negative score the stronger is the anti-Nazi belief. This means that the experimental group showed a slight *decrease* in its anti-Nazi beliefs. The control group, on the other hand, showed an *increase* in its anti-Nazi beliefs, starting with a score of −0.95 and ending with a −1.94. It should also be noted that the control group showed a greater absolute change (.99) than did the experimental group (.38). Collier interprets these surprising results in the following way:

The experimental factor may be thought of here as counteracting in a small group a trend in the restructuring of attitude in the total social group. The C-group is taken as a sample of this field and we may infer that had the experimental factor been absent the E-group would have shown the same direction of change. It is important to note that at the time of this study the German drive into the Balkans was in progress. British participation in Greece, Crete, and in the Mediterranean area generally was not only changing the public apathy toward Britain which had been obvious since Dunkirk, but was operating to stiffen attitudes in sharper opposition to the Axis . . . . It is, therefore, of interest that the attitudes of the E-group were not only prevented in participating in such a shift, but that there was some change, even though small, in the direction more favorable to the Nazi viewpoints.

That this shift in attitudes which the control group displayed was generally true of American students at that time is indicated by the test scores Collier obtained with various groups of students tested at different dates, the data of which are given in Table 6.

TABLE 6.—CHANGES IN PRO-NAZI ATTITUDE TESTS DURING FOURTEEN-MONTH PERIOD.*

	April, 1941	May, 1941	October, 1941	June, 1942
Average score........	−0.95	−1.94	−2.24	−2.64
Sigma...............	1.45	1.42	1.02	0.86
Number of cases......	75	75	125	72

* Adapted from Collier (1944), Table 3, p. 11.

Collier suggests that what probably happened among the students in the experimental group was that at the beginning of the study, when they had relatively confused and perhaps contradictory beliefs and opinions about the Germans and the Allies (*e.g.*, "Germany got a raw deal after the last war in the Versailles Treaty and cannot now be blamed for attacking the oppressors" vs. "The ruthlessness of the Nazi leaders is real and designed to intimidate all non-Nazi people"), exposure to material that supported the former of these already existing beliefs and attitudes was effective enough to strengthen them at the expense of the latter.

Thus it appears that even though people may be warned against propaganda, may spend some time studying its characteristics, etc., their beliefs and attitudes can still be shaped by the propaganda if such propaganda fits in with existing frames of reference.

The above conclusion, though in harmony with the theoretical analysis outlined in this chapter, does not follow unambiguously, however, from Collier's data. It might be argued, for example, that the subjects of Collier's experimental group, because of their study of propaganda, had become more immune to all persuasion in this area—Allied as well as German propaganda—and would therefore tend to resist a shift toward pro-Allied attitude (see the discussion on page 189, Chap. VI). This would account for the differences between his two groups. Obviously additional experimental data are required before we can assess the value of propaganda training in providing propaganda immunity.

"PRINCIPLES" OF PROPAGANDA

We can now answer the general question that was asked at the beginning of the chapter. The experimental data available from the investigations of propaganda and suggestion are congruent with the general laws of perception, cognition, and motivation which were reviewed in Part I of this book. No special basic "principles of propaganda" are necessary to account for persuasion through propaganda. Man's reaction to propaganda is on the same level of rationality as is his reaction to other forms of persuasion. Language, when used by the propagandist, has no added power that it lacks in other speech events. The emphasis on the adjustive and rational character of man's responses to suggestion, the necessity of viewing propaganda effects as a function of both structural and functional factors operating in the individual's psychological field all permit us to assess the efficacy and limitations of propaganda realistically. We can agree with Zilboorg (1938) who points out, in his discussion of war propaganda,

There are situations in which no propaganda is of any avail . . . . We must conclude that where social changes are concerned, propaganda in general is a secondary phenomenon and not a real tool . . . . War propaganda is somehow hopelessly inefficient when people have enough to eat and when they are not afraid and when they are permitted to be socially angry.

Guides for the Propagandist.—However, the term *propaganda* has some practical value in helping us to label and isolate certain instances of persuasion—even if the term does not isolate a basically different process from other cognitive reorganizations. It might be useful, therefore, to summarize some of the generalizations that can be drawn concerning persuasion through propaganda specifically in terms of the usual practices of propagandists as we know them. Such principles of propaganda—or guides for the propagandist—must necessarily bear strong resemblances to the basic principles of cognitive reorganization we have already discussed at length in previous chapters, but the specific illustrations that can be used and the immediately practical implications that can be drawn may differ sufficiently to justify a listing.

1. *A suggestion that seems to meet an existing need will be more readily accepted than one that does not meet a need.* The effective propagandist will seek to "tie in" his propaganda with any existing need, no matter how illogically related. Thus the suggestion that we vote Republican may be tied in with our need for a postwar dishwasher. Where there is no need

that can be successfully tied in with the suggestion, the propagandist will first attempt to create a need.   Since speech events, in so far as they can change man's environment, can thereby cause new needs to appear, the propagandist may first direct his activities toward the creation of imbalances and tensions in the psychological field of man and only later will he propose his "suggestion."   This is sometimes called *delayed propaganda*.   Thus, if no need exists on the part of the people that can be used to support antilabor legislation, the propagandist will first see to it that newspapers, radio, and political discussions emphasize and magnify every "labor incident"— especially cases of strikes and violence—no matter how small or how infrequent.   If successful, he will have created a fear on the part of the citizen of labor tie-ups and a need for labor peace.   At that point the propagandist may offer his suggestions concerning his antilabor legislation.   *He views with alarm, shakes his head, and then gives the answers.*

2. *A suggestion concerning an ambiguous situation will be more readily accepted than one concerning a clearly structured situation.*   The good propagandist will watch his timing very carefully.   He will be ready to take advantage of every critical social situation when man's needs for new and clearer meanings are great because of the changing and confused nature of man's real world.   In taking advantage of such critical situations, he will offer his suggestions as "clarifying explanations" for the ambiguous situation and will, if at all possible, prevent alternative suggestions from coming to the attention of people.   The effective propagandist can permit the luxury of free access to information and different "explanations" and viewpoints during a peaceful period, but not during a period of crisis—for he runs the danger of suggestions other than his own being just as readily accepted.   Closely related to the first principle, a good propagandist may first seek to create confusion and ambiguity in order to increase the effectiveness of his propaganda.   *He fishes in muddy waters.*

3. *A suggestion that fits in with other systems of beliefs and frames of reference will be more readily accepted than one that does not.*   The good propagandist will first seek to discover what the generally held beliefs, attitudes, ideologies, and life philosophies of his target group are.   He will pattern his suggestions so as to make them congruent with these enduring organizations.   In one situation he may present communistic suggestions (for example) as congruent with the ideals of Christianity; in the next situation he may present the very same suggestions as congruent with a purely "rational, scientific, and atheistic" philosophy.   Where he cannot find such congruence, he may first attempt to change the larger system of beliefs before making his specific suggestions.   This is sometimes referred to as *long-range propaganda*.   He might advocate general scientific training in the schools or

"vocational" curricula as opposed to "cultural" curricula, for example, and then fit his specific suggestions to belief systems that are basically scientific or basically antiintellectual. *He is a man who looks toward the future.*

4. *A suggestion that can readily induce new attributes in the perception of a familiar object will be more readily accepted than one that does not have that advantage.* The good propagandist will attempt to orient his suggestions with respect to the object of the belief rather than attacking the belief itself. This can be facilitated by a proper way of describing the object and by explicit "pointings" to the elements of the object that he wishes accentuated in the perception of the person or that he wishes the person to "discover." Thus, instead of offering a direct suggestion that the public support a universal conscription bill, the propagandist may discuss and emphasize the educational opportunities offered in Army service or the health benefits involved in Army training or the morale value of Army discipline. Where possible, he must permit the citizen to draw his own conclusions. This is sometimes referred to as *indirect propaganda.*

If the technique of accentuation of certain elements in the objects is not possible or is very difficult, the propagandist can attempt to change the meaning of the object by presenting it in a new *context.* Thus, he may present the proposal to maintain the secrecy of the atom bomb in the context of military preparedness and *war* or in the context of *peace* by arguing that through a monopoly of the know-how it will be impossible for other nations to use it and therefore they will be afraid to start a war and therefore peace will be preserved.

Finally, as a last resort, the propagandist can literally coerce the subject's action and supplement this physical coercion with propaganda in the knowledge that where there is a need to put up with or come to terms with an object, there is also a tendency to seek to discover favorable aspects about the object. Thus, if an individual is forced into the Army, and if this is accompanied by suitable propaganda, the draftee, by virtue of his new group identifications, may become more susceptible to the propaganda and will discover values in Army life that, without such enforced contact, he might have missed. The good propagandist, then, continues to propagandize even where he must use more direct methods of social control. In other words, a perceptual change in an object may be induced through accentuating certain aspects of the original perception and minimizing others, by presenting the object in a different context, or by forcibly modifying the environment of the individual who is perceiving the object. *The propagandist can "push people around" and sometimes make them like it.*

5. *A suggestion that can be phrased so as to be congruent with the need of people to identify with or be in harmony with other people will be more readily*

accepted than one that does not draw upon such social support. The good propagandist will seek to have his suggestions come from prestige figures, or he will seek to give the impression that "most people" agree with his suggestion or that the "best" people do so. He will use the "band-wagon" technique with respect to issues of general social import, the "expert" technique with respect to issues of a technical nature, the "personality" technique with respect to issues of emotional import. He will vary his prestige technique not only in terms of the issues involved but also in terms of the characteristics of his target group. If necessary, he may first direct his efforts to establish identification between the public and the individual who will later be used for prestige suggestion, or he will first attempt to establish that individual as an acceptable authority. *This is sometimes referred to as public relations.*

6. *A suggestion that makes effective use of the principles of stimulus presentation will be more readily accepted than one that neglects these considerations.* The good propagandist will exploit all the values that can inhere in the external structure of the material. He will use words with the proper invariant feeling tones where that is possible and where it does not violate the acceptable speech patterns of his target group. He will pick speakers and writers whose voice, appearance, dress, word usage, intonation, pronunciation, etc., are most acceptable to the target group. He will seek to make his final suggestions brief, simple, "level," "sharp," and attention getting. He will use repetition as a device not only to bring his suggestions into the perceptual field of the members of his target group but also to "freeze" the cognitive structure of the individuals who have already accepted his suggestion. *Propagandizing those who already believe has its values.*

7. *Propaganda can be fought most effectively with counterpropaganda.* The good propagandist will not spend a great deal of his energy in exposing the techniques of the propagandist of whom he disapproves but will, instead, offer effective countersuggestions. The effectiveness of his countersuggestions will depend upon the observance of all the foregoing principles, but especially the first principle, which involves meeting the existing needs of people. *The best kind of counterpropaganda, therefore, is a social and economic system that satisfies most of the needs of most of the people most of the time.*

SUMMARY

Man's appreciation of the function of speech in the creation and transmission of culture is equaled only by his awe at the power of language to mislead him. There is the popular feeling that in propaganda man has a unique force. The purpose of this chapter is to examine persuasion through propaganda to determine whether propaganda effects involve special kinds of psychological processes or are describable in terms of the basic propositions of cognitive reorganization already covered in previous chapters. This special treatment of propaganda is merited because, it is pointed out, propaganda plays so important a role in modern life that it is essential to have a sound understanding of the processes involved and of the limitations of propaganda.

Since language is the chief medium of propaganda, some of the characteristics of language are examined first. Attention is given to the patterned nature of language. Two types of patterns are distinguished: *individual patterns* and *cultural patterns*. Experimental evidence is examined which indicates that listeners judge personality traits of speakers in terms of their individual speech patterns. Both patterns influence the effectiveness of speech in persuasion, and the generalization is suggested that the efficiency of speech in influencing beliefs and attitudes is somewhat dependent upon the comparability of speech patterns employed by the speaker and that usually accepted by the listener.

An examination is then made of what determines the meanings of words. Several types of words are differentiated: (1) words with relatively invariant meanings because of their *physical* characteristics, (2) words with relatively invariant meanings for a people of a given *culture*, and (3) words whose meanings depend upon the *immediate psychological field of the listener*. On the basis of a theoretical analysis and the experimental data cited, it is suggested that words can be understood as *genuine objects in the person's environment*. The similarities and differences between words and other environmental objects are outlined, and it is concluded that through changing an individual's environment by the manipulation of words, one can accomplish the same kind of changes in his beliefs and attitudes as by changing his environment through the manipulation of other objects. This suggests that we should expect to find that the same principles which apply to cognitive reorganization in general apply to cognitive reorganization brought about by language. At this point the experimental studies dealing specifically with propaganda are examined to see if the data substantiate such a conclusion.

A preliminary consideration of some data indicates that there is no basic difference between the processes involved in education and propaganda or between unconscious and conscious propaganda. The reasons for the assumption that basic differences do exist are traced to the historical treatments of "suggestion" and "suggestibility." Two alternative descriptions of suggestion are outlined, and the data are then examined. A review of the data indicates that the concept of a unique personality trait describable as suggestibility is unsupported by experimental evidence. These data, by denying suggestibility as an acceptable explanation of suggestion and pointing, instead, to the conditions of the psychological field of the person as the locus for explanatory principles, lead next to an examination of such conditions.

The phenomenon of prestige suggestion is first examined, and it is concluded, on the basis of experimental data, that rather than treating suggestion by prestige as though it results in grafting on an otherwise unchanged object a new value, prestige suggestion operates in one of two ways: (1) By changing the person's environment (through words) the person's *perception* of the object undergoes a change. Consequently, his beliefs and attitudes about the object may change. (2) The prestige source may be such as to call forth a need for agreement on the part of the recipient of the suggestion. Consequently, the recipient will first change his judgment and then seek to rationalize the object perceived so that it is congruent with his changed judgment. The net result in both sequences is a change in the perceptual qualities of the original object. Both of these sequences, then, are seen as congruent with the generalized description of the conditions of cognitive reorganization described in Part I of this book.

An examination of the data pertaining to forms of suggestion other than prestige leads to the same conclusions. In addition, these data point to the importance of the relationship between the ambiguity of the original perception or belief and the effectiveness of the suggestion. This observation is then related to the discussion of the role of "crises" in the "normal" process of belief and attitude change. Finally, the data concerning the effectiveness of suggestion as a function of the needs and major belief systems of the individual are examined, and it is concluded that the efficacy of propaganda and suggestion is dependent not only upon the same perceptual principles but also upon the same tension factors that are involved in all forms of belief and attitude change.

In completing the analysis of propaganda and suggestion, the special techniques used by propagandists are examined, and several typical studies are abstracted. It is concluded that these special tricks of the trade help determine the effectiveness of propaganda. But it is emphasized that these are also important in other forms of persuasion—"reasoned persuasion" or "education."

The next section is devoted to propaganda prophylaxis, and some of the data are examined in an attempt to formulate an efficient program of propaganda immunization. While the available experimental data are not unambiguous in their implications, it is suggested that sound propaganda prophylaxis would involve, in addition to exposing current techniques of propaganda and education in rules of evidence, (1) aggressive counterpropaganda and (2) meeting the needs and demands of people. Of all these steps, the last is emphasized as the most significant.

At this point the answer to the general question raised at the beginning of the chapter is formulated as follows: The experimental data indicate that suggestion and propaganda operate in accordance with the same principles as have been discussed for all cognitive reorganization. Man's reaction to propaganda is on the same level of rationality as is his reaction to other forms of persuasion or environmental change. The emphasis upon the perceptions, beliefs, and needs of man in understanding propaganda effects permits us to assess the efficacy and limitations of propaganda realistically.

However, the term propaganda has some practical value in labeling and isolating certain instances of persuasion. It is suggested that to summarize the discussion of propaganda in terms of guides for the propagandist might therefore be helpful. The following seven guides are then listed, discussed briefly, and illustrated by specific propagandistic techniques and incidents: (1) A suggestion that seems to meet an existing need will be more readily accepted than one that does not meet a need; (2) a suggestion concerning an ambiguous situation will be more readily accepted than one concerning a clearly structured situation; (3) a suggestion that fits in with other systems of beliefs and frames of reference will be more readily accepted than one that does not; (4) a suggestion that can readily induce new attributes in the perception of a familiar object will be more readily accepted than one that does not have that advantage; (5) a suggestion that can be phrased so as to be congruent with the need of people to identify with or be in harmony with other people will be more readily accepted than one that does not draw upon such social support; (6) a suggestion that makes effective use of the principles of stimulus presentation will be more readily accepted than one that neglects these considerations; (7) propaganda can be fought most effectively with counterpropaganda. In considering this last guide, it is pointed out that in the last analysis, the best kind of counterpropaganda is a social and economic system which satisfies most of the needs of most of the people most of the time.

BIBLIOGRAPHY

ALLPORT, G. W., and CANTRIL, H.: 1934. Judging personality from voice. *J. soc. Psychol.*, **5**, 37–55.

ALLPORT, G. W., and VERNON, P. E.: 1933. *Studies in expressive movement.* New York: Macmillan.

ANNIS, A. D.: 1939. Relative effectiveness of cartoons and editorials as propaganda media. *Psychol. Bull.*, **36**, 638.

ASCH, S. E., BLOCK, H., and HERTZMAN, M.: 1938. Studies in the principles of judgments and attitudes: I. Two basic principles of judgment. *J. Psychol.*, **5**, 219–251.

ASCH, S. E., BLOCK, H., and HERTZMAN, M.: 1940. Studies in the principles of judgments and attitudes: II. Determination of judgments by group and by ego standards. *J. soc. Psychol.*, 12, 433–465.

ASHER, R., and SARGENT, S. S.: 1941. Shifts in attitudes caused by cartoon caricatures. *J. gen. Psychol.*, 24, 451–455.

BELLAK, L.: 1942. The nature of slogans. *J. abnorm. soc. Psychol.*, 37, 496–510.

BIDDLE, W. W.: 1931. A psychological definition of propaganda. *J. abnorm. soc. Psychol.*, 26, 283–295.

BIDDLE, W. W.: 1932. Propaganda and education. *Teach. Coll. Contr. Educ.*, No. 531.

BOAS, F., EFRON, D., and FOLEY, J. P.: 1936. A comparative investigation of gestural behavior patterns in "racial" groups living under different as well as similar environmental conditions. *Psychol. Bull.*, 33, 760.

BRIDGES, J. W.: 1914. An experimental study of decision types and their mental correlates. *Psychol. Monogr.*, 17, No. 1.

CANTRIL, H., and ALLPORT, G. W.: 1935. *The psychology of radio.* New York: Harper.

COFFIN, T. E.: 1941. Some conditions of suggestion and suggestibility. *Psychol. Monogr.* 53, No. 4.

COLLIER, R. M.: 1944. The effect of propaganda upon attitude following a critical examination of the propaganda itself. *J. soc. Psychol.*, 20, 3–17.

CUSHING, H. M., and RUCH, G. M.: 1927. An investigation of character traits in delinquent girls. *J. appl. Psychol.*, 11, 1–7.

DUNCKER, K.: 1938. Experimental modification of children's food preferences through social suggestion. *J. abnorm. soc. Psychol.*, 33, 489–507.

ESTABROOKS, G. H.: 1929. Experimental studies in suggestion. *J. genet. Psychol.*, 36, 120–139.

FREEMAN, E.: 1936. *Social psychology.* New York: Holt.

HARTMANN, G. W.: 1936a. A field experiment on the comparative effectiveness of "emotional" and "rational" political leaflets in determining election results. *J. abnorm. soc. Psychol.*, 31, 99–114.

HARTMANN, G. W.: 1936b. The contradiction between feeling-tone of political party names and public response to their platforms. *J. soc. Psychol.*, 7, 336–355.

HULL, C. L.: 1933. *Hypnosis and suggestibility.* New York: Appleton-Century.

KANTOR, J. R.: 1936. *An objective psychology of grammar.* Bloomington: Indiana Univ. Press.

KNOWER, F. H.: 1935. Experimental studies of changes in attitudes. *J. soc. Psychol.*, 6, 315–347.

KNOWER, F. H.: 1936. Experimental studies of changes in attitudes. *J. abnorm. soc. Psychol.*, 30, 522–532.

KROUT, M. H.: 1942. *Introduction to social psychology.* New York: Harper.

LASSWELL, H. D.: 1935. In *Encyclopedia of the social sciences.* New York: Macmillan.

LEWIS, H. B.: 1941. Studies in the principles of judgments and attitudes: IV. The operation of "prestige suggestion." *J. soc. Psychol.*, 14, 229–256.

LINDBERG, B. J.: 1940. Suggestibility in different personality types. *Amer. J. Psychol.*, 53, 99–108.

LUCHINS, A. S.: 1945. Social influence on perception of complex drawings. *J. soc. Psychol.*, 21, 257–273.

LUNDHOLM, H.: 1938. Mark Antony's speech and the psychology of the persuasion. *Character & Pers.*, 6, 293–305.

McGEHEE, F.: 1944. An experimental study of voice recognition. *J. gen. Psychol.*, **31,** 53–65.

MEYERS, G. C.: 1921. Control of conduct by suggestion. An experiment in Americanization. *J. appl. Psychol.*, **5,** 26–31.

ORR, J.: 1944. On some sound values in English. *Brit. J. Psychol.*, **35,** 1–8.

ORR, J.: 1945. Note on Professor Thorndike's paper. *Brit. J. Psychol.*, **36,** 14.

OTIS, M.: 1924. A study of suggestibility of children. *Arch. Psychol.*, No. 70.

PEAR, T. H.: 1931. *Voice and personality.* London: Chapman & Hall.

REYMERT, M. L., and KOHN, H. A.: 1940. An objective investigation of suggestibility. *Character & Pers.*, **9,** 44–48.

SARGENT S. S.: 1939. Emotional stereotypes in *The Chicago Tribune. Sociometry,* **2.** 69-75.

SARGENT, S. S.: 1942. *In* Watson, G. (ed.) *Civilian morale.* Boston: Houghton.

SHERIF, M.: 1937. The psychology of slogans. *J. abnorm. soc. Psychol.*, **32,** 450–461.

SMITH, G. H.: 1947. Beliefs in statements labelled fact and rumor. *J. abnorm. soc. Psychol.*, **42,** 80–90.

TAYLOR, H. C.: 1934. Social agreement in personality traits as judged from speech. *J. soc. Psychol.*, **5,** 244–248.

THORNDIKE, E. L.: 1946. The psychology of semantics. *Amer. J. Psychol.*, **59,** 613–632.

TOLMAN, E. C.: 1932. *Purposive behavior in animals and men.* New York: Century.

TRAVIS, L. E.: 1922. Studies in dissociation. *J. exp. Psychol.*, **5,** 338–346.

WOLFF, W.: 1943. *The expression of personality.* New York: Harper.

ZILBOORG, G.: 1938. Propaganda from within. *Ann. Amer. Acad. Pol. Soc. Sci.*, July 1938.

ZUCKER, L.: 1946. Psychological aspects of speech-melody. *J. soc. Psychol.*, **23,** 73–128

CHAPTER X

THE STRUCTURE AND FUNCTION OF SOCIAL GROUPS

Every society consists of interrelated social groups. These groups within any given society may be ephemeral and come into being and pass out of existence within a matter of minutes, or they may last over thousands of years. They may be very simple and involve in their functioning no more than the loosely coordinated behavior of several individuals, or they may be extremely complicated and operate through the highly specialized and formalized action patterns of thousands of people under a monolithic leadership. But no matter how short-lived or enduring, how simple or complicated, such social groups influence the needs, beliefs, attitudes, and actions of the people involved, and the structure and function of such groups are in turn determined by the dynamic interactions of their constituent members. When social groups become elaborated, enduring, and inclusive of many people, their importance in understanding and predicting the behavior of the individual becomes absolute. They determine the structure of his society, the nature of his goals, and the range of his behavior possibilities.

Society as Arbuthnot knows it today can be described as an *interrelated system of social groups*—ranging from the informal friendship groups to the most formal political, economic, educational, and religious groups within whose grooves Arbuthnot moves and by whose enforcement agents he is pushed around. But all of these groups are not static, unchanging "institutions." To understand Arbuthnot's behavior we must not only examine the structure and function of his groups in a descriptive manner but also seek to understand the tensions and relationships and forces within these groups. We must, in other words, seek to examine the dynamics of group structure and functioning. These are the purposes of this and the following chapter.

DEFINITIONS AND GENERAL CONSIDERATIONS

We have seen in Chap. I (page 20) that there is nothing in social psychology that is not logically explicable at the level of the psychology of the individual. The study of groups as a whole can reveal nothing new beyond what is given by a synthesis of all the data pertaining to each of the group members. There is nothing superordinate to the individual, no "group mind."

But we have also seen in Chap. I that although it is theoretically possible to learn all we need to by an understanding at the individual level, it is in practice difficult or impossible to proceed in this way. Consider a group, such as a committee, made up of nine people. Assuming that we know all the pertinent characteristics of each of these nine people and that we know all the principles governing individual behavior, we should, theoretically, be able to predict just what the behavior of this group would be under given circumstances. But by proceeding on the level of the individual we would be faced with an impossibly complex synthesis, requiring the solution of not one but nine equations simultaneously. Even for the simplest group action, the necessary prediction (based upon a synthesis of predictions of the behavior of each single individual) would be more complex than that of determining the new orbits of the nine planets of the solar system if a new planet of given dimensions were suddenly to appear in it.

The complexity is caused by the fact that the members of a committee or any psychological group are in dynamic relationship[1] with one another, just as through the operation of gravitational forces the planets are in dynamic relationship with one another. The behavior of each one affects all the others, these effects rebound on the original member who in turn influences all the others anew, and this complex of effects is taking place simultaneously among all members. To trace these many effects through the behavior of each of the separate members may be practically impossible, even if theoretically possible in the "divine mind" or in the most elaborate of electronic computers.

Fortunately, we do not have to work at the individual level. If our interest is in the *end result* rather than with the details of how this result comes about, we may dispense with an analysis of what happens to each of the constituent members. We may state that, under given conditions, this group structure will lead lawfully to that group structure, though the behavior and role of any specific individual in the group may be indeterminate. Thus, for example, if we throw a number of chickens together in a coop, we may with considerable assurance predict that a fairly stable pattern of dominance behavior will sooner or later emerge—there will develop an orderly arrangement of which chicken pecks which.[2] There

---

[1] See Chap. I, p. 19, for a discussion of dynamics.

[2] For an account of experimental study of dominance behavior in chickens and other animals in "social group" situations, see Murchison (1936), Winslow (1938), and Nowlis (1941).

will undoubtedly be a great deal of mutually adjustive behavior in the chicken coop before this stable pattern emerges; but if we are not interested in the details of how the pattern develops or in the fate of any particular chicken in the lot, we may deal with the group as a whole without predictions of the behavior of the individuals.

Very frequently in social psychology our interest is with the action of a group as a whole, and not with its specific members. We may wish to be able to predict, for instance, that under such and such conditions a leader will appear (not caring about the particular identity of the leader) or that under specified rules and regulations a group will develop good or poor morale or that in the face of given circumstances a group will tend to split into antagonistic subgroups or will tend to develop a more homogeneous ideology, etc.

All these behaviors of a group depend upon the individually lawful behaviors of the constituent members. But the group behavior need not be stated in individual terms. As we have said in Chap. I, "A scientifically mature approach to group dynamics must seek out new concepts, new properties, new variables with which to characterize the group as a whole."

Psychological Groups and Social Organizations.—A psychological group has been defined as "two or more people who bear an explicit psychological relationship to one another" (page 18). As was indicated at the time, a group is different from a *class* of people or an aggregate of people who may be seen as grouped simply because the individuals are in close spatial proximity. It should also be clear that a group is not the same as a "perceived group," which may exist for an individual. A person may think of himself and "see" himself as connected with other persons; yet for them he may not exist psychologically, and hence we cannot speak of these people as a group. On the positive side, it was pointed out that the criteria for establishing whether or not a given set of individuals constitutes a psychological group are mainly two: (1) All the members must exist as a group in the psychological field of each individual, *i.e.*, be perceived and reacted to as a group; (2) the various members must be in dynamic interaction with one another.

May groups, as here defined, be of any size whatsoever, of any duration, and of any degree of informality? May we, for instance, think of the hundreds of people who work together in a factory as one group or, more extremely, of the 135 million people of the United States as one group? A collection of people at a dinner party may form a group for the duration of the evening. Is such a group of the same order as the Catholic Church, which has existed for hundreds of years? Is the informal grouping of a collection of teen-age "best friends" to be differentiated from such a formal grouping as a military unit? For reasons that will become clear in the following discussion, it is helpful to differentiate social groups on the bases of size, duration, and informality. In general, the definition we have already given for a psychological group refers to collections of people that meet the two criteria listed above and that are relatively small, of relatively short duration, and relatively informal. The other kind of social groupings we will refer to as "social organizations."

Social organization defined.—The term *social organization*, as it will be used in this chapter, has much in common with the term *social institution* as used by many social scientists. A consideration of the reasons for preferring the former term to the latter will help place the concept of "social organization" in its proper psychological and sociological context and will facilitate its definition.

In the first place, the term *social institution* is an inconvenient one to use because it suffers greatly from a lack of precision in definition. Hobhouse (1924), for example, has pointed out that, "The term is so variously used that it is doubtful if it has a single root meaning common to all of its applications," and Hertzler (1929), in his attempt to draw up a composite definition based on the common usages of most sociologists, ends with a statement that contains approximately 27 different clauses or subsidiary concepts. The use of such a term, then, might result in more confusion than clarity in our attempt to differentiate among the different kinds of groupings.

In the second place, in so far as there is any core of common agreement in its usage by sociologists, the term refers to a more abstract kind of concept than the one that we will find most useful. Some of the common definitions of the term suggest that it is used to refer to a sort of disembodied set of stable relationships among people but does not include the specific people involved or the specific instrumentalities used by these people. It is not a "substantive concept," in Allport's (1927) phrasing. Thus, for example, the family is a social institution, but any specific family is not considered a social institution. In contrast to this general concept, *social organization* is a specific one. The term *social organization* refers to specific groupings of actual people, which are characterized by the possession of the following: (1) cultural products (such as buildings, robes, prayers, magic formulas, songs); (2) a collective name or symbol; (3) distinctive action patterns; (4) a common belief system; and (5) enforcing agents or techniques.

Relationships among different social groupings.—It is just as important to isolate the above defining characteristics of a social organization as it is to be clear about the definition of a psychological group. Each of these social groupings has its own unique effects upon the behavior of the individual, and each has its own special generalizations. Thus we can make certain generalizations about a friendship group which do not apply to such a social organization as United States Steel; and similarly, we can generalize about the behavior of an organized church in a way that is different from our generalizations about a group of religious people praying together.

Although we can distinguish between psychological groups and social organizations, these two have much in common. In the first place, the very same social group can, at certain times and under certain conditions, simultaneously qualify as either. The Arbuthnot family is not only a psychological group but also a social organization—it may own such cultural products as stoves and family Bibles, it has a collective name, it may have unique eating patterns and a commonly shared belief about the sanctity of father's decisions, and the elder Arbuthnot acts as an enforcing agent as far as the other members of the family are concerned. In the second place, and this is of the greatest significance for our discussion in this chapter, many of the most basic generalizations about psychological groups apply to social organizations. This is merely a reflection of the fact that both kinds of groups are special instances of social groups. It is because of this that many features of the social organization can be experimentally studied by the device of creating, under controlled conditions, smaller groups and studying the structure and function of these smaller groups. Throughout this chapter, then, the word "group," unless otherwise indicated, will refer to both a psychological group and a social organization.

GROUP STRUCTURE

An examination of the dynamics of groups must start with an examination of the basic structural characteristics of groups. In connection with the structure of groups we must take up such matters as the size of the group, individual "roles" within the group, subgrouping, methods of describing structure, and relationships among groups.

Size of Groups.—The smallest group is made up of two people—a husband and wife, an employer and his worker, two people conversing. With a membership of three—the first step in increased size—the group already increases its potential complexity significantly. In the pair, there is but a *single* interrelationship possible, which we can symbolize by (a)-(b). With a group of three individuals, there are no less than *six* potential relationships. There are the three simple ones: (a)-(b), (a)-(c), and (b)-(c). In addition, there are the relationships among the subgroupings:

$(a)-(b, c)$, $(b)-(a, c)$, and $(c)-(a, b)$. These latter are extremely important for the study of group behavior, since some of the most interesting problems arise in connection with the subgroupings of parts of the whole group and their relation to other members of other subgroups. With a group of four people, to carry the process of increase only one step further, the possibility of interrelationship becomes enormously complicated, and the number increases to 25 as follows:

$(a)-(b)$	$(a)-(b, c)$	$(c)-(a, b)$	$(a)-(b, c, d)$	$(a, b)-(c, d)$
$(a)-(c)$	$(a)-(c, d)$	$(c)-(b, d)$	$(b)-(a, c, d)$	$(a, d)-(b, c)$
$(a)-(d)$	$(a)-(b, d)$	$(c)-(a, d)$	$(c)-(a, b, d)$	$(a, c)-(b, d)$
$(b)-(c)$	$(b)-(a, c)$	$(d)-(a, b)$	$(d)-(a, b, c)$	
$(b)-(d)$	$(b)-(a, d)$	$(d)-(a, c)$		
$(c)-(d)$	$(b)-(c, d)$	$(d)-(b, c)$		

Whether or not all the potential relationships within a group play a significant role in the analysis of the group's behavior will depend upon the nature of the group, its "morale," the kind of leadership characteristic of the group, etc. In a family of three, for example, all six potential relationships are important: mother to father, mother to child, father to child, mother and father to child, mother and child to father, and father and child to mother. In other groups, as in the case of the millions of people in the Catholic Church or the Communist party or the workers in the United States Steel Corporation, only certain of the potential relationships will have any importance; the others will not have the opportunity to emerge, crystallize, and influence the action of the group. Under some conditions the existence of certain of the potential relationships preclude or inhibit the appearance of others. But the main point of relevance here is that groups do differ in size, and the larger the group the more potentially complex can its structure be. Furthermore, this relationship is not a simple one, but potential complexity increases much more rapidly than size.

The determination of size of groups.—Because there is a limit to the number of persons that the individual can perceive and react to as group members, there is a limit to the size of a psychological group. This limitation does not apply with equal force to a social organization. This difference suggests that some of the principles of group dynamics will apply only to psychological groups and not to social organizations. The analysis of how small face-to-face groups reach a decision, for example, cannot be applied to the problem of how a nation decides to go to war.

The actual size of many groups is determined by the operation of arbitrary external factors. Thus the size of a family may be determined by the number of births and deaths; the size of a committee, by the number appointed by the chairman; the size of an industrial plant, by the productivity rate of the workers and the effective demand for its products. But there are also internal group determinants of optimal size. For certain functions groups must be small; for others, large. Certain "atmospheres" determine the optimal size of groups. If a committee is too large, some members "run the show" and the others may drop out; if a party is large, it almost inevitably breaks up into subgroups or even into separate groups, completely independent of one another. A poker game that is too small is likely to attract others until it becomes optimally large. Several studies are available that have demonstrated a constant relationship between the size of the group and certain external and internal factors. Thus Chevaleva-Janovskaja (1927) has demonstrated a relationship between the "natural" group size and the age of its members.

The importance of group size—an illustration from the family group.— The significance of group size for intragroup relationships is clearly demonstrated in the changing nature of the family group structure as a consequence of the marked decline in the size of American families. Gruenberg (1947) points out several of these changes in her discussion of the changing conceptions of the family. Among these she points to the relative isolation in which the child of a small city family grows up, the lack of own-age groups for the growing child and its consequences on the child's opportunity for acquiring certain social skills, etc. But perhaps the most significant, for our present interest, are the effects on the interpersonal relationships that develop within the group:

> In small families the parents are called upon to do for their children . . . what in the old-fashioned family the other children of various ages and other adults did casually and incidentally. Parents have to double as friends and playmates while remaining fathers and mothers . . . . To parents of one or very few children, the individual child is naturally more precious . . . [they] not only shower the child with all the "advantages" and services they can afford, but they focus upon him also all their anxieties. It is very difficult to let the child be himself and to mature into freedom from parental domination . . . . Having so few, they have no margin for error as had parents of larger broods . . . . The pressure upon the child to make good is then the source of severe strains . . . .

Individual Roles within Groups.—When a man takes a new job or joins a fraternity or enters a military unit, his relations to his superiors, inferiors, and associates are, to a very considerable extent, predetermined for him. How an individual behaves toward other members of the group depends partly upon the personality of the individual and partly upon the nature of the group structure and his role within that structure. Similarly, how the individual is perceived and reacted to by the others is also partly dependent upon his role.

Who fills a certain role in a group may be entirely arbitrary and may bear no relation to the personality or abilities or interests of the individual. The more rigidly established and more formal the group the more likely is it that group interaction is guided along predetermined lines and the perception of and reaction to other group members is related to the defined role rather than to the individual per se. In informal groups, on the other hand, the very absence of predetermined interpersonal relations means that the group structure depends more upon the individual characteristics of the members. In other words, in *social organizations*, there is a marked tendency to channel interpersonal relations along routinized lines; in *psychological groups*, the dynamic interactions among people have much more significance in determining the role of the individual.

But the distinction is not absolute. Even in quite rigid social organizations there is considerable latitude for individual differences within a given role. Different people placed in the same formal role may behave quite differently, as the individual differences found among second lieutenants testify. For another thing, the group as defined formally may not represent the group as it functions in reality. Thus the formal leader may be only a figurehead, the servant may rule the master, the real intercommunication within the group may not travel via official channels. And even in quite informal psychological groups there is not complete spontaneity in the way the group forms and the individuals function. In the first place, the roles of members of many psychological groups are to some degree predetermined. Thus, in a given culture when a man and a woman marry and have a child, the pattern of interpersonal relations among the family members will tend to assume the form typical of that culture. In the second place, people coming together for the first time as a psychological group bring with them beliefs and attitudes concerning interpersonal relations that they have developed out of past group experience, and these beliefs, attitudes, and interpersonal skills will shape their behavior in the new group to a considerable extent.

Limitations on group determination of individual's roles.—The fact that a person's behavior in the group is not determined *entirely* by the structure and nature of the group—whether psychological group or social organization—has significant practical implications and testifies to the dangers that may inhere in completely disregarding individual considerations when dealing with groups. This is attested to by the disappointing experiences of many people in administrative, supervisory, and leadership functions who have attempted to improve individual morale by making changes in the *group situation* that, theoretically, should be conducive to improvement. Often they have discovered that the individual fails to respond properly to the changed situation. What they have overlooked is that the individual is not completely flexible, nor is he newborn with every new group. He may have habits of group living that may make it difficult for him to adjust to new group interpersonal relations. The "democratic" leader may thus find it difficult to function in a group that is so structured as to demand "autocratic" leadership; the German who has never been encouraged to behave democratically vis-a-vis officialdom will find it difficult suddenly to "make like a democrat" when the American Military Government creates a democratic setup.

This fact that the over-all past group experiences of the individual affect his current group relationships is a reflection of the proposition discussed in Chap. IV that the major cognitive organization will determine the nature of the specific methods of solution attempted by the individual in various situations (see especially the discussion on pages 123 *ff*.). It is in consideration of this that many have emphasized the view that in dealing with large-scale problems of intergroup behavior, where the groups come from different cultures, it is necessary to go back to the individual's experiences in primary (or original) group living, as in his family, in order to discover the basis of his present group role.[1] As one observer has commented, "The basic patterns of interaction are laid down in primary groups and are carried over into secondary. For instance, the reactions of the child to parental authority furnish an important basis of the later adult attitudes of obedience to law and leadership in public life." And Peak (1945), on the basis of data collected in postwar Germany by the United States Strategic Bombing Survey, concludes, "Persons reared in the authoritative family, which is common in Germany, typically find greatest security and satisfaction where they are dominated by superior authority on the one hand, and where they can, on the other, 'lord it over' someone else of lower status."

Group Relations.—The most obvious fact about most groups is that they are made up of subgroups. Groups are not usually homogeneous within but are characteristically divided into parts that are relatively homogeneous and tend to differ from the other parts. Thus, the leaders

---

[1] When some United States social psychologists canvassed psychologists from other countries on what they thought were the important problems for research on the psychology of internationalism (Bruner, 1947), Dr. Costa Pinto of the University of Brazil urged that studies of different philosophies of child rearing throughout the world be carefully investigated as a prerequisite to such study.

and followers are differentiated, and the members of a work group have different responsibilities. Often the subgrouping is not on the basis of such formal functional grounds, but on other more subtle ones. In a group discussion some people are dominant and others submissive; some coalesce into a subgroup that upholds one opinion as opposed to other subgroups that champion different opinions. The criteria for determining the existence of subgroupings are the same as those for determining the major groupings. Thus we would expect that members of a subgroup will perceive the other members of the subgroup as somewhat separated from the remaining group members, and we would expect that the amount of interaction *across* subgroup boundaries would tend to be less than *within* the subgroup.

Relationships among subgroups.—Similarly, there are both *horizontal* and *vertical* relationships among subgroups. That is, some subgroups are on an equal level, having equivalent power and status; others are in a hierarchical relationship, some being superior to others, having more power and status. And both vertically and horizontally, the different subgroups vary in the closeness or remoteness of relationship to one another. In a military unit, for example, there may be a vertical differentiation into commissioned officers, noncommissioned officers, and men. The relationship between the first and third is remote, being mediated by the second. And there may also be horizontal differentiation among the men into MP's, cooks and bakers, headquarters staff, field personnel, etc. Some of these will be (and feel) more closely related than others. Thus, the MP's, for obvious reasons, may be "psychologically distant" from most of the other subgroups.

Smaller subgroups.—We cannot, of course, stop with a classification of social organizations, groups, and their subgroups. To be complete, the "map" of group structure must incorporate all groupings from the largest to the very smallest. The final step is the subgrouping into units of two. Just as in all larger groupings, the groupings of two individuals may be based on many different kinds of interpersonal relations. These include such things as feelings of friendship, love, admiration, respect, identification, loyalty, cooperation as well as dislike, hatred, sadism, masochism, dominance, submission, rivalry, and just sheer indifference. It is only when we have a complete description of all the interrelationships and subgroupings within a social organization or a psychological group that we have what is essential to a complete understanding of the structure and functioning of a group.

Sociometric Method.—To determine and portray the exceedingly complex network of interrelationships that exist within even the very simple groups requires some systematic method. To this end, Moreno (1934) has developed what he calls "sociometric" methods. As originally used by Moreno the objective of these methods is to establish the pattern of feelings of acceptance and rejection, like and dislike (or "tele," as Moreno calls it) that exist among the members of a group. It is Moreno's thesis that the most significant social groupings are those based on such feelings rather than those based on formal structures. The understanding of group life, he argues, can best be accomplished through a study of these "spontaneous" groupings and the way in which they harmonize or conflict with the formal group structure that is imposed externally.

As used by Moreno, the sociometric method involves simply asking each member of a group to specify (privately) which other members he likes or wishes to work or eat or live beside and which ones he dislikes or wishes to avoid. Such data obtained from all group members make it possible to construct a *sociogram*, which pictures for the whole group all the patterns of mutual like, dislike, and indifference. This makes it easy for the investigator to see at a glance what the "tele" structure of a group actually is—the cliques, the people who are much liked and disliked and by whom, the social "isolates," etc.

Sociometric methods have been extended to include other ways of discerning the interpersonal relationships of people, beyond what is revealed in their reported feelings about others. Another approach is to observe the *frequency of contact* (or the total amount of time of contact) between pairs of individuals. Where such contacts are largely voluntary, it is assumed that their frequency may provide a good measure of grouping. Loomis (1941), for example, has made an elaborate sociometric study of a New Mexican village. He ascertained the frequency of visiting, eating meals together, and lending farm equipment among the families and on the basis of such data was able to construct a sociogram of the village which revealed the essential social groups in it.

That sociometric patterns do in fact tend to coincide with patterns of dynamic interaction within the group has been demonstrated in several ways in Moreno's (1934) elaborate sociometric mapping of a reformatory for girls at Hudson, N. Y. Fourteen girls who ran away within a two-week period were found in terms of their sociometric positions to constitute a network. Cases of single runaways who were not psychologically related to other girls did not cause a similar epidemic of runaways. Rumor was also observed to travel more rapidly within networks. A girl was caught stealing, and the spread of rumor about her misconduct through the community of girls was observed at intervals of 24 hours, one week, and six weeks. After 24 hours it was found that the only girls who had heard the rumor were members of the culprit's sociometric network; after one week *all* the girls in her network knew of it, and it had filtered into parts of two other networks; after six weeks no further spread was noted.   The significant fact about these dynamic interactions was that they did not follow along the lines of the formal structure of the community, such as by cottages in which the girls lived or by racial (white-colored) lines, but tended rather to follow sociometric lines.

Moreno stresses the importance of this distinction between what he calls the "social organization" and the "psychological organization."

The colored population is housed in cottages separate from the white.   But in educational and social activities white and colored mix freely.   These and similar aspects can be termed the "social organization" of the community. And whatever the "social structure" of a particular cottage may be it is necessary to ascertain the psychological function of each of its members and the "psychological organization" of the cottage group.   The social function of a girl, for instance, may be that of supervising the dormitory, but her psychological function may be that of a housemother pet who is rejected by the members of her group and isolated in it.   These emotional reactions and responses among the girls of the group must result in a dynamic situation, its "psychological organization."

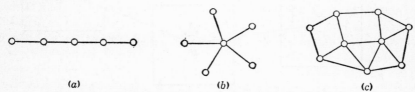

(a)   (b)   (c)

FIG. 9.—Types of sociometric relationships: (a) chain (b) star, (c) network.

Typical sociometric patterns.—The extensive sociometric investigations of Moreno and many others have uncovered a large variety of sociometric patterns which are likely to turn up repeatedly.   We shall note a few of the more interesting ones here.

Isolates are members who are not liked or accepted by other members or who have little or no contact with them.   *Pairs* are groups of two who are mutually attracted, *triangles* are groups of threes, etc.   Larger groupings may form *chains* (Fig. 9a) or *stars* (Fig. 9b) or interlocking *networks* (Fig. 9c).

Each of these patterns will be significant in determining how the group as a whole behaves under various conditions.   Isolates may tend to break away from the group under pressure.   Networks, which have many interlocking connections, are likely to be stronger and more resistant to change. Star patterns make for a centralization of the subgroup around one person; without him the subgroup may collapse.

Another interesting pattern has to do with "power." It can be ascertained which individual or individuals in the group occupy positions where they can be particularly influential. Figure 10a shows the sociogram of a

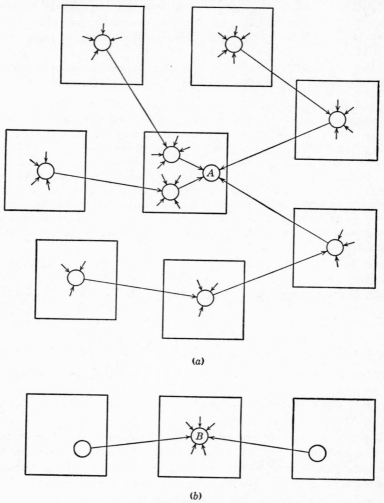

(a)

(b)

Fig. 10.—Sociometric diagrams revealing a "powerful" and a "popular" person. (a) A is directly chosen by four individuals who in turn are chosen by many others both inside and outside their groups; thus A is in a highly influential position; (b) B is more popular, being directly chosen by seven individuals, but is less influential, since those who choose B are not themselves popular. (*Adapted from Moreno*, 1934.)

"powerful" individual as contrasted to a merely "popular" person in Fig. 10b.

Relationships among Social Organizations.—There are a number of compelling reasons why we must give special attention to the interrelationships among social organizations. These reasons are of three different orders, or levels, of analysis. In terms of the most general of these levels, any survey of social organizations must be made from the vantage point of the particular society in which it is functioning. Each society, as was indicated in Chap. II, has a character and "flavor" of its own. The American religious, economic, educational, political, and family organizations will differ from the corresponding Japanese or German or French social organizations because each of these national groups of organizations will reflect their peculiar over-all cultural pattern. Sometimes this cultural pattern can determine even such matters as the specific membership of social organizations or social groups. Thus, for example, the common belief that every individual in our country has the legal right to choose his own marriage partner is literally wrong. Every state in the union has some prohibition against marriage. These prohibitions are most commonly based on the wealth of the intended marriage partners, mental or physical health, blood relationships, and race.[1] In some states paupers, drug addicts, and criminals are denied the right to marry; in 14 Northern states and in all the Southern states Negroes are prohibited from marrying whites.

From a slightly more specific level, the interrelationships among social organizations are seen as deriving from their hierarchical relationships, communality of organizational goals, or mutual dependencies. Thus, the United States Army is a social organization which is subsidiary to another social organization—the United States government. As an illustration of the second type of interrelationship, the First Church of Christ, Scientist, of Chicago can be related to the Upper Bronx Orthodox Synagogue because both are religious social organizations and the general goals and policies of the former may be influenced by the latter—as, for example, in presenting a "united front" for or against Federal legislation dealing with religious training in the schools. Finally, a social organization can be related to another because of certain kinds of dependencies. Thus, for example, because it takes money to operate almost any social organization, most social organizations in our society stand in a dependent relationship to *economic* organizations. The continued existence of churches, universities, labor unions, or government is almost directly dependent upon the solvency of insurance companies, banks, investment houses, mines, and steel corporations. It is because of this that so many social organizations

---

[1] For a critical discussion of current marriage and divorce laws in the light of the changing society in which we live, see Daggett (1947).

concern themselves with economic organizations. They may seek to avoid conflict with them and abide by their demands, or they may, on the other hand, seek to change and control these economic organizations, but it is almost impossible for any social organization to neglect and be uninterested in economic organizations. As a consequence the current beliefs and rituals of economic organizations are reflected in the beliefs and activity patterns of other social organizations within our society—sometimes to the point where conflicts within the social organization may arise. For example, the university or hospital may adopt such economic beliefs as "balanced budgets," such economic rituals as "clock punching," and such leadership patterns as are presumably necessary for "efficient business management." These beliefs and practices may seem, to some members of the organization, as subverting the original functions of the organization and eventuate in interorganizational irritations and conflicts. This is especially true in government organizations. The tendency on the part of some government leaders and officials to run the government as if it were a "business" frequently runs counter to the needs and demands of many of the general members (citizens) of the government.

From the point of view of the individual level of analysis, the fact of multiple membership necessitates our giving due attention to interrelationships among social organizations. The religious organizations, for example, are composed of people who are also members of economic, political, and other social organizations. Although not all man's belief systems are highly integrated, neither are they, as we have seen, completely "watertight." There seems always to be a tendency toward integration. The "interlocking" membership which is characteristic of various social organizations, will therefore reflect itself in the attempts of one social organization to become integrated with or congruent with the functions, belief systems, and action patterns of other social organizations. The changing belief systems of the Protestant church with the rise of Capitalism provides a good illustration of this kind of interaction.

A FUNCTIONAL ANALYSIS OF GROUPS

The membership of an individual in a particular group may come about through external circumstances that compel or enforce his membership. Thus, a child is, through biological accident, a member of a given family group; a soldier becomes a member of a military unit by being drafted; a man may be forced to join a labor union. Or the individual may freely choose his membership in a group. He selects friends, joins a preferred club, decides to become a Republican. Whether membership is externally imposed or freely chosen will undoubtedly have considerable influence on the nature of his relations to the group. A person's attitude toward a group will be different if he is free to leave it when he wishes than if he is not free to do so. However, the significant fact is that the nature of the membership of any group determines the function of the group. In analyzing the functional nature of a group we must keep the two standard cautions in mind: (1) The apparent or avowed needs of group members are not always the real needs, and, therefore, the apparent or avowed functions of groups are not always the real functions, and (2) the needs served by any group may differ from the needs served by the same group in times past.

The Function of Groups and the Needs of Its Members.—As was indicated previously (page 32, Chap. II), we cannot admit as psychologically valid any "survival" theory with respect to groups—informal or formal, psychological groups or social organizations. For most groups it can be safely generalized that group membership serves a function for the individual. Through it he satisfies needs and demands. It may serve to provide food and shelter and sexual satisfaction. It may be the avenue for achievement of social goals which require cooperative effort. It may be protective against external threats. It may serve gregarious needs and desires for recognition and prestige. The needs and demands that a given group serves for some of its members may differ from those of other members. In order to understand a group and predict its behavior under various conditions, it is necessary to have a picture of the needs and demands that this group serves for all of its different members. However, in addition to the basic generalization that groups serve to meet needs and demands of its members, we can specify the functional nature of groups with the following characterizations: (1) Most groups serve to meet the current needs of its *dominant* members more adequately than of its less dominant (or rank-and-file) members; (2) most groups can be seen as having "unique" and "accessory" functions; (3) most groups, in addition to other functions, serve to meet the dominance and "belongingness" needs; and (4) most groups induce new needs among their members.

Differential satisfaction of needs.—We have seen that some group members are members involuntarily. This is especially true of many social organizations—nations, prisons, armies, etc. We also know that some social organizations (*e.g.*, industrial plants) do not respond equally to the needs of all its members because of the very nature of the belief systems that control the operation of those organizations. Finally, in most groups (and again particularly in large social organizations) there is a vast and complicated hierarchy of membership—some members have more influence in making group decisions than others. It is therefore more accurate to say that the function of any group can be better understood in terms of the major needs of its more dominant members than in undifferentiated terms for all of its members. The distribution of dominant and non-dominant members varies for different groups, but the above generalization holds for all groups. Thus, in a purely democratic group we should expect to find the group reflecting the major needs of its dominant members in one way, in a purely autocratic group in another way, but in neither case should we find all the needs of all the members equally reflected in the group function.

"Unique" and "accessory" functions of groups.—Almost every group comes into being as a special social device to meet certain specified needs of its members. This is most clearly seen in social organizations, and it is for this reason that we can categorize groups and social organizations in terms of their major, or "unique," functions. Thus we can speak of friendship groups, religious organizations, family groups, political organizations, etc. However, such a functional analysis can be misleading. Frequently, groups accrue to themselves "accessory" functions as they continue to exist over time. These additional, or accessory, functions may sometimes be unrelated to the unique function of the group and may even completely overshadow the unique function to the point where it disappears entirely.

Douglass's (1926) analysis of the changing functions of the Protestant Church in the United States presents a very good illustration of this group phenomenon. He found that in 357 Protestant churches which he examined there existed 33 different kinds of nonreligious "church activities." Among these were general social events, boy scout activities, orchestras and bands, girls clubs, dramatic clubs, gymnasium classes, sewing classes, domestic science classes, employment offices, visiting nurse associations, day nurseries, dispensaries and clinics, civics and economics classes, etc. These activities represent a change in the very nature of the functions of these religious organizations. Religious organizations have always concerned themselves with nonreligious functions—with medicine, farming, warfare, education, etc.—but always in a religious sense. That is, since the supernatural entity was all-powerful, the healing art could not be conducted except in accordance with religious practices; the fields could not be sown or harvested except in accordance with religious ceremonies; wars could not be conducted except with the blessings of the priest and the presence of the Cross. But the picture that Douglass presents is that of a religious organization concerning itself with *nonreligious functions in a nonreligious manner.* In our society we may very well see the accessory functions of some churches grow in such proportions as to illustrate the development of a social organization whose accessory functions overshadow its unique functions.

One of the reasons for this process of accretion of function lies in the fact that as the needs and demands of its members change, the functions of the group show corresponding change. Another reason is found in the interrelationships that exist among groups. Thus, the functions of the local Communist party will reflect not only the needs of its dominant members but also the changing needs of the top policy members of the Cominform. The organizational needs of one group, in other words, can determine the accessory needs of another. Still a third reason for the growth in number and kinds of functions served by a group derives from the fact that groups, by virtue of their very existence, can induce new needs among their members—a significant characteristic of groups which we shall discuss presently. But whatever the reason, it is important to remember that in any functional analysis of groups, it is just as necessary to examine the accessory functions as the unique functions of the group, and the ability to discriminate between the two functions can sometimes lead us to understand apparent inconsistencies in the belief systems and action patterns of groups.

"Dominance" and "belongingness" needs.—Perhaps the most generally valid statement that can be made about the nature of the accessory functions of groups is that all groups serve to meet the dominance needs of some of their members and the belongingness needs of most of their members We have already seen that every group, even where there is no formal recognition of leadership, provides for different roles for its various members and permits different individuals to display their different capacities. In so far as this is true, every group will provide for the gratification of power and dominance needs for some of its members. While power and dominance needs characterize many people, the need to belong to some activity or group larger than one's self, to be "accepted," to be a part of something significant characterizes most people in society. This driving need is frequently found behind the "joining" activities of many people. By joining a union the individual worker seeks to satisfy not only his economic needs but also his need to "belong." The church member, the member of a college fraternity, of a scientific association, of the Knights of Pythias, of the American Veterans Committee—all may find gratification of this need in these groups. These common needs, even though accessory to the major functions of the group, are served by all groups and are in part responsible for the belief systems, rituals, and ceremonies that are common to all social organizations, whatever their histories and whatever the nature of their unique functions.

Creations of new needs.—We know that man's needs are not static but grow and develop as the psychological field of the individual changes. The membership in any significant group must necessarily reflect itself in various changes in the individual's psychological field and, therefore, in his need structure.   The new needs that are created by groups are many and varied.   They are conditioned by whether it is a psychological group or a social organization, by its permanency or its temporary nature, by the unique function it serves for the individual, etc.   Thus, in social organizations, the specific cultural products of the organization; its developing ideologies, ceremonials, and rituals; its powers; and the resistances and antipathies it arouses among nonmembers all are significant.   The effects are frequently of an interactional nature.   The unique functions, for example, determine the nature of the tangible property the organization will acquire, and the acquisition of the tangible property will, in turn, induce new accessory needs.

Perhaps among the most socially important accessory needs that a group can induce are those needs which its members acquire with respect to the continued existence of the group.   This is especially true for the dominant members and is in part responsible for what Hertzler (1929) has called the "grewsome immortality" of social groupings.   As we have pointed out in Chap. II (page 70), the normal process of socialization of the individual is one of self-involvement in groups and the continued existence and growth of the group becomes identified with the continued existence and welfare of the individual member.   Consequently these members seek to ensure the continued existence of their groups, and in many instances this need becomes an autonomously functioning one without any reference to the services that the group can perform.   Frequently the existence of such a driving need on the part of its members results in a *conscious effort to increase the functions of the group* and to add to it accessory functions. This may be done either as an attempt to expand the powers of the group or as a defensive tactic in recognition of the fact that the unique needs which the group has served are no longer important ones for most of its members. The guiding hypothesis here is that the more needs of its members a group can serve the longer will it continue to exist and the stronger will it be.

Group Functions and Membership Loyalty.—Even though every group may serve a number of different functions for the individual, no one group can satisfy all of his needs and demands.   This means that the same individual is perforce a member of many different groups.   His pattern of group memberships will not be identical with other people's. Sometimes he finds himself grouped together with one set of people, such as his coreligionists; at other times he finds himself grouped with other people, such as his fellow members of a political organization and in opposition to his coreligionists. In that sense we can say that the membership of any specific group consists of "part personalities." The single member's loyalties to his various groups and to their members will be divided and often conflicting.

It is because of this that the degree to which the members of a group are also members of other groups is particularly significant in determining group structure and functioning. We have already indicated that the greater the number of functions served by a single group for its membership the more stable and strong will that group be. That is one reason why family groups are among the strongest and most stable in our society. Cultures differ in the degree to which they foster single groupings that serve over-all functions, and this is sometimes responsible for conflict among various groupings and social organizations. The Church, for example, may seek to function as an educational organization, a religious organization, a cultural organization, and even a political organization. This is frequently resented in a culture like that of present-day America, where there is a great diversification of overlapping group memberships and a great degree of specialization of groups.

Pressures toward diversification and unification.—The pressures toward diversification of group membership arise out of at least three sources: (1) the very multiplicity of the constantly developing needs and demands of the individual, (2) the trend toward specialization of function which makes given groups apply to specific objectives, (3) the failure of any given group to satisfy the changing needs of the individual—especially in a rapidly changing world.

Countering these influences toward diversification, there is a strong tendency toward unification of group function. We have already discussed one of the reasons—the deliberate attempt of the dominant members of any group to increase the functions of any one group and thus make unnecessary multiple-group membership. Another reason arises from an attempt of the individual to escape from conflicts involved in competing group memberships and the enormous emotional pulls toward making a single group the focus of loyalty and identification. The closely knit group of teen-age girls who strive "to do everything together" is an example of this reaction.

The special case of the dominant member.—The dominant member, or leader, of a group does not show so varied a multiple membership as does the general member. For the former, the "entire personality" may be wrapped up with the single group. Thus the church leader, priest, minister, or rabbi finds in the religious group an agency for expressing his entire personality, and the religious group becomes the object of all his strivings and aspirations. Unlike the general member the leader does not find it necessary, for example, to belong to another group for physical maintenance—the church provides. He does not have to seek out still another group to satisfy his needs for power—the church offers that too. The leader, therefore, is not under any pressure to accept nongroup ideologies which are demanded by other groups. His belief systems are therefore more easily integrated, his loyalties and identifications more specific and simple, his conflicts less bothersome.

In this connection it is of some interest to note that the "personality differences" which are sometimes discovered between leaders and followers in any group may not be primary in the sense that because of these personality differences one becomes a leader and the other a follower, but these personality differences may be a consequence of the differential membership characteristics of the two.

General Comments.—We have seen that the needs and demands which a given group serves for some of its members may differ from those of other members. For one person the group may provide vicarious satisfactions through identification with the successes of the group; for another person the group may be mainly a vehicle for satisfaction of his need to be a leader. But despite this diversification of function both within and among groups, there are several generalizations with respect to function that apply to all groups. However, one of the implications of the fact that any one group can serve a variety of needs and demands in each member is that the *structure* of the same group may vary according to the *particular function* that it plays in a given situation. Thus, even though the group may consist of precisely the same members, the pattern of interrelations among the members and the status role of any single individual in the group may vary depending upon the function being performed by that group. A family group when facing a serious decision may be structured differently from when it is playing or when it is eating dinner. This general consideration emphasizes the significance of paying attention to the *functional* meaning of a group when discussing any other group characteristic—the *role* of members, the *structure* of groups, or the *dynamic* relationships.

GROUPS AND BELIEF SYSTEMS

The interrelationship among needs, beliefs, and action is intimate and complicated. The double role of beliefs—in shaping action designed to satisfy needs and in creating new tensions which must be released—becomes particularly important in an analysis of group behavior of people. This is true for all groups but is especially true for social organizations, since, as we have indicated, one of the defining characteristics of a social organization is the possession by its membership of a common belief system. We have seen that the individual needs which induce people to affiliate themselves with various groups may vary but the existence of a common belief system tends to eliminate otherwise expected behavior differences by inducing a common method of expressing these different needs and by creating common needs among the members.

Group Beliefs and Group Functions.—To argue, as some do, that the official ideology of a formal group is merely a network of rationalizations and myths to justify the existence of the group or organization is to misunderstand the multitude of roles that beliefs play in human behavior. Group beliefs as *effects* of the needs of the members and as *causes* of needs require serious consideration in studying the structure and function of groups. It is true that a group belief system may be more clearly related to the needs of the dominant members of the group than to the needs of the other members and that some of these beliefs may be properly described as "rationalizations," but probably in no case can group beliefs, or "official ideology," be dismissed as of little consequence for the understanding of group behavior.

Patterning of group beliefs.—There are several reasons why a well-structured and relatively long-lasting group has a core of beliefs held in common by its various members with their various need structures. In the first place, most members of groups do have needs in common, and these will predispose, to a certain extent, a communality in beliefs. In the second place, we must remember that many groups are joined by people as a result of a free choice among a field of similar groups. Thus, there is nothing that compels most members of political groups to join a Republican club, a Democratic club, or a Communist club. People may join any one of these groups for the same purposes, to achieve power, to express dominance, to sell insurance—but the reasons any specific club is picked are frequently because the belief systems of the chosen club are more nearly congruent with the beliefs of the individual. Thus there is a *selective* factor which is operative to ensure a common set of beliefs among diverse members of a group. In the third place, as was indicated in Chap. VI, many of our beliefs are necessarily based upon facts and information given to us by "authorities." It is necessary to point out in this connection only that almost all groups have within them certain members who function as authorities or "experts"—especially the leader.[1] The expert role of the leader is frequently one of the attractions of a group and one of the reasons why some groups are joined by individuals. In so far as the members of

[1] See Chap. XI for a further discussion of the role of the leader as an "expert."

a group *receive their facts from the same expert*, or authority, the different members will tend to acquire common beliefs. Finally, in so far as the members of any group are constantly stimulated with a common and specifically limited range of opinions and judgments (through the group-controlled, group-approved, group-censored propaganda and educational media), we must expect a common standard of judgments and values to occur. This is a consequence of the processes described in Chap. III, which determine the individual's judgment as a function of the range of the stimulus objects to be judged. Thus, as Tresselt and Volkmann (1942) have pointed out,

> Each person in a group says what he does not only because he has been persuaded by argument, induced by reward, compelled by pressure, guided by his own past beliefs, or influenced by the voiced opinions of other people: he says it also because he faces a restricted range of social or non-social stimulation, and this range has determined his scale of judgment.

In other words, *even without direct indoctrination* concerning any specific issue, the various members of a group will tend to make the same judgment about any issue that is of interest to the group.

As a consequence of the four factors listed above—and others—most members of groups will have individual belief systems and make individual judgments which will overlap greatly with those of their fellow members.

Group beliefs and resistance to change.—There are several reasons why group beliefs are more resistant to change than beliefs that are not shared by members of the same group. One of these reasons derives from our first principle of cognitive organization (page 84), which indicates that man will organize and integrate discrete perceptions and facts. When it is realized that the very essence of a group belief is its *integrating nature* (that is why one speaks of "ideologies," for example, when referring to the official beliefs of a social organization), we can see why people will hold on to group belief systems despite a world that presents them with "new" and frequently contradictory facts. Second, primarily as a consequence of intermembership communication difficulties which are characteristic of large groups, there occur certain processes which result in the maintenance of group beliefs *despite profound and universally felt changes in the social environment*. We have already referred to the importance of social support in the maintenance of beliefs and attitudes of people (see especially page 192). There it was pointed out that because "proper" beliefs and attitudes can smooth the way to group acceptance, the degree to which a given belief is held by the other members of a group will influence the strength of the belief within any one person's mental structures.

When an individual's needs and psychological field are undergoing change, we can expect a tendency on his part to change his beliefs—and among them his group beliefs. But if this individual is under the impression that he alone, among all of his fellows, is in the position of questioning the group belief, if he feels that he will not receive social support for any new and "heretical" beliefs and that he may even lose group membership, then a reorganization of his beliefs will be inhibited. Furthermore, the fact that he feels that all the rest of his fellow group members find the original belief valid will, in itself, give positive support to the old beliefs that he already holds. The impression that all of one's fellow members do not question the old group beliefs may not correspond to the facts, but in groups with large membership the individual members are rarely in direct communication with each other, and the communication that does take place is frequently through rigid channels. Therefore a condition of "pluralistic ignorance" may obtain (see Katz and Schanck, 1938); *i.e., no one believes, but everyone believes that everyone else believes.*

Finally, there is the factor of coercion. Many psychological groups and all social organizations are characterized by the possession of enforcing agents or enforcing techniques. Some social organizations extend their coercive activities to the *beliefs* of their members; and as we have seen in Chap. IX (especially pages 341, 359), force and coercion applied to the individual may frequently result in effective control of percepts and beliefs.

An illustrative example.—The large corporation presents a striking picture of a social organization whose official ideologies have not yet caught up with the major changes that have occurred in its structure, method of operation, and the general social milieu in which it exists. It can therefore serve as a profitable illustration of many of the foregoing characteristics of group beliefs or organizational ideologies. Brady (1945) has described the discrepancy between the belief systems of the corporation and the real world in the following way:

Lacking any rationally verifiable principles, or any popularly acceptable arguments for identifying monopoly-oriented practices with the popular well-being, business . . . [is] ever more persistently driven towards the development of an ambivalent propaganda that attempts to at once justify the tenets upon which the private enterprise system rests *per se* and to represent monopoly practices as consistent with these tenets . . . . It seeks to prove that business is based on the "free enterprise" principle, when in fact it is increasingly organized on a monopoly footing. It favors *laissez faire* while talking on behalf of *carte blanche.* It says "free competition" when it means cartel types of price-fixation. It eulogizes "private property" when privately held productive property is rapidly disappearing down the throats of the corporate giants. It glorifies the system of "free contract" as contracts become increasingly lopsided, with the large and organized dictating the terms to the small and unorganized . . . .

The preceding discussion of the nature of group beliefs can help us to understand this peculiar nature of the belief systems of our large corporations and monopolies. For one thing, it must be remembered that the official ideology of "private enterprise and competition" has had a valuable integrating function for many business people over a period of many years. It is a well-developed, satisfying belief system, which gives desirable status and meaning to many different kinds of discrete business activities. In terms of that belief system the activities of the advertising "huckster," the salesman, the producer, and the speculator are all seen as parts of a patterned whole which functions to ensure both "progress" and "stability." It is an ideology that integrates the strivings for personal wealth and power, with the culturally accepted ideals of democracy, freedom, and service to one's fellow men. No matter how many facts can be brought to the attention of the business man that such a belief system is no longer in accordance with actual practice, he will tend to interpret these facts as "exceptional cases" and will find it difficult to reorganize his thinking completely. Many members of corporations and businesses believe in their group ideology quite honestly. Business groups, and especially big business, have yet to develop an integrated belief system that can be substituted for the old one. A new economic ideology may be needed, and the probability is that it will be developed and adopted; but until such a new belief system is achieved by the economic groups themselves, the group members will hold on to the old one.

While all of the above is true, we must also remember that "a group belief system may be more clearly related to the needs of the dominant members of the group than to the needs of the other members, and that some of these beliefs may be properly described as 'rationalizations' . . ." (page 387). For a realistic understanding of the official ideologies of our corporations and monopolies we must realize that many corporation and monopoly leaders do not believe in competition, private enterprise, and the other beliefs of Adam Smith, despite their violent and insistent assertions that they do.

We have examined in so much detail the reasons for the patterned nature of group beliefs and the resistance of these beliefs to change because of the profound social importance of these characteristics of group beliefs. To understand the role of social groups in social change, we must give proper weight to the static nature of group beliefs, to the forces that inhibit cognitive reorganization among the members of groups and that eventually tend to result in the nonadaptive behavior (sociologically or technologically viewed) of groups.

The "institutional fiction."—The members of almost any well-structured group frequently regard their group as transcending the immediate members of the group or the real property of the social organization or even the space-time coordinates in which the group seems to exist. A university, our commencement speakers never tire of telling us, is "something more" than its students and faculty and buildings and laboratories and books and anything else one can see, hear, smell, taste, or feel; a nation is "more than" its inhabitants and rocks and rills. There are a number of perceptual and motivational reasons for this common characteristic of the beliefs of group members about their own group.

In the first place, the very process of perception predisposes the individual to regard his group as existing in a superordinate manner. When a person perceives several people acting together or praying together or working together or fighting together, the resulting perception will be organized and certain properties of these groups of people will be perceived that are different from the perceived properties of the individuals comprising the group. That is, as far as perception is concerned, and as far as the individual's own psychological field is concerned, a group of people is something other than the sum of the individuals comprising the group. But to argue from this that because the group is *perceived* as superindividual, it therefore exists "out there" as superordinate is to confuse perceptual reality with objective reality.

Not only do we perceive this superordinate reality because we see many individuals in proximity or having significant traits in common or behaving in coordination, but also the very material property possessed by many social organizations (buildings, stoves, uniforms, weapons, prayer books) serves as environmental supports that predispose us toward perceiving the group as a transcending reality. Thus, as Katz and Schanck (1938) point out,

Great buildings and extensive grounds are the visible symbols of a great institution. The fiction of the institution as a super-personal reality is aided by the magnificent structures which single individuals and sometimes a single generation of individuals could not have produced. Men come and go, but the continuity of the institution is preserved in its most obvious form in the buildings which endure for centuries . . . . Judicial robes, priestly garments, and military uniforms serve to set apart their wearers as something more than individual human beings.[1]

[1] Every veteran of the American Army will remember how he was admonished, during his basic training, that in saluting an officer he was not saluting an *individual* but the *uniform*. And the uniform, he was told, represented something more than any individual —living or dead—it represented the traditions and spirit and glory of America.

In addition to the above factors there are the motivational factors which reinforce these beliefs. We have seen that members of a group tend to identify themselves with the group. If identification is to serve its functions, that with which the person identifies himself must be greater than the person himself—it must have virtues beyond any virtues of his own or his obviously imperfect fellow members. Only where a belief exists in the reality of a superlative group, in other words, can that group become a wholly satisfying object of a person's identification. Because of this many members of groups, in their beliefs about the group, consider their own group as the best of all similar groups and believe that their group is righteous in its aims and must, in the long run, achieve those aims and conquer all other competing groups.

Not only do the individual members of groups have needs in common and beliefs in common, but they also display common *action patterns*. In the next section, then, we must concern ourselves with this attribute of groups.

GROUPS AND COMMON ACTION PATTERNS

Not all patterned action is determined by an individual's group membership. We must distinguish between patterned action that can properly be called group determined and that which is more general in origin. The first of these is that patterned behavior which is *peculiar to members of a given group;* the latter (usually referred to as "fads," "mores," "folkways," "fashions") is that which is displayed by most members of a given culture. Thus, instances of group-determined patterned behavior would be the ritual of Mass in the Catholic Church, the secret handclasp of a college fraternity, the cadenced step of soldiers on the march, the formula used by presidents of universities in granting honorary degrees, the parliamentary procedure corresponding to the special bylaws of an organization. The culturally determined pattern refers to such acts as hat tipping when meeting a lady, handshaking, driving on the right side of the road, the wearing of trousers by men, and skirts by women.

As we have already seen, most groups induce two kinds of patterns among its members; there are those patterns which all members show in common, and there are those patterns which differentiate one member from another, one role from another. Thus the leader has a different activity pattern from the follower, the foreman from the worker, the head of the family from the child.

Action Patterns and Functional Significance.—Many social scientists, in discussing group-determined action patterns, distinguish between "technological" patterns and "ritualistic" or "ceremonial" patterns. This distinction is presented clearly in an illustration that Benedict (1935) gives in her discussion of "ritual":

Ritual according to the accepted usage of the term does not include acts of routine provision of physical necessities. Traditional ways of building a house or of grinding and leaching acorns may be elaborating and exacting, but they are technological and not ritualistic. Ritual is always extra-necessitous from the technological point of view: it has reference, for example, to the act of killing slaves to bury under the house posts or to fertility ceremonies that employ the symbolism of eating or of impregnation to further the growth of fields.

It must be strongly emphasized, however, that this distinction is of doubtful psychological validity. To an anthropologist who has his own technological beliefs as to what does and what does not determine a firm foundation for a house, killing and burying a slave underneath the house post may seem extra-necessitous; but to the person who carries out these rituals and who has different technological beliefs, such action may be just as utilitarian and just as technologically required as any other of his construction activities. What was said in Chap. V (see pages 170) concerning the relationship between superstitions and other forms of *belief* holds with equal validity for rituals and other forms of patterned *actions*. *Rituals, ceremonies, or any kind of standardized action patterns that are group determined must be seen as organically related to the goals of the group.*

Patterning of actions.—While all group-determined action patterns can be seen as functional, we must understand why such actions show the high degree of communality and patterning that they do among different members of the same group. Perhaps the major reason lies in the fact that patterning is frequently demanded by the very nature of the group's goal objects. Typically, many of the primary goals sought by the members of the same group require the coordinated action of many people. Thus the work patterns in a modern industrial plant must display a minimum of individual differences if production is to proceed "efficiently." The actions of the individual soldier must likewise be standardized if the army is to achieve any military objective.

Another compelling force toward standardization of action derives from the fact that groups are frequently the repository of all the expert skills and knowledge for achieving certain goals. Groups also provide for communicating any new skill developed by one member to many other members. Any single group member, therefore, by availing himself of a *common fund of knowledge* will end with a way of doing things that is similar to the way others do the same things. Furthermore, the different members of groups have access to the same material possessions of the group (tools, equipment, etc.), and these common tools impose a certain uniformity in the action of the person using them.

In addition, the knowledge that he is going through a specialized and elaborate routine in common with the other members of "his" group can go a long way toward satisfying the individual's need for feeling that he is an integral part of something larger than himself. The participation in the same ritual in common with his fellows serves as not-to-be-denied evidence to the participant and others that he does belong and that he is accepted. The youngster who gets his first job in the factory not only performs his particular work task in a patterned way but also gets great satisfaction in adopting the same dress, carrying the same kind of dinner pail, and walking along with the same stride as his fellow employees.

Group-determined differentiating patterns.—We have seen that different individuals play different roles in any group. These roles are reflected not only in the "social status" of the individual but also in his patterned action. This is especially true for larger and more formal groups. As a group becomes larger, the degree of specialization in function and in "appropriate" action patterns is increased. Rules and regulations concerning intermembership communications and relationships become at the same time more and more standardized and more and more differentiated. The greater the degree of such differentiation the greater the vested interests that the different individuals acquire in their special action patterns. What seems to happen is that within each group of such special activity patterns, subsidiary social organizations come into being—within each of which the same forces operate to "freeze" beliefs and action patterns that operate for all groups. The leaders of these "suborganizations," or "bureaus," establish their own hierarchies of membership, tend to center their needs and aspirations within their particular "department," seek to increase the power of their own bureau, etc. These are usually referred to as problems of bureaucracy, and these problems, it should be noted, are not restricted to any single type of group or social organization. They are found in business, education, religion, and government.[1]

GROUP DYNAMICS

Having reviewed some of the principal aspects of group structure, group functions, group beliefs, and group action, we must now turn our attention more directly to group dynamics—to the changes that take place within groups.[2] We must examine, in terms of many of the characteristics of groups

[1] For a discussion of some aspects of the psychology of bureaucracy, see the special issue of the *J. Soc. Issues*, **1**, No. 4, 1945.

[2] The outstanding name in the study of group dynamics is that of Kurt Lewin who provided this new field of inquiry with many of its basic theoretical principles and many of its major methods of research. For a discussion of this field, its theoretical orientation, its objectives, and its techniques, see Lewin's (1945) paper describing the founding of the Research Center for Group Dynamics.

that we have already discussed, what kinds of groups tend to change, under what conditions they change, and what the direction of change is likely to be.

Stable and Unstable Groups.—Some groups are more *stable* than others; *i.e.*, their structure tends to remain unchanged over a period of time. Other groups, on the contrary, undergo progressive changes *even in the absence of significant variations in the external situation.* Groups are especially apt to be unstable during the process of formation or of reformation as the aftermath of some significant change in the external environment. Instability arises out of conflict among individuals and among subgroups within the whole group, *i.e.*, out of a lack of balance among all the internal forces of the group. Several different subgroups may be seeking to increase their power at the expense of the others; the leader of the group may be trying to broaden his authority, and other members may be trying to displace him; the functional roles of the various group members may not be harmoniously established; the attitudes and beliefs of the various members as to group objectives and means of accomplishing these objectives may be in conflict.

The resolution of intragroup tensions.—As a consequence of the lack of balance among the internal forces in the group, changes in group structure occur. In general, these changes seem to tend in the direction of a reduction of the tensions, a balancing of the forces, and hence a more stable group structure. It is as though there were something of the nature of a self-distribution of forces within the group toward an equilibrium state. It is noteworthy that this generalization about resolution of *group tension* closely resembles the treatment of resolution of *individual tension* in Chap. II. But this does not mean that we assume principles of group dynamics to be necessarily identical with principles of dynamics of the individual psychological field. It is often provocative to try to transpose the latter principles to the analysis of groups, for instance, in connection with the variety of avenues through which tension may be reduced. But whether or not individual and group dynamics may ultimately be expressible in one set of principles is a question for future study.[1]

The kinds of changes in group structure that work toward increased stability are many. *Subgroupings* may change, and new ones appear, and there may be mutual interaction and adjustment among them until they come into a more balanced relationship of power, function, and responsibility. To bring and maintain various subgroups in a balanced state is, we shall presently see, one of the critical functions of the leader. *Dissident elements*—individuals or subgroups—may be forced out of the group altogether, thus achieving more harmony within the group. The *leadership*

[1] For a discussion of constancy and self-regulation in group behavior, see Lewin (1944).

structure may undergo drastic change, with the old leaders deposed and new leaders established. Important *ideological shifts* may occur so that the group achieves stability by redefining its objectives, its beliefs, and its plans.

There may also be temporary expedients in tension reduction. One is *scapegoating*, in which the internal group tensions become manifested (and, apparently, temporarily alleviated) through aggressions centered on certain individuals or subgroups within the group. Another is *external aggression*, in which group tensions become expressed in attacks upon individuals and groups outside the group.

The most extreme consequence of intragroup tensions is complete *dissolution of the group*. Thus, a divorce or the abandonment of a club or the demise of a political action committee may be seen as a dissolution of a group.

Cohesive and disruptive forces.—Complete dissolution such as that above means that the cohesive forces tending to hold the group together are over-balanced by the disruptive forces tending to pull the group apart. The degree of strength or stability of a group can be viewed in terms of the relative strength of the cohesive and disruptive forces. We have already discussed some of the sources of disruption and cohesion, but it may be of value to review them briefly here.

Groups are held together because of common objectives of the members and common beliefs that the objectives can be reached through the group. The objectives may be either positive or negative. Groups are also held together by emotional bonds—the identification of the individual with the group and its members. And groups are held together in general because of the main different needs and demands they serve for the individual. We shall see the importance of these matters in connection with group morale.

Groups sometimes dissolve not because the disruptive forces are so great but because the cohesive forces are so slight. Thus, groups often break up because they have no genuine objectives or functions or because they are not believed in by their members as ways of achieving objectives or because they command little emotional identification.

External Determinants of Group Change.—We have discussed above the kinds of changes in group structure that occur as a result of internal imbalances and tensions. Once such tensions have been resolved and a stable group structure achieved, the structure can be expected to exist unchanged until "external" influences are brought to bear on it. Under external influences are included those arising out of the environment of the group, those arising in connection with the change in membership of the group, or the changes that take place within the original members of the group.

The rigidity of groups.—Groups differ in the degree to which they respond to such external influences. Some groups have very rigid structures, which resist changes. Others are more flexible. If a group structure is overly rigid, it is likely to be rendered less adaptable to the exigencies of external change; tensions arising within the group may fail of resolution; the level of tension may rise continuously until the "brittle" group disintegrates. Slavson (1943), in discussing children's groups, comments on the need for flexibility in group structure:

In a wholesome group, equilibrium is reestablished whenever there is conflict or imbalance. This occurs when other children *neutralize* the emotional drives of the contestants, reinforce the weaker against the stronger, or exert pressure upon the disturbing individual, when a compromise is struck, or when a common interest proves stronger than the cause of the cleavage.

Organized and unorganized groups.—The degree of organization of a group will also help to determine its reaction to external influences. Thus, in a study by French (1944), organized groups were compared with unorganized under conditions of fear and frustration. The organized groups in this experiment were boys' clubs and athletic teams; the unorganized groups were previously unacquainted sets of college students who were brought together as a group for the first time during the experiment. The different groups were observed by French when they were working as a unit on extremely difficult problems and when exposed to what they believed to be a "dangerous" situation (a simulated fire in the locked experimental room). The organized groups as compared with the unorganized demonstrated "definitely *more* social freedom, we-feeling, interdependence, equality of participation in the group activity, motivation, frustration, and aggression against other members of the group." Thus, we see that an organized group not only can be more strongly motivated in the cooperative effort but can, as a consequence, also be more frustrated and aggressive. And in the fear situation, the organized groups tended to behave more homogeneously, with reactions of either panic or skepticism. A group leader or other dominant member could show the way for the group as a whole, while in the unorganized groups there was less chance that the individuals were affected by what the others did.

Group changes caused by situational changes.—As the situation in which a group exists undergoes changes, there are likely to be significant changes in the group structure. The appearance of threats or attack against the group arising from outside the group has often been observed to induce important changes in group structure.   Under the external dangers, group unity often seems to be increased and inner differences to diminish.   Subtly employed, however, external forces can be divisive if they seek to split some subgroups from others, to breed mutual suspicion and distrust, to cause one faction to blame others, etc.   This is particularly important in the analysis of group morale during a national catastrophy or during international conflict.[1]

The group may be required to serve a different function, and we have already seen that the group structure relating to one function may differ from that relating to another function.   The normal structure of a family group may change drastically when in an emergency.   After the emergency is passed, the structure may shift back to its original state or may continue in its new form.   Some dramatic illustrations of this are found in the study by Koos (1946) of the group dynamics among families living in one block of a New York tenement district.   Thus, in discussing the dominance of the father under situational change, Koos writes:

If, *in the opinion of the family*, the father failed to meet the demands of a trouble situation, a loss of dominance followed in every instance, regardless of the adequacy of the family.   This is best illustrated in the Eduardo family, where the Italian-born father prevented the early hospitalization of the daughter, and in so doing, lost his dominance.   The changes in dominance are shown in the following diagram:[2]

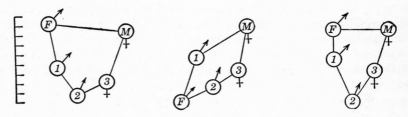

Koos quotes the older son as describing this change in dominance in the following words:

[1] For a further discussion of this, see Chap. XV.

[2] The biological symbols ♂ and ♀ represent the sexes, the father and mother are designated with the letters (*F*) and (*M*), and the siblings as (1), (2), and (3) in the order of birth. Koos indicates the relative dominance of each member by the individual's relation to the positional scale at the left of the diagram.   Thus, in the above figure, the first group structure indicates that the father was dominant, the mother next, the oldest son next, the daughter next, and the youngest son last.

"The old man is always boss in our place. That's o.k., he's got a right to be the boss. But, Christ, he wasn't the boss after he belted that one around. When he raised hell, and wouldn't let Agnes go to the hospital (and she sure was sick) everybody forgot he was the old man. None of us paid any attention to what he said . . . . Yea, he's boss again, but not the way he was before. If you didn't forget so easy, he'd never been boss again. If she'd a died, we'd have run him out of the house. Hell, he wasn't worth two cents in our family for a while."

Group changes caused by membership changes.—Although it may be argued that a group is defined by the particular people who constitute it and that any change in group personnel necessarily means that a different group exists, it is still practicable to discuss groups as persisting in much the same way, even when old members leave and new ones enter. A military unit may retain the same general structure and may even seem completely unchanged to its members when one of its officers is replaced. There seems to be, in fact, a remarkable amount of substitutability of personnel in a group without producing appreciable changes in its structure. This is particularly true of social organizations where many of the interpersonal relationships have become stereotyped and the dominance relationships are determined by the official role of the individual rather than by his own characteristics.

But there is a limit to the replaceability of personnel. Sometimes the loss of a member or the entrance of a new one produces considerable readjustment in the group. This can again be illustrated from Koos's study. Among the causes of changes in family structure Koos lists deaths in families, addition of relatives to families, etc. Thus:

In the Walther family, the death of the breadwinner placed the responsibility for family support upon the eighteen year-old son, who left school and took a shipping clerk's job in order to support his mother and two sisters. Because of his new position in the family as breadwinner, the son felt himself entitled to the headship of the family, which the mother refused to accept . . . . The result for this family was trouble—a trouble which was resolved only through the continued pressure by the son and the two daughters which overwhelmed the mother's striving to hold the dominant position in the family.

And again:

In one family, when Mrs. Mark's mother was taken into the family because another family could no longer care for her, trouble was initiated. The grandmother immediately began to "side" with her daughter against the son-in-law in small matters which would have been resolved under other circumstances, and troubles resulted.

But even without any loss or addition of members, group changes can occur as a consequence of changes within the original members of a family.

Thus, for example, the aging of members of a group will produce restructuring. As a gang of boys gets older, the group relationships change as the interests and personalities of the members develop differentially and as the special capacities that were important for a teen-age group become relatively less important for an older group.

Group changes caused by socioeconomic changes.—The structure of a group can change as the general social milieu in which it exists changes. Thus, Lazarsfeld's (1933) study of families in an economic depression indicates clearly how the group structure changes and how the group as a whole tends to withdraw from active contact with the outside world. Different members of the same group may hold different political views, and some critical political event in the outside world may thus result in the creation of internal group tensions which sometimes can lead to radical group restructuring or even dissolution. This is no less true of family groups than it is of political, religious, and economic groups.[1]

General Comments.—The detailed analysis of structural, functional, cognitive, and activity characteristics of groups is significant only in so far as they can permit us a better understanding of group *changes*. The study of how and why groups change is fundamentally the study of *social dynamics*, just as the study of the motivational, perceptual, and cognitive processes are important because they can permit us understanding of the *adjustment* of the individual. The social scientist must seek to answer the following questions as Lewin (1945) has formulated them:

. . . what forces are keeping this type of group life? What type of change would be brought about by what type of action? What forces would resist what changes? Under what conditions would a change be permanent and when will group living bend quickly back to previous designs? . . .

These questions can be only partially answered at this stage in the development of group dynamics. *To achieve more satisfactory answers and to formulate general laws and principles of social dynamics experimental procedures and scientific theorizing with groups must become an integral part of social psychology.*

SUMMARY

In every society there exist smaller social groupings. No matter how ephemeral or "permanent," small or large, simple or complicated, these groups influence the needs, beliefs, and actions of people. The purpose

[1] For a brief and clear discussion of the changes that have occurred and are occurring in the family group as consequences of sociological and technological changes, see Gruenberg (1947).

of this chapter is stated as an analysis of *group* structure and function. Although it is pointed out that there is nothing in social psychology which is not logically explicable at the level of the psychology of the individual, nevertheless it is difficult in practice to restrict analysis to that level. It is suggested that if our interest is in the *end result* rather than in the details of how this result came about, we can work on the level of groups as a whole. Two social groupings are differentiated and defined as the major concern of this chapter—the "psychological group" and the more formal and permanent "social organization." Although these two groups differ in some important respects, it is emphasized that they are closely related and many of the basic considerations of the one apply to the other.

The first section of analysis is given over to group *structure*. Such matters as (1) the size of the group, (2) individual roles within the group, and (3) methods of describing group structures are discussed and illustrated, and (4) relationships among groups are examined. With reference to the first of these it is concluded that the larger the size of the group the more potentially complex can the group structure be, that this relationship is not a simple one but that potential complexity increases much more rapidly than does size, and that there are dynamic factors which limit the size of most groups, especially of psychological groups. With respect to the second, it is pointed out that for most groups the interindividual relationships *within* a single group are determined by the structure of the group to a considerable degree rather than by the personality of the individuals. However, even for social organizations, where this is most true, allowances must be made for individual differences and other extra-group factors. Among these extra-group factors one of the most important is the over-all past group experiences of the individual that affect his current group relationships. The "sociometric method" is described as a systematic method to determine and portray the exceedingly complex network of interrelationships that exist within even the very simple groups. Typical sociometric patterns are illustrated by reference to various studies. With respect to the fourth, relationships among groups, the reasons for stressing this question are given from three different levels of analysis, and it is concluded that to gain a full understanding of group structure, the "map" of group structure must incorporate all groupings from the largest to the very smallest.

The second section of analysis concerns itself with the *functions* of groups. In addition to the basic generalization that group membership can always be seen as serving a function for the individual, the following characterizations are discussed and illustrated as further specifications of the functional nature of groups: (1) Most groups serve to meet the current needs of their *dominant* members more adequately than of their less dominant (or rank-

and-file) members; (2) most groups can be seen as having unique, or major, functions as well as accessory, or minor, functions; (3) most groups, in addition to other functions, serve to meet the dominance and belongingness needs of its members; and (4) most groups induce new needs among their members. Each of these generalizations is illustrated, and its significance for social dynamics is discussed. Finally, the relationship between group functions and membership loyalty is examined, and the latter is seen to be partly dependent upon the number, kind, and variety of functions performed by the group. A concluding point is made to the effect that the structure of the group may vary according to the *particular function* that the group plays in a given situation.

The third section of analysis discusses the *belief systems of groups*. It is first pointed out that the group beliefs can be seen as related to the functions of the group and the needs of its members in a dual capacity—as *effects* of the needs of the members and as *causes* of new needs. The reasons why various members of the same group have a core of beliefs in common and why such common beliefs are resistant to change are discussed, and this discussion is illustrated with reference to the official ideology of some economic groups and organizations. Finally some characteristics of group beliefs that are common to most groups are examined.

The fourth section is given over to group-determined *action patterns*. The basic generalization made is that any kind of group-determined action patterns (whether labeled "ritual" or "technological") must be seen as organically related to the goals of the group. The reasons why such actions show the high degree of communality and patterning that they do among the different members of the same group are discussed, and a differentiation is made between two kinds of group-determined action patterns: (1) those patterns which all members of a group show in common and (2) those patterns which differentiate one member from another within the same group. The problem of bureaucracy is briefly discussed in connection with the latter type of group-determined action pattern.

The final section of analysis is given over to group dynamics—to the *changes that take place within groups*. Among the topics discussed are the factors that make for stable and unstable groups, the methods of resolving intragroup tensions, the major cohesive and disruptive forces, and the external determinants of group change. In connection with this last topic illustrations are given from the changes that occur in the dominance relationships in families under various conditions. It is concluded that to achieve any insight into *social dynamics*, experimental procedures must become an integral part of social psychology to the end that we shall be able to answer such questions as what forces operate to maintain certain forms of group life, what type of change would be brought about by what type of action, what forces would resist such changes, under what conditions would a change be permanent, and under what conditions would group living quickly return to its previous design.

BIBLIOGRAPHY

ALLPORT, F. H.: 1927. The nature of institutions. *Social Forces*, **6**, 167–179.

BENEDICT, R.: 1935. Rituals. In *The Encyclopedia of the social sciences*. New York: Macmillan.

BRADY, R. A.: 1945. *Bureaucracy in business*. J. soc. Issues, **1**, 32–43.

BRUNER, J. S.: 1947. International research on social issues: a world survey. *J. soc. Issues*, **3**, 38–53.

CHEVALEVA-JANOVSKAJA, E.: 1927. *Les groupements spontanes d'enfants a l'age pre-scholarire*. Arch. de Psychol. **20**, 219–233.

DAGGETT, H. S.: 1947. Reflections on the law of the family. *Ann. Amer. Acad. Polit. Soc. Sci.*, **251**, 120–127.

DOUGLASS, H. P.: 1926. *1000 city churches*. New York: Doran.

FRENCH, J. R. P.: 1944. Organized and unorganized groups under fear and frustration. In *Studies in topological and vector psychology*. Iowa City: Univ. Iowa Press.

GRUENBERG, S. M.: 1947. Changing conceptions of the family. *Ann. Amer. Acad. Polit. Soc. Sci.* **251**, 128–136.

HERTZLER, J. O.: 1929. *Social institutions*. New York: McGraw-Hill.

HOBHOUSE, L. T.: 1924. *Social development*. London: G. Allen.

KATZ, D., and SCHANCK, R. L.: 1938. *Social psychology*. New York: Wiley.

KOOS, E. L.: 1946. *Families in trouble*. New York: King's Crown Press.

LAZARSFELD, P. F.: 1933. *Die Arbeitslosen von Marienthal*. Leipzig: S. Hirzel.

LEWIN, K.: 1944. Constructs in psychology and psychological ecology. *Univ. Ia. Stud.*, **20**, 1–29.

LEWIN, K.: 1945. The research center for group dynamics at Massachusetts Institute of Technology. *Sociometry*, **8**, 126–136.

LOOMIS, C. P.: 1941. Informal grouping in a Spanish-American village. *Sociometry*, **4**, 36–51.

MORENO, J. L.: 1934. *Who shall survive?* Washington: Nerv. Ment. Dis. Publ. Co.

MURCHISON, C.: 1936. The time function in formation of social hierarchies of different sizes in *Gallus domesticus*. J. soc. Psychol., **7**, 3–18.

NOWLIS, V.: 1941. Companionship preference and dominance in the social interaction of young chimpanzees. *Comp. Psychol. Monogr.*, **17**, No. 1.

PEAK, H.: 1945. Observations on the characteristics and distribution of German Nazis. *Psychol. Monogr.*, **59**, No. 276.

SLAVSON, S. R.: 1943. *An introduction to group therapy*. New York: Commonwealth Fund.

TRESSELT, M. E., and VOLKMANN, J.: 1942. The production of uniform opinion by non-social stimulation. *J. abn. soc. Psychol.*, **37**, 234–243.

WINSLOW, C. N.: 1938. Observations of dominance—subordination in cats. *J. genet. Psychol.*, **52**, 425–428.

CHAPTER XI

GROUP MORALE AND LEADERSHIP

Two characteristics of social groups of great interest for the student of group dynamics and for the man of affairs are group morale and leadership. The industrialist, the army officer, the director of a playground, the head of the gang, the churchleader, the father of a family, the department chairman in a university, the political leader, and every other leader of a social group is concerned, at one time or another and whether or not he phrases it in that way, with the "morale" of his group. Morale refers to the level of group functioning, the unity and solidarity of the group, its *esprit de corps*. And it is significant that it is the leader of a group who is primarily concerned with this problem of morale. More than any other member of the group it is within his power and it is his responsibility to increase and sustain group morale.

The purpose of this chapter is to extend the discussion of group structure and functioning, the study of group dynamics, to a detailed examination of the principles involved in group morale and group leadership.

GROUP MORALE

There have been various attempts made to define group morale more precisely than by such general terms as *esprit de corps* or *unity of the group*. But the term can perhaps be defined best by the various criteria that are used to determine whether or not a given group has "high" or "low" morale—and these criteria are many.

Criteria of High and Low Morale.—The signs of high morale in a group are frequently clear even to the untrained observer, and either these signs can be in terms of direct actions of the group members, or they can be more subtle and be "sensed" by the observer without his being able to put his finger on any specific group act that leads him to rate the morale as high. In terms of the concepts of group structure and functioning developed in the last chapter, the signs of high morale can be listed as follows: (1) a tendency for the group to hold together through internal cohesiveness rather than through mere external pressures, (2) a minimal level of divisive frictions, (3) the adaptability of the group to changing circumstances in such a way as to enable the group itself to handle inner conflicts and to produce the necessary inner readjustments of an interpersonal nature, (4) substantial amounts of "tele" among group members (see page 376), (5) communality of the goals of the individual members, (6) positive attitude by group members concerning the objectives of the group and the group leadership, (7) desire of the group members to retain the group and a regard for it as a positive value.

The converse of the above conditions characterizes a state of low morale. A group can be said to have low morale when it falls apart easily or breaks up into antagonistic subgroups once the external pressures holding it together are reduced, when interpersonal frictions arise out of distrust and destructive criticism, when the group fails to be self-governing of its internal tensions, when there is a lack of friendly emotional currents among the group members and appreciable amounts of feeling of unfriendliness and rejection, when the goals of the individual members conflict and are out of harmony with the group objectives, when the members have negative attitudes toward the group objectives and its leadership, and when the members have little feeling of identification and involvement in the group.

An illustration.—As an example of several of the above distinguishing features of a good and a poor morale state in groups having the same formal structure and the same general objectives, we may look at the cases reported by Jenkins (1947) of two naval air squadrons during the war in the Pacific. One of them had many distinguishing marks of high morale; the other was definitely in the opposite direction in the morale dimension. Both squadrons were made up of a commanding officer, an executive officer, and 17 flying personnel. Following the sociometric method (page 375), the 17 men in each squadron were asked to state anonymously their personal preferences as to men they knew (inside the squadron or outside it) whom they would like to have fly beside them. They were also asked to name men they would not like to have fly beside them. The results for each squadron were plotted in a sociogram as shown in Fig. 11. A solid line with arrow indicates a choice, and dotted line a rejection. Persons named outside the squadron are shown outside the enclosing square.

In Squadron A it is notable that the commanding officer (CO) was named favorably by eight men and the executive officer (XO) by six. In Squadron B, in sharp contrast, the CO was named by no one, either positively or negatively, and the XO received no favorable mentions and nine rejections. On this evidence alone of differential attitude toward the leaders of the two groups, it is easy to recognize the superiority of morale of Squadron A over Squadron B.

There are other equally revealing indications. In Squadron B we see the existence of two subgroups or cliques within the whole—one made up

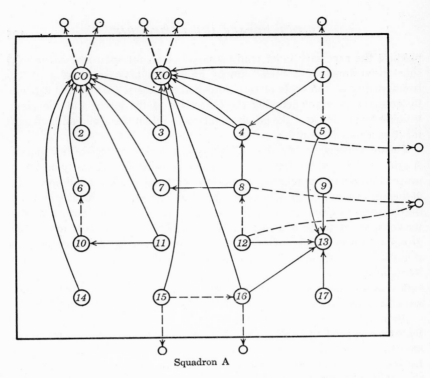

Squadron A

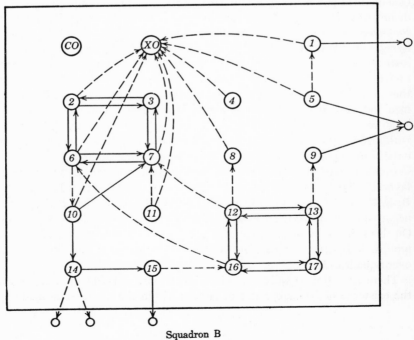

Squadron B

FIG. 11.—Sociograms of two naval air squadrons. (*Jenkins, 1947.*)

of individuals 2, 3, 6, and 7; the other of 12, 13, 16, and 17. In each of these squares we have a sort of "mutual-admiration society," each individual being chosen and choosing in return. And note that no member of either of these cliques chose anyone outside the tight little group. Squadron A, in contrast, contains no apparent segregated subgroups of this sort, the polarity of the whole group centering mainly in the formal leaders.[1]

A third interesting indication of the difference in morale of the two groups is seen in the relative incidence of favorable and unfavorable mention of people outside the squadron itself. In Squadron A there were no choices of men outside the squadron and ten rejections; in Squadron B the proportions were reversed, there being four choices outside and only two rejections. High morale is distinguished by preference of one's own group members over outsiders, and Squadron A showed up best here too.

Misleading indicators of morale.—Sometimes *orderliness* has been mistakenly assumed to demonstrate a healthy morale state. Thus a quiet and neat classroom is the ideal of many unprogressive schoolteachers, and an "efficient" and "businesslike" office atmosphere the ideal of many business executives. Actually, such orderliness is frequently brought about through the application of external pressures, through arbitrary rules and regulations, through penalties and punishments for violators. Orderliness and efficiency may be symptomatic of high morale, but not if produced through the operation of external authoritarian pressures.

The same thing is true of *productivity*. There is obvious danger in ascribing the quantity of work output of a group endeavor directly to the level of morale of the group. Productivity, like orderliness, may be increased through measures of regimentation. The reports of the United States Strategic Bombing Survey (1946) reveal a remarkable ability of the German workers to produce at a high level even under desperate hardships resulting from Allied bombing. Yet these people were also shown to have been at the same time in a state of materially lowered morale, as expressed in feelings of despair and defeatism and in criticism of Nazi leadership. The two facts can be reconciled only by recognizing that the German people were working in a repressive atmosphere in which heavy external pressures were brought upon them at all times to keep going. The question is not will people continue to strive even when things look hopeless but rather will they continue to work on and fight on if allowed to decide for themselves, *without* external pressures. There seems little doubt from the data collected by the United States Strategic Bombing Survey that

---

[1] It is of incidental interest that individual 13 in Squadron A, a junior officer, commanded favorable choices only second in number to those of the formal group leaders. This may be prognostic of high leadership capacity in this individual.

great numbers of the German people were ready to quit long before their leaders permitted them to do so.   This, then, was low morale.

A third misconception lies in identifying bad morale with the existence of a considerable degree of interpersonal tension in the group. Level of tension cannot alone differentiate between good and bad morale. Some conflicts among group members are healthy ones; others are unhealthy. Tensions between the leader and the others is a dangerous symptom; so is tension arising out of conflicting self-interests of the group in connection with needs and goals not directly related to the group objective.   On the other hand, conflicts that arise concerning how the group should achieve its ends and with criticism of the performance of other members can often be demonstrative of a high *esprit de corps*.

Determinants of Morale.—In analyzing the bases of group morale it is important that we examine not only relevant features of the group structure and function as a whole but also certain details of the attitudes, beliefs, and needs of the constituent members. We are concerned here with *group* morale rather than the morale of the individual, but an understanding of group morale depends partly upon an understanding of the individual psychology of the members.   It is also of interest that many generalizations about group morale seem closely parallel to those about the morale of an individual when not functioning as a member of a group.

Morale, we shall find, depends upon the proper integration of certain motivational, emotional, and cognitive factors in each of the individuals making up the group.   In order that group morale be high, the member must have strong needs, he must believe that the group can function so as to satisfy these needs, and he must feel a sufficient degree of emotional involvement with the group.

Positive goals.—One essential of good morale is a positive goal. As Watson (1942) has put it, "Morale, first of all, demands a magnetic pole toward which the aspirations of men are drawn."   In the absence of clear over-all objectives, groups cannot hope to achieve a high order of synthesis and will easily deteriorate. One of the most serious morale problems of men in the military forces during the war was the nonexistence for large numbers of them of any clear-cut goal for which the war was being fought. Much of the unity that was achieved in the nation at war was on the basis of essentially negative motivation—the presence of an active threat from the enemy or the attack on Pearl Harbor.   As we shall see, such negative factors as fear, hatred, and anger are important motivations in morale, but they are not usually sufficient in the absence of positive goals as well. It is also probable that the kind of morale based on negative motivations differs in some critical aspects from that based on positive motivations.

Satisfaction of "accessory" needs.—Quite apart from the primary purpose of group membership for the attainment of some common objective, there are usually, as we have seen, secondary satisfactions which the individual gets from group activity. Many people feel a strong wish to participate in activities with others, and such desire for participation may be related to needs for self-expression, prestige, recognition, and the like. These "accessory" functions of groups are extremely important. Better group morale can be expected, other things being equal, in groups that so function as to permit the optimal degree of feelings of participation, self-expression, and recognition on the part of its members. In military units, in industrial and business employee groups, in school groups, in political associations, it is often notable how morale of group members deteriorates in an atmosphere in which they feel they have little voice in determining the destiny of the group, in which their suggestions or ideas are not solicited or used, in which they are accorded no opportunity to distinguish themselves in any special way in the activities of the group.

Sense of advance toward goal.—It is not sufficient that a group goal exists and that there are techniques available for attaining it. It is also necessary to have some feeling of moving toward the goal. As laboratory and clinical studies have shown, very small amounts of encouragement and success and small steps toward the goal are frequently effective in sustaining and enhancing motivation. It is a truism that to maintain the morale of people in a dictatorship it is essential to signal progress toward the main national objective by a continuous series of "successes." It was partly in this way that Hitler, through a long series of successful repudiations of the Treaty of Versailles and successful aggressions against neighboring countries, built up the morale of his Nazi state. In a democracy the same may hold true. The phenomenal political strength of Roosevelt over a long period of years was accounted for partly by the series of economic advances and reforms perceived by his supporters as continuous steps toward the goal of the New Deal.

Whenever group members can see or believe they can see evidences of advance toward the group objective, morale is thereby likely to be strengthened. The converse is also true. Just as "nothing succeeds like success," so "nothing fails like failure."

Level of aspiration and level of achievement.—In connection with the necessity for a sense of advance toward the goal it is essential to understand the critical significance of the *level of aspiration* and the *level of achievement* of the individual group members for the morale of the group. Lewin's (1942) comments on this point are particularly helpful:

A successful individual typically sets his next goal somewhat, but not too much, above his last achievement. In this way he steadily raises his level of aspiration. Although in the long run he is guided by his ideal goal, which may be rather high, nevertheless his real goal for the next step is kept realistically close to his present position. The unsuccessful individual, on the other hand, tends to show one of two reactions: he sets his goal very low, frequently below his past achievement—that is, he becomes intimidated and gives up reaching out toward higher goals—or he sets his goal far above his ability. This latter conduct is rather common. Sometimes the result is a gesturelike keeping up of high goals without serious striving; it may at other times mean that the individual is following blindly his ideal goal, losing sight of what in the present situation is possible. To develop and to maintain high goals, and at the same time, to keep the plan for the next action realistically within the limits of what is possible, seems to be one of the basic objectives for and a criterion of high morale.

The implications of these remarks for the problem of group morale are obvious. Groups may often become demoralized even though they possess the requisite high objectives toward which they are cooperatively striving because of a failure to plan their actions with sufficient realism to promise an actual step forward. Thus, we observe that well-intentioned groups with high ideals, such as peace groups and social reform groups, frequently disintegrate because their perspective, in being too remote, interferes with the realistic planning of immediate action which will serve as the next concrete step toward the final goal.

Time perspective.—Other aspects of time perspective, *i.e.*, the psychological past and future as they exist for and influence the individual at the present moment, are intimately related to morale. For optimal conditions of morale the group members should understand clearly the relevance of present activities to the main ultimate group objective. The future steps to be taken in achievement of the goal should be explicitly laid out, so that the person has a clear cognitive structure concerning the general plan of action to be followed. Leadership, as we shall see, differs markedly in the degree to which it provides the individual group member with an adequate cognitive structure of the present group activities and those which are to follow. It is a commonplace observation that when people are kept in the dark, when the work they are doing is not meaningfully related for them to ultimate objectives, when the successive activities of the group are, from the point of view of the individual, separate and unrelated parts without coherent pattern, then morale is likely to deteriorate. Conversely, it is sometimes remarkable how the morale climate of a group can radically improve when care is taken by the leadership to explain the necessity for what previously have seemed to be trivial, wasteful, or "stupid" activities.

Another aspect of time perspective important for morale is concerned with feelings of insecurity or uncertainty as to what the future holds. Many soldiers were seriously demoralized by the uncertainty as to what would happen to them next, where they would be sent, what sort of duties they would be assigned. Usually a sense of relief and better spirits followed their discovery of what was in store for them even if this was not particularly pleasant. The lack of morale of many groups of college students frequently reflects their uncertainty as to the type of future jobs open to them and their fear of depressions and hard times. The same is true of groups of the unemployed. And for groups of people who band together to work for a common ideal of peace and international order, an increasing uncertainty about the possibility of avoiding future wars often leads to severe demoralization. What is probably the best antidote for the lowered morale of this kind is a facing up to the grim realities and a refusal to permit the effects of insecurity and uncertainty to extinguish hope. Roosevelt's famous phrase as he assumed the presidency, with the country in a state of severe economic and psychological demoralization, is apropos: "The only thing we have to fear is fear itself."

Lewin (1942) has pointed out that the relationship between high morale and long-range time perspective is reciprocal; *i.e.*, not only does a long-range time perspective help maintain high morale in a group, but a group that has high morale, for whatever reason, also tends to develop a long-range time perspective. Thus, in an experiment by Bavelas and Lewin (1942) a children's group that had existed for only one hour but that had been so organized by the experimenters as to result in a high state of morale for the group spontaneously demanded the continuation of that group. When the experimenters told the children that no adult leader was available for the continuance of this group, the children decided to organize themselves and carry on alone. Their morale, in other words, was high enough to broaden the time perspective of their own group, they wanted to continue to exist for more than one hour, and, in fact, they set themselves a group project that extended over weeks, and later they included a half-year project.

Equality of sacrifice or gain within the group.—One of the deadliest weapons in the arsenal of psychological warfare is propaganda aimed at convincing some segments of the enemy group that they are suffering more hardships or are gaining fewer benefits than other segments of the group. Thus, the soldier may be brought to believe that he is sacrificing more than the industrial worker, that he gets soldier's pay while the worker gets rich on war wages; those who obey the rationing regulations may come to believe that others are profiting on the black market; the poor may come to feel they are being taxed more than the rich in support of the war. Such beliefs in inequality of sacrifice and gain within the group are among the most divisive forces in group morale. It is significant that during the war considerable attention was paid, even in the armies of the authoritarian states, to reducing the apparent differentials of privilege among soldiers of various ranks. In the first stages of the bombing of London, the poorer districts of the East End were attacked almost exclusively, and the resentment of the people in this section toward the more favored in other parts of the city grew dangerously ugly. With the bombing of Buckingham Palace, however, there was swift change in morale, the people now feeling that all were in it equally.

Feelings of solidarity, identification, and involvement.—Equally important with the various cognitive and motivational factors affecting morale which we have examined above are those factors of an emotional sort having to do with feelings of group solidarity, identification, involvement, and the like. These emotional factors are inseparable, of course, from all the other morale determinants. Morale is not a summation of effects from different sources but a characteristic of the whole individual and of the whole group.

The sense of "togetherness," of joining with others in a common enterprise, seems by itself to make for stronger morale. As Watson (1942) points out, convictions are firmer when it is felt that other people join in them. An individual who, alone, might easily become discouraged or intimidated can sustain his faith and keep fighting if he is with his gang. An experiment by Wright (1940) demonstrates that a pair of strong friends among children is less affected by frustrating circumstances than a pair of children who are not friends. The feeling of solidarity in the group seems to provide a defense against demoralization. In Wright's experiment the group solidarity derived from strong feelings of friendship which already existed among the pairs of children. It might be safe to conclude, therefore, that a group formed on the basis of a deep emotional attachment, as in friendship among its members, will demonstrate a higher morale in all sorts of activities even though these activities have nothing to do with the basis of friendship as such.

Another way to talk about the emotional forces enhancing group morale is in terms of *identification.* It can be expected that, other things being equal, the more closely the individual members identify themselves with the group the higher the morale of the group will be. By identification is meant the tendency of the individual to feel the group to be "his" group, the welfare of the group to be "his" welfare, the achievements of the group to be "his" achievements. The psychological mechanism underlying group identification is presumably no different from that underlying an individual's identification with his family, his children, his possessions, the fruit of his work. Yet there is, at least superficially, a difference. For these personal things are in a real sense his; they are recognized by others as belonging to him, as identified with him and no one else. But in the case of identification with a group, the group is not in any real sense any more his than it is any other group member's. Group identification, then, requires the development of something more in the direction of "we" and "our" feelings than of mere feelings of "I" and "mine."

Identification with the group is a complex and not well-understood process. We have seen in Chap. II (page 59) that identification is one of many different possible avenues to the satisfaction of thwarted needs, by virtue of the fact that vicarious prestige or other satisfactions may accrue to the individual through his identification with people or groups who themselves have prestige or other positive values. An individual citizen is likely to feel emotional satisfactions in the power and success of his country. But group identification is not simply something to be utilized when it is need fulfilling and ignored when it is not. It is also important that when there are no positive benefits accruing to the group, as when it is being subjected to criticism or punishment, the individual member may still remain thoroughly identified and may willingly suffer the criticism and punishment that he could otherwise escape by breaking away from the group. Need satisfactions may be essential for the initial formation of groups through identification, but it seems that they are not always necessary for the maintenance of groups once established. It is as though the group once strongly established for the individual becomes an external and demanding force, often in conflict with the immediate personal wishes and interests of the individual. There is nothing necessarily mysterious in this; it bears a striking resemblance to another phenomenon, *viz.*, the development of *values*. Values for the individual also come to have what seems to him an external existence; they too demand on his part action that is often at variance with his immediate personal desires. At an even earlier stage in the person's growth we are reminded of the existence of parental authority, which again carries for the child the character of an external demanding force overriding immediate wishes.

Groups may function for the individual in a way remarkably parallel to values; groups may even, indeed, *become* values, and in this case group loyalty is certainly no more surprising than loyalty to one's other values.

This does not mean, of course, that all groups to which the individual belongs exist as permanent and objectified values or ends in themselves for him. Sometimes this does seem to occur: "My country right or wrong"; but more usually the group derives its influence from the fact that its objectives are perceived by the individual as fulfilling or being congruent with his basic values. The loyalty to the group, then, is most often a means to an end, not an end in itself.

Group identification and time perspective.—There is a very significant relationship between group identification and time perspective which can be an effective determinant of group morale and which deserves special consideration. Frequently a long-range time perspective is impossible without group identification, without the development of the "we" or "our" feelings that have been mentioned. As we have previously pointed out, group beliefs commonly include the perception of one's group as existing in a superordinate manner—not restricted by the limitations that determine the existence and behavior of the individual member. Where there is strong group identification, this group belief can operate so as more readily to give the individual a long-term time perspective for *his* group. An illustration of this relationship is found in Lewin's (1942) description of how the Zionists in Germany, after Hitler came to power, were less demoralized than other Jews because the Zionists, a strong group with all the usual group beliefs about the superordinate nature, the essential righteousness and inevitable success of their group, were able to achieve a long-term time perspective. Most of the Jews, including the Zionists, had not believed that Hitler could come to power and that pogroms could occur in Germany. When these things happened, many of them became desperate, lost their morale entirely, and committed suicide—they could see nothing in the future to live for. The Zionists, on the other hand, were able to go on and were able to maintain their morale because they had a broader time perspective—with reference to both the past and the future. The past, in the Zionist's perception, included a knowledge of their (*i.e.*, their superordinate group) having survived for thousands of years under adversity, and *their* future looked toward a definite objective of a national home for the Jews which, despite all, would inevitably come into being. Lewin writes,

As a result of such a time perspective, this group showed high morale—despite a present which was judged by them to be no less foreboding than by others. Instead of inactivity and encystment in the face of a difficult situation, the Zionists with a long-range and realistic time perspective showed initiative and organized planning.

Encouraging group identification.—How may group identification be produced and enhanced? Quite apart from the critically important matter of the community of the group goals and ideals and the goals and ideals of the individual, there are other important factors in the development of group identification. For one thing the group must be made to stand out clearly for the individual. It must be a clear structure in his cognitive field. To this end the formal organization and paraphernalia are useful: a group name, group symbols, ritual, uniforms, flags, etc. Also significant in this connection is official group leadership, which provides an important cognitive and emotional focus for the group identification. At the same time the integration of the individual with the group must be made explicit and cognitively clear, by dressing him in uniforms, by adorning him with badges, by assigning him definite roles in the group structure. For another thing, the psychological boundary between the group and the nongroup must be accentuated. This is accomplished by some of the above devices, which mark off members from nonmembers, as well as by initiation ceremonies.

In the third place, the participation of the individual in the group activities must be encouraged. Requiring the individual to assume responsibilities ensures that he will feel more deeply involved and identified than if he is permitted to exist passively in the group. To this end some political organizations use the technique of placing new members immediately in positions of responsibility, thus forcing quicker involvement.

Finally, group identification can be enhanced by involving the individual in the group in as many different aspects of his personality as possible. Allport (1942) has spoken in this connection of "segmental" morale, which mobilizes only certain segments of the personality at the risk of severe conflict with other segments, and "integral" morale, in which the whole personality is involved in the group and the pursuit of critical social goals is possible without conflict (see page 385, Chap. X). In this connection, Allport's (1945) insistence on distinguishing between "activity" and "participation" is valuable. As he points out,

Activity alone is not participation. Most of our fellow citizens spin as cogs in many systems without engaging their own egos even in those activities of most vital concern to them . . . . When the ego is not effectively engaged the individual becomes reactive. He lives a life of ugly protest, finding outlets in complaints, strikes, above all in scapegoating; in this condition he is ripe prey for a demagogue whose whole purpose is to focus and exploit the aggressive outbursts of non-participating egos.

The person who is merely "acting" is differentiated from the person who is "participating" in that the former's activity is not geared to such strong needs as status seeking, self-regard, self-respect, etc. Where the activity of the individual that is demanded of him by the group is of the participant sort, group identification is enhanced.

Positive vs. Negative Morale Determinants.—Thus far we have examined determinants of morale that are of a *positive* nature, *i.e.*, those concerned with the positive goals of the individual, his emotional affiliations, etc. There are also *negative* factors that can produce high morale. It is well understood, for example, that unity may develop in the face of a common threat or danger to the group. But as French (1942) has pointed out, ". . . fear and rational expediency are not adequate motives to weld together a people in cooperative effort even in the face of common danger. If a people has not already some sense of solidarity, then fear is apt to result in panic rather than in common action."

This qualifying limitation on the effectiveness of negative factors in producing high morale has been dramatically demonstrated in the last war. The Japanese committed a serious psychological blunder, even if a strategic military move, in their attack on Pearl Harbor. And Dunkirk welded the British people together into a state of almost incomparably high morale. Hostile pressures from without do serve to reduce internal dissensions and to unify people in their defense against and attack upon the enemy outgroup. But that common danger alone is not enough is seen in the example of France in 1940, when invasion produced demoralization rather than the reverse. Here the internal forces of disruption were too great, produced by long years of strife and antagonism between economic and political groups (and exacerbated by the Nazi fifth column), no "sense of solidarity" existed, and the unifying forces stirred up by hostile external pressures were insufficient to overweigh the internal disruptive forces.

The glib and frequently cynical belief held by many leaders that all that is necessary to heighten morale or decrease intragroup antagonism is to find a suitable and "dangerous" out-group is a false belief, and practice based on such a belief may boomerang disastrously. Hostile external pressures *may* increase morale, but only under certain conditions of group structure.

Differential nature of positively determined and negatively determined morale. Not only is the effectiveness of a negative factor limited in its capacity to induce high group morale, but the morale that is thus produced differs from that produced by positive factors. Lippitt (1942) has suggested that

Whether the group's interpersonal unity is derived from mutual resistance to external pressures or from spontaneous inner sources of cohesion is a fact of considerable importance both in determining the extent to which the group will resist disrupting forces and persist in its efforts toward goal attainment, and in determining what channelization the tension resulting from group frustration will take.

In support of this conclusion, Lippitt adduces several pieces of evidence drawn from experimental comparisons of groups of children positively organized on the basis of positive goals and positive interpersonal relationships and those negatively organized on the basis of external pressures of an authoritarian adult leader. Gordon (1940) has shown that positively organized groups resisted the attempts of the experimenter to set up lines of cleavage within the group—cleavages that would result in group disruption under frustration. Lewin, Lippitt, and White (1939) have evidence that negatively organized groups, on the other hand, tended to develop frictions along the potential lines of cleavage and aggression toward scapegoats made spontaneous appearance. In positively organized groups, the aggressions arising out of experimentally created frustrations tended to be channeled toward the source of the frustration itself or toward "depersonalized" objects; in the negatively organized groups the aggressions were more likely to be directed inwardly toward other group members or toward the group leader or outwardly toward other organized groups. And recriminations and reactions of personal blame so disrupted the group effort as to destroy the goal-directed motivation.

GROUP LEADERSHIP

It was pointed out in the introduction that the group leader is of central importance to the morale of the group. By virtue of his special position within the group structure he serves as the primary agent for the determination of group structures, group atmosphere, group goals, group ideology, and group activities, and we have now seen that the level of morale depends intimately upon these various group properties. It is therefore essential, if we are to understand how to increase group morale, that we understand how to select good group leaders. In order to understand that, we must examine in some detail the functions of a leader, the various types of leadership that can be employed, and, finally, how to train good leaders.

Functions of the Leader.—As will presently be shown, the specific functions of a leader vary somewhat with the kind of group being led. Thus, a leader functioning in an "authoritative" group may stress certain functions, whereas a leader in a "democratic" group may stress others. However, whatever the nature of the group, all leaders must partake to some degree of the functions of executive, planner, policy maker, expert, external group representative, controller of internal relationships, purveyor of rewards and punishments, arbitrator and mediator, and examplar.

The leader as executive.—The most obvious role of the leader in any group is as coordinator of the activities of the group. Whether or not he assumes the direct role of determining policies or objectives of the group, it is almost invariably his responsibility to oversee the execution of these policies. The effective chairman of a committee guides the committee discussion along the appropriate lines, appoints subcommittees, etc. The foreman of a work group lays out the work plans and supervises its general execution. The captain of a military unit is responsible for having the orders of the day carried out.

In his executive capacity the leader does not himself ordinarily carry out the necessary work; he assigns it to other group members. Occasionally, a person in a leadership role suffers from an inability to delegate responsibility and work; he feels the necessity of being personally involved in each group activity and invariably in this way produces either or both of two difficulties in group operation: (1) He becomes a bottleneck; (2) he interferes with the healthy involvement and feeling of group responsibility on the part of the other members.

The leader as planner.—Intermediate between the determination of objectives and policies and the execution of them lies the planning function. The leader often assumes this role of planner—deciding the ways and means by which the group shall achieve its ends. This may involve not only immediate steps but long-range planning of all the future steps to the goal. And frequently the leader is the sole custodian of the plan, he alone knowing the entire pattern and other group members being apprised only of segments—often apparently unconnected—of the whole plan.

The leader as policy maker.—One of the most important of all leader functions is the establishment of group goals, objectives, and policies. In general, group goals may arise from three sources: (1) from "above," *i.e.,* dictated by authorities superordinate to the given group, such as commands passed down from higher military officers to lower, or policies established at the top level of the business hierarchy and unquestionably accepted as directives by lower levels; (2) from "below," *i.e.,* dictated by the decision of the group membership as a whole; (3) from the leader himself, he being provided with mandates from neither above nor below and being autonomous in his policy decisions.

The leader as expert.—Aside from functions of policy making, planning, and execution, the leader is often distinguished as a source of readily available information and skills for the group membership. In this sense, the leader is the one who is regarded as the best qualified for the technical requirements of the group activities. With continued specialization of function, of course, leaders of formal groups can less and less be expected to supply by themselves the necessary technical information; hence they come to lean more and more heavily upon technical assistants and advisers. In many informal and spontaneous groups, on the other hand, it is often the man who demonstrates the highest technical knowledge, relevant to the group's needs, who becomes leader. Thus, in a camping expedition the guide may come subtly to assume the real (though not formal) leadership of the group, and in a boys' gang the best athlete or best marksman may become leader. Adults often automatically enforce their leadership upon children's groups by mere virtue of their superior knowledge. Wherever the only avenue for cognitive clarification for the group members is through the person with technical knowledge, there is likely to be a tendency of polarization of power around him, and, depending upon other factors, he may exploit this power to consolidate his role as leader.

The leader as external group representative.—Since it is manifestly impossible for all members of a large group to deal directly with other groups and other people outside the group, the leader characteristically assumes the role as representative of the large group in its external relationships. He is the official spokesman for the group. Not only are the outgoing demands and contacts of the group channeled through him, so are the incoming demands and contacts. He is in this special sense what Lewin has called a "gatekeeper."

The leader as controller of internal relationships.—Not only may the leader function as the gatekeeper of psychological relationships between group members and the out-group. he may also function as the controller, or gatekeeper, of internal interpersonal relations among the group members themselves. More than any other member, the leader governs the specific details of group structure and by so doing affects the nature of in-group relations. There are those types of groups, as we shall presently see, in which the channels of in-group relationship are primarily through the leader himself; there are others in which the leader is remote from all but a few contacts with special group members; there are still others where the leader's relations with other members are of the same order as those of the others. Groups that are not spatially proximal may often carry on almost all in-group relations through the central "switchboard" of the leader. In such cases, particularly, the leader finds himself in the strategic position where he may operate as a "censor" of in-group relations.

The leader as purveyor of rewards and punishments.—Particularly significant from the individual member's point of view is the leader's power of reward and punishment, which enables him to exercise strong disciplinary and motivational control over the group member. Sometimes the rewards and punishments are concerned with relatively external things, such as when a gang divides up stolen loot or when a worker is given an unpleasant task by his foreman.   Often, however, the rewards and punishments have to do directly with the role of the individual in the group—he may be promoted to a more important rank in the group hierarchy, he may be given special group honors, he may be reduced in rank or deprived of a coveted group position, in extreme disciplinary action he may even be ousted from the group altogether.   These latter types of rewards and punishments are mainly concerned with the seeking by the individual of satisfaction of subsidiary needs, such as desires for participation, recognition, and self-expression.

The leader as arbitrator and mediator.—Somewhat associated with the leader's function as a purveyor of rewards and punishments is his role as an arbitrator and mediator of intragroup conflict and dissension.   It is his task not only to act as an impartial judge and to render decisions but also to act as conciliator in reestablishing good group interrelations.   It is within the power of the leader in this role to reduce or to encourage factionalism within the group, depending upon what his personal aims may be.

The leader as exemplar.—In some kinds of groups the leader may serve as a model of behavior for the group membership, in order to stimulate them to follow his lead in a desired activity and to provide them with a concrete indication of what they should do.   A military leader who bravely precedes his troops into battle serves as such an exemplar; so does the leader of the church who must, at least in his public life, exemplify all the moral virtues he would inculcate in the church members.

The leader as symbol of the group.—Group unity is likely to be enhanced by any factors that make for cognitive clarity and outstandingness of the group for its individual members.   And as we have pointed out, to this end groups equip themselves with various identifying paraphernalia—badges, uniforms, names, etc.   The leader plays something of a similar role by standing for the group as a single concrete person.   The King of England is a classic example of this function of a symbol providing a kind of cognitive focus for group unity.   In still another way the leader as a symbol provides for group continuity in that he may exist in "office" over a prolonged period, even though the individual membership constantly changes.

The leader as surrogate for individual responsibility.—Not uncommonly in certain types of group organization, the leader plays an extremely important psychological role for the individual in relieving him of responsibilities for personal action that he wishes to avoid.   In return for allegiance, the leader frees the individual from the necessity of making decisions.   Instead of endeavoring to clear up areas of cognitive confusion for himself, the

individual puts his trust in the leader and lets him make the decisions.
Fromm (1941) has written cogently about the tendency of people to delegate
critical responsibilities to their leaders in an attitude of fear of and "escape
from freedom."

The leader as ideologist.—The leader may in some circumstances serve
functions far more extreme in their implications than some of those described
above. Sometimes it is the leader who furnishes the ideology of the group
membership; he acts as a source for the very beliefs of the individual members. The "official" ideology of a group, as was indicated in Chap. X,
frequently reflects the beliefs of the leadership more accurately than those
of the rank-and-file membership. There is often marked discrepancy, for
instance, between the opinions of farmers as reported by the leaders of
farm organizations and the opinions as reported by the farmers themselves.
Unquestionably, the official ideology, no matter how discrepant with the
beliefs of individual members, will tend to percolate down and influence
the individual's beliefs. This will be particularly the case where the
leadership exercises the function of gatekeeper of flow of information from
the outside into the group.

Not only, of course, may the leader provide the group membership with
beliefs of a more factual nature, he may also act as a fountainhead of values.
Gandhi served in this sense as a "spiritual" leader, the living conscience,
and moral guide of millions of Hindus.

The leader as father figure.—A number of the preceding functions of the
leader are incorporated in a more general emotional role of *father figure*
for the individual member. The leader serves as a perfect focus for the
positive emotional feelings of the individual; he is the ideal object for
identification, for transference, for feelings of submissiveness. Psychoanalytic theorists have stressed this exceedingly significant feature of the
relationship of the leader to his followers, and there seems to be no doubt of
the major role that it plays in accounting for the tremendous power of
certain leaders in special group circumstances. Roosevelt and Hitler undoubtedly served as compelling father figures for many of their followers.

In probably any group that endures with any permanence and whose
activities are concerned with matters of deepest importance to the individual,
the leader is to some degree the pole for the positive emotionality of the
members.

The leader as scapegoat.—The ambivalence characteristic of father figures
in general is markedly true of leaders. It is astounding to see the savageness
with which a previously loved leader may be repudiated and excoriated by
the group. Just as the leader may constitute an ideal object for positive
emotional feelings, so may he serve as a perfect target for the aggressions

of the frustrated, disappointed, disillusioned group. Group members often feel "betrayed" by a leadership that fails, as witness the violent denunciation of the Nazi leadership after the war by many Germans who were probably loyal and devoted followers while all was going well.

The leader functions as an admirable scapegoat for the group's feelings of guilt and failure, which can be projected safely onto the discredited leader. This is the opposite side of the coin: To the extent that the leader assumes responsibility, he may in the event of failure expect blame.

Types of Leadership.—Although leadership tends in any group to partake of all of the above functions, the degree of importance of each function, the pattern of interrelations of functions, and the particular manner in which each function is carried out depend upon the type of group and the type of leadership. In informal, temporary groups which are formed on the basis of some immediate circumstance that throws a number of people into close dynamic relationship over a period of short duration, *e.g.*, a group of guests at a party, many or most of the above functions of leadership have no opportunity to emerge. In somewhat more stable and more formal groups existing for longer periods of time—such as people working together in an office or serving on a jury or living together in a dormitory— many but not all of these leadership functions may operate. In the most formal and stable groups of long duration, in social organizations such as family or religious groups, political societies, military units, etc., all the various leadership functions may be expected to play a role.

Social organizations are also likely to imply *formal leadership*, *i.e.*, leadership whose functions and characteristics are established by law or custom and the identities of the leaders being determined arbitrarily or externally, rather than through the unhindered operation of dynamic forces within the group itself.   The details of the process by which a previously unorganized group comes together and, through a process of interaction as a group, gradually produces a leader will be considered at a later point.   Here we wish to note only the fact the leadership which is imposed is almost certain to be different from leadership which arises spontaneously and freely.   The difference is seen as a difference between "ascribed" and "achieved" status (Linton, 1936).   A military officer has an ascribed leader status.   He has been chosen externally and placed into the leadership role; he has not achieved the role through the process of dynamic interaction within the group itself.   The functions of such a military leader are carefully established for him; his job is simply to fulfill these specified functions.   That we have here a clear case of ascribed rather than achieved status is demonstrated by the adjuration to the soldier, "You are not saluting the man but the uniform."

Even if imposed on the group in such an external and arbitrary manner, the formal leader may be intelligent enough to develop and guide his relations with the group in such a way as to make his dynamic position equivalent to his formal position. In other words, if the group were then to be given a free choice of leadership, the same leader would emerge.

Imposed vs. freely chosen leadership is intimately related to the contrast between authoritarian and democratic leadership, which we shall consider next.

Authoritarian vs. democratic type of leadership.—Perhaps the most fruitful and socially significant comparison to be made of types of leadership is that between what we may call "authoritarian" and "democratic." At the outset it should be emphasized that these terms are used simply as a convenient way of distinguishing two very different types of leadership. Whether the particular names authoritarian and democratic are the most precise ones is questionable, and it is wise to be cautious in identifying these two types as directly descriptive of the kind of leadership to be found in what are called, in the world today, democracies and authoritarian states. Nonetheless, we do feel some confidence that what we shall describe as authoritarian leadership is more like that to be found in dictatorship states, and democratic leadership more like that found in democracies.

Another caution should be indicated All the experimental evidence to be reported has been obtained by the study of so-called "authoritarian" and "democratic" leadership situations *in our democratic culture.* It is entirely possible that similar studies in other cultures might yield different results. The advantage for morale, the experiments find, seems to lie with the democratically led group, but in an autocratic culture the reverse might possibly hold true. But even granting this possibility, the significance of these data are not diminished. The fact is that in our own culture all types of leadership are to be found, from the most extremely authoritarian to the most extremely democratic. It is of highest relevance, therefore, to compare the effectiveness of these two leadership types as they operate within our culture.

Authoritarian leadership.—The authoritarian leader wields more absolute power than the democratic leader; he alone determines policies of the group; he alone makes major plans; he alone is fully cognizant of the succession of future steps in the group's activities; he alone dictates the activities of the members and the pattern of interrelations among the members; he alone serves as the ultimate agent and judge of rewards and punishments for the individual members and hence of the fate of each individual within the group structure.

The authoritarian leader deliberately develops these absolute functions

and actively resists changes in them. The techniques by which he reinforces and protects his leadership status are various. By preventing the
involvement of individual members in the setting of the group goals and
by imposing what often seem to them irrelevant subgoals, the autocratic
leader guarantees that his guidance will be indispensable for the sustained
motivation of the group as a whole. Under this type of control, the motivation of individual members is segmental and dependent. To anticipate one
of the experimental findings of a study of authoritarian and democratic
groups which will later be described, it is observed that striking differences
appear in these two types of groups during the absence of the leader. The
work morale of the democratic group maintains itself at a high level, whereas
that of the authoritarian group deteriorates rapidly.

An illustration of how the leader may deliberately insulate the group
members from the cognitive future of their activities can be taken from
the protocol of a boys' club for the making of masks which was led in an
experimentally induced authoritarian manner (Lippitt, 1940):

Leader: We are going to start making a mask for the club.

Jim: How do we do that?

Leader: I'll show you how as we go along. John, you take this board
and pound ten nails in it, and Jack go get a pail of water.

John to Jim: I wonder what this board is for?

The authoritarian leader encourages a segregated group structure in
which the intercommunication among the parts is held to a minimum and
wherever possible the avenues of intercommunication are through him or are
under his immediate supervision. In this way he ensures the indispensability of himself to the group, which serves his own personal motives of control,
but this may have unfortunate effects on the group as a whole. For one
thing, there is less opportunity for the development of close interpersonal
relations among all group members, and this means that the morale of the
group cannot be so firmly founded. For another thing, the withdrawal
of the leader (for whatever reason) may precipitate chaos in the group.
With the leader as keystone removed, the group structure may simply fall
apart, since there is little else in the way of cohesive forces among the
remaining group members.

The sociometric picture of an authoritarian group is thus more likely to
be star-shaped (see page 377) with the leader at the center of the radial
strands and with little circumferential relationship among the strands.
Experimental illustration of this group structure is given in the authoritarian boys' club. Here it was observed that the boys made many more
approaches to the leader than they did to other group members. The
nature of the approaches was either "direction demanding," *i.e.,* asking

for directions or help, or "attention getting," *i.e.*, seeking approval and recognition from the leader. This latter kind of relationship also points to the fact that in the authoritarian group the leader particularly exploits his role as the purveyor of rewards and punishments. It is to him rather than to other group members that the individual is motivationally oriented.

In very small face-to-face groups the authoritarian leader may be personally in relation to each of the members in the above fashion. As the group grows larger, however, the leader perforce becomes more remote from the rank and file, and a hierarchical organization tends to develop in which the authoritarian leader is directly in contact with the second-rank leaders, who are in turn in contact with the next rank, etc., down to the most

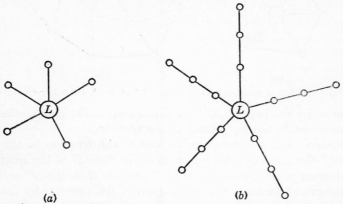

(a) *(b)*

Fig. 12.—Structure of authoritarian leadership in small group (*a*), and in larger group (*b*).

inferior members. But the important point is that the authoritarian leader still is able to retain the star-shaped structure and to minimize the degree of interpersonal contacts among the rank and file. Figures 12*a* and 12*b* indicate this type of structure in the very small and in the larger groups.

The hierarchical organization of the authoritarian group can be seen, then, as a natural consequence of the aim of the leader to maintain his position of central power. With it automatically goes the development of the "palace guard," the "teacher's pet," and the leader's personal deputies and lieutenants who seek to maintain and extend their own status at the expense of other group members. And with it goes the development of an atmosphere of rivalry for status within the group and jockeying for position. This atmosphere is conducive to frustration and aggression and to the rise of intragroup tension and conflict.

Democratic leadership.—The democratic leader does not differ from the authoritarian in the amount of power but in the nature of his role in the group structure. The democratic leader seeks to evoke the maximum involvement and the participation of every member in the group activities and in the determination of objectives. He seeks to spread responsibility rather than to concentrate it. He seeks to encourage and reinforce interpersonal contacts and relations throughout the group structure so as to strengthen it. He seeks to reduce intragroup tension and conflict. He seeks to avoid hierarchical group structure in which special privilege and status differentials predominate. The sociometric picture of a democratically led group tends to be of the form shown in Fig. 13. Although the

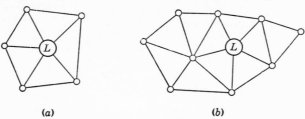

(a)   (b)

Fig. 13.—Structure of democratic leadership in small group (*a*), and in larger group (*b*).

leader occupies the position of focal importance in the group, other individuals also are intimately related to one another.

Much more than the authoritarian leader, who tends to be the group "dictator," the democratic leader serves as the "agent" of the group. He seeks wherever possible to carry out the "mandate of the group" or, better, to encourage and facilitate the carrying out of this mandate by the group members themselves. Whereas the authoritarian leader is the keystone of the group, without whom the whole structure may collapse, the democratic leader may judge his success in terms of the degree to which the group is able to go along without him when he is temporarily removed from the group structure.

An experimental comparison of authoritarian and democratic groups.—In order to investigate some aspects of group functioning under different types of leadership and different types of group "atmosphere," Lippitt (1940) and others, under the general direction of Kurt Lewin, have conducted a series of experiments with children's groups.[1] The objective was to set up small, genuine groups of children who were led by adults in such a way as deliberately to induce different types of group atmosphere. The activities of the groups were mask making and other similar tasks. Meetings were held regularly over a period of weeks. The behavior of the groups was

[1] The most detailed experimental account is found in the Lippitt paper. Other relevant references to this work are Lewin, Lippitt, and White (1939), Lippitt (1939), and Lippitt and White (1943).

under intensive observation, with particular attention to the nature of the group structure, the attitudes and morale of the members, their relations to the leader and to one another, etc.

The comparisons of which we shall speak are those between an authoritarian atmosphere and a democratic atmosphere, although a study was also made of groups characterized as "laissez faire." The adult leader (the experimenter) in each group adjusted his behavior so as to produce the desired atmosphere. This was done in the two types of groups by employing the following leadership techniques (see Fig. 14):

Authoritarian	*Democratic*
1. All determination of policy by the leader	1. All policies a matter of group determination, encouraged and drawn out by the leader
2. Techniques and steps of attaining the goal dictated by the leader, one at a time, so that future direction was always uncertain to a large degree	2. Activity perspective given by an explanation of the general steps of the process during discussion at first meeting. Where technical advice was needed, the leader tried to point out two or three alternative procedures from which choice could be made
3. The leader usually dictated the particular work task and work companions of each member	3. The members were free to work with whomever they chose, and the division of tasks was left up to the group.
4. The leader was "personal" in his praise and criticism of the work of each member without giving objective reasons. He remained aloof from active group participation except when demonstrating	4. The leader was "objective" or "fact-minded" in his praise and criticism and tried to be a regular group member in spirit without doing too much of the actual work

Differences in the behavior of the groups were striking. Some of the most interesting differences were as follows:

1. The authoritarian groups tended to be more aggressive or more apathetic than the democratic groups. When aggression was expressed, it tended to be directed toward other group members rather than toward the authoritarian leader. In the authoritarian groups two scapegoats were the targets of such concentrated group hostility that they left the club. In the apathetic authoritarian groups it seemed that the lack of aggression was due merely to repressive influence of the leader; for when he temporarily left the group, aggressive outbursts occurred.

2. In the authoritarian groups there were more submissive approaches to the leader and also more attention-demanding approaches. The approaches to the democratic leader were more friendly and work-minded.

FIG. 14.—Boys' club with an "authoritarian" adult leader (*above*), and a "democratic" adult leader (*below*).   (*Lippitt*, 1940.)

3. In the authoritarian groups the relations with other group members tended to be more aggressive and dominating than in the democratic groups.

4. There seemed to be more "we-feeling" in the democratic groups and more "I-feeling" in the authoritarian. Group unity appeared higher in the democratic groups, and subgroups tended to be more stable than in the authoritarian atmosphere where they tended to disintegrate.

5. Constructiveness of work decreased sharply when the authoritarian leader temporarily absented himself, whereas it dropped only slightly when the democratic leader was absent.

6. Under experimentally induced frustrations in the work situation, the democratic group responded by organized attacks on the difficulty, whereas the authoritarian groups tended to become disrupted through recriminations and personal blame.

General comments.—These experimental findings would seem to argue for superior morale under democratic-type leadership than under authoritarian leadership. But several reservations must be noted. Not all the autocratically led children's groups in the Lewin experiments reacted poorly to authoritarian leadership. Though most children expressed secret preference for the democratic leader, not all did. The submissive groups seemed perfectly satisfied to take orders. That some of these children came from homes which were autocratic in structure is probably revealing. Even in our culture, it seems, authoritarian leadership may often be accepted. Democratic leadership may in the long run be preferred, but the techniques of democratic group living may require a process of learning and growth.

There is some evidence to indicate that people will tend to react favorably to authoritarian leadership patterns especially when they are emotionally insecure or when they find themselves in an ambiguous and critical social situation. It will be remembered that one of the functions of leadership is in the leader's capacity to relieve the individual of responsibilities and decision making. In this connection the findings of Peak (1945) that proportionally more German Protestants than German Catholics adopted the views and ideology of the Nazi party are relevant. In the United States Strategic Bombing Survey (upon whose data Peak based her analysis) a total of 2,033 German Protestant civilians and 1,265 German Catholic civilians were interviewed on various beliefs and attitudes, using the open-end question technique. Forty-three per cent of the Protestants and 31 per cent of the Catholics were found to have pro-Nazi political beliefs and attitudes. Peak suggests that one of the reasons for this difference might be stated as follows: The emotionally insecure German Catholics, in the unstable social order of Germany after the First World War, could find their security needs met by submitting to the monolithic and authoritarian leadership hierarchy of the Catholic Church—a leadership that prescribes precisely and in detail the authoritative course of conduct for all its members. Such a leadership is most efficiently designed to furnish feelings of stability and security for the emotionally insecure and immature individual, for the confused individual living in a confused and changing world. On the other hand, the emotionally insecure and confused German Protestant did not have so elaborate and authoritative a leadership in his church to meet his needs and so he more frequently "found solace in the submission to a *Fuehrer* who left little to individual choice and mapped a clear course to salvation."[1]

However, in most situations and from a long-term point of view, democratic leadership patterns are more conducive to high group morale than are authoritarian patterns. But it is not sufficient, in order to ensure democratic group life, that the formal group situation be set in a way that supposedly meets the democratic roles. The members of such a group, as was indicated in Chap. X, must know how to behave in a democratic atmosphere, how to assume responsibility, how to behave toward other members. Good intentions are not enough; techniques are also necessary. What is true for the members of a group is even more important for the leaders of democratic groups. They must know how to be democratic leaders. To provide the proper atmosphere is the first essential, but more than that the group members and leaders must know *what* to do.

Leadership Training.—There has been traditionally in America and in other democracies a neglect of the problem of leadership training. This has been based on two things: (1) a suspicion of leadership, a feeling that the idea of leadership is somehow incompatible with democracy; (2) a belief that there is no need for leadership training in any case, that "leaders are born, not made." Both notions seem to be giving way to a more positive attitude toward the need for leadership training. It is being more widely recognized that it is not leadership which is incompatible with democracy, but one *kind* of leadership, *viz.*, authoritarian leadership, that, in fact, strong leadership of the right kind is indispensable in a democracy. And it is being more widely appreciated, at least by those who deal directly with the problem of leadership in government, in business, in education, and in all sorts of organizational activity, that the success of a person in a leadership capacity depends less upon inherent features of his personality

[1] Peak points out, however, that ". . . it is an interesting question whether members of Protestant Churches would have been more susceptible than Catholics to a fascist appeal in a nation where submission to authority was a less common national tradition and where individuals had been taught to stand on their own feet." In this connection the student is referred to the discussion of the influence of early (or "primary") group roles upon the individual's new intragroup relations (see especially p. 374, Chap. X).

than upon the skills and attitudes that he possesses and the kind of group atmosphere in which he functions.

The impetus for leadership training comes from many sources. Industry has its problems of foremen and supervisors; business its problems of executives, office managers, etc.; government its various administrative officers; labor its union leaders; education its principals and teachers; the Boy Scouts of America its scout masters. In every organization in our organization-rich society, the problem of leadership training arises.

Much attention has been paid to problems of selection of leadership personnel and the *evaluation* of their performance. Relatively less has been given to *training*. And the emphasis on training has, on the whole, been one-sided. As Bradford and Lippitt (1945) comment:

> It is unfortunate that the majority of books and articles on supervision and group leadership have laid almost their entire stress upon the techniques of group leadership and but little emphasis upon understanding the causes of varying degrees of group productivity and morale resulting from different patterns of leadership . . . . They have turned the attention of the supervisor only toward what he does and not toward the effects of his actions on what the group does.

The training of the supervisor may also, they point out, tend to concentrate on his relations with individuals rather than with the group as a whole:

> Any efficient work group, whether in an industrial establishment or an office, is more than a collection of individuals. It has a personality and unity that grows and changes according to the pressure upon it . . . . It is important to note that frequently supervisors' actions, correct for the individual, prevent rather than develop work efficiency of the group.

Obstacles to retraining.—There are several important obstacles in the retraining of an inadequate leader, assuming in this discussion that inadequacy means failure to employ the kinds of democratic leadership techniques previously described.

1. The leader may fail to recognize that he is in *need of training*. He may not realize that there is anything wrong, that the morale and productivity of the group are not all that they should be. And even if he does know that all is not well, it may not occur to him that he is at fault, that he has it within his power to rectify the group difficulties. He tends often to ascribe the apparent difficulties to outside factors over which he has no control or to the lack of motivation or lack of ability of the people in his group. To put it another way, the leader lacks perspective on his actions.

2. The leader may not have the proper attitudes conducive to the re-

training process. He may not feel that it is desirable for a group to participate in all policy decisions; he may feel that the leader should make the decisions and pass them down to the subordinates; he may regard "democratic" methods in his group as being nothing more than wasteful talk, even though at the same time he subscribes wholeheartedly to the principle of democracy as it applies on the national level. It is one of the greatest obstacles to a retraining of supervisors, teachers, and parents that they have no deep-seated conviction that the work unit, the school, or the family should be run democratically. And, as we have noted above, even when the leader does seem to have the right attitudes, he may, in practice, fail to measure up to them. The supervisor or the parent is often incredulous when it is pointed out to him that he is not running his group on democratic principles. He overlooks the fact that what may from *his* point of view seem democratic may from the other group members' point of view seem the reverse.

3. The personality of the leader may prevent him from being easily retrained. The leader often feels extremely status conscious; he feels a basic sense of personal insecurity which he allays by the demonstration to himself and others of his own leadership role and power. Or he may feel fundamentally inadequate in his responsible position and behave in a particularly dominating and inaccessible way as a cover for this feeling of inadequacy. These feelings of insecurity may be brought out into the light by any retraining attempt. The leader may be ashamed to acknowledge that anything is wrong; he may actively resist the proferred aid of the trainer.

4. The leader may *lack the necessary skills* that are required in the new leadership role. He may recognize the failures of his present method of leadership, he may wish to improve, and he may be unafraid of exposing himself to the personal difficulties involved in changing techniques. But all these will not suffice to make him a democratic leader until he has developed certain basic skills in handling intragroup relations.

The prime job of leadership training is to overcome each of these obstacles. We shall turn now to a discussion of some of the training methods that have proved effective.

An experiment on leadership training.—Bavelas (1942) describes a study in which three WPA supervisors of children's play groups were given training in leadership. Their behavior with the children before and after training was compared with that of a control group of three supervisors who were not given the training. Before training, the leadership of all six supervisors showed various degrees of inadequacy, as demonstrated by several symptoms. The morale of the children was low; the morale of the leaders themselves was low; the method of group control tended to be authoritarian rather than democratic, in the sense that the leaders relied mostly on direct commands as to what the children should do rather than placing responsibility on the children to make wise choices.

After the training program, which lasted three weeks, the three retrained leaders showed marked improvement as compared with the nontrained leaders. They now relied much less on authoritarian methods of control and much more on democratic methods; the morale of the children was improved, as evidenced by increased enthusiasm for the work, more participation in the group activities, higher quality and output of work, and tendency to form larger subgroups within the group (a sign of increased group unity); the morale of the retrained leaders themselves was appreciably raised.

The training process was designed to train "on the job" and to make the training process itself an experience in democratic group activity for the trainees. As Bavelas comments, "It is not an unusual thing to find groups being taught democracy in a completely authoritarian manner." The trainer assumed the role of group leader for the trainees and thus illustrated proper techniques of democratic leadership. In a real degree, the trainee group decided as a group how the details of their training program should be carried out, though, of course, the trainer had a general program in mind.

The aspects of the training program were as follows: (1) the discussion of the attitudes and objectives of recreational group work so that the trainees were able to get a perspective on underlying principles rather than learning a "bag of tricks" which would not be flexible in meeting all sorts of group situations; (2) "sensitizing" the leaders by discussion of what qualities a leader should have, what different possibilities of alternative actions were available to him, etc.; (3) learning of concrete techniques through various processes, such as observing the trainer in handling a group, observation of each other followed by criticism and discussion, having the experience in the training of being the led rather than the leader and thus coming to appreciate morale problems, being shown films of how they themselves had previously conducted groups.

Bavelas emphasizes that this experiment shows, among other things, the danger of assuming that personality traits of leadership are the most significant determining features in how successful the leader is. In a period of three weeks, leaders who had been poor leaders for years were converted into good leaders.

Role playing as a training technique.—The complex skills involved in handling intragroup relations cannot hope to be developed on a verbal level. Here, as with any complex skill, "learning by doing" seems essential.

This presents, however, a technical difficulty in training, for the leader cannot ordinarily be trained in his actual group. One solution to this problem is the use of *role playing* as a training device. In this method, the trainer asks the trainee to act out a role simulating that involved in the actual group leadership situation.[1] In a study reported by Bradford and Lippitt (1945), for instance, supervisors in a business organization met in training groups to discuss the problems they faced in handling the employees under them. After preliminary agreement as to what some of the major problems were, the trainers asked several of the supervisors to assume the role of the supervisor in talking to an employee, *e.g.*, a filing clerk. Another supervisor assumed the employee role. As the incident was acted out, the supervisors as a whole were enabled to see aspects of the problem they had not before appreciated and to gain new perspective on the nature of the relationship with the employees and on their own leadership techniques.

Following such diagnostic role-playing episodes, other role playing was done in order to find solutions to the problems. Here the trainers asked questions and made suggestions as they seemed called for.

The advantages of the role-playing technique are several. It enables the supervisor to gain new perspective on the problems and on his way of handling them. It helps him, by assuming the reverse role of the employee, to get insight into the employees' attitudes and behavior. It dramatizes the points of difficulty in a way that mere verbal discussion cannot do. And it enables the leader to try out the new techniques and become familiar with them in a mock group situation before he must use them in the genuine group situation.

How Leadership Develops.—Under what circumstances does group leadership appear? For one thing, it may be imposed from without, as a product of established social organization. For another thing, it may emerge spontaneously as a product of dynamic group interaction. The latter is the more interesting psychologically and will occupy our attention here.

The emergence of leadership in group formation and growth.—From the very beginning of formation of a group, some members are almost certain to take a more active role than others, to be preferred in interpersonal relations within the membership, to be cast into a relatively more dominating position vis-à-vis other members. This is the beginning of leadership differentiation. Moreno (1934) describes sociometric studies of groups of babies who were observed when placed in close spacial proximity at various

---

[1] "Role playing" as a leadership-training technique is an adaptation of the "psychodrama" to a special purpose. Moreno (1940) originally developed the "psychodrama" technique for purposes of individual diagnosis and therapy in psychiatric cases. For a general discussion of the psychodrama in leadership training see Lippitt, 1943.

ages from birth to three years. The pattern of organization of the group progressed from *isolation* (up to twenty to twenty-eight weeks of age), with virtually no interaction among the individuals, through *horizontal* differentiation (up to forty to forty-two weeks), in which there was interaction with one's immediate neighbors but without clear-cut dominance relations appearing, to *vertical* differentiation (after forty to forty-two weeks), in which several infants began to command disproportionate attention from the group and a "top" and a "bottom" began to develop. This progression (though with some stages much abbreviated or elongated) probably is characteristic of all new group formations. With the stage of "vertical" structuring, leadership emerges. At the very beginning of such differentiation, the personal characteristics of the individuals may be expected to play a much larger role in determining leaders and followers than they will later in the group life. Immediate feelings of like and dislike, for example, will help determine initial group organization, though later these feelings may change and they may not be so absolutely important.[1]

The emergence of leadership in unstable group structures.—Leadership is most likely to develop and to change in states of unstable group structure. We have seen that group structure tends to modify itself naturally in the direction of a more stable structure, and one means by which stability can be increased is through the development of a leader. Conflicting forces among subgroups can sometimes be brought into equilibrium by the addition of forces from the leader, who thus achieves a "balance-of-power" status.

The emergence of leadership in problem situations.—The emergence of leadership is particularly demanded in situations where the progress toward the group goal is blocked or when the group suffers external threats to its security. In such cases there is likely to be lack of cognitive clarity on the part of the group membership as to what steps to take to achieve the goal or to ward off the danger. If at this point, for whatever reason, an individual in the group is *perceived by the group as a means* to the goal or the escape from danger, because of his personal characteristics of bravery or skill or knowledge or self-confidence or anything else, he is then likely to emerge in a leadership status. The leader gains his position, in other words, through a process of reorganization in which he is perceived and reacted to as the means to the group goal.

The emergence of leadership in satisfaction of individual needs.—In listing the functions of leadership, we indicated the importance of the leader as

---

[1] For an experimental study showing, on the other hand, that the sociometric patterns which are formed at the first meeting of a group may sometimes be remarkably similar to those which exist after the group has become well acquainted and stabilized, see Barker (1942).

purveyor of rewards and punishments within the group, as exemplar, as symbol of the group, as surrogate for individual responsibility, as father figure, and as scapegoat. We have also spoken (page 382) of the various accessory needs, beyond mere attainment of the group goal, which group membership serves in the individual. Whenever there arise such individual needs for prestige and recognition and participation and for identification with and vicarious satisfaction in the group, and whenever emotions of fear and love and anger become intense in the members of a group, the time is auspicious for the appearance of a leader who can serve these various needs and emotions.

The emergence of leadership in response to the needs of the leader.—The appearance of group leadership, like all aspects of group functioning, is a dynamic process. Leadership is a *relationship* between subparts of the whole structure, and in understanding it we must, therefore, consider not only the factors in the group situation as a whole and in the needs and perceptions of the individual members but also *the psychology of the leader*. There are situations in which the group is developing, its structure is unstable, it faces problems in achievement of its goals, its members have pressing needs and emotions, which in all ways are auspicious for the emergence of leadership and yet in which no leadership does appear. In such circumstances the group is likely to disintegrate. The reason that no leadership makes its appearance is that one significant factor has been left out of consideration—the potential leader himself. To understand fully the emergence of leadership we must, then, consider the needs of the leader.

Like any member, the leader seeks achievement of the group goal and seeks also the satisfaction of personal or accessory needs. But what marks off the leader from the nonleader is the urgency of certain kinds of needs that are especially well served by the leadership role. Such needs are those of dominance, power, and prestige. If the group situation is one that requires leadership (for the reasons cited above), and if there are members of the group who have needs that will be satisfied through the leadership function, then we can assuredly expect that leadership will emerge.

The Characteristics of Leaders.—When leadership in a group does emerge, it makes its appearance in the person of some members and not others. What are the characteristics of the leader that set him off from the nonleader?

(1) It should be emphasized that there is not a true dichotomy of leaders and nonleaders. Every individual may, given the proper group and the proper situation, come to serve as a leader. (2) There is not a perfect correlation in the relative potentialities of leadership among people in all types

of groups and situations. An individual who is a leader in some groups and situations may not be a leader in others. However, it is true that there is a substantial correlation. People who are leaders in one group and situation tend more than the average to be leaders in other groups and situations. There do seem to be certain personal characteristics that serve rather generally to differentiate people in leadership potentiality.

Personality and needs of leaders.—Other things being equal, those persons who have insistent needs for dominance, power, and prestige may be expected to have higher potentiality for leadership. And this is particularly true to the extent to which these persons have developed personalities that are characterized by certain ways of satisfying these needs, *viz.*, in dominating interpersonal relations with others.

Skills and attitudes of leaders.—Aside from personality and needs, the potential leader must have the skills in interpersonal relationships, the techniques for handling people and groups, and the capacities for planning, making decisions, and executing them that are an integral part of leadership functioning. Leaders may need high intellectual abilities as well as a fund of expert information and technical competence. And the attitudes of the leader must fit the group and the situation in which he is to operate. Thus, a democratic leader requires certain attitudes about democratic leadership, just as an authoritarian leader requires appropriate attitudes about authoritarian leadership.

Perceived qualities of leaders.—And finally, not only must the leader need the leadership role and be actually qualified in skill and attitudes to occupy it, he must be *perceived by the group members* as having the appropriate leadership qualities. Thus, it has been shown that imposing physical stature, a "strong" face, a persuasive voice and manner, an air of self-confidence and competence all predispose the group to accept an individual as leader. And to the extent that he has perceived qualities which call out feelings of love, liking, respect, admiration, submissiveness, and sometimes even fear, the leader is likely to be more successful.

SUMMARY

Two characteristics of social groups of great interest for the student of group dynamics and for the man of affairs are group morale and group leadership. The purpose of this chapter is stated as the analysis of group morale and leadership and the extension of the principles of group dynamics that were examined in Chap. X.

It is suggested that the term *group morale* can best be defined by the criteria used to determine "high" or "low" morale. These criteria are listed and illustrated by reference to a morale study of two naval air squadrons. Seven "positive" determinants of high group morale are discussed and illustrated. These are (1) positive goals, (2) satisfaction of accessory needs, (3) sense of advance to the goal, (4) relations between the level of aspiration and level of achievement, (5) time perspective, (6) equality of sacrifice or gain within the group, (7) feelings of solidarity, identification, and involvement. In connection with the last of these, several suggestions are made concerning methods of increasing group identification. Finally, some discussion is given to "negative" determinants of high morale, and it is pointed out that although fear and danger from an out-group may sometimes make for high morale within a group, this will usually happen only when the members of the group already have some cohesiveness and sense of solidarity. It is further suggested, on the basis of some experimental evidence, that the morale induced by negative factors differs in several respects from that induced by positive factors.

The second major part of the chapter is given over to a discussion of group leadership. It is first pointed out that the group leader is of central importance to the morale of the group and that to understand the characteristics of a good leader it is necessary to examine the functions of a leader, the various types of leadership that can be employed, and how to train good leaders.

Fourteen different common functions of leaders are briefly described. These include the leader as an executive, as planner, as policy maker, as expert, as external group representative, as controller of internal relationships, as purveyor of rewards and punishments, as arbitrator and mediator, as exemplar, as group symbol, as surrogate for individual responsibility, as ideologist, as father figure, and as scapegoat.

In discussing the types of leadership, two major patterns are differentiated—the authoritarian and democratic. These two types are compared with respect to the resulting group motivation, group morale, and group structure. The conclusion is made, on the basis of this examination and with reference to the available experimental material, that in general a superior group morale is found under democratic-type leadership than under the authoritarian type. However it is also pointed out that when people are emotionally insecure or when they find themselves in ambiguous and critical social situations, they will tend to react favorably to authoritative leadership patterns. This is illustrated by reference to the differential receptivity of the German Protestants and Catholics to Nazi ideology. Finally, it is emphasized that in order to ensure democratic group life both the members and leaders of the group must possess certain democratic skills.

In discussing the *training* of democratic leadership, four major obstacles to the retraining of an inadequate leader are examined. These are the failure of the leader to recognize that he is in need of training, the necessity of changing the social attitudes of the individual, personality difficulties which may prevent the individual from being easily retrained, and the lack of certain specific skills. Role playing as a technique for training leaders is then described and illustrated with a study that reports the training of a group of supervisors in a business organization.

The next section of the chapter is given over to a discussion of how leadership develops in groups. The emergence of leadership in various group situations and in response to various group and individual needs is examined, and in the final section the characteristics of leaders are discussed. It is emphasized here that there is not a true dichotomy of leaders and nonleaders, and it is suggested that every individual, given the proper group and the proper situation, may come to serve as a leader. However, it is pointed out that, other things being equal, those persons who have insistent needs for dominance, power, and prestige and certain interpersonal skills may be expected to have higher potentiality for leadership. Finally, it is also pointed out that the leader must be *perceived* by the group members as having the appropriate leadership qualities for the particular group.

BIBLIOGRAPHY

ALLPORT, G. W.: 1942. The nature of democratic morale. *In* Watson, G. (ed.), *Civilian morale*. Boston: Houghton.

ALLPORT, G. W.: 1945. The psychology of participation. *Psychol. Rev.*, **52**, 117–132.

BARKER, R. G.: 1942. The social interrelations of strangers and acquaintances. *Sociometry*, **5**, 169–179.

BAVELAS, A.: 1942. Morale and the training of leaders. *In* Watson, G. (ed.), *Civilian morale*. Boston: Houghton.

BAVELAS, A., and LEWIN, K.: 1942. Training in democratic leadership. *J. abnorm. soc. Psychol.*, **37**, 115–119.

BRADFORD, L. P., and LIPPITT, R.: 1945. *Supervisory training for group leadership.* Cambridge: Publ. Research Center Grp. Dynamics.

FRENCH, T. M.: 1942. The psychodynamic problem of democracy. *In* Watson, G. (ed.), *Civilian morale*. Boston: Houghton.

FROMM, E.: 1941. *Escape from freedom.* New York: Farrar & Rinehart.

GORDON, M. M.: 1940. Discriminatory leadership and its effect on the relations between the more and the less privileged sub-groups. Department of Psychology, Univ. Iowa (Unpublished Doctoral Dissertation).

JENKINS, J. G.: 1947. The nominating technique, its uses and limitations. Paper delivered at Eastern Psychological Association Annual Meeting, Atlantic City, April.

LEWIN, K.: 1942. Time perspective and morale. *In* Watson, G. (ed.), *Civilian morale*. Boston: Houghton.

LEWIN, K., LIPPITT, R., and WHITE, R. K.: 1939. Patterns of aggressive behavior in experimentally created social climates. *J. soc. Psychol.*, **10**, 271–301.

LINTON, R.: 1936. *The study of man.* New York: Appleton-Century.

LIPPITT, R.: 1939. Field theory and experiment in social psychology: autocratic and democratic group atmospheres. *Amer. J. Sociol.*, 45, 26–49.

LIPPITT, R.: 1940. An experimental study of the effect of democratic and authoritarian group atmospheres. *Univ. Ia. Stud.*, 16, No. 3, 43–198.

LIPPITT, R.: 1942. The morale of youth groups. *In* Watson, G. (ed.), *Civilian morale.* Boston: Houghton.

LIPPITT, R.: 1943. The psychodrama in leadership training. *Sociometry*, 6, 286–292.

LIPPITT, R., and WHITE, R.: 1943. The "social climate" of children's groups. *In* Barker, Kounin, and Wright (eds.), *Child behavior and development.* New York: McGraw-Hill.

MORENO, J. L.: 1934. *Who shall survive?* Washington: Nerv. Ment. Dis. Publ. Co.

MORENO, J. L.: 1940. Psychodrama and mental catharsis. *Sociometry*, 3, 209–244.

PEAK, H.: 1945. Observations on the characteristics and distribution of German Nazis. *Psychol. Monogr.*, 59, No. 276.

United States Strategic Bombing Survey: 1946. *The effects of bombing on German morale.* Washington: Government Printing Office.

WATSON, G.: 1942. Five factors in morale. *In* Watson, G. (ed.), *Civilian morale.* Boston: Houghton.

WRIGHT, E.: 1940. The influence of frustration upon the social relations of young children. Department of Psychology, Univ. Iowa (Unpublished Ph.D. Dissertation).

PART THREE

APPLICATIONS

CHAPTER XII

RACIAL PREJUDICE IN THE UNITED STATES

Large numbers of Americans agree that the problem of racial prejudice is a pressing national problem. The elimination of this prejudice has served as the subject of innumerable books and tracts; has provided the theme for many of our novels and dramas; has enlisted the efforts of civic, political, labor, religious, educational, and cultural groups; and has become an official government concern. Racial prejudice has been characterized as "the myth that threatens America" and has been diagnosed as "the disease of hate." Almost every ill that can beset a nation has been ascribed to its baneful influence, ranging from debilitating economic waste to the ultimate danger of social chaos. Pearl Buck, the writer, prophesies, "race prejudice is not only a shadow over the colored—it is a shadow over all of us . . . . The world will close down on us some day if race prejudice goes on dividing us."[1] These forebodings and concerns motivate the thinking and acting of many Americans. There are today, in the United States, perhaps as many civic organizations devoted to wrestling with this one problem as with any other single problem on our social scene.

Racial prejudice has been a concern not only of the citizen but also of the social scientist. It has received more concentrated scientific study by social psychologists and sociologists than almost any other aspect of our social behavior. As a consequence we have better observational, clinical, psychometric, and experimental data about racial prejudice than about any other kind of belief and attitude found among the American people.

As was pointed out in Chap. I, a major problem of society becomes a major problem of applied social psychology. The fact that racial prejudice is a current problem of deep concern for so many members of our society demands that any treatise of social psychology give it serious consideration. The added fact that so much research has been done on racial prejudice makes possible a detailed application of the general principles discussed in Parts One and Two of this book to this specific problem. As we have seen, an analysis of specific social problems requires both general principles and data specific to the problem—and we have both.

[1] Quoted by Baruch (1946) in her *Glass House of Prejudice.*

The present chapter, then, will present an analysis of racial prejudice in the United States today. The following chapter will present a program designed to eliminate this prejudice from among our people.

GENERAL CONSIDERATIONS

In Chap. V the term *prejudice* was defined as referring "to attitudes and beliefs that serve to place the objects of the attitudes and beliefs at an *advantage* or *disadvantage*." As a specification of that general definition, the term *racial prejudice* is to be defined as referring to attitudes or beliefs concerning any minority racial, ethnic, or national group that are *disadvantageous* to the members of that group. In such a definition, therefore, the word "racial" is used in its popular and not anthropological or scientific meaning. It covers such groups of people as Negroes, Jews, and Irish. These groups and others are minority groups in the United States in the sense that they differ from the dominant group with respect to race, culture, or nationality origin. The use of the term *racial* does not necessarily imply any fundamental biological differences between these minority groups and the dominant group. The general principles discussed in this chapter are also applicable to other forms of minority-group prejudices.

As was also pointed out in Chap. V, when we talk about the "same" attitude or belief of different people, we are, strictly speaking, discussing different beliefs and attitudes. Although the general aspect of a commonly held belief may be the same, the specific contents of the same belief vary tremendously from person to person. This is particularly important to keep in mind when discussing racial prejudice among the people of the United States. The beliefs and attitudes of racial prejudice currently held by millions of Americans vary significantly not only in content but also in clarity, specificity, strength, importance, and verifiability. Racial prejudice has different functional meanings for the different people who hold such beliefs and results in widely different actions. Racial prejudice need not always, for example, involve active aggression. In many cases (and perhaps most) it results in passive avoidance of the minority group by the prejudiced person or in the withdrawal of certain privileges (privileges common to the rest of Americans) from the members of the minority group or in scarcely noticeable discriminatory behavior of all kinds. But what is common to all racial prejudice is the *direction* of the belief or the *sign* of the attitude. The net effect of these beliefs and attitudes is that the object of the prejudice (the Chinese, the Italian) is placed at some disadvantage. The diverse nature of beliefs and attitudes of racial prejudice, however, makes the problem of diagnosis an extremely difficult one, as we shall soon see, and, correspondingly, makes the problem of therapy even more difficult.

The Problem of Diagnosis.—On the basis of the theoretical considerations in Chaps. V and VI it is obvious that any diagnosis of racial prejudice must be a multidimensional one. We must examine the motivational, emotional, perceptual, and cognitive processes involved. This sets the problem, at the outset, as *a problem in the psychology of the individual.* We must seek primarily to diagnose *individuals*, not American *culture* or American *people as a whole.* We must diagnose the contemporary and infinitely varied needs, emotional experiences, demands, frustrations, problems, and larger belief systems of millions of individual Americans. This is not to deny, of course, that it is essential to know a great deal about the American cultural pattern, for we have seen in Chap. VI that cultural factors play a very significant role in determining the development of beliefs and attitudes. Without appreciating this fact no amount of individual analysis can give us an adequate etiology of racial prejudice in the individual. We shall therefore include in this chapter an examination of some sociological data. But the critical point to remember is that American history, American culture, American economic organizations and practices are relevant for our present problem only in terms of how they are perceived by the prejudiced individual, how they influence him in creating and satisfying his needs and demands, how they expose him to emotional experiences, and how they provide him with environmental supports for his perceptions. In other words, to state our problem as a problem in the psychology of the individual is not to limit the kind of data we will examine but is to specify the unit of analysis (see pages 13 *ff.*, Chap. I, for a further discussion of this problem).

In the analysis in this chapter, the diagnosis will be limited to two major questions: (1) How and why does the American, here and now, acquire beliefs and attitudes of racial prejudice, and (2) what cultural and psychological factors operate to maintain such beliefs and attitudes once they are acquired? We will leave relatively unexplored a third area in the etiology of racial prejudice—the *historical* development of racial prejudice in the United States—because such an analysis is only of peripheral interest to our present problem.

Significance of historical origin of racial prejudice.—The *origins* of the causative conditions of racial prejudice can frequently be traced to political, geographic, legal, and economic accident and are, essentially, of little psychological interest. We might illustrate this by the early history of anti-Negro attitudes in the United States. There is no doubt that our present complex racial problem with respect to the Negro started with a simple and primary economic practice. Africans were brought here as slaves to labor in the fields and create wealth for the white planter. What happened once the Negro came here is again, in large part, ascribable to "historical accident." Tannenbaum (1947) has proposed the thesis that the reason the Negro become a problem of racial prejudice in the United States, while he did so to a much smaller extent in South America, is primarily due to the different laws and customs with respect to slavery that existed in these two areas *before the first Negro ever appeared in either area.* There are many historical and economic reasons why these laws and customs differed in these two areas; but in a sense, it was sheer accident that north of the Rio Grande the imported African found himself a "victim" of such laws and south of the Rio Grande a "beneficiary" of such laws. In turn, then, it can be seen as accidental that in the United States the Negro became the "Negro problem" whereas in Brazil he did not. There was, in other words, nothing inherent in the biology or psychological processes of the Negro, North American, or South American, that has brought about that difference. Thus, as Tannenbaum points out, slaves were not new to the Spanish dominated countries.

At the end of the fifteenth century there were numerous slaves in Portugal and Spain . . . among them not only Negroes, but Moors, Jews, and apparently Spaniards as well.... But the mere survival of slavery in itself is perhaps less important than the persistence of a long tradition of slave law that had come down through Justinian Code . . . the slave had a body of law, protective of him as a human being, which was already there when the Negro arrived and had been elaborated long before he came upon the scene. And when he did come, the Spanish law and *mores* knew him as a slave and made him the beneficiary of the ancient legal heritage.... Slavery had thus from a very early date... moved from a "status" or "caste," "by law of nature," or because of "innate inferiority," or because of the "just judgment and provision of holy script," to become a mere matter of an available sum of money for redemption.

This situation which confronted the African slave in South America is compared with that confronting him in the British-dominated colonies up north:

. . . the experience of nations other than those of the Iberian Peninsula was very different. They had long since lost all vestiges of slavery and a slave code. In neither tradition, policy, nor law was there room for the slave . . . . The fact that the slave was a Negro merely added to the confusion; it did not create it . . . . In the absence of either religious or legal provision for the slave, it was not illogical for the planters . . . to settle the legal issue involved by legally defining the slave as chattel . . . . This legal definition carried its own moral consequences and made ultimate redefinition of the Negro as a moral person most difficult. If only the Negro could be a slave—only the Negro and no one else—the question soon arose: Why the Negro? A whole series of explanations was soon devised to justify slavery for the Negro.

To summarize, Tannenbaum proposes the thesis (which his analysis and data seem to support in a compelling way) that because of the differences in law and custom existing among the Spanish-dominated countries in America, as compared with the British-dominated countries, even before the Negro ever appeared on this continent as a slave, he was considered as the moral and biological equal of the master in South America but in North America as "chattel property" with none of the human attributes. Because of these differences in the legal status of the Negro, the resulting attitudes and beliefs about him differed tremendously in the two parts of the continent. One of the reasons, therefore, why Brazil does not have a Negro problem, while the United States does, stems from this historical accident.

But the above analysis is an historical one; and although it may help tell us why the American of the eighteenth century was racially prejudiced, it is of very little aid in telling us why an American of the twentieth century develops and maintains anti-Negro beliefs and attitudes. Whatever the historical process, in other words, we must look at the United States as it is now and examine the American as he behaves today if we are to make a psychologically meaningful diagnosis of his beliefs and attitudes of racial prejudice.

THE FUNCTIONAL CHARACTER OF RACIAL PREJUDICE

It should be clear from Chaps, V and VI that all beliefs and attitudes are functional in character. Our first step in diagnosis, therefore, must concern itself with a motivational analysis of racial prejudice. We must ask what needs and demands are being satisfied for the individual by his beliefs and attitudes of racial prejudice—how does racial prejudice serve the person in the solution of his own problems?

The specific needs that can be served by racial prejudice are as varied as man's needs themselves. This forces the analyst to take two different approaches to the motivational analysis of prejudice. If he is interested in diagnosing the prejudice of a single individual, the most fruitful approach would be to make a detailed and specific analysis of the need structure of the particular person concerned. This is, essentially, the method of the clinician treating a patient. On the other hand, if he is interested in analyzing the prejudices of millions of Americans, such a detailed approach is impossible, and he must resort to a kind of statistical classification. The only feasible thing to do is to list the types of need-prejudice patterns—the major categories of functions served by beliefs and attitudes of prejudice. In other words, instead of dealing with specific demands and needs, we can deal only with general classes of demands and needs.

In considering such major categories, it is essential to keep two cautions always in mind if the listing of such general categories is not to be misinterpreted. In the first place, many prejudices cannot be assigned to any one category. There may be no pure types in nature. Any one belief or attitude of prejudice may serve several functions. In listing these different categories we are admittedly abstracting and purifying for purposes of exposition and analysis. The second caution to remember is related to our basic proposition that the diagnosis of any belief or attitude must be multidimensional. It is tempting and easy, when listing the various needs served by racial prejudice, to exaggerate the explanatory value of the functional nature of racial prejudice. But *a motivational analysis presents only one aspect of the problem and is only the beginning of a diagnosis.* The failure to pay adequate attention to this limitation has led to many incomplete "explanations" of racial prejudice. Clinical literature is replete with such theories of prejudice. The behavior of man is explicable only in terms of his entire psychological field, not in terms of any one process characteristic of such fields. That is exactly why, as was pointed out in the introduction to Chap. V, a psychological analysis must have recourse to higher order units of analysis—units that involve motivational, emotional, and cognitive processes.

With these two cautions in mind, then, we can turn to a consideration of the major functional types of racial prejudice among the American people today.

Racial Prejudice and Pathological Personality Systems.—Although beliefs and attitudes of prejudice describable as attributes of the mentally sick are relatively rare—since many more than the mentally sick have such prejudices—there can be no doubt that they exist. Racial prejudice is found among the sadists, the patients with "free-floating aggressions," the paranoiacs. It must be emphasized, however, that not all such mentally sick people necessarily develop racial prejudice, nor, of course, are all racially prejudiced people sadists or paranoiacs. We have seen in Chap. VI that there can be no simple correlation between personality structure and specific beliefs and attitudes. The point is, however, that the pathological individual can, and sometimes does, develop beliefs and attitudes of racial prejudice that rationalize and support his deviant behavior, and any account of the motivational and emotional tensions that lie behind racial prejudice must take this functional type (and, as we shall soon see, socially important type) of prejudice into account.

Free-floating aggressions and racial prejudice.—As was pointed out in Chap. II (pages 41 *f.*), the conscious correlates of tensions frequently exist as uncrystallized emotions which have no specific reference to particular objects. Clinical practice abounds with cases of people who experience intense and almost continuous free-floating aggressions, which are likely to spread into all aspects of the individual's personality and to influence all of his behavior. The tensions of these people can be dissipated only through attack on others. And since, as we have also seen, characteristic modes of tension reduction may be learned and fixated by the individual (Proposition V, page 62), these people, in a given culture, can learn to direct their aggressive behavior against a specific racial group. The beliefs and attitudes lying behind and rationalizing such directed aggression in these people can be seen as racial prejudice in the service of pathological aggression.

Paranoia and racial prejudice.—Closely related to the above functional type of racial prejudice is that which may develop in individuals suffering from the mental disease of paranoia. The paranoiac has been described as a person who is not capable of understanding other people and who continually attributes all sorts of sinister motives and deeds to other people. The paranoiac lives in a world of dire suspicions; and, again, *if and when* he fixates these suspicions (or "delusions") on members of a specific racial group, we have beliefs and attitudes in the service of the peculiar needs of the pathological paranoiac. These beliefs and attitudes give meaning to his actions and justify his behavior.[1]

General comments.—Though perhaps insignificant in number, the people who have racial prejudices of this type can occasionally be strong in influence. Because of the intensity and high saliency of their attitudes, these people are frequently found among the leaders of antiracial mobs, organizations, movements, and even ideologies. Because, in other words, of the structure of their psychological fields, their racial prejudices have very low thresholds (see page 164), and these are the people who seek out targets against which to aggress. They do not wait for the "incident" to occur; they help create incidents. They constitute the "lunatic fringe" of the racially prejudiced.

Racial Prejudice in Support of Aggression Induced by Frustration of Various Needs.—Not all aggressive impulses, however, are free floating and experienced almost continuously. We have seen, in the discussion of Proposition IV in the chapter on dynamics of behavior, that accumulated tensions arising out of persistent frustration of almost *any* significant need often find expression in aggressive acts which seem temporarily to allay the frustrated state. The targets of such aggression are not necessarily related logically to the frustrating situation. When the aggression is directed against a racial group as the target, the conditions are created for the development of a belief or attitude of racial prejudice that will rationalize such normal aggression.

[1] For a brief statement of the possible role of paranoia in racial prejudice, especially in anti-Semitism, see Allport (1944).

An experiment by Miller and Bugelski (described in Dollard, Doob, et al., 1939) indicates how even the frustration of a relatively unimportant and casual need—one that is altogether unrelated to racial factors—can display itself in increased feelings of racial antipathy. These experimenters took advantage of a frustrating situation in a natural setting at a boys' camp for their investigation:

> By chance it was known that, as a part of a general testing program, boys at camp were going to be forced to sacrifice a portion of their leisure activity in order to take long, dull examinations composed of questions which, on the whole, were too difficult for them to answer. At the outset the boys were relatively unaware of what was in store for them. Later it became obvious that the tests were running overtime and preventing them from . . . attending Bank Night at the local theater; thus they were compelled to miss what they considered to be the most interesting event of the week. In order to exploit this situation . . . all of the boys were given brief attitude tests before and after the main examination. Half of them rated Mexicans before and Japanese afterwards. As would be expected, the attitude toward either set of foreigners was more unfavorable after the frustration of taking the examinations and missing Bank Night than before.

Man's possible frustrations range from the rather trivial one illustrated above to the more profound ones that affect his most basic and most permanent needs. Thus beliefs and attitudes of racial prejudice which serve to support aggressions induced by frustration can derive from economic, social, political, or sexual frustration. As some psychologists have pointed out, the history of growing up and living as an adult in modern society is a history of continuous and persistent frustrations.[1] For some individuals this frustration may be chronic and may be seen as an almost inevitable reflection of their status in society. Thus Doob, in Dollard's book (1937) *Caste and Class in a Southern Town*, characterizes the "poor whites" of the South as "a frustrated class" and presents some convincing data in support of such an analysis. For some people, the experience of significant frustration may be intermittent and give rise to acute but temporary aggressive impulses. But the universality of some degree of frustration among people in our culture suggests that the incidence of aggressive impulses deriving from such frustration is probably very great.

Limitations of frustration-aggression hypothesis.—This situation has so impressed a number of social psychologists as to lead them to espouse the theory that *all* racial prejudice can be ascribed, from the motivational point of view, to the frustration-aggression sequence. Although such a

---

[1] For one such analysis, see Dollard, Doob, *et al.* (1939), Chap. 4, titled "Socialization in America."

theory is a tempting one and superficially plausible, it does not appear to be consistent with everything we know about racial prejudice or frustration. It is, in a sense, another illustration of the error that was warned against in Chap. VI (see especially page 197)—the attempt to find *one* motive or emotion, common for all people, behind any commonly held belief or attitude.

The arguments against such a motivational theory are many. For one thing, not all beliefs and attitudes of prejudice involve aggression—unless we strain our definition of aggression. In many of the more subtle and socially more significant prejudice patterns, withdrawal from a minority group is accompanied by genuinely felt "good wishes" for its welfare. In many such cases there is no evidence of aggressions. In the second place, it is extremely difficult, if not impossible, to demonstrate that all people who are racially prejudiced have suffered more frustrations than people who are not racially prejudiced. Finally, as we have seen in Chap. II, frustration does not always lead to aggressive tendencies—a number of alternative tension-reduction techniques are commonly found in frustration. Although we need not accept the frustration-aggression sequence as an all-explanatory motivational analysis of racial prejudice, nevertheless there can be no doubt that beliefs and attitudes of racial prejudice in the support of frustration-induced aggression are very common.

Racial Prejudice and Culturally Disapproved Behavior.—Clinical studies have amassed a wealth of data to substantiate the conclusion that, at least within our culture, many people have strong impulses of cruelty, greed, sexual aggression, etc., which society indicts and which, therefore, the individual is forced to control because of his fear of social repercussions and because of his need to maintain his self-regard as a member in good standing in his culture. Similarly, there are many needs and demands that society regards as desirable but that the individual may attempt to satisfy through means that are socially disapproved. In the attempt to solve either of these difficulties, cognitive reorganizations can take place that will eventuate in beliefs or attitudes of racial prejudice.

Racial prejudice and culturally disapproved needs.—When an individual finds himself in a situation where some of his persistent needs are culturally disapproved, the resulting blocking or conflict of needs can lead, as we have seen, to a cognitive reorganization where the nature of the act that can satisfy these needs is so reinterpreted as to remove the "baseness" from the need behind the act. And when such reinterpretation necessitates certain disadvantageous ways of regarding the members of a specific racial group, then we have an instance of racial prejudice in support of culturally disapproved needs. As Redl (1946) points out,

These suppressed impulses must find an outlet, and frequently express themselves in ways for which there is presumptive alibi. A common way is for a person to say to himself, "You couldn't do this to a 'white man' (a person of your own group), but when I do it to a person of another group it doesn't count (because he isn't really a person at all)"! For such suppressed impulses of greed, cruelty, and so forth, prejudice may serve as a good disguise.

Racial prejudice and culturally disapproved means.—Many Americans may have strong needs for political eminence or for wealth. These needs are recognized by our society as good needs, as needs that all enterprising Americans might have.   When the individual, in the service of such socially approved needs, engages in socially disapproved action and rationalizes this action by ascribing undesirable or disparaging attributes to racial groups, we have another instance of beliefs and attitudes in the support of socially disapproved behavior.   Thus, for example, the Southern politician who prevents the Negro from voting (through fear that the Negro's vote may block the Southerner's political aspirations) on the grounds that "The mental level of those people renders them incapable of suffrage"[1] may be using a belief of racial prejudice to rationalize behavior in the service of a socially approved need.   Or the businessman who cheats the Mexican laborer (in order to increase his own wealth) on the grounds that "Mexicans would only use the money to get drunk" may similarly be using prejudice in the service of what is basically a culturally approved need.

An illuminating illustration of a deliberate attempt to reinterpret socially disapproved behavior so as to make it socially acceptable by appealing to beliefs and attitudes of religious antipathy is found in the recruiting speech of Pope Urban II in the eleventh century to the people at Clermont, France:

Let those who have formerly been accustomed to contend wickedly in private warfare against the faithful, fight against the infidel. Let those who have hitherto been robbers, now become soldiers. Let those who have formerly contended against their brothers and relatives fight against the barbarians as they ought.

Racial Prejudice in the Service of Repressed Tensions.—Culturally disapproved needs may find expression through building up "presumptive alibis" for their expression, and this may result in beliefs and attitudes of racial prejudice as we have seen above.   But sometimes, culturally disapproved needs—especially those which conflict with the moral ideology of the person—are repressed.   In other words, as was pointed out in Chap. II,

[1] This is a direct quotation from a speech of a Democratic senator of a Southern state, delivered during the first session of the 80th Congress.

unsatisfied needs may be subjected to forces that render them inaccessible to consciousness, "the individual 'forgets' the unsatisfied need." However, as was also pointed out in that discussion, this does not mean that the repressed tensions are made impotent or that the tensions are resolved. The further fate of such repressed effects is to be seen in projection, among other ways. When the projection is of such a sort as to ascribe uncomplimentary attributes to a specific race, we have an instance of a belief or attitude of prejudice in the service of repressed tensions.

An illustrative study.—The study of Frenkel-Brunswik and Sanford (1945) to which we referred in Chap. II is rich with illustrations of this functional pattern in prejudice. After administering a test of anti-Semitism to a group of approximately one hundred University of California students (76 per cent of whom were women), they selected out for intensive clinical study those students who earned extreme scores on the anti-Semitic scale (at either end of the scale). Among the techniques and devices they used were clinical interviews, the Thematic Apperception Tests, and the Rorschach test. On the basis of the resulting data, the investigators felt that they were able to get a fair picture of the need structures (including the repressed needs) of their anti-Semitic subjects.

The anti-Semitic girls "declared without exception that they liked their parents" and tended to show, on the surface, an uncritical devotion to their parents. However, in the Thematic Apperception Test of these same subjects, *aggressive* themes were found to stand out. The writers give the following illustrations of the aggressive themes against parents and men that occurred:

In story No. 1, of Case 6, a murder is being committed; in story No. 3, the husband has lost both legs, and the father is mentioned only to tell us that he has been killed; in story No. 4, a man is being foiled and captured; in No. 5, a man has been killed; in story No. 6, the hero is being convicted and severely punished. Very similar are the stories of Case 4, in story No. 3, the father and son are both killed; in story No. 4, the man is a traitor; in story No. 5, he is sent to the concentration camp; in story No. 6, the hero is electrocuted; and in story No. 10, the hero is burned to death and the father killed in battle . . . . By way of contrast, in the stories of Case 1 and Case 13, both extremely low on anti-Semitism, nobody gets murdered or killed. On the whole, little aggression is manifested.

In general, then, the anti-Semitic girls' Thematic Apperception Test responses indicated repressed hatred, meanness, jealousy, and suspicion toward parental figures. And, Frenkel-Brunswik and Sanford suggest, these repressed tendencies and tensions find outlet in feelings and attitudes of antipathy against various racial groups which serve as scapegoats.

There are other indications of the mechanism of repression in the anti-racial beliefs and attitudes of these girls. "For instance, in responding to the question 'what would you do if you had only six months to live?' the girls high on anti-Semitism never mention sensual pleasures, while the low ones frequently do . . . . Sexual strivings which are kept repressed have acquired a dangerous and sadistic connotation." And the authors conclude, "An important tendency of the girls high on anti-Semitism is thus to keep one's basic impulses repressed, to keep oneself pure and reputable. *Primitive needs are rendered ego-alien and projected onto an alien group.*"[1]

General comments.—The implications of this study, however, must be realistically evaluated. It must be emphasized that the picture drawn above is based on a very selected sample. In the first place, the subjects were all college girls coming from a fairly restricted group and family background. In the second place, the above description is based on only those girls who were high in anti-Semitism, *i.e.*, who had intense attitudes of racial prejudice. And finally, the description is essentially a composite one and does not do justice to the individual differences among the subjects. This description, then, is not to be interpreted as a description of "the personality" of the anti-Semitic individual. We must guard constantly against overgeneralization from such data. However, these data do indicate the very real possibility that the mechanisms which the personality adopts in reaction to repressed tensions—in the effort to reduce the tensions—may involve projecting onto minority groups certain "base" attributes or may involve the diverting of aggressions from parental figures to these minority groups. *If and when* that happens, we have an instance of beliefs and attitudes in the service of repressed tensions.

Racial Prejudice in the Service of Meaning in Ambiguous Crisis Situations.—We have seen in Chap. V that man must make sense out of any situation that is close to him and involves his way of life, his circumstances, his daily behavior. And so he does. The fundamental processes of cognitive organization and reorganization operate so as to make the development of beliefs inevitable. When his usual stock of beliefs can no longer encompass his recurrent experiences, then he will frequently seek and adopt new beliefs that do. In such "crisis" situations, the individual, frequently in response to the only available interpretation offered to him by the educational and propagandistic media of our culture, may resort to beliefs and attitudes of racial prejudice. Thus, for example, in a period of economic crisis, when the small businessman and the worker suddenly find themselves in such a crisis situation, when they see a country rich in natural

[1] Italics our own.

resources and general know-how slump into a depression, when their own homes and businesses and jobs are threatened, the relatively vague beliefs they have held about the economic operation of the country are no longer adequate. They seek "understandable explanations" of the depression.

If at such time they are provided with a concrete "explanation" that "the international Jew" has created this situation by his "monopolistic and wicked machinations," and if they are offered no alternative explanations, they may be quick to accept such an interpretation.

Historical studies of anti-Semitism, for example, have shown a fairly clear correlation between such periods of social crisis and anti-Semitism. Periods of unrest when corruption in government appears on a large scale or when caste and class lines are drawn more closely; periods of national calamity, especially after a disastrous war; periods of economic depression; and periods of political instability are periods when anti-Semitism has flourished, grown in scope and intensity.[1]

The beliefs and attitudes of prejudice adopted at such times, it must be stressed, do not necessarily involve any suppressed or repressed needs, pathological aggressive tendencies, etc.—although they may do so; and where they are present, the beliefs and attitudes are more readily adopted. Fundamentally, however, beliefs and attitudes of prejudice of this sort operate *in the service of meaning.* Man, as we have repeatedly stressed, is an organizing animal, and the "best" of men, emotionally mature and with no more than the "normal" share of repressed aggressions, can end up with beliefs and attitudes of racial prejudice as a consequence of this need for meaning when they lack other information and interpretations. People in a crisis situation cannot long stand ambiguity. In such a situation, no one is immune to propaganda, as was clearly emphasized in the chapter on propaganda. To interpret racial prejudice that occurs in such a situation as "latent aggression" or as an instance of the "scapegoat" phenomenon is frequently unwarranted. In these cases the individual is seeking not an *alibi* but a *reason.*

Racial Prejudice, Self-regard, and Conformity.—The self, as was pointed out in Chap. II, is likely, under normal conditions, to be one of the strongest structures in the psychological field, and it has, therefore, a role of unparalleled significance in the determination of the organization of the field. It is therefore not strange to find that many of the beliefs and attitudes of racial prejudice operate in the service of the specific needs that are induced by the person's conception of his self and those which are induced

---

[1] For one such historical summary see the article on "Anti-Semitism" in the *Encyclopaedia Britannica*, 1946, by Pinson.

by his perception of a connection between various objects, individuals, and groups and himself. We can distinguish two somewhat different functions that racial prejudice can serve in this regard: (1) There are the beliefs and attitudes of racial prejudice that serve in *defense of the self*, and (2) there are the beliefs and attitudes of racial prejudice that serve to maintain the individual's *identification with society*.

Pride and prejudice.—Some of the most potent of all needs have to do with the defense of the self. Many of our perceptions, cognitions, beliefs, and attitudes are so organized as to enhance feelings of self-esteem or to remove any threat to such feelings. We know that in our culture the need for superiority feelings is a strong and driving need in many individuals. But we also know that enormous socioeconomic barriers are interposed among the various classes of American society, which make such feelings difficult to maintain. Differences in language, manners, clothing, education, income, and place of residence mark off one class from another in the American social hierarachy. Resulting rejections of the lower class in the hierarchy by the superior class are commonly experienced phenomena. Each individual who has strong needs for superiority feelings will frequently attempt to gratify them by finding other individuals who can be relegated to a still lower class and with respect to whom he can then feel superior. If and when this need for superiority feelings is satisfied through the perception of a minority racial group as being "inferior," we have a belief or attitude of prejudice in the service of the need for a feeling of superiority in the social hierarchy. The individual who is on the lowest rung of the social ladder can get ahead by creating a still lower rung—by placing the Mexican or Negro or Jew at the very bottom.

Another manifestation of this prejudice pattern may be caused by a temporary threat to the individual's feelings of pride and self-regard through a situational change, with the resulting operation of the mechanism of "displacement of fears." Thus, for example, a man may be threatened with the loss of his job. If he does not know the real reason for this impending calamity, he may feel that the loss of his job will demonstrate that he himself is "no good." Unable to tolerate such a conclusion, he will seek some other explanation—one that will not threaten his feelings of self-regard or pride. In the course of such active seeking for a different explanation he may eventually (if all the other conditions are such as to encourage such a solution) achieve the belief that the unscrupulous actions of the Jew have resulted in his dismissal from the job. Such an explanation or belief meets his needs. His pride has been saved, but an anti-Semite has been created.

Prejudice and conformity to a way of life.—In Chap. II we have pointed to the fact that the normal process of socialization of the individual is one of development and multiplication of various self-involvements with objects, people, groups, and social organizations in the world about him. Most people, in other words, have needs for group acceptance. This specific need may frequently be supported by beliefs and attitudes of racial prejudice—especially where the group with which the person wishes to identify is characterized by such beliefs and attitudes. Thus, for example, without holding certain racial prejudices, the person may not be accepted as a member of a firm or a university faculty or a staff of a hospital or a country club or a fraternity or a gang. To have different beliefs and attitudes from those of the group may result in such charges being leveled against him as "Nigger-lover" or "Communist." Prejudice, in this case, as Redl (1946) has phrased it, serves as a "social entrance ticket."

But perhaps more frequently than in the above direct way, beliefs and attitudes of racial prejudice in subtle ways serve the function of maintaining an individual's identity with his society. We all have many common, seemingly unimportant and perhaps nonsalient beliefs induced by and in turn supporting the accepted mores, practices, knowledge, superstitions, and habit patterns of society. Thus we are taught that freedom from trichinosis is an important desideratum in our lives, that children should be taught to avoid lockjaw, and that our homes should be decorated in "good taste." Because of this we believe that eating uncooked pork is undesirable, that rusty nails are not proper toys for young children, and that one does not hang "calendar art" in one's home. We have "directed" beliefs about uncooked pork, rusty nails, and calendar art. We do not aggress against them, we may not have attitudes about them, but we avoid them, and we try to protect our children from exposure to them.

Beliefs about members of minority racial groups may serve the very same function and be of the very same order. "Nice" people do not have Italians and Irishmen for friends, do not have Jews as fellow club members, do not invite Negroes to house parties. These are seen by some of us simply as the "facts of social life." If we are to satisfy our needs for behaving in good taste and avoid being pointed out as "queer" or as "nonconformist," we will avoid the Irishman, the Italian, the Jew, the Negro. We will not aggress against them, we may be perfectly content to see these people happy and prosperous, we may even honestly believe them to be valuable members of society—but we will see to it that they do not live on our streets, do not enter our homes, and do not come into contact with our children. No pathology or aggression or repression is involved. These beliefs of racial prejudice, however, direct much of our daily comings and goings and may be found among the gentlest, least aggressive, and best adapted of people.[1]

General Comments.—We have seen that the answer to the questions— What do beliefs and attitudes of racial prejudice do for people? What needs do they serve?—can almost be described as an inventory of all the needs of man. Prejudice patterns function all the way from justifying some men's pathological aggressive tendencies to serving people's need for "good taste." Racial prejudice can be used to rationalize culturally unacceptable needs, to rationalize culturally unacceptable behavior in the service of culturally acceptable aspirations, to reduce repressed tensions, to build up feelings of self-regard, to protect the self against threats to such feelings, to grow wealthy, to find a reasonable explanation of why one remains poor, and to achieve the "good life" as one has been taught to regard it. In the service of these functions, racial prejudice can be characterized as a scapegoat phenomenon, as vicious and aggressive, or as passive and "tolerant" avoidance. Prejudice can be all things to all men.

What we do not find is that there is a single need which lies behind all racial prejudice. In that sense there can be no "motivational theory of racial prejudice." Beliefs and attitudes of racial prejudice are special kinds of beliefs and attitudes, in the sense that they are socially important, but that does not mean that there must be a special motivational theory to account for them. To seek for a unique "theory" here is to make the same sort of error as those who seek for a special psychological process to account for "propaganda" or "suggestion." The motivational theory or analysis of racial prejudice is the same as the motivational analysis of any belief or attitude as far as the fundamental processes are concerned.

However, one additional general point should be made. Beliefs and attitudes of racial prejudice, perhaps more than any other kind of belief and attitude, may be accompanied by or lead to deep emotional tension. It must be remembered that racial prejudice does run counter to many avowed beliefs held in our society—the beliefs of individual freedom, equality, fraternity, democracy. Holding a belief or attitude of racial prejudice, no matter in what form and no matter which needs are thereby supported, can frequently result in emotional conflict in the American. For we must remember that needs and beliefs interact dynamically. We must concern

[1] In New York City the Jews have a phrase for one type of this pattern of prejudiced belief: "Five o'clock anti-Semitism." This refers to the situation where a Jew and a non-Jew are business partners and work in perfect harmony and friendship during business hours. But as soon as five o'clock strikes, the non-Jew goes his way and the Jew his. The non-Jew business partner would never think of inviting his Jewish partner to become a member of his club, to spend a weekend at his home, or to have their children "mix" socially or in marriage.

ourselves not only with the function of beliefs for the need structure but also with the function of beliefs in *affecting* the need and tension systems of the individual (see the discussion of this latter point with reference to the study by French, page 185). Not only, then, do beliefs and attitudes of racial prejudice frequently arise out of emotional experiences and needs, but they result in guilt feelings, emotional conflicts, aggressive defense reactions, etc. Beliefs and attitudes do something *for* the person who harbors them, but they also do something *to* the person.

Finally, the student must again be warned that a motivational analysis of racial prejudice does not explain racial prejudice. It merely points to the wide range of motive power for these special cognitive organizations. To understand how all of the above needs come to be served by beliefs and attitudes of racial prejudice, we must next turn our attention to the real world in which the individual seeks to work out ways and means of satisfying his various needs.

THE ENVIRONMENTAL SUPPORTS FOR RACIAL PREJUDICE

Racial prejudice, whether attitudes or beliefs, involves cognitive structures and therefore involves an organization of various specific objects or percepts. To know what needs racial prejudices *support*, therefore, is only half the story. We must also know how these beliefs and attitudes themselves are supported. We know, in other words, that the perceptions and cognitions which an individual experiences are related in a systematic manner to the nature of his real world. We perceive trees, partly because there are real trees "out there." The continued existence of a tree can be seen as an environmental support for our perception of a tree. That is why the perception psychologist is interested in describing the physical world as well as the perceptions evoked by the physical world, and that is why the social psychologist is interested in describing the world sociologically, in order to understand the environmental supports for percepts, beliefs, and attitudes.

We can differentiate between two kinds of environmental supports: (1) actual objects, events, and relationships and (2) the beliefs, attitudes, and verbalizations of other people as independently existing in the environment. Thus, if the Negro lives in a broken-down shack, that is an actual, objectively describable event which can operate as an environmental support for Arbuthnot's perception of the Negro as a poor, economically inferior individual. If Arbuthnot's teacher or preacher or congressman *believes* the Negro to be an inferior person (even if Arbuthnot himself has never seen a Negro), that also may serve as an environmental support for Arbuthnot's cognition of the Negro as an inferior being.

In addition the ambiguity of many objectively existing things, events, and relationships makes possible certain kinds of perceptions which then give these ambiguous objects such attributes as to permit them to function as environmental supports of racial prejudice. Thus the business behavior of a Jew, by being perceived as "shrewd," can serve as an environmental support for the belief that Jews are shrewd. The shrewd attributes of his behavior are there only because the meanings of any complicated behavior are frequently ambiguous and can be seen in a number of ways, and the particular meaning we give it will depend on various personally determined factors.

Objective Events as Environmental Supports for Racial Prejudice.— We have seen in Chap. III that discrete items which are organized together into a single cognitive structure must, among other things, be perceived as being either similar or in proximity. Before we can have a racial prejudice, then, we must be able to perceive the different individuals of the given racial group as having certain constant characteristics, as being similar to other individuals of the same group, and as being different from individuals not of that racial group. This, on reflection, seems a self-evident fact, yet it is the failure to appreciate the importance of this basic requirement that has resulted in many inadequate and superficial theories of racial prejudice. Our cognitive structures of racial groupings—a prerequisite, or course, to a belief or attitude of racial prejudice—depend upon the perceived similarities among the individuals of such a racial group. The more compelling these similarities are perceptually the easier it is to arrive at such a grouping. The more environmental supports for such similarities in perception the more compelling will these perceptual similarities be. Our first task, then, is to determine the nature of such environmental supports.

Heterogeneity of the American people.—Racial prejudice is not unique to the United States, but it is probably more prevalent and exists in a more virulent form here than in most other large countries of the western world. One of the factors that makes this condition *possible* is the "melting pot" nature of the American population. Rose (1947) presents the relevant data for the size of minority groups in the United States (Table 7).[1]

One out of every three Americans, therefore, differs in some way—in racial, religious, cultural, or national background—from the dominant group in the United States! A brief survey of the population of New York City itself gives us a dramatic example of the wealth of "discriminanda" [to use Tolman's (1932) term for possible perceptual differences among

[1] Rose's sources included the U. S. Bureau of the Census statistics, Linfield's (1945) study of the Jewish population of the United States, and the data of the department of research of the Federal Council of the Churches of Christ in America (1945).

objects] available for our groupings of people in this country. New York City, capital of the United Nations, is actually more representative of the world than the United Nations. Living within its five boroughs are people of some 60 different nationalities. More than two million of its residents are foreign born, another two and a quarter million are natives of foreign-born or mixed parentage, and almost a half million are colored. A few more than one million of all the city's residents come from Italy; just under one million from Russia; and close to half a million from Germany, Ireland,

TABLE 7.—SIZE OF MINORITY GROUPS IN THE UNITED STATES.*

	Year	Per cent	Number
1. Roman Catholics 23,419,701, exclusive of Filipinos, Mexicans, other Latin Americans, and French Canadians.....................	1943–1944	16.4	21,640,837
2. Negroes (inc. 83,941 foreign-born).............	1940	....	12,865,518
3. Indians (inc. 4,491 foreign-born)..............	1940	....	333,969
4. Chinese (inc. 37,242 foreign-born).............	1940	....	77,504
5. Japanese (inc. 47,305 foreign-born)...........	1940	....	126,947
6. All other races (inc. 2,779 foreign-born; 45,563 Filipinos; 2,405 Hindus; and 2,499 Koreans, Polynesians, other Asians).................	1940	....	50,467
7. Foreign-born Mexicans......................	1940	....	377,433
Native-born whites with one or both parents from Mexico.......................	1940	....	699,220
8. Foreign-born French Canadians...............	1940	....	273,366
9. Foreign-born whites from Central and South America and West Indies.................	1940	....	66,942
Native-born whites with one or both parents from Latin America.......................	1940	....	66,340
10. Puerto Ricans.............................	1940	....	250,000
11. Jews......................................	1937	....	4,770,000
Subtotal (exclusive of nonduplicated Catholics)..	....	15.2	19,957,706
Total..	....	31.6	41,598,543
Total population of United States............................... 131,669,275			

* From Rose (1947), Sec. VII, p. 17.

and Poland each. New York is the world's largest Negro metropolis, the world's third largest Irish city, and the largest Italian city outside Italy itself. The average New Yorker or any other American would have no difficulty in finding objective cues of similarity and difference on the basis of which he could organize his cognitive field in terms of distinct and separate racial groupings.

But what specific cues are used for such perceptual differentiation?

What are the specific discriminanda that Americans use for perceiving as "different" the members of the "Jewish" group, "Mexican" group, etc.? It would be impossible to list every such cue. In some cases it is the color of the skin; in others, the shape of the nose; in still others, the manner of speech, the type of food eaten, the occupation, etc. However, we can divide the cues into *physical* cues, *psychological* cues, and *sociological* cues. Skin color would be an instance of the first type, a personality trait would illustrate the second type, and a specific occupation the third type.

Physical cues as environmental supports for perceived racial groupings.— There can be no doubt that actual physical signs are of tremendous importance in making ethnic groupings possible in the mental world of the perceiver. The Negro, the Oriental, the Caucasian have fairly easily observable physical characteristics which permit differential perceptions and hence groupings. There is greater doubt about the more detailed racial and ethnic groupings that are found in the cognitive structures of people. Does the average Jew, Irishman, or Italian have differentiating physical characteristics? Frequently in attempting to answer this question, analysts have confused this problem with the problem of stereotypes. It can be demonstrated again and again that the average Jew, Irishman, or Italian does not correspond to the American's stereotype of the Jew, Irishman, or Italian, but that does not answer the question. It must be remembered that a stereotype, like any belief, does not do justice to all the details of the object (see discussion on page 171). Perception is selective, and from that point of view we should expect to find that the stereotype of the Jew or Irishman does not apply universally to Jews and Irishmen. But most stereotypes do bear some relation to the objects stereotyped. Proof that very few Italians have *all* the characteristics ascribed to them by the stereotype does not rule out the possibility that many Italians have one or more of those physical characteristics. There are some data (see especially Lund and Berg, 1946, and Allport and Kramer, 1946) that suggest that the identifiability of the Jew, from physical characteristics alone, is greater than would be expected by chance. In the absence of definitive data, we can only guess that the tenacity of the stereotype of what a Jew or Italian or Irishman looks like suggests that differentia exist *in fact* which can support differential perceptions.

However, whether or not that is altogether true, the significant point is that the existence of any discriminable differentia and the commonly held belief of the existence of many such discriminanda play an important role in supporting the perceptions of the prejudiced person. In the first place, we must remember that attention and perception are responsive to needs. The person who has been told that Jews look different from other people and who is also prejudiced against Jews has an induced need, or mental set, that requires him to be able to recognize a Jew from a non-Jew. We would therefore expect him to be more alert and more attentive to possible "Jewish signs" than one who had no such need to guide and organize his perceptions. As Bruner and Goodman (1947) have pointed out in their statement that we referred to on page 82. (Chap. III), the stimuli habitually selected for major attention tend to become progressively more vivid and achieve greater clarity. Therefore the existence of any cues, no matter how minor or how ambiguous, will be detected by the prejudiced person more frequently and with more certainty than by the nonprejudiced person. The discovery of such discriminanda will, in turn, help to maintain his cognitive structure of the Jews as a race apart. The prejudiced person, in other words, will tend to maximize the perceptual usefulness of minor differentia. An experiment by Allport and Kramer (1946) presents some interesting evidence on this point.

Two hundred and twenty-three students at Harvard and Radcliffe (who had previously been given an anti-Semitic attitude test) were shown 20 slides, each a photograph of a male college student, and were asked to say whether they thought the photograph was that of a Jew or of a non-Jew. They were also permitted to say "Don't know." The pictures were selected from a five-year-old edition of the Harvard senior-class album, and an equal number of Jews and non-Jews were included in the series of 20. The order of presentation was random, and the subjects did not know how many Jews were represented in the photographs. The two most significant findings from this experiment were:

(*a*) Students with higher total prejudice scores judge *more* faces to be Jewish than do students with lower scores. In other words, they are more suspicious of the identity of the photographed subjects . . . .

(*b*) Students with higher anti-Semitic prejudice scores are more *correct* in their judgments. They are better able to identify Jewish and non-Jewish faces.

These results, in spite of the selected sample of Jewish faces used in the experiment (admittance to Harvard may have depended upon the relative "non-Jewish" appearance of the person), are impressive confirmations of the point made above. As the experimenters write:

Many people, free from anti-Semitism, have felt bewildered and uncertain when someone asks if a friend (whom they have known for years) is or is not Jewish. The reply often is, "Why, I don't know—I never thought about the matter." The question of racial identity is of small importance to the person free from prejudice. Yet it is of considerable importance to the bigot, and for this reason the bigot apparently learns to observe and interpret both facial features and expressive behavior so that he can more easily spot his "enemy."

Because, then, of the selective influence of need on perception and the role of attention in learning (see Chap. III, Chap. VI), the importance of any physical cue that can help support a differential perception as among people of different "races" must not be minimized.

Psychological cues as environmental supports for perceived racial groupings.— The cues available for differentiating different peoples are not limited, of course, to physical ones. Some people may and do distinguish a Jew from a non-Jew by such traits as "shrewdness," "ambitious," etc.; some people distinguish a Negro from a non-Negro by such traits as "sensuousness" and "loudness"; and some people may distinguish an Italian from a non-Italian by the "volatile temper" or "emotionality" of the person.

The distinction between psychological traits and physical traits is not a clear-cut one as far as their status as environmental cues is concerned. It is frequently assumed by the prejudiced person that the psychological traits are just as *biologically determined* as are the physical traits. Presumably, then, one of the questions we must answer in considering the environmental supports for psychological-trait differentia is whether or not different psychological traits reflect different biologically determined racial characteristics.

The relevancy of this question is not, however, as direct as it may appear at first glance. For our analysis here, we must know whether the different ethnic groups do, in fact, differ in psychological traits—*regardless of whether the differences are hereditarily determined or culturally determined.* The *cause* of any differences that may exist is of significance only if we should be interested in changing the perceptions of people who observe the differences, but not in accounting for the perceptions in the first place. Failure to recognize this has led to theories of racial prejudice that exemplify the historical error. That is, some analysts have shown that since it cannot be demonstrated that psychological differences among ethnic groups are biologically determined, therefore the "assumed" psychological differences among these groups cannot be considered as environmental supports for prejudiced beliefs and attitudes but must be written off in all cases as "rationalizations" which the prejudiced person uses to justify his prejudices. Such an analysis may be valid in some instances but is invalid in others.

For example, if a white Southerner says that Negroes should not be given certain responsibilities because they are intellectually "under par," it may be quite irrelevant (even if true) to analyze the case of the white Southerner by pointing out that, *biologically considered,* the Negro's intelligence is equal to the white's, that the difference is only apparent and is due to inequalities of educational and cultural opportunities, and that therefore the white man is only rationalizing without factual support for his rationalization. The point is, however, that the Negro in the South, *today*, does score lower on intelligence tests and is less prepared to take on certain intellectual responsibilities. *In many cases, therefore, the white man has true, real, objective environmental supports for his beliefs and attitudes concerning the Negro's inferiority.* If, on the other hand, the Southerner should argue that the Negro will always be intellectually inferior, because there is an innate difference between the Negro and the white, then, of course, the question of the biological or cultural determination of intelligence becomes immediately relevant.

Race, biology, and psychological traits.—There are no unambiguous and scientific answers to the two questions we have raised. This is not due to the lack of interest or the lack of effort on the part of the psychologist. There are perhaps over a hundred studies that have investigated the comparative intelligence, for example, of various ethnic groups in this country, but every one of those studies can be attacked on one basic ground or another. However, the over-all *trend* of the results from these studies may be summarized as follows:

1. Using typical and well-standardized tests, statistically reliable differences in intelligence have been found to exist between the *average* scores made by one ethnic group and the average scores made by other groups. Thus, the Negro is fairly consistently found to be at the bottom of the list, the Pole and Italian some place in the middle, and the Englishman, German, and Jew at the top.

2. Although these groups differ in average score, the extent of *overlap* is tremendous, and it is consistently found that some Negroes score higher than some Englishmen and some Jews score lower than some Poles, etc.

3. When such cultural factors as socioeconomic status, education, general cultural surroundings, urban or rural domicile, etc., are equated, the obtained differences in averages tend to diminish.[1]

It appears then that differences in psychological traits (at least as far as intelligence is concerned) can be demonstrated to be present among different racial and ethnic groups and that these differences seem to reflect cultural rather than biological factors. In addition to the available psychometric data, however, there are general observations and theoretical considerations that strengthen the conclusion that objectively observable psychological cues exist which can serve as environmental supports for beliefs and attitudes of prejudice.

[1] For some specific studies, criticisms, and discussions on this whole question, the student is referred to the following: Feingold (1924), Hirsch (1926), Goodenough (1926), Brigham (1930), Klineberg (1935), Bice (1938), Jenkins (1940), Hollingworth and Witty (1940), and Garrett (1945).

Prejudice, culture, and psychological traits.—In the first place it appears that *actual differences* in psychological traits among people *can be induced* by behavior that is racially discriminatory. This operates in several ways, and Dollard (1937), in his study of class and caste in the South, illustrates some of these mechanisms. Thus, he shows how the caste conditions can create a psychological situation that brings out certain behavior patterns and traits in the Negro which then serve to differentiate him from the white man:

> Southern white informants believe that there is much more aggression and violence within the Negro caste than there is in the white caste . . . . Some are inclined to charge it to the emotional instability among Negroes . . . . A preferable view would seem to be that, since the hostility of the Negroes against the whites is violently and effectively suppressed, we have a boiling of aggressive affect within the Negro group.

As a specific illustration of this mechanism, Dollard analyzes the causes of the frequent fights that occur among Negroes in connection with sexual matters:

> . . . part of the jealousy which motivates the fights between Negro men is actually directed against the whites who take Negro women or have them accessible; this jealousy cannot be expressed and must be suppressed so far as the whites are concerned, but is vented with additional fury against any Negro aggressor of the same kind.

Not only do these caste conditions, then, create a psychological state in the Negro that results in aggression, but the prejudiced beliefs and attitudes of the white man may be such as to encourage the Negro to aggress by "letting him get away with it" if he does aggress.

> It is impossible to see the more violent patterns of Negro behavior in the right perspective unless one understands that there are different standards of justice for the two castes. White persons are held much more strictly to the formal legal code; Negroes are dealt with much more indulgently . . . . This is true only under one condition, however—when Negro crimes are committed on Negroes . . . . The result is that the individual Negro is, to a considerable degree, outside the protection of white law . . . . It is clear that this differential application of the law amounts to a condoning of Negro violence and gives immunity to Negroes to commit small or large crimes so long as they are on Negroes.

The creation of psychological traits that differentiate one group from another by discriminatory behavior holds for most minority groups who are victims of racial prejudice. Racial prejudice, in other words, affects the personality not only of the holder of the prejudice but also of the victim.

If the Chinese or the Jew is not allowed to mix with other groups, is not accepted by them, then the Chinese or the Jew must seek the satisfaction of his need for "belongingness" within his own group. This, in turn, can make him "clannish," "secretive," and even "furtive." The use of quotation marks is not meant to suggest that these traits are only apparent. They may become genuine traits, which can frequently and easily be observed. Baruch (1946) presents an insightful account of how racial prejudice among the whites of the West Coast operates to induce all sorts of undesirable personality characteristics in the Mexican boys and girls of Los Angeles—the *Pachucos*, or "zoot-suiters"—who figured in the California "zoot-suit riots" of 1944.

Prejudice, selective contact, and psychological traits.—Quite a different mechanism, which helps fill the perceived world of the prejudiced person with ethnic groups all wearing the psychological stigmata of their "difference," is the selective nature of the contacts with people against whom he is prejudiced (see the discussion of the "sampling error of experiences" in Chap. IV, page 133).

The wide range of individual differences in psychological traits and characteristics is one of the most firmly established psychometric findings. There are Jews who are intelligent, Jews who are low-grade imbeciles; Negroes who are illiterate, and Negroes who write best sellers; violent Irishmen and gentle Irishmen. But the prejudiced person does not seek out a representative sample of Jews, Negroes, or Irishmen. He may seek to avoid them altogether. His experiences with these people will therefore be limited to only those individual members of such groups whom he cannot avoid. He hires the illiterate Negro to tend his furnace because he can get him to work cheaply—but he does not invite the Negro author to his home. He knows the Jewish pawnbroker because he must avail himself of his services, but he does not have the Jewish professor as a fellow club member. His true, real, objective world, in other words, consists of illiterate Negroes and Jewish pawnbrokers.

We find, then, that partly as a consequence of prejudiced behavior itself, some of the ethnic groups in this country do have psychological differentia which serve as environmental supports for perceptual groupings. These differences, whatever their cause, are used to the maximum by the prejudiced person in his perceptual behavior. Thus again do we find that the prejudiced person is living in a real world which offers a wealth of environmental supports for his beliefs and attitudes of prejudice.

Sociological cues as environmental supports for perceived racial groupings. We perceive people not only in terms of their physical characteristics or psychological characteristics but also in terms of certain sociological cues—

their occupations, schools, places of residence, church membership, etc. These sociological cues, through the operation of the principles of similarity and proximity, serve as environmental supports for beliefs and attitudes of racial prejudice.   Thus, there is a tendency to perceive as one group laundry-men or pullman porters or shoeshine boys, etc.   Similarly, if we notice a number of people living in one part of a community, segregated from the rest of the community, there is a tendency to perceive them as members of one group.

The most superficial sociological analysis of the United States is adequate to confirm the hypothesis that strong forces are at work operating to segregate various races into distinct and objectively different groupings and forcing them to behave in distinct patterns.   These forces have legal status, are supported by the dominant American churches and other social organizations, and are demanded by custom.   A brief review of these sociological environmental supports for beliefs and attitudes of prejudice and of the method of their operation will make their importance clear.

1. *Legal segregation.*—Legal segregation of people in the United States is founded on the doctrine promulgated by the Supreme Court in 1896 in the case of *Plessy v. Ferguson* (163 U.S. 537), which maintained that *separate* accommodations for the residents of a state did not violate the Fourteenth Amendment.   Thereafter the term "equal" was defined as "separate but substantially equivalent."   This rule has been applied to Indians, Negroes, Chinese, and Mexicans and to such accommodations as railroad seats, schools, parks, places of amusement, hotels, restaurants, and drinking fountains.[1]   As Reid (1947) has pointed out, "The chief device of racial segregation in the South is law.   In all southern states the law defines one's racial identification and then proceeds to define status and rights in relation to race."   Although separation of races has no direct legal status in states above the Mason-Dixon line, various individual and business legal devices are used to enforce segregation.   It would be impossible to find a single kind of segregation that is not supported by law in some part of the United States.   From birth through death and burial the law segregates the people in the United States in terms of race.

2. *Religious segregation.*—Liston Pope (1947), associate professor of Social Ethics at Yale Divinity School and a leading figure of the Federal Council of the Churches of Christ in America, sums up the story of segregation in the Church with these words, "Christian teaching about race transcends the practices of the Christian churches in America.   This is especially true of the Protestant churches, on which most of the responsi-

[1] For a brief but clear review of the legal aspects of segregation, see Cushman (1947).

bility for racial segregation in religious groups, and for its abolition, must fall."

In his discussion of caste in the Church, Pope singles out the Negro for special attention, although, he points out, ". . . patterns of treatment in his [Negro] case would, in most particulars, apply equally well to minorities in general—Japanese Americans, Mexicans and other groups." Pope, further, reports little difference between Northern and Southern denominations in the matter of segregated churches. Almost all of the 6,500,000 Negro Protestants in the United States are forced to worship in segregated churches; and of the 300,000 Negro Catholics, about 200,000 are similarly segregated.

3. *Segregation in business.*—Either through law, legal "devices," or business policy, various ethnic groups are forced into certain specified forms of employment and into specified areas where they can rent or buy housing facilities.

Despite recent governmental efforts to minimize open and flagrant segregation in employment, the practice of individual employers and corporations is such as definitely to limit the employment opportunities for members of various racial and religious groups. This is true even in government employment. It is in the light of this that Lohman and Embree (1947) have characterized Washington, D.C., as a ". . . travesty on the politics and culture of our American democracy."

"Race-restrictive covenants" are the most frequently used devices by the real-estate business to create racial or ethnic ghettos in the United States. A "race-restrictive covenant" is an agreement entered into by property owners not to sell or rent their property to any member of a given racial or ethnic group.[1] Such covenants exist in thousands of American communities (it is estimated, for example, that 80 per cent of the residential area of Chicago is covered by such restrictive covenants) and only recently have been held by the United States Supreme Court to be unenforceable in courts.

4. *Segregation in labor unions.*—Segregation on the basis of race has always existed in the American labor movement. Some labor unions (notably the International Ladies Garment Workers Union) discourage such practices, some encourage them, but almost all, at one time or another, have practiced segregation. This sometimes takes the form of outright refusal of admittance to membership, and sometimes segregation is accomplished by forming independent Negro unions or "Jim Crow" auxiliaries.

---

[1] Miller points out (1947) that these covenants frequently employ "delicacy" in their wordings. Thus, a recent Virginia covenant, which included an agreement obviously directed against Jews, proscribed land use by "persons who customarily observe the seventh day of the week as the Sabbath." Ironically enough, the first person to become enmeshed in the toils of this delicately worded covenant was a Seventh-Day Adventist!

Thus some of the railway unions limit their membership to white workers, while the Brotherhood of Carpenters and Joiners organizes the Negro carpenters into separate locals.[1]

5. *Segregated education and health facilities.*—In the South, public schools practice legal and open segregation as far as the Negro is concerned. In the North, educational segregation comes about through various extra-legal means. Some cities deliberately build "Negro schools" despite any legal right to do so and encourage all Negroes to attend these special schools where they can receive "special" attention. And McWilliams (1947) points out that "Throughout the Southwest, Mexican Americans have long been segregated. Separate facilities for Spanish-speaking children is the practice of many local school systems in Texas. The present school code of California permits segregation of Mexican children." Private schools and colleges employ "quota" systems and do not permit more than a very small percentage of Negroes, Italians, or Jews to enter. In reaction, the result is such preponderantly Jewish colleges as City College of New York and such segregated Negro colleges as Howard University.

Even in matters of disease, sickness, and death, the pattern of segregation is maintained in the United States. Jewish or Negro doctors are not permitted to practice in some hospitals—or else a "quota" system is enforced. Negroes are not accepted as patients in many hospitals—North or South. Even when viewing dead people, many Americans find objective environmental support for their beliefs and attitudes of racial prejudice— Negro corpses are not permitted to lie in the same morgue with white corpses, and it was only in 1946 that the National Cemetery at Arlington permitted the burial of Negro veterans on equal terms with whites.

6. *Segregation in the armed forces.*—Even when drafted out of the civilian world into the military world, the American finds the same environmental supports. The Second World War inductees were classified by race, and the Negro soldiers were sent to special companies at induction centers. Most training centers had segregated facilities for Negro soldiers. Thus Dollard and Young (1947) report that camp theaters had segregated seats available for "certain units only," Negro officers were discouraged from entering officers' clubs, Negro sailors were typically assigned to mess-boy duties, etc. When the   American draftee returned to civilian life as a veteran, he again found environmental supports for his prejudice. The

---

[1] Lohman and Embree (1947) report the following instance of segregation on the picket line, "An interesting sidelight on the recent hotel strike in Washington was the variation in picket lines at the several hotels. At one Connecticut Avenue hostelry, segregated picket lines prevailed, with white workers picketing the front entrance and Negroes picketing the rear."

Negro veteran was not permitted membership in the older and well-established veteran organizations, or else he could apply for membership only in segregated "Jim Crow" posts.

We have devoted so much discussion to these segregation practices which provide sociological cues to support beliefs and attitudes of prejudice because of all the cues that can reinforce those beliefs and attitudes, the sociological ones are the most important. There are three major reasons for this:

1. These indices provide the clearest cues for perception. The perception of a man's intelligence or shrewdness or emotionality is frequently dependent upon the idiosyncratic interpretation of the perceiver, and different perceivers will not observe the same psychological or even physical trait in any one individual. Whether or not a jaw is "apelike" is not unambiguously given, but the perception of a Negro as a "special" kind of person when he is seen as forced to sit in the rear of a bus is simple and unambiguous. Because of the greater clarity of the cues involved, the resulting tendency to group as distinct peoples the Negroes, Jews, Mexicans, Italians, Chinese is frequently more compelling when based on these sociological cues than when supported by either physical or psychological cues.

2. As we have seen, many of these sociological stigmata are *forced* upon the ethnic groups by *civil* law, *religious* policy, and *military* practice. This means that the possibility of any specific Negro's or Jew's escaping the differentiating stigmata is very low. In addition, these stigmata are saturated with acceptability for many people. That is, anything that is legal, written into state laws, official contracts, and land deeds; accepted by the Church; and condoned by the Army is seen as "good" and "is as it should be." These sociological differentia, in other words, are not seen as happenstance attributes of the minority group members but as necessary and appropriate attributes.

3. Occupation and place of residence in a class society like ours carry with them fairly definite implications about ability, personality, and character. Such associations are a definite part of our cultural pattern. The occupation of a shoeshine boy, pawnbroker, or hand-laundryman or attendance at an "unrespectable" college is seen, by many, as reflecting on the ability or character of the shoeshine boy, pawnbroker, laundryman, or college student.

Environmental supports in the fictitious world.—As was pointed out in Chap. IX (page 327), our real world consists of word objects as well as other objects. In the present connection, this means that our social world does not consist only of "real" people but also of characters of literature, history, and fable. We experience men, women, soldiers, Negroes, Jews, priests, and diplomats not only "in the flesh" but also through our reading, on the motion-picture screen, and through radio broadcasts. We react to these fictitious characters in much the same way that we react to living characters. The cues these people of fable and story carry with them can be just as effective environmental supports as can the cues of living people. To obtain a complete description of environmental supports, therefore, we must examine the attributes of these fictitious people who inhabit our world in much the same manner that we have examined the real people.

During 1944 the Writers' War Board and its Committee to Combat Race Hatred commissioned Columbia University's Bureau of Applied Social Research to make a study of the fictional characters who inhabit the magazine short story, the stage, radio, and advertising copy. The following is a brief digest of the report taken from the Writers' War Board account:

1. *Magazine short stories.*—Eight nationally circulated magazines were selected to provide representative short story samples. These were the *Saturday Evening Post, Collier's, American, Cosmopolitan, Woman's Home Companion, Ladies' Home Journal, True Confessions,* and *True Story.* One hundred and eighty-five short stories (1937 through 1943) were analyzed.

Of 889 identifiable characters 90.8% were Anglo-Saxons . . . whereas only 9.2% . . . were drawn from all other racial stocks in the United States . . . .[1] And where the authors brought in menials, racketeers, thieves, gamblers, shady night club proprietors, crooked prize fight managers, such non-sympathetic characters were seldom Anglo-Saxon . . . . The overwhelming attention is given to the Anglo-Saxons. The stage and the spotlight belong to them. They were habitually pictured as the salt of the earth. Their superiority, wealth, and prestige were usually taken for granted, whereas in the few instances where a minority character was represented as rich or important the author offered an elaborate explanation—he had inherited wealth, married well, worked hard, been lucky, or come by his gains through crooked dealings . . . . The evidence is clear, American short story writers have made "nice people" synonymous with Anglo-Saxons. Such characters are written as intelligent, industrious, esthetic, democratic, athletic, practical, frank, lovable . . . the non-Anglo-Saxons were usually pictured as the "villains," domineering, immoral, selfish, unintelligent, cowardly, lazy, sly, cruel, stubborn, non-esthetic, weak . . . . *The behavior of these fictional characters could easily be used to "prove" that the Negroes are lazy, the Jews wily, the Irish superstitious and the Italians criminal.*

2. *The stage.*

Under modern conditions the legitimate stage appears to be by far the most liberal of all media of entertainment in avoidance of racial stereotypes . . . . Oddly enough, however, some obnoxious and persistent racial stereotypes have been popularized in the theatre—notably the "Uncle Tom" type of Negro, the quarrelsome Jewish business man and the "stage Irishman."

[1] Compare this with the percentages given in Table 7, p. 461

3. *Motion pictures.*—An analysis of 100 motion pictures involving either Negro themes or characters produced this score: stereotyped and disparaging, 75; neutral and unobjectionable, 13; favorable, 12.

4. *Radio programs.*—All of the American networks have an official policy which presumably prohibits offense to minorities. But nevertheless, the heroes and heroines in radio drama tend invariably to be white, Protestant, Anglo-Saxons. Frequently the treatment of the Negro "comic" is stereotyped on all the usual counts—"addiction to drink, dice, wenching and razors."

5. *Advertising.*—Typical of the results of the research here is this quotation from an advertising man, "You'd lose your audience if a colored man appeared in the ad. However, in a picture of the Old South, whiskey ads and so forth, one puts in an Uncle Tom for atmosphere."

The significant point of the above research is not that short-story writers, script writers, and advertising men have racial stereotypes but that as a consequence of their work, not only is the American's world peopled with living ethnic groups that carry with them physical, psychological, and sociological stigmata, but the fictional people are similarly marked for special perception.

Beliefs and Attitudes of Others as Environmental Support for Racial Prejudice.—In our discussion of the cultural determinants of beliefs and attitudes it was pointed out that the current beliefs and attitudes of one's neighbors, parents, teachers, schoolmates, colleagues, ministers, etc., are just as genuine environmental supports for one's own beliefs and attitudes as are the more "objective" supports we have discussed in the preceding section. We shall therefore have to examine (1) the extent of beliefs and attitudes of racial prejudice in the United States and (2) the content of these beliefs and attitudes.

Extent of racial prejudice in the United States.—Despite the number of public opinion polls which have attempted to measure the extent of racial prejudice in the United States, we cannot depend upon their data in estimating the prevalence of such prejudice. The polls that have been made suffer from all the difficulties discussed in Chap. VIII—ambiguous wordings of questions, the possible bias of the interviewer,[1] the truthfulness of the respondents' answers, etc. Thus, for example, one public opinion poll (Fortune, 1946) indicated that 8.8 per cent of the American people were anti-Semitic, and another (National Opinion Research Center, 1943) that 49.7 per cent were anti-Semitic. But these conclusions are questionable.

---

[1] It will be remembered that the study by Robinson and Rohde (1946), which was discussed on p. 290, Chap. VIII, demonstrated the significant influence that the interviewer can have on polls of anti-Semitism.

The first estimate is based on the number of respondents who took one or both of two opportunities to express hostility to Jews in answer to the following questions:

Are there any organizations or groups of people in this country who you feel might be harmful to the future of the country unless they are curbed? [If "Yes"] Name: [Here 5.1 per cent named Jews.]

Are there any groups of people you think are trying to get ahead at the expense of people like you? [If "Yes"] Name: [Here 6.5 per cent named Jews.]

The estimate of 49.7 per cent is based on the number of respondents who replied "Too much" to the question, "Do you think that Jewish people in the United States have too much influence in the business world, not enough influence, or about the amount of influence they should have?"

To infer the absolute amount of anti-Semitism from one or even two questions is an unjustified procedure, as was indicated in our discussion of the interpretation of percentages from opinion polls (see especially page 276). Katz (1946), in discussing the results of the Fortune poll cited above (which estimated that 8.8 per cent of the American people were anti-Semitic), points out,

Merely because 91.2 per cent of the people did not name the Jews on either of the two questions does not establish their complete lack of anti-Semitism. Anti-Semitism is a complex set of attitudes and practices which varies both in intensity and in qualitative aspects.... Obviously, if other types of questions had been used the percentages might have been higher or lower, depending upon the questions employed. To say that there is 8.8 per cent of anti-Semites in the United States is to assume that we have a single yardstick to measure this complex attitude and that we know its zero point.

While the above objections also hold for polls that attempt to measure anti-Negro attitudes, the results are somewhat more consistent, perhaps because of the greater social acceptability of anti-Negro attitudes and therefore lesser reluctance of the respondents to reveal their racial prejudices. Thus Horowitz (1944) reports a Fortune poll indicating that 80 per cent of the American people favor residential segregation for the Negro, while another Fortune poll (among high-school students, 1943) indicates that 91.6 per cent of white Protestants have anti-Negro beliefs and attitudes.

Turning to the data obtained through more intensive and sensitive techniques of measurement than is possible with the public opinion poll, the indications are that beliefs and attitudes of racial prejudice are extremely prevalent in the United States. Thus Allport and Kramer (1946) have suggested that

It would seem a safe estimate that at least four-fifths of the American population lead mental lives in which feelings of group hostility play an appreciable role . . . . This estimate, necessarily rough, is based on various types of evidence. (*a*) In a hundred typical life-histories obtained from college students, 80 per cent contained admissions of group prejudice; (*b*) recent unpublished research of the Commission on Community Inter-relations shows that of a random sample of the population drawn from Times Square pedestrians, only about 17 per cent gave virtually unprejudiced replies to the anti-Semitic questions contained in the scale . . . (*c*) only 22 per cent of the Harvard and Radcliffe students in the present study[1] reported that they did not feel uncongenial toward any group at all. Also, only 16 per cent of the 437 students in the present study showed prejudice scores of 10 or lower, that is to say, so low as to be of no practical account.

When it is remembered that the above estimate is based on a sample that does not include, in proper proportions, the anti-Negro whites of the South, the anti-Mexicans and anti-Oriental whites of the West Coast, etc., it is highly probable that the estimate by Allport and Kramer is too low. On the basis of all the data available, it is fairly safe to say that in the realm of racial prejudice we are dealing with an experience with which most Americans are personally familiar. At least four out of five of our people have it.

Sociological distribution of beliefs and attitudes of racial prejudice.—There have been numbers of studies that have attempted to determine whether racial prejudice is more prevalent among rural or urban people, Northern or Southern Americans, individuals from low vs. high socioeconomic levels, etc. Again the data are not unambiguous, but again they indicate the universality of this kind of belief or attitude. Thus, the study of Sims and Patrick (1936) indicates that white Northern college students are more favorable toward Negroes than are white Southern college students; Horowitz (1936) found little or no difference in the anti-Negro beliefs and attitudes of grade-school children in New York City, urban Tennessee, urban Georgia, and rural Georgia; while Katz and Allport (1931) report that Northern college students were more anti-Negro than Southern white college students. Merton (1940) and Allport and Kramer (1946) found anti-Negro prejudices among Catholics, Protestants, and Jews with the intensity of the prejudice in the order named. While Zeligs and Hendrickson (1933) found a slight correlation (.31) between racial tolerance and intelligence among sixth-grade pupils, Bolton (1935) found no such relationship. Where Minard (1931) reports no class difference in attitudes toward minority groups among high-school students, Levinson and Sanford (1944) conclude that anti-Semitism among college students increases with reported

[1] See p. 463 of this chapter for a description of that study.

income of parents, membership in sororities, and affiliation with the Republican party.[1]

In general, then, all the above results strongly indicate that no American can escape being in intimate contact with some other American who has a belief or attitude of racial prejudice. All Americans can find support for such beliefs and attitudes among the beliefs of their friends—whether their friends are intelligent or stupid; from the North or the South; Catholic, Protestant, Jewish, or Negro; rural or urban; old or young.

Contents of beliefs and attitudes of racial prejudice.—Racial prejudice as a mental structure is a significant environmental support not only because of its great incidence among Americans but also because of its apparent stability and the communality in the content of these beliefs and attitudes among different Americans. We have pointed out that the contents of the "same" belief or attitude among different people frequently vary but that usually these beliefs and attitudes have in common some general content (see page 159). As far as the beliefs and attitudes of racial prejudice among Americans are concerned, studies have repeatedly demonstrated that despite the varied personal experiences, needs, socioeconomic status, and cultural backgrounds of Americans, their racial prejudices show two major common characteristics: (1) a firmly fixed *hierarchy of racial preference* and (2) agreement of the psychological traits ascribable to the various ethnic groups inhabiting our country ("stereotypy"). In addition to these common characteristics, every individual probably has in his beliefs and attitudes of prejudice specific contents that are unique to him or to his particular group, but the impressive uniformity found in terms of these common attributes goes far to establish racial prejudice as one of the most dependable and uniform characteristics of the mental life of the average American.

Hierarchy of racial preference.—In 1931 Guilford reported one of the first of the studies that sought to determine the degree of correlation existing among various groups with respect to racial preferences. He examined the preferences of about 1,100 college students drawn from seven widely separated institutions in this country—Florida, Kansas, Nebraska, Northwestern, Washington, Wells, and New York University. Using the method of paired comparisons (see page 224) Guilford was able to assign to each of 15 nationalities and races a scale value that indicated its relative standing in the preferences of the students from each university separately. When the scale values for the different ethnic groups obtained from the

---

[1] For a good summary of many of these studies, see Rose's (1947) valuable assembly of the vast amount of scattered literature reporting the results of investigations of attitudes toward minority groups.

different universities were compared one with another, an extremely high series of correlations was found. As Guilford points out, "The intercorrelations are nearly as high as the self-correlations, with exception of those involving N.Y.U. They range from .843 to .894 for N.Y.U., but they are between .975 and .991 for all the other universities."

In other words, the students from Wells College, from Nebraska, from Florida, and from Washington, all gave almost identical rankings in racial and nationality preferences. The fifteen different ethnic groups ranked as follows, from most preferred to least preferred: *English, German, French, Swedish, Spanish, Italian, Russian, Jewish, Greek, Japanese, Mexican, Hindu, Negro, Chinese, Turkish.*[1]

Guilford's findings seem to have set a pattern for future research in this area. Again and again his investigation has been repeated with substantially the same results. Meltzer (1939a) reported a similar study with school children in St. Louis and found not only that the preferences of these children were patterned after those of the college students but that when he studied different groups of children—Jews, Catholics, Protestants, Negroes, whites, rural, urban—he obtained similar patterns.

Of particular interest are Meltzer's data (1939b), which indicate a good correspondence between the pattern of racial preferences of the Negro and white children. The rank-order correlation for these two sets of ratings is .60. Thus both Negro and white children ranked the English and the French on top, the Italian and Russian in the middle, and the Turkish and Hindu at the bottom of the list. The relatively low figure of .60 that was obtained was due primarily to the fact that the Negro children rated their own race first in preference whereas the white children rated the Negro second from the bottom (note the close correspondence between these results and those of Guilford). The significant degree to which the Negro children reflect the general American pattern in their racial preferences is demonstrated by the correlation we get when we remove the "Negro" item from the list of nationalities used by Meltzer. Doing this, the correlation of .60 is raised to .83.[2]

The most recent study that substantiates the above results is that of Hartley (1946). Using a slightly modified form of the Bogardus social distance scale (see page 221), he determined the racial preferences of students from eight different colleges and universities chosen because of the diversity

---

[1] These results do not include the data from New York University which, because of the preponderance of Jewish students at that university, gave slightly atypical results.

[2] This treatment of Meltzer's data assumes that had Meltzer omitted the "Negro" item in his series of paired comparisons, the resulting preference patterns would not have changed significantly.

of the backgrounds, ethnic stock, socioeconomic status, and professional interests of the students. These institutions were Bennington College, Columbia University, College of the City of New York (Arts), College of the City of New York (Business), Howard University, Princeton, a state normal school, and a state teachers college.[1] The comparison of the results obtained from these different groups indicates high agreement among them, the correlation coefficients ranging from .68 to .95. In other words, the boys at Princeton, at C.C.N.Y., at Howard University, and at Columbia display the same pattern of racial preferences as the girls at Bennington, the students at state teachers colleges, and commercial students at C.C.N.Y.

As an indication of the stability, over time, of the pattern of racial preferences, Hartley's comparison of his results with those of Bogardus (1928), obtained over ten years earlier, is illuminating. Bogardus obtained the preference ratings of a sample of 1,725 Americans, representing a general cross section of the country, for 40 different nationalities and races, among which were included 26 of the groups used in Hartley's study. Hartley has computed that the per cent of students unwilling to admit each of these 26 nationalities to citizenship correlates .78 with the comparable index from Bogardus' study. As Hartley points out, "This coefficient demonstrates a highly significant relationship between the two patterns of preference. The students are responding in the pattern generally prevalent a decade earlier."

Common content ("stereotypy") of racial prejudices.—Although not so many studies have concerned themselves with the detailed contents of the attributes assigned to the different minority-group members, there are some data to indicate that here, too, we are dealing with a common pattern. Among the first of these studies was the one by Katz and Braly (1933) in which 100 Princeton students were asked to give the five traits that they considered most characteristic of each of the following ten groups: Germans, Italians, Negroes, Irish, English, Jews, Americans, Chinese, Japanese, and Turks. The traits were to be selected from a list of 84 adjectives, but the students were allowed to add trait names of their own choosing if they wished. The following lists (prepared from the data of Katz and Braly) present the five characteristics that were most frequently assigned to four of the groups by the Princeton students (the numbers next to each trait indicate the percentage of students assigning that particular trait):

Germans:	Per Cent	Jews:	Per Cent
Scientifically minded	78	Shrewd	79
Industrious	65	Mercenary	49
Stolid	44	Industrious	48
Intelligent	32	Grasping	34
Methodical	31	Intelligent	29

[1] In deference to the wishes of the authorities at these last two institutions, Hartley does not specify which ones they were.

Negroes:		Chinese:	
Superstitious	84	Superstitious	34
Lazy	75	Sly	29
Happy-go-lucky	38	Conservative	29
Ignorant	38	Tradition-loving	26
Ostentatious	26	Loyal to family ties	22

Despite the fact that these students had some 84 adjectives to choose from, it will be noticed that there is an extremely high degree of agreement in ascribing psychological attributes to the four ethnic groups. That this communality in content of the beliefs and attitudes about these four ethnic groups was not limited to Princeton students is indicated by Bayton's (1941) study of the racial stereotypes of Negro college students. Using the very same techniques, instructions, and material used by Katz and Braly seven years earlier with Princeton students, Bayton obtained the following comparable data from 100 Negro students (80 per cent of whom came from Southern states) at Virginia State College.

Germans:[1]	Per Cent	Jews:	Per Cent
Scientifically minded	78	Progressive	38
Intelligent	52	Shrewd	34
Ambitious	35	Ambitious	32
Highly nationalistic	25	Grasping	27
Cruel	21	Industrious	27
Negroes:		Chinese:	
Superstitious	62	Superstitious	38
Very religious	53	Tradition-loving	37
Musical	43	Loyal to family ties	29
Happy-go-lucky	38	Physically dirty	27
Loud	32	Quiet	25

In many respects there is a striking similarity between the specific contents of the beliefs of the white Princeton boys of 1933 and the Negro Virginia State College students of 1940. The Negro students seem to be somewhat less stereotyped in their thinking than do the Princeton students (as is indicated by lower agreement among the Negro subjects than among the white subjects), but it is of interest to note that both groups paint very much the same pictures: For both groups is the Negro happy-go-lucky, superstitious, and loud ("ostentatious" seems to be the Princeton word for "loud"). For both groups is the Jew shrewd, grasping, and industrious. For both groups is the Chinese superstitious, tradition-loving, and loyal to family ties, and for both groups is the German scientifically minded and intelligent.

[1] It should be remembered that some of the attributes ascribed to the Germans by Bayton's students (*e.g.*, highly nationalistic, cruel) may reflect the specific influence of the war and the Nazi activities, Bayton's study being done in 1940.

Ambiguity of Objects and Events as Environmental Supports for Racial Prejudice.—In addition to the various objects, events, relationships, and the beliefs and attitudes of others that can serve as environmental supports for perceptions involved in racial prejudice are those objects or events which, because of their *ambiguity*, are easily perceived in such a manner as to give them attributes that then establish those objects and events as environmental supports of racial prejudice. In a sense, the perceptual processes "create" these environmental supports.

It will be remembered that the perceptual characteristics of a substructure are determined in large measure by the major structure of which it is a part (see page 94). Thus, the prejudiced person whose stereotype of Irishmen includes the attributes of a broad, apelike face may perceive these attributes in any person who, he is told, is an Irishman. In many instances such a perception will come about readily (whether the person is Irish or not) because faces are frequently ambiguous with respect to structure; and in that sense, the very ambiguity of a face, a nose, complexion, and other anatomical characteristics makes possible a whole host of environmental supports for differentiating people one from another. This is not restricted, of course, to physical cues. Psychological traits are notoriously ambiguous, and so, to perhaps a somewhat lesser extent, are sociological traits and the beliefs, opinions, and verbalizations of others.

Such ambiguity of physical traits, behavior traits, etc., and the resulting distorted perceptions can have an additional effect in supporting racial prejudice. As a consequence of the factors involved in cognitive *re*-organization, the particular Irishman (in the example used above) will be remembered not only as a broad-faced, large-jawed person, but gradually, over time, other attributes of the man will "fall into line," and he will be remembered as a "typical" Irishman in *every* detail (see page 132). Such a "memory" will then give additional support to the original stereotype.

General Comments.—Because the United States is a "melting pot" of races and our population is made up of so many different ethnic stocks, the *possibility* of finding environmental supports for cognitive structures in which different peoples are segregated is greatly increased. This possibility is further strengthened because the various ethnic groups carry with them objective, differentiating cues—physical, psychological, and sociological. These differentiating cues accrue to these people because of biological, innate factors or because of the effects of discriminatory and repressive practices to which they have been subjected in this country or because of historical accident. Where such cues exist in fact, the prejudiced person, through the operation of various perceptual processes common to all people, maximizes the utility of these cues as supports for his beliefs and attitudes. Where such cues do not exist in fact, the prejudiced person, again through the operation of lawful perceptual processes, "invents" such cues, and the perception of such invented cues again supports and reinforces his beliefs and attitudes of prejudice. These environmental cues are found not only among the real people who make up our social world but also among the fictional people—in song and story. This fictional part of our real world is consistently, unambiguously, and deliberately peopled with ethnic groups displaying various physical, psychological, and sociological stigmata.

In addition to the above environmental supports, beliefs and attitudes of prejudice find support in the beliefs and attitudes of other people. It is almost impossible for any American to avoid coming into frequent and intimate contact with many other Americans whose perceptions, beliefs, and verbalizations are colored by racial prejudice. Whatever specific belief and attitude of prejudice any single American adopts—whether it includes the belief that the Negro is dirty, unintelligent, and superstitious; the Jew is grasping, shrewd, and ambitious; or the Chinese is sly, clannish, and strange—he will find social support in the beliefs and attitudes of many of his friends, teachers, coreligionists, fellow workers, and neighbors. This applies to a member of a minority group who is prejudiced against other minority groups (*e.g.*, the Negro vis-a-vis the Jew) as well as to members of the dominant groups.

The above data are of great help in our understanding of the formation of beliefs and attitudes of prejudice in the United States *today*. We have already seen, in our analysis of the functional nature of racial prejudice, that the American people, like people everywhere, have a wide variety of tensions, needs, and demands which can be served by beliefs and attitudes of racial prejudice. We have now seen in the present section that there exist in the real world of these people easily identifiable and appropriately constituted stimulus patterns which can evoke and support such beliefs and attitudes. To account for many instances of racial prejudice, we do not have to assume that any instruction in prejudice is necessary. We have seen in Chap. IV that not all cases of cognitive reorganization come through "training" or teaching. Just as we have seen that a person's goals and needs can change without specific training, so can his beliefs and attitudes undergo change through the operation of the basic organizing forces. Thus, for example, if an individual has a strong aversion to uncleanliness, *and if all the Negroes he sees fail to meet this person's standards of cleanliness* (for the various reasons we have discussed above), then it is highly likely that he will develop an anti-Negro attitude. In many cases this correspondence between need and object is enough to create prejudiced behavior. This is not an instance of circular reasoning, as long as we restrict this explanation to the contemporary person's racial prejudice and do not extend it to "explain" the prejudice of this person's grandfather who created the unclean Negro in the first place and clothed him with the psychological and sociological stigmata that our contemporary person now observes.

However, although many instances of prejudice are thus explainable, not all prejudices are. As we have repeatedly pointed out in this section, many of the perceptions of the prejudiced person are not based on objective fact. In many cases, the very perception of an "environmental support" for the belief of prejudice *presupposed prejudice to begin with*, and for these cases we cannot use the perception to account for the development of the belief—the causal sequence is the other way around. The only explanatory value of such perceptions is to help explain why and how racial prejudice can maintain itself once it exists. Furthermore, we have also seen that even where there is some basis in fact for the perception of a physical, psychological, or sociological stigma, such environmental supports are effective because of the *selective nature* of perception, and the cause of the selectivity of perception is in many instances due to the already existing belief or attitude of prejudice. Frequently, in other words, an individual selects out *because he is prejudiced*, he is not prejudiced *because he selects out*. Finally, it is also obvious that not all the environmental supports and the beliefs and attitudes of Americans are of such a nature as to support racial prejudice. The average American is exposed to stimulus patterns that support democratic beliefs and attitudes as well. To understand the role of the environmental supports we have discussed, we must realize that our culture is not homogeneous, and we must therefore understand how and why one set of environmental supports appears to be winning out over another set, as far as the development of beliefs and attitudes about minority groups is concerned.

To answer all the above problems we must next turn our attention to the third and last section of our analysis of racial prejudice in the United States today—the role and process of education, guidance, training, and propaganda in the development of beliefs and attitudes of racial prejudice.

TEACHING RACIAL PREJUDICE

The problem in this section of our analysis is to determine the processes by which the educational agencies of America, through teaching, training, guidance, and propaganda, induce beliefs and attitudes of racial prejudice. We must examine the techniques that are used to encourage the individual to *pay attention to* the environmental supports we have discussed in the preceding section and those which encourage the release of tensions through *racially discriminatory action*. This statement of the problem does *not* imply that the educational agencies do all this deliberately. In many cases it is completely unintentional and, as a matter of fact, contrary to the sincerely avowed aims of the agency. But as we have seen in Chap. IX, the cognitive reorganization that results from "conscious" propaganda or education is no different from that which accompanies "unconscious" efforts. Nor does the above statement of the problem refer only to formal educational agencies. As was pointed out in Chap. VI, "educational agencies" not only refer to our schools and colleges but also refer to our parents, children, friends, the neighborhood gang, the office mate or the man at work on the next bench, the union leader, the straw boss, the newspaper editor, the motion-picture producer, the advertising copy writer, the congressman, the priest, minister, or rabbi, and many others. The term *educational agencies* includes ". . . every functioning, stimulating person and object. . . within the individual's ken" (page 179). It is in this general sense that the term will be used in the following discussion.

The Role of "Teacher."—The significant influence that the teacher plays in the development of beliefs and attitudes of racial prejudice is indicated by the well-authenticated fact that contact with *ideas* about race may be just as influential as contact with members of the race itself in the formation of beliefs and attitudes in this area.

This conclusion can be drawn from some of the data we have already examined. As many writers have pointed out, the ethnic group that consistently is found at the bottom of the racial preference list represents an extreme of unfamiliarity. Thus not many Americans can have come into contact with Hindus, who, it can be seen from Table 7, page 461, represent but *two-thousandths of one per cent of the American population*, but the Hindu is consistently placed at the bottom of racial preference lists. It is the ideas about the Hindu that are important here.

Horowitz (1936), on the basis of his study of the development of attitudes toward the Negro among Northern and Southern white children, points out,

Young children were found not to be devoid of prejudice; contact with a "nice" Negro is not a universal panacea; living as neighbors going to a common school was found to be insufficient; Northern children were found to differ very, very slightly from Southern children. It seems that attitudes toward Negroes are now chiefly determined not by contacts with Negroes, but by contact with the prevalent attitude toward Negroes.

And more recently, Radke (1946a) found children ranging in age from nine to eighteen who had not had any personal experiences with either Jews or Negroes but who, nevertheless, had beliefs and attitudes of prejudice, the contents of which were characterized by the same pattern that we have already described.

The point of the above data and observations is not that the "teacher" of racial prejudice (the individual who is the "carrier" of prevailing ideas about Negroes and Jews and Chinese and Irishmen) is more important than contact with Negroes and Jews and Chinese—as Horowitz's last sentence seems to indicate—but that it may be just as important an influence.

That the racial beliefs and attitudes of one's associates must be considered as important sources of data for the learning process of the individual not only is supported by the above data but also follows from what we have already seen to be generally true for the development of all beliefs and attitudes. The "data" for beliefs are very rarely restricted to those which can be collected first-hand. We "know" and believe many things because of the say-so of authorities (see page 187).

The estimate, then, that at least 80 per cent of Americans hold beliefs or attitudes of racial prejudice (and in our terms all Americans are "teachers" of all other Americans), coupled with the observation that the teacher has a signficant role to play in determining the development of beliefs and attitudes of prejudice, indicates immediately one of the reasons why such beliefs and attitudes develop. However, this merely characterizes the nature of the personnel who staff our educational agencies. We must know much more before we have an adequate account of the teaching process involved.

Teaching Techniques.—How does the teacher present his data to the pupil, and why does the pupil incorporate the teacher's data into his own beliefs—many times in preference to contradictory data supplied him by other teachers? There are almost as many different answers to this question as there are teaching and learning individuals. The method of teaching racial prejudice ranges from the most simple and direct use of corporal punishment to the subtle (and frequently "unconscious") creation of a situation where the learning of racial prejudice takes on many of the aspects of problem solving. It might be said that the champions of any educational procedure, any learning theory, can find effective demonstrations of their positions in education for racial prejudice in the United States. Some of the techniques in vogue seem to be patterned after the "conditioning" theory, some seem to be guided by the "learning by doing" principles, some demand that the pupil "redintegrate," generalize, induce, deduce, etc.

"Direct" training.—Horowitz and Horowitz (1938), in the study already referred to on page 180, have shown that among some groups of whites in Tennessee the child is taught to regard the Negro in a derogatory fashion by the use of insistent exhortation accompanied by the use of force. Every

time a white child is found playing with a Negro child, he is told that the Negro is dirty and breeds disease, and then the child is whipped for having played with the Negro child. He is led to understand that he will be continued to be whipped as long as he persists in playing with Negro children. As he grows older, he may rationalize his behavior; he may say that he stays away from Negro children for the "reasons" his mother originally gave him—only this time claiming the reasons as his own and as self-evident. He may even have different needs being served by his prejudice, but the original learning took place under the lash of the whip and in the service of the need to avoid a "whupping."

No less direct and straightforward is much of the anti-Negro, anti-Chinese, anti-Japanese, anti-Catholic, anti-Jewish propaganda put out by a large number of organizations in the United States. Strong (1941), who has made a study of organized racial prejudice in this country, has counted 119 anti-Semitic organizations alone in the United States—the first one of which was organized in 1915.

At this point it is relevant to consider the instances where racial prejudice develops in apparent response to an unpleasant experience that a person might have with a Negro, a Jew, or any other minority-group member. Here, it might appear, there is no "teaching" in the sense that some educational agency has had any influence, but the actual, objective experience itself has induced a lasting effect. Thus, for example, Allport and Kramer (1946) found that most of their prejudiced subjects reported unpleasant memories of experiences with minority-group members against whom they were prejudiced, and it might therefore be assumed that they were prejudiced because of these experiences—no "teaching" being involved. There are several points to be made here, however.

In the first place, such memories may reflect either "creative forgetting" (see page 134) or the rationalization of present beliefs by "selective forgetting" (see page 132). However, this probably does not account for all such cases. In a number of instances, a belief or attitude of racial prejudice may have developed as a consequence of an actual unpleasant experience with a member of a minority group. But an unpleasant experience by itself will not usually result in an enduring and generalized belief or attitude. As we have seen in Chap. IV, the cognitive reorganization process cannot be described as a process of "conditioning." The mere sequence of event A and effect B does not guarantee that an "association" will be established. It is not "the objective sequence of cause and effect that determines the nature of the resulting cognitive organization. . . only those things which are perceived and attended to will play a role in the new cognitive organizations. . ." (page 120). Thus, if an individual is badly treated by a Negro, that in itself does not explain why he should adopt an anti-Negro attitude. In most cases he will adopt an anti-Negro attitude *only if he has been previously "set" to regard Negroes as a specially bad group or if the Negro stands out as a special percept from all other people.*   It is for this reason, for example, that an individual who is badly treated by a man with glasses does not adopt a generalized "antiglasses" attitude as readily as a man who is badly treated by a Negro would adopt an anti-Negro attitude.   The cognitive structure will be reorganized in terms of the particular objects or attributes that are dominant in the perceptual field at the moment.

The reason why simple and direct teaching (whether of the type illustrated by the Tennessee mother or the anti-Semitic organization) is relatively efficient derives from the following considerations: (1) Genuine and important needs and demands are appealed to; (2) the objects of the to-be-induced beliefs are easily apprehended by the pupils and already stand out as prominent objects in his field; and (3) social support is available for the beliefs that are being taught.

Not all direct education of this sort is as obvious, straightforward, and brutal as the instances cited above.   More sophisticated mothers and propagandists may use gentler methods.   Children are told that it is not "nice" to play with Negroes, or it may be suggested that "Our kind of people don't associate with Jews."   But the teaching is as directed as the previous cases, and the reasons for its "taking" are the same.

"Indirect" training.—Midway between such direct teaching and the development of beliefs and attitudes of racial prejudice through creative thinking is the situation where the child hears the mother or father or friend refer to the Jew or the Mexican or the Negro in derogatory terms.   The child hears that the "Jewish grocer is untrustworthy," that "Jim, the porter, probably uses all of his money to get drunk—like all colored people." Frequently, of course, these comments are not intended for the child's ears; they are not made as part of a conscious and directed educational program, but racial prejudice being so universal a phenomenon of the thinking of the people around him, the child cannot help hearing such comments.   The same is true of much of the content of the reading matter of the adult.   The omissions and inclusions of certain data in school and college textbooks[1] or the humorous anecdotes about Negroes in *The Reader's Digest*[2] need not be conscious attempts to induce beliefs and attitudes of racial prejudice, but

[1] See Eleazer's (1937) and Carpenter's (1941) studies.

[2] See the publication prepared by the National Association for the Advancement of Colored People, "An analysis: Negroes in anecdotes. *The Reader's Digest*: January, 1942, May, 1944."

people read them, just as the child overhears the remarks of his elders, and they become part of the child's or adult's world. Here the "training" is effective, not because any strong need is appealed to, not because the child or adult is threatened with punishment, but because, as we have seen, cognitive reorganization can occur when the stimulus pattern in the real world is strong enough or outstanding enough as to evoke a perception. What the adult says is interesting. The anecodote about "Rastus" is funny. In the absence of contradictory data and with the support of many other similar stimulus patterns, racially prejudiced beliefs will be formed. They may not become attitudes, they may not be important, salient, or intense—but they may remain as beliefs.

Formation of prejudice as problem-solving.—At the other extreme is the educational pattern that provides the individual with an over-all approach to his social adjustmental problems and that, almost inevitably, leads to the acquisition of beliefs and attitudes of racial prejudice. We have seen in Chap. IV that the learning process frequently consists of a series of hierarchically related structures, where the most general organization determines the nature of the successive solution attempts. Once the over-all approach is laid down, the subsequent attempts to solve problems will reflect that over-all approach (see page 117). Many individuals in our society are taught a general "way of life" that emphasizes the value of patterning behavior on the accepted and the conventional—to lean for support on external, institutionalized sanctions. Once having been taught that, the individual will attempt to solve many of his interpersonal problems in those terms. And that means, as the studies of both Frenkel-Brunswik and Sanford and Allport and Kramer have suggested, a hostility toward groups who do not subscribe to the same institutional pattern. For example, both those studies indicate that, at least for the University of California students and the Radcliffe and Harvard students, emphasis on religion and nationalism is characteristic of people with intense racial prejudices. "Connected with the conventional moral code is an emphasis on *religion and nationalism as a source of support that could substitute for genuine effort and achievement. . .* our high extremes are *overconformist;* they adhere rigidly to middle-class values and are made anxious by the appearance, in themselves or in others, of tendencies of an opposite character" (Frenkel-Brunswik and Sanford, 1945). In the Allport and Kramer study, confirmatory evidence of this pattern is indicated by the analysis of the subjects' racial prejudice as related to religious training. To the question, "To what degree has religion been an influence in your upbringing?" the students divided themselves in the following way: Those who said that religion had a marked or "moderate" influence had among their number a considerably larger percentage of racially prejudiced people than those who said that religion had a slight or zero influence.

It should be emphasized, however, that the above data do not mean that religion per se teaches racial prejudice or even that religious training neces- sarily predisposes the person to racial prejudice. The crucial point is that the type of education which overemphasizes the importance of conformity, of institutionalized patterns of behavior, of the "value" of leaning on rigidly functioning religious or nationalistic patterns for personal support may lead the individual to hostility toward other people or groups who depart from these standards. It is not religion or even nationalism that is necessarily bad, then, but how religion and nationalism are taught and the role that these beliefs play in the person's life.

Closely related to this sequence is the kind of cognitive reorganization leading to racial prejudice that frequently occurs among members of the "middle class" and the members of minority groups themselves. American society is a relatively mobile society. Not only is an individual legally permitted to move upward in the social hierarchy (at least if he is white, Protestant, Anglo-Saxon), but he is encouraged to do so by his teachers, parents, and national song and story. An individual who has recently arrived at a higher stratum in society, who is relatively insecure about his social status, or who aspires to the next rung has been described as a "mar- ginal man"—a person "who stands on the boundary. . . between two groups. . . . He does not belong to either of them, or at least he is not certain about his belongingness" (Lewin, 1939). In response to these insecurity feelings, the marginal man reacts by overemphasizing conformity to the cultural pattern of the group with which he wishes to establish strong identification. It is the marginal parent who will attempt to inculcate in his children the approved patterns of behavior with a rigidity that allows for no deviation. It is the marginal person who will, himself, adopt such a general outlook or "functional solution" with respect to social problems.

Similarly, many members of minority groups can be seen as marginal people. Many members of minority groups wish to identify themselves with the dominant members of the country. They, too, wish to partake of the mobility characteristic of American society. And, thus, as Lewin (1941) points out, "It is recognized in sociology that the members of the lower social strata tend to accept the fashions, values and ideals of the higher strata. In the case of the underprivileged group, it means that their opinions about themselves are greatly influenced by the low esteem the majority has for them." In other words, the very process we have described for the "middle-class" person holds for the member of the minority group with the result that, in his striving for conformity, the minority-group member will frequently develop beliefs and attitudes of racial prejudices directed against other minority groups *and even against members of his own group.*

We have already examined some data that support this conclusion. Thus, it will be remembered, the Negro college students of Bayton's study (see page 479) held the same stereotyped beliefs about the Negro as did the white students of Katz and Braly's study. And Radke (1946*b*) has shown in a study in which Jewish children matched descriptions with pictures of Jews and non-Jews that the older Jewish children were more inclined to ascribe negative traits to Jews than were the younger children. Radke also found that upper-class Jews were more inclined than the poorer Jews to feel that the undesirable traits of the Jews themselves were responsible for anti-Semitism. The Negro, the Jew, the Irishman, the Catholic, the Mexican, the foreign-born all show the same cognitive reorganization process that the middle-class white, Protestant Anglo-Saxon does. The result, as Rose (1947) points out, is that "The line-up in America is not majority *vs.* minorities, but whites *vs.* Negroes, Gentiles *vs.* Jews, native-born *vs.* foreign born, New Englanders *vs.* 'Canucks,' and so on." And he might have added, "Jews *vs.* Negroes, 'Canucks' *vs.* Jews, Negroes *vs.* foreign born, etc."

Learning Patterns.—The varied educational techniques for the inculcation of racial prejudice discussed above result in various learning patterns on the part of the pupil. In the light of the variability of the training techniques, it is rather futile to seek *one* pattern of racial prejudice development. That is, some children start with a generalized racial prejudice where the members of a given race are "bad" on every count and end up with a more differentiated, precise, and stabilized set of beliefs or attitudes. Other children seem to start with fairly differentiated belief systems. The pattern that will characterize any given child's development of these beliefs and attitudes is a function of what the child was taught, by whom, and under what general circumstances.

The study by Blake and Dennis (1943) illustrates the first pattern. These experimenters tested 324 pupils from grades 4 through 11 in a Virginia school for white children. The pupils were asked to compare Negroes and whites in regard to each of 60 traits (such as cheerful, cruel, easygoing, religious, emotional, etc.). For many of these traits the high-school seniors showed a high agreement as far as the *differentiated* content of their beliefs about the Negro was concerned. The younger subjects, however, showed an *undifferentiated* communality in content—they agreed that the Negro was "bad" on all counts. The younger white child, in his undifferentiated prejudice, even attributed certain traits to white people that the older child attributed to the Negro, *e.g.*, "more religious." For the younger child, being religious was "good" and therefore not attributable to the Negro. This undifferentiated belief, Blake and Dennis found, persists until about the fourth or fifth grade—after which, in response to more specific training and increased differential perceptions, the beliefs become differentiated until at last the Negro is seen in the generally stereotyped fashion common to the members of adult society in Virginia.

Horowitz' (1936) study, on the other hand, showed the opposite developmental pattern. Using as his subjects Northern white boys from kindergarten age through eighth grade, Horowitz presented them with a set of photographs of individual white and Negro boys, of groups of white and Negro boys at play, and of mixed groups at play. His subjects were then asked to make three judgments: (1) to indicate their preferences from among an assortment of white and Negro faces, (2) to indicate which individual boy pictured they would like to take home with them for luncheon or with whom they would like to play ball, and finally, in the photographs of the white boys alone at play and the mixed groups at play, they were asked (3) to indicate which groups they would like to join. When Horowitz correlated the results of one choice against the others, he found low correlations at the kindergarten level but increasingly higher correlations as his subjects grew older. In other words, a kindergarten child might show prejudice in one situation but not in another—a Negro child might be perfectly acceptable as a member of a ball team but not as a luncheon companion, etc. But an eighth-grade child was relatively consistent in his attitudes toward the Negro in all situations. In this case, then, the child starts off his educational career by learning one "bad" thing about the Negro. As his experiences increase, as he comes into more and more contact with more and more prejudiced people, he learns more and more bad things about the Negro; and by the time he has reached the eighth grade, he, too, has the full-blown, integrated, precise stereotype characteristic of the members of adult society in New York.[1]

Teaching "Prejudice-prone" Needs.—We know that the cultural pattern is influential in inducing specific tensions and needs in individuals (see page 47, Chap. II). We have also pointed out that some tensions and needs are more prejudice-prone than others (see page 199, Chap. VI). Any discussion of the role of teaching in the development of racial prejudice

---

[1] For additional investigations that have studied the pattern of formation of beliefs and attitudes of racial prejudice in children, see Moreno (1934) and Criswell (1937), who used sociometric techniques (see p. 375, Chap. X) to measure racial prejudice of school children.

must take into account the effects of our educational agencies on the need structures of people.

Here, as in so many places throughout this analysis, it would prove either fruitless or impossible to examine the cultural etiology of each need and emotion separately. What may be valuable, however, is to examine certain statistically common tension-belief complexes. There are at least two such groups of complexes that merit brief attention: (1) prejudice associated with repressed needs and (2) prejudice associated with frustrated needs. How, and to what extent do our educational agencies induce repressed and frustrated needs?

Repressed needs.—Repressed needs are not unique to the people of the United States. It is perhaps true that every society creates conflict situations among the basic needs of the individual which result in the repression of one of the conflicting needs. But there is some clinical evidence for the hypothesis that in certain segments of our society the educational and training procedures in vogue are such as to encourage a fairly high incidence of repressed needs. This is the segment we have already discussed in some detail—the "middle class." We have already seen that many members of the middle class teach and are taught the desirability of *conformity* as a way of life. The need to conform is taught with such rigidity as, in many instances, to prohibit even deviating *thoughts*. As Frenkel-Brunswik and Sanford point out,

The mischief is done when those trends which are taboo according to class standards become repressed, and hence no longer susceptible to . . . control. This is most likely to happen when the parents are too concerned and too insistent with respect to the positive aims for the child and too threatening and coercive with respect to the "bad" things. The child is thus taught to view behavior in terms of black and white, "good" and "evil"; and the "evil" is made to appear so terrible that he cannot think of it as something in himself which needs to be modified or controlled, but as something that exists in other "bad" people and needs to be stamped out completely.

As we have already pointed out, America is a class society, but also a mobile society. This sociological pattern—a class society wherein each class has a fairly well-defined list of "goods" and "bads" and a mobile society which produces a large number of "marginal" individuals—defines a psychological situation that encourages the creation of repressed-need structures among a large section of American society.

Frustrated needs.—In discussing need blockage in Chap. II, it was seen that perhaps the most common fate of all needs, in all societies, is that they be blocked in their expression at one time or another. But social orders can differ in the extent to which they frustrate needs and in the type of needs they most frequently block. Societies like ours, which are characterized by educational attempts to induce certain economic and social needs on the one hand and, on the other, make it impossible or very difficult to satisfy these needs, must, necessarily, create widespread and significant experiences of need frustration (see page 52, Chap. II).

Characteristic of our economic pattern are two aspects that almost guarantee the creation of whole groups or classes of people experiencing daily, chronic economic frustration interspersed with periods of acute frustration. These aspects are the maldistribution of wealth and the periodic economic depressions. Our educational agencies do not attempt to induce economic needs differentially; and even if they attempted to do so, it would be almost impossible. The lower economic third of our population, as well as the upper third, is told that it needs two automobiles, television sets, U.S. Steel garbage cans, Monel-metal bathroom fixtures, and membership in after-shaving lotion clubs. In the light of these educational influences almost any significant spread between the incomes of the lower third and the upper third that does not permit the economically unfavored group to gratify these induced needs is potentially frustrating. Economic depressions, of course, with wholesale cuts in the income of the lower third, intensify this process.

But this process is not a function only of our economic system. Many of our other needs follow the same pattern. Thus, our educational philosophy attempts to induce in all of us the need to go to college—and to the best colleges. Our patterns of prejudice or our economic patterns make that impossible of fulfillment for many of us. Our literature, magazines, motion pictures, advertisements (educational agencies) all extol the delights and glories of "forbidden sex." Our religious, legal, and moral laws (educational agencies) say "Don't touch!" Our educational agencies, in other words, are inconsistent in what they teach and are therefore frustration inducing. They create veritable never-never lands which abound with frigidaires, yachts, television sets, glamorous exotic women, and men of distinction. We are taught to want them, and to want them, we are taught, is proof of our enterprise and our sound Americanism. And then we are prevented by our economic organizations and practices, by our church and our parents and our neighbors from getting them. There is much in our culture that induces frustration.

General Comments.—Beliefs and attitudes of racial prejudice develop not only in response to the perception of the objective nature of our world—a world peopled with groups of individuals many of whom carry with them objectively definable cues which set them apart as a special people—

but also in response to the efforts of our educational agencies. These educational agencies are staffed with "teachers" who themselves have beliefs and attitudes of racial prejudice, and contact with ideas about race can be effective in inducing beliefs or racial prejudice. These teachers and agencies use a number of different educational and training techniques to teach racial prejudice, and the learning patterns of the "pupils" are correspondingly varied. Despite all this variation, and despite the fact that many Americans are also exposed to democratic beliefs and education, racial-prejudice teaching is extremely effective and frequently (and perhaps usually) wins out over counterteaching and propaganda.

There is a number of reasons why racial-prejudice teaching is so effective: (1) The *objective situation* is, by and large, more favorable for the prejudice pattern than for the democratic pattern; (2) it is easier to find *social support* for the prejudice pattern than for the democratic pattern; and (3) our educational agencies tend to induce some *prejudice-prone needs*—needs that are more readily supported by beliefs and attitudes of prejudice than by beliefs and attitudes of democracy. As our analysis of the learning process has indicated, and as any educator will readily see, under these circumstances the cards are stacked in favor of the teachers of racial prejudice.

However, no matter how stacked the cards may be, a very good possibility remains for changing the situation to one where beliefs and attitudes of democracy can prevail. The reasons for this possibility inhere in the fact that beliefs and attitudes of democracy can also be taught, that our educational agencies are staffed with democratically minded people as well as prejudiced-minded, that our society is not homogeneous in terms of the kinds of beliefs and attitudes for which social support can be found, and that there are aspects of the objective situation that can serve as environmental supports for democratic beliefs. To this question of controlling racial prejudice we shall turn in the next chapter. The reason we have spent so much time on an analysis of the dark side of the picture lies in the fundamental proposition that a realistic diagnosis of a situation is demanded before a sound cure can be proposed

SUMMARY

The fact that racial prejudice is a current problem of deep concern for so many members of our society demands that any treatise of social psychology give it serious consideration. The added fact that so much psychological and sociological research has been done on racial prejudice makes possible such consideration. The objective of the present chapter is stated as an analysis of racial prejudice in the United States in terms of general psychological principles and the specific data relevant to the problem.

Racial prejudice is defined as referring to beliefs and attitudes (no matter how significant or intense) that are disadvantageous to members of minority groups. The word "racial" is thus used in its popular and not scientific sense—no fundamental biological differences among these minority groups being implied. In characterizing the analysis to be made in this chapter as a problem in the psychology of the *individual*, it is pointed out that this does not limit the kind of data to be examined (sociological as opposed to psychological) but specifies only the unit of analysis. However, except for an illustrative example, the historical development of racial prejudice in the United States is not explored.

In illustrating the proposition that the origins of racial prejudice can frequently be traced to historical "accident," the thesis advanced by Tannenbaum is outlined. This thesis suggests that the reason the Negro became a problem of racial prejudice in the United States, while he did so to a far less extent south of the Rio Grande, is due to the different laws that existed in these two areas before the first Negro ever appeared in either area. However, it is pointed out that such an analysis is of little aid in telling us why the American of the twentieth century is anti-Negro.

The first section of the analysis proper is given over to the functional character of racial prejudice. The relations between racial prejudice and (1) pathological personality systems, (2) aggressions induced by frustration of various needs, (3) culturally disapproved behavior, (4) ambiguous crisis situations, (5) repressed tensions, and (6) self-regard and conformity needs are discussed, and experimental as well as clinical data concerning these relationships are examined. It is concluded that racial prejudice can function to support most of man's needs; and in the service of these needs, racial prejudice can be sometimes characterized as vicious and aggressive and sometimes as passive and "tolerant" avoidance. It is emphasized that no single need or personality structure lies behind all racial prejudices, and in that sense there can be no "special" motivational theory of racial prejudice. However, it is also pointed out that racial prejudices, in the American culture, can frequently result in guilt feelings, emotional conflicts, and defense reactions for the person harboring these prejudices. Finally, the student is cautioned that a motivational analysis does not "explain" racial prejudice—it merely points to the range of motive power behind these beliefs and attitudes. To understand how needs come to be served by racial prejudices it is necessary to know something about the real world in which the individual seeks to satisfy his needs and meet his demands.

The second section of the analysis is then given over to a survey of the environmental supports for beliefs and attitudes of racial prejudice. Two major kinds of environmental supports are differentiated: (1) observable objects, events, and relationships and (2) the beliefs and attitudes of other people. In addition the ambiguity of many objects and events is also discussed as contributing environmental supports. In discussing the first of these, three different sets of cues characteristic of minority-group members are described which serve as environmental supports for racial prejudice: physical, psychological, and sociological. The statistical, psychometric, and experimental data relating to each and the processes involved in the perception of these cues are examined (the examination being extended to the "fictional" world as well). Of the three, it is concluded that the sociological cues, which accrue to minority-group members as a consequence of widespread segregation practices, are the most significant environmental supports of racial prejudice. In discussing beliefs and attitudes of other people as environmental supports of racial prejudice, data taken from polling surveys and more intensive studies as well as a number of experimental investigations are examined in some detail. It is concluded that at least 80 per cent of the American people harbor beliefs and attitudes of racial prejudice, that such prejudices are found among all classes and conditions of men, that the content and nature of these beliefs and attitudes are highly stereotyped and stable. In summary it is pointed out that because of the wealth of environmental supports for such prejudices, many instances of these prejudices can be explained without recourse to any active "teaching." However, not all racial prejudices can be thus explained. For a complete understanding of racial prejudice in the United States, it is also essential to investigate the role of education in the development of these beliefs and attitudes.

The final section of the analysis, then, concerns itself with an examination of the techniques that are used by our "educational agencies" to encourage the individual to pay attention to the environmental supports discussed in the preceding section and to encourage the release of tensions through racially discriminatory action. Educational agencies are defined broadly so as to include every stimulating person and object within the individual's environment. It is first pointed out that contact with ideas about race may be just as influential as contact with members of the race itself in the formation of beliefs and attitudes in this area. Some experimental evidence is adduced for this statement, and it is concluded that the role of the "teacher" can be important. The various teaching techniques employed are then discussed, including direct training, indirect training, and the formation of prejudice as problem solving. This last process is seen as specially applicable to certain segments of American society as well as to members of the minority groups themselves, who also display racial prejudice. These various teaching techniques are seen as leading to various learning patterns on the part of the pupil, and two general patterns are illustrated from experimental work with the development of racial prejudice in children. Finally a brief discussion follows of the role of our educational agencies in the development of certain prejudice-prone need structures—especially in the creation of repressed and frustrated needs.

In concluding the chapter the reasons for the effectiveness of the teaching of racial prejudice are outlined, but it is also pointed out that no matter how the cards are stacked in favor of racial prejudice in the United States, there still remains the possibility of controlling beliefs and attitudes of racial prejudice. To this question of controlling racial prejudice the next chapter will be devoted.

BIBLIOGRAPHY

ALLPORT, G. W.: 1944. The bigot in our midst. *Commonweal*, Oct. 6, 2–3.

ALLPORT, G. W., and KRAMER, B. M.: 1946. Some roots of prejudice. *J. Psychol.*, **22,** 9–39.

BARUCH, D. W.: 1946. *Glass house of prejudice.* New York: Morrow.

BAYTON, J. A.: 1941. The racial stereotypes of Negro college students. *J. abnorm. soc. Psychol.*, **36,** 97–102.

BICE, H. V.: 1938. A comparison of white and Negro pupils in North Carolina. *Proc. Amer. Ass. Stud. ment. Def.*, **43,** 72–77.

BLAKE, R., and DENNIS, W.: 1943. The development of stereotypes concerning the Negro. *J. abnorm. soc. Psychol.*, **38,** 525–531.

BOGARDUS, E. S.: 1928. *Immigration and race attitudes.* Boston: Heath.

BOLTON, E. B.: 1935. Effect of knowledge upon attitudes toward the Negro. *J. soc. Psychol.*, **6,** 68–90.

BRIGHAM, C. C.: 1930. Intelligence tests of immigrant groups. *Psychol. Rev.*, **37,** 158–165.

BRUNER, J. S., and GOODMAN, C. C.: 1947. Value and need as organizing factors in perception. *J. abnorm. soc. Psychol.*, **42,** 33–44.

CARPENTER, M. E.: 1941. *The treatment of the Negro in American history school textbooks.* Menasha: Banta.

CRISWELL, J. H.: 1937. Racial cleavage in Negro-white groups. *Sociometry*, **1,** 81–89.

CUSHMAN, R. E.: 1947. The laws of the land. *Survey Graphic*, **36,** No. 1, 14ff.

DOLLARD, C., and YOUNG, D.: 1947. In the armed forces. *Survey Graphic*, **36,** No. 1, 66ff.

DOLLARD, J.: 1937. *Caste and class in a Southern town.* New Haven: Yale Univ. Press.

DOLLARD, J., DOOB, L., et al.: 1939. *Frustration and aggression.* New Haven: Yale Univ. Press.

ELEAZER, R. B.: 1937. *School books and racial antagonisms*, 3d ed. Atlanta: Executive Committee, Conference on Education and Race Relations.

Federal Council Churches of Christ in America: 1945. *Information Service*, **24,** No. 42.

FEINGOLD, G. A.: 1924. Intelligence of the first generation of immigrant groups. *J. educ. Psychol.*, **15,** 65–83.

Fortune Survey, III: 1946. *Fortune Mag.*, January, p. 157.

Fortune Survey: 1943. Fortune survey among high school students—Nov., 1942. *Publ. Opin. Quart.*, **7,** 167.

FRENKEL-BRUNSWIK, E., and SANFORD, R. N.: 1945. Some personality factors in anti-Semitism. *J. Psychol.*, **20**, 271–291.

GARRETT, H. E.: 1945. "Facts" and "interpretations" regarding race differences. *Science*, **101**, 404–406.

GOODENOUGH, F. L.: 1926. Racial differences in the intelligence of school children. *J. exp. Psychol.*, **9**, 388–397.

GUILFORD, J. P.: 1931. Racial preferences of a thousand American university students. *J. soc. Psychol.*, **2**, 179–204.

HARTLEY, E.: 1946. *Problems in prejudice.* New York: King's Crown Press.

HIRSCH, N. D. M.: 1926. A study of natio-racial mental differences. *Genet. Psychol. Monogr.*, **1**, 231–406.

HOLLINGWORTH, L. S., and WITTY, P.: 1940. Intelligence as related to race. *Yearb. nat. Soc. Stud. Educ.*, **39**, 257–269.

HOROWITZ, E. L.: 1936. The development of attitudes toward the Negro. *Arch. Psychol.*, **28**, No. 194.

HOROWITZ, E. L.: 1944. *In* Klineberg, O. (ed.), *Characteristics of the American Negro.* New York: Harper.

HOROWITZ, E. L., and HOROWITZ, R. E.: 1938. Development of social attitudes in children. *Sociometry*, **1**, 301–338.

JENKINS, M. D.: 1940. Racial differences and intelligence. *Amer. Teach.*, **24**, 12–13.

KATZ, D.: 1946. The interpretation of survey findings. *J. soc. Issues*, **2**, No. 2, 33–44.

KATZ, D., and ALLPORT, F. H.: 1931. *Students' attitudes.* Syracuse: Craftsman Press.

KATZ, D., and BRALY, K.: 1933. Racial stereotypes of one hundred college students. *J. abnorm. soc. Psychol.*, **28**, 280–290.

KLINEBERG, O.: 1935. *Race differences.* New York: Harper.

LEVINSON, D. J., and SANFORD, R. N., 1944. A scale for the measurement of anti-Semitism. *J. Psychol.*, **17**, 339–370.

LEWIN, K.: 1939. Field theory and experiment in social psychology: concepts and methods. *Amer. J. Sociol.*, **44**, 868–896.

LEWIN, K.: 1941. Self-hatred among Jews. *Contemp. Jewish Rec.*, **4**, 219–232.

LINFIELD, H. S.: 1945. The Jewish population of the United States. *In Amer. Jewish Yearb.* 5706. Philadelphia: Jewish Publication Society of America.

LOHMAN, J. D., and EMBREE, E. R.: 1947. The nation's capital. *Survey Graphic*, **36**, No. 1, 33ff.

LUND, F. H., and BERG, W. C.: 1946. Identifiability of national characteristics. *J. soc. Psychol.*, **24**, 77–83.

McWILLIAMS, C.: 1947. Spectrum of segregation. *Survey Graphic*, **36**, No. 1, 22ff.

MELTZER, H.: 1939a. Group differences in nationality and race preferences of children. *Sociometry*, **2**, 86–105.

MELTZER, H.: 1939b. Nationality preferences and stereotypes of colored children. *J. genet. Psychol.*, **54**, 403–424.

MERTON, R. K.: 1940. Fact and factitiousness in ethnic opinionnaires. *Amer. sociol. Rev.*, **5**, 13–28.

MILLER, L.: 1947. The power of restrictive covenants. *Survey Graphic*, **36**, No. 1, 46ff.

MINARD, R. D.: 1931. Race attitudes of Iowa children. *Univ. Ia. Stud. Charact.*, **4**, No. 2.

MORENO, J. L.: 1934. *Who shall survive?* Washington, D. C.: *Nerv. Ment. Dis. Publ. Co.*

National Opinion Research Center: 1943. Attitudes toward Jews. *Publ. Opin. Quart.*, **7**, 313.

PINSON, K. S.: 1946.   Anti-Semitism.   *Encyclopaedia Britannica*, **2**, 74–78.

POPE, L.: 1947.   The Protestant experience.   *Survey Graphic*, **36**, No. 1, 59*ff.*

RADKE, M.: 1946*a*.   Children's attitudes toward minority groups.   *In* New trends in the investigation of prejudice.   *Ann. Amer. Acad. Polit. Soc. Sci.*, **244**, 168*ff.*

RADKE, M.: 1946*b*.   Unpublished study.   Reported in *The Christian Science Monitor*, July 17, p. 4.

REDL, F.: 1946.   The clinical approach.   *Intercult. Educ. News*, **7**, No. 4, 3–5.

REID, I.   DE A.: 1947.   Southern ways.   *Survey Graphic*, **36**, No. 1, 39*ff.*

ROBINSON, D., and ROHDE, S.: 1946.   Two experiments with an anti-Semitism poll. *J. abnorm. soc. Psychol.*, **41**, 136–144.

ROSE, A. M.: 1947.   *Studies in reduction of prejudice*.   Chicago: American Council on Race Relations.

SIMS, V. M., and PATRICK, J. R.: 1936.   Attitude toward the Negro of northern and southern college students.   *J. soc. Psychol.*, **7**, 192–204.

STRONG, D. S.: 1941.   *Organized anti-Semitism in America*.   Washington: American Council on Public Affairs.

TANNENBAUM, F.: 1947.   *Slave and citizen*.   New York: Knopf.

TOLMAN, E. C.: 1932.   *Purposive behavior in animals and men*.   New York: Century.

ZELIGS, R., and HENDRICKSON, G.: 1933.   Racial attitudes of 200 sixth-grade children. *Sociol. and Social Res.*, **18**, 26–36.

CHAPTER XIII

CONTROLLING RACIAL PREJUDICE

The social psychologist has a dual role when considering socially significant problems. He must be a diagnostician and a therapist—at least to the extent of ascertaining what people's attitudes and discriminatory behavior would be like under different social circumstances and by what change in the present social situation the desired attitudes and behavior could be engendered. This sets the problem for the present chapter. Having devoted a chapter to the analysis of racial prejudice in the United States, we must now address ourselves to the problem of controlling racial prejudice.

This chapter can deal with a control program only in a limited manner. What we can do is state the over-all psychological considerations and the most general strategy involved in controlling and changing racial prejudice. We cannot deal with all aspects of the problem, since that requires the data and principles of other social scientists—economists and political scientists, for instance—nor can we write a manual of tactics or a guide that will detail the specific measures even of a purely psychological nature to be taken by individuals wrestling with the problem of racial prejudice among their friends, their organizations, or their communities. In the first place, as we have seen in Chap. II (page 39), the scientist cannot make concrete predictions, he can make only conditional ones, since "alien" factors can always interfere with predictions based upon general principles. As Lewin (1946) has pointed out,

. . . lawfulness in social as in physical science means an "if so" relation, a linkage between hypothetical conditions and hypothetical effects. These laws do *not* tell *what* conditions exist locally, at a given place at a given time . . . . In social management, as in medicine, the practitioner will usually have the choice between various methods of treatment and he will require as much skill and ingenuity as the physician in regard to both diagnosis and treatment.

In the second place, not only do beliefs and attitudes of racial prejudice differ with respect to their specific contents, there is also a wide and significant variability in the role such beliefs and attitudes play in the personality structure of individuals. And we know that any effective program for

499

changing beliefs and attitudes must be "tailored," above all else, to these motivational factors.

All of this means that the application of any principle enunciated in this chapter must be *carefully examined in the specific context in which it is to be applied before putting it into practice.*

GENERAL CONSIDERATIONS

In addition to the above general precaution, the following specific considerations must be kept in mind by the field worker when he formulates a program designed to control racial prejudice.

1. *Each proposed step must be evaluated in terms of its "absolute" as well as its "relative" effectiveness.* We have pointed out in Chaps. VI and XII that the effectiveness of any one procedure in the attempt to change beliefs and attitudes will depend, to a large extent, on the simultaneous and integrated application of other procedures. Beliefs and attitudes are multidetermined, and their control requires a multidimensional program. Too frequently, however, the recognition of this principle leads to an undervaluation of the effectiveness of any one step. Thus, to argue that the racial quota system in colleges is only a "symptom" of prejudice and that, therefore, there is not much point in expending a great deal of effort in eliminating it is to underestimate the value of the single step. Of course, the removal of the quota systems from colleges, by itself, does very little to change the basic reasons that lie behind the racial prejudice of the college president or chairman of the Board of Regents or the college students, and its removal, therefore, will not accomplish everything we might like to see accomplished, but it can have a number of beneficial effects in the desired direction. The principle of the multidimensional approach, as we have indicated previously, is not the same as the "all-or-none" principle. The field worker must always do the most that he can, but he must also realize that any single step has its "absolute" value as well as a relative value.

2. *The effectiveness of any specific step will frequently vary with the size of the target group.* Some procedures may be quite valuable and feasible where an attempt is being made to change the racial prejudices of a single person or of a small neighborhood group but may be quite ineffective where an attempt is being made to change the racial prejudices of an entire city, state, or nation. It does not follow, either theoretically or practically, that when we deal with larger masses of people we need merely increase the size of the operation. As we have seen in Chap. X, the degree of intimacy of interpersonal relationships is an important factor in group dynamics, but large masses of people, in our complex society, are frequently organized together in such a manner as to make intimate interpersonal contact almost

impossible. This means that the theoretical principles applicable to a small group may not be applicable to a large mass of people. There are also limitations of feasibility. Thus it may be effective, in trying to change the prejudices of a group of graduate students at Teachers College, to take them on several week-end tours through Harlem (see page 195), but it would be quite unrealistic to suggest that some such program of interracial "parties" be promoted among 135 million people. The field worker must carefully evaluate any program that has been "pretested" on a small scale (no matter how carefully and scientifically) before he enthusiastically attempts to put it into practice on a large scale.

3. *Action research must be continuously applied at every stage of an action program.* That the social manager or field worker cannot take over, without further testing, any "action research" results which come from the laboratory of the social scientist suggests that evaluation and assessment research must be continued at every point of action. The results of this research must be used to determine both the general nature of the program in action and the planning of the next specific steps. The field worker and the researcher must cooperate throughout the action program. Lewin (1946), who first popularized the term *action research*, has clearly indicated the intimate relationship that must exist between action research and action in the following analysis of planning for social management:

Planning starts usually with something like a general idea. For one reason or another it seems desirable to reach a certain objective . . . . The first step then is to examine the idea carefully in the light of the means available. Frequently more fact-finding about the situation is required. If this first period of planning is successful, two items emerge: namely, an "overall plan" . . . and secondly, a decision in regard to the first step of the action. [The execution of the first step is followed by certain fact-finding which has several functions.] First it should evaluate the action . . . . Secondly, it gives the planners a chance to learn, that is, to gather new general insight, for instance, regarding the strength or weakness of certain weapons or techniques of action. Thirdly, this fact-finding should serve as a basis for modifying the "overall plan" . . . . [The above procedure is repeated again and again so that a scientifically sound program of action] proceeds in a spiral of steps each of which is composed of a circle of planning, action, and fact-finding about the result of the action.

This formulation of the relationship between the field worker and the researcher points the way to the solution to some of the problems that we have already listed. Where action research is closely geared to a program of action, the field worker can determine the "absolute" effectiveness of any single step, and he can evaluate the applicability of his program in terms of the size of his target group. Such research can also help him measure what seems to be an almost inevitable consequence of any social action—undesirable "side effects" or "kickbacks."

4. *Calculated risks must frequently be taken.* Most procedures designed to change beliefs and attitudes of people may have side effects that are undesirable and in the direction opposite from the one intended. From everything we know about the complex and indirect nature of cultural determinants of beliefs and attitudes, it is obvious that no procedure involving environmental change will induce the same cognitive changes in all people. Thus, to return to our previous example, a campaign to remove the quota system from a college may, if successful, remove one environmental support for prejudice; but in addition, it may provoke resentment on the part of some members of the college community, and this resentment may express itself in increased attacks on the racial or ethnic group in question. Frequently, there is no way to avoid such kickbacks, *but this cannot be ground for failing to put such procedures into effect.* There can be no psychologically perfect and foolproof program, and the social manager must be prepared to take a "calculated risk." He must weigh the expected benefits of any one step against the possible detrimental effects—and he must continually check on his predictions through action research. Such questions as long-term vs. immediate effects and the number of people who will be changed in one direction vs. the number of people who will be changed in the opposite direction must be considered.

Plan of This Chapter.—The present chapter is primarily addressed to the social field worker or the social manager—to the man of action rather than to the student of society. Because of this it is necessary to emphasize again that the reader must keep constantly in mind the above four cautions, or *caveats*, as he considers the general principles that follow.

These principles will be presented under three major groupings, which correspond to the groupings used in the analysis of racial prejudice: (1) changing racial prejudice through controlling and changing the motivational and emotional factors involved, (2) changing racial prejudice through controlling and changing the environmental supports of such beliefs, and (3) changing racial prejudice through educational and learning procedures.

CHANGING RACIAL PREJUDICE THROUGH MOTIVATIONAL CONTROL

While it is true that almost any need can be served by racial prejudice, we have also seen that some need structures are more prejudice prone than are others. It would be desirable, therefore, to remove, change, or otherwise control those specific needs and tensions—specifically, the repressed and frustrated needs.

Eliminating Repressed, Frustrated, and Socially Unacceptable Need Structures.—To eliminate the patterns of racial prejudice involving repressed tensions, aggressive impulses induced by the frustration of other needs, and actions engendered by culturally disapproved needs is not simply a negative program but is a "positive" program as well. First, steps must be taken to provide for the *adequate satisfaction* of man's common and socially acceptable needs; and second, the psychological insights of all people—especially parents—must be increased, and provision must be made for psychological therapy wherever it is indicated and no matter on how large a scale it may be necessary.

The positive approach.—With reference to the first of these objectives it should be clear that any economic, social, technological, or political policy or device that can minimize the frustration of any significant need is an important weapon in the control of the motivational forces leading to prejudice.

Different groups of people at different times are blocked from the satisfaction of different needs. No one measure can prove to be a panacea. To attack racial prejudice for one group or for one individual may involve raising the *economic* level of the person or persons concerned[1]; for another group or another person it may involve creating a freer *political* situation; and for still another group it may involve a more permissive situation for *leadership* expression. Such steps should not be regarded as "indirect" attacks on racial prejudice but as among some of the most direct attacks possible. An adequate minimum wage law or the abolition of the poll tax may be immediate contributions to the elimination of racially directed aggressive impulses induced by the frustration of economic or political needs.[2]

In addition to the needs that can be met by economic and political actions, there are many needs that can be met by the establishment of various cultural, fraternal, and recreational organizations. Such organizations should provide the individual with opportunities for fulfilling his need of a sense of vital participation in community affairs, for self-expression, leadership, and the many aesthetic, cultural, and recreational demands that characterize

---

[1] See, in this connection, the various correlations that have been reported by Raper (1933) and by Hovland and Sears (1940) between lynchings of Negroes in the South and per-acre value of cotton. Although the absolute values of these correlations have been questioned on statistical grounds by Mintz (1946), even he agrees that some relationship (about —.25) exists between the two variables; *i.e.*, when the economic level of the South drops, the number of lynchings tend to rise. The complex nature of the environmental determinants of beliefs and action would support Mintz's suggestion that the correlations cannot be linear or high, but it would also support the finding of some relationship between business indices and racial prejudice.

[2] In the next chapter the role played by the economic level in the frustration of various needs is detailed, and the student is referred to that chapter, especially p. 541.

people in the United States. In this connection the student is again referred to Chap. XIV for a discussion of how the labor union, for example, can (and in some instances does) serve as a social organization that provides socially accepted paths and goals for the satisfaction of many needs of the worker which would otherwise be blocked from acceptable expression. What is true of these labor unions is also true of other social organizations—the possibilities inhere in most social organizations and should be exploited.

The Therapeutic Approach.—The above program does not concern itself with countermeasures against need but rather with measures directed toward the satisfaction of existing needs. However, many needs are repressed and frustrated not only because the appropriate goals are unavailable but because of the profound and disturbing emotional experiences that have become attached to the expression of such needs and that, in turn, can create culturally unacceptable behavior. Thus, for example, we have seen in the preceding chapter how the very training of our children may be such as to promote fears and insecurities in the expression of such simple needs and demands as sex, elimination, group acceptance, conformity. The mechanisms of repression, projection, and displaced fears are not peculiar to individuals of any one economic, political, or religious class. Therefore, in addition to the economic, political, and social measures suggested above, we must have a program of prophylaxis and therapy designed to create emotional security and maturity in the individual as well as to remove the effects of past traumatic emotional experiences.

Such a program must concern itself with the psychological education of people from their infancy up, with parent-child relationships, with group behavior, with methods of indoctrinating our approved ideologies, morals, and ethics and, finally, with the provision of medical care for the neurotic and mentally sick of our population. The history of the two fields of *psychological guidance* and *psychotherapeutic counseling*[1] has indicated the possibilities of carrying on these activities on a wide scale. Parental, vocational, industrial, educational, and marriage-guidance centers have already established themselves as socially useful and acceptable institutions. They are no less demanded and no less feasible than public milk stations for babies from underprivileged homes or national, state, and local information services for business enterprises. These latter, when opened to the public, have decreased rickets and bankrupcies; the former can decrease beliefs and attitudes of racial prejudice. As far as psychotherapeutic counseling is concerned, although it may be true that "we cannot hope to

---

[1] Snyder (1947) presents a comprehensive review of the literature on psychotherapeutic counseling as of 1947, to which the student is referred.

psychoanalyze everybody" (as Frenkel-Brunswik and Sanford remark), much can be done, nevertheless, for the many people who need professional help in solving emotional problems and modifying emotional attitudes. Recent developments of interest here are those in the areas of "brief psychotherapy," "brief psychoanalysis,"[1] and "group therapy"—the last of which holds particular promise. Group therapy, though first adopted because of necessity—there not being enough therapists to supply each patient with an individual therapist (especially in military installations during the war)—has been demonstrated to have many significant advantages over individual therapy and is now generally acknowledged as an effective and relatively inexpensive psychotherapeutic counseling procedure. But what is most important is that it makes possible the provision of psychotherapeutic counseling service to much larger numbers of people. For our present concern, group therapy is also especially significant because it is perhaps the best form of therapy for such cases where the patient needs to gain social experience, where group relationships outside the family must be developed, or where he must learn to express personality traits in harmony with other persons.[2] All of these are directly relevant to helping change social beliefs and attitudes of the maladjusted person.

Just as it is correct to say that the establishment of an adequate minimum-wage law can serve as a direct attack on racial prejudice, so is it correct to say that the establishment of parent-training centers, child-guidance clinics, and public psychotherapeutic counseling services are also direct attacks on racial prejudice. Inadequate wage levels and unsound toilet training can both result in tension systems that can become the basis for racial prejudice, and both can be remedied by appropriate economic or psychotherapeutic procedures.

General Comments.—The entire program we have discussed in this section is of crucial importance in controlling many beliefs and attitudes of racial prejudice. However, it touches only upon some of the motivational forces behind racial prejudice—not all. Some of the need patterns involved in racial prejudice have very little to do with frustration, repression, or socially unacceptable behavior; for such patterns of prejudice other tech-

---

[1] See especially the article by Amster and Amster (1944), which gives a description of single-meeting therapies practiced in some USO centers during the war. Of the more orthodox psychoanalytic school, the book by Alexander, French, *et al.* (1946) presents the best account of "brief psychoanalysis."

[2] For a more comprehensive discussion of the applicability of group therapy, see Slavson (1943). For a brief description of various techniques involved in group therapy, see the bulletin issued by the War Department (1944).

niques than those involving manipulation of the need structures can be resorted to. Beliefs and attitudes can be changed through the manipulation, for example, of the perceptions of the individual. Not only must these other means be used concurrently with motivational control measures, but frequently these other means are more readily available and sometimes more feasible. We must, therefore, turn our attention now to the problem of controlling racial prejudice through controlling the perceptual attributes of the individual's psychological field and to the environmental supports for these perceptions.

CONTROLLING THE PERCEPTIONS INVOLVED IN RACIAL PREJUDICE

We have seen that an important prerequisite for racial prejudice is the existence of environmental supports that permit the individual to perceive members of minority groups as having certain "unique" attributes which set them apart from other people. Any step that will remove these environmental supports, therefore, will contribute to the control of racial prejudice. Before discussing the various steps that might be taken, however, several qualifying considerations must be stated. First, the *grouping* of people in perception does not, in itself, make for racial prejudice—it merely makes such beliefs and attitudes possible. Thus, perceptual grouping may result in favorable beliefs and attitudes. The Anglophile or Russophile, for example, must be able to group Englishmen or Russians together as a people apart just as much as the Anglophobe or Russophobe. This leads to our second consideration that not all types of groupings are equally conducive to the formation of racial prejudice. What is important is *the nature of the cue that supports the grouping.* For example, if we were to group all Negroes together only on the basis of their skin color and nothing else, the resulting cognitive organization would be a stable and a strong one, but it would not be any more conducive to derogatory beliefs and attitudes than grouping people on the basis of whether or not they wore glasses or whether they were taller or shorter than five feet five. For our present problem, then, the significant concern is not only with the environmental supports that lie behind groupings of people in the perception of the individual but with the kinds of cues that support such groupings. The significance of this formulation lies in the suggestion that in our attempt to control racial prejudice through changing the percepts involved, we are not necessarily forced to adopt a program that will eliminate all racial differences. Although it is true that if such an end were achieved, racial prejudice would also necessarily disappear, nevertheless racial prejudice can be eliminated through a process far short of such an "expunging solution" of the problem. Racial prejudice can be eliminated through the differential elimination or control of cues without erasing all the perceptible differences among races—in skin color, speech patterns, food habits, name endings, etc.

Fundamentally, the varied techniques that can result in the person's changed perception of an object involve (1) the changing of the objective qualities of an object, (2) the presentation of the unchanged object in a new context, or (3) the underlining or stressing of previously unobserved attributes of the object.[1]

Changing the Objective Qualities of Minority-group Members.—We have seen that the *objective qualities* of minority-group members range all the way from the slanted eyes of the oriental or the "clannishness" of the Jew to the "typical" occupations of the Negro. Anything, therefore, that would remove the physical, psychological, or sociological environmental supports for the resulting perceptual groupings would result in a change in the way the minority-group members would be perceived. Among the steps that might achieve such removal are intermarriage, acculturation, improving educational and other services for the minority group, and abolition of segregation practices. The first two involve steps that the minority-group members themselves can take; the latter two, steps that can best be taken by the dominant-group members. Of all four steps, however, the last—abolition of segregation practices—is the most significant and will be discussed in greatest detail.

Intermarriage.—Intermarriage among the different stocks in this country would tend to eliminate many of the physical cues that set people apart into discriminable groups. Should such a process continue long enough and on a universal scale, all consistent physical differentiae characteristic of racial or ethnic groups would disappear completely. However, there are several obvious difficulties and barriers to such a proposal. As many writers have pointed out, intermarriage can be seen more realistically as a consequence of the elimination of racial prejudice than as a technique to achieve such an end. A man or a woman who is anti-Negro, anti-Jewish, anti-Chinese, or anti-Irish will usually not take a Negro, Jew, Chinese, or Irishman as a mate. Thus although it is true to say that intermarriage can contribute to the solution of the problem of racial prejudice, we cannot expect many such marriages to take place until there are many people without racial prejudice. Second, many barriers to intermarriage exist even where the individuals concerned have no racial prejudice. Such barriers are sometimes legal (see page 468, Chap. XII), but the most significant ones derive from the beliefs and attitudes of the rest of society. While there are no trustworthy data to indicate that *biologically* considered race mixtures

---

[1] See p. 338 in the chapter on propaganda for a further discussion of these techniques as used in "prestige suggestion."

are either beneficial or detrimental to the progeny,[1] there is sufficient evidence to indicate that *sociologically* the situation is such that children resulting from some mixed marriages in our society find themselves rejected by the very groups with which they would normally seek identification, and they are consequently faced with many difficulties of adjustment. The realization of what is in store for children of mixed marriages serves as a deterrent to such marriages.

For the above reasons and others, intermarriage as a step toward the elimination of physical cues that support racial prejudice has only limited value. It is of significance when it occurs, but it can occur only slowly and sporadically.

Acculturation.—There are some steps that the minority-group member himself can take toward eliminating some of the sociological cues that identify him as a "different" person. Many minority groups, for instance, have distinctive surnames, food habits, and recreational patterns, which help set them apart from other people. In many cases, the dominant group makes it difficult for the minority group to eliminate such cues (by shutting them out from certain restaurants, resorts, etc.), but frequently the maintenance of these distinctive cues is due to the free choice of the minority-group member. Thus, for example, it is possible for the Chinese to change his name from "Wong Chi Wei" to "Wilson" and for the Jew to shave his beard without running into any effective resistance.

This suggestion, however, presents several difficulties which must be considered. In the first place there is the *cultural* objection. Each one of these steps should be evaluated in terms of not only whether or not it will "erase" an environmental support but also whether or not the loss of such characteristics is desirable in terms of cultural and aesthetic considerations. Would American life be the poorer if the various people in this country gave up their distinctive patterns, foods, dress, speech, literature, music, games, etc? This is a question of general social value and probably does not concern the specific individual who must make his own decision, but it is a consideration that the social manager, who would persuade the minority-group member to make such a change, must take into account.

Second, there is the *psychological* argument. Many minority-group members resist taking these acculturation steps because of strong feelings of pride and self-respect. This is a difficult barrier to overcome, and some psychologists have argued (notably Lewin, 1946) that it may be psychologically unsound to encourage such acculturation and the consequent loss of group morale in the minority group. They point out that one of the side

---

[1] See Klineberg (1940), p. 306–311, for a discussion of the data relevant to the biological characteristics of children of mixed marriages.

effects of changing an old family name or any traditional behavior pattern, in order to conform to the practices of the dominant group, may be the induction of feelings of oversubmissiveness and loss of self-esteem. These feelings, in turn, will tend to make the person maladjusted and will eventually lead to increased intergroup tensions. It may even induce new differentiating psychological cues in the minority-group member—extreme self-assertiveness, aggressiveness, etc.—in overcompensation to feelings of submissiveness. In addition, it has been pointed out that even though the foreigner takes over the superficial American habit patterns—using slang, eating "hot dogs," and worshiping baseball or movie stars—he may nevertheless still find himself unaccepted and again may end up as a baffled, dissatisfied individual.

Several points must be made in connection with this objection. (1) The supposed side effects will differ in intensity and significance for different individuals. Not all members of a minority group have strong feelings of belongingness to such groups. We must always avoid confusing *psychological belongingness* with sociological or *ethnic belongingness*. (See the discussion of what constitutes a genuine psychological group as opposed to a sociological class, page 18, Chap. I.) Many people will therefore gain more emotional security by conforming to the dominant group (which may be their real psychological group) than they will by endeavoring to live out their lives within the confines of their own minority sociological class. (2) In so far as side effects do occur, they may have to be considered as part of a calculated risk. The long-term effects of such a program must be weighted against the temporary ill effects that might eventuate. (3) Not all behavior patterns are equally ego-involved. Some types of acculturation can be made by most minority group members without any ill effects at all. The social manager, in proposing this step to minority-group members, must weigh all the above arguments and considerations and make his decision in terms of the specific situation. In so far as acculturation is possible, it can be extremely helpful in removing some supports for beliefs and attitudes of racial prejudice.

Improving the services available to minority-group members.—The above steps, however, may be regarded as dealing with the less significant cues. The cues that would be eliminated by intermarriage or by acculturation do not, in themselves, easily support racial prejudice, even though they do support differential groupings. The cues to be discussed in connection with the last two steps, however, are of quite a different character, since these cues carry with them evaluations as to the character, capacity, or personality of the minority-group member. Thus, for example, physical or psychological cues that permit us to perceive the Mexican as less educated than the North American or the Negro as a slow, lazy ne'er-do-well are of this character. Any step that can be taken to remove such cues from the minority-group member becomes immediately significant.

Intermarriage is not the only way in which certain "typical" physical characteristics of people can be eliminated. Some of the physical cues are not genetically determined but are environmentally controlled. They reflect the consequences of malnutrition, different diets, inadequate access to recreational facilities, or the unavailability of good medical advice. The studies of physical anthropologists (see especially Lasker, 1946) make it clear that the size of the body, the proportion of the limbs, the shape of the head, the form of the face reflect environmental influences. Changes in the glandular structure or functioning due to environmental factors may reflect themselves in changes in such psychological traits as "slowness," "laziness," "nervousness," etc. Any program, therefore, that makes for equal nutritional, medical, and recreational care for all people in this country might constitute a step in the direction of reducing the number of physical and psychological cues that support beliefs and attitudes of racial prejudice.

In addition, any step that will increase the educational level of the minority-group member is a step in the direction of removing some of the psychological cues that lie behind racial prejudice. We are here concerned not with the program of eliminating segregation practices (which will concern us next) but with such steps that may even increase segregation tendencies. Thus, the support of Negro colleges in the South, where the establishment of nonsegregated schools is impossible for the immediate present, may be psychologically justified on the grounds that it will aid in removing a psychological stigma from the Negro. As we have indicated many times before, we cannot seek for only the "perfect" measure. Each step must be realistically considered on its own merits.

Abolition of segregation practices.—Of the four steps discussed here, the abolition of segregation practices is by far the most significant. But this program is as difficult as it is necessary. We have seen in the preceding chapter that the segregation of people in the United States is accomplished through legal means, religious and economic practices, and accepted custom. To abolish segregation is a program of tremendous proportions. It requires changing legal interpretations supported up to now by the Supreme Court; it requires passage of new legislation on a state and Federal basis; it requires the abolition of quota systems from some of the most powerful educational institutions in the world; it requires doing away with "gentlemen's agreements" and race-restrictive covenants in the real-estate business; it requires changing time-honored practices of most of the American churches, many American labor unions, and business-management policies.

In addition to all these legal and other difficulties there are certain psychological barriers and resistances to any attempt to abolish segregation practices. It is these psychological problems which we must now examine.

Minority-group resistance.—A program to abolish segregation will meet with resistance *from among some of the very people it is aimed to benefit.* This barrier must be fully appreciated by the social manager who sets out to carry through such a program, and steps must be taken to overcome or circumvent such resistance.

As a consequence of many years of segregation practices some minority-group members have acquired vested interests in segregation. Just as long as racial prejudice exists, the members of minority groups who have achieved wealth or political power or social status in segregated businesses, professions, or churches realize that with the abolition of these segregated organizations their own favored positions would also disappear and that they would find it difficult to find equivalent positions in the "outside" prejudiced world. These persons might favor the abolition of segregation after the elimination of racial prejudice on the outside but would oppose it as a means toward elimination of prejudice. For them the "cure" would be worse than the "disease." Frazier (1947) summarizes the nature of these vested interests in his revealingly titled article, "Human, all too human":

In the separate schools, as in the separate churches, many Negroes have found a field for leadership. Some of the separate schools in the South have enabled their heads to accumulate means . . . . In border states and even in Northern cities, some Negroes have regarded separate schools as an opportunity to acquire exclusive rights to employment . . . . Negro physicians may advocate separate hospitals on the grounds that in them they would have more opportunities to develop their skill and to serve their "own people." But this, too, is a rationalization because there is abundant evidence that the standards of medical care in segregated hospitals . . . is lower than in unsegregated institutions. It is scarcely necessary to point out that to abolish segregation would create technological unemployment for Negroes who secure a living from the existence of segregation . . . . If segregation were eliminated, the social justification for the existence of Negro business would vanish and Negro businessmen would have to compete with other businessmen. Undoubtedly many Negro enterprises would disappear, along with the sentimental justification which helps support them . . . . The status of a Negro college professor in the Negro community bears little or no relation to his professional achievements. In fact he is relieved of competing with white men in the same profession . . . . He enjoys rewards and advantages solely because of his social position in the Negro world.

In this connection it is significant to point out that in accordance with our whole-part principle (see page 96) the white man judges the Negro scholar or scientist not in terms of the achievements of the Negro but in terms of the supposed lack of capacity of the Negroes as a group. Consequently, by contrast, the Negro scholar of mediocre ability is regarded as a "great scholar," and his achievements are likely to be overevaluated by the white man. This process results in another source of personal advantage which some Negroes gain from racial prejudice.

What is true for the Negro minister, doctor, college professor, newspaperman, businessman, and social worker is also true for the man of wealth and status among Jewish, Catholic, or other minority groups. The minority-group members who have gains to make from segregation may judge a program to eliminate segregation in terms of their personal fortunes, not in terms of "class" fortunes, and may therefore oppose such a program. However, it must be pointed out that such advantages as do derive from segregation affect only a small proportion of the minority-group members, and most members of the minority group, as well as most of the farsighted leaders of such groups, have little to gain from segregation. The opposition of the few, then, can be overcome, but it must be reckoned with by the realistic social manager.

Abolition of segregation by force.—Segregation practices are so definite and all-pervasive a characteristic of American culture that the abolition of these practices frequently requires the use of legal force. And it is because of this that the social manager frequently comes up against a seemingly strong "psychological" argument against his program. The argument is frequently phrased in the following terms: "You can't change beliefs and attitudes of people by legislation and by force." This has been one of the major arguments used against the passage of a permanent Fair Employment Practice Act, for example, and has acted as a deterrent on the activities of many people who would otherwise support such an act. But the validity of this argument is questionable both on theoretical grounds and in the light of empirical evidence. *The use of legal force in changing beliefs and attitudes is frequently a psychologically sound procedure.*

In the first place, the use of legal force, apparently against the wishes of many of the people in the community, *will occasionally not meet any significant resistance.* This is particularly true where a condition of "pluralistic ignorance" obtains (see page 389). In some instances segregation practices *seem* to be supported by the beliefs and wishes of most of the people, but in actuality a condition exists where no one is in favor of segregation but everyone believes that everyone else is in favor of segregation. In such cases all that is needed is for someone or for a small minority to break through this apparent but nonexistent resistance. Fact-finding research widely publicized would be extremely helpful in detecting such pluralistic ignorance situations (see page 307). In the second place, we must remember that the American culture pattern and ideology is an inconsistent one. Consequently, as we have pointed out, many Americans have definite guilt feelings about their racial prejudice and segregation practices. Although they approve of such practices, they could not easily bring themselves publicly to oppose the elimination of segregation. They frequently assuage their guilt feelings by the rationalization that they themselves did not institute such practices, but such a rationalization would not enable them to take an active part in opposition to any group that attempted to do away with segregation.

At least three states now (1947) have laws against racial and religious bias in employment—New York, New Jersey, and Massachusetts. To date, very little difficulty has resulted from the attempts to enforce these laws—most businesses, newspapers, labor unions, and individuals find it advisable to avoid offering public resistance and, when pressed, comply with the law. There are also available several accounts of how segregation practices have been broken down, on a community level, by the action of small groups of citizens, without incurring any reactions on the part of those who were opposed (see, for example, the accounts in *Soc. Action Mag.*, vol. 13, No. 1, 1947).

However, even where genuine and significant resistance does appear, legal force in abolishing segregation may still be effective. Theoretically, *any change* in the environment that removes an environmental support for certain perceptions—whether this environmental change has come about naturally, through happenstance, or by force—may eventually result in changed perceptions and changed beliefs. This theoretical consideration is borne out by a number of empirical demonstrations.

Some empirical demonstrations.—There have been several successful experiments with the use of force, *in the face of expressed opposition*, in breaking down segregation practices and consequently decreasing racial prejudice. This has been especially true in the labor field. Northrup (1947) gives the following account of the effect of legal force when used against the segregation practices of the Machinists' International:

The whole pattern of racial segregation in the labor movement was challenged by the Executive Order creating the Fair Employment Practice Committee, expressing the Federal government's antidiscrimination policy in war industry. . . . Two important early cases (October 1941) charged the machinists' local lodges No. 68 and 741 with refusing to admit Negroes to membership or clear them for employment . . . . It was these cases which . . . finally broke the racial barriers of the Machinists' International . . . . Two years later, local lodge No. 54, apparently with the approval of the International, accepted Negro workers . . . into full membership. At that time, the organizing chairman of the shop committee of the plant told the colored employees: "I remind you that no matter where you go, if you have your union card with you then you will be recognized as a member of the machinist lodge No. 54 .... There will be no separate meetings of white and Negro. You will sit in our regular meetings, with full voice and voting rights" ....

But perhaps the most significant story is found in the experiences of the National Maritime Union. This union, almost from birth, has insisted on equal rights for all seamen regardless of race. Not only has it succeeded in abolishing segregation practices, but there is evidence that it has helped change the racial beliefs and attitudes of many of its members. It has succeeded in doing this by *frequent recourse to sheer force*—economic force or threat of force applied to its own members. A revealing description of how this force is applied is found in the account that its president, Joseph Curran (1947) gave of the "educational" procedures the union used in situations involving opposition on the part of its own members:

Let us say that a seaman objects to sailing with a Negro brother. Here is the approach used by a union patrolman who services that vessel: the first step is to call a meeting of the entire crew, except those needed for safe navigation of the ship.

At this meeting the problem is presented: a union member refuses to accept a Negro brother. The patrolman asks all members who object to the Negro to stand up. Each is asked to state his reasons.[1]

The arguments—invariably fallacious and easy to expose—are answered point by point. If the men refuse to accept logic, they are asked whether they believe in the NMU constitution. They invariably say yes. They are asked whether they believe in *all* the constitution, not just parts of it. They again say yes. Then they are asked whether they believe in the clause that states that there will be no discrimination. If they say no, obviously they do not believe in all of the constitution. If they say yes, then what is all the arguing about?

If that isn't successful, the brothers are told that they are not obligated to sail with a Negro; they can get off the ship. And they can leave their union books behind because their books will be of no further use to them.

The effectiveness of the National Maritime Union's policy is borne out by a study of Brophy (1946), which investigated the prejudice of white merchant seamen toward Negro seamen. Brophy interviewed approximately 500 white seamen at canteens operated in New York City by the United Seaman's Service. The interview consisted of asking each seaman 10 questions dealing with racial prejudice situations. On the basis of these interviews Brophy assigned a "prejudice index" to each respondent. In

[1] Note how the opportunity for "pluralistic ignorance" to be effective is decreased.

addition, Brophy obtained the usual sociological data and other information for each respondent.

In correlating the prejudice index against sociological variables, Brophy found that the commonly assumed cultural determinants of racial prejudice were not operative. That is, he found no correlation between the prejudice index and the place of birth of the seamen (men born in the South did not differ from those born in the Middle West or England, etc.), nor did he find any correlation between racial prejudice and educational level. However, Brophy did find two variables that correlated highly with the prejudice index. These two were (1) *the trade union to which the seaman belonged* and (2) *the number of times the seaman had shipped with Negroes.*

Thus, of the seamen who were members of the National Maritime Union, only 4.1 per cent earned a high prejudice score; whereas of the seamen who belonged to other unions, the percentages were 71.6 (for "craft" unions), 40.7 (for British unions), and 65.8 (for "others"). Similarly, of all the seamen who had never shipped with Negroes, 54.1 per cent earned high prejudice scores; of the seamen who had shipped once with Negroes, 44.2 per cent earned high scores; of the seamen who had shipped *twice* with Negroes, the percentage dropped to 23.7; and this trend continued until when all the seamen who had shipped *five or more* times with Negroes were tabulated, only 9.5 per cent earned high prejudice scores. All these data seem to support the conclusion that contact with Negro seamen is correlated negatively with anti-Negro prejudice, *i.e.*, the more contact the less prejudice—even where such contact is *enforced contact*, as in the case of the National Maritime Union.

During the war there was an even more crucial opportunity to test the effect of enforced contact between Negroes and whites *against opposition from the whites*. Rose (1946) reports the results of the following experiment. At one point of the war there was a great need for replacement of combat troops in the European Theater of Operations. Due to the man-power shortage, the American General Staff adopted a new policy with regard to the utilization of Negro combat troops. Instead of attempting to form all-Negro infantry units, Negro soldiers who volunteered for combat were formed into platoons led by white commissioned and noncommissioned officers and assigned to 11 white combat divisions. Attitude surveys were made before and after the institution of this policy. The first survey showed that the majority of the white soldiers and two-thirds of the white officers who were to lead the Negro soldiers were opposed to this mixing of troops. Nevertheless the General Staff went through with its decision. Two months after the Negro troops had joined the white outfits, a second survey indicated that (1) 77 per cent of the white officers had become more favorable to the mixed companies while none said he had become less favorable, (2) more than 80 per cent thought that the Negro soldiers had performed well and that the white and Negro soldiers were getting along well with each other, (3) in comparing the attitudes of the white soldiers in the mixed and "pure white" companies only 7 per cent of the former said that they disliked very much the policy of mixing Negroes and whites whereas 62 per cent of the latter were opposed to the policy.

General considerations.—Any program designed to eliminate segregation practices in the United States will meet resistance—both from some members of the segregated groups and from members of the segregating groups. In some cases this resistance is more apparent than real; but even where real, the attempt to eliminate segregation by force is frequently justified on both theoretical and empirical grounds. However, the studies cited above must be assessed realistically. They do not prove that contact per se will result in a diminution of racial prejudice. In both Brophy's study and Rose's study the contact was of a specific kind. In both instances the enforced contact between the Negro and white (seaman or soldier) was of the type where the actions of the Negro were of vital importance for the white man. The performance of a Negro seaman, during the war, or a Negro combat soldier could mean the difference between life and death for his white companion. Each had to depend upon the other, and each had to react to the other as a seaman or as a soldier and not as a "brother under the skin." The interracial contact was a *functional* one, and therein lies the crux of the matter. Once the white man was forced to perceive the Negro in a functional role, he could then see many characteristics that he had previously not observed and that could change his beliefs and attitudes.

However, it still remains true that any step which can be taken to break down segregation—in industry, in education, in recreation, in churches, in fraternal organizations, in housing regulations, in labor unions, in government, and in every phase of social life—can make a significant contribution to the removal of racial prejudice in this country. In addition to removing environmental supports for prejudiced beliefs and attitudes, the elimination of segregation would operate in two other beneficial ways: (1) It would help eliminate the "sampling error" which lies behind many beliefs and attitudes of racial prejudice (see page 467); and (2) it would tend to modify the mental set of the perceiver and encourage him to look for desirable traits in the minority-group member (see page 359, chapter on propaganda). To illustrate: If Negroes were, by force of law, enabled to live in the same neighborhoods and apartment houses with whites, the abolition of Negro ghettos would eliminate one of the sociological environmental supports—a support for the cognition that Negroes are "slum people." Second, some of the Negroes' white neighbors would at least have the opportunity to meet and know a more representative sample of Negro people than they have now. Although it is true that many of the white neighbors would not avail themselves of such an opportunity, the probability of their doing so would be greater than if there were no Negroes in their neighborhood. Finally, we have seen that "where there is a need to put up with or come to terms with an object, there is also a tendency to seek to discover favorable aspects about the object" (page 359, Chap. IX), and some of the white neighbors might insist that "Negroes aren't so bad after all," in situations where the whites found themselves on the defensive because of their "mixed" neighborhood. Even if this should be only a rationalization at first, it could eventually become part of the individual's belief system and influence his subsequent perceptions. Thus the effects of elimination of segregation not only might destroy current perceptions but could also build up more favorable ones.

Here again, however, the standard caution must be mentioned. Before any steps are taken to eliminate segregation by force, a great deal of attention must be paid to the possible harmful side effects, and careful consideration must be given to the calculated risk. Where such abolition would result in more resentment than good, forced abolition of segregation practices must be avoided. Second, the abolition of segregation by force should always be accompanied by appropriate "education" and "propaganda" (see page 359). The point of importance to remember, nevertheless, is that not every use of force is *ipso facto* psychologically unsound.

Changing Context and Emphasis of Observable Qualities of People.— The above section has concerned itself with changing the actual observable qualities of minority-group members (by removing physical, psychological, and sociological stigmata from them) to the end of changing the percepts involved in racial prejudice. It will be remembered, however, that there are other methods of changing the way in which people will perceive members of minority groups—by presenting these minority-group members in new contexts or by underlining and stressing previously unobserved characteristics which inhere in the individuals of minority groups. These two steps attempt to take advantage of the fact that minority-group members already have, in great measure, good, desirable characteristics which, if perceived by the individual of the dominant group, would result in changed beliefs and attitudes about the minority member. In our preceding discussion we have already referred to several ways in which this can occur, *i.e.*, when, for example, the white is forced to perceive the Negro as a comrade in arms or as a neighbor and, in that new context, begins to perceive the Negro in his "true light." We can, however, list additional specific steps directed toward this objective.

Newspaper reporting practices.—Changing the perception of an object by underlining certain qualities is a common practice among those who propagandize for racial prejudice. This has sometimes been called the "stacked cards" technique. Certain characteristics or attributes of people are reported (accurately enough, to be sure), but other characteristics are not mentioned. A variation of this technique (perhaps unconsciously) is common to most newspapers of this country. The almost universal practice of newspapers, in identifying as "Negro" any Negro who happens to be involved in a crime while failing to identify as "white" or as "Protestant," for example, any white Protestant who is involved in a crime, is an instance of using this loaded technique (or stacking of cards) in pointing to the supposed "criminal" tendencies of the Negro. Daily reading of the newspaper, because of this practice, can function as an effective environmental support for beliefs and attitudes of racial prejudice. It is therefore obvious that one simple but effective step would be the elimination of national or racial identity in reporting crime stories by newspapers.

Portrayal of racial characters in fiction and advertising.—Closely allied to this is the demand that steps should be taken to prevent the presentation of minority-group members—in motion pictures, radio broadcasting, fiction, advertising, comic strips, etc.—in their "worst" light.

In addition to the above "don'ts" which must be demanded of those responsible for the production of our mass communication and entertainment material, there must also be a list of "dos." A broadcasting station that never presents the Negro as lazy, the Jew as wily, the Irish as superstitious, and the Italian as criminal cannot be given a clean bill of health by the social manager who is interested in eliminating racial prejudice. Place must be found for reporting the activities of the Jewish war hero, the Negro chemist, the Irish pacifist, and the Italian judge. The inclusion, in the fictional world, of a few "Anglo-Saxon, white, Protestant" villains is not enough either; these "villains" must be accompanied by an occasional minority-group "hero." Further illustrations of the important role that "context" can play in changing one's perception of a minority-group member will be given in the following section on controlling racial prejudice through education.

Up to this point we have outlined the steps that can be taken with respect to the object of perception—the minority-group member himself. But we know that one's perception of people is a function not altogether of the people perceived but also of the perceiving person. To change the percept involved in racial prejudice, therefore, we must also change the perceiver. This, in broad terms, is a problem in learning and education, and to that problem we must now address ourselves.

CONTROLLING RACIAL PREJUDICE THROUGH EDUCATION

As we have pointed out previously (see especially page 200, Chap. VI), any measure designed to change the motivational structure or perceptions of an individual involves manipulation of the person's environment for specified ends. That, broadly defined, is the educational process. In a very true sense, therefore, we have been discussing "education" throughout this chapter. What we can discuss in this section, however, are certain specific techniques and the use of certain specific agencies whereby the steps already listed can be organized and put into effective operation. Among these will be a discussion of the role of the school, the community education program, and some aspects of mass publicity activity.

Education through the Schools.—Much attention has been paid recently to the possibilities of controlling racial prejudice through school activities and formal educational programs. This is in recognition of the fact that although the school is not the only educational device used by our society, it is, obviously, an important formative agency for most American children. Among the general principles that must be kept in mind when initiating an educational program to control racial prejudice are the following:[1]

1. *The over-all content of the child's education must be carefully synchronized with the objective of teaching for democracy.* When we speak of an educational program designed to "teach democracy," we cannot mean a "course" in democracy which the pupil is required to attend three times a week or so but rather a well-integrated and all-pervasive program of education. It will be remembered that beliefs and attitudes very rarely grow up in isolation one from another (see page 161). Every subject and course taught to a child must be examined from the point of view of what it contributes to the child's social beliefs and attitudes. What the student learns in his history course, economic course, civics course, biology course, arithmetic course, and reading class must be consistent with the over-all objectives of inculcating democratic beliefs and attitudes. In this connection the discussion of "unconscious propaganda" and textbooks (see page 331) is relevant, and

[1] A number of helpful reports are now available on the experiences of schools in teaching democracy and in controlling racial prejudice. Among these may be mentioned *The Story of the Springfield plan* (Chatto and Halligan, 1945), *A report of a study on practical democracy* (Chenowith, 1947), *Education for cultural unity* (Myers, 1946), *The school's responsibility for the improvement of intergroup relations* (Hughes, 1946), and *Education for unity* (Wiley, 1947).

of especial significance is the kind of books used by the children for their reading exercises and their introduction to the enjoyment of literature. The world of the modern individual, we have emphasized, is peopled not only with "real" persons but also with personalities created by writers and story tellers. Instead of the usual children's books, which either do not touch upon the existence of the problem of racial prejudice in the United States (or any other real social problem with which the child inevitably comes into contact) or serve to perpetuate the stereotypes about minority-group members, other and more psychologically sound and useful books should be provided to children. Such books should present the problems involved in the adjustment of foreign-born children in America, in racial prejudice, in social and economic differences, and in the translation of democratic ideals in everyday terms. Such books must contain stories in which the children are interested per se, they must not stress the "glamorous" *differences* among people of varying ethnic and racial backgrounds, and they must avoid the reinforcement of the stock racial characters. Such books are now available and should be given an important place in the educational process.[1]

2. *The educational program must be carried out under appropriate general conditions.* The realization that educating for beliefs and attitudes of democracy is a multidimensional task points to the significance of other than "content" factors in the child's education. That is, not only must the subject matter of his various courses be congruent with democratic beliefs and attitudes, but the general "social atmosphere" of the school must also be consistent with such beliefs and attitudes. It is psychologically unsound, for example, to expect democratic beliefs and attitudes to be taught by teachers who themselves are racially prejudiced or in a school system that practices racial prejudice. The social manager, therefore, who would use the school system to educate for democracy must first seek the attainment of the following objectives: (1) The school system itself must have a policy in which no segregation is permitted—neither teachers nor pupils being accorded discriminatory treatment on account of race or ethnic origin. A school that has both Negro and white teachers, for example, is in a much better position to "put across" its democratic educational program than is a segregated school. (2) It must be made certain that the teachers who teach

[1] The Child Study Association of America, through its Children's Book Committee (1945), has issued an extremely useful list of selected books for boys and girls, the books being grouped for different age levels. "In selecting this list," the committee states, "the Children's Book Committee does not suggest that children's reading be confined to realism or 'books with a purpose.' The list includes some non-fiction, vividly presented, as well as books with a compelling story which gives a true picture of the world today.'' See also the review of children's books by Fisk (1947).

the youngsters believe in what they teach. A teacher, this would suggest, should not be chosen only in terms of her technical preparation but also in terms of her beliefs and attitudes. This means that frequently, before an educational program can be instituted, the teachers themselves must first be "educated." That this is a factor of some consequence is indicated by Manske's (1935) study, where certain factual material on race and minority problems was used in a high-school course. All teachers at the high school, presumably, taught the same material. It was found that when the teacher's own attitudes and beliefs were "liberal," the students in her course showed some change in the direction of liberalism. When the teacher herself, however, was racially prejudiced, the same material had no effect on the attitudes or beliefs of the students. It will be remembered that the content of educational material is not the only factor that determines the persuasiveness of the material. The personality of the teacher, her beliefs and attitudes, and other "peripheral" matters are also significant variables.

3. *A school program, in so far as possible, must enlist the support of the children's parents.* In recognition of the fact that the child's educational experiences are profoundly influenced by the beliefs and attitudes of his parents (see page 180), many school programs designed to teach democracy have attempted to use the home as an important adjunct of the school. This again may involve an adult education program prior to the institution of a child education program. Where the parents are consulted by the school, are informed of the objectives of the program, and are given a direct role to play, the probability of success is greatly increased. The importance and effectiveness of this have been well demonstrated in the experiences of the organizers of the well-known Springfield plan (Chatto and Halligan, 1945).

4. *Specific "intercultural" education must avoid emphasizing or creating differences.* While it is true that educational control of racial prejudice should be furthered through every course and subject taught, there have recently been developed specific programs of education called "intercultural education" programs. Thus, for example, in New York State six courses relating to intercultural relations are used in the secondary schools. The titles of these courses are Community Life (Grade 7), Our American Heritage (Grade 8), Our Economic World (Grade 9), World History (Grade 10), American Institutions (Grade 11), and American Life (Grade 12).[1] In so far as such specific programs attempt to familiarize the pupil with the different cultural backgrounds of the American people, make him more appreciative of the contributions made by many people of many nations to our pres-

[1] Detailed content outlines and specific teaching suggestions have been developed for each of these courses, and the materials are available in separate bulletins published by the New York State Education Department.

ent living, and make him realize the necessity of cooperative activity among many different kinds of people and many different nations for the best functioning of the economic and political order of any one nation, such programs have great value. But frequently an "intercultural" program may emphasize differences unnecessarily, and the effect can be regressive and aid in perpetuating stereotypes. Fisk (1947) gives the following examples of a bad and a good intercultural program:

... the typical "I Am an American Day" program brings out the various nationality and ethnic groups wearing their own costumes and singing their own songs. In one high school on such an occasion, it was suggested that the Negro children give an exhibition of jitterbugging and sing Negro spirituals. The principal was amazed when the Negro students refused to participate. Contrast with that another school's handling of this occasion where students of various backgrounds worked out creatively together a program on the war effort and the participation of the functional groups in society (farmers, factory workers, nurses, servicemen, etc.) some of whom happened to be Negro, others Chinese Americans, and others still different in nationality backgrounds. As Negro and Chinese and white students worked side by side in creating the program, a spirit of oneness was built up which is the essence of America, and the mixed groups of Americans in various settings gave a more valid picture of American democratic living than any series of ethnic groups.

This is another illustration of the necessity of paying attention to the context in which we place members of minority groups. To present Negroes or Mexicans or Chinese or Jews in the context of special groups, with special dress, special songs, and special foods, is presenting them in the wrong context. They should be presented in their context of functional groups and as American groups. The purpose of intercultural programs should not be primarily the building up of self-regard in the minority groups through attempts to identify them with their "quaint, beautiful, and different" behavior but rather to make all Americans aware of the beauty or utility in all cultural patterns and to identify the members of the minority group with this common heritage. Thus, for example, to ask a Mexican child to report on the culture of the Chinese and a Protestant child on the religious practices of the Jews would be more effective and more genuine "intercultural" education than to ask the Mexican child to come dressed to school in *his* quaint dress or to ask the Chinese child to tell the other children how to prepare "bird's nest soup."

5. *Education for democracy must include training in the techniques of democracy.* Educating for beliefs and attitudes of democracy does not involve merely the reiteration of democratic philosophies, ideologies, and concepts. This is important and should be done, but in addition it involves

teaching the kinds of behavior that are demanded by such concepts and beliefs. This means that a large part of the program should be given over to the teaching of the specific skills required by democratic beliefs and attitudes. We must remember that beliefs and attitudes are characterized by their functional utility. Usually an individual will hold on to beliefs and attitudes because they help direct his behavior and solve his many problems in interpersonal relationships. To attempt to inculcate such beliefs and attitudes without providing the student with techniques that can help him express these beliefs and attitudes in his action is to attempt the very difficult. Lippitt (1946a), in discussing the problem of changing beliefs and attitudes, has stressed this point when he says,

Another important barrier which has become increasingly clear in recent training research is the insecurity about making the change, even when the desirability of such a change has been perceived and accepted. A motivation to change, and even a decision to change, *must frequently be coupled with the acquisition of certain new inter-personal skills before natural insecurities and inadequacies can be overcome.*[1]

What is true for changing beliefs is equally true for the initial inculcation of beliefs. Thus, for example, it is necessary to help every pupil grow in understanding social relationships through experiencing them at school, it is necessary to provide means for developing the ability to meet and work with other children, to encourage working in small groups in cooperation with other groups, to teach the skills and provide for practice in group discussion and group decision making, so that the child can act in accordance with majority opinion but with due respect for minority rights. These skills and techniques are as complicated and as teachable as any other highly developed techniques. To depend upon "innate" capacity in interpersonal relations which will be congruent with democratic beliefs and attitudes is unwarranted. A number of psychologists have given special attention to this problem and some of their studies (see especially, Lippitt, 1946b, and Benne, Bradford, and Lippitt) are especially valuable in suggesting the principles behind such techniques and the methods of teaching these techniques. Quite apart from any deliberate reference to racial prejudice, such training and education can help control beliefs and attitudes of racial prejudice by giving the pupil an effective set of beliefs and corresponding behavior patterns that are inherently opposed to racial prejudice patterns.

Education through Community Programs.—Recent developments have seen an ever-widening series of programs designed to control racial prejudice through community activities and education. These programs are designed primarily for the adults of the community. Some of these programs are

[1] Italics our own.

carried on through educational, fraternal, and religious organizations, and some of them are sponsored by municipal governmental agencies.   In terms of the size of the problem of racial prejudice, such community programs are essential.   However, to be effective, these "educational" programs must be specifically designed in terms of action programs.   Exhortation and propaganda (as adult education is too frequently conceived) will usually not be effective.   Among the various suggestions that can be made to guide the formulation of a community program, the following two are basic.[1]

1. *Community self-surveys are valuable prerequisites for a program of action.* Any community program is increased in effectiveness if behind it are the community leaders and a representative section of the community.   In so far as possible attempts should be made to avoid the situation where ". . . those who lead the campaign for intergroup understanding become a small cult whose interests are usually enough to brand them as visionaries" (Weaver, 1947).   A technique that is valuable in this respect and has many other merits is the *community self-survey.*

A community self-survey can be described as action research in which the *members of the community themselves*, under the expert guidance of applied social psychologists, are responsible for the collection and analysis of community data.   Three important objectives can be achieved by such community self-surveys: First, the facts collected will permit the realistic planning of a program of action.   It was pointed out earlier in this chapter that no program of action, no matter how carefully it is based on sound general psychological principles, can dispense with action research that is carried on concurrently with the program (see page 501).   Second, the facts thus uncovered by the citizens of the community will be more readily accepted by the community than if those facts were supplied to them by an outside research agency.   We pointed out in Chap. VI that effective education designed to change or create attitudes must seek, wherever possible, to do its work by creating new group identification for the people it would educate (see page 200).   One significant implication of this principle is that the effectiveness of facts in bringing about changes in beliefs and attitudes is frequently dependent upon the degree to which those whose attitudes we would change *are themselves responsible for discovering the facts*, for as Lewin and Grabbe (1945) point out,

This principle of in-grouping makes understandable why complete acceptance of previously rejected facts can be achieved best through the discovery of these

[1] Among the various publications that can be helpful in designing community educational programs for democracy are *Centerville Studies Itself* (Zander, 1941) and the *Community Relations Manual* (Weaver, 1945).

facts by the group members themselves . . . . Then, and frequently only then, do the facts become really *their* facts (as against other people's facts). An individual will believe facts he himself has discovered in the same way that he believes in himself or in his group.

We must remember that "facts, just facts," no matter how valid and scientifically obtained, are frequently not enough to evoke changes in beliefs and attitudes. The community self-survey, for the reason indicated above, gives the resulting facts the added dimension of acceptability that can increase their effectiveness.

Finally, there is a third merit inherent in self-surveys as opposed to surveys by outside organizations. Quite apart from the facts collected, the intimate contact with the problems of minority-group members may have a powerful motivating effect on the surveyors. As Weaver (1947) points out,

. . . self-surveys expose a large number of citizens to a face-to-face acquaint-anceship with existing human problems in the community. This experience with primary data is significant, and as a result of it and the facts that are collected, there is developed a body of representative citizens who can be recruited to support and reinforce remedial programs.

2. *Interracial contacts, as parts of community programs, must be geared to basic objectives and action.* Common to most community educational programs are provisions for interracial meetings and interracial contacts. Although such "intercultural" contacts are essential and potentially valuable, they can frequently in practice be quite valueless in their effects. We have already pointed out that striking evidence exists for the proposition that contact (even if enforced) among individuals of different racial groups can result in decreasing racial prejudice (see page 515) but such contact must occur under fairly well-defined conditions. Intergroup meetings whose only objective is the furtherance of good will and brotherhood have limited value. Each intergroup meeting must be called to consider and act upon specific, well-defined issues in which the various individuals (of whatever racial or ethnic group) act and are seen in the context of *community members* rather then in the context of *minority-group members* to whom the dominant-group members are being "sweet and democratic" for this one evening. Attention to specific community issues, which are the genuine and natural concern of *all* the people attending the meeting, demands that during the meeting itself the members of one group work with the members of the other group. In that way the Negro or the Jew or the Mexican is seen in the context of a member of the community interested in the local school or the garbage-removal program or the community-wide small-pox inoculation

program or the housing problem.   Attention is forced on those problems and the contribution each member of the community can make to solving those problems rather than on the member's skin color or quaint ways.

Such interracial meetings will have the value of actually doing something toward the elimination of environmental supports behind racial prejudice, in addition to presenting the minority-group member in a more desirable context.   Each community must attempt, in such a meeting, to tackle its own segregation problem—whether involving the use of public facilities, education, housing, or employment.   In other words, attention must be paid to both the *context* and *content* of interracial meetings.

Controlling Racial Prejudice through Mass Publicity Programs.—In addition to the various specific and local programs that schools, churches, civic bodies, and community-wide organizations can carry on, these educational procedures must be reinforced by a nation-wide program of publicity and propaganda.   The heterogeneity and interrelationships that exist among the various cultural determinants of beliefs and attitudes suggest that it is extremely difficult to create "islands" of democratic beliefs and attitudes in this country—or any country where intercommunications among communities are so efficient and widespread.[1]

The obstacles to effective mass publicity are imposing.   Quite aside from the results that can be expected from such publicity, there is the specific problem of reaching the target groups aimed at.   As we have already pointed out, the prejudiced person, through the process of withdrawal, can frequently evade exposure to such propaganda (see page 191).   Thus, Lazarsfeld and Merton (1943) have reported that radio and film propaganda reach the people who are in the least need of the "messages" carried by such propaganda.   As a more specific illustration, there are studies (Lazarsfeld, 1947) indicating that radio broadcasts designed to promote friendly intergroup relations among the Poles and Italians, for example, were listened to chiefly by the members of the specific group being discussed rather than by the group to whom the discussion was addressed.

But despite these obstacles, there is definite merit in the use of mass communication media.   For one thing it is essential continually to reinforce the beliefs and attitudes of those who already hold democratic beliefs, as was indicated in our discussion of the merits of "propagandizing the believers"

---

[1] A number of studies are available that indicate the relative effectiveness of various communication media for different segments of the population.   These studies can be helpful in enabling the social manager to make the most efficient use of public information media in his mass educational activities.   Among such studies can be mentioned the following typical investigations: Lazarsfeld and Wyant (1937), "Magazines in 90 cities— who reads what?"; Clark (1940), "Radio listening habits of children"; Lazarsfeld (1940), *Radio and the Printed Page;* and Meine (1941), "Radio and the press among young people."

(see page 360). For another thing, there is always the possibility that the public reiteration of the strongly democratic views of national, educational, and cultural leaders, through the adaptation level phenomenon, can result in shifts of public opinion (see page 102).

Needs for group-acceptance and understanding and public reiteration of democratic views.—The public reiteration of the strongly democratic views of American leaders becomes a particularly significant educational device when we realize that *democratic beliefs, no less than racial prejudice, can serve as social entrance tickets.* Group acceptance, in other words, can operate in two ways. If the accepted leaders of the culture are racially prejudiced and make their views known, then the desire to become identified with the leaders may be served by racial prejudice; but if the accepted leaders have democratic beliefs *and their views become known*, then the desire to become identified with the leaders may be served by democratic beliefs.

There is another technique which also uses auxiliary needs to bring about democratic beliefs and attitudes. We have seen, in discussing the functional nature of beliefs and attitudes, that much of man's behavior can be described as a striving after meaning, and in crisis situations or in frustrating situations beliefs and attitudes are more amenable to change than in other situations. This suggests that the social manager who would induce democratic beliefs must be alert and take advantage of every blocked need or crisis situation. Frustrations and confusions, too, can operate both ways. Wherever possible the educator or propagandist who is interested in promoting democratic beliefs must point out to the frustrated person the *barrier* characteristics of beliefs and attitudes of racial prejudice and the *adaptive* values of democratic beliefs. He should not, in other words, lose the battle to the opposing propagandist by default. Thus, for example, the worker who is blocked in his attempt to unionize his plant must be shown that his own anti-Negro beliefs and attitudes make possible management's access to nonunion Negro labor and thus help break a strike. The businessman who sees a depression just around the corner must be shown that extending democratic practices to the economic, racial, and political field might avert a malfunctioning of the economic system. *Almost any frustration or ambiguous crisis situation offers opportunities for inducing beliefs of democracy no less than beliefs of racial prejudice.*

SUMMARY

This chapter, addressing itself to the problem of controlling racial prejudice, can present only the most general principles and strategy involved. It is therefore emphasized that the social manager, for whom this chapter is primarily written, must carefully examine the specific context in which he attempts to apply these principles before putting them into practice. In addition to this most general precaution, four specific considerations are also presented. These relate to the absolute and relative effectiveness of any specific step, the size of the target group involved, the role of action research, and the necessity for taking calculated risks.

The first major section of this chapter is devoted to the motivational control of racial prejudice. Steps designed to eliminate repressed, frustrated, and socially unacceptable need structures are discussed. It is pointed out that this involves both a preventive and a therapeutic approach. For the first, the necessity of more adequately satisfying man's economic, political, and other common needs is stressed as having direct relevancy to eliminating racial prejudice. For the second approach, it is pointed out that many people require such professional help and that recent developments in psychological guidance and psychotherapeutic counseling can make these services available to people on a mass scale.

The second major section concerns itself with the control of the perceptions involved in racial prejudice. It is first pointed out that this does not necessitate a program which will eliminate all differences among men but one where *differential* elimination of differences among men is involved. The program is then divided into three parts: (1) changing the objective attributes of minority-group members, (2) presenting minority-group members in new contexts, and (3) underlining or stressing previously unobserved attributes of minority-group members. To achieve the first objective, four specific steps are considered: (1) intermarriage, (2) acculturation, (3) improving educational and other services for the minority groups, and (4) abolition of segregation practices. Of these four steps the last is pointed out as the most significant, and the major part of the discussion revolves about that one step. In connection with this, the resistance to abolition of segregation practices *from some of the minority-group members themselves* is first discussed, and it is concluded that this resistance is one which the social manager must take into account and circumvent. The next barrier that is discussed is the argument that "You can't change attitudes by force or legislation." This is an important argument, since the abolition of segregation frequently involves the use of legal force. Theoretical and empirical considerations are then examined (the latter from the experience of labor unions and the armed forces during the war), which lead to the conclusion that the use of legal force in abolishing segregation practices is sometimes justified psychologically and can lead to the reduction of racial prejudice. Finally some specific steps are suggested that can lead to changing the context and emphasis of observable attributes of minority-group members— steps that can also lead to a reduction of racial prejudice.

The final section of this chapter concerns itself with the control of racial prejudice through educational techniques. The role of the public school, the community education program, and some aspects of mass publicity activities are discussed. In connection with the first, five guiding principles are listed and illustrated. These refer to the over-all content of the child's education, the social atmosphere of the school, the role of the parents in such education, the nature of "intercultural education" programs, and the necessity for training in *techniques* of democracy. In connection with the second, two basic suggestions are made. These stress the value of community self-surveys as prerequisites for a program of action and the importance of gearing interracial contacts to basic objectives and action. In considering the use of mass publicity programs, the obstacles to effective mass publicity are first discussed, but it is concluded that despite these obstacles there is merit in the use of mass communication media in the attempt to reduce racial prejudice. It is pointed out that these media can be especially valuable in reinforcing the democratic beliefs that are already held, in shifting the zero point in public opinion about racial prejudice, and in making effective use of the need for social and group acceptance toward the end of inducing democratic beliefs and attitudes. All of this is especially significant during periods of social crisis.

BIBLIOGRAPHY

ALEXANDER, F., FRENCH, T. M., et al.: 1946. *Psychoanalytic therapy: principles and application.* New York: Ronald.

AMSTER, F., and AMSTER, S.: 1944. Spot therapy (short-term) for soldiers and implications for long term treatment. *Amer. J. Orthopsychiat.*, **14**, 505–509.

BENNE, K., BRADFORD, L., and LIPPITT, R. Discussion-method and reality-practice. (In press).

BROPHY, I. N.: 1946. The luxury of anti-Negro prejudice. *Publ. Opin. Quart.*, **9**, 456–466.

CHATTO, C. L., and HALLIGAN, A. L.: 1945. *Story of the Springfield plan.* New York: Barnes & Noble.

CHENOWITH, A. S.: 1947. *A report of a study on practical democracy.* Atlantic City: Atlantic City Public Schools.

Children's Book Committee: 1945. *Let them face it: today's world in books for boys and girls.* New York: Child Study Association of America.

CLARK, W. R.: 1940. Radio listening habits of children. *J. soc. Psychol.*, **12**, 131–149.

CURRAN, J., 1947. How we did it. *Survey Graphic*, **36**, No. 1, 57ff.

FISK, A. G.: 1947. Stereotypes in intercultural education. *Common Ground*, Winter, 28–33.

FRAZIER, E. F.: 1947. Human, all too human. *Survey Graphic*, **36**, No. 1, 74ff.

HOVLAND, C. I., and SEARS, R. R.: 1940. Minor studies in aggression: VI. Correlation of lynchings with economic indices. *J. Psychol.*, **9**, 301–310.

HUGHES, M.: 1946. *The school's responsibility for the improvement of intergroup relations.* Los Angeles: Los Angeles County Superintendent of Schools.

KLINEBERG, O.: 1940. *Social psychology.* New York: Holt.

LASKER, G. W.: 1946. Migration and physical differentiation. *Amer. J. Phys. Anthrop.,*
N. S. 4, 273-300.

LAZARSFELD, P. F.: 1940. *Radio and the printed page.* New York: Duell, Sloan & Pearce.

LAZARSFELD, P. F.: 1947. Some remarks on the role of the mass media in so-called tolerance propaganda. *J. soc. Issues,* **3,** No. 3, 17-25.

LAZARSFELD, P. F., and MERTON, R. K.: 1943. Studies in radio and film propaganda.
Trans. N. Y. Acad. Sci., **6,** 58-79.

LAZARSFELD, P. F., and WYANT, R.: 1937. Magazines in 90 cities—who reads what?
Publ. Opin. Quart., **1,** 29-41.

LEWIN, K.: 1946. Action research and minority problems. *J. Soc. Issues,* **2,** No. 4,
34-46.

LEWIN, K., and GRABBE, P.: 1945. Conduct, knowledge and acceptance of new values.
J. Soc. Issues, **1,** No. 3, 53-64.

LIPPITT, R.: 1946a. Techniques for research in group living. *J. Soc. Issues,* **2,** No. 4,
55-61.

LIPPITT, R.: 1946b. Discussion—practicing ideas and preparing for action. *The Campfire Girl,* May.

MANSKE, A. J.: 1935. *The reflections of teachers' attitudes in the attitudes of their pupils.*
Teachers College, Columbia University (Ph.D. Thesis).

MEINE, F. J.: 1941. Radio and the press among young people. *In* Lazarsfeld and
Stanton (ed.), *Radio research.* New York: Duell, Sloan & Pearce.

MINTZ, A.: 1946. A re-examination of correlations between lynchings and economic
indices. *J. abnorm. soc. Psychol.,* **41,** 154-160.

MYERS, N. D.: 1946. *Education for cultural unity.* California Elementary School
Principal's Association.

NORTHRUP, H. R.: 1947. In the unions. *Survey Graphic,* **36,** No. 1, 54ff.

RAPER, A. F.: 1933. *The tragedy of lynching.* Chapel Hill: Univ. North Carolina Press.

ROSE, A. M.: 1946. Army policies toward Negro soldiers. *Ann. Amer. Acad. Polit. Soc
Sci.,* **244,** 90-94.

SLAVSON, S. R.: 1943. *An introduction to group therapy.* New York: Commonwealth
Fund.

SNYDER, W. U.: 1947. The present status of psychotherapeutic counseling. *Psychol.
Bull.,* **44,** 297-386.

Social Action, 1947. Toward racial integration. *Soc. Action Mag.,* **13,** No. 1.

War Department: 1944. *Group psychotherapy.* TB Med. 103.

WEAVER, R. C.: 1945. *Community relations manual.* Chicago: American Council on
Race Relations.

WEAVER, R. C.: 1947. Community action against segregation. *Soc. Action Mag.,* **13,**
No. 1, 4-24.

WILEY, G. M.: 1947. *Education for unity.* Albany: State Education Department.

ZANDER, A.: 1941. *Centerville studies itself.* Ann Arbor: Univ. Michigan.

CHAPTER XIV

INDUSTRIAL CONFLICT

The dominant theme of labor-management relations in this country during the last several decades has been that of strife and tension. Although there have been instances of labor-management cooperation and eras of good will and peace, the frequency and intensity of labor-management conflict gives more urgency to the need for a psychological analysis of this aspect of labor-management relations than of any other aspect. It is in common recognition of these tensions that people so frequently phrase the questions of labor-management relations in terms of the emotionally loaded word, "problem"—the "labor problem," the "union problem," the "labor-management problem." Most of the energy of labor organizations, management organizations, and related governmental agencies is directed toward dealing with conflict between labor and management.

The major concern of this chapter will be with the individuals most directly involved in industrial conflict—with workers, union leaders, management. Such an analysis, it is hoped, will give us an understanding of the basic psychological processes concerned and will permit us to indicate some psychologically sound procedures which might reduce the frequency and intensity of industrial conflict. The task for this chapter differs from another common objective of psychologists who concern themselves with industrial problems. Many psychologists have worked on problems of industrial efficiency—selection and placement of employees, reduction of fatigue and accidents, increase in output per hour per worker, design of machines to "fit" the human organism, etc. These are typical problems of the *industrial* psychologist. Such problems will concern us in this chapter only in a general way. The problem confronting us is a problem of the *social* psychologist—the fundamental understanding of the behavior of people involved in a specific form of social conflict.

THE SOCIOLOGICAL BACKGROUND

Conflict among individuals must be analyzed in terms of the needs, beliefs, and attitudes of the specific individuals involved. That has been the consistent theme of our treatment of all social behavior. However,

531

we have also pointed to the importance of paying attention to the specific social context in which individuals behave (see especially Chaps. VI and X) for an understanding of social activity. In an analysis of industrial conflict we are dealing with formalized and institutionalized behavior of people that occurs within the confines and patterns laid down by an economic system called "capitalism" and by such social organizations as the industrial plant and the labor union. Before starting our psychological analysis, therefore, it might be desirable to sketch briefly the nature of capitalism and the characteristics of these two types of social organizations.

The Nature of Capitalism.—The pattern of capitalism is one that is supported by legal, religious, and educational practices and concepts in this country. It is all-pervasive in its effects and conditions almost every kind of social conflict. A thorough analysis of capitalism, therefore, would require extended treatment from the point of view of every social science. However, for our purposes, we can summarize the most important characteristics of capitalism in the following propositions: (1) The capitalistic system is an economic pattern of activities and social organizations that carry out the functions of production, transportation, distribution, and manipulation of credit units. Its industrial and business elements are the major agencies responsible for supplying the great variety of wants of large heterogeneous populations. (2) The "corporation," which is the major type of economic organization within the capitalist system, consists typically of a large number of investors who supply the needed capital for the enterprise, who seek interest and dividends from their investments, who are liable for debts incurred by the corporation only up to the value of the shares they hold, and who delegate the responsibility of management to a committee that chooses a president or manager. In large corporations, therefore, the "owners" are many in number, have little feeling of personal responsibility, and are usually completely divorced from management and from contact with workers. (3) Under capitalism, management is relatively free to hire or fire workers in accordance with production schedules. It has no responsibility, in time of "depression," to keep the worker on its pay roll or otherwise to provide for his support. The worker, similarly, is legally free to accept or refuse a job and owes no lasting loyalty to management. (4) Management is relatively free to withhold or increase production, set prices for its commodities, and seek an individually determined profit level, limited only by competitive and certain governmental restraining forces. The worker, theoretically, is also free to set prices on his labor, again limited by competition from other workers, the relative cost of labor-saving devices, and labor-union activities. (5) Capitalism *in practice* (as opposed to some theoretical descriptions) is strongly monopolistic. Monopolies typically require large investments and have effective control of the employment, production, and price practices in any industry. The consequences of this are a general decrease of new competitive industries, a tendency to keep prices constant and production limited—with decreased consumption—and a lowering of the opportunities for the worker to "shop around" for other jobs. (6) Under capitalism, as practiced in the United States, a tremendous inequality of income exists. This inequality is periodically intensified by occurrence of economic depressions and unemployment. Modern capitalism is a complexly integrated system depending for smooth functioning on the synchronization of many parts. When purchasing power of the unemployed worker drops, prices do not drop correspondingly, but production is limited instead, and more workers are dropped from the pay roll (a consequence of monopoly control of production and prices).

Maldistribution of income.—This last characteristic of capitalism, as it has operated in the United States, is of sufficient importance for our analysis to warrant more detailed consideration. The amount of income an individual receives is related to the adequacy with which he can satisfy many of his major needs and demands. The question, therefore, of how capitalism, in practice in the United States, distributes the income of the country is immediately relevant to any psychological analysis of the behavior of management and workers.

The first and most obvious fact is that there is a very large differential in the incomes received by the people of the United States. Roughly, the upper 10 per cent of the American people receives as much income (in aggregate) as the lower 60 per cent.[1] The second important fact is that a large section of the country does not receive the minimum income necessary for even a "bare subsistence level." In 1942, for example, when employment was high as a consequence of war production efforts, 40.6 per cent of all American families and single consumers received an annual income of less than $1,500, and only 25.6 per cent of the families and single consumers received an income of $3,000 or over per year. In 1939 about 15 million workers received less than $10 per week, and 23 million workers less than $20 per week.

Social Change and Social Insecurity.—The economic system described above has been functioning in a very special social atmosphere. It is no mere rhetoric to say that the outstanding characteristics of our age are the confusion and lack of security exhibited by almost all people as a consequence

[1] These data and the following, unless otherwise indicated, are based on the information available from the *Statistical abstract of the United States*, 1946, published by the U. S. Department of Commerce, Bureau of the Census (1946). See especially pp. 270–281.

of the extensive and rapid social change that has occurred during the last forty years or so.   These years have seen two world wars, a universal and devastating economic depression, significant realignments in international political power relationships, revolutionary changes in government forms and practices, and unprecedented technological advances—culminating in the promise and threat inherent in atomic fission.   Most people, therefore, have been living through several decades of "crises"; and as we have seen in Chap. VI, crisis periods are periods of rapid changes in individual beliefs and attitudes, since at these times old beliefs are frequently found inadequate to give meaning to the person's daily behavior.   This is true of beliefs about personal security and personal worth, about group standards, about opinions, about faiths, and even about matters of "knowledge."   Social change, no matter how desirable, almost always results in individual feelings of insecurity, confusion, and doubt.   And this is true for those people whose lot is seemingly being improved by the social change as well as those whose former prerogatives are being withdrawn.   The antagonistic beliefs and attitudes, the incompatible behavior techniques, and the frustrated needs and demands of both labor and management which are involved in industrial conflict must be viewed against this background.

In addition to this general "atmospheric" effect of social change, there are three specific correlative consequences that are of immediate relevancy to our analysis.   These are the changes that have taken place in the nature of industrial conflict, the changes that have occurred within the industrial plants, and the developments that have characterized labor unions.

Expansion of area of industrial conflict.—Industrial conflict today is rapidly becoming widespread social conflict.   As a consequence of the growing interdependence of one industry upon another (due to the increasing complexity of manufacture and distribution and of the increasing industrialization of our society), any industrial conflict in one area of our economic life has an almost immediate effect on other areas.   Thus, a strike in the coal-mining industry is reflected in the cessation of work in the steel, automobile, chemical, power, and transportation industries, as well as in a decrease in the essential heating, lighting, and recreational services to the individual citizen.   The normal activities and well-being of the public become dependent upon labor-management peace in every major industry.   As a consequence, industrial conflict in one industry almost immediately evokes public support for the suggestion that the government step in and "do something about it."   Labor and management are no longer permitted to fight it out between themselves.   Labor and management, when in conflict, therefore find it wise to bring pressure upon the government officials who have now become immediate parties to the conflict. Neither labor nor management, of course, will wait until the moment of conflict but will anticipate such action and will attempt to elect government officials who can be "counted upon." The result is that the area of industrial conflict becomes widened and so takes on the attributes of widespread political and sometimes even "class" conflict.

Changes in industrial organizations.—The personnel of any factory, plant, shop, yard, or mine comprise a *social organization* with all that that involves. Technological advances will reflect themselves not only in a new relationship among cranes, presses, stamping machines, and conveyor belts but also in a new relationship among managerial personnel, foremen, skilled workers, unskilled laborers, maintenance men, etc. The most general effect of modern production changes has been noticed in the area of interpersonal relations among the people who work in any one plant.

In the first place, as the complexities of new methods of production increase, and as technical education becomes a prerequisite for management, *the social cleavage between workers and management within the industrial organization becomes more and more marked*. The worker finds it increasingly more difficult to become a manager, and the manager, trained to assume a technical job, can no longer afford to start at the "bottom of the ladder" and consequently has little opportunity to become intimately acquainted with the job and outlook of the worker at the bench. The social cleavage between workers and management within the industrial organization becomes more and more marked and can contribute to growing tensions between the two. In the second place, there are factors that also lead to difficulties of communication, decreased mutual understanding, and deterioration in the interpersonal relationships within the plant. Top management is frequently far removed from any direct contact with the workers. The communication between the two is necessarily indirect and through go-betweens—supervisors, department heads, foremen, personnel officers, etc. In addition to the top management, which decides on general policy and over-all production schedules, there are "efficiency experts," "rate setters," and many other specialized groups, each of which has its own objective in the plant. These objectives are technical and "nonhuman" in nature. Top management may decide on the production schedule only in terms of *units of production;* the technician may scrutinize his problems only in terms of the *logic of efficiency*. On the basis of these considerations, orders are given to the foremen—the only group that has daily face-to-face relations with the worker. In many cases the foremen do not understand the reasoning that lies behind the orders they must see carried out, and the foremen's superiors do not appreciate the personnel problems involved in having those orders carried out. The result is that the relationship between foremen and workers frequently takes place in an atmosphere of arbitrariness, and the interpersonal relations take on many of the attributes of dictatorial leadership and followership. Thus as a consequence both of the differences in social origins of workers and management and of the nature of the interpersonal relationships established within the plant, a situation is created that can intensify and complicate any tensions that may exist among the workers vis-a-vis management.

Developments in labor organization.—Labor unions, in response to the same social, political, and technological changes we have mentioned, have also shown significant changes in structure and functioning—changes that have their own sociological and psychological effects. The last fifteen years have seen a tremendous growth of labor organizations. From a membership of approximately 2 million prior to 1933 (or approximately 1 out of every 24 gainfully employed persons), labor unions now claim a membership in the neighborhood of 15 million, or 1 out of every 4 gainfully employed persons in both the agricultural and nonagricultural fields. In America's basic industries—steel, automobile, rubber, electrical equipment, coal, etc.,—the typical worker is a union member. The existence of these large workers' organizations has resulted in changes in the nature and frequency of industrial conflict, in changes in the interpersonal relationships between labor and management, and in the formation of groups that have basic social significance.

As frequently happens to all functioning organizations, the membership and leaders of labor unions acquire new aspirations and demands peculiar to the organization itself and apparently essential for the continued existence of the organization (see page 384, Chap. X). Without denying the possibility that the existence of a strong labor union may result in an overall decrease in the number of strikes within any one industry, *these new aspirations and demands frequently result in new sources for industrial conflict.* The labor leaders and members must seek to increase the power and influence of their unions, and consequently sources of conflict for organizational reasons come into being, as, for example, in the case of a strike for closed shop agreements. Because of the wide ramifications of labor unions and the wide distribution of their memberships, the industrial conflict of one worker becomes the conflict of another—and frequently the two individuals may not know each other, may be separated by hundreds of miles, and may even be employed in different industries, as, for example, in a "sympathy" strike. Finally, the existence of many competing labor organizations may sometimes lead to conflict *among labor unions,* and this competition can also eventuate in industrial conflict, as, for example, in the case of "jurisdictional" strikes.

Labor unions *deepen the depersonalization of worker-management contacts*—induced in the first instance by the nature of capitalist economy and technological growth. The union member no longer even *seeks* for personal contact with management when he wishes to discuss grievances, wage increases, or better working conditions. This is done for him by his union leaders or "grievance committees" and through regularized channels. Frequently, even the recognition that a grievance exists or the determination of what is a just and adequate remedy for the grievance is not determined by the needs and beliefs of the worker concerned. The majority vote of the union membership or the decisions of the top union leadership may determine these matters for the individual.

Finally, *labor unions have changed many of the off-the-job behavior patterns of workers.* Again, as is typical of all social organizations, the labor unions have sought to increase the loyalty and interest of its members by deliberately seeking to meet more and more of the needs and demands of its membership within the confines of the labor unions (see page 385, Chap. X). Thus labor unions have established banks, recreation centers, educational institutions, health clinics, housing projects, insurance companies, retail cooperatives, publishing houses, etc. All this has tended to encourage the emerging of genuine psychological groups among workers.[1] A member of a labor union not only meets with fellow members to discuss union matters but plays ball with them on the union baseball team, attends the same union dances, serves on the same political action committee, and helps his fellow union members to organize a civic movement for more efficient removal of garbage from the streets.

General Comments.—The growth and development of the large industrial plant and the labor union—both social organizations that operate within the capitalist pattern of economy—in a social atmosphere of rapid and far-reaching change have had *compounding dynamic* effects. As a consequence of the nature of both the industrial plant and the labor union, the stratification of the social origins of labor and management personnel has become sharper, the insulation of managerial personnel from workers' outlooks and the insulation of labor personnel from managers' outlooks have become more pronounced, the depersonalization of labor-management contact has been increased, and the nature and intensity of industrial con-

---

[1] See the discussion in Chap. I, p. 18, on the difference between a psychological group and a sociological class.

flict has changed profoundly. It is important that these considerations be kept in mind when attempting to make a psychological analysis of industrial conflict.

INDUSTRIAL CONFLICT AND MOTIVES OF PEOPLE

Just as we have found that there is no one need which lies behind racial prejudice, so must we expect to find that there is no one need or demand which lies behind industrial conflict. We must be careful to avoid the error of looking for a universal basic "cause." To say that workers have a need or desire for "social change" and management for the maintenance of the *status quo* is to make an analysis that is neither theoretically sound nor supported by empirical data. It is neither helpful nor accurate to say that the labor "agitator" or the "reactionary" manager—the two kinds of individuals frequently assumed to be responsible for industrial conflict— are "defective personalities." In an analysis of the motivational processes involved in industrial conflict we must bear clearly in mind that we are analyzing individuals (whether these individuals are "workers" or "managers") with many varied needs, demands, aspirations, frustrations, and emotions. With this as a point of departure we must seek to answer such questions as the following: What are the special conditions under which the individual as a worker and the individual as a manager operate that bring about conflicting needs and demands between them, and how does this relate to industrial conflict?

Needs of the Worker.—We have seen from Chap. II that the needs of men are varied in kind and potentially limitless in number and derive from the nature of the psychological field of the person. This is no less true for the worker than for his boss. Although it is true that differences in the specific needs and demands of the two will exist because of their different socioeconomic origins, nevertheless there will be large and important overlapping areas in their needs and demands, since both workers and managers are exposed to significantly common cultural influences. It was suggested in Chap. II that it is legitimate to talk about need patterns that are characteristic of certain cultures. Every need and demand that characterizes our social scene will be found among most workers and among most managers: the need for food, sex, shelter, social approval, self-expression, power, self-esteem, etc. The needs of the American worker will be much more similar to the needs of the American capitalist than they will be, for example, to the needs of the French worker or the Russian worker or the Chinese worker. The reason why, given this large area of communality of needs and demands, there is conflict rather than cooperation between the American worker and the manager derives in part from the conditions under which both seek to satisfy their varied needs.

Methods of satisfying needs.—To understand the importance of work conditions in relation to the needs of man, we must realize that the job situation is not a "happenstance" within our culture but is a defining characteristic of our culture. That is, it is wrong to consider the job situation as an appendage of the cultural environment where an individual works and then, after hours, reenters his "real" cultural environment to seek satisfaction of his needs and to express himself as a member of his culture. Within our culture much of the waking time of both management and labor is spent on the job. For these people the job is a major part of their cultural environment, and both management and labor, therefore, *will seek to satisfy many of their needs in and through their work.* It is true that different areas of our culture may be best adapted for the satisfaction of different needs, but the successful operation of such a division of function is possible only within certain narrow limits. It depends upon the nature and strength of the need and the availability to the individual of such functionally different areas. For some needs, however, such a division of function is altogether impossible. Some needs and demands must be satisfied in every area of man's activities. Thus, for example, the need for "decent treatment" must be provided for at work, at play, in the family, in the social group, etc. This and many other needs and demands are not operative only in certain sociologically defined situations. As we have pointed out in Chap. II, needs are the products of imbalances and deficiencies in the current psychological field; and wherever these imbalances occur, needs and demands will be operative. If the job conditions create these imbalances, then the needs will be operative in the job situation. It is therefore important to determine which tensions are created by the job situation and whether or not the job situation typically allows for the reduction of the resultant tensions.

Tensions as a Function of On-the-job Situations.—The tensions created among workers in the industrial plant can be grouped into two major categories—those which derive from technological changes per se and those which derive from the nature of the interpersonal relationships typical of modern industrial plants.

Technology and tensions.—Technological changes in and of themselves (although frequently compounded by unskilled or inconsiderate action on the part of management) frequently operate so as to block the expression of many important needs of the worker on the job. Merton (1947) has listed a number of such technologically determined factors, among them being the rapid *obsolescence of skills, subdivision of labor,* and *assembly-line production methods.*

The worker whose painfully acquired skill has suddenly become useless and meaningless by some new invention or improvement in production method finds himself facing very serious psychological problems. Not only must he learn new skills and routines of work, but his feeling of personal worth and self-esteem, based in many instances on his mastery of the now-obsolescent skill, is threatened. Technological development has resulted in the frustration of strong needs formerly expressed on the job—and *best expressed* on the job.

The splintering of work tasks, also characteristic of technological advance, frequently results in a loss of social status to many workers. The growth of subdivision of tasks to the point where the label attached to the worker in any one of these "splinters" has no social meaning outside of his plant (and very little inside) leaves the worker with no easy means of satisfying this need for status in a civilization of craftsmen, "experts," and technicians. Thus, as Merton points out,

Who but a chosen few, for example, can distinguish a fin-sticker in an automobile plant from other radiator-core assemblers? Or to take a more homely instance, what distinguishes the pride in work of a doughnut sugarer from that of a doughnut pumper, who successfully injects jelly into fried doughnuts with a jelly pump? To the outside world, these esoteric specializations are all of a piece, and consequently, for the outside world there must be other marks of status and significant work activity that count.

The worker, then, as a further consequence of technological development, is left with a complete absence of social meaning that can be attributed to the task at which he spends most of his active waking hours.

Finally, the assembly-line production methods, technologically valuable perhaps, demand not only that each piece of machinery in the line function with a minimum of variation but also that the variation in tempo of the worker be reduced to a minimum. This results in the necessity of imposing more and more discipline on the behavior of the worker. Under some conditions this not only robs the worker of any interest in his monotonously repeated movements but results in a definite feeling of coercion on his part. The assembly line creates tensions and does not permit their reduction.

Interpersonal relations in the plant and tensions.—In addition to the above tension-creating factors, the indirect and circuitous contact between top management and workers, which is involved in the translation of economic demands of the plant into personal directives to the workers (see page 535), is such as to create situations that lead to tensions between those who give the orders (*e.g.*, foremen) and those who carry out the orders (*e.g.*, workers). As far as the worker is concerned, he is being "pushed around" by management in a manner that disregards his needs for understanding, feelings of security, and "decent human treatment." Changes imposed upon the worker without his prior knowledge, consent, or even understanding are regarded by him as a threat to his well-being.[1] Such arbitrariness is inconsistent with the pattern of behavior that he has been taught by his society is the proper one for every "self-respecting American."

In this connection the following reply of H. J. Ruttenberg, research director of the Steel Workers Organizing Committee, in answer to a question asked of him at an industrial conference (National Research Council, 1941) is of particular interest:

> I live in a district where the workers live, and spend almost all of my time with them, and they are emotionally dissatisfied, intellectually dissatisfied, and economically dissatisfied . . . because of having to respond to technical changes which they do not originate, and in contrast to (workers) who increased production when they were consulted on technical changes . . . . One of the most fundamental impulses in a man in a shop is self-expression. If he is denied that in determining his wages, he feels much dissatisfied. If he is permitted expression in the production set-up, then he feels that he has made a contribution to the whole.

Tensions and Frustrations Indirectly Related to the Job.—In our society the satisfaction of many needs depends upon the material wealth or income of the individual. In so far as the man's job does not provide him with an adequate income, the consequent blocking of needs and demands can be seen as frustration that is indirectly related to the job situation. This indirect effect frequently intensifies the frustration of needs *on* the job. Some needs can be expressed either on the job or off the job. Where the lack of money prevents the expression of needs off the job and the job situation does not permit their expression at work, then we have a compounding effect—all of it traceable to the job situation.

Psychological definition of an adequate wage.—There is a positive correlation (though not a perfect one) between the wage level of the worker and his "satisfaction." This may seem an obvious statement, requiring no further analysis, but the difficulty stems from the failure to realize what determines an "adequate" wage. We have already seen that the incomes of millions of Americans fall below the level necessary to provide for minimum essentials (page 533). From this purely *economic* consideration the

---

[1] Merton suggests that in this respect the worker is in the same position as the businessman who feels threatened by and resents the "unpredictable decisions by those bureaucrats in Washington."

wages earned by many American workers are inadequate and are constant and important sources of need frustration. But even if these incomes were raised to a level sufficient to enable the gratification of nutritional, shelter, and health requirements, wages could still serve as a major source of need frustration. Essentially, the adequacy of wages is determined by *psychological* factors.

Psychologically, wage rates must be seen from the perspective of all of man's needs. An adequate wage rate is not a static wage, nor is it, as some economists have suggested, a wage that is pegged to cost-of-living price levels. To say, for example, that when the price of tomatoes, bread, housing, and clothes rises 5 per cent, the wage rate should also rise 5 per cent is to assume that man's needs remain static. We have seen that man's needs are almost constantly growing and proliferating—the achievement of one goal merely sets the stage for a higher level of aspiration. Each wage rise, by permitting the worker access to new interests and by raising his socioeconomic level, induces new needs. The relationship between wages and needs is a spiraling one; and just as long as the worker's needs change, the definition of what is an adequate wage must also change. It is false to argue that "inadequate wages" cannot be an important cause of worker dissatisfaction, since the worker today is receiving twice as much money (or even twice as much real income) as the worker of yesterday or the worker of Britain, France, or Russia. If the American worker's level of aspiration has increased fourfold, then he is today receiving only half as much as he did yesterday, not twice as much. *A wage rate is psychologically inadequate, no matter how large in absolute amount, if it results in a wide discrepancy between the worker's level of aspiration and his level of achievement.*

Income satisfaction and income aspiration.—The importance of the above considerations is borne out by a number of studies that have investigated the relation between income satisfaction and income aspiration. In one such study, by Centers and Cantril (1946), some 1,200 persons, representing a cross section of the American population eighteen years or over, were asked to indicate their average weekly income and their answer to the following question: *"About how much more money than that do you think your family would need to have the things that might make your family happier or more comfortable than it is now?"* Although the phrasing of this question is "loaded" (it assumes that the respondent wants more money), nevertheless there is some reason to believe that the answers represented genuine aspirations of the respondents. Thus, for example, although Centers and Cantril did not solicit discussion as to whether or not the respondents were satisfied with their present incomes, a large proportion volunteered comments that indicated the existence of genuine and salient feelings of dissatisfaction. The data of that study suggest the following conclusions:

1. Sixty-eight per cent of the sample was definitely dissatisfied with its income, and these people wanted, on the average, an 86 per cent *increase over their present incomes*.[1]

2. The relative discrepancy between the level of achievement and level of aspiration of the lower income groups was much larger than that of the higher income groups—although all groups indicated such discrepancy.

3. A correlational analysis indicated that income is a more reliable index to satisfaction than either occupation or education. However, the writers point out that there is a tendency "for persons in those occupations providing greater personal independence to be more satisfied in all income levels."

Worker morale studies.—The general validity of the analysis presented in the preceding pages relative to on-the-job and off-the-job causes of tensions among workers has been demonstrated by almost every worker morale study made in recent years. French, Kornhauser, and Marrow (1946) have compiled the following summary list of factors that have been found by the various studies as "underlying causes" of worker satisfaction or dissatisfaction:

Factors in the individual: Ability, health, age, temperament, desires and expectations, neurotic tendencies, unconscious conflicts, etc.

Factors in life away from work: Home conditions; recreation; consumer problems; labor union activities; social, economic, and political conditions; etc.

Factors in employment relations: Wages or earnings; steadiness of employment; transfer, lay-off, and rehiring procedures; kind of work performed; supervision; training; conditions of work; opportunities for advancement; opportunity to use ability; social relationships on the job; recognition and fair evaluation of work; opportunities for participation; free interchange of ideas; prompt and fair settling of grievances; understanding and respect by employer

This list indicates that the "causes" of worker dissatisfaction are not restricted to wages but run the whole gamut of man's needs and aspirations. The data indicating that the neurotic and "unadjusted" individual has low worker morale do not demonstrate that job conditions are of little consequence in determining the dissatisfaction of these workers. As Watson

---

[1] This 86 per cent figure, it should be noted, is far greater than any increase in cost-of-living index that had taken place at the time of the study. This again emphasizes that people's aspirations are not in terms of keeping up with the "market basket."

(1939) has pointed out in discussing such conclusions, "which is cart and which is horse" is not shown by any correlation between a person's dissatisfaction with his life outside the plant and his life inside the plant. As we have suggested, dissatisfactions arising from outside the job are frequently reflections of job conditions.

While the above list is fairly exhaustive, the specific factors will vary from time to time, from place to place, and from one group of workers to another. For illustrative purposes we shall consider a few specific studies.

Hull and Kolstad (1942), using the polling technique, attempted to determine the "morale" and "specific attitudes" of various employee populations. Employee morale was "assumed to be a function of the worker's general attitude toward his job and toward his company as an employer." "Specific attitudes" referred to such matters as wage policies, supervision, foreman-worker relationships, etc. The results of their polling survey indicated that

Perhaps the most important conclusion . . . is that industrial morale as defined here . . . is not determined simply by such material considerations as pay, hours, working conditions, vacations, and miscellaneous company benefit plans. The extent to which the employee enjoys the psychological satisfactions that come with recognition of and respect for his own personality, day by day, and hour by hour on the job is equally important . . . . The second outstanding conclusion is that foremen, department managers, and others having direct supervision over workers play a tremendously large part in the determination of employee morale[1]. . . . The quality of immediate supervision, furthermore, appears to create a mental set which carries over to and influences attitudes on factors of the job situation which are not controlled by the supervisor.

In January, 1946, the British Institute of Public Opinion polled the British people on the following question: *"Apart from wages and security, what do you need most in a job for making you feel contented whilst at work?"* Forty per cent of all the respondents gave such answers as "cooperation between management and employee," "appreciative employer," etc. Most of the other answers referred to "good working conditions," "shorter hours," etc.

Studies that use the open-end question method (see Chap. VIII) find essentially similar results. Illustrative of such studies are those conducted in war industries by such governmental agencies as the Program Surveys Division, U.S. Department of Agriculture, and the Surveys Division,

---

[1] Hull and Kolstad found marked variation in "morale scores" for many departments in the same plant working on essentially the same type of operation and with identical hours and pay. The only variable that they could discover to account for this variation was the nature and quality of the immediate supervision.

Office of War Information. In those studies the morale of the workers was measured on both the subjective and objective side—the former being measured in terms of "satisfaction with working conditions, with wages, with upgrading or promotion, confidence in management, feeling of participation in the plant's production, etc. . ." (Katz, 1946). The objective side was measured by absenteeism records, labor turnover, plant and worker productivity. Some of these studies indicated that the over-all "in-plant" conditions—wages, conditions of the job, the interpersonal relationships between workers and supervisors, the feeling of participation in the plant's production—were frequently *more important* in determining worker morale than were living conditions outside the plant. Although this would probably hold only for relatively short periods of time and only during such national crises situations as war, nevertheless the importance of the general plant atmosphere is emphasized.

General Comments.—The job conditions under which people work are responsible, directly or indirectly, for the creation of many tensions and the frustrations of many needs and demands. It must be continuously emphasized that there is no one need which lies behind worker dissatisfaction and no one need which is inadequately met by job conditions. A good summary of this view is the following statement by French, Kornhauser, and Marrow (1946):

What do working people want? Perhaps the best answer is that of the labor leader who replied: "More." They want more of whatever they feel especially deprived of—more security, more income, more personal appreciation and decent human treatment, more individual self-expression, more say in whatever affects them, more freedom "to tell the boss to go to hell." Their wants focus upon the matters which are most frustrating or forbidding at the time.

And, as we have seen, the typical job conditions of the American worker are such as to frustrate all of these needs and demands. However, it is important to remember that in giving appropriate stress to these various needs of social status and recognition, self-expression and group identification, we should not undervalue the crucial importance of wage rates as a job condition that frustrates the worker.

Because of all these factors, then, work conditions and wage level, the people in our society who occupy the role of "workers" suffer more from a general feeling of frustration than do the individuals who occupy the role of management. As Kornhauser (1939) concludes on the basis of his study of the attitudes of major business executives and manual workers in Chicago,

A sketchy analysis of people's major motivations and the opportunities for their gratification at the several income levels suggests that personal maladjustment, frustration and unrest are likely to be greater, on the whole, as one descends the socio-economic scale.[1]

We know that when major needs are frustrated over any lengthy periods of time, various frustration reactions occur. What we must now examine are the following questions: What opportunities for expressing frustration reactions are available to the man who works? Are there any factors in the job situation that force certain types of frustration reactions to appear? How is all this related to industrial conflict?

Frustration Reactions and Industrial Conflict.—Before discussing the frustration reactions of workers, it is essential to remind ourselves that not all frustration reactions are "bad," "unhealthy," "pathological" or involve aggression and conflict. As was pointed out in Chap. II, "Frustration is a bad word. It has come, for most people, to connote unhappy, tortured experience and neuroticism. This is unfortunate . . . . Most blockages can, as a matter of fact, be regarded as *beneficial* and *adaptive,* for they energize the individual's efforts toward achievement of his goals and cause him to reorient, learn, and grow" (pages 53–54). The frustrated worker whom we have described above will, as do all men, find many ways of successfully resolving his tensions in *constructive* activity, in creating new social inventions which will meet his blocked needs. But, and this is particularly important for our main concern in this chapter, some of these *adaptive, healthy, and constructive reactions can lead to increased industrial conflict.* One section of our present analysis, then, will concern itself with the constructive frustration reactions of workers and their relation to industrial conflict.

Another major proposition we must keep in mind about frustration reaction is that no matter how seemingly bizarre and "illogical" the reaction may be, it must be regarded as being in the direction of tension reduction (see page 55). The second section of this analysis, therefore, will concern itself with the "indirect" and frequently illogical frustration reactions of workers and their relation to industrial conflict.

Constructive reactions to frustration and industrial conflict.—Action directed intelligently and effectively against the barriers intervening between

[1] Thus, for example, he found the following percentages of respondents who answered "Yes" to these questions:

"Do you feel that your children (or those of your friends and neighbors) have as much opportunity as they should have?" Major business executives, 91 per cent; manual skilled workers, 49 per cent.

"Do you feel that you have as much opportunity to enjoy life as you should have?" Major business executives, 85 per cent; manual skilled workers, 52 per cent.

"Do you feel that you have a good chance to get ahead in life and become fairly well-off?" Major business executives, 98 per cent; manual skilled workers, 55 per cent.

the individual and his goal object is one of the most constructive and healthy types of frustration reaction. Although good statistics are not available, it is safe to hazard a guess that most instances of industrial conflict can properly be characterized as constructive and healthy frustration reactions. That is, specific, consciously identified needs are frustrated. The worker, thus frustrated, recognizes management policies as the barriers intervening between him and his goals, and he reacts by direct action against these barriers through striking or other forms of industrial conflict.[1] Although it is true that all behavior is multidetermined and that no single factor is completely adequate to describe such complicated action as going out on strike, nevertheless this analysis presents the fundamental factors involved. It might, however, be desirable to point out that in so far as a strike involves *aggressive* behavior against management, the readiness with which different workers will resort to a strike will depend upon many personality factors within the individual. Thus, because it is aggressive action, it will have an added appeal to the "aggressive" person and it will have a negative valence for the person who shrinks from all forms of aggression. But it must be stressed that for the type of strike we are here considering, these factors have only a contributing role to play. The major factors, to repeat, are the frustration of current, on-the-job needs; the recognition of specific managerial policies as the barriers to the satisfaction of these needs; and the belief that the strike is a legitimate and efficient method of overcoming these barriers.

But as we have seen in Chap. II, constructive reactions to frustration situations frequently occur that do not involve action against the barrier. Thus, as we pointed out there, the successfully adaptive individual, in reaction to frustration, may sometimes seek and find alternative paths to goals or alternative and equally satisfying goal objects. The dissatisfied worker, blocked from fulfilling his needs for feelings of personal worth, power, companionship, or leadership on the job, will seek to satisfy those demands elsewhere. One way that readily suggests itself to him is through fraternal association with other workers.

Alternative paths to goals, labor unions, and industrial conflict.—While it is true that the individual worker may find substitute satisfactions in many different kinds of social organizations (see page 503)—in fraternal, religious, or other types—it is highly probable that he will seek many of them in

[1] In 1944, 3,946 of the 4,958 strikes and lockouts, or approximately 80 per cent, occurred in connection with issues having no relation to union activity but around such immediate matters as wages, hours, and other working conditions (Bureau of the Census, 1946). Although, as we shall see later, we cannot assume that all of these 3,946 strikes and lockouts were reactions to direct and consciously recognized frustrations, it is highly probable that most of them were of this nature.

labor unions.   There are various reasons for this.   Under present conditions almost every worker is familiar with labor unions, comes into contact with them, and sometimes is even forced to join them.   On the other hand, the opportunity and compulsion to become acquainted with or join other types of social organizations is not so great.   Second, the labor union, by and large, can better meet most of the worker's needs and demands than can other organizations.   As we have seen in Chap. X, most social organizations will generally reflect the major needs of its members, and labor unions will therefore be more "tailored" to the needs of workers than will religious organizations or other less homogeneously composed social organizations.

How do labor unions provide alternative paths to goals blocked by the job conditions, and how do they provide satisfying substitute goals?   The reasons for joining labor unions are varied, but among them might be listed the following major ones (in addition to the purely "economic" reason):

1. Labor unions frequently provide the individual worker with a *sense of participation in deciding vital issues*.   We have seen that under the typical work conditions of the large industrial plant the individual is not consulted even on minor decisions, let alone on major, over-all decisions.   In the labor union the worker who feels a need for such social expression finds a possible outlet.   Especially is this true in the early stages of union organization.   The excitement of organizing, and the first decisions for demanding recognition give the participants a sense of responsibility and an opportunity for important action.

2. Labor unions frequently provide the individual with an opportunity to *express himself in speech and action with much more freedom from fear of reprisal than is possible on the job*.   There are various techniques adopted by unions which deliberately attempt to meet this need for free expression.   Educational classes conducted by unions, for example, are usually of the discussion type, where each person is urged to "speak his piece."   Meetings and rallies offer him an opportunity to appear on public platforms; labor newspapers seek his letters and his articles and allow him to appear in print; labor radio programs provide still another medium through which the individual can say what he thinks, say it publicly and freely.

3. Labor organizations provide the worker with *opportunities to achieve positions of leadership and authority*—opportunities that are denied him on the job.   As Watson (1942) has pointed out in discussing the ways open to working class people for the achievement of leadership positions,

The average young man or woman from a working class home once had two avenues open.   One was through rising to the top in the business hierarchy—a ladder which has now been largely blocked off for those youths without college training or family position.   A second has been the ladder of politics, but elections, too, are expensive nowadays. The labor movement now offers another line of promotion. Some twenty thousand men and women have risen to full-time positions in leading their fellow workers. Some of these officials sit in at the top conferences of government and industry. It may well be that today the average boy has a better chance of reaching a post where he can mold American life, if he becomes a labor leader, than he would have if he aspired to be a legislator or a business mogul.

In addition to the above, labor unions provide opportunities for the multitude of activities denied the worker either on his job or in his life outside the job. Through the establishment of credit unions and banks, they help give the worker a sense of economic security; through their many educational, recreational, and cultural programs he is provided with opportunities to get in touch with art, music, literature, dramatic activities, and sport events, which can enrich a life made monotonous by the assembly line; through the political programs of many unions, he can participate in local, state, and national politics in a more personal and genuine sense than would otherwise be possible. The modern labor union, like the modern drugstore, caters to almost every need of its public.

It should be pointed out, however, that no one worker seeks to satisfy all these needs—people vary in the saliency and kinds of needs they have. Nor does every union offer opportunities for the satisfaction of these needs. Some unions, whose battles are in the far past, no longer offer their members an exultant sense of progress toward an increasing share in controlling the conditions of their work; a number of unions are dictatorial in their procedures and are not adverse to using violence and "goon squads" to silence their members who would participate in free speech; other unions operate as a tight bureaucracy, and opportunities for leadership are limited to a selected and self-perpetuating few; many unions concern themselves only with the purely economic needs of their members; and the leadership of even the best of unions frequently is motivated to provide the services we have been discussing only because of a need for power and control. But nevertheless, most unions offer the individual worker roundabout, constructive, healthy solutions to the blockages of many needs—blockages that he can trace either directly or indirectly to his job.

In so far as this is true, the labor union tends to reduce the tensions and dissatisfactions that can erupt into industrial conflict. But there is a "side effect" that can lead to an increase in industrial conflict. As we have already pointed out, the labor union, because it does all this for its members, becomes an increasingly strong organization. The workers, because they find so many satisfactions in the union, become increasingly loyal to and jealous of their organization. Strong in-group feelings are engendered, and the grievance of one member becomes the grievance of another. Individuals within the labor movement, seeing it as a source wherein to gratify their needs for power, will compete with other leaders and use the labor union as their tool of battle. All this can increase the number of industrial conflicts by bringing about "sympathy" strikes and "jurisdictional" strikes. But the incidence of these strikes accounts for a small fraction of all the strikes and lockouts.[1] Of more significance is the fact that genuine grievances against management that, without a union, would have no way of expressing themselves in strikes can, with a strong union on the scene, result in organized industrial conflict. In addition, a strong union can operate so that grievances which, in other circumstances, would be "below the action threshold" can now eventuate in conflict. Another factor to take into account is that in so far as unions do satisfy many of the workers' needs and do permit higher aspiration levels to emerge in the individual worker, new needs are created that can again eventually result in industrial conflict. Finally, the existence of strong unions provide increasing opportunities for the "illogical" and "bizarre" frustration reactions to be translated into labor-management conflict.

Nonconstructive frustration reactions and industrial conflict.—Despite the existence of labor unions which can serve as a medium for adaptive and constructive frustration reactions, many needs of millions of workers must still remain unsatisfied. This is due to several factors: (1) Some needs, as was pointed out on page 539, must by their very nature be satisfied *on the job.* Degradation of one's personality eight hours a day on the job cannot always be adequately compensated for by any off-the-job activity; (2) labor unions are not equipped and perhaps can never be equipped to provide substitute means of need satisfaction for a whole category of "personal" needs; (3) not all unions make provisions for such satisfactions as they might properly and adequately do; and (4) labor unions themselves create needs that can be easily expressed in "illogical" aggressions against management. As was pointed out in Chap. II, page 54, "Sometimes the nature of the psychological situation in frustration does not permit the reduction of tension through the various adaptive means . . . . The barriers to goal achievement may be impermeable, even in the face of the most intensified efforts of the person to overcome them; the problem of locating a path to the goal may be actually unsolvable; there may not exist within the psychological purview of the individual any possible goal substitutes.

[1] Thus, of the 4,958 strikes and lockouts in 1944, only 204 were listed by the U. S. Department of Labor as being due to "interunion or intraunion matters." In terms of number of workers involved this accounted for about 5 per cent (Bureau of the Census, 1946). And this number, it should be made clear, includes management-initiated lockouts as well as worker-initiated strikes.

In such cases, the frustration persists and intensifies; and eventually, consequences of a less adaptive sort occur."

These "consequences of a less adaptive sort" frequently take the form of strikes. One of the major reasons for this is that the strike and the demand for "higher wages" or "shorter hours" are the only patterns of aggression with which the worker is familiar or the only patterns that are readily accessible. Thus, for example, the worker whose job has been robbed of social meaning through technological development may react by demands for "more money." Here the demand for more money might be seen as an instance of compensatory behavior in reaction to loss of social status. Sometimes the granting of more money may act as an adequate substitute for the loss of social status, but very frequently it may not. The original need for status recognition may persist, and the relief afforded by an increased wage may be only temporary, and very soon the worker will again make "demands" on management. That these demands are all beside the real point may frequently be unknown to either management or the worker.

Or, again, the continued frustration of a need on or off the job (whether it be due to the intolerable personality of the foreman, the worker's own marital difficulties, sexual frustration, or what not) will express itself in aggression against management simply because that is one of the socially approved *aggression* techniques. Although aggression as a consequence of frustration does not always occur, it is a common reaction. Where a strong labor union exists, and where *some* grievances against management also exist, aggressions consequent upon any kind of frustration can be channeled through a strike against management.

Occasionally the power relationships within the union may lead to persistent frustration of the individual, and he sometimes may see an industrial conflict as an adequate way to alter the internal union situation.

There can be no doubt that a number of instances of industrial conflict are to be viewed as "blind" aggressions, regressions, and rationalizations in reaction to frustrations and tensions induced by on-the-job conditions, off-the-job conditions, biological factors within the individual, factors in the person's physical or social environment, or conditions of internal psychological conflict.

Management and Industrial Conflict.—Up to this point we have concerned ourselves with the motivational analysis of the worker and what drives him to conflict against his employer. Obviously we must also examine the motivations of the employer and management. In the first place, if management were not motivated to resist the worker's demands, there would be no conflict; and in the second place, many instances of conflict are initiated by management—as in the "lockout."

There are a number of motivational and emotional reasons why management accepts such conflict or provokes such conflict; and in general, the motivational analysis would follow the one we have indicated for the worker. In the first place, owners and management see in many of the demands of the workers a threat to the satisfaction of their own needs. These demands, as we have seen, frequently express themselves in terms of "more wages." Every rise in wages is seen by management as a potential threat to its own immediate profits. With management, as with workers, it is psychologically irrelevant to point to the absolute income already enjoyed by management and to argue that it is obviously large enough to satisfy their money needs. A hundred dollars per week, a thousand dollars per week, or several thousand dollars per week may not be a psychologically adequate income. As Centers and Cantril found in the study referred to previously, "The more money a person has, the more money he wants." This does not hold for all people, by any means, but it is a significant factor for many. Money, in our society, represents more than purchasing power. It is also a mark of social status and power. This is especially true for those individuals who have not learned other ways of achieving the goals of social recognition, and for them, as for everyone else, the level of aspiration is usually higher than the level of achievement—irrespective of the absolute height of either level.

In the second place, the demands of unions for "closed shops," the "check-off," control of "hiring halls," etc., are seen by management personnel as a threat to their own feelings of self-regard—feelings that they share with workers or labor leaders or politicians or clergymen. The identification between the owner and "his" plant is frequently very strong. As we have pointed out in Chap. II, "The nature of the relationships of the self to other parts of the field . . . is of critical importance in understanding the individual's motivation." The plant, the mine, or the business is frequently to be understood as part of the owner's "self"—intimately identified with him. Just as the worker may have a need to "tell the boss to go to hell," so does management or owner have a need to tell anyone else who presumes to "interfere" with his business to "go to hell."

In the third place, many of the demands of the workers seem entirely bizarre and illogical to the owners, and some of those demands cannot possibly be met without jeopardizing the very existence of a given enterprise. The owner in such cases will obviously resist the worker.

Finally, we must remember that the owners and management of industry are subjected to the same psychological pulls, pressures, and conflicts to which workers are subjected. Owners and management will frequently welcome industrial conflict because it gives them an opportunity to engage in aggressive action in reaction to tensions induced by climate, marital discord, political frustrations, or biological inadequacies.

General Comments.—A word of caution is necessary at this point. The preceding pages have concerned themselves with frustrated and dissatisfied workers and with owners and management who see threats to the satisfaction of their own needs or who are also frustrated and dissatisfied. This does not mean, of course, that all workers or owners at all times are in a state of profound dissatisfaction or suspicion. We have emphasized this aspect of their life patterns only because we are here concerned with the behavior of these people when in a *conflict* situation. However, this motivational analysis does not hold for every individual actively involved in such conflict. Frequently both the worker and management may engage in industrial conflict *without any significant background of personal frustration.* That is, some workers may go out on strike simply because they are forced to by their coworkers. It would be gratuitous to assume that in modern industrial conflict every worker who goes out on strike wants to do so— consciously or unconsciously. Industrial conflict is a highly organized form of action, and the individual, through threat of punishment, through desire to conform, through "social pressure," may be forced to join the strike.

This is also true for many owners. They, too, are frequently forced to resist workers' demands and precipitate conflict—through the pressure of their friends and colleagues and through their management associations. Both labor unions and the National Association of Manufacturers, like all social organizations, have coercive power over the actions of their individual members.

While all of the above is true, it still remains that most people involved in industrial conflict are reacting to personal frustrations, threats, and dissatisfactions. In this connection we must remember what was pointed out earlier in this chapter—that these personal frustrations and threats are being experienced in a changing confused world, in a general atmosphere of insecurity and doubt. The dissatisfied worker of today is a man who remembers the mass unemployment of several years ago, who is subjected to screaming headlines in today's newspaper with its forebodings of new international tensions, inflationary periods, and general unrest. These serve as contributory factors which make recourse to aggressive action on the worker's part more probable.

Similarly, uncertain political situations, unpredictable markets and government regulations, the memory of wholesale bankruptcies in past depressions, and the dreaded future—all help to create in the individual owner marked anxieties and uncertainties. This increases his fears and his tendency to strike out against any immediately perceived threat. As French, Kornhauser, and Marrow (1946) have pointed out,

> ... the industrial magnate who explodes emotionally against what he considers the "threat of unions" and "impending communism" is moved largely by his own uncertainties regarding his personal status and power in a vague, forbidding future in which almost anything can happen. The breakdown of old sanctions and traditional controls leads . . . to intensified resistance to the threat of further change.

INDUSTRIAL CONFLICT AND BELIEFS OF PEOPLE

To understand industrial conflict, which is a highly formalized and organized form of behavior, not only is it necessary to know the motivational forces operating among the individual parties to the conflict, but it is also essential to examine the processes by which these motivational forces are channeled into such formalized expression. In other words, we must now concern ourselves with the educational (or propaganda) influences that are brought to bear upon the individuals involved in industrial conflict and to examine their beliefs and attitudes. Such an examination must give some attention to the perceptions, beliefs, and attitudes of the "public" as well as of labor and management, for, as we have seen, industrial conflict involves many more people than the owners and workers of a given plant.

How Labor and Management Perceive Industrial Conflict.—The most obvious manifestation of industrial conflict is a labor strike. There are many economic and legal definitions of what constitutes a strike, but what is of immediate interest to us, as psychologists, is how the people involved in a strike perceive the strike. It is essential to know what constitutes a strike *as viewed by the worker and the owner* if we are to understand many of the actions of the individuals involved.

We pointed out in the introductory section to this chapter that one of the acknowledged rights of a worker, under capitalism, is to refuse to work for any employer. Unlike the serf of feudalism or the laborer under Fascism, the worker under capitalism is not bound, legally or morally, to any specific employer or plant. All Americans accept this view, and many Americans, therefore, regard a strike as merely an expression of this traditional right of the worker. But the worker, viewing the strike in an altogether different context, perceives an altogether different thing.

Discrepancies in the perception of a strike.—In terms of our motivational analysis, a strike is not *withdrawal* in the face of frustration but is an *active* attempt to overcome a barrier. The worker does not perceive a strike as a passive refusal to work—he sees it as a *positive technique of force*. The worker who goes out on strike is not only refusing to work himself but must refuse to permit anyone else (including management) to work in the plant until his demands are met. The citizen who perceives the strike as a manifestation of the worker's legal right to refuse to work, therefore, judges as "unreasonable" and "illegal" the worker's insistence on throwing an impregnable picket line about the plant. On the other hand, the worker who is told that he has a legal right to strike must, for similar reasons, see as equally unreasonable and illogical any constraints on his efforts to shut down the plant completely. The many recriminations and misunderstandings that occur during a strike can be traced to the fact that both groups perceive different things in a strike. They have different frames of reference, different contexts, or different over-all cognitive organizations within which they view this particular phenomenon.[1]

Specific and general objectives of industrial conflict.—Usually, strikes are seen by most workers in the context of the specific industrial conflict under way, and most industrialists see the strikes in which they become involved in the very same way. But some radical labor leaders (who do so hopefully) and some industrialists (who do so with fear and trembling) see the strike as an indication of the worker's readiness to "overthrow the system." This is another illustration that the strike, just as any other event, is seen in the context of the larger belief systems of the perceiver.

The assumption that workers on strike have larger ends in view than the immediate issues involved is based either on an a priori "class consciousness" analysis typical of both the naive Marxist and the reactionary industrialist or on the misinterpretation of public opinion data. Although it is true, as Williams and Mosteller (1944) point out, that such data suggest that "There is . . . at least some ground for the inference that the population tends to form two classes and that demarcation between them can become marked under some circumstances . . . ," to argue from this that the American worker is "class conscious" is unwarranted. For one thing, as the same authors point out, the role of economic status in determining opinions is ". . . enormously affected by events . . . . Immediately after Pearl Harbor . . . economic status seemed to disappear as a determinant of opinion and unity along economic class lines was clear. Even class differences in attitude toward President Roosevelt seemed, after Pearl Harbor, to have been rubbed out, at least temporarily . . . ." For another thing, even though it might be demonstrated that the opinions of workers, defined as a *sociological class*, tend to be relatively homogeneously different from that of management, much more than that is necessary before we can speak of the existence

---

[1] Compare this analysis with that given of the perception of the angles of Fig. 2 (Chap. III, p. 95) and the reactions of the hypothetical judges described there.

of a class-conscious group of workers all viewing the strike as a means to "overthrow the system." The behavior of workers in labor unions and during industrial conflict suggest very definitely that they see the strike in specific and not general, sociological, revolutionary, or historical contexts.

The frequent instances of discrimination against one set of workers by another set of workers because of racial differences (see Chap. XII) are indications of a lack of "class consciousness." The care taken by labor unions to assign a maintenance crew to keep furnaces and pumps in working order during a strike or the cases where labor unions make money loans to employers in order to tide them over temporary economic difficulties or the instances where labor unions and industry both support the same tariff legislation—all testify dramatically to labor's concern for maintaining the *status quo*. Labor may regard management as class conscious; management may regard labor as class conscious, but neither labor itself nor management itself is radical or Fascist in the sense of wanting to make fundamental changes in the economic pattern of the country. The militant striking worker will usually reject, with honest and righteous indignation, the preferred helping hand of the radical. Such group feelings as may exist among members of a given union are usually centered around immediate and specified objectives and very rarely around a "revolutionary program and purpose."

Channeling Dissatisfactions.—The strike is only one of a number of possible forms of expressing dissatisfaction. We must therefore concern ourselves now with the question of why the many tensions of the worker are so frequently channeled into industrial conflict rather than, say, aggressions against racial groups, political groups, etc.[1] We can isolate six general reasons for this tendency.

The strike as an accepted social technique.—Most strikes, as was indicated previously, are to be understood as specific attempts to remove barriers. The first thing to be emphasized, therefore, is that the strike is a *social technique*—a social means-end-readiness, to use one of Tolman's terms—which is applied to certain social problem situations. Two characteristics of a strike as a social technique merit discussion. In the first place, as is true for any means-end-readiness, the strike will be resorted to in proportion to which the striker believes it effective in solving his problems. In the second place, it will be resorted to in proportion to which it is socially approved. In our present society, as a consequence of some of the factors to be discussed soon, the strike meets both of these major criteria. Should the strike become an ineffective technique or socially condemned, then

---

[1] Sometimes, of course, these tensions are channeled into just these forms of aggression. This is especially true where the factors to be discussed are not operative.

recourse to the strike will tend to disappear and other forms of expressing dissatisfaction or attempting to solve problems will appear. But as of today the strike qualifies as both an effective and accepted social technique.

Management as the perceived cause of dissatisfaction.—In addition to the above factor, the strike makes what might be termed "good perceptual sense" to the worker, because it is a form of action directed against *management*. As we have noted, most of the dissatisfactions of workers can be seen by him as stemming from an inadequate wage level. He receives his wages from management. Many of his tensions that lead to dissatisfaction are created on the job. Management is responsible for work conditions. Management and management policy, therefore, can be perceived as the "cause" of the worker's dissatisfactions. This cause-and-effect relationship is convincing enough to the average worker even without further guidance but is emphasized by the continued practice of labor unions in "exposing" the huge profits made by management and drawing the moral that these profits are made at the expense of the worker's wage and that therefore management is to be blamed for the worker's frustration.

Economic determinism as a major structure in thinking.—The easily perceived environmental supports for the above cause-and-effect structure are aided by still another factor. The influence of the school of thought that ascribes most of man's ills to his economic exploitation at the hands of the wealthy must not be underestimated. This belief is popularized by many writers, philosophers, educators, and even clergy—it is by no means restricted to the radical. Consequently this belief has seeped through to many people and serves as a major conception which conditions the nature of the specific reactions to all sorts of problem situations. It becomes highly probable, in other words, that any frustration will be ascribed to low wages or the machinations of management.

Existence of organizations capable of carrying on industrial conflict.—As of today, most labor unions and management associations are specifically designed to carry on industrial conflict rather than, say, street fighting. These organizations, ready to do something about any dissatisfaction of their membership, do what they are best designed for, and thus predispose the channeling of the aggressions and dissatisfactions of their membership into industrial conflict—into strikes and lockouts. As the nature of these organizations change, as they become better equipped, for example, to carry on political conflict, the dissatisfactions of their membership may be increasingly channeled into that form of conflict rather than industrial conflict.

Narrowing the field of possible aggressive behaviors.—Many alternative forms of expressing dissatisfaction and aggression have lost social acceptance or are losing it. For many workers, and especially "friends of labor," the excitement of the strike and all its manifestations provide the only accept-able and easily available form left for venting personal aggressions or engag-ing in "exciting and dangerous" action. The same is true for management and the various "citizens' committees" and "vigilantes" organized by management. Industrial conflict, in other words, may in some instances be considered as the modern equivalent of witch burnings, crusades, etc. It is one of the approved forms of being socially angry.

The hope and fear of revolution.—Finally, many industrialists (in common with radicals) see the economic structure of our society as the focal point for attack or defense of our present social system. Therefore the radical will attempt to focus most of the worker's discontent into attacks against management and will thus seek to provoke strikes, and the reactionary management leadership will attempt to focus management's discontent and fears against labor unions and will thus also provoke strikes and lockouts.

As a consequence of all of the above factors, it is readily seen why so much of the frustration and dissatisfaction of labor and management is channeled through industrial conflict. This particular mode of tension reduction is frequently effective, is socially approved, is congruent with the perceived cause of the dissatisfaction, is in accordance with current ideol-ogies, and the necessary organizations to facilitate such behavior patterns are available.

Industrial Conflict and the Public.—We have pointed out that indus-trial conflict in any major industry is almost immediately translated into deprivation of goods and services for a large segment of the public. This in turn brings pressure upon the government to take a hand in labor-man-agement disputes, with the result that both labor and management antici-pate this by seeking to win over public support. Both labor and manage-ment, in other words, engage in propaganda directed at the public. In understanding the nature and consequences of such propaganda, we must first recall the point made previously that neither the typical worker nor manager considers himself a member of a special psychological group. It is because of this that the appeal of labor and management to the "public" is not to be understood only as a "diabolic tactic"—an attempt to use some "outside group" for their "own" selfish ends. Of course, many labor leaders and top management leaders do so conceive of the public; but as far as many individual workers and owners are concerned, they seek support from the public in the firm belief that they are thus seeking the common good.

The worker considers himself a member of the American people whose welfare he identifies with his own, and so does the owner. Therefore both seek and expect to find support from other members of American society—from workers, priests, politicians, clerks, doctors, housewives. No matter how the conflict may appear from an economic, historical, or sociological vantage point, each contestant does not see himself as battling for a special group, but for "America."

Objectives and techniques of industrial conflict propaganda.—Because of these considerations the nature of the propaganda engaged in by both sides of the conflict becomes understandable. In their propaganda to the public each side usually has three major objectives in view: (1) to strengthen or create the impression that the general interests of the employer (or of labor) are the interests of all of society, (2) to create an unfavorable sentiment toward labor unions (or industrialists) as a class apart from the rest of the public and having interests inimical to the social interests, and (3) to stimulate public support for a particular company (or a particular union) especially just before or during industrial conflict.

In seeking to attain these objectives, every device listed on pages 357 *ff.*, Chap. IX, is resorted to by both management and labor. They will attempt to "tie in" their suggestions with almost any need of the rest of society; and where such a need does not exist they will seek to create a need. They will engage in "long-term" propaganda aimed at changing the major belief systems of the public. They will time their efforts carefully and wait for the critical social situation to "spring" their major propaganda efforts. They will picture the labor leader as a thug, foreigner, or hoodlum and the industrialist as a bloated profiteer. They will seek to exploit prestige personalities. They will invent and popularize slogans, rallying cries, etc.[1]

In using such devices no segment of society is spared, since both labor and management feel that all of society is or should be on "their side." Both industry and labor deliberately attempt to get their material into the public-school system, motion-picture houses, colleges, etc. The Church is not left alone either. Thus, for example, the National Association of Manufacturers has a Committee on Cooperation with the Churches, while the CIO has its Religious Associates. The central purpose of the former is the "development of better understanding between clergymen and managers of business to the end that the public interest be furthered"; and the Credo of the Religious Associates sets forth the following statements: "We believe that the labor movement is one of the major democratic forces in America. We believe that the religious forces and the labor movement have in common the desire to strengthen and hasten democratic trends in

---

[1] For some striking illustrations of many of the above propaganda techniques as used by both labor and management, see Menefee (1939).

America, and should therefore more closely associate themselves together to this end."[1]

The significance of all this lies in the apparent paradox that just because neither labor nor management is class conscious, conflict between them tends to become class conflict. From the point of view of labor, the conflict is presented as that between all of society vs. the special class of management; from the point of view of management, it is all of society vs. the special class of organized labor. Each side identifies itself with the rest of society, and because of this the propaganda of each side is addressed to every segment of society. The area of conflict becomes broadened, more people are drawn into the conflict, and eventually industrial conflict may become social conflict in the widest and most significant sense of the word.

The public's receptivity to labor-management propaganda.—There are several factors that operate to make the public more receptive to the propaganda of the owner than to that of the labor union. While it is obvious that the "public" does not consist of a homogeneous group of people and that the receptivity of any individual to propaganda material varies tremendously and is a resultant of the specific needs, belief systems, moods, and personality of the individual, *statistically* considered there is reason to believe that the employer's propaganda is more readily acceptable by the general public than is the worker's propaganda. The major reasons for this are (1) the greater availability of mass propaganda media to management, (2) the greater ease with which labor union activity can be perceived as the "cause" of the deprivation of the needs of the public, and (3) the nature of the over-all belief systems of large segments of the public.

1. Public education, or "propaganda," involves a great expenditure of money. While the propaganda budgets for both labor and industry are large, there can be no doubt that, on the whole, management can buy more propaganda than can labor. Among the other reasons for this is the fact that propaganda designed to create the impression that the general interests of the employer are the interests of all of society is technically not called propaganda but goes by the name of "institutional advertising." As such, institutional advertising is a deductible item from tax returns and thus represents a lower actual outlay than might be indicated by the absolute cost of such propaganda. Labor's institutional advertising is not subsidized in that way by government. But, in addition, even where equal amounts of money are available to both sides, some media are simply not "for sale" to labor where they are available to management. The policies

---

[1] Quoted from an illuminating discussion of the dilemma in which the American church leader finds himself in this connection, in Lendbeck, Lefevre, and Pope's (1945) special issue of the Congregational Church publication, *Preachers under Pressure.*

of radio stations and newspapers, in other words, reflect what the Commission on the Freedom of the Press (1947), headed by Chancellor Hutchins of the University of Chicago, has called "the bias of owners":

The agencies of mass communication are big business and their owners are big business men.... The newspapers alone have more than 150,000 employees. The press is connected with other big businesses through the advertising of these businesses, upon which it depends for the major part of its revenue. The owners of the press, like the owners of other big businesses, are bank directors, bank borrowers and heavy taxpayers in the upper brackets.

This "bias of owners" not only selects the propaganda it will print or broadcast but may frequently distort the views and propaganda of labor. Finally, management has available to it a great deal of "free" propaganda. Newspapers, radio commentators, lecturers, motion-picture newsreels, etc., will give more space and time to pronouncements of industry than to pronouncements of labor. The significance of all this is clear when we recall, as was pointed out in Chap. VI (page 187), that in our modern complex world the facts upon which we all base our beliefs and attitudes are inevitably obtained from secondary sources and the most common secondary source of facts is the newspaper and the radio.

2. As has been indicated several times in this chapter, an industrial conflict frequently results in an immediate cessation of the flow of essential goods and services to many people. It is much easier for the people thus deprived (whether of a new automobile, streetcar service, milk deliveries, or coal) to perceive the unwillingness of the worker to work as the cause of their deprivations than the unwillingness of management to accede to the workers' demands. The connection between the decision of the labor union to stop working and the stoppage of goods and services is simple and direct. To see the "cause" of this deprivation as inherent in management policies requires much more sophistication. Consequently it is much easier for management propaganda to be "tied in" with a real need of the public than it is for labor propaganda. And, as we have seen in Chap. IX, those suggestions which seem to meet a real need will be more readily accepted than those which do not.

3. Finally, to review what has already been indicated, it is difficult for many people, not familiar with the way the worker perceives a strike, to see why the worker thinks he is within his "rights" in preventing non-union members from working. To many people who perceive strikes in terms of the frame of reference we have outlined, the labor union member's picket-line behavior appears to be a violation of democratic rights and privileges, and the worker appears to assume coercive powers not in keeping with the frame of reference of many Americans. The worker, on the

other hand, does not perceive his action in this manner, and much antagonism between the "public" and the worker is thus engendered—antagonism due to the failure of either side to perceive a given event in the same way because of different frames of reference. Industrial propaganda that attempts to exploit this misunderstanding is apt to be effective, since it more easily fits into the major belief systems of the nonlabor public.

General Comments.—All of the above considerations emphasize the necessity of viewing industrial conflict from the point of view of *social conflict*. There is hardly an individual in our society who does not get caught up, in one way or another, by any large-scale strike or lockout. The needs and beliefs of the "innocent bystander" are no less relevant to a psychological analysis of industrial conflict than the needs and beliefs of the labor union member or the employer. What is true for diagnosis is also true for therapy. In the next, and concluding, section of this chapter, which is devoted to suggestions for reducing industrial conflict, the major attention will be given to the worker and the employer, but these suggestions should always be seen in their total social context.

REDUCING INDUSTRIAL CONFLICT

The preceding analysis can provide us with a number of suggestions that might reduce the intensity and frequency of industrial conflicts, but we cannot hope to outline a psychological program that will eliminate these conflicts within the present structure of our society. It must be emphasized that *psychological considerations alone are not sufficient to deal with the problem of industrial conflict*. Perhaps more basic than psychological considerations are economic and political factors. The following psychological suggestions can be only of contributory value to an adequate program.

In considering the psychological suggestions that might be made, two major approaches must be taken. A good psychological program must address itself to the motivations and frustrations of workers and employers—no matter how these tensions are created—and to the educational techniques necessary to permit workers, employers, and the public to enjoy a greater area of common experience and mutual understanding. And it must do all this with constant reference to the realities of our production and distribution system.

Reducing Tensions Deriving from Technological Development.—It is highly probable that the introduction of every laborsaving device will result in job insecurities and anxieties in individual workers, in enforced obsolescence of skills or lowering of wage levels or loss in status, and yet it is clear that such technological development cannot be put off permanently because of these possibilities. However, certain procedures are available that can minimize or reduce these undesirable effects.

Consulting the worker.—To develop any adequate program designed to deal with the problem of the technologically displaced worker, it is essential for management to realize, above all else, that *the worker has a stake in the question of whether or not new technological developments are to be installed in his plant.* One of the major implications for such a guiding principle is that management's decision to make the technological change must be made in consultation with the worker or his representative—the union.

The reasons for the proposed changes in production method must be made amply clear to the worker as well as to his supervisor. The possible resulting immediate dislocations must not be avoided in such a discussion. The timing and rapidity of the changes must be carefully considered, and the views of the workers should be given significant weight, even if—from the short-term point of view—this may delay the installation. If changes are to be introduced in one department only, this must also be made clear so that not every worker, of every department, will remain in insecure ignorance of where the axe will fall next. Sufficient time must be allowed for placing the displaced workers in other jobs or in retraining them for other types of work.

Even with the greatest care, however, the installation of laborsaving devices may result in a number of frustrated and dissatisfied workers; but in so far as they have had prior knowledge of the event, have had some voice in determining the details of such a change, have been given some opportunity to prepare for the change, and have adequate assurance of the limits of the proposed change, the tensions consequent upon the installation of laborsaving devices can be reduced considerably.

The logic of efficiency.—We have pointed out that the assembly-line production method, demanding a minimum of variability in the work pattern of the individual, frequently leads to the creation of tensions. This is inevitable as long as efficiency is measured in hypothetically possible output units produced under hypothetically possible work patterns. But such "logic of efficiency" is illogical simply because not all the important variables are thereby taken into account. A production line that operates with 100 per cent efficiency when it is in operation but breaks down periodically through strikes, absenteeism, slowdowns, etc., *is not an efficient production line.* A production line that operates with only 90 per cent "efficiency" but does so all the time is far more efficient. The determination of what is an efficient production system must take into account as one of its variables the total behavior of the workers involved. If this variable demands something less than a rigid predictability of work patterns, then the efficiency engineer must provide for such flexibility. *A plant remaining idle because of a strike must be charged up to the inefficiency of the production method that helped bring about that strike through the creation of tensions.* The application of such a concept to cost accounting will give more realism to the whole matter of the "logic of efficiency" and more significance to efficiency research. The efficiency expert cannot be an engineer only; he must also be a social psychologist and sociologist.

Roethlisberger (1944) in his discussion of the research in industrial psychology done at the Hawthorne plant of the Western Electric Company makes a convincing case for the assertion that even the traditional problems of the industrial psychologist must be attacked as problems in social psychology. After discussing some of the Hawthorne researches on the effect of lighting on worker output and their ambiguous results, he writes,

In the illumination experiments . . . we have a classic example of trying to deal with a human situation in non-human terms. The experimenters had obtained no human data; they had been handling electric-light bulbs and plotting average output curves. Hence their results had no human significance. That is why they seemed screwy.

Reducing Tensions Resulting from Interpersonal Relationships on the Job.—It was pointed out that one of the major sources of tensions in the on-the-job situation derives from the nature of the worker's contact with management. Usually this contact is through the supervisor, the foreman, or department head. It would be unrealistic to suggest that ways and means should be devised for more direct and intimate contact between management and workers. Such personal contact is not feasible in a large plant and would probably work to the disadvantage of the individual worker. His union "grievance committee" can represent him in better strength than he can himself in individual bargaining. But the day-to-day contact does not involve only discussion of grievances, and the unfortunate relationships that frequently exist between workers and foremen usually reflect the inadequate attention given by top management to preparing the foremen for their roles.

To establish a more satisfying interpersonal relationship between worker and supervisor (and, therefore, between worker and management) the following two points represent the minimum essentials of an adequate program.

Qualifications of supervisors.—In the selection of its supervisors, top management must consider seriously the *personality* of the supervisor and his *capacity to deal with people* as well as his technological experience and training. Too frequently this is neglected, and the task of "personnel management" is given over to a central office. But the function of personnel management cannot be relegated to any single "staff officer"; *it must be exercised every moment of every day by the "line officer."* A plant cannot rest content with a good personnel man; it must have good personnel men *in every one of its supervisors.*

In addition to a proper selection program, it is essential that an extensive, vigorous, and psychologically sound "leadership training" program be maintained for every supervisor in the plant. As was pointed out previously, the skills and techniques required in leadership are as complicated and as "teachable" as any highly developed skill. To depend upon "innate" capacities or idiosyncratic hunches in interpersonal relations is as unwarranted as to depend upon "innate mechanical ability" alone in choosing supervisors for highly technical jobs. As we have seen from Chap. XI, training in supervisory skills frequently involves changing some basic social attitudes and ways of thinking of supervisors. This is a task which can be accomplished only by a highly specialized and skillfully conducted educational program.

Briefing the supervisors.—A foreman who does not know and approve the reasoning behind the order he must transmit to the worker cannot be expected to avoid irritations between himself and the worker. Before any major change in policy is contemplated, extra precautions have to be taken by top management to make certain that its direct representative to the worker understands completely what the change is all about, can transmit such understanding to the worker, and can defend the change in terms that make sense to the worker. To accomplish this, much more than a series of "pep talks" or "educational talks" is frequently necessary. Sometimes this may even mean that the supervisor cannot be *told* the facts but must *participate in discovering the facts.*

A very good illustration of a psychologically sound way of preparing supervisors for policy changes in industry is found in the study by Marrow and French (1945). This study is of particular interest because it demonstrates the value of approaching problems in industry from the vantage point of the social psychologist with his concern about beliefs, attitudes, prejudices, group dynamics, etc. The specific problem that these investigators attacked was that of preparing the foremen of the Harwood Manufacturing Corporation to carry out a change in policy toward the employment of women over thirty years of age. In most mass industries it was usually assumed that for skilled jobs, women over thirty were inferior to younger women. Most of the foremen at this plant held this belief and were reluctant to take older women into their departments. However, the tightening of the labor supply during the war years necessitated that this be done, and the plant psychologist was given the task of convincing the supervisors.

The first step taken was the carrying out of research to determine the facts of the case with respect to women over thirty. The results indicated quite clearly that older women were able to learn new skills no less rapidly than younger women, had a better attendance record and a much lower turnover record. The psychologist, armed with these facts, was now prepared to convince the supervisors. But he soon discovered that this was no easy matter. The supervisors believed firmly that older women were inferior despite all the facts the psychologist could muster. To "brief" the supervisors on this new policy, then, became a problem in the changing of beliefs and attitudes, not merely a problem in giving information. Consequently, a method of group education was set up for the supervisors:

. . . it was apparent that the supervisory employees could not be convinced individually and that re-education would be necessary throughout the plant. Therefore the findings were presented to groups of sub-leaders. Discussions followed, centering around the origin of the stereotype and the possible motivations for believing in it. In the course of these meetings, insights into the original bias gradually developed. What is more, group decisions were reached recommending that an experiment be made in the training of older women. In this way the idea of hiring older women workers was gradually established. Only with this group shift in attitude did the new policy become a reality.

A supervisory group that is selected on the basis of leadership skill in the first place, given adequate leadership training, and prepared in a sound way to put management policy into effect can do much to reduce worker dissatisfaction deriving from the day-to-day, hour-to-hour personal contact between worker and supervisor—the only kind of personal contact possible in modern industry where management itself is necessarily so far removed from the worker.

The first two major steps of the program we have thus far discussed (reducing tensions consequent upon technological change and those resulting from the nature of the interpersonal relationships) are dictated by the necessity of viewing the plant as a very important part of the workers culture—not merely as a place where he happens to work. As Roethlisberger and Dickson (1943) point out, on the basis of their work in industrial problems,

For the employee in industry, the whole working environment must be looked upon as being permeated with social significance . . . . To understand the meaning of any employee's complaints or grievances, it is necessary to take account of his position or status in the company. This position is determined by the social organization of the company: that system of practices and beliefs by means of which the human values of the organization are expressed, and the symbols around which they are organized.

Reducing Tensions Resulting from Inadequate Wages.—No amount of wise application of all of the above principles and specific suggestions, however, will remove the major dissatisfactions of workers if their wages are inadequate to permit them the satisfaction of their major needs. *This still remains the crux of the matter.* Here, because of the difficulty of establishing a psychologically adequate wage (see page 542), there are perhaps the most grounds for pessimism in considering attempts to reduce worker frustration completely. Because of this it might be argued that any program short of extensive change in our economic system which will do away with the profound variations in income among the people of our country is doomed to eventual failure.

Some suggested procedures.—There have been many suggestions for steps that can be taken in this direction short of giving each worker an adequate wage as defined psychologically. If a policy of equal wages for equal work is established by industry, some dissatisfactions stemming from wage levels may be lessened. If government provides ways and means of satisfying certain of the needs of workers (*e.g.*, "free" education, health facilities, etc.), the distance between aspirations and the achievement made possible by inadequate wages is reduced. If government agencies make provisions for unemployment insurance, old-age pensions, etc., again the pressure for more wages may drop. But it must be pointed out immediately that all these proposals are merely indirect ways of raising wages, and the money for these government services must eventually be reflected in a lower income for management and owners through increased tax rates and will thus be resisted as vigorously and for the same reasons as will direct wage demands. Just as long as workers are permitted to live in a culture that results in ever-expanding needs, just so long will they continue to be dissatisfied with any wage rate that is not continually and rapidly increasing. Their dissatisfactions may be channeled off into other forms of expression than industrial conflict, but the dissatisfactions will remain. If these dissatisfactions are drained off into political activity, such political activity may eventually and gradually be designed to bring about profound changes in the economic structure of the country. Whether through industrial conflict or political conflict, attempts will probably always be in progress to equalize the distribution of income in the country.

However, we must remember that some wage demands arise simply because that is the only kind of demand with which the worker is familiar and making demands on his employer is the most accessible technique he has for being "socially angry." In so far as the worker's demands can be made more "rational" and more adequate to his real needs, frustrations *apparently* due to inadequate wage rates can be lessened. We now turn to a consideration of this problem.

Reducing Off-the-job Tensions and Providing Substitute Paths and Goals.—We have seen that some cases of industrial conflict can be considered as maladaptive expressions of the personal frustrations of workers and management—frustrations that may have little to do with conditions of work or wages. To minimize these frustrations the nation-wide program of guarding the psychological health of every member of society which was suggested in Chap. XIII (see especially pages 504–505) must be established. An appreciation that *individuals* are involved in industrial conflict leads clearly and directly to the view that psychological guidance and psychotherapeutic counseling are essential tools in reducing industrial conflict. The sick personality or the unadjusted individual is frequently an initiating and sustaining factor at the bottom of any type of social conflict—political, religious, or industrial. And maladjusted personalities are not restricted to the members of any one socioeconomic group.

Recently several efforts have been made to apply psychotherapeutic counseling techniques to labor-management problems. Thus Roethlisberger and Dickson (1943) have developed a program of personnel counseling in the Western Electric Company that has been characterized by Snyder (1947) as "nondirective therapy." Similarly, Cantor and Bonning (1944) and Gardner (1945) have used the same techniques in other industrial plants. Of particular significance is the work of the Tavistock Institute of Human Relations, established in England, to provide "social therapy" to various community groups. Among the specific projects undertaken by this social therapeutic organization is the treatment of industrial conflict.[1]

It might be in order to repeat, however, that such psychotherapeutic services and clinics should be available to management and ownership personnel as well. These people need the services provided no less than do workers.

It must be clear that psychotherapy of almost any kind depends for its effectiveness on the availability to the patient, after treatment, of an environment in which healthy substitute paths and goals abound. To provide such a world will involve a difficult and extensive series of changes in our system of values, social practices, and the operation of many of our social organizations. In so far as we can make any progress in that direction, we shall be making a contribution to industrial peace.

Increasing Mutual Understanding.—The problem of controlling the

---

[1] For an interesting account of the group therapy techniques employed by the Tavistock Institute of Human Relations in dealing with the morale problems among young textile workers, see Sutherland and Menzies (1947).

behavior of both the worker and the employer so that each may be prevented from an excessive amount of autistic thinking, misunderstandings, and vicious and debilitating propaganda activities may be approached in several ways. Steps can be carried out to eliminate some of the *barriers to communication* between labor and management; provisions can be made to *clarify the specific issues* involved in any labor-management dispute; and precautions can be taken *to "protect" the public from one-sided or biased authority sources for its information* concerning labor-management disputes.

Barriers to communication.—A contributing factor in many cases of industrial conflict lies in the difficulties of communication. These difficulties are of two major kinds. The first, and the most obvious one, is simply the refusal of either party to the conflict to engage in discussion of any kind. Alleged grievances are not discussed, but management or labor immediately prepare to "fight it out" and industrial conflict is in full sway. In a sense, a failure to meet one's adversary and discuss matters with him is an instance of the type of *withdrawal* behavior we described on page 59. And it will be remembered that we pointed out there that one of the consequences of withdrawal is the tendency to engage in autistic thinking. The labor leader and, similarly, the employer must guess at what the other side thinks, wants, and feels. This guessing, not checked by direct communication with the person involved, must necessarily reflect the guesser's fears and hopes and biases more accurately than it does the behavior of the person whose thoughts and wishes are being "guessed at." Such autistic thinking can serve only to intensify conflict—not solve it. The only feasible cure to this communication barrier is legal coercion which will force discussion and negotiation prior to a strike or lockout.

The second barrier to communication, which also leads to increased tensions in industrial conflicts, derives from the fact that effective group discussion is a highly technical skill which is beyond the capacity of many labor-management discussants and negotiators. The capacity to understand what an adversary is attempting to convey, to be aware of his frame of reference and his motives is not a simple one. Frequently discussion and negotiation increase and strengthen prejudices and stereotypes rather than lessen them. Here, as elsewhere, the only proper cure is the institution of a psychologically sound training program for both labor leaders and management personnel involved in such negotiation.[1]

Clarifying the issues.—We have seen that the issues involved in industrial conflict may frequently not be recognized correctly by either labor or management. When the worker does not know what is behind his dis-

[1] For some helpful studies on methods of increasing the skill involved in group discussion, see Elliot (1932), Walder (1933), Lippitt (1946), and Benne, Bradford, and Lippitt.

satisfaction, he cannot formulate demands that can be remedied nor can management meet those demands.   There is only one solution to this cause of misunderstanding—the *facts* about worker dissatisfaction must be obtained.   Such attitude and belief research must take as its objective the determination of specific sources of irritation and the understanding of the dynamics of tensions as they operate in the particular industrial situation concerned.

To achieve these objectives best, the attitude research must make use of the intensive type of opinion and attitude reasearch discussed in Chap. VIII as well as the group dynamic research discussed in Chap. XI.   To increase the effectiveness of the kind of research needed here, the investigation of the beliefs and attitudes of employees should be carried out under the *joint control of labor and management*.   There is one practical reason and a number of theoretical considerations that demand this.   As French, Kornhauser, and Marrow (1946) have pointed out, in some situations employee attitude research could not possibly be carried out unless the research was jointly sponsored by the labor union and management.   If this were not done, the labor union might, on the grounds that all expressions of employee feelings should be channeled through union leadership or on the grounds that management could not be "trusted," effectively block the study by preventing its membership from participating.   But perhaps more significantly, the joint planning of such research by both labor and management would increase the insightfulness of the study (since both parties could contribute their understandings and hypotheses to the original planning) and would tend to make the resultant findings more acceptable to labor and management—for the reasons we have already discussed in connection with community self-surveys (see page 524).

In so far as such studies are well done, their results might have decisive influence in preventing some cases of industrial conflict either by redefining issues and demands so as to make them more amenable to negotiation or by permitting management to take remedial action before minor irritations develop into stronger feelings of dissatisfaction.

Improving the public's information sources.—If the public is not to be propagandized to the point where most of its beliefs and attitudes are based on one-sided, biased "facts" and where its major belief systems become so distorted as to be completely unrealistic with respect to labor-management problems, a minimum threefold program of action is required.

1. In so far as possible, public information sources should not disseminate "concealed propaganda" of either side.   This means that school boards, colleges and universities, motion-picture houses, and churches must avoid the attempt of either management or labor to infiltrate their propaganda

into school textbooks, "sponsored" lectures, "free" educational material, "educational movies," etc. Where such material appears to have value, the source should be clearly indicated.

2. Provisions must be made to make mass communication media equally available to both management and labor. This means, frequently, the legal control of newspapers and broadcasting chains to the end that space and time be for sale to both sides of any industrial controversy on equal terms. The recognition that newspapers and radio broadcasting stations are public services justifies some measure of public control over their policies.

3. Finally, whenever and through whatever means possible, the sound education of the public in economic matters should be promoted. "Controversial issues" should occupy an acknowledged and important place in school curricula. We cannot leave the education of the public about economic matters to the activities of either the National Association of Manufacturers or the Congress of Industrial Organizations.

In so far as the public has now become an immediate party to industrial conflict and its support is needed by both the labor union and management, increasing the extent and reliability of the public's information about labor-management problems can lead to a decrease in the intensity and to a more reasonable resolution of this significant social conflict of our time.

SUMMARY

The frequency and intensity of labor-management conflict, it is pointed out, gives more urgency to the need for a psychological analysis of this aspect of labor-management relations than of any other aspect. The major concern of this chapter is therefore defined as the analysis of the basic psychological processes involved in industrial conflict and the indication of some psychologically sound procedures (based on such an analysis) which might reduce the frequency and intensity of such conflict.

This statement of the problem as a problem of the psychology of the individual, however, does not preclude the necessity of first discussing the sociological context within which industrial conflict—a highly formalized action pattern—occurs. The first section of the analysis is therefore given over to a discussion of this sociological background. The nature of capitalistic economy is first reviewed briefly, and special attention is given to the maldistribution of income characteristic of this economy as it has operated in the United States. Then a general survey of the social changes that have occurred in the last thirty years is sketched out, followed by a discussion of the developments that have taken place in the nature of industrial conflict, industrial plants, and labor unions. It is concluded that as a consequence of all these developments, the stratification of the social

origins of labor and management personnel has become sharper, the depersonalization of labor-management contact has increased, and the nature and
intensity of industrial conflict have changed profoundly.

The second section of the analysis is given over to the motivational processes that lie behind the individual worker's participation in industrial
conflict. It is first pointed out that many needs of the workers are created
on the job and must be satisfied on the job—especially in a culture where
so much of a man's time is spent at work. The tensions that are created
among workers in the industrial plant are discussed in terms of those deriving from technological changes and those deriving from the nature of the
interpersonal relationships typical of modern industrial plants. Then the
tensions and frustrations that are indirectly related to the job are discussed,
and some data relating to all these factors, taken from various "worker
morale" studies, are examined. It is concluded that the job conditions
under which people work are responsible, directly or indirectly, for the
creation of many tensions and the frustrations of many needs and demands.
However, it is stressed that in giving appropriate weight to the variety of
needs that are thus frustrated, one should not undervaluate the crucial
importance of wage rates as a job condition. Following the above analysis,
an examination is made of the various methods of reacting to frustration
that can lead to industrial conflict. Two major categories of frustration
reactions are isolated: constructive and nonconstructive reactions. Among
the former are listed such activities as striking for increased wages, better
working conditions, shorter hours, etc., and it is also pointed out that many
labor unions provide avenues of substitute satisfactions to the worker
frustrated on the job. Although these satisfactions are psychologically
healthy and socially useful, they may result in creating conditions that can
lead to increased industrial conflict. Among the nonconstructive reactions
to frustration are listed such behaviors as strikes called for avowed causes
that are not the real causes and interunion or intraunion reasons for striking.
The above motivational analysis is then applied to management, and reasons
are adduced for management's resistance to workers' demands as well as
management's initiation of some industrial conflicts. Finally it is pointed
out that some workers and some employers engage in industrial conflict
simply because they are forced into such action by their fellow workers
or fellow employers.

The third section of the analysis concerns itself with the perceptions and
beliefs of the people involved in industrial conflict. First some discussion
is given over to the different ways that management, labor, and the public
perceive industrial conflict. It is concluded that where the public sees the
strike as the passive refusal of the worker to work, the union member sees
the strike as an active technique of force. This discrepancy in perception

leads to many recriminations and misunderstandings. Second, it is empha-sized that neither the typical worker nor the typical employer views the strike in historical, sociological, or "revolutionary" terms, but only in terms of the immediate issues involved. The next part of the discussion concerns itself with the reasons why tensions of workers are so frequently channeled into industrial conflict rather than into other forms of aggression. Finally, the objectives and techniques of industrial conflict propaganda are examined, and it is concluded that the propaganda of both sides is aimed at all sections of society (for reasons that are indicated), that such propaganda activity may eventually convert industrial conflict into widespread social conflict, and that because of various reasons, the propaganda of the employer finds greater acceptability among the public than the propaganda of the labor union.

The last major section of the chapter makes several suggestions designed to reduce the intensity and frequency of industrial conflict. However, it is first emphasized that psychological considerations alone are not suffi-cient to deal with the problem of industrial conflict but that economic and political factors are more basic. The specific suggestions involve steps designed to reduce tensions deriving from (1) technological development, (2) interpersonal relationships on the job, (3) inadequate wages, and (4) off-the-job conditions, together with some suggestions for (5) increasing the area of mutual understanding among labor, employers, and the public. The steps suggested to meet the first two objectives are characterized as those demanded by the necessity of viewing the plant as a very important part of the worker's culture. In connection with the third objective it is pointed out that the difficulty of establishing a psychologically adequate wage rate (for reasons given) warrants ground for pessimism, and it is con-cluded that attempts will probably always be in progress to equalize income distribution and that this may continue to be a constant source of indus-trial conflict. For the fourth objective the same nation-wide program of guarding the psychological health of every member of society as was in-dicated in Chap. XIII is suggested. Finally, for the fifth objective a minimum three-point program is outlined. This consists of steps designed to remove the barriers to communication between labor and management, methods of clarifying the issues involved in industrial conflict, and improving the public's information sources. In this connection it is pointed out that we cannot leave the economic education of the public to the National Association of Manufacturers or the Congress of Industrial Organizations. In so far as the public has now become an immediate party to industrial conflict, increasing the extent and reliability of the public's information about labor-management problems can lead to a decrease in the intensity of such conflict and to a more reasonable resolution of this significant conflict of our time.

BIBLIOGRAPHY

BENNE, K., BRADFORD, L., and LIPPITT, R.   Discussion-method and reality-practice techniques.   (In press.)

Bureau of the Census: 1946.   *Statistical abstract of the United States.*   Washington: U. S. Dept. of Commerce.

CANTOR, N., and BONNING, J. C.: 1944.   Functions of personnel counselors.   *Person. J.,* **23,** 104–110.

CENTERS, R., and CANTRIL, H.: 1946.   Income satisfaction and income aspiration.   *J. abnorm. soc. Psychol.,* **41,** 64–69.

Commission on the Freedom of the Press: 1947.   *A free and responsible press.*   Chicago: Univ. Chicago Press.

ELLIOT, H. S.: 1932.   *The process of group thinking.*   New York: Association Press.

FRENCH, J. R. P., KORNHAUSER, A., and MARROW, A.: 1946.   Conflict and cooperation in industry.   *J. soc. Issues,* **2,** No. 1.

GARDNER, B. B.: 1945.   Employee counseling in private industry.   *Publ. Person. Rev.,* **6,** 6–8.

HULL, R. L., and KOLSTAD, A.: 1942.   Morale on the job.   *In* Watson, G. (ed.), *Civilian morale.*   Boston: Houghton.

KATZ, D.: 1946.   Survey techniques and polling procedures as methods in social science.   *J. soc. Issues,* **3,** No. 4, 62–66.

KORNHAUSER, A.: 1939.   Analysis of "class" structure of contemporary American society.   *In* Hartmann, G., and Newcomb T., (eds.), *Industrial conflict.*   New York: Cordon.

LIPPITT, R.: 1946.   Discussion—practicing ideas and preparing for action.   *The Campfire Girl,* May.

MARROW, A. J., and FRENCH, J. R. P.: 1945.   Changing a stereotype in industry.   *J. soc. Issues,* **1,** No. 3, 33–37.

MENEFEE, S. C.: 1939.   Propaganda and symbol manipulation.   *In* Hartmann, G., and Newcomb, T., (eds.), *Industrial conflict.*   New York: Cordon.

MERTON, R. K.: 1947.   The machine, the worker, and the engineer.   *Science,* **105,** 79–84.

National Research Council: 1941.   *Fatigue of workers—its relation to industrial problems.*   New York: Reinhold.

ROETHLISBERGER, F. J.: 1944.   *Management and morale.*   Cambridge: Harvard Univ. Press.

ROETHLISBERGER, F. J., and DICKSON, W. J.: 1943.   *Management and the worker.*   Cambridge: Harvard Univ. Press.

SNYDER, W. U.: 1947.   The present status of psychotherapeutic counseling.   *Psychol. Bull.,* **44,** 297–386.

SUTHERLAND, J. D., and MENZIES, I. E.: 1947.   Two industrial projects.   *J. soc. Issues,* **3,** No. ?, 51–58.

WALSER, F.: 1933.   *The art of conference.*   New York: Harper.

WATSON, G.: 1939.   Work satisfaction.   *In* Hartmann, G., and Newcomb, T. (ed.), *Industrial conflict.*   New York: Cordon.

WATSON, G.: 1942.   Labor unions and morale.   *In* Watson, G. (ed.), *Civilian morale.*   Boston: Houghton.

WILLIAMS, F., and MOSTELLER, F.: 1944.   Education and economic status as determinants of opinion.   *In* Cantril, H. (ed.), *Gauging public opinion.*   Princeton: Princeton Univ. Press.

CHAPTER XV

INTERNATIONAL TENSIONS

In the atomic age the ultimate question facing the social psychologist, like all individuals in the world, is that of sheer survival. All other social problems, no matter how acutely important under usual circumstances, become irrelevant in the face of total atomic warfare. Racial prejudice, industrial conflict, propaganda and political persuasion, group morale and leadership have no significance in the midst of radioactive rubble. The possibility for the solution of these problems depends in an absolute way upon the solution of the problem of international tensions and war.

In this, the final chapter of the book, we shall discuss the nature and problem of international tensions, their psychological bases, the obstacles to international unity and understanding, and a program for the reduction of international tensions. The emphasis throughout will be, of course, *psychological*, with the principal aim of ascertaining the psychological factors underlying international tensions and the psychological means by which these tensions may be reduced.

GENERAL CONSIDERATIONS

International tensions arise among nations—the largest, most highly organized, and most autonomous political organizations of people. The tensions among nations take many forms—feelings of hatred and aggressiveness, attacks in the press and on the radio, diplomatic strife, persecution of other countries' citizens, economic conflict and sanctions, and, ultimately, war. War, it should be emphasized, is only the last step in tensions. As Stagner (1947) has put it, "the specific pattern of violence called war is an expression of trends clearly observable during peace."

In analyzing the problem of international tensions there are three common errors one must seek to avoid. In the first place, there may be danger of concentrating too exclusively on the problem of *war*. Tensions that exist in times of "peace" must be given at least equal consideration. Not only are they often the forerunners of war, but also they may have destructive consequences in their own right, less dramatic than those of war, yet no less serious for the individual. They may produce widespread fear, hatred and maladjustment, economic and political exploitation, and disintegration of personality and constructive living.   Moreover, it can be argued that war is not necessarily the greatest of all possible evils in the world.   The loss of democracy, freedom, and human dignity, the repression of thought, science, and art; the enslavement, exploitation, and systematic murder of millions of peoples are worse.   There is no such thing as a "good" war, and war is never more than a "stupid" solution to international tensions, but there are times when war in the absence of constructive solutions seems to be a lesser evil than doing nothing at all.   The danger of absolute pacifism may lie in the failure to recognize this fact.   It is true, however, that with the advent of atomic warfare the defensibility of war even in these extreme circumstances becomes less valid.   With the use of atomic weapons, those on the "right" side may be destroyed as completely as those on the "wrong" and the positive values they were fighting to protect may be obliterated in the process.

The second common error in analyzing the problem of international tensions lies in a tendency to concentrate too exclusively on conflicts among *nations*, as total social organizations, at the expense of attention to the *individuals* who make up these nations.   Thus, it is analyzed why France and Germany fight, why Britain and the United States form an alliance, why the nations of the world impose economic sanctions on Spain.   But there may be less attention to the behavior of the individual Frenchmen, Germans, British, Americans, and Spaniards who constitute these nations and who in the last analysis determine relations with other peoples.   The convenience in talking about nations as a whole may lead to carelessness in thinking about international relations; it may lead, for instance, to the imputing to nations of motives, perceptions, attitudes, behaviors that are, in fact, the motives, perceptions, attitudes, behaviors of a very few individual persons of these nations.

The third common error in analyzing international tensions is the over-emphasis on war as the expression of *aggressive acts* of the individual. Modern war is not the physical combat of two individuals multiplied by millions, nor is it simply a large-scale version of ancient wars in which bands of enemy warriors came into hand-to-hand combat.   Modern war is the most stupendous mass effort of organized peoples; it incorporates virtually all functions and behaviors of modern life; and only small proportions of a people at war actually engage in fighting or other directly aggressive actions. War is not the direct expression of the feelings of every individual involved. Many, perhaps most, people are forced to engage in war despite their own lack of desire for it or even active opposition to it.

To avoid the above errors an adequate treatment of the problem of international tensions must take account of all kinds of tensions, in addition to those eventuating in war; it must study the relationships among nations as whole social organizations but with equal emphasis upon the perceptions, needs, attitudes, and behavior of the individuals who make up these nations; and it must view war in such a way as to allow for the wide diversity of individual roles and motives in it. The first part of the chapter will, accordingly, be concerned with international tensions as analyzed among nations as whole social organizations. The second part of the chapter will take up the individual psychological bases of international tensions. The third part will discuss important obstacles to international unity. And the final part will present a program for reducing international tensions.

INTERNATIONAL TENSIONS AMONG NATIONS

In order to analyze the problem of international tensions on the level of nations as whole social organizations, it will be necessary first to say something about nations as organizations of people, about extra-national groupings of people, and about organization among nations. Following this "structural" analysis, there will be considered dynamic interaction and international tensions, the relation of international tensions to internal conditions within nations, and the effects of tensions on change of international structure.

Nations as Organizations of People.—International tensions, we have said, occur primarily among nations. This is because the most important lines of structural division within the present-day world are *national boundaries*. By national boundaries we refer not so much to the geographical frontiers that separate nations as to the lines of social organization that differentiate one political state from another, though to a remarkable degree these tend to coincide. Nations are *social organizations* as we have discussed them in Chap. X (see especially page 369). They have cultural products, collective names and symbols, distinctive action patterns, common belief systems, and enforcing agents and techniques. They command identifications and loyalties from their citizens and belief in the transcendence of the state. They satisfy many different needs of their citizens and create new needs. They have relatively stable and unique forms of internal organization.

These various characteristics of nations as social organizations are too well understood to merit detailed discussion here, but we shall mention several points that are especially relevant in the analysis of international tensions.

Differences among nations.—The people of various nations may be differentiated in a number of ways, no one of which is perfectly correlated with nationality: language, culture, religion, political ideology, typical names,

customs, ways of dress, etc.   They tend also to be spatially (*i.e.*, geographi-
cally) segregated from one another.   And nations, too, may be differentiated
in many ways: names, flags, laws, leadership, national history, national
products, etc.   The differentiation is strengthened by sharpening the
boundaries between nations by secondary means, such as by frontier guards,
immigration rules, custom duties, or passports.

In accordance with the principles of perception discussed in Chap. III,
all these factors make for a clear cognitive separation in any individual's
thinking not only of his own nation but of other nations as well.   And this
cognitive separation makes possible the operation of all the motivational and
emotional processes (Chap. II) that result in strong national identifications,
loyalties, fears, hates, and rivalries.

Differences in internal structure of nations.—All nations do not enter the
world scene on equal footing, nor do they have equal influence on international tensions.   This is partly a function of population, economics, and
geography.   Some nations are small, some large; some are industrial, others
agricultural; some are adjacent, others are widely separated.   But aside
from these obvious factors, the significance of the role of any nation in
creating or resolving international tensions is intimately bound up with the
internal structure of the nation as a social organization.   Some nations are
strongly or stably or rigidly organized; others are weak and unstable.
Some are authoritarian in structure, others democratic (see Chap. XI).
Some are monolithic, others diversified.

When we see the representatives of 11 nations sitting around a table in the
Security Council, we may get an illusory impression that here are 11 nations
in dynamic interaction.   To a certain extent this is actually true, but there
are very wide variations among the nations in the *way* in which these diplomats are representing their countries.   The position taken by the representative of an authoritarian state will directly and unambiguously reflect
the international position of all the dominant members of that state, whereas
what the representative of a democratic state says often represents a compromise of several different points of view within his country And the
people of a democratic state may come into dynamic interaction with other
peoples of the world in a variety of ways, whereas the people of authoritarian
states are severely limited and regulated in their interaction with the world.

Manifold functions of nations as organizations.—We have seen in Chap. X
that social organizations tend to assume more and more functions for their
members.   This is especially true of nations, which seek to serve *all* necessary functions for their citizens—political, economic, educational, social.
This functional unification of each nation helps to reinforce its cognitive and
emotional differentiation from other nations in the minds of its citizens.

But we have also seen in Chap. X that social organizations do not meet the needs of all their members equally. Consequently, it may be expected that other types of organization, in addition to organization by nations, will occur among the people of the world.

Extra-national Groupings of People.—Divisions along racial, religious, political, economic, cultural, and other lines, which exist within every nation, may cut across the national boundaries. Thus, the Catholics in all countries may be somewhat unified in opposition to non-Catholics; organized labor in many countries may also hold membership in the World Trade Union Congress; the Communist International supersedes national boundaries; and scientists, artists, chess players, Rotarians, and many other types of people form international bodies.

Just as all people are members of many overlapping groups within a nation, so are great numbers of them members of groups that overlap national boundaries. The crucial significance of this fact for the problem of international tensions will presently become clear.

Organization among Nations.—In Chap. X (see especially page 379) it was pointed out that there are important interrelationships *among* social organizations. These are clearly manifested on the level of nations. The relationships among some nations are closer than among others, and the types of relationship differ. Nations tend to form blocs (formal or informal), and the basis of such blocs may be geographical, cultural, ideological, economic, racial, religious, etc. For example, America and the British Commonwealth, the Latin-American countries, Russia and the pro-Soviet countries of eastern Europe, Egypt and Pakistan may be drawn together and work together on the international scene. The form of such international organization may be either "horizontal" or "vertical" (see page 375). Thus, the relations within a bloc may be on a basis of relative equality of power and status, as in the Scandinavian group or in the Arab Federation, or the relations may be such that one or more countries dominate others in the bloc who are in a dependent relationship, such as the economic dominance of the United States in the Pan-American group and the political dominance of Soviet Russia over her satellites.

Nations may tend to be drawn together as a function of certain extra-national groupings (see foregoing) which include all or substantial parts of the populations of the several countries. Thus, predominantly Catholic countries may be drawn together more closely, and England and America may be drawn together on the basis of common language and cultural heritage. But this may not be true if the overlapping membership includes only a small part, and not a dominant part, of one or several of the countries. For example, the existence of a considerable number of people in the United

States who feel strong loyalty to Communistic principles shared by the people of Russia does not therefore make for closer relationship between the United States and Russia. In fact, a reverse effect is produced; since there is tension already existing between Russia and the United States, the presence of a minority group of Communist sympathizers in the United States serves merely to exacerbate the tensions.

Organization of nations along emotional lines.—In mapping the structure of psychological groups it has been found convenient to state relationships among individual members on the basis of feelings of like and dislike, acceptance and rejection (see Chap. X, page 376). The organization of nations along such emotional lines could be profitably studied in the same way. It is obvious that for the majority of people in a country there are differential feelings of like and dislike, acceptance or rejection of the peoples of other countries. On a world-wide scale, therefore, all the lines of emotional relationship among the various nations could be mapped out. In this way it would be possible to inspect the "sociogram" and ascertain constellations of nations, friendly and unfriendly pairs, isolated nations, etc. This would be a worth-while project, but what would be even more significant would be such a sociometric analysis as applied to the differences in feelings *of various groups within each nation toward groups in other nations*. Not all Americans feel equally well disposed toward different groups within France. This detailed sociometric picture might prove of the highest value in predicting future lines of cleavage in international tensions.[1]

It is certain that the "sociogram" of nations would in many critical respects vary markedly from the structure of relationships of nations as seen in terms of economic interests or political interests. That is, nations are often drawn together for ulterior reasons in the face of mutual feelings of antipathy, and those who are emotionally close may be in conflict on other grounds. This fact is reminiscent of the observation of Moreno (see Chap. X, page 377) that the formal groupings of people may often be at variance with their psychological relationships. His inference was that the lines of psychological relationship are likely to be more significant for the behavior of the group than are the lines of formal structure. Translated to the international scene the implication would be that the emergence, the effects, and the resolution of international tensions may be more readily understandable in light of the feelings of like or dislike among peoples of the world than upon lines of organization based upon other kinds of factors. Neither,

---

[1] The nearest approach to this kind of study with which we are familiar is that of Dodd (1935), who employed the social distance technique (see Chap. VII, p. 221) to establish the feelings of psychological affinity among 15 national, 11 religious, 5 economic, and 3 educational groupings of people in the Near East.

of course, must be overstressed. To neglect either is likely to lead to an erroneous analysis and prediction of international behavior.

Dynamic Interaction and International Tensions.—The structure of nations and of supra-national relationships has been examined in light of the discussion of social organizations in Chap. X. It may also be profitable to analyze international tensions in terms of principles of group dynamics. The justification for such a method of analysis lies in several considerations: (1) It is theoretically plausible that, with some appropriate modifications, the dynamics of relatively small groups of individuals will be similar to those of much larger social organizations on an international scale; (2) it can be observed, in fact, that there does seem to be something in the nature of dynamic interaction among nations and other international groupings of people; (3) to the extent that *relationships among nations are channeled almost exclusively through small numbers of leaders*, who carry out the personal negotiations with other nations and who possess enormous power in determining the policies and actions of their respective countries, the facts of dynamics of smaller groups do directly pertain to the international problem. It is also likely that many of the facts about group morale and group leadership reviewed in Chap. XI are applicable to questions of morale and leadership in the international organizations of nations.

Tensions and Change of International Structure.—The causes of tensions among nations are many: conflicting interests and objectives, mutual suspicion, fear and hatred, overlapping loyalties and identifications, etc. These tensions have various effects on international structure and relations. They may lead to decreased unity among nations, which is often exhibited in withdrawal and isolation from one another, or they may lead to the realignment of relationships and creation of "blocs" among nations, or, finally, they may lead to war. These three reactions can be understood as in the direction of tension reduction and are similar in many respects to tension-reductive reactions of smaller social groups.

The reaction of withdrawal and isolation is, however, limited in its effectiveness. Because of economic factors—raw materials, trade, technological changes, population pressures, etc.—nations are required to carry on many diverse relationships with one another and cannot be cut off in a complete fashion. Moreover, there is an ever-growing "world-mindedness" among the people of the world which makes for necessary interaction. The psychological fields of many people in the world today are expanding to include more and more of the whole world. The recent war has necessarily broadened the cognitions of millions of Americans and of millions of people in other countries. It is true that the effective horizons of the psychological worlds of most Americans and most Chinese and most Frenchmen are still exceedingly narrow, extending not beyond the immediate "valley" in which they live and work and die.[1]   But there is everywhere a steady pressure for growth and enrichment of people's views of the world.   This increasing world-mindedness does not in itself determine the kind of international interaction that it produces.   World-mindedness can be reflected in fears and hatreds of other nations and in desires to dominate and conquer them, as well as in feelings of friendship and desires to cooperate.   The road from isolationism may lead to imperialism rather than to international unity.

In addition to economic necessities and world-mindedness among people, another limiting factor on isolation and withdrawal among nations is the existence and growth of membership in the various kinds of extra-national groupings of people we have mentioned above.   Pressures for isolationism run counter to pressures for maintaining the world-wide unity of the Catholic Church, trade unions, and scientists, artists, and chess players.   For these various reasons, therefore, tensions among nations can be reduced or resolved only in a minor way, if at all, by withdrawal and isolation.

Another effect of tensions among nations on international structure is the realignment and regrouping of blocs of nations.   Thus, in the face of a common threat, two or more nations previously unallied may form a unified opposition.   The presence of tension in some parts of the world may reduce dissensions and disunity in other parts of the world.   For example, the unity of Britain and the United States was markedly raised by the threat of Nazi Germany and Imperial Japan, and even more dramatically the relationship between Soviet Russia and the United States, who had long been in covert conflict, achieved an unexpectedly high unity during the war on a common enemy.

It is in the realignment of nations as a consequence of international tensions that the interactive character of international relations becomes most obvious.   A change in constellation of nations in one part of the world is likely to have effects that spread rapidly throughout the world and may produce at remote places changes in structure that seem to bear no direct relation to the original change.   A new pact between two nations or a break in relations may have immediate repercussions on the relations of all other nations, either strengthening or weakening them.   And these changes in turn rebound on the original effect and modify it.   This continues until a

[1] Studies on international thinking of a cross section of the American public made during the war by the Program Surveys Division of the U. S. Department of Agriculture clearly demonstrated that for large segments of the population, the world outside the United States or even outside their own immediate community was virtually nonexistent.   Not only was there a lack of emotional and motivational connection with anything beyond these narrow borders, there was for large numbers of people only the haziest conception of what lies beyond.

new equilibrium state is at least temporarily established or until war or other extreme forms of conflict eventuate. This dynamic picture of the interplay of forces among nations has been dramatized by the political scientists and historians in the concepts of "balance of power," "power vacuum," etc. Although the changes in international organization are reflected most vividly in the form of political pacts and rupture of diplomatic relations, it is to be understood that the really important lines of interaction may be less obvious, being concerned with matters of trade, raw materials, military inventions, technological changes, and population shifts, whose effects on international structure may be more gradual and less easily discerned.

The third major effect of international tensions is war itself. *It is not that the very activity of war is itself tension reductive.* To apply the frustration-aggression hypothesis as it operates in the *individual* directly to the behavior of *nations* would be meaningless. It is rather that the *consequences* of war may sometimes be tension reductive. Intense rivalry of two nations over raw materials or control of populations may be resolved by one nation's aggressing against and obtaining the raw materials or the control over the people. Perceived threats to national security and the fear thus engendered may be reduced through war. It can be argued that in the long run, for example, the Civil War in the United States did produce a higher unity in the nation than had previously been achieved (though, of course, war was not the only conceivable way in which this might have been brought about). More frequently, however, war simply sows the seeds of future conflict and tension. But the long-term consequences of war are, for our immediate discussion, somewhat irrelevant. What is significant is the fact that under some circumstances war is *perceived* by the people of a country or by its leaders as the only available way of resolving conflicts. When this is the case, and when the international tensions reach a level where they are no longer held in check by such means as isolation and withdrawal or realignment of power among nations, then war can be expected to occur.

The relation of international tensions to internal conditions.—The lines of dynamic interaction in the world cut across national boundaries. This means that the problem of international tensions must be viewed in a general framework that includes events and conditions *within* as well as among nations. International tensions affect the internal policies and structure of nations, and, conversely, internal policies and structure can affect international relations.

It has already been pointed out (Chap. X, page 398) that the presence of a hostile out-group tends to unify the in-group. Hence, tension between two countries frequently increases the cohesiveness and unity within each country. This commonplace phenomenon requires no illustration. But there is a highly significant qualification to this effect.   If lines of cleavage within the nation are such that the out-group is not perceived by the various groups within the country as a common threat, then outside pressure may produce internal dissension rather than unity.   Thus, the leaders of a nation may perceive another nation as threatening, whereas the people as a whole may not.   In order that unity shall prevail, the leaders must convince the people that there is a threat to them.   This was one objective of Hitler's propaganda to the German people; another example is seen in the persistent stress of the Soviet leaders on "capitalistic encirclement" or the efforts of some American leaders to convince all Americans of the "Communist" threat.   And also, special interests within the nation may perceive other nations as economic competitors, and it is necessary to gain backing from the people as a whole by arranging or magnifying "incidents" that prove the threatening character of the out-group.   Whether or not the *basis* of perception of external threat among all the groups within the nation is identical is irrelevant.   What is essential is that there be a *common perception* of danger.

Not only may there be a failure of common perception of danger, there may be serious roots of internal dissension in the face of international conflict.   It has been pointed out that many people in every country are members of overlapping groups which transcend national boundaries. This overlapping membership is the source of conflicting loyalties.   Sometimes, therefore, groups within a nation have strong loyalties to groups within the "enemy" nation or even to the "enemy" nation as a whole.   Communists in America would be less likely to support a war against Russia; business interests may oppose a war with a good "customer"; Catholics resist sanctions against the Franco regime in Catholic Spain.[1]

In international conflict one nation may seek to exploit these lines of potential cleavage within the enemy nation.   We have already spoken (see Chap. XI, page 411) of the use of propaganda to accentuate divisive forces within a country.   This may be done even more directly by the use of groups within the enemy country who have loyalty and identification directed outside: the fifth column.

---

[1] An interesting sidelight on how conflicting identifications may reduce support of a war was seen in the observation based on public opinion surveys of the American public at the beginning of the last war which indicated that among Negroes there was somewhat less enthusiasm for war against Japan than against Nazi Germany.   The inference was that the Negro had something of a feeling of identification with other dark-skinned people who had also suffered white man's oppression.   Although the wartime record of Negroes was one of high morale and loyalty to the Allied cause, it is significant that this morale was jeopardized by the existence of an undemocratic class structure in the United States, which predisposed the Negro to identify with elements of the enemy out-group.

Internal dissension resulting from international conflict may have several different consequences, depending upon the relative power of the dissenting groups. Dissension may lead to a state of weakened resistance, permitting the enemy country to take over. Or the country may be delivered to the enemy if the friendly dissident group can assume power. More frequently, such internal dissension in times of international conflict leads to stern repressive measures against the dissident groups. Thus, as relations between the United States and Soviet Russia grow worse, it can be expected that there will be stronger repressive pressures brought to bear against radical groups in the United States and those who are or are perceived by most Americans as being sympathetic toward Soviet Russia.

Even when the nation itself is not directly engaged in international conflict, the existence of tensions in other parts of the world may have its influence on internal conditions. The succession of events involved in the signing of the German-Russian pact in 1939, the Nazi attack on England, and the eventual attack on Russia produced a succession of changes in structure and alignment of groups within the United States. The Communists, for instance, bitterly opposed the Administration's desires to aid Britain in the early part of the war, but the situation reversed itself with dramatic suddenness on June 22, 1941, when Russia was invaded. The leadership of a country may stand or fall in terms of conditions existing in other parts of the world. Thus, a sudden increase in tension between the United States and Soviet Russia may bring about the resignation of the French cabinet.

We have considered the influence of international tensions on internal policies and structure; the reverse type of influence is equally important. What happens within a single country may upset international equilibrium. A change in leadership, a revolution, the electoral victory of one political party over the incumbent party, the repression or exploitation of one minority group by dominant groups, a bumper wheat crop, devaluation of the dollar, and many other internal events may be expected to have influences that reach out into all corners of the world. When internal tensions reach the explosive stage of civil war, international repercussions are in the present world almost inevitable. As Murphy (1945) comments,

. . . civil wars threaten to disturb even a stable international system. For there are strong impulses to take sides; there are economic as well as political temptations to intervene; and civil war on a large scale, where military power is seized by those who have been kept under the thumb of another power bloc, can introduce all the evils and dangers of international war.

Indeed, one might go one step further and say that if we actually achieve a single world sovereignty, any local war can tend to become a spreading civil war within the world structure, one area under its own political, economic, and military system striking out against the rest, with repercussions of rebellion on other parts of the earth.

One other effect of internal conditions on international stability must be noted. We have seen how the unresolved tensions of the individual may be manifested in outward aggressions (Chap. II, page 55) and how the tensions in a group may find expression in aggression toward an out-group (Chap. X, page 396). Similarly, on an international scale internal tensions may be channeled outward toward other nations. This is especially true to the extent that the emotions and perceptions concerning another nation involve fear and hatred and the belief that it is a threat, and hence that it constitutes a target toward which aggression is predisposed. It is a traditional device of the leaders of a country stirred by internal dissensions and discontent to foment aggressions outwardly and, if need be, to go to war.

In light of the above observations, it may be concluded that the world is truly a dynamic whole. What happens among nations in one part of the world cannot be insulated from what happens elsewhere, and what happens within a nation cannot be separated from what happens on the international scene. International tensions are not merely tensions among nations; they are also tensions among racial, religious, economic, and ideological groups.

INTERNATIONAL TENSIONS AND THE INDIVIDUAL

Up to this point our discussion of international tensions has been cast in terms of an analysis of the dynamic interaction of nations and other international groups. But just as we found it necessary when studying the dynamics of psychological groups to take account of the psychology of the individual (see Chap. X, page 381), so in studying international tensions we must consider the individual. The problem of international tensions is ultimately a problem of the psychology of the individual. War is declared by and fought by individuals; peace and international unity are the products of the actions of individuals.

This is not meant to deny the critical significance of economic, political, and other such factors in international tensions. We have tried to indicate the relevance of these factors in our foregoing discussion. But the point is that the manner in which these economic, political, and other such influences work in international tensions is psychological; i.e., they become effective through and are guided and channeled by the needs, perceptions, beliefs and attitudes of the individual.

Much of what we shall have to say about the individual will pertain most directly to the individual American. We have more available psychological data on Americans, and the application of basic principles concerning international tensions must be made by us mainly through Americans. But what we say about the individual American is probably also true, in principle, of the individual Russian, Frenchman, and Chinese. There is, of course, no typical American. The needs, perceptions, beliefs, and attitudes of individuals differ widely depending upon the groups to which they belong. There are in America many groups, having different interests, different functions in the structure of the nation, and different effects on international tensions. These differences must be considered.

The leaders of a nation play a particularly crucial role in determining international relations. It is usually through them that the psychological forces among the people as a whole become coalesced and translated into national action. And the leaders are, as we have seen in Chap. XI, the external representatives of the group and the "gatekeepers" of relations with other countries. How the leadership position is used, to what ends it is exploited, and whether international tensions are thereby heightened or diminished depend upon the psychology of the individual leaders—their needs, their perceptions, and their beliefs and attitudes. The psychology of the leader must, therefore, be given special attention.

The prime psychological questions to be considered in connection with the bases of international tensions are: (1) What needs of the individual are served by international conflict? (2) How do the beliefs and attitudes of the individual come to make international conflicts seem appropriate ways of satisfying these needs?

Needs and International Tensions.—The needs underlying international tensions are manifold. They may be considered in seven categories: (1) frustrated needs leading to aggressiveness, (2) needs for direct gain, (3) needs for power and prestige, (4) patriotic and nationalistic needs, (5) needs for "escape from peace," (6) needs for resolving ambiguous crisis situations, (7) needs for group belongingness and conformity, (8) needs for war itself.

Frustrated needs leading to aggressiveness.—One of the most important ways of reducing unresolved tensions that result from thwarted goal achievement is through aggressive behavior (see Chap. II, page 55). The critical social significance of the frustration-aggression sequence has already been discussed in connection with racial prejudice and industrial conflict. It is equally important in the creation of international tensions.

The crucial facts about the frustration-aggression sequence are that frustrations arising from many *different* needs may be reflected in aggression and that the target of the aggression may be *unrelated* to the source of frustration. People who are thwarted in their everyday needs for subsistence, economic security, personal status, self-expression, etc., may become aggressive, and this aggression may frequently be directed at accessible and socially approved targets, such as "foreigners" or "enemy countries." *Given the appropriate belief and attitude systems*, it is likely, other things being equal, that the higher the level of frustration among the people of a country the greater will be the feelings of aggressiveness toward other countries. Whether or not these aggressive feelings are translated into actual aggression depends upon *how effectively the leaders of the country organize and channel its people's feelings and upon the availability of instruments of aggression, such as armies or economic sanctions.*

The various groups of people in a country are frustrated for many different reasons, but all these frustrations may be commonly served by external aggression. Such aggression is, of course, only one of many ways to reduce frustration, and international tensions and war, as we shall see, need not be inevitable consequences of frustration.

Needs for direct gain.—International tensions and war often arise out of direct needs for gain. For the wealthy, they may have to do with desires for more wealth. For the farmer, with desires to protect his markets. For the industrialist, with desires to obtain raw materials and to protect and maintain his operations. For the munitions maker, with desires to sell armaments. For the organized worker, with desires to prevent labor competition. For the military man, with desires to put his training into use. For the politician, with desires to maintain his position. For everyone, with desires to protect his life and property and to maintain and extend his "way of life."

War is often seen as and frequently proves to be a way of satisfying these diverse needs. But many or most of them can also be satisfied in other ways.

Needs for power and prestige.—Other sorts of direct needs served by international tensions and war have to do with desires for power and prestige. These motives may be as potent as or in some individuals more potent than those of direct economic gain, etc., which we have mentioned just above. The leaders of a nation, particularly, are likely to have strong needs for prestige and power—this is one reason why they have become leaders (see page 436)—and in their face-to-face relationships with the leaders of other nations and in their uniquely prominent identification with the countries they represent, they are likely to behave in such a way as to encourage international tension and war rather than preventing them.[1]

Aside from the leaders, all citizens have identification with the prestige,

---

[1] For a provocative statement of the thesis that the desire for personal power may be much more significant in many leaders of modern society than the desires for personal economic gain, see Burnham (1941), *The Managerial Revolution.*

power, and successes of their nation. Through such identification (see Chap. II, page 59) they achieve vicarious satisfaction of their needs for prestige and power which may be thwarted in their own personal lives.

Patriotic and nationalistic needs.—For some people under some circumstances the most insistent and intense needs involved in international tensions and war are those deriving from love of and loyalty toward their country. Identification with and involvement in a group creates new needs in the individual (see Chap. II, page 70) that have to do with the welfare, protection, and enhancement of the group and that may compete with and take precedence over other "self-centered" needs. The "nation" may, like one's family or one's ideals, become something to be defended, to be sacrificed for even with one's life. Nationalism and patriotism are unquestionably among the most powerful motivations in the world today.

It has become fashionable to discount patriotic and nationalistic needs and to regard them as intrinsically dangerous. Yet it should be emphasized that it is not these needs as such which are dangerous but the fact that they have too often tended to become channeled into international tensions and war. These needs are, in their essential nature, the very kind of needs of love and loyalty that it is hoped can come to be engendered among people of the world with respect to a total organization of nations. There is nothing necessarily incompatible with needs of nationalism and patriotism and a condition of international peace and unity.

Needs for escape from peace.—International tensions culminating in war may serve a quite different sort of need in people—the desire to escape from the tedium of their everyday existences, the desire for excitement and activity, the wish to be caught up in something dramatic and large with other people. It is not so much in these cases that men love war as that they dislike the circumstances of peace. William James was so impressed with the functional significance of warlike behavior in satisfying these needs that he stressed the necessity for finding a "moral equivalent of war."

Needs for resolving ambiguous crisis situations.—The extraordinary significance of "crisis" situations in the life of the individual has been stressed at several points (see Chap. V, page 154, and Chap. XII, page 454). When there is confusion and ambiguity in the individual's world, especially in reference to areas of salient importance to him, he seeks meaning and undertakes action that will resolve the ambiguity. It is often in this way that warlike behavior seems to the individual to fulfill the requirements of clarification in a complex world situation which he regards as important but does not understand.

Needs for group belongingness and conformity.—As a citizen of the nation and a member of various groups within the nation the individual is susceptible to pressures of conformity. His belongingness to the group and his status in it depends partly upon his readiness to conform to the behavior of the group. Thus, when his nation is at war and the various political, occupational, social, religious, and other groups of which he is part are supporting the war, it is difficult for him to resist social pressures to join in. Many people given a secret choice would prefer not to go to war, but in the searching light of public opinion they enlist in the war effort. Back of public opinion there is, of course, more drastic pressure that can be brought to bear on the reluctant individual. The draft resister, for instance, may be sent to prison.

Sometimes the needs for group conformity run counter to war. Thus a member of a pacifist religious group may be more responsive to the pressures of "public opinion" of his immediate group than of the nation at large. This provides for internal dissensions within the national framework and may lead to heavy reprisals against the dissenting groups by the dominant part of the nation.[1]

Needs for war itself.—All the needs served by war that have been discussed above may be thought of also as capable of satisfaction through other means than war. Beyond these, however, is there also a need for war itself, *i.e.*, a need that can be satisfied *only* by the aggressive behavior of war? The question may be phrased in several ways—is there an instinct of war, is war an ineradicable part of human nature, etc.—and it has been the subject of endless debate. On the basis of the discussion already made in Chap. II of the potentialities of growth, modification of needs, and the changeability of "human nature," it may be asserted unreservedly that *war is not an instinctive part of human behavior*. People are not born with nor do they automatically develop a need for war or for any form of aggressiveness. This is not to deny that aggressiveness as a function of appropriate psychological conditions, such as frustration, may be universally observed, but it is not the same thing as a need for aggressiveness *as an indispensable end in itself*. As Murphy (1945) has remarked: "There is, I think, a universal tendency to fight back when blocked, thwarted, interfered with; but if the individual is not blocked or thwarted or interfered with, he has no intrinsic tendency to aggression."[2]

To argue that need for aggressiveness is neither universal nor intrinsic is

[1] See Crespi (1944, 1945) for an intensive study of wartime attitudes toward conscientious objectors and their psychological correlates.

[2] For a more detailed statement of the problem of war and human nature the student will profit by Chap. 2 in Murphy's book, which is, as a whole, one of the most satisfactory available discussions of the psychology of war and peace. See, also, the extremely provocative remarks by Kluckhohn (1947) on certain anthropological aspects of the problem.

not, however, to maintain that there is no such thing as a genuine need for aggressiveness. For some people and under some circumstances war exists as a positive value, irrespective of whatever functions it may serve. War may be glorified by a society and surrounded with all sorts of positive emotions to such an extent that a genuine need for war is created in the members of the society. This was probably the case in certain warlike Indian societies and more recently among Nazi youth, for whom war was brought to appear uniquely desirable as a thing in itself. Most societies that are faced with the necessity or the likelihood of war may find it expedient to inculcate martial virtues in its people.

National character and international tensions.—What has been said just above concerning the existence of genuine needs for aggressiveness among some people in some societies raises the important question of "national character" as related to international tensions. This question may be phrased in the following way: Is the national psychology of some countries such that they are particularly prone to aggressiveness? Many people believe that there are such tendencies in typical Germans and typical Japanese as contrasted with, say, typical Swiss, and they believe that much of the responsibility for war rests upon the fact of those nations having an aggressive "character." From their point of view, the solution to world strife is to quarantine aggressive nations and—depending upon how dim a view of human nature they take—to exterminate them or to reeducate them to peaceful ways.

It is to be suspected that which nations are characterized as "aggressive" and which "peace-loving" depends somewhat upon who does the characterizing. The Russians may regard the national character of the Turks as typically warlike, and the Turks may return the compliment; the American finds it hard to believe that other nations can regard us as anything but "peace-loving," atomic bomb and all. There is here something of the "projective" phenomenon also illustrated by the characterization of syphilis by Italians as the "French disease," by the French as the "Italian disease," etc.

Even allowing for this projective effect, it does seem probable that some nations exhibit a lower threshold for aggression than do others. Germany and Japan appear to be good recent examples. What is to be inferred from this fact?

First, it is necessary to clarify the concept of "national character." In one sense this is a statistical concept, having reference to distribution of various traits in the population of a nation. Thus, it may be ascertained that *on the average* there is more reserve among Englishmen than among Americans, more submissiveness among Germans than among Norwegians, etc. In another sense "national character" refers to the typical patterns of social behavior within the organization of a given nation. Thus, it may be ascertained that the behavior in one country tends to fall into democratic patterns and that of another country into authoritarian patterns, that children in one country tend to be raised in a permissive atmosphere and those of another country in an atmosphere of severe control, etc.

As Klineberg (1944) has pointed out, both meanings of the concept are useful, and they are not independent: The traits of the individuals in a nation help shape its social organization, and the social organization shapes the development of traits of its members.

A wealth of anthropological data seems to support the view that there are striking differences in the "character" of various primitive cultures. These societies are much smaller and more homogeneous, however, than nations of the world today, and it is not safe to generalize from primitive cultures to large nations. Nations are complex and highly heterogeneous, made up of many groups within the whole population. It is not unlikely that important differences in the character of such groups within a nation do exist, and these may be more marked than differences among nations as a whole. The variance within the nation may be greater than the variance among nations.

Some observers feel certain that they have detected critical differences in the national character of national groups. Brickner (1943) attributes an enduring characteristic of "cultural paranoia" to the German nation as a whole. Through an analysis of recent events in Nazi Germany and of German history and literature over a long period of time, he concludes that the characteristic behavior patterns of Germans are compounded of aggressiveness, delusions of persecution, megalomania, and all the other symptoms of the paranoiac. Aside from the questionable validity of applying a concept of individual abnormality to a whole nation, Brickner's argument may be criticized on a number of grounds: It fails to allow for possible wide differences in the characteristics of various groups and classes of people within Germany; it may reflect only the tendencies of temporarily dominant and highly aberrant groups, such as the Nazi leaders; it may have been based on a biased sampling of German history and literature; it may fail to make sufficient allowance for the possibility that the "paranoid" behavior is a function not of "national character" but of certain external conditions such as economic insecurity, etc.

Gorer (1943) goes a step further in his analysis of the "character" of the Japanese, by trying to account for the apparently greater aggressiveness of these people in terms of the personality development within the culture, especially as related to the early rigid training of the child. Here again there are many technical questions to be raised concerning the adequacy of sampling, the accuracy of the appraisal of the presumed trait of aggressiveness, the distinction between enduring features of the "national character" and behavior produced by immediate circumstances, etc.

On the basis of the meager data now available, it does not seem possible to conclude with assurance that there are genuine and important differences in national character. And even if differences were assumed to exist, there is virtually nothing that can be said definitively about the *specific nature* of such presumed differences.

Differences in national character, if they exist, will certainly not be found to depend upon *innate* differences among national peoples. What they will depend upon are three factors: (1) varying level of general frustration of needs among nations, which leads to differences in the incidence of such tension-reductive behaviors as aggression; (2) variations in cultural patterns among nations, which predispose toward the development of characteristic personality patterns for most people in the nation; (3) variations among nations in patterns of beliefs and attitudes held by most members based on cultural tradition, education, national experiences, etc. In the next section we shall turn our attention to the importance of beliefs and attitudes in determining different modes of behavior in connection with international tensions and war.[1]

General comments.—International tensions and war serve many needs, but it is important to be clear about the way in which such conflict serves these needs, for we know that the relation between needs and the activity of the individual in the service of these needs is not always simple and direct. It is of some value to differentiate between two kinds of relationships that seem to exist between the needs of men and international tensions and war in the service of these needs. In some instances international conflict is a *direct and logical* way of satisfying needs; in other cases (and perhaps in the majority of cases) international conflict can best be understood as an *indirect and maladaptive* way of satisfying needs whose more direct solution is

[1] Comprehensive research on national character is urgently needed. If there are significant differences among nations or among large segments of national groups, it is essential to understand them as fully as possible, so that intelligent planning for international harmony can take them into account. Consideration of the question is bound to be hampered by preconceptions, prejudices, and emotional partisanship from one extreme by those who extoll the superiorities of their own way of life and find most of the world's ills resulting from the "evil" personalities and cultural patterns of other nations and from the other extreme by those who, because of the exploitation of theories of racial and national differences to bad ends in the past, are unable to acknowledge the possibility that genuine differences do exist. But the question of national character is too critical to be dodged. It is essentially a matter of objective scientific appraisal, and many of the available methodological techniques for such an appraisal have been outlined by Klineberg (1944).

frustrated. Thus, for the individual whose business interests would be benefited by national conquest or for the person for whom war exists as a positive value, international conflict is a direct and logical means toward need satisfaction. On the other hand, for the person whose many "personal" needs—none of them having to do with war, aggression, expansion, etc.—are frustrated because of social, economic, biological, or psychological barriers, international tensions and war are indirect and maladaptive tension-reductive reactions.

The needs served by war among some of the dominant members of a nation are likely to be different from and more direct than those among the people as a whole. Since it is in the interests of some dominant members that war be resorted to by the entire nation, these dominant members are likely to try deliberately, through propaganda and other means of persuasion, to channel all people's frustrations toward war. However, this formulation should not be interpreted to mean that the citizens of a nation are led into war through evil and wily warmongers against their own will. In the first place, the needs that are directly served by war are not only the needs of the "dominant" members. People of various economic and sociological levels may have such needs. In the second place, war propaganda is successful precisely because among many people of a nation there is a substratum of frustration that can be channeled into war. If this condition did not exist, the probability of war, no matter how intense the activities of warmongers might be, would be greatly diminished. And finally, war persuasion can be successful to the extent that most of the people of a nation already have the appropriate ethnocentric beliefs, negative attitudes concerning other nations, etc. In other words, those who can benefit from international conflict are successful in taking a nation into war because the vast majority of people are both motivationally and cognitively prepared for such activity before the prowar propaganda is initiated.

One important qualification on the above analysis is, however, necessary. The fact that a nation goes to war does not necessarily mean that all or even an overwhelming majority of the people in the nation have frustrated needs or "appropriate" beliefs and attitudes. Modern war is an activity of the total social organization of the state, and all citizens are required to take part. Even without the appropriate beliefs and attitudes and without the predisposing needs, many people may still be coerced into participating in war. They are drafted into the army, they are "shamed" into buying war bonds, they are forcibly prevented from talking against the war policy of the controlling group. For many people, in modern war, the psychological analysis of why they go to war is no more profound than that they are forced to at the point of the bayonet and by the police agencies of the state.

Beliefs and Attitudes and International Tensions.—The needs served by war are manifold, and most of them are capable of being satisfied in other ways than through international conflict. That raises our second main question: How do the beliefs and attitudes of the individual come to make international conflict seem an appropriate way of satisfying these needs? The answer may be traced through the following cognitive and emotional factors: (1) ethnocentric beliefs, (2) stereotyped beliefs concerning other nations, (3) negative attitudes toward other nations, (4) predominance of nationalist over internationalist attitudes, (5) oversimplified perceptions of causes and cures of international tensions, (6) belief in the inevitability of war, (7) cognitive "set" toward international tensions and war, (8) "wishful thinking" about the outcome of war, (9) emotional blocks to cognitive re-organization concerning international tensions.

The explanation of the way these cognitive and emotional factors operate in the individual's thinking about international relations is to be found, of course, in the discussion of the earlier part of the book, especially Chaps. V and VI on the nature and development of beliefs and attitudes.

Ethnocentric beliefs.—The beliefs of all individuals tend to be ethnocentric; *i.e.*, the individual believes that the ways of his culture and his nation are the "right" ways and that the ways of other peoples, being different, are thereby "wrong." The individual's perspective is narrow, and he is not easily able to "see" things from the point of view of other peoples of the world. The average American has virtually no conception of how he is regarded by Russians and Argentinians and Burmese. Just as we have seen (Chap. XI) that a supervisor of a group is often unable to correct poor group morale because he is unable to assume the perspective of the other members, so on an international scale nations are often in conflict because they are unaware of problems as they exist for others. To the American it seems natural and proper that for reasons of national security the United States should control the Panama Canal, yet he deplores Russian attempts for similar reasons to control the Dardanelles. He has bitterly indicted the British for economic exploitation of India while defending the American business interests in Latin America.

Stereotyped beliefs concerning other nations.—We have already at considerable length (see Chap. XII) reviewed the facts about "stereotyping" of beliefs about other nationalities and the reasons for such stereotyping. People in America tend to have a remarkably high consistency and uniformity in their beliefs about the other peoples of the world. Certain traits are widely believed to characterize given nationalities, and there is relatively little differentiation made among the people of a country. For large numbers of people in America, in fact, there is even less differentiation than this—

all "furriners" are alike (and usually bad).   Evidence on the beliefs of people in other countries about the rest of the world is meager, but it seems certain that extreme "stereotyping" is the rule.

Negative attitudes toward other nations.—This is a fertile soil for the development and maintenance of negative attitudes toward other nations. Frustrations of many of the individual's needs lead to emotional reactions that, because of the sterotyped beliefs about alien peoples, may be directed against them as accessible targets.   Feelings of insecurity may lead to generalized fears that become associated with perceptions of other nations. It may even happen that feelings of guilt arising out of a failure of one's own nation to live up to certain ideals, such as democracy, peacefulness, etc., may be rationalized and projected onto foreign nations.   The growth of such negative attitudes is strengthened by the various factors we have discussed in Chap. VI, including selectivity of perception, the attitude "climate" of the nation as a whole, the social support for attitudes, etc. Negative attitudes toward foreign countries are, moreover, frequently reinforced through the persuasion of leaders of the nations or special interest groups who wish for ulterior reasons to consolidate the attitudes of the people against the foreign country.

Irrespective of the state of international tensions at any moment, relations among the nations of the world are characterized by negative attitudes, which vary from a mere feeling of "social distance" to the most violent hates.   In America, for instance, numerous studies of public opinion reveal widespread negative attitudes toward Russia and, to a lesser extent, toward most other foreign countries.

Predominance of nationalist over internationalist attitudes.—Coupled with the negative attitudes toward foreign countries (and possibly as a partial function of these negative attitudes) tend to be strong positive attitudes toward one's own country.   These nationalist attitudes are intimately related, of course, to the patriotic and nationalistic needs discussed above (page 589).   As we have already said, the existence of nationalist attitudes is not necessarily incompatible with world unity; but when these attitudes are found together with intense negative attitudes toward other countries and *in the absence of strong internationalist attitudes*, the situation is conducive to international tensions and war rather than to peace and unity.

It is the unfortunate fact that among the people of all nations today strong internationalist attitudes are rare.   In many respects, the people of the United States are in the most favorable position of any people—because of the dominant political role in world affairs, because of military power, and because of economic security and prosperity—to entertain genuine inter-nationalist attitudes.   Yet as a recent nation-wide intensive survey of the

American public reveals, such attitudes are not strong.[1] As this study points out,

Most Americans want to be friendly with all countries; they believe their country should take part in the United Nations; they agree that America cannot remain aloof from the rest of the world, though some wistfully wish that she could. On the level of generalities the people seem friendly, cooperative, and even international in outlook. However, when specific issues are raised they are apt to deviate from this position. Frequently they fail to see the relation between specific action and the general values they have expressed. The majority did not approve the loan to Britain and failed to see any relation between it and American economic stability. Most are opposed to yielding exclusive control of atomic power. The most common criticism of American foreign policy is that we have been too lenient. Although the people are beginning to admit to themselves that their country is inextricably involved in world affairs, they seem unaccustomed to thinking of America as playing an international role . . . . It seems clear that for many Americans the principles of international cooperation which they are now willing to endorse will be placed under severe strain if specific developments in the United Nations seem to place the interests of the United States in a disadvantageous position.

A number of the determinants of internationalist attitudes have already been indicated (Chap. V, page 155) as well as some sociological correlates (Chap. VI, page 176). Queener (1947) makes the important point that the development of nationalist attitudes is more easily fostered than that of internationalist attitudes because the "rewards" to the individual for the former are more direct and immediate than for the latter and because the "prestige" sources for nationalist attitudes are stronger and more numerous than for internationalist attitudes.

Oversimplified perceptions of causes and cures of international tensions.— Ethnocentric and sterotyped beliefs about other nations, negative attitudes toward them, and the predominance of nationalist over internationalist attitudes, all set the stage for the needs of the individual to be seen as capable of satisfaction through international tensions and war. This trend is strengthened by the very nature of the individual's perceptual and cognitive processes (Chap. III) which lead him to perceive the sources of international problems and their solutions in an oversimplified and inadequate way. It is obviously easier to make sense out of a complex world situation by ascribing the world's ills to the "evil" intentions and actions of a foreign country than to achieve real insight into the complex political, economic, and social factors involved. Thus, the "devil theory" of history. And it is easier

[1] The study referred to is by the SSRC (1947): *Public Reaction to the Atomic Bomb and World Affairs.*

to "solve" the problem by exorcizing the "devil," *i.e.*, by going to war, than it is to work out a true solution.

Belief in the inevitability of war.—Another important contributing condition for the recurrence of international tension and war is the widespread belief that war is inevitable. War never really surprises anyone; it is the occasional period of international harmony that is apt to be considered remarkable. The path to war is cut deeply in men's minds. This fatalistic acceptance by millions of international tension and war as the "natural" state of human relations cannot but render the outbreak of international conflict that much more certain, for it serves as a comforting rationalization for the leaders and people of a country that they have done everything possible to avert war and it saps the courage and persistence of those who seek a permanent formula for peace.

That pessimism about future war is, in fact, widespread among Americans has been repeatedly demonstrated in public opinion surveys. In October, 1943, in the midst of a war to halt aggression, a National Opinion Research Center poll of the nation revealed that only 27 per cent considered it "likely that we will prevent future wars after this." And in December, 1946, 63 per cent of the American public replied "yes" to the NORC question, "Do you expect the United States to fight in another war within the next 25 years?" Since the beliefs of young people in America may ultimately have more to do with future war or peace than those of present adults, it is interesting to determine their beliefs about the inevitability of war. In December, 1947, the Purdue Opinion Poll for Young People reported that in a sample of 10,000 high-school students drawn from all over the United States, 48 per cent expect the United States to fight in another war within 5 years. There is small room for comfort here.

Cognitive set toward international tensions and war.—Pessimism about avoidance of future wars is made more deadly by the fact that so much of the average person's thinking about international relations is set in the context of tensions and war rather than unity and harmony. History books dramatize wars at the expense of perhaps more significant cooperative advances in international relations; the same is true of newspapers, commentators, the radio, etc.

"Wishful thinking" about defense and war.—In the face of these various cognitive and emotional tendencies predisposing the individual toward war in service of his many needs, there is an insufficient restraining force in his fear of the outcome of war. Wishful thinking may interfere decisively with his realistic appraisal of the success of war in accomplishing whatever he wishes it to. Thus, the Japanese leaders might not have precipitated the war in the Pacific had they not been so utterly misled by wishful thinking

in their appraisal of the military strength and will to resist in the American people.

Wishful thinking also plays a deadly role in fostering a defensive isolationist state of mind, which inhibits a positive attempt to forestall and peacefully resolve the growing international tensions. Thus, the French withdrew passively behind their Maginot Line, and at the present time the American people feel secure in their possession of the atomic bomb and their conviction that they will develop a defense against other nations who may later try to use it against them.

Emotional blocks to cognitive reorganization concerning international tensions.—The achievement of harmonious international relations is a *problem* for each individual, and it requires of him problem-solving behavior that, though on a grander and more complex scale, involves the same principles of cognitive reorganization as those involved in solving a problem in the laboratory or in social relations among a small face-to-face group. We have reviewed in the above paragraphs the various factors that come to make the individual tend to "see" international conflict as an appropriate solution to his problems and needs. The significant fact is that he often seems blind to the fact that international conflict is really not a solution and that even if he becomes aware of the inadequacy of this behavior, he seems unable to find a more adaptive solution. He is, in a word, "fixated."

In order to understand the failure of a cognitive reorganization that will permit him to achieve his ends through international unity rather than through conflict, we can draw upon our discussion in Chap. IV. Proposition IV asserted that "the ease and rapidity of the cognitive reorganization process is a function of the differentiation, isolation, and rigidity of the original cognitive structure." The applicability of this proposition to the immediate question is evident in several respects. For one thing, the area of international relations is poorly structured for most people; there is relatively little differentiation on cognitive content. With this goes a high degree of isolation of problems of international relations from other parts of the individual's cognitive world. He does not usually see relationships between international problems and the immediate domestic problems about which he is most concerned. For the average individual, the basic facts and relationships that are necessary to make a cognitive reorganization possible may simply not be existent. Thus, if he understands nothing about international economics, if he is ignorant of the relationship between the level of prosperity of other countries and that of the United States, it is unlikely that he will arrive at a solution to some aspects of international tensions requiring that the United States extend liberal economic aid to other nations in order in the long run to help herself as well as the others.

To yield an immediate and direct economic gain in order to achieve an ultimate economic stability is a high order of *umweg* behavior which will occur to the individual only if the necessary facts and relationships are accessible to him.

For another thing, the very fact that certain kinds of solutions to problems of international relations have been used over and over—*viz.*, those involving withdrawal, imperialism, conflict, etc.—tends to "fixate" these solutions as the only available ones. In approaching new international crises and seeking for solutions, the individual's thinking is already predetermined in its "direction" by the basic way of thinking about international problems that he has previously established. Certain basic "assumptions" condition the kinds of specific solutions that will occur to him; and if these basic "assumptions" are inadequate, as they so frequently are in the area of international relations, the subsequent solutions will also be inadequate. We have seen an illustration of this in Chap. IV (page 124), where preconceptions about "national sovereignty" inhibit successful cognitive reorganization in the solution of the problem of international peace.

And finally, cognitive reorganization is likely to be hindered by high levels of emotionality. When the needs are very strong and the emotions intense, cognitive structure is rigid. Unfortunately, strong needs and intense emotions are invariably characteristic of people facing international crises. People in any country who are starving or are deeply frustrated are not in an auspicious state of mind to discover healthy, adaptive solutions to world problems. Neither are people who hate foreigners, who fear aggression from without, who are fanatically attached to national symbols. We have spoken already (Chap. II, page 60) of how an international fear psychology engendered by the atomic bomb may serve to rigidify people's thinking about world affairs. It is an accelerating process—the greater the fear the less adaptive the solutions, which in turn causes greater fear, and so on. This chain reaction must be broken at some point, or else it necessarily leads to international conflict.

OBSTACLES TO INTERNATIONAL UNITY

In light of the above discussion of the variety of individual needs served by international tensions, of the beliefs and attitudes that predispose people toward international conflict as a means of resolving these needs, and of the psychological factors that make difficult the discovery of more adaptive solutions to the problems of international relations, it is now possible to state the principal obstacles that lie in the way of international unity.

High Level of Frustration the World Over.—In every country—even in the United States, the most favored—large masses of people are at present subject to frustration of intense needs. The needs may be of sheer subsistence (for food, clothing, and shelter), or they may be needs of economic security and security from attack, or they may be needs of personal opportunity, self-expression, prestige, and power. And the sources of frustration may be various—inadequate level of industrialization and economic development in a country, monopolistic economic practices, class discrimination and lack of social democracy, authoritarian government and the failure of political democracy, etc. Whatever the needs and whatever the sources of frustration, it is clear that the widespread frustration is almost inevitably translated into aggressions that find readiest expression in international tension and conflict. The existence of this widespread frustration is, then, an almost insurmountable obstacle to international unity.

Supports for Distorted Beliefs about Others.—We have seen above how people's beliefs about other countries and other peoples are likely to be distorted in such a way as to encourage international misunderstanding and disunity. Such misconceptions are supported by a number of factors. *Inaccessibility* of peoples from one another is a major factor. This is caused by geographical separation, by the absence of a common language, and by all the barriers to international communication, such as restrictions on free world travel and the restricted circulation of books and other information from other countries. Misconceptions are also deliberately fostered by *propaganda*. Control of the media of communication by the leaders and dominant interests of a country makes it possible not only to reduce access to the real facts but also to distort and invent "facts" for ulterior ends. The average citizen of any country in the world today is in virtually complete dependence upon the media of mass public information for his information about other countries. Another major "support" for distorted beliefs is the *beliefs of others*. Thus, the individual may have nothing to turn to in the development of his beliefs about foreign countries but the widely held beliefs of the people with whom he is in direct contact—his parents, friends, teachers, business associates, fellow workers, etc. The stereotypes that universally prevail are thus self-perpetuating, being supports to the growth of new beliefs.

Dominant Role of National Leaders and Special Interests.—As more and more responsibility for the conduct of international relations devolves upon the leaders of each nation, the personal needs, beliefs, and attitudes of these individual leaders play an increasingly disproportionate part in determining international relations. The personal power and prestige drives of individual leaders may be served better by international tension and conflict than by international harmony. Not only may the leaders of a nation assert their dominance over other nations, they may also seek to maintain and extend their prestige and power within the nation by directing internal conflicts and dissatisfactions outwardly toward other nations. Even with the best of intentions, moreover, and assuming that the nation's leaders are not striving to achieve selfish ends or to satisfy needs for power and prestige, the dominating position of the leaders in directing international relations can be a serious obstacle to international unity because their personal beliefs and attitudes may have a deleterious effect.   Career diplomats may often be expected to hold prejudiced beliefs and attitudes that predispose them to distrust other nations, to misunderstand them, and to be impervious to modification of their inadequate conceptions.   The stultifying effects of bureaucratic development in national government may likewise be expected to inhibit the kind of cognitive reorganization and adaptation of techniques necessary to solve the problems of international relations. To an alarming extent in all countries, the fate of international relations is determined by the entrenched bureaucratic core of civil servants who run ministries of foreign affairs and departments of state.

National leaders may also be susceptible to the influences of special interest groups within the country who wish to direct international relations toward the satisfaction of their own needs for direct gain.   Thus, oil interests may promote an imperialistic adventure in oil-rich foreign lands, and farm groups may lobby for high tariffs which seriously disrupt international trade relations.

The Dependence of International Relations on National Politics.— In the United States, as in many countries, international issues have traditionally been an instrument of partisan politics.   Domestic issues have been the primary focus of concern and international relations of only incidental importance.   This has been possible for the United States because it has seemed to most Americans that they could travel a course independent of the rest of the world.   However true this may have been at various periods in the past, it is not true today.   Internal and external policies are becoming ever more intimately interwoven, and no country can hope to keep its internal problems segregated from its external relations.

What is called for if a condition of international unity and understanding is to be achieved is a high order of statesmanship by the various national leaders, and this requires that they be permitted to behave in a statesmanlike way.   They must be enabled to make decisions on foreign policy that transcend the particular political aspirations and demands of the political party to which they happen to belong.   Unfortunately the situation is such that the voting of members of Congress on international issues is more likely than not to follow party lines, the actions of the Administration in power are often guided by political necessity, and the public approval or censure of the Administration's foreign policy often rests upon irrelevant matters of domestic issue rather than upon the international issues themselves.

Woodrow Wilson underrated the importance of national politics in determining American foreign policy after the First World War, and American participation in the League of Nations was thereby prevented. A government that makes honest attempts to arrive at international cooperation opens itself to the attack of its political opponents, who out of mere expediency accuse it of endangering national sovereignty and honor.

Another dangerous consequence of the indiscriminate mixture of national politics and international relations is that the people of a country may be afforded little or no opportunity to express themselves directly on international affairs. National elections are always compounded of a great variety of political issues. A vote for a presidential candidate can never by itself be construed as a vote for isolationism or internationalism, for tariff protection or the "good neighbor" policy. Although the position of the candidate on such international issues may have some effect on the votes he receives, it is more usual that the determinants of voting refer to traditional party preference and to specific domestic issues, such as taxation or attitude toward organized labor. A presidential candidate must take a position on all matters of importance, and his subsequent election or rejection provides no clear-cut mandate for any single policy.

The dependence of international policies upon internal partisan politics also makes for instability in international relations. As Administrations change, largely on the basis of domestic issues, foreign policy may undergo drastic shifts. This interferes with any real continuity in foreign policy and makes long-range planning impossible. As unfortunate as this may be from the nation's own point of view, it is even more disastrous from the point of view of other countries. For they cannot depend upon their future relations with the country, which may be radically upset on the basis of the next national election and for reasons that have nothing whatever to do with the real international problems. Nor can they feel confidence in the foreign commitments of the other nation, which may be repudiated by the next political administration that comes along.

The Lack of Certain Prerequisites for International Unity.—Even assuming that all the foregoing obstacles to international understanding— widespread frustration leading to aggressions, "supports" for distorted beliefs about others, dominant role of leaders and special interests, and the dependence of international relations on national politics—were reduced or eliminated, international unity might still fail of accomplishment because of the very lack of certain positive prerequisites. For a group to develop and to persist there must be something more than mere absence of divisive forces. There must be positive forces of cohesion. And there must also be essential skills and mechanics of group functioning. Both these positive forces and these skills and mechanics are lacking in international relations, and their lack is a serious obstacle to world unity.

There is, for one thing, no common motivation that serves to bind the peoples of the world together. National unity can be built on the common desire to resist aggression from other nations, but for the world as a whole there is no common enemy, no men from Mars. A common desire for peace may help, but it can hardly be expected to provide a real basis for unity, being essentially a negative aim rather than a positive one. It is difficult to imagine, for instance, that a group could hold together purely by reason of the desires of its members to avoid conflicts with one another.

Another lack is a world organization that can command emotions of loyalty and identification of comparable intensity to those toward nations. The United Nations provides what may become the structure of such a world organization, but at present it has not sufficient reality for the people of the world and is not equipped with sufficient paraphernalia of group organization—flags, uniforms, cultural products, etc.—to encourage deep identification.

An effective organization of people requires a great deal of inter-communication among them, and here again is a serious shortcoming of the present world situation. Physical distance, the lack of a common language, and the deliberate restrictions by national leaders who act as "gatekeepers" of interrelations with other peoples, all make for inadequate communication.

And finally, there is a serious lack of skills of international cooperation. We have mentioned previously in connection with the behavior of groups (see page 430) that no amount of good intention can ensure group unity unless the necessary skills and experience in group living and action are available. There is discouragingly little in the way of such skills and experience on the international level, to say nothing of the level of national groups and even primary groups such as the family. The effectiveness of groups of any size depends upon the ability of the members to engage in group discussion and group decision, to employ democratic procedures, and to fall back upon genuine attitudes of toleration and compromise. If small groups of people who are commonly motivated and who have high identification with the group are unable to operate effectively because of the absence of these skills, it is not surprising that nations also fail in international cooperation in their absence.

Basic Ideological Conflicts.—The final obstacle to international unity that we shall mention is of a somewhat different order from those described above. It is the existence in the world of profound ideological differences that are such as to admit of no meaningful compromise, no possible synthesis within a comprehensive world order. Ideologies that in their very essence require the destruction of other ideologies cannot exist side by side in "one world." Either perpetual conflict or the complete suppression by one of all the others is the only possible outcome.

Historically, the most important of such profound ideological clashes were along lines of religious cleavage. Thus, in some societies religious dissenters, or "heretics," were completely wiped out or forcibly converted, and holy wars were among the most bloody of conflicts among peoples. The significant fact was that the religious ideologies concerned carried in them a necessary intolerance for opposing views, and hence conflict among religious groups was almost inevitable. Although unity under these conditions was impossible, tensions among the large groups of people having different religious ideologies were sometimes avoided through physical separation. The opposing groups could not live peaceably side by side, but they could live in different parts of the world and could, as did the Puritans and the Mormons, seek out new places in which to live unhindered. As the world has become smaller and dynamic interaction among all parts of the world has grown, the tensions arising out of intransigent ideological differences can no longer be readily resolved by the segregation of the conflicting groups. It is because of this that the relative importance of ideological differences as a basis of international tensions becomes greater and greater.

In the present world the most critical ideological conflicts are no longer in religious terms. Tensions still arise between Protestants and Catholics and between Moslems and Hindus, etc., but on the whole opposing religions have gradually found it possible to live side by side in mutual tolerance even if not in positive cooperation. This is a function of both a lessening of the fanaticism of religious beliefs and changes in the ideologies themselves.

Aside from the abortive "master-race" ideology of the Nazis, the most profound ideological conflicts of the world today are in the areas of economic and political philosophy. Cleavages of capitalism and Marxism and of totalitarianism and democracy show danger of becoming the source of the most intense international conflicts the world has experienced. Already these cleavages have given rise to serious tensions and to war. And the potential strength of these ideological positions and the numbers of people to be reached by them are still far short of fullest achievement. There are those who with cautious optimism hope that there need be no final issue drawn, that even if the world divides into two sharply separated ideological camps, it will still be possible to avoid ultimate conflict and to achieve something in the way of international harmony. But the prospect is indeed dubious, for the struggle for the mind of man is ever bloodier than for his body or his goods. It is more than a superficial matter of a different form of government or different cultural habits; it is a difference in the most fundamental values and ideals that men have.

There are also those who tend to discount the ideological differences as merely symptomatic of other kinds of conflicting interests among peoples, such as territorial interests or demands for raw materials, which if resolved will automatically remove the threat of ideological conflict. This view seems to underrate the genuine motivational power of the ideologies, which, though nourished by frustrations of various kinds and even deliberately fostered by national leaders for ulterior ends, may acquire a demanding character for people that far exceeds the power of the initiating sources and becomes entirely independent of them. A man's loyalty to the ideal of human freedom may far transcend narrow self-interest and loyalty to his country.

The problem of ideological conflicts is infinitely complicated by the fact that the lines of ideological cleavage tend to coincide with other lines of world cleavage, particularly with national boundaries. Thus, the ideological and national identifications become joined, and both are thereby vastly strengthened. And where ideological and national lines do not coincide, that, too, may be the source of greater tensions, since the opposing ideological groups within the nation come into conflict and severe repression or civil war may eventuate. We have already seen (page 585) that such internal repression and civil strife can, in our dynamically interactive world, spread beyond the national borders to intensify international tensions.

A PROGRAM FOR REDUCING INTERNATIONAL TENSIONS

In light of the foregoing discussion about the nature of international tensions, their psychological bases, and the obstacles to world unity, it is now possible to state the elements of a comprehensive program for reducing international tensions. The execution of this vast undertaking requires the skills of all the social sciences—political science, economics, law, education, history, and all the others. And the problems involved are manifold, requiring attention to industrial concentration, transportation, commerce, international monetary funds, population shifts, forms of government, international political bodies, world courts and law, science, education, and the arts.

The social psychologist can contribute to this vast undertaking in certain essential ways. He can advise on aspects relating to human behavior—on needs, perceptions, beliefs and attitudes, principles of group functioning, morale, and leadership. The economic and political factors operate *through people,* and the ultimate solution to the problem of international tensions is not found in economics or politics or geography or science, but in psychological considerations. As the preamble to the constitution of the United Nations Educational, Scientific and Cultural Organization asserts, "Since wars begin in the minds of men, it is in the minds of men that the defences of peace must be constructed." The objectives of a program for peace are psychological objectives; in order to achieve these objectives various economic and political programs may be called for.

Preliminary Considerations.—Before stating the elements of the program, it is necessary to point out several preliminary considerations. For one thing, the objectives of the program are ideal objectives. The achievement of some of them must of necessity be much more gradual than of others. None can be hoped to be put into effect immediately. But they do serve to indicate the direction toward which efforts should be made in the problem of international tensions.

Second, the problem of international tensions is multidimensional, and its solution must be multidimensional. There is no one cause of international tensions and no one cure. And the various factors underlying tensions are mutually interactive and reinforcing. An intelligent attack on the problem requires an attack on many fronts.

Third, every step in such a program must be evaluated in terms of its *absolute* as well as its relative effectiveness. Although the contribution of a single step toward ultimate peace may seem discouragingly small, it should nevertheless be taken along with other simultaneous steps. To design and display international symbols, to ease restrictions on free world travel, to establish international institutes for health may seem trivial steps in a program for world peace. Yet they each contribute and, taken together with many other steps, may in the end prove vitally important. At the same time, this does not mean that the easy steps should be pursued first and the truly profound and difficult ones postponed indefinitely. Along with these separate steps must go a continuous attack on the basic economic and political obstacles to international harmony.

And finally, such a program, like any social program, involves the necessity of taking some "calculated risks." Some measures may have side effects that are themselves deleterious, that increase rather than decrease tensions. Yet the over-all effect may be a gain. Such calculated risks often enter in the negotiations of a country with other countries. The people of the United States are now at a point where they may have to take a calculated risk in connection with the internationalization of atomic energy. It may seem temporarily safer to retain monopoly of the bomb as long as possible, yet this action may serve to incite a world-wide atomic armaments race that cannot be halted short of total atomic war. Although there is risk in sharing the secrets of atomic energy, it may be only by assuming this risk now that atomic warfare can be averted later.

We have said that the proposed steps are *ideal* steps. It may with considerable justice be argued that for these steps to be achieved or to begin of achievement would first require a much greater degree of international good will and mutual confidence than exists. This is unquestionably true. Still, tentative beginnings can be made on all of these steps, some more readily than others, and the fruits of these small beginnings make that much easier further steps toward these objectives. It is an accelerating process.

It is also argued that not all countries have a genuine desire for international unity. This, too, may be true, and it is likely that universal striving toward international unity can be expected to occur only after some of the first steps toward improved international relations have first been taken by some leading nations.

America's role in promoting peace.—A recognition of the above difficulties leads some people to the fatalistic view that there is nothing one country— no matter how genuinely devoted to the ideal of international unity—can do. Many Americans seem to take refuge in the comforting view that we as a nation have done all we can do to promote world peace and that it is up to other nations to cooperate with us. This point of view is probably not unique to the American. Frenchman, Russians, Englishmen, and the people of all other nations may hold similar opinions. Each nation is waiting for the others to cooperate.

Earlier in this chapter the point was made that since the world is a dynamically interactive whole, the actions of any single nation must be expected to have effects throughout the world. Any nation can alone behave in such a fashion as to make for better possibilities of international harmony. This is particularly true of the United States in light of its dominating economic, political, and military position in the world. America may alone have it in its power to avert World War III (atomic) and to behave in world relations in such a fashion as to reduce international tensions and eventually to achieve world unity. One nation, no matter how powerful, cannot, of course, do the job alone. But one nation may be able to establish the direction that other nations will eventually follow.

Because of this potentially decisive role of America in world affairs and because this book is addressed primarily to American readers, the proposed program for achieving peace is cast largely in terms of what America can do. The workability of such a program is based on the assumption that there is a sufficiently sincere desire of Americans to accomplish this end. This assumption seems not unduly optimistic. Unquestionably there are large numbers of the American people and many national leaders who do have this sincere desire, and it seems perfectly possible that many others can be brought to see that these proposed measures are realistic, that they need not jeopardize the security or welfare of the United States, and that they are worth while in their own right even if they fail in their prime objective of increasing international harmony.

A note on pacifism.—The program for peace to be stated does not include the techniques of pacifism. Pacifism addresses itself primarily to the evil of war rather than to the underlying dynamics that produce war. It is essentially a negative rather than a positive approach. It is equivalent to telling a child not to behave in a certain way, without providing the child with alternative and understandable ways of behaving. Aside from an unimportant minority of people in the world for whom war itself may be directly attractive, war for the great majority of people is regarded as evil, costly, and futile. It is pointless to reiterate endlessly to them the evils of war and the joys of international peace. Unless they have available some other way of satisfying the needs served by war, they will go to war when the level of international tensions become sufficiently high, whether or not they hate war. This is as true of many pacifists as it is of other people. For they, too, find themselves caught in the inexorably mounting tensions and ultimately find no other way out than through war.[1]

Ten Steps in a Program for Peace.—The objectives of a program for reducing international tensions are to eliminate or circumvent the various obstacles to international unity that we have discussed above. This can be accomplished in the following ways: (1) reducing people's frustrations, (2) making democracy work, (3) improving mental health, (4) educating for international thinking, (5) changing attitudes, (6) developing nonpartisan foreign policy, (7) assuming democratic world leadership, (8) providing the positive prerequisites for international unity, (9) reducing ideological conflicts, (10) using techniques short of war in international conflict.[2]

Reducing people's frustrations.—To reduce widespread aggressions which can readily be channeled into war, the general level of frustration of all the American people must be alleviated. This means raising the standard of living of all classes of Americans; it means providing economic security; it means maintaining full production and full employment; it means breaking monopolies and protecting economic opportunity for all.

But not only must America see to its own people, it must also be prepared

---

[1] For a discussion of the nonadaptive character of pacifism, see Sanford (1945). See also Glover (1933).

[2] Tolman's (1942) *Drives toward War* states some rather similar requirements to achieve peace. His book also offers an interesting analysis of the motivational bases of war.

to extend aid to the limit of its enormous capacities to other peoples of the world. It means encouraging free international trade, making loans, participating in international monetary funds, etc. Through such means America can help to remove the blockages to satisfaction of such major needs of people all over the world as those of sheer subsistence. And this is an indispensable step in preventing the aggressions of all peoples.

Making democracy work.—Together with such an economic program must go a sustained effort to improve the working of democracy in the United States. People must be encouraged and given the opportunity to participate in local and national affairs. Just as provision of an adequate standard of living for all people is the major economic task of the world today, so the provision for adequate participation and representation of all people in their governments is the prime political task of the world today. Both are indispensable to enduring peace, and both are exceedingly difficult of accomplishment. Without such popular participation and control of government, the power structure of nations is such that the *personal needs and attitudes of leaders and special interests dominate national action in international affairs.* And this, we have seen, is likely to predispose toward war rather than toward peace.

Barriers to individual advancement must be lowered for all classes of Americans. By making democracy work better, it will be possible for needs of self-expression, prestige, and participation to be satisfied through constructive channels rather than indirectly through war.

What is equally important is that wherever American influence reaches in the world, it should be used to foster the growth of democracy in other countries. One critically important feature of such democratic practice is that it helps to convince the world of America's good intentions. It is hard for other nations to trust America when it fails to operate democratically at home or when it fails to support democracy in foreign countries. Denial of democracy to the Negro at home and dalliance with undemocratic regimes in foreign countries weaken America's psychological position in international relations.

Improving mental health.—In connection with the reduction of racial prejudice in the United States we have already discussed at some length (Chap. XIII, page 504) the general methods for prophylaxis in connection with antisocial needs. The fostering of widespread group psychotherapy among the American people and attention to the healthy personality development of American children can do much to reduce and prevent the occurrence of antisocial needs, which are easily translatable into aggressions and war.

It is exceedingly significant that all three of these measures—reducing frustration, making democracy work better, and improving mental health—can be expected to yield wide social benefits in reducing not only aggressions that may lead to war but also those which may be channeled into racial tensions and industrial conflict within the nation.

Educating for international thinking.—All the educational agencies of the nation must be utilized to raise the level of information of the American people about international affairs, about other peoples and other nations, about the causes and cures of war. It is essential to make clear for people the relations that exist between their own narrower interests and issues on an international scale. Scientific thinking should be encouraged about the origin of aggressiveness, the basis of "scapegoating," etc. The ignorance about and particularly misconceptions about other peoples and other nations must be corrected. This requires the abolition of the various "supports" to distorted beliefs that we have previously mentioned. Better communications, a common language, free travel, etc., will all help to enrich understanding of others and to reduce stereotyped thinking. Stress must be laid on the basic communality among national characteristics, and the differences must be seen as "good" rather than "bad."

And serious attention should be given to informing the American people about how they are perceived by the people of other countries, what the stereotypes about Americans held by Frenchmen, Chinese, Russians, and others actually are. This can serve to correct the ethnocentrism of the American people and to give them some understanding of the point of view of other peoples, which is essential to ultimate world cooperation.

A necessary part of such an educational program is an allied program of research by public opinion techniques and other techniques which will aim to discover the content of people's international beliefs and attitudes and the bases of them. Such research data can be used to plan information and educational programs more effectively.

Changing attitudes.—It is not sufficient to operate on the level of people's information and understanding about international issues. It is also essential to undertake programs of changing negative attitudes toward foreign countries and international relations to positive ones and to encourage the growth of positive attitudes toward international participation and international organizations. All the best techniques for attitude change and development discussed in Chap. VI must be utilized, including the enlistment of group supports, the use of ambiguous and "crisis" situations, the methods of persuasion through propaganda (Chap. IX), etc.

Identifications of the American people with international symbols, such as the United Nations, must be fostered by continued strong support of this and other international bodies. In conjunction with this, the United States should take the lead in the development of international institutes of medical research, agriculture, science, the arts, public opinion research, and the like, which not only can give the American people a sense of participation in international activities but can also give the world as a whole a concrete demonstration of American readiness to participate cooperatively in world enterprises.

Developing nonpartisan foreign policy.—Serious efforts should be made to establish a nonpartisan (or at least bipartisan) position on foreign policy, which will make possible long-range continuity in the international actions of the United States and a clearer perspective for other countries of what the United States can be counted on to do.   This poses a national political problem of grave dimensions.

Assuming democratic world leadership.—If it were possible to achieve something approaching a nonpartisan foreign policy, this would have the added critical value of making it possible for American leaders to function more like world statesmen.   The United States more than any nation in the world today is in a position to assume a role of democratic leadership in world affairs.   But this is possible only if national leaders are relatively unhindered by dissensions and special pressures at home.

The behavior of the United States in international relations should be guided among other things by attention to principles of group morale and leadership discussed in Chap. XI.   We have already pointed out that these principles on a grand scale probably have some relevance for the way in which nations behave toward one another.   The way in which the United States conducts itself in respect to other nations may be such as to strengthen international unity or to weaken it.   It can, for example, use its dominant position in an "authoritarian" manner or in a "democratic" manner, and each of these will have its own consequences for the fate of international relations.

Providing positive prerequisites for international unity.—Aside from elimination of divisive forces in international relations there are certain positive prerequisites for the achievement of international unity.   For one thing, it is necessary to establish whatever common motivation is possible among the peoples of the world.   This seems most feasible in connection with the abolition of poverty and disease and the creative advances in science, thought, and the arts.

Another necessity is the development of widespread feelings of identification with the people of the world as a whole and with groups all over the world which transcend national boundaries.[1]   What is needed is for such

[1] For a more detailed discussion of the problem of developing identifications with world organizations, see Tolman (1943).

international organizations to be made to stand out clearly in people's psychological fields by supplying the organizations with all manner of symbols, membership identification, etc. It is also important that international leaders begin to emerge who can be identified by most people primarily as leaders of the international groups and only secondarily as citizens of given nations. There are in the world virtually no international figures of this sort, though there are tiny beginnings in the person of the Secretary-General of the United Nations and a few other such officers. Identification with international organizations can also be enhanced by the gradual accumulation of successful products of their activities. It is important to bring people the world over to feel that they have had a part in prevention of aggression in some part of the world, in the establishment of scientific cooperation on some world-wide project, etc.

Still another prerequisite for international unity is the general development of skills and experience in group activity of all kinds. Much study is needed in every nation and in every type of group in every nation of how groups can best function, how morale can be sustained, how leadership can be most effective. If people are to be able to function cooperatively in international relations, they must first know how to function cooperatively and harmoniously in family groups, in work groups, in national political groups, etc. The methods of group discussion, group decision, encouragement of individual participation, etc., are not naturally given but must be painfully learned like any other skills. Leadership training is a particularly urgent need. It is only through effective leadership that the positive forces which can contribute to world unity can be channeled in appropriate directions.

Statesmen and diplomats, too, need training in methods of group functioning, for it is not infrequent that international cooperation fails not out of irreconcilable differences among nations but sheerly out of inability of the statesmen and diplomats to understand one another, to be able to discuss problems constructively, and to be able to reach decisions as a group.

Reducing ideological conflicts.—This is in some ways perhaps the most difficult step of all, for it requires a program of reeducating some of man's basic values or, at least, of reorienting them in such a way that they need not conflict with those of other people in the world. The most direct and immediate step that can be taken is in the direction of increasing people's understanding of other people's values. Often, the root of ideological conflict is in failure to understand; often in different ideologies there may be areas of communality that can be stressed rather than stressing points of difference. Different religious groups have often found it possible to work together in spite of what originally seemed to be insurmountable differences of opinion. The same may prove true of certain economic and political ideologies, which at present split the world.

Using techniques short of war in international conflict.—There are many forms of international conflict other than war, and no matter how evil their form or their consequences they are less destructive than war. If international tensions cannot be avoided, it still may be possible for countries such as the United States to make a choice of techniques for carrying out international conflict that are short of war. Even if the differences between two countries seem irreconcilable, war need not be the only outcome. Economic sanctions and trade warfare and political action directed at isolating the other country or building up opposing blocs may be effective forms of conflict. And bad as they are, they are to be preferred to war itself. These very forms of international action may serve a preventive purpose and force a change in international relations and reduction of tensions before war can become a reality.

In view of the enormous economic and political power of the United States, American leaders should seek all avenues of international persuasion through these means before even considering the ultimate necessity of war.

A United Nations Institute of the Human Sciences.—In June, 1945, the Society for the Psychological Study of Social Issues prepared, at the request of the Department of Social Affairs of the United Nations, a draft proposal for a . . . "United Nations Institute of the Human Sciences. . . ." Since this proposal has direct implications for the advancement of international understanding, since it provides a way of implementing some of the measures for promoting peace that we have discussed above, and since it envisages a concrete step forward on international cooperation in the study of human relations, it is worthy of description in some detail at this point.

The purpose of the proposed institute is to establish cooperative work by social scientists of all nations on the general problem of understanding human relations. It envisages the cooperative planning and implementation of basic research in the human sciences. The specific objectives of the institute would include the following: provision of comparative data on problems of human relations from various cultures and various nations, joint planning of international research projects, collation of research data on a world-wide basis, broadening scientific perspectives of the scientists of various nations, facilitation of communication among scientists, cultivation of interdisciplinary research, defining uniform research standards, establishment of central archives of research data, equalization of research facilities among the various countries, provision for training facilities for younger scientists, formation of consultation and information services on problems of human relations for national and international bodies in quest of expert advice.

The report also presents a number of illustrative research projects, all of which have direct bearing on the search for international peace and unity:

1. *The development of constructive human relations in childhood.* The research in this critical area might proceed by the collection of basic data on the group life of children, study of the process of development of social ideals in children, and study of the growth of international awareness and attitudes of nationalism and internationalism in the child.

2. *Psychological requirements for living in the United Nations.* The problem of how to bring people to be prepared psychologically to behave as world citizens may take the form of studies of the bases of feelings of loyalty to the United Nations, the means by which international symbols can be developed, the sources of confidence in the United Nations and its lack, the level and content of people's information about the United Nations, methods for stimulating interest in international affairs, and historical studies of successful federations.

3. *The study of national character.* Procedures for research in this important area could include study of different peoples in various experimental situations, through projective and personality tests, through field observation, and through comparisons of child development in various cultures.

4. *Social and psychological security.* International unity depends upon the maintenance of a necessary level of psychological security in the peoples of the world. Research is needed here to discover among other things the genesis of psychological security and insecurity and the psychological consequences of economic and social insecurity.

5. *Integration of research on intergroup relations.* Studies of the causes and consequences of satisfactory and unsatisfactory intergroup relations are already being carried out in many parts of the world. There is serious need for close coordination of such important research.

6. *Research on international committee procedures.* Since in international relationships, major decisions are often made by small face-to-face groups of mixed nationalities, it is important to understand more about such problems of group dynamics as group discussion, group work, and group decisions. Relevant research might take the form of studies of methods of chairmanship of committees, of maintaining productive open-mindedness, etc.

Whether or not an institute of this proposed form comes into existence, it is a highly encouraging sign that social scientists the world over are beginning to come to some agreement about the kinds of basic problems in human relations that must be solved if international unity is to be achieved.

The Leverage of Atomic Energy for Peace.—We come finally to the question of atomic energy.   Atomic fission has radically altered some dimensions of the problem of international tensions.   It makes the destructive potentiality of war infinitely greater; it engenders deep fears and suspicions and hostilities among nations; it makes dangerously short the period of grace in which international harmony must be achieved.   But by the very virtue of its frightful potential destructiveness, it can, with intelligent planning, be brought to exert an enormous leverage for peace.   Atomic energy can, as we have said once before, lead to panicky, destructive fear and maladaptive behavior, or it can lead to healthy, action-goading fear and successfully adjustive behavior.   Which kind of fear and action will eventuate depends upon many factors—upon the trust or distrust of the various nations of international control of atomic energy, upon the degree to which the various nations can make a realistic appraisal of the problem, upon the success they may have in carrying out the complex and delicate negotiations involved in internationalization of atomic energy.   These are at the present moment imponderables.   As far as the United States is concerned, the fate of atomic energy lies mainly in the beliefs and attitudes of the American people about the danger of atomic energy, the desirability of keeping the secret, the prospect of internationalization, the possibility of development of defenses against atomic bombs, etc.   Even if the American people are fully cognizant of the dangers and are heartily in support of international controls, the problem may fail of solution because the world will not succeed in working out the necessary agreements.   But if the American people do not understand the danger and if they will not support international controls, then such a plan is clearly doomed regardless of what other nations want to do.   This circumstance makes it especially important to review what we know about the present beliefs and attitudes of the American people concerning the problem of atomic energy.   And, incidentally, these beliefs and attitudes also throw considerable light on the outlook of the American people on international affairs and the problem of international tensions in general.

A nation-wide survey of beliefs and attitudes.—In June and again in August, 1946, a nation-wide survey was conducted under the auspices of the SSRC (1947) of the beliefs and attitudes of the American public concerning the problem of atomic energy.   Altogether, 5,984 adults were questioned on a poll-type schedule, and 1,177 on an intensive open-end schedule.   The people were carefully selected to represent a cross section of the whole adult population.   The principal findings concerning beliefs and attitudes on the problem of atomic energy were as follows:

   1. Virtually all Americans, even those who have never heard of the United Nations and know nothing and care nothing about international affairs,

know about the atomic bomb. And with few exceptions they are convinced of its enormous destructive power.

2. Worry about the problem of the bomb is not salient in the minds of most Americans. The lack of worry seems to stem from several different reasons: a belief that the United States will develop a defense against the bombs other countries might later develop, a fatalistic acceptance of its danger, an unwillingness to think about it, a feeling that the problem is in the hands of the "authorities." But coupled with this lack of personal worry or concern goes a real recognition that the bomb is dangerous. Thus, to the question, "Do you think there is a real danger that atomic bombs will ever be used against the United States?" almost two-thirds said yes.

3. There is fairly general confidence that the United States will be able to work out a defense against the bomb. In answer to the question, "Do you think the United States will be able to work out an effective defense against the atomic bomb before other nations could use it against us?" 56 per cent said yes, 19 per cent said no, and 25 per cent said they did not know.

4. A large majority of the American public opposes putting the bomb under international control. To the question, "Do you think the secret of making atomic bombs should be put under the control of the United Nations, or should the United States keep the secret to itself?" 75 per cent expressed a belief that the United States should keep the secret.

5. Although people are not prepared to yield control of the bomb to the United Nations now, the great majority of them (73 per cent) do favor the attempt to work out a system of international control to prevent any nation including our own from using the bomb. Yet only slightly more than a third (37 per cent) believe that such international control could be successful.

6. Consistent with this lack of faith that international control can work, most people (69 per cent) believe that the United States should continue manufacturing atomic bombs at least for the time being.

7. There appears to be a rather general attitude that the rest of the world has no reason to be apprehensive about American possession of the bomb. Quoting from the SSRC report:

> ... Americans tend strongly to identify American security with world security. They reason ... that as long as America alone holds the atomic bomb the world will be safe from atomic warfare, for it is inconceivable that this country would take the initiative in provoking international conflict .... Very few people see any suggestion of hostile action in an American monopoly of the bomb.

8. By far the most powerful correlate of these various beliefs and attitudes

proved to be the individual's *level of information* about international affairs and about atomic energy.   Again quoting from the SSRC report:

The poorly informed, as compared with the well informed, are most pessimistic about avoidance of future war, but perhaps take comfort in the firmer beliefs that the U.S. alone now has the secret of the atomic bomb, and will be able to work out a defense against it.   Rather than a policy of working for friendly relations with Russia, they seem to prefer the route of national security and preparedness, wanting a large peacetime Army, Navy and Air Force, and having a stronger belief that the U. S. should retain control of the bomb rather than internationalizing it . . . the above set of attitudes appears to have the possibility of forming a somewhat consistent and self-reinforcing pattern which might be characterized as "defensive" or "non-internationalist" in nature.

Some additional support for the existence of this sort of a defensive pattern of thinking, especially among the poorly informed, is given by the fact that a belief that the United States should control the bomb and continue its manufacture tends to be correlated with pessimism about avoidance of future war, less concern about friendly relations with Russia, doubt that international control of the bomb could be successful, belief that the bomb secret is held exclusively by the United States, and belief that the United States will be able to work out a defense against it.

General comments.—The above findings clearly reveal many of the dangers in present American thinking about international affairs.   There seems to be widespread escapist thinking about the threats of atomic warfare.   Attitudes of "defensiveness" and "security" seem to predominate over attitudes of "internationalism."   Pessimism about avoidance of future war and the success of international organization inhibits willingness to support international controls.   And with this autistic thinking goes a deadly ethnocentrism that prevents the average American from realizing that American possession of the atomic bomb may be regarded by the people of other countries as a serious threat to their national welfare.

This is a somber picture, but it is relieved somewhat by certain implications of the above findings.   A continued and accelerated educational campaign devoted to "telling the facts of atomic life" to the people of America can be expected to encourage internationalist thinking to the extent that it can destroy such illusions as that there can be a defense against the bomb.   An educational campaign that strives to make clear to the American people how the other peoples of the world view our possession of the atomic bomb and our continued manufacture of bombs may aid in developing a broadened perspective in connection with international control.   Concerted attack on the pessimistic view that war is unavoidable and international organization cannot work may help to free people of their defensive, security-minded, preparedness psychology. And above all else, as the findings of the above study demonstrate, a campaign designed to raise people's level of information about international affairs can be expected to predispose them more fully to international cooperation.

SUMMARY

The purpose of this chapter is the discussion of the nature and problem of international tensions, their psychological bases, the obstacles to international unity, and a program for the reduction of international tensions. The emphasis throughout is *psychological*.

International tensions arise among nations, and the tensions take many forms. War is only the last step in tensions. Three common errors to be avoided in analyzing the problem of tensions are overemphasis on the problem of war, overemphasis on tensions among nations as whole social organizations without reference to the individuals who make them up, and overemphasis upon the behavior of individuals who participate in war as aggressive acts.

Nations are social organizations of people. They differ in numerous respects, which makes it easy for them to be perceived as separate. They differ in internal structure, and this has its consequences for their international behavior. They have manifold functions for their citizens, but they do not serve the needs of all their citizens equally. For this reason and others, there are also *extra-national* groupings of people in the world, which cut across national boundaries. The relationships among nations are of different types, depending upon various functions of "blocs," political or economic dominance, overlapping membership in extra-national groups, etc. The *emotional* relationship among nations is also important, and a "sociogram" of nations might reveal potential forms of international structure.

Nations are shown to be in dynamic interrelation with one another throughout the world. Tensions that appear among nations arise out of conflicting interests and objectives, mutual suspicion, fear and hatred, overlapping loyalties and identifications, etc. The effects of tensions on international relations are threefold: They may lead to withdrawal and isolation from one another, to realignment of relationship and creation of blocs, and, finally, to war. But the reaction of isolation and withdrawal is shown to be ineffective on the whole as a way of reducing tensions.

It is shown that international tensions affect internal policies and structure of nations and, conversely, that internal policies and structure can affect international relations.

The problem of international tensions is ultimately a problem of the psychology of the individual.   The manner in which economic and political and other such important influences work in connection with international tensions is determined by the needs, perceptions, beliefs, and attitudes of the individual.   Different individuals in a nation have different interests and different functions and hence have different effects on international tensions. Leaders of a nation have especially significant effects.

The prime psychological questions to be considered in connection with international tensions are the following: What needs of the individual are served by international conflict?   How do the beliefs and attitudes of the individual come to make international conflict seem the appropriate way of satisfying these needs?   The needs underlying international tensions are discussed in the following categories: (1) frustrated needs leading to aggressiveness, (2) needs for direct gain, (3) needs for power and prestige, (4) patriotic and nationalistic needs, (5) needs for "escape from peace," (6) needs for resolving ambiguous crisis situations, (7) needs for group belongingness and conformity, (8) needs for war itself.

In connection with the last, it is asserted that war is not an instinctive part of human behavior, that there is no intrinsic need for aggressiveness. But it is also argued that cultures can induce genuine aggressive needs in people.   This leads to a discussion of "national character" wherein the meager evidence on national differences is examined and the probable bases of any observed differences are discussed.

The cognitive and emotional factors that predispose people to accept war as a way of satisfying their many needs are discussed in the following categories: (1) ethnocentric beliefs, (2) stereotyped beliefs concerning other nations, (3) negative attitudes toward other nations, (4) predominance of nationalist over internationalist attitudes, (5) oversimplified perceptions of causes and cures of international tensions, (6) belief in the inevitability of war, (7) cognitive set toward international tensions and war, (8) wishful thinking about the outcome of war, (9) emotional blocks to cognitive reorganization concerning international tensions.   In connection with the last, there is discussion of the factors that make it difficult for people to arrive at new and more adaptive solutions to the problems of international relations.

The following obstacles to international unity are discussed: (1) high level of frustration the world over; (2) "supports" for distorted beliefs about others, such as inaccessibility of people from one another, propaganda, and the beliefs of others; (3) dominant role of national leaders and special interests, who encourage war in satisfaction of their own personal needs; (4) the dependence of international relations on national politics, which makes it difficult for national leaders to behave in a farsighted and statesmanlike way; (5) the lack of certain prerequisites for international unity, such as a common motivation for all the peoples of the world, widespread feelings of identification with international symbols, intercommunication among the peoples of the world, and skills of international cooperation; (6) basic ideological conflicts, which make international unity difficult.

A psychological program for the reduction of international tensions is presented with special application to what America can do. Certain cautions and difficulties in implementing such a program are indicated. The 10 steps in the proposed program for peace are (1) reducing people's frustrations, (2) making democracy work, (3) improving mental health, (4) educating for international thinking, (5) changing attitudes, (6) developing nonpartisan foreign policy, (7) assuming democratic world leadership, (8) providing the positive prerequisites for international unity, (9) reducing ideological conflicts, (10) using techniques short of war in international conflicts.

A proposal for a United Nations Institute of the Human Sciences is described, and its implications for international understanding and certain illustrative types of research activities are indicated.

Finally, the importance of the potential leverage of atomic energy for peace is discussed, and the critical role of the beliefs and attitudes of the American people about the problem of atomic energy is indicated. The results from a nation-wide public opinion survey show that there are serious dangers in present American thinking about atomic energy. There tend to be widespread escapist, wishful and defensive thinking, reluctance about international control of the atomic bomb, and pessimism about the future of international relations. On the positive side, however, there does seem promise that the right kind of informational and educational campaigns can help to predispose people more favorably to international cooperation.

BIBLIOGRAPHY

BRICKNER, R. M.: 1943. *Is Germany incurable?* Philadelphia: Lippincott.

BURNHAM, J.: 1941. *The managerial revolution.* New York: John Day.

CRESPI, L. P.: 1944. Attitudes toward conscientious objectors and some of their psychological correlates. *J. Psychol.*, 18, 81–117.

CRESPI, L. P.: 1945. Public opinion toward conscientious objectors: II. Measurement of national approval-disapproval. *J. Psychol.*, 19, 209–250. III. Intensity of social rejection in stereotype and attitude. *J. Psychol.*, 19, 251–276. IV. Opinions on significant conscientious objector issues. *J. Psychol.*, 19, 277–310. V. National tolerance, wartime trends, and the scapegoat hypothesis. *J. Psychol.*, 20, 321–346.

DODD, S. C.: 1935. A social distance test in the Near East. *Amer. J. Sociol.*, 41, 194–204.

GLOVER, E.: 1933. *War, sadism, and pacifism.* London: G. Allen.

GORER, G.: 1943. Themes in Japanese culture. *Trans. N. Y. Acad. Sci.*, 5, 106–124.

KLINEBERG, O.: 1944. A science of national character. *J. soc. Psychol.*, 19, 147–162.

KLUCKHOHN, C.: 1947.   Anthropological research and world peace.   *In* Newcomb, T. M., and Hartley, E. L. (eds.), *Readings in social psychology.*   New York: Holt.

MURPHY, G.: 1945.   *Human nature and enduring peace.*   Boston: Houghton.

QUEENER, L.: 1947.   The development of internationalist attitudes directed toward peace. Graduate School, Yale Univ. (Ph.D. Dissertation).

SANFORD, R. N.: 1945.   Relapse into old habits.   *In* Murphy, G., *Human nature and enduring peace.*   Boston: Houghton.

Social Science Research Council: 1947.   *Public reaction to the atomic bomb and world affairs.*   Ithaca: Cornell Univ.

STAGNER, R.: 1947.   War and peace.   *In* Harriman, P. L. (ed.), *Encyclopedia of psychology.*   New York: Philosophical Library.

TOLMAN, E. C.: 1942.   *Drives toward war.*   New York: Appleton-Century.

TOLMAN, E. C.: 1943.   Identification and the post-war world.   *J. abnorm. soc. Psychol.*, **38**, 141–148.

NAME INDEX

A

Adams, D. K., 112, 113, 145
Adler, A., 51, 74
Alexander, F., 505, 529
Allport, F. H., 20, 236, 270, 369, 403, 475, 497
Allport, G. W., 45, 62, 74, 130, 131, 145, 154, 174, 183, 208, 209, 238, 239, 270, 318–319, 320, 350, 363, 364, 415, 439, 444, 462, 463, 474, 475, 485, 487, 496
Alper, T. G., 133, 145
Amster, F., 505, 529
Amster, S., 505, 529
Annis, A. D., 350, 363
Asch, S. E., 85–87, 99, 109, 246, 270, 338, 339, 346, 363, 364
Asher, R., 350, 364

B

Barker, R., 55, 56, 74, 136, 145, 435, 439
Bartlett, F. C., 127–129, 145, 153, 174, 188
Baruch, D. W., 443, 467, 496
Bavelas, A., 411, 432, 433, 439
Bayton, J. A., 479, 489, 496
Bellak, L., 350, 364
Benedict, R., 392, 403
Benne, K., 523, 529, 569, 574
Berelson, B., 297, 314
Berg, W. C., 462, 497
Bice, H. V., 465, 496
Biddle, W. W., 316, 347, 353, 364
Birch, H. G., 114, 117, 141, 145
Blake, R., 489, 490, 496
Blankenship, A. B., 290, 313
Block, H., 246, 270, 338, 339, 363, 364
Boas, F., 321, 364
Bogardus, E. S., 194, 210, 221–224, 262, 270, 477, 478, 496
Bolton, E. B., 475, 496
Bonning, J. C., 568, 574

Bradford, L. P., 431, 434, 439, 523, 529, 569, 574
Brady, R. A., 389, 403
Braly, K., 478, 479, 489, 497
Brickner, R. M., 592, 621
Bridges, J. W., 337, 364
Brigham, C. C., 465, 496
Brophy, I. N., 514–515, 516, 529
Browder, E., 341
Brown, J. F., 21, 28
Bruner, J. S., 82, 88, 89, 109, 249, 272, 284, 313, 374, 403, 463, 496
Buck, P., 443
Bugelski, B. R., 450
Burnham, J., 588, 621
Bush, C., 311

C

Cahalan, D., 295, 313
Caldwell, O. W., 170, 174
Campbell, A., 304, 308, 309, 313, 314
Cannon, W. B., 60, 66, 74
Cantor, N., 568, 574
Cantril, H., 70, 75, 101, 109, 154, 174, 252–253, 254, 270, 272, 282, 284, 288, 290, 291, 292, 303, 314, 318–319, 320, 350, 363, 364, 542, 552, 574
Carlson, H. B., 176, 203
Carlson, H. S., 168, 174
Carmichael, L., 127, 129, 145
Carpenter, M. E., 486, 496
Carson, C., 195
Cartwright, D., 309, 310, 314
Carver, G. W., 195
Centers, R., 542, 552, 574
Chatto, C. L., 519, 521, 529
Chave, E. J., 214, 262, 272
Chein, I., 83, 89, 109
Chenowith, A. S., 519, 529
Chevaleva-Janovskaja, E., 372, 403
Clark, W. R., 526, 529

SUBJECT INDEX

A

Acculturation, 508–509

Action research, 501

Adaptation level, 101–102, 388

Advertising and racial prejudice, **473**

Aggression, and catharsis, 61–62
free-floating, 42, 448–449
and frustration, 55, 449–451
and industrial conflict, 547, 551, 557–558
in Negroes, 466
and projection, 58
and racial prejudice, 55, 448–451
and war, 576, 583, 588, 590

Alien factors in prediction, 39, 499

American Institute of Public Opinion (*see* Gallup poll)

American Jewish Committee, 192

American Jewish Congress, 175

The American Magazine, 472

American Veterans Committee, 383

Analysis, levels and units of, higher order units, 26
individual vs. social group, 13, **14–18,** 21–25, 28, 366–368, 576
in motivation, 30–33
in perception, 84–87

Animal groups, 14–16, 367–368

Animism, 10

Army, race segregation in, 470–471, **515–** 516
as social group, 17, 379

Assimilation (perceptual), 95–97, 130, 191

Atomic energy, attitudes and beliefs about, 279, 287, 616–618
and international tensions, 575–621
and peace, 616
SPSSI statement on, 60–61
sources of information about, 187–188

Attitudes and beliefs, 149–315
as adaptive acts, 32
and autism, 59

Attitudes, characteristics of, 158–167
content, 159–160, 210, 247–250, 476–479
importance, 163–164, 210, 251–257
kind, 158–159, 210, 247–250
precision, 160–161, 210, 247–250
specificity, 161–163, 210, 247–250
strength, 163, 210, 250–251
verifiability, 164–167, 210, 257–258
crystallization of, 285–286
and cultural influences, 176–182, 451–452
definitions of, 149–153
development and change of, 175–204
diagnosis of, 196–198
and emotion, 64, 196, 199–200
and "facts," 167–168, 186–190, 306–307, 387–388
as higher order processes, 26
individual differences in, 178–179
and judgments, 157–158
measurement of, indirect methods of, 245–247
problems in, 205–306
indirect nature of, 206–208
individual and private, 209–210, 220
measurable attributes, 210, 247–258
momentary situation, influence of, 208
precision of, 208, 297–299
reliability of, 208–209, 214, 216–217, 219–220, 226, 233, 258–262, 289–292, 300–302
validity of, 209, 239, 262–267, 280–284
and motivation, 153–157
polarization of, 227–230, 253
public opinion measurement of, 273–306
coding of data, 279–280, 299–302
community self-survey, 524–525
international applicability of, 292–293
interpretation of data, 280–285, 302–305